A National Bureau
of Economic Research
Project Report

Privatizing Social Security

Edited by Martin Feldstein

The University of Chicago Press

Chicago and London

The University of Chicago Press, Chicago 60637
The University of Chicago Press, Ltd., London
© 1998 by the National Bureau of Economic Research
All rights reserved. Published 1998
Paperback edition 2000
Printed in the United States of America
07 06 05 04 03 02 01 00   2 3 4 5
ISBN: 0-226-24101-7 (cloth)
ISBN: 0-226-24102-5 (paperback)

Library of Congress Cataloging-in-Publication Data

Privatizing social security / edited by Martin Feldstein.
     p.   cm. — (A National Bureau of Economic Research project
report)
   Includes bibliographical references and index.
   ISBN 0-226-24101-7 (cloth : alk. paper)
   1. Pension trusts — Cross-cultural studies. 2. Pension trusts — United
States. I. Feldstein, Martin S. II. Series.
HD7105.4.P75   1998
332.67′254—dc21   98-43851
                                                                          CIP

Relation of the Directors to the
Work and Publications of the
National Bureau of Economic Research

1. The object of the National Bureau of Economic Research is to ascertain and to present to the public important economic facts and their interpretation in a scientific and impartial manner. The Board of Directors is charged with the responsibility of ensuring that the work of the National Bureau is carried on in strict conformity with this object.

2. The President of the National Bureau shall submit to the Board of Directors, or to its Executive Committee, for their formal adoption all specific proposals for research to be instituted.

3. No research report shall be published by the National Bureau until the President has sent each member of the Board a notice that a manuscript is recommended for publication and that in the President's opinion it is suitable for publication in accordance with the principles of the National Bureau. Such notification will include an abstract or summary of the manuscript's content and a response form for use by those Directors who desire a copy of the manuscript for review. Each manuscript shall contain a summary drawing attention to the nature and treatment of the problem studied, the character of the data and their utilization in the report, and the main conclusions reached.

4. For each manuscript so submitted, a special committee of the Directors (including Directors Emeriti) shall be appointed by majority agreement of the President and Vice Presidents (or by the Executive Committee in case of inability to decide on the part of the President and Vice Presidents), consisting of three Directors selected as nearly as may be one from each general division of the Board. The names of the special manuscript committee shall be stated to each Director when notice of the proposed publication is submitted to him. It shall be the duty of each member of the special manuscript committee to read the manuscript. If each member of the manuscript committee signifies his approval within thirty days of the transmittal of the manuscript, the report may be published. If at the end of that period any member of the manuscript committee withholds his approval, the President shall then notify each member of the Board, requesting approval or disapproval of publication, and thirty days additional shall be granted for this purpose. The manuscript shall then not be published unless at least a majority of the entire Board who shall have voted on the proposal within the time fixed for the receipt of votes shall have approved.

5. No manuscript may be published, though approved by each member of the special manuscript committee, until forty-five days have elapsed from the transmittal of the report in manuscript form. The interval is allowed for the receipt of any memorandum of dissent or reservation, together with a brief statement of his reasons, that any member may wish to express; and such memorandum of dissent or reservation shall be published with the manuscript if he so desires. Publication does not, however, imply that each member of the Board has read the manuscript, or that either members of the Board in general or the special committee have passed on its validity in every detail.

6. Publications of the National Bureau issued for informational purposes concerning the work of the Bureau and its staff, or issued to inform the public of activities of Bureau staff, and volumes issued as a result of various conferences involving the National Bureau shall contain a specific disclaimer noting that such publication has not passed through the normal review procedures required in this resolution. The Executive Committee of the Board is charged with review of all such publications from time to time to ensure that they do not take on the character of formal research reports of the National Bureau, requiring formal Board approval.

7. Unless otherwise determined by the Board or exempted by the terms of paragraph 6, a copy of this resolution shall be printed in each National Bureau publication.

(Resolution adopted October 25, 1926, as revised through September 30, 1974)

784981

Contents

Preface

This volume focuses on the possible methods and problems involved in shifting from an unfunded system of social security retirement benefits to a system based on mandatory saving in individual accounts. The research project that led to the current volume began several years ago. It is interesting to note that, when the project began, there were many who were quite skeptical about whether this was even a subject worth studying since the idea of such a radical change in the form of social security financing seemed so politically implausible. Much has changed since then. The official 1994–96 Advisory Council on Social Security appointed by President Clinton recently presented its recommendations for social security reform in which a majority of the members called for a shift from the current unfunded system to a system in which some portion of the benefits would be financed by a funded system. Whatever the outcome of those recommendations, it seems likely that the future public policy debate will carefully consider the proper role of funding and individual accounts of the type studied in this volume.

The first part of the volume examines the experience with privatizing social security in five very different countries—Chile, Australia, the United Kingdom, Mexico, and Argentina. The second part looks at a variety of issues that will have to be resolved if the United States chooses to adopt such a privatized system.

This project brought together experts on social security from several countries as well as from many universities and research institutes in the United States. I am particularly grateful to the Reserve Bank of Australia, the British Treasury, and the Ministry of Finance of Argentina for permitting senior officials to prepare studies for this project. These papers were presented and discussed at a conference held in Cambridge, Massachusetts, in August 1996. Professors Jeffrey Liebman and Andrew Samwick prepared the summary of the very interesting and lively discussion at the conference.

The research benefited from frequent interaction among members of the NBER research group on social security and from discussions of this research at meetings of the NBER programs on public economics and on the economics of aging.

I am grateful to the Smith Richardson Foundation for the funding that made this project possible. I also want to thank the members of the NBER staff for their assistance with all the details involved in the planning and execution of this research and of the many meetings that took place during the project. In addition to the researchers and research assistants named in the individual chapters, my thanks go to Kirsten Foss Davis, Rob Shannon, Mark Fitz-Patrick, Deborah J. Kiernan, and Norma J. MacKenzie for providing logistic support with the meetings and with the preparation of this volume.

Martin Feldstein

Introduction

Martin Feldstein

Reforming the social security retirement program is an issue of enormous practical importance. Although elected officials are still unwilling to confront the serious problems of our social security system, its deteriorating financial condition will eventually force major reforms. Whether those reforms are good or bad, whether they deal with the basic economic problems of the system or merely protect the solvency of existing institutional arrangements, will depend in part on whether economists provide the appropriate intellectual framework for analyzing reform alternatives. The papers presented in this volume represent an attempt to contribute to that framework.

Major policy changes that affect the public at large can happen in our democracy only when there is widespread public support for the new direction of policy. In the field of economics, the views of the media, of other private-sector opinion leaders, and of politicians and their advisers depend very much on their perception of what economists believe is feasible and correct. Fundamental policy reforms in a complex area like social security also require the development of technical expertise, both in and out of government, about the options for change and the likely consequences of alternative reforms. Fortunately, as the papers and discussion reported in this volume show, an expanding group of economists is now thinking and writing about social security reform.

Part 1 of this volume contains studies of the actual experience with priva-

Martin Feldstein is the George F. Baker Professor of Economics at Harvard University and president of the National Bureau of Economic Research.

Much of this introductory chapter borrows directly from the author's 1996 Richard T. Ely Lecture to the American Economic Association, which was published as "The Missing Piece in Policy Analysis: Social Security Reform" (*American Economic Review* 86, no. 2 [May 1996]: 1–14) and is used with the permission of the American Economic Association. The introduction also draws on a prior technical paper on the conditions under which privatizing social security would raise economic welfare (Feldstein 1995d).

tizing social security in five very different countries: Chile, Australia, the United Kingdom, Mexico, and Argentina. Part 2 deals with a variety of practical issues that the United States will have to face if we as a nation want to make a similar transition to a system of individual funded accounts. This introduction provides background for the subsequent chapters by discussing the economic costs imposed by an unfunded social security system and the nature of the gains that would be achieved by switching to a funded system. It then summarizes the questions that are considered in the individual country studies and reviews the subjects of the chapters that deal with the United States.

Before going further, a word about the term *privatizing social security* is in order. The term *privatize* is ambiguous and raises political objections if it suggests an abrogation of government responsibility for the income of the aged. In this volume, *privatizing social security* refers to the shift from unfunded pay-as-you-go programs to mandatory funded programs with individual accounts. Because the contributions are mandatory, the government retains responsibility for assuring retirement income to all. The benefits of a funded system that are discussed in this volume refer to capital accumulation and to the resulting reduction in labor market distortions. I take the essence of privatizing to be whether individuals are also given control over their own investments. In a funded but not privatized system, the government would have to invest in private stocks, bonds, and mortgages. There are obvious reasons for not wanting the government to acquire very large investments in individual private companies. Although the administrative costs may be higher when individuals have control over their investments, major U.S. mutual funds have reduced their expenses to less than one-quarter of 1 percent of assets. Even in a privatized system, the government might constrain the mix of assets in which individuals are permitted to invest and might provide a general safety net to protect individuals whose investments did not produce adequate retirement income. The chapters in part 1 of this volume consider the way that different countries have dealt with these issues, while Mitchell (chap. 10) discusses administrative issues in more detail.

The Magnitude of the Problem

The social security program of retirement, disability, and survivor benefits is the largest program of the U.S. government, with outlays of more than $350 billion in 1997. The 12.4 percent employer-employee payroll tax that is earmarked for social security exceeds the income tax obligations for most taxpayers. An alternative measure of the magnitude of the social security program is *social security wealth,* the present actuarial value of the social security benefits to which the current adult population will be entitled at age sixty-five (or to which they are already entitled if they are older than sixty-five) minus the present value of the social security taxes that they will pay before reaching age sixty-five.[1] Social security wealth had grown by 1995 to about $7 trillion, equal to the size of the GDP.[2] Since that is equivalent to more than $35,000 for every adult in the country, the value of social security wealth substantially exceeds all other financial assets for the vast majority of American households. In the aggregate, social security wealth exceeds the combined value of pension and life insurance reserves and equals nearly half of all private financial wealth as conventionally measured.

Social security wealth is of course not real wealth but only a claim on current and future taxpayers. Instead of labeling this key magnitude *social security wealth*, I could have called it the nation's *net social security liability*. Like ordinary government debt, social security wealth has the power to crowd out private capital accumulation. And social security wealth will continue to grow as long as our current system remains unchanged, displacing an even larger stock of capital.

The $7 trillion social security liability in 1995 was twice as large as the official national debt. Even if the officially defined budget deficit is eliminated in 2002 so that the traditional national debt is no longer increasing, the real national debt in the form of the social security liability is currently scheduled to increase in that year by more than $300 billion.[3]

Looking further into the future, the aggregate social security liability will grow as the population expands, as it becomes relatively older, and as incomes rise. Government actuaries predict that, under existing law, the tax rate required to pay each year's social security benefit will rise over the next fifty years from the present level of slightly less than 12 percent to more than 18 percent and perhaps to as much as 23 percent.[4]

The financial problems of the social security system are therefore very serious indeed. But even more fundamental are the economic effects of continuing with an unfunded system. The next section discusses the large deadweight loss that an unfunded system causes by distorting the supply of labor and the form

1. The concept of *social security wealth* was introduced and defined explicitly in Feldstein (1974).

2. This estimate is based on the disaggregated model presented in Feldstein and Samwick (chap. 6 in this volume), which has been calibrated to the aggregate benefits projected by the social security actuaries. An earlier calculation reported in Feldstein (1996a) was based on a simpler estimation procedure that assumed a faster growth of future benefits.

3. These increases in social security wealth and its liability twin are the core of the massive intergenerational transfers that Auerbach, Gokhale, and Kotlikoff (1991, 1994) have warned us about in their important studies of generational accounting.

4. The 18 percent rate is based on what the social security actuaries call their intermediate alternative II assumptions, while the 23 percent rate is based on the somewhat more pessimistic alternative III assumptions. Experience suggests that even these alarming predictions may be too optimistic. In 1983, the social security actuaries calculated that a 12 percent rate would be enough to finance social security benefits until the year 2065. A dozen years later, these projections have been revised to show that the social security fund will be exhausted by 2031 if the tax rate is not increased or benefits reduced.

of compensation. I then discuss the intertemporal welfare loss that results from depressed capital accumulation and the potential gain from shifting to a funded system.[5]

A common feature of all the foreign systems discussed in this volume is the provision of a universal system of retirement benefits for the aged. The analyses of the United States in this volume also assume that the nation is politically committed to such a universal system. An alternative would be a means-tested system that provides benefits only to those individuals who, through inadvertence, bad luck, or strategic behavior, reach old age with income and assets that are below some specified level. Although I believe that such an alternative deserves careful consideration, this possibility has not been studied in the current project.[6]

The Deadweight Loss of the Labor Market Distortions

The social security payroll tax distorts the supply of labor and the form of compensation.[7] Moreover, although the link between the social security taxes that individuals pay and their subsequent benefits means that the statutory payroll tax rate overstates the effective individual marginal tax rates, the mandatory social security contributions are nevertheless real taxes with very substantial deadweight losses. These losses are inevitable because of the low return implied by the pay-as-you-go character of the unfunded social security system.

Unlike private pensions and individual retirement accounts, the social security system does not invest the money that it collects in stocks and bonds but pays those funds out as benefits in the same year that they are collected.[8] The rate of return that individuals earn on their mandatory social security contributions is therefore far less than they could earn in a private pension or in a funded social security system. As Paul Samuelson (1958) first taught us forty years ago, an unfunded social security program with a constant tax rate provides a positive rate of return that, in equilibrium, is equal to the rate of growth of the social security payroll tax base. The 2.6 percent average annual rate of

5. For an earlier discussion of the potential effect of a social security fund on national capital accumulation, see Feldstein (1975, 1977).
6. For an analysis of the conditions under which an unfunded means-tested system would provide a higher level of social welfare than an unfunded universal program, see Feldstein (1987a). It would be desirable to extend this analysis to include the possibility of funding both alternatives. The foreign programs described in pt. 1 of this volume generally provide an unfunded safety net in addition to the mandatory funded accounts.
7. I do not discuss the distortion to the retirement decision because that could be remedied by eliminating the retirement test and by other changes within the unfunded system.
8. Although the social security system has been accumulating a fund since 1983 to smooth the path of tax rates, more than 90 percent of payroll tax receipts are still paid out immediately as benefits, and the assets in the social security trust fund are only about 5 percent of the social security liabilities.

growth of real wages and salaries since 1960 can therefore illustrate the yield of an unfunded social security program.[9]

I might just note that, in contrast to this 2.6 percent potential future yield, the rate of return on social security contributions since the inception of the program has been kept artificially high by the sharp increase in the social security tax rate.[10] The combined employer-employee tax rate rose from just 2 percent in 1940 to 3 percent in 1950, 6 percent in 1960, 10 percent in 1980, and 12 percent since 1988. Thus, those who got in on the ground floor of the social security program and are now retired paid taxes at relatively low rates but are receiving benefits that are financed by a much higher tax rate on current employees. The resulting very high real return on social security contributions has sustained political support for the existing system. But such a sixfold increase in tax rates cannot happen again.[11]

In contrast to the 2.6 percent "equilibrium" return on social security contributions, the real pretax return on nonfinancial corporate capital averaged 9.3 percent over the same thirty-five-year period since 1960.[12] That is the return that each individual's retirement saving could have earned in a fully funded government system or in a privatized system if the government credited the corporate tax receipts back to each account. The difference between the 2.6 percent social security return and the 9.3 percent real return implies that mandatory contributions to an unfunded social security plan are real taxes with a very substantial deadweight loss.[13]

A simplified example will indicate the magnitude of the implied tax wedge. Consider an employee who contributes $1,000 to social security at age forty-five to buy benefits that will be paid at age seventy-five. With a 2.6 percent yield, the $1,000 grows to $2,160 after the thirty years. In contrast, a yield of 9.3 percent would allow the individual to buy the same $2,160 retirement in-

9. The social security actuaries now contemplate an even lower long-term real rate of return of about 2.0 percent because of the slower growth of the population and of real wages.

10. Samuelson's (1958) analysis shows that the rate of return is equal to the rate of growth of the tax base plus the rate of growth of the tax rate.

11. The increases in the payroll tax rate that are projected for the next fifty years are needed just to offset the changing demographic structure and the lower growth of earnings; they do not imply higher rates of return. As noted above, the rapid aging of the population and other recent changes imply that the return would be significantly lower than 2.6 percent for the current younger generation of employees.

12. This 9.3 percent return combines profits before all federal, state, and local taxes with the net interest paid. The method of calculation (described in Feldstein, Poterba, and Dicks-Mireaux 1983) has been applied to the more recent data in Poterba and Samwick (1995) and Rippe (1995).

13. In practice, individuals do not earn the full 9.3 percent pretax rate of return even on retirement saving. Individual retirement accounts and private pension plans earn that return net of federal, state, and local corporate taxes. Since those taxes averaged 42 percent of the pretax return (Rippe 1995), the real net yield available to savers has been about 5.4 percent. In principle, however, a funded retirement system could deliver the full 9.3 percent pretax return to each individual saver. But even the lower 5.4 percent net return implies that the social security contributions are a substantial tax.

come for only $150.[14] Thus, forcing individuals to use the unfunded system dramatically increases their cost of buying retirement income. In the current example, a funded plan would permit individuals to buy retirement income at just 15 percent of the price that they must pay in the unfunded program, allowing the 12.4 percent social security tax rate to be replaced by a 1.9 percent contribution. The remaining 10.5 percent excess mandatory contribution is a real tax for which the individual gets nothing in return.[15]

The deadweight loss caused by this 10.5 percent tax is much larger than the "small triangle" that typically comes to mind when we think of deadweight losses. This is true for two distinct reasons.

First, because the social security payroll tax is imposed on top of federal and state income taxes, the deadweight loss is not a small triangle but a much larger trapezoid. With a federal marginal tax rate of 28 percent (for single individuals with taxable incomes over $23,000 and married couples with combined incomes over $38,000) and a typical state income tax rate of 5 percent, the social security tax comes on top of an initial 33 percent marginal income tax rate.[16] A little arithmetic shows that the incremental deadweight loss that results from the additional 10.5 percent net social security tax is equal to 4.6 percent of the product of the payroll tax base and the compensated elasticity of that tax base with respect to the net of tax share.[17] That is about ten times as large as the deadweight loss that would result if the social security tax were the only tax.

The second reason that the deadweight loss is substantially larger than is commonly assumed is that the payroll tax distorts much more than the number of hours that individuals work. More specifically, it affects such other dimensions of labor supply as occupational choice, location, and effort. It also distorts the form in which compensation is taken, shifting taxable cash into untaxed fringe benefits, nice working conditions, etc. These distortions to the

---

14. With a 5.4 percent net rate of return, the individual can buy the $2,160 retirement income for $446, less than half the cost with the unfunded social security program.

15. The extent of the effective tax depends on the taxpayer's age (or, more generally, on the amount of time that will elapse between the payment of the tax and the receipt of the benefit). Replacing the forty-five-year-old in the example with a thirty-five-year-old who has forty years until retirement raises the net tax from 10.5 to 11.4 percent, while raising the age of the individual to sixty reduces the net tax to 7.6 percent.

16. The combination of the 33 percent rate and the 10.5 percent net social security tax implies a 43.5 percent rate. However, since employers pay half the 15.3 percent statutory payroll tax, the marginal tax rate on the full pretax marginal product of labor is (43.5/1.0765 =) 40.4 percent.

17. Edgar Browning (1987) showed that, when the relevant behavioral elasticity is measured in the presence of the tax, the original Harberger (1964) formula for the deadweight loss of a tax with marginal tax rate t on a wage base of wL must be modified to DWL $= 0.5 \, \varepsilon t^2 wL/(1 - t)$, where ε is the compensated elasticity of the tax base (wL) with respect to the marginal net of tax share, $1 - t$. The increase in the deadweight loss because the marginal tax rate is at t_2 rather than t_1 is therefore ΔDWL $= 0.5\varepsilon(t_2^2 - t_1^2)wL/(1 - t_2)$. Thus, a pure payroll tax of (10.5/1.0765 =) 9.8 percent with no other tax present would induce a deadweight loss of $0.0053\varepsilon wL$. But, in the presence of a preexisting income tax of 33 percent, the 10.5 percent payroll tax raises the deadweight loss by ΔDWL $= 0.046\varepsilon wL$.

form of compensation are in effect distortions to the individual's pattern of consumption. They are, dollar for dollar, as important as the distortions to labor supply. In a recent paper (Feldstein 1995c), I showed that the deadweight loss caused by this full range of distortions—the number of working hours, the broader dimensions of labor supply, and the pattern of consumption implied by the form of compensation and by the use of tax deductions—can be evaluated quite simply in the traditional Harberger framework by using the compensated elasticity of taxable income (with respect to the net of tax share) in place of the usual compensated elasticity of labor supply. Because there are so many aspects of behavior that affect taxable income, this elasticity (and therefore the associated deadweight loss) is much larger than the traditional supply elasticity of working hours.

To estimate the elasticity of total taxable income with respect to the net of tax rate, I studied the tax returns of a panel of taxpayers before and after the 1986 Tax Reform Act (Feldstein 1995a). These data imply a range of elasticity estimates between 1 and 1.5, all much larger than the traditional labor supply elasticity.[18]

This elasticity of the income tax base is likely to exceed the elasticity of the social security payroll tax base because itemized deductions and changes in portfolio income do not influence the base of the payroll tax. To be very conservative, for the current calculation I assume that the relevant compensated elasticity of the payroll tax base with respect to the net of tax share is only 0.5.

Putting these pieces together implies that the deadweight loss due to the net social security tax is about 2.3 percent of the social security payroll tax base—about $67 billion in 1995.[19] This deadweight loss is about 1 percent of GDP and about one-fifth of total social security payroll tax revenue.

In practice, the deadweight loss of the payroll tax is exacerbated by the haphazard relations between benefits and taxes that result from existing social security rules. For example, because benefits are based on the highest thirty-five years of earnings, most employees under age twenty-five receive no additional benefit for their payroll taxes. Because many married women and widows claim benefits based on their husbands' earnings, they also often receive no

18. These estimates relate to the experience of taxpayers with 1985 incomes over $30,000 and may not be appropriate for the entire population. A similar study by Gerald Auten and Robert Carroll (1994), using a much larger set of panel data that is available only inside the Treasury Department, estimated the elasticity to be 1.33, with a standard error of 0.15. In a more recent study (Feldstein and Feenberg 1996), Daniel Feenberg and I used the 1993 tax rate increases to estimate the elasticity implied by the experience after the 1993 tax rate increases. We found a short-run compensated elasticity of 0.74, although the interpretation of this is clouded by the lack of panel data and by transition issues.

19. Total wages taxable by the OASDI payroll tax in 1992 were $2.5 trillion. Scaling this up to the 1995 level by the increase in total wage and salary disbursements implies a 1995 tax base of $2.9 trillion. Since the payroll tax applied only to wages up to $61,200 per person in 1995, this $2.9 trillion should be reduced by the entire income of the individuals who earn $61,200 or more (for whom the payroll tax has no marginal tax consequence), not just by the portion of their incomes over $61,200.

benefit in return for their payroll taxes. Because there is no extra reward for taxes paid at an early date, the effective tax rate on younger taxpayers can be a substantial multiple of the effective tax rate of older employees. Indeed, older men who are married can actually face a negative marginal social security tax rate, receiving more than a dollar in actuarially expected future benefits for every dollar that they pay in payroll taxes (Feldstein and Samwick 1992). The social security rules are so complex and so opaque that many individuals may simply disregard the benefits that they earn from additional working, therefore acting as if the entire payroll tax is a net tax no different in kind from the personal income tax.

The extra deadweight loss that results from these very unequal links between incremental taxes and incremental benefits would automatically be eliminated in a privatized funded system with individual retirement accounts. It can, however, also be eliminated within the existing unfunded system by creating individual social security accounts for each taxpayer (as James Buchanan [1968] suggested many years ago), crediting the account with the individual's tax payments and imputing the average pay-as-you-go return of 2.6 percent.[20] But the labor market distortions and the resulting deadweight loss that result from the low rate of return in an unfunded system cannot be eliminated without shifting to either a funded public system or a privatized system of individual retirement accounts.[21]

The Welfare Loss of Reduced National Saving

The deadweight loss that results from labor market distortions is not the only adverse effect of an unfunded social security system or even the largest one. Even if there were no distortions to the labor supply or to the form of compensation (i.e., even if the compensated elasticity of the tax base with respect to net of tax rate were zero), each generation after the initial one would lose by being forced to participate in a low-yielding unfunded program, that is, by being forced to accept a pay-as-you-go implicit return of 2.6 percent when the real marginal product of capital is 9.3 percent. Even though capital income taxes now prevent individuals from receiving that 9.3 percent on their own savings, the public as a whole does receive that full return; what individuals do not receive directly they receive in the form of reductions in other taxes or increases in government services.

20. Tax payments or mandatory contributions of husbands and wives could be pooled and divided into two separate accounts, thereby providing protection in case of divorce. A fraction of the contributions could be automatically devoted to the purchase of life insurance. I do not explore these important issues further here.

21. Auerbach and Kotlikoff (1987) and Kotlikoff (1996) examine a special model in which the labor market distortions can be eliminated in an unfunded system by having a higher *marginal* link of benefits to taxes than the average benefit-tax ratio. They achieve this with a lump sum tax on all employees. This creates no problem in their analysis since all employees are assumed to have the same income. In practice, however, a lump sum tax that is large enough to eliminate the marginal payroll tax distortion would make the social security payroll tax very regressive.

The extent to which an unfunded social security system causes a decline in national capital income and economic welfare depends on how individual saving responds to social security taxes and benefits and on how the government acts to offset the reductions in private saving.

Consider first the effect on individual saving. Individuals who have had average earnings during their entire working life and who retire at age sixty-five with a "dependent spouse" now receive benefits equal to 63 percent of their earnings during the full year before retirement. Since the social security benefits of such individuals are not taxed, those benefits replace more than 80 percent of peak preretirement net-of-tax income. Common sense and casual observation suggest that individuals who can expect such a high replacement rate will do little saving for their retirement. Such saving as they do during their preretirement years is more likely to be for precautionary balances to deal with unexpected changes in income or consumption. Not surprisingly, the median financial assets of households with heads aged fifty-five to sixty-four were only $8,300 in 1991, substantially less than six months' income. Even if we look beyond financial wealth, the median net worth (including the value of the home) among all households under sixty-five years of age was only $28,000.

To get a sense of the order of magnitude of the resulting annual loss of aggregate income, it is helpful to begin with the simplest case in which each dollar of social security wealth reduces real private wealth by a dollar.[22] Since the forgone private wealth would have earned the marginal product of capital while the unfunded social security system provides a return equal to the growth of aggregate wages, the population incurs a loss equal to the difference between those two returns. With a marginal product of capital of 9.3 percent and a social security return of 2.6 percent, the annual loss of real income is 6.7 percent of social security wealth. The social security wealth of $7 trillion in 1995 implies an annual loss in that year of $470 billion, or more than 6 percent of total GDP.

Of course, this loss is not directly comparable to the deadweight loss associated with the distortions to labor supply and to the form of compensation. Although this loss of investment income affects all generations that pay social security taxes, a full welfare evaluation requires comparing these losses to the gain of the initial generation of retirees who received benefits without making any contribution and the gains of subsequent retirees who received windfall benefit increases as tax rates rose.

More generally, this massive potential loss must be qualified by addressing three questions. First, how much does the social security system actually depress real capital accumulation? The capital income loss occurs only to the extent that the capital stock would be higher with private saving or a funded program. Second, how should risk be taken into account in evaluating the loss of real income per dollar of forgone capital accumulation? Third, how should the windfall gain to the initial generation that received social security benefits

---

22. I discuss the evidence about the effect of social security on saving below.

without making any contribution be balanced against these subsequent losses? I deal briefly with each and then turn to the potential benefit of shifting to a privatized funded social security program.

The Induced Change in National Saving

To assess the effect of the existing social security system on national saving we must recognize that social security affects public saving as well as private saving. Consider first the effect on public saving. The official surplus of the social security fund in fiscal year 1995 was $69 billion. To what extent does this social security surplus actually increase real national saving and investment? The common criticism, that such a surplus does not raise real investment because it is invested exclusively in government bonds, is incorrect. If the social security trust fund buys government bonds that would otherwise have been sold to the public, it prevents an equal amount of crowding out and thereby does raise the level of real investment.

The critical issue is therefore how the existence of the social security surplus affects the size of the overall (unified) budget deficit. The current budget discussions about achieving a balanced budget in the year 2002 use the projected social security surplus of $111 billion in that year to offset projected deficits elsewhere in the budget. If the goal of a balanced budget in 2002 would have been set even if there were no projected social security surplus, then the existence of the surplus does not reduce the projected total budget deficit and therefore does not affect the projected future national savings available for investment. But, if, as seems more likely, in the absence of a social security surplus Congress and the president would have targeted a deficit in 2002 (with the budget balanced in some later year), then the projected social security surplus does increase projected national saving to some extent, although less than the full amount of the projected surplus.

Similarly, the actual deficit in 1995 would probably have been larger without the $69 billion social security surplus, but not $69 billion larger because Congress and the president would have enacted other legislation to reduce the budget deficit. Thus, some part, but only some part, of the $69 billion current social security surplus probably does help offset the decline in private saving. But, since the $69 billion annual surplus is only one-sixth of social security receipts and the entire social security trust fund is now less than 10 percent of social security wealth, the offsetting effect of public saving is not a major consideration.

The key issue is therefore the extent to which social security wealth reduces private saving. Economic theory alone cannot provide an unambiguous answer. Even if all individuals were rational life-cycle savers, each dollar of social security wealth would not necessarily replace exactly a dollar of real wealth. To the extent that the income-tested character of social security benefits induces earlier retirement, individuals will save more than they otherwise would.

The relative importance of this induced retirement effect and of the more basic wealth replacement effect will vary from individual to individual (Feldstein 1974). Social security also affects private saving through an income effect and by providing a real annuity.[23] Finally, an unknown number of individuals who are irrational or myopic may not respond at all to the provision of social security benefits.

Thus, the extent to which social security wealth substitutes for private real wealth accumulation is an empirical issue. A substantial amount of research has been conducted on this question. Like every other important and complex issue in economics, different studies do not all point to the same conclusion. That is inevitable in empirical economics. As I have argued in a different context (Feldstein 1982), all empirical specifications in economics are false models, oversimplifications that cannot be literally true. Statistical estimates must therefore be interpreted with a sensitivity to potential biases, simplifications, data quality problems, and the like. In the end, the researcher must make a judgment based on all the evidence rather than by applying traditional theories of statistical inference to any individual study.

What, then, does the evidence tell us about the effect of social security on private saving? At the most basic level is the fact, to which I have already referred, that most households accumulate little or no financial assets. This is consistent with a rational decision to substitute social security benefits for private wealth accumulation (Diamond 1977), but it could also be interpreted as evidence that individuals are completely myopic, providing nothing for their old age whether or not there are social security benefits. However, studies based on cross sections of household data (including Blinder, Gordon, and Wise 1983; Diamond and Hausman 1984; and Feldstein and Pellechio 1979) support the substitution hypothesis. Although there remain serious problems of statistical identification and data quality and a wide range of parameter estimates, I interpret the cross-sectional evidence as implying that each extra dollar of social security wealth replaces about fifty cents of private wealth accumulation. Finally, there are the time-series studies linking social security wealth to aggregate private saving and consumption (see, e.g., Barro 1978; Esposito 1978; Feldstein 1974; and Leimer and Lesnoy 1982). I recently reestimated the specification presented in Feldstein (1974) using time-series

---

23. In principle, individuals who have operative utility-maximizing bequest motives might offset fully the effect of social security wealth by increasing their saving in order to compensate future generations for the tax burdens implied by the social security liabilities (Barro 1974). I doubt that that effect is empirically very important. My own judgment on this "Ricardian equivalence" issue is that very few of the individuals who are affected by social security have operative bequest motives. Because future generations can be expected to have higher real incomes, even parents who include their children's consumption or utility in their own utility functions may prefer to receive gifts rather than to make bequests. If children do not wish to support their parents, the result is a corner solution in which loving parents do not compensate their children when the value of the social security liability increases. On the empirical irrelevance of Ricardian equivalence, see, e.g., Altonji, Hayashi, and Kotlikoff (1992). See also Bernheim (1989).

data through 1992 and tested some of the specifications that others had examined with earlier data (Feldstein 1996b). The new parameter values are remarkably close to my original estimates and imply that the existing social security wealth reduces overall private saving by nearly 60 percent.

Although none of these studies establishes definitively a precise substitution of social security wealth for other household wealth, I believe that, taken together, these studies do imply that the social security program causes each generation to reduce its savings substantially and thereby to incur a substantial loss of real investment income.[24]

That the displacement of private saving by social security is less than complete reduces the loss that each generation incurs from the imposition of an unfunded program. But, even if each dollar of social security wealth displaces only fifty cents of private wealth accumulation, the annual loss of national income would exceed 4 percent of GDP.[25]

In assessing the aggregate welfare effect of a social security program, the loss that results from the depressed level of real capital accumulation must be balanced not only against the windfall gain of the earlier retirees but also against the gain in protection to those myopic individuals who would otherwise have saved too little for their old age.[26] Such an analysis is not necessary, however, to assess the loss that results from using an unfunded instead of a funded program to provide benefits. But, in order to do so, it is necessary to consider

24. The decline in the size of the domestic capital stock depends also on the extent to which a lower rate of saving induces an increased net inflow of capital from abroad. If capital flowed internationally to maintain the same rate of return everywhere, a decline in the U.S. saving rate would induce an equal offsetting inflow from abroad. Although the net-of-tax return on this capital would go to the foreign suppliers of this capital, the U.S. government would collect taxes on the equity portion of this investment, and the U.S. public would gain a corresponding amount. The evidence suggests, however, that the international capital market is sufficiently segmented that relatively little capital flows to replace the lost U.S. saving (see Feldstein and Horioka 1980; Feldstein 1994; and Mussa and Goldstein 1993).

25. Increasing the capital stock by half the 1995 net social security wealth of $7 trillion would raise capital income by more than $300 billion, or 4 percent of GDP, if the rate of return remained unchanged at 9.3 percent. Such a large increase in the capital stock would of course reduce the marginal product of capital. If all the increase in the capital stock went into the domestic capital stock (i.e., if there were no change in international capital flows), a Cobb-Douglas production function with a labor coefficient equal to the share of compensation in national income implies that the marginal product of capital would be depressed from 9.3 to 7.9 percent if the incremental capital went only into the business sector (i.e., excluding owner occupied housing) and to 8.3 percent if the entire capital stock were increased. Of course, the lower return to capital would be matched by a higher return to labor. An increase in the capital stock equal to half of net social security wealth would raise the capital stock by about 16 percent and would therefore raise national income by 3.8 percent.

26. If public policy is committed to an unfunded social security program, setting the appropriate level of benefits requires balancing the protection of the myopic undersavers against the loss to others that results from replacing high yield real capital accumulation with the low implicit social security yield. I have examined this optimization problem with the help of some simple models (Feldstein 1985) and concluded that, with realistic estimates of the yield on capital and the return on the pay-as-you-go social security system, the replacement ratio of social security benefits to past earnings should be very much lower than it is in the current system.

first how the returns on real capital and on social security contributions should be adjusted for risk.

Adjusting Returns for Risks

Since the portfolio returns to the owners of real capital and the returns to participants in a pay-as-you-go social security system are both subject to risk, it would be appropriate to evaluate the income loss of an unfunded system by considering the lower certainty equivalent values for both the real capital and the pay-as-you-go returns.

The certainty equivalent social rate of return on real capital depends on how the risk in that return is shared through the tax system between individual savers and the broader public.[27] Taxes paid by corporations have equaled about 42 percent of the 9.3 percent real pretax return over the past thirty-five years (Rippe 1995), implying a net 5.4 percent average return to savers before personal taxes[28] and a 3.9 percent return collected by the government. Variations in this source of government revenue are reflected in the short run in the budget deficit and, in the longer run, in changes in taxes on all incomes (most of which are employment incomes) and in government spending.

I believe that most individuals who have small amounts of financial assets do not invest in stocks and bonds because the costs of learning how to make such investments outweigh the incremental income that would result relative to the yield on bank deposits on their very limited financial assets. The very small variations in net income imposed on them through their sharing in the tax revenue derived from investment income can therefore be ignored, taking the mean value of that income as the certainty equivalent.[29] It is reasonable therefore to use the mean value (of 3.9 percent) as the relevant certainty equivalent for the part of the return to capital that is collected by the government.

What is the appropriate certainty equivalent for the 5.4 percent return that accrues to individual savers? A relatively conservative choice is the real yield on ten-year government bonds, a return of 2.5 percent between 1960 and 1994. Combining the 3.9 percent return collected in taxes and this 2.5 percent certainty equivalent return received by individuals gives a total certainty equivalent return of 6.4 percent instead of the expected return of 9.3 percent.

27. This issue is discussed in Feldstein (1995d). Arrow and Lind (1970) explain that the fundamental principle for the evaluation of risky public expenditures is that the value of benefits should be reduced if a substantial risk is borne by the individual but that the expected value is an appropriate certainty equivalent for the part of the benefits and costs that the government spreads to all taxpayers through the tax system.

28. I assume that the alternative to the unfunded program would be a funded program in which the individual saver would get a return net of the corporate tax but not subject to any personal taxes. If additional personal taxes were levied, the certainty equivalent would get even closer to the expected value.

29. This implicitly assumes that the variation in portfolio income is uncorrelated with shocks to their income and consumption.

It is less clear how the 2.6 percent return of the unfunded social security program should be adjusted for risk. The future return that individuals will receive on their social security taxes depends on the growth of aggregate real wages, on the changing age structure of the population, and on political decisions about taxes and benefits. During the period since 1960, the forward-looking increase in aggregate real wages for completed twenty-year periods varied from a low of 1.5 percent to a high of 3.0 percent. Changes in demographic structure added to the fluctuations in available returns. And, in recent years, the value of future social security benefits has been decreased by subjecting them to tax and by increasing the retirement age at which full benefits are paid.

One possibility would be to assume that the return on social security is as uncertain as the real return on investment in plant and equipment, suggesting that the appropriate difference between the two certainty equivalents may be the same as the difference between the two mean values, or 6.7 percent. An alternative extreme assumption would be to adjust the return on real capital for risk but to make no adjustment in the return on the social security program, implying a risk-adjusted difference of only 3.8 percent, that is, the difference between the 6.4 percent certainty equivalent yield on real capital and the 2.6 percent expected return on social security wealth. Note that even this low 3.8 percentage point difference in returns implies that substituting the existing $7 trillion unfunded social security wealth for a funded program of equal size implies a risk-adjusted income loss of nearly 4 percent of GDP.[30]

In short, while risk adjustment might change the specific magnitude of the annual loss, even with a very conservative risk adjustment, the loss of having a funded rather than an unfunded program remains very substantial.

Initial Gains and Subsequent Losses

I turn now to the issue of how to balance the gain to those generations of beneficiaries in an unfunded system who receive benefits without contributing a corresponding amount and the losses to all future generations who forgo the higher yield that would be earned on real capital.[31]

When a social security program first begins, the government collects an amount in taxes that it distributes to the then current retirees, if the program is unfunded, or that it invests in the national capital stock, if the program is to be funded. The same thing happens again whenever the tax rate is increased to

30. See n. 25 above. A $7 trillion increase in the 1995 capital stock would raise the capital stock by about 33 percent and, assuming a Cobb-Douglas technology with a capital coefficient of 0.25, would raise national income by 7.4 percent. Labor would receive about three-fourths of this increase. This calculation ignores the risk adjustment and the offset for the implicit pay-as-you-go return on social security wealth. A 2.6 percent pay-as-you-go return on social security wealth would be about 2.5 percent of GDP.

31. A more formal analysis of this issue is presented in the appendix.

finance a relative increase in benefits or an expansion of coverage. To simplify the current discussion, I ignore the role of subsequent expansions and consider only the windfall benefits to the initial generation.

If each dollar collected by an unfunded program reduces national saving, each generation after the initial one incurs a loss that reflects the difference between the marginal product of the displaced capital and the return on the unfunded program (i.e., the growth rate of aggregate wages). The key question is whether the present value of the losses to all future generations exceeds the windfall benefit that the initial generation received without having paid any tax.

To compare these magnitudes, the future losses must be discounted at a rate that reflects the rate at which the marginal utility of consumption declines over time. The dollar loss to each subsequent generation grows at the same rate as aggregate wages. Discounting this growing stream of losses at a constant discount rate is therefore equivalent to applying a growth-adjusted discount rate—that is, the difference between the discount rate and the growth rate—to a constant perpetual loss at the level incurred by the first generation of losers. Thus, the present value of the losses is equal to the amount of capital displaced by the initial transfer of taxes multiplied by the ratio of the reduced rate of return—that is, the difference between the risk-adjusted marginal product of capital and the risk-adjusted social security return—to the growth-adjusted discount rate.

To simplify this discussion, assume now that the unfunded program reduces national saving by a dollar for every dollar that it collects in taxes.[32] Since the initial generation receives a benefit equal to the initial amount of the tax, the adoption of an unfunded plan rather than a funded plan causes a net present value loss if the return difference per dollar of forgone investment exceeds the growth-adjusted discount rate. This condition is satisfied for any plausible values of the parameters, implying that the present value of the future losses exceeds the value of the initial transfer.

Consider the following example. If one adopts the very conservative procedure of risk adjusting the return to private capital but making no adjustment to the return on social security taxes, the lost rate of return is 3.8 percent. The present value of the future losses therefore exceeds the value of the initial generation's windfall if the growth-adjusted discount rate is less than 3.8 percent. Since the growth rate is 2.6 percent, this is satisfied if the real discount rate itself is less than 6.4 percent, a condition that is certainly warranted.

With a more plausible but still very conservative high discount rate of 4 percent,[33] the risk-adjusted annual loss of 3.8 percent of displaced investment

---

32. The assumption of one-for-one substitution simplifies by abstracting from income effects and individual myopia. Alternatively, the alternative to an unfunded program might be considered to be a funded program. The more general case of less than one-for-one substitution is discussed in the appendix.

33. The discount rate should reflect the decline in the marginal utility of per capita consumption that results from the growth of per capita real wages. With per capita real wage growth at about

implies a present value loss of an unfunded program that is nearly three times as large (when discounted back to the start of the program) as the windfall benefit to the initial retirees.[34]

The Potential Gain from Privatization

This framework for thinking about the cost implied by an unfunded program can be used to assess whether a gain in economic welfare could be achieved by shifting to a privatized system in which each employee has a retirement account into which the employee and/or the employer must make regular periodic contributions that are then invested in stocks and bonds. The government may recognize its obligations to existing retirees and employees at the time of privatization by depositing in these retirement accounts new government bonds equal to the present value of the benefits to which the individual is then entitled on the basis of past contributions to the unfunded system. Funds in these new retirement accounts can be used to purchase annuities, or withdrawn gradually when the individual reaches retirement age, or bequeathed to a spouse or other heirs.[35]

A skeptic might ask whether this "privatization" really accomplishes anything since it merely converts the existing unfunded social security obligations into explicit government debt with the same present value. That skepticism would be warranted in a static economy but is not appropriate when economic growth is continually enlarging the size of the social security liability. Shifting from an unfunded to a funded program is an application of the general principle that, when you discover that you are in a hole, the first thing to do is to stop digging. Shifting to a funded system eliminates the future losses associated with future increases in the size of social security wealth.

In the first year after the privatization of a pay-as-you-go system, there is no increase in the capital stock because the government would have to borrow all the mandatory saving to pay benefits to existing retirees. But, as time passes,

---

1.6 percent a year, the appropriate discount rate is less than the critical value of 6.4 percent if the elasticity of the marginal utility function is less than the extremely high value of 4. An elasticity of 2, e.g., which is high enough to imply that the marginal utility of consumption is halved about every forty-five years, corresponds to a discount rate of 3.2 percent. With aggregate wage growth of 2.6 percent, this implies a growth-adjusted discount rate of only 0.6 percent.

34. Recall that, to simplify the discussion, I have assumed that there was only one initial windfall. The actual loss reflects all subsequent program expansions as well.

A discount rate of 4 percent implies a growth-adjusted discount rate of 1.4 percent. The present value of the losses is thus $(3.8/1.4 =) 2.7$ times the initial transfer. With a more plausible discount rate of 3.2 percent, the corresponding loss would be 6.3 times the initial transfer. And, if the return to social security is given the same risk adjustment as the return to real capital, the loss becomes $([9.3 - 2.6]/0.6 =) 11.2$ times the initial transfer.

35. An alternative to explicitly creating these "recognition bonds" is to provide future retirement benefits based on past contributions but to stop accruing any further entitlements to pay-as-you-go benefits. That is the approach developed in Feldstein and Samwick (chap. 6 in this volume).

the amount of net capital investment grows (because the mandatory saving rises with the number of employees and their average incomes), while the net social security debt that is explicitly recognized at privatization remains constant. As a result, the capital stock grows and, with it, the incremental income.[36]

The net effect in each year consists of two parts: a gain equal to the real risk-adjusted return on the increase in the capital stock and a loss of the implicit social security return on the taxes paid. As the incremental capital stock grows, the net effect shifts from negative to positive and then increases without limit. The magnitude of the gain depends on the form of the transition. In the long run, if the risk-adjusted return on capital is 6.4 percent, the implicit return on the unfunded social security 2.6 percent, and the appropriate consumption discount rate 4 percent, the present value gain is nearly equal to the current value of the unfunded program. Approximating the current value of the unfunded program by the social security wealth implies a potential present value gain of nearly $7 trillion.

It is hard to put such a large sum in perspective. It may help to note that, with the assumed discount rate and GDP growth rate, that present value gain from privatization is equivalent to 1.4 percent of GDP starting immediately and continuing in perpetuity. Although this way of scaling the magnitude of the benefit may be useful, when thinking about the political economy of reform, it is also worth bearing in mind that the potential gain from the one-time political act of shifting to a funded program has such an enormous positive present value.

This is just the gain from increasing real capital accumulation. In addition, the shift to a funded program would also reduce the deadweight losses that are now caused by a payroll tax that distorts labor supply and the form of compensation. Recall that this reduction in deadweight loss is the portion that cannot be obtained by redistributing the existing implicit return but depends on raising the rate of return on social security contributions from the rate of growth of wages to the real return on capital. This $68 billion deadweight loss for 1995 corresponds in the long run to an additional 1.0 percent of GDP.

Foreign Experience with Privatization

The five individual country chapters in part 1 of this volume show how very different countries have managed the transition from systems based on unfunded government programs to systems that depend primarily on individual funded accounts. It is clear that no two systems are identical, reflecting differences in starting conditions, demographic circumstances, and political oppor-

---

36. In the transition presented in Feldstein and Samwick (chap. 6 in this volume), the pay-as-you-go benefits decline over time as retired individuals are able to rely more on the mandatory savings that they had accumulated during their working years.

tunities. Despite these differences, however, there is a core of common structural features.

In order to compare the evolution of the different systems and the structure of the privatized programs, I asked the authors of each of the country papers to address a common set of questions. Each country paper therefore begins by describing the social security pension system before the reform. It then discusses the reasons that the change was made and the steps that were needed to make the shift politically possible. The main part of each country paper is a detailed description of the new system, dealing with such issues as whether participation is mandatory, the contribution rate and base, the nature of the fund management and selection of investment options, and the ways that benefits are paid. Careful attention is given to the transition to the new system and the way that employees and retirees are treated in the transition. Although some of the systems are relatively new, the authors also discuss the likely effects of the new system on saving and capital markets in their respective countries.

Privatization Issues for the United States

Part 2 of this volume contains five papers that explore issues that are relevant to the consideration of privatization in the United States. Feldstein and Samwick (chap. 6) examine alternative feasible transitions from the existing U.S. social security program to a system of funded individual accounts, calculating the changes in the age-specific contributions that would occur along the transition path if current tax rate or benefit schedules were preserved and no change was made in the government borrowing requirements. Kotlikoff (chap. 7) extends the Auerbach-Kotlikoff multiperiod overlapping generations model to study the general equilibrium effects on capital accumulation, wages, and welfare of alternative ways of financing the obligations to existing employees and retirees if the current system were replaced with voluntary funded contributions to individual accounts. Gustman and Steinmeier (chap. 8) focus on the retirement decisions and explore how alternative transitions rules would affect retirement behavior. Poterba and Wise (chap. 9) study the investment choices of employees with 401(k) and IRA accounts to assess how individual asset allocation decisions might be made in the accounts created by a privatized social security system. They also examine some of the issues associated with the choice between annuities and other methods of paying benefits over time. Finally, Mitchell (chap. 10) discusses the issue of administrative costs and the experience of U.S. and foreign fund managers and pension programs.

As I noted in the preface, the papers in this volume are part of an ongoing research program. The countries that are switching to privatized systems are still in the process of transition, and their problems and achievements merit continued study. Although the papers dealing with the issues that the United States would confront in considering a shift to individual accounts provide substantial new information, they also help focus on issues that are not yet well enough understood. These are the subjects of NBER research currently under way.

Appendix
The Effect of Privatizing Social Security on Economic Welfare

This appendix presents a more formal analysis of the economic gains that result from shifting from an unfunded pay-as-you-go system of retirement benefits to a funded system.[37] The analysis clarifies the way that the welfare gain from privatization depends on the productivity of capital, the rate of growth of real wages, and the rate at which future consumption is discounted to the present. To simplify the analysis, I focus on the comparison of future consumption gains and current short-term consumption losses, ignoring the sizable deadweight losses associated with labor supply distortions that would be eliminated in the process of privatization.

The first section of this appendix reviews the simple analytics of replacing private saving with an unfunded social security system. The second section then builds on this to examine the potential gain from shifting from an unfunded system to a funded system, bearing in mind the obligations to existing retirees and employees. The analysis assumes that the shift to the funded system raises the national saving rate by the full amount of the taxes collected by the unfunded system, thereby substantially increasing the level of real benefits. The third section repeats the analysis of the second section with the alternative assumption that the funded system has a smaller contribution rate that is selected to provide the same level of benefits as the existing unfunded system.

There are a variety of possible mechanisms for dealing with the obligations to existing employees and retirees. The current analysis assumes that these obligations are converted to an explicit national debt (the so-called recognition bonds) that is then serviced in perpetuity. Alternative assumptions would implicitly involve different schedules for repaying the recognition debt without the formal creation of recognition bonds.

Surprisingly, there has been no explicit analysis of the conditions under which privatizing social security would increase economic welfare.[38] The po-

---

37. An earlier version of this appendix appeared as Feldstein (1995d).

38. Samuelson (1958) showed that the introduction of a pay-as-you-go program would raise the welfare of every generation in an economy in which there can be no capital stock (because all goods are perishable) and therefore no opportunity to earn a return greater than the rate of increase of the tax base. Aaron (1966) noted that a dynamically inefficient economy that is producing with a capital intensity greater than the golden rule level (i.e., in which the marginal product of capital is less than the rate of aggregate economic growth) could also raise economic welfare by introducing an unfunded social security program because doing so would reduce the initial excessive level

tential ambiguity of the effect occurs because, while each future generation would benefit from earning the higher return on real investments instead of getting a return equal to the rate of increase of the payroll tax base, these future generations would also be obligated to pay taxes to finance the interest on the extra national debt created in the process of privatization.[39] The question of whether privatizing social security raises economic welfare is therefore equivalent to asking whether the burden of financing the extra debt is less than the gain from the return on the incremental real saving.

The Welfare Loss of Introducing an Unfunded Social Security Program

Consider a simple overlapping generations (OLG) model with no social security program in which individuals live for two periods, earning w_t in the first period and saving s_t. If the marginal product of capital is ρ, the individuals consume $s_t(1 + \rho)$ in retirement.

Now introduce an unfunded social security program at time $t = 0$ financed by a payroll tax at rate θ. The proceeds of the tax are paid to the current retirees. In the next period, the population has increased by a factor of $1 + n$ and the common wage rate by a factor of $1 + g$. The taxes collected in that next period are therefore $\theta w_0(1 + n)(1 + g) = \theta w_0(1 + \gamma)$, where w_0 is the wage when the social security program is introduced. The members of the initial generation of employees thus receive $1 + \gamma$ dollars of benefits in retirement for every dollar of tax that they paid while working.

If the requirement to pay a social security payroll tax induces individuals to reduce their saving by an equal amount,[40] the loss of income in retirement is $(\rho - \gamma)\theta w_0$. The present value of this loss to the individual at the time that the social security program is introduced is $(1 + \rho)^{-1}(\rho - \gamma)\theta w_0$.

---

of the capital stock. But, in the empirically relevant case in which the marginal product of capital exceeds the growth rate, the substitution of an unfunded social security program for capital accumulation can reduce economic welfare. Feldstein (1987b) presented an explicit formula for the welfare cost of social security's adverse effect on private saving similar to the analysis in the first section of this appendix. Feldstein (1985) derived the optimal level of benefits in an unfunded system and showed conditions under which that optimum would be zero. Feldstein (1995a) states the potential loss in present value consumption from introducing an unfunded program but does not discuss the consequences of switching from an unfunded to a funded system. Analyses by Auerbach and Kotlikoff (1987) and by Seidman (1983, 1986) have discussed the effects of reducing the benefits of existing retirees but not those of privatizing the existing system with benefits unchanged. Auerbach and Kotlikoff (1987) and Corsetti and Schmidt-Hebbel (1996) show that shifting to a funded system would raise welfare by reducing the distortions to labor supply caused by existing payroll taxes.

39. More fundamentally, future generations would lose the income generated by the capital stock that is crowded out by the creation of the new debt. This is equivalent to the interest on the national debt when the rate of interest paid by the government is equal to the marginal product of capital in the private economy.

40. Because the program reduces the present value of lifetime income, it would be expected to cause a fall in first-period consumption and therefore a less than one-for-one displacement of private saving by the social security tax. This effect reduces the magnitude of the loss from introducing an unfunded program.

If the number of employees is initially N_0, the loss to future generation t when the wage rate is $w_0(1 + g)^t$ and the labor force is $N_0(1 + n)^t$ is

$$(1 + \rho)^{-1}(\rho - \gamma)\theta w_0(1 + g)^t N_0(1 + n)^t = (1 + \rho)^{-1}(\rho - \gamma)\theta w_0 N_0(1 + \gamma)^t$$

$$= (1 + \rho)^{-1}(\rho - \gamma)T_0(1 + \gamma)^t,$$

where T_0 is the initial aggregate payroll tax and therefore the initial transfer to the first generation of retirees. If the appropriate rate for discounting consumption of future generations is δ,[41] the present value of the loss to employee participants of all generations (i.e., ignoring the gain to the initial generation of retirees) is

(A1) $$\text{PVL} = (1 + \rho)^{-1}(\rho - \gamma)T_0 \sum_0 [(1 + \gamma)^t / (1 + \delta)^t]$$

$$= [(1 + \delta)/(1 + \rho)][(\rho - \gamma)/(\delta - \gamma)]T_0,$$

Note first that, if the economy is at the golden rule level of capital intensity (i.e., that $\rho = \gamma$), there is no loss to any generation of employees. The transfer to the initial retirees is a clear Pareto improvement.

In reality, of course, $\rho > \gamma$, and each generation of employees incurs a loss.[42] Note, however, that, if $\delta = \rho$, the loss to future retirees just balances the transfer to the initial retirees ($\text{PVL} = T_0$) regardless of the difference between ρ and γ. In this case, the present value of the loss to all future generations is exactly equal to the value of the transfer to the initial retirees. If, however, the intergenerational consumption discount rate is less than the marginal product of capital, the loss exceeds T_0, and the introduction of an unfunded social security program reduces the present value of future incomes by more than the value of the transfer to the initial retirees T_0.[43]

The condition $\delta = \rho$ implies that the marginal rate of substitution between consumption in one generation and consumption in the next is equal to the marginal rate of transformation. Equivalently, the existing level of capital is optimal in the sense of maximizing the intergenerational social welfare function subject only to the constraint of the intergenerational production function. Equation (A1) implies that, if the economy is operating at this first-best optimum level of capital intensity, there is no loss from a small shift of consumption from future generations to the current generation. In the more relevant case in which tax rules or other distorting factors cause $\rho > \delta$, shifting a dollar from investment to current consumption reduces the present value of the total

41. The appropriate rate for discounting consumption across generations is discussed on page 25.

42. The relation of ρ and γ is discussed on page 24. See also Feldstein (1965) and Abel et al. (1989).

43. Equation (A1) implies $\text{PVL} > T_0$ if $\gamma > -1$ and $\rho > \delta$. Since γ is the growth rate of aggregate real labor income, $\gamma > 0 > -1$.

consumption stream. Such a shift from investment to current consumption is exactly what the introduction of an unfunded social security program does and why, if $\rho > \delta$, it causes the present value of consumption to fall.

Whether the introduction of an unfunded social security program does in fact reduce the present value of consumption depends also on the extent to which it provides benefits that raise the consumption of retirees who would otherwise have saved "too little" for their own retirement.[44] Such myopic behavior would be precluded by the assumption that $\theta w_t < s_t$, that is, that each individual's social security payroll tax is less than the amount that the individual would otherwise save. But, if some individuals would have saved less than the payroll tax, the evaluation must go beyond the present value calculation of equation (A1) to reflect the utility gain from providing benefits to "myopic" retirees in each generation. When there are enough myopic individuals, the gain from helping them by even an unfunded social security program can outweigh the loss associated with giving a lower return to rational savers.[45]

Although the balancing of this gain to myopes against the loss to rational savers is important in deciding whether to introduce a mandatory retirement program and in setting the scale of benefits, it is not relevant for deciding between a funded and an unfunded program since myopes would be protected at least as much under a funded program as under an unfunded program.[46]

The Welfare Gain from Privatizing Social Security

Privatizing social security requires recognizing the obligation to existing retirees and to others who have already paid payroll taxes under the pay-as-you-go system. This appendix models that recognition as the explicit creation of additional national debt of equal value that is serviced in perpetuity.[47] Each future generation therefore bears a burden because of the additional national debt that must be balanced against the higher retirement income[48] that results from substituting real saving for the pay-as-you-go program. Since a debt-financed privatization of social security does not reduce the benefits of existing

44. Feldstein (1985) analyzed the issue of inadequate individual saving by modeling the representative individual in a two-period OLG model as having a true lifetime utility function $u(c_1) + u(c_2)$ but acting while young to maximize $u(c_1) + \lambda u(c_2)$ with $\lambda < 1$ for "partial myopia" and $\lambda = 0$ for "complete myopia."

45. Feldstein (1985) derives the optimal level of social security benefits in an unfunded system by balancing the gains to myopes against the loss to those who would otherwise have saved optimally.

46. If the mandatory saving level in the funded program is as large as the tax in the pay-as-you-go program, retirement benefits are even higher in the funded program.

47. Feldstein and Samwick (chap. 6 in this volume) assume that the debt is not explicitly stated but that the retirees and existing employees receive the benefits that they have accumulated on the basis of past contributions to the unfunded program. No additional national debt remains after the last of these employees has died. This is equivalent to creating explicit national debt and amortizing it over the life of the youngest current employee.

48. The third section considers the alternative of lower pension contributions (instead of higher retirement benefits).

Table A.1   **Receipts and Payments of Overlapping Generations**

	t	$t + 1$	$t + 2$	$t + 3$
Social security program and participants:				
Unfunded:				
Retirees (benefits)	$+T_t$	$+T_t(1 + \gamma)$	$+T_t(1 + \gamma)^2$	$+T_t(1 + \gamma)^3$
Employees (taxes)	$-T_t$	$-T_t(1 + \gamma)$	$-T_t(1 + \gamma)^2$	$-T_t(1 + \gamma)^3$
Net	0	0	0	0
Privatized:				
Retirees[a]	$+T_t$	$+T_t(1 + \rho)$	$+T_t(1 + \gamma)(1 + \rho)$	$+T_t(1 + \gamma)^2(1 + \rho)$
Employees[b]	$-T_t$	$-T_t(1 + \gamma)$	$-T_t(1 + \gamma)^2$	$-T_t(1 + \gamma)^3$
Debt	0	$-\rho T_t$	$-\rho T_t$	$-\rho T_t$
Net receipts	0	$-\gamma T_t$	$[(1 + \gamma)(\rho - \gamma) - \rho]T_t$	$[(1 + \gamma)^2(\rho - \gamma) - \rho]T_t$

[a]Under the privatized funded plan, retirees receive benefits at time t and then receive the principal and earnings on their savings for all $t > 0$.
[b]Under the privatize funded plan, employees save these amounts.

retirees, the welfare effect depends on the relative magnitude of the future retirement income gains and the future debt service requirements.

In the OLG model of the first section, the privatization process that begins at time t is equivalent to reducing the payroll tax on the current generation of employees by T_t and issuing national debt of T_t. If that generation of employees increases saving by the amount of the tax reduction, this incremental saving is just enough to absorb the additional national debt.[49] The debt service during each period in the future is ρT_t.[50]

Table A.1 shows the first four periods of the sequence of income and saving under the existing unfunded plan and the alternative privatized funded plan. With the unfunded system, taxes and benefits are equal to each other in each period and increase at the rate of growth of aggregate wages (γ). With the privatized funded system, (mandatory) saving is by assumption the same as the employees would otherwise have paid in payroll taxes. Retirees continue to receive transfer funded benefits only in the first period of the transition (at time t) and then receive the income and principle from their private saving. In

49. Although the initial employees are required to save T_t in the mandatory private saving fund, they may reduce (or increase) other saving in response to the income effect of privatization. If capital income taxes distort the lifetime distribution of each individual's consumption, a change in saving induced by these income effects will have a first-order effect on individual lifetime welfare. Taking this into account explicitly would not alter the condition under which privatizing an unfunded social security program raises the present value of consumption, but it would alter the magnitude of the gain.

50. Although the government may pay a net interest rate that is less than the marginal product of capital, the fact that national debt absorbs the private saving (and thereby displaces an equal amount of investment) implies that the lost return is the marginal product of capital. I return in the next section to the relation between the marginal product of capital and the net of tax yields on private securities and government debt.

addition, the existence of the government debt reduces real income (by crowd-ing out private capital) in each period by ρT_t.

Note that, at time t, there is no difference between the outlays and receipts of retirees and employees under the existing unfunded plan and under the alter-native debt-financed funded plan. At $t + 1$, the retirees receive $T_t(1 + \rho)$, an improvement of $(\rho - \gamma)T_t$ in comparison to the unfunded system. But some combination of retirees and employees must also bear the cost of debt service ρT_t. The net effect of privatization on consumption at time $t + 1$ is therefore $-\gamma T_t$.

Table A.1 shows that, while the negative effect of debt service remains con-stant at $-\rho T_t$, the retiree's gain from shifting to a funded plan increases in proportion to the growing level of aggregate wages $(\rho - \gamma)(1 + \gamma)^t$. The effect of privatization eventually shifts from negative to positive. Privatizing the sys-tem raises the present value of consumption if the discounted value of the in-creased retirement consumption $(\sum_{s=1} [\rho - \gamma]T_t[1 + \gamma]^{s-1}[1 + \delta]^{-s})$ exceeds the present value of the debt service $(\sum_{s=1} \rho T_t[1 + \delta]^{-s})$. The present value gain from privatizing is

(A2) $$PVG = \sum_1 (\rho - \gamma)T_t(1 + \gamma)^{s-1}(1 + \delta)^{-t} - \sum_1 \rho T_t(1 + \delta)^{-s}$$

or, equivalently,

(A3) $$PVG = [(\rho - \gamma)/(\delta - \gamma) - \rho/\delta]T_t.$$

Thus, PVG > 0, and privatization raises the present value of consumption only if three conditions are met: $\rho > \gamma$ (the return on capital exceeds the im-plicit return in the unfunded program), $\rho > \delta$ (the capital intensity of the econ-omy is below the welfare-maximizing level), and $\gamma > 0$ (the economy is grow-ing). Why does privatization raise the present value of consumption only when all three conditions are satisfied? First, an unfunded system has an inferior return to employees in each generation only if $\rho > \gamma$. If $\rho \leq \gamma$, the economy is dynamically inefficient, and consumption can be raised permanently by re-ducing the initial capital stock. Even if $\rho > \gamma$, the annual gains $([\rho - \gamma]T_0$ $[1 + \gamma]^t)$ have a present value that exceeds the initial transfer to retirees only if the marginal rate of transformation between present and future consumption exceeds the marginal rate of substitution between consumption in different generations $(\rho > \delta)$. Both are also the necessary conditions for the introduction of an unfunded program to reduce welfare. If they are not satisfied, an un-funded program raises welfare (even if there are no myopic individuals), and replacing it with a funded private program is therefore welfare decreasing.

The additional condition $(\gamma > 0)$ is now required to make the gain from increased retirement income exceed the cost of the additional national debt. A positive rate of growth is important in this context because the annual gain to retirees grows with the size of the economy while the cost of the increased national debt remains constant. If the economy did not grow, the annual gain to the retirees would remain constant at $(\rho - \gamma)T_t$, which, with $\gamma = 0$, is ρT_t, exactly the same as the cost of debt service.

Privatizing social security raises economic welfare only if the economy is growing because only in a growing economy does the shift to a funded program avoid the rising loss of an increasingly large unfunded program in the future. The privatization at time t just substitutes national debt for the existing social security liabilities with no net present value gain, but, in a growing economy, privatization prevents the automatic impositions of a larger inefficient social security program in the future.

For any realistic economy, all three inequalities are likely to be satisfied, and therefore a shift to a funded program is likely to raise economic welfare. The next section discusses the evaluation of γ, ρ, and δ and the implied present value gain from a debt-financed privatizing of the existing U.S. social security retirement benefits.

Parameter Values and the Estimated Net Gain

The values associated with the three key parameters (γ, ρ, and δ) that were discussed in the text of this introductory chapter imply the critical inequalities ($\rho > \delta$ and $\delta > \gamma > 0$) and provide the basis for calculating a theoretical estimate of the net gain from privatizing social security. More specifically, the experience in the United States since 1960 implies $\gamma = 0.026$ and $\rho = 0.093$. The text suggests that the certainty equivalent rate of return that replaces the return to portfolio investors with the yield on government bonds is 6.4 percent, which will be denoted $\rho^* = 0.064$. Finally, the corresponding certainty equivalent for the return on the unfunded program will be written γ^*. If the risk of the social security program is ignored, $\gamma^* = \gamma = 0.026$, while, if social security is deemed to be as risky as portfolio investments, $\rho^* - \gamma^* = \rho - \gamma = 0.093 - 0.026 = 0.067$.

The derivation of equation (A3) for the present value gain from privatizing social security implies that

(A4) $$PVG = [(\rho^* - \gamma^*)/(\delta - \gamma) - \rho^*/\delta]T_0.$$

Note that the γ^* in the numerator refers to the certainty equivalence return in the unfunded social security program. The value of γ in the denominator refers to the effect of the economy's growth on the future size of the program and therefore is not a rate of return subject to a certainty equivalence adjustment.

There are two conceptually different approaches to defining the appropriate rate of intergenerational discounting (δ). The first begins with the view that the generations are linked by family altruism so that the appropriate rate of discount between generations is the same as the rate of discount within generations. This implies that the relevant discount rate is the real net yield that individuals receive. If considerations of risk are ignored, this implies $\delta = (1 - \tau)r_N$, where τ is the marginal individual tax rate, and r_N is the return after corporate taxes but before individual taxes. With a relatively conservative estimate of $\tau = 0.2$, and with $r_N = 0.055$, this approach implies $\delta = 0.044$. If the real net return on government bonds is regarded as a more appropriate risk-adjusted measure, $\delta = r_{GN} = 0.010$. In either case, it is clear that $\rho > \delta$. Using $\delta = r_{GN}$ implies that $\delta < \gamma$ and therefore that the appropriate discount rate is less than the rate of growth of the social security program. In this case, the present values in equations (A1), (A2), and (A3) do not exist; the loss of income of an unfunded social security program $(\rho^* - \gamma^*)T_t(1 + \gamma)^s$ grows faster than the discount factor. But, although the present value is not defined, it is clear that the discounted loss of introducing an unfunded social security program exceeds the value of the initial transfer within a finite number of years. Similarly, the discounted gain from a debt-financed transition to a funded program exceeds the cost within a finite number of years.

The second approach to defining δ rejects the use of a market rate for intergenerational discounting on the grounds that the generations are not linked by operative bequest motives and that the preferences of the current generation should not determine the relative values to be put on consumption in future generations. The rate of discount must therefore be derived from the structure of the utility function. The common assumption of an additive separable constant elasticity utility function implies that $\delta = (\gamma - n)\eta$, where $\gamma - n$ is the rate of increase of per capita incomes, and η is the absolute elasticity of marginal utility.[51]

Between 1960 and 1994, the population growth rate was $n = 0.011$, implying $\gamma - n = 0.015$. Plausible values of the elasticity of the marginal utility function are generally taken to be about $\eta = 2$, implying that $0 < \gamma < \delta < \rho$, the condition that implies a positive but finite discounted value of the gains from a debt-financed shift from an unfunded to a funded social security program. Values of $\eta < 1.7$ imply $\delta < \gamma$ and therefore that the gains from shifting to a funded program grow faster than the discount rate. In this range, the present value gain from a debt-financed shift to a funded program increases without limit as the time horizon is extended. Only an implausibly high $\eta > 4.2$ would imply $\delta > \rho^* = 0.064$ and therefore a net loss from a debt-financed shift to a funded system.

Effect of Constant Benefits and Reduced Taxes

The calculations in the second and third sections may be regarded as unrealistic because they assume that the mandatory saving in a funded system would be as large as the contributions to the unfunded system. That may not occur because it would imply a much higher level of retirement income with no increase in net income during working years. An alternative "extreme" assump-

---

51. Let the social welfare function be $\sum u(c_t)$, where c_t is mean per capita consumption at time t and $u(c_t) = kc_t^{\eta+1}$. Then $1 + \delta = \text{MRS}(c_t, c_{t+1}) = (1 + \gamma - n)^\eta \cong 1 + (\gamma - n)\eta$.

tion is that contributions in the funded program are set to produce the same benefits as in the current unfunded system.

With this assumption, each generation of employees saves the fraction $(1 + \gamma)/(1 + \rho)$ times what it would pay as payroll tax with an unfunded system. This implies that the analogue to equation (A3) is

$$(A5) \quad PVG = \{[(1 + \delta)/(1 + \rho^*)][(\rho^* - \gamma^*)/(\delta - \gamma)] - \rho^*/\delta\}T_t.$$

The difference is that the gross gain (before taking into account the debt service cost) is reduced by a factor of $(1 + \delta)/(1 + \rho^*)$, reflecting the fact that, with the smaller saving, the gain is reduced. If individuals were permitted to supplement mandatory saving and earn the return ρ^*, this reduction could be eliminated.

Other variations on the basic theme could be considered, including debt amortization instead of a perpetual increase in the debt. These have consequences for the intergenerational distribution as well as for the net present value gain.

Rather than consider more such possibilities in this simplified theoretical framework, it is better to study them with actual parameter values (as in Feldstein and Samwick, chap. 6 in this volume). But the current analysis has been sufficient to indicate why gains occur and how, in a qualitative sense, they are related to the rates of growth of wages, the productivity of capital, and the rate of consumption discount.

References

Aaron, Henry. 1966. The social insurance paradox. *Canadian Journal of Economics and Political Science* 32:371–74.

Abel, Andrew, N. Gregory Mankiw, Lawrence H. Summers, and Richard J. Zeckhauser. 1989. Assessing dynamic efficiency: Theory and evidence. *Review of Economic Studies* 56, no. 1 (January): 1–20.

Altonji, Joseph, Fumio Hayashi, and Laurence Kotlikoff. 1992. Is the extended family altruistically linked? Direct tests using micro data. *American Economic Review* 82, no. 5 (December): 1177–98.

Arrow, Kenneth, and R. C. Lind. 1970. Uncertainty and the evaluation of public investment decisions. *American Economic Review* 60:364–78.

Auerbach, Alan, Jagdish Gokhale, and Laurence Kotlikoff. 1991. Generational accounts: A meaningful alternative to deficit accounting. In *Tax policy and the economy*, vol. 5, ed. David Bradford. Cambridge, Mass.: MIT Press.

———. 1994. Generational accounts—a meaningful way to assess the stance of fiscal policy. *Journal of Economic Perspectives* 8:73–94.

Auerbach, Alan, and Laurence Kotlikoff. 1987. *Dynamic fiscal policy.* Cambridge: Cambridge University Press.

Auten, Gerald, and R. Carroll. 1994. Taxpayer behavior and the 1986 Tax Reform Act. Washington, D.C.: Treasury Department, Office of Tax Analysis, July.

Barro, Robert. 1974. Are government bonds net wealth? *Journal of Political Economy* 82 (6): 1095–1118.

———. 1978. *The impact of social security on private saving.* Washington, D.C.: American Enterprise Institute.

Bernheim, Douglas. 1989. A neoclassical perspective on budget deficits. *Journal of Economic Perspectives* 3, no. 2 (Spring): 55–72.

Blinder, Alan, R. Gordon, and David Wise. 1983. Life cycle savings and bequests: Cross-sectional estimates of the life cycle model. In *The determinants of national savings and wealth,* ed. F. Modigliani. New York: Macmillan.

Browning, Edgar. 1987. On the marginal welfare cost of taxation. *American Economic Review* 77, no. 1 (March): 11–23.

Buchanan, James. 1968. Social insurance in a growing economy: A proposal for radical reform. *National Tax Journal* 21 (December): 386–95.

Corsetti, Giancarlo, and Klaus Schmidt-Hebbel. 1996. Pension reform and growth. In *Pensions, privatization, funding and macroeconomic policy,* ed. S. Valdés-Prieto. Cambridge: Cambridge University Press.

Diamond, Peter. 1977. A framework for social security analysis. *Journal of Public Economics* 8:275–98.

Diamond, Peter, and J. Hausman. 1984. Individual savings and retirement behavior. *Journal of Public Economics,* pp. 81–114.

Esposito, Louis. 1978. The effect of social security on saving: Review of studies using time-series data. *Social Security Bulletin,* May, 9–17.

Feldstein, Martin. 1965. The derivation of social time rates. *Kyklos* 18:177–287.

———. 1974. Social security, induced retirement and aggregate capital accumulation. *Journal of Political Economy* 82, no. 5 (September–October): 75–95.

———. 1975. Toward a reform of social security. *Public Interest,* no. 40 (Summer): 905–26.

———. 1977. The social security fund and national capital accumulation. In *Funding pensions: The issues and implications for financial markets.* Boston: Federal Reserve Bank.

———. 1982. Inflation, tax rules and investment: Some econometric evidence. (1980 Fisher-Schultz Lecture of the Econometric Society). *Econometrica* 50, no. 4 (July): 825–67.

———. 1985. The optimal level of social security benefits. *Quarterly Journal of Economics* 10 (May): 303–20.

———. 1987a. Should social security be means tested? *Journal of Political Economy* 95, no. 3:468–84.

———. 1987b. The welfare cost of social security's impact on private saving. In *Modern developments in public finance: Essays in honor of Arnold Harberger,* ed. M. Boskin. Oxford: Blackwell.

———. 1994. Tax policy and international capital flows (1994 Bernhard Harms Prize Lecture). *Weltwirtshaftsliches Archiv* 4:675–97. (Reprinted as Working Paper no. 4851 [Cambridge, Mass.: National Bureau of Economic Research, June 1994].)

———. 1995a. Behavioral responses to tax rates: Evidence from TRA86. *American Economic Review* 85, no. 2 (May): 170–74.

———. 1995b. Fiscal policies, capital formation and capitalism. *European Economic Review* 39:399–420.

———. 1995c. Tax avoidance and the deadweight loss of the income tax. Working Paper no. 5055. Cambridge, Mass.: National Bureau of Economic Research, March.

———. 1995d. Would privatizing social security raise economic welfare? Working Paper no. 5281. Cambridge, Mass.: National Bureau of Economic Research, November.

————. 1996a. The missing piece in policy analysis: Social security reform. The Richard T. Ely Lecture of the American Economic Association. *American Economic Review* 86, no. 2 (May): 1–14.

————. 1996b. Social security and saving: New time series evidence. *National Tax Journal* 49:151–64.

Feldstein, Martin, and Daniel Feenberg. 1996. The effects of increased tax rates on taxable income and economic efficiency: A preliminary analysis of the 1993 tax rate increases. In *Tax policy and the economy,* ed. J. Poterba. Cambridge, Mass.: MIT Press.

Feldstein, Martin, and Charles Horioka. 1980. Domestic savings and international capital flows. *Economic Journal* 90:361–68.

Feldstein, Martin, and Anthony Pellechio. 1979. Social security and household wealth accumulation: New microeconometric evidence. *Review of Economics and Statistics* 61, no. 3 (August): 361–68.

Feldstein, Martin, James Poterba, and Louis Dicks-Mireaux. 1983. The effective tax rate and the pretax rate of return. *Journal of Public Economics* 21:129–58.

Feldstein, Martin, and Andrew Samwick. 1992. Social security rules and marginal tax rates. *National Tax Journal* 45, no. 1: 1–22.

Harberger, Arnold. 1964. Taxation, resource allocation, and welfare. In *The role of direct and indirect taxes in the Federal Reserve System,* ed. John Due. Princeton, N.J.: Princeton University Press.

Kotlikoff, Laurence. 1996. Privatization of social security: How it works and why it matters. In *Tax policy and the economy,* ed. James Poterba. Cambridge, Mass.: MIT Press.

Leimer, Dean, and Selig Lesnoy. 1982. Social security and private saving: New time series evidence. *Journal of Political Economy* 90, no. 3 (June): 606–29.

Mussa, Michael, and M. Goldstein. 1993. *The integration of world capital markets, changing capital markets: Implications for monetary policy.* Kansas City, Mo.: Federal Reserve Bank of Kansas City.

Poterba, James, and Andrew Samwick. 1995. Stock ownership patterns, stock market fluctuations and consumption. *Brookings Papers on Economic Activity,* no. 2:295–357.

Rippe, Richard. 1995. Further gains in corporate profitability. *Economic Outlook Monthly,* August. New York: Prudential Securities.

Samuelson, Paul. 1958. An exact consumption loan model of interest with or without the social contrivance of money. *Journal of Political Economy* 66:467–82.

Seidman, Lawrence. 1983. Social security and demographics in a life-cycle growth model. *National Tax Journal* 36 (June): 213–24.

————. 1986. A phase-down of social security: The transition in a life-cycle growth model. *National Tax Journal* 39, no. 1 (March): 97–107.

I   Country Studies

1 The Chilean Pension Reform: A Pioneering Program

Sebastian Edwards

For decades, the Chilean economy was characterized by a lukewarm performance. Growth was modest, inflation was among the highest in the world, and the degree of social conflict was high. Already in the nineteenth century international observers argued that, despite its natural beauty, the country's economy was unexciting. Some even blamed this state of affairs on the lack of creativity and work ethics in Chileans. This view was vividly expressed in 1885 by H. W. Bates, the assistant secretary of the Royal Geographic Society, when he argued that the typical Chilean was a "half breed of the Spaniard and Indian, and like the inhabitants of all the warmer climates, . . . love[s] best the *dolce far niente*" (p. 379).

Throughout most of the twentieth century the role of the state grew relentlessly in Chile. Regulations were piled on top of regulations, and state-owned enterprises became increasingly important. This heightened government intervention was supposed to accelerate growth and help reduce inequality. Nothing of the sort happened, however. In fact, during the first seven decades of the twentieth century, Chile was a timid performer, experiencing one of the lowest rates of growth in Latin America.

And then in the late 1980s things changed dramatically. As a result of a deep and daring market-oriented reform program initiated in the mid-1970s, the country began to grow at increasingly rapid rates—between 1986 and 1995, the average rate of growth has bordered on 7 percent. Not only has Chile be-

Sebastian Edwards is the Henry Ford II Professor of International Business Economics at the Anderson School, University of California, Los Angeles, and a research associate of the National Bureau of Economic Research.

This is a revised version of a paper presented at the NBER's conference on Privatizing Social Security, held in Cambridge, 1–2 August 1996. The author is grateful to Stephen Zeldes, Martin Feldstein, and the participants of a preconference meeting for helpful suggestions and comments. He thanks Daniel Lederman for his assistance. The author has benefited from discussions with Juan Andrés Fontaine.

come a star performer, but her reforms have attracted considerable attention around the world. More and more analysts are studying the Chilean experiment in order to understand how to move successfully toward a market orientation. Perhaps one of the most admired aspects of the Chilean program has been the reform of the pension system, which replaced an inefficient pay-as-you-go system with a privately administered defined-contribution one.[1] This reform has been credited with helping develop Chile's capital market, with reducing government contingent liabilities, and with helping boost Chile's traditionally anemic saving rate. A large number of pension reforms around the world are now being tailored after Chile's pioneering program. For example, by the mid-1990s, six other Latin American countries had followed Chile's lead and had reformed (to different degrees) their social security systems. More important, perhaps, enough time has elapsed since implementation of the reforms, allowing for an evaluation of the program.

The purpose of this paper is to analyze the most salient aspects of the Chilean program and to evaluate its achievements to date. The paper is organized as follows: Section 1.1 provides a brief background of the Chilean reform effort. Section 1.2 deals with Chile's old pay-as-you-go system, including its degree of (in)efficiency, its distributive characteristics, and its fiscal consequences. Section 1.3 is the core of the paper; it deals with the reforms per se, focusing on the functioning of the system. Section 1.4 concentrates on the system's results to date. Section 1.5 discusses transitional issues, including the fiscal consequences of the reforms. Section 1.6 deals with the effects of the reforms on labor markets and saving. Finally, section 1.6 contains concluding remarks.

1.1   The Chilean Market-Oriented Reforms: A Brief and Selective Overview

The Chilean market-oriented structural reform program was initiated in 1975, ten years prior to the launching of the rest of the Latin American reforms. The program was based on three basic policy measures: (a) a drastic opening of the economy; (b) an ambitious privatization and deregulation program; and (c) a stabilization based on a predetermined nominal exchange rate anchor, supported by (largely) restrictive fiscal and monetary policies. Table 1.1 contains a summary of the policies undertaken during the first ten years of the Chilean reforms.[2]

Chile opened up its economy to international competition in the mid-1970s. After decades of protectionism, import licenses were fully abolished, and import tariffs were reduced from an average that exceeded 100 percent to a uni-

1. As I point out in sec. 1.1, as is the case with most Latin American systems, the Chilean system was not created as a pay-as-you-go system. Originally, the accumulation of reserve funds was contemplated. In reality, however, it quickly became a de facto pay-as-you-go system. Throughout the paper, thus, I will refer to it as such.

2. On the Chilean reforms, see Harberger (1985), Edwards and Edwards (1991), and Bosworth, Dornbusch, and Labán (1994).

Table 1.1   **Chile's Structural Reforms: An Overview**

Item	Description
Trade liberalization	Major unilateral opening during 1975–79. All quantitative restrictions eliminated; uniform import tariff of 10% established. Temporary hike in tariffs in mid-1980s; since 1987, uniform import tariff of 11%.
Privatization	Two rounds of privatization: 1974–79 and 1984–89. During first round, banks were privatized first, followed by manufacturing firms. First round ended in crisis in 1982, with a number of major banks being nationalized. During second round, efforts made to establish regulatory framework before firms and banks were sold. By 1994, approximately 96% of state-owned enterprises had been privatized. Some major firms, including the giant copper producer CODELCO, remain under government control.
Fiscal reform	Major tax reform in 1975. Value-added tax introduced. Personal and corporate income taxes consolidated. Significant improvement in administrative capacity. Fiscal accounts balanced since 1977. Tax rates revised in mid-1980s in order to encourage saving.
Financial reform	Sweeping reform was begun in 1975 with privatization of banks. Interest rate controls and forced credit allocation were eliminated. Reserve requirements were drastically reduced, and entry into banking sector was encouraged. Securities markets received a major boost as a result of social security reform. Supervisory framework weak until mid-1980s; significantly strengthened since then.
Social security	Insolvent pay-as-you-go system replaced by individually capitalized system run by private administrators. Health system transformed into a two-tier system: a basic one for lower-income people and an insurance-based system for most workers.

form 10 percent level. As a result of Chile's integration with the rest of the world, local firms were forced to increase their degree of productivity. By the early 1990s, Chile's exports were booming and had clearly become the country's engine of growth.

Between 1974 and 1992, the Chilean government privatized more than five hundred firms. This process was carried out in two rounds—the first during the mid- and late 1970s and the second during the mid- and late 1980s. These two efforts were separated by a brief interlude, between 1982 and 1984, when there was a partial reversal in the process and the government had to take over more than fifty banks and firms.

The first round of privatization (1974–82) had two distinct components. The first was the return of firms seized by the Unidad Popular during 1970–73 to their original stockholders.[3] The second consisted of the sale of a large number

3. These firms had not been nationalized. The Allende administration used an obscure piece of legislation from the 1930s to "intervene" in the business of companies whose products were in "short supply." For details, see Edwards and Edwards (1991). See also Larraín and Meller (1991).

of banks and firms to the private sector. Some of these companies had been nationalized during the Allende administration, while others had traditionally been under government control. In an effort to sell large number of companies fast, the government made no effort to restructure them before offering them to the public. Many of these firms were in serious financial difficulties, and all of them had major productivity problems. It was expected that buyers would implement the necessary steps to improve efficiency. To that effect, the government placed very few restrictions on the buyers' ability to lay off redundant workers.

During the second round of privatization, started in 1985, the authorities' main objectives were to reduce very significantly the size of the government and to spread ownership. The first step in this second round consisted of reprivatizing those firms that had failed during the financial crisis of 1982. This time, however, the government did not provide credit and carefully checked the financial credentials of prospective buyers. Financial institutions (including two of the largest banks) were privatized through a scheme known as "popular capitalism," under which private individuals were allowed to buy a limited amount of shares—up to U.S.$7,000 at a discounted value.[4]

In the late 1980s, the Chilean government greatly broadened the scope of privatization by selling large public utilities and firms that had always been in government hands, including the largest steel mill, the national airline, and most utilities—telephones, electricity, water. During this phase, the government exercised great pragmatism, combining different modes of privatization even for a given firm. Shares were sold—usually at a discount—to workers, to foreigners, to local private companies, and to the newly created pension funds.

During the second phase of privatization, the Chilean government introduced sweeping regulatory reforms. Particularly important were the laws establishing operating and servicing rules for utilities. The main principle behind this new set of regulations was that entry and price setting would be left to the market in those areas with a high degree of competition or contestability. The government would regulate technical aspects—including those related to safety—and price setting in areas where markets were imperfect.

In an effort to shield the real sector from the effects of inflation, in the 1970s the Chilean authorities developed a comprehensive indexation program for the financial sector. At the heart of this mechanism was the creation of a unit of account called *unidad de fomento* (UF), whose value changes daily according to (one-month) lagged inflation. Starting in the mid-1980s (and until the time of this writing), virtually every financial contract exceeding ninety days has been expressed in terms of UFs. As a result of this, interest rates on longer-term securities are generally expressed (and negotiated) in real terms in an ex ante fashion. This, as will be seen below, has added an important component of predictability to Chile's capital market and to the privately managed pensions system.

---

4. For details, see Lüders (1991).

Many observers forecasted that the new Chilean democratic government that took over in 1990 would put an end to the divestiture process and would even repeal some of the privatizations of the military regime. However, nothing of this kind happened. In fact, after some heated debate on the subject, the government of President Aylwin decided to *continue* the privatization process (see *El mercurio* [international edition], 7–14 January 1993).

By the mid-1990s, Chile's market-oriented reforms had become consolidated, as the leaders of virtually every political party agreed with the merits of the new system. The country was growing at a rapid and steady rate, unemployment was around 5 percent, and poverty was in retreat. Foreign observers, marveling at the country's transformation, continued to analyze the sources of this success story. More often than not, they pointed to the pension reform as one of the central elements of the Chilean miracle.[5]

1.2 Chile's Traditional Pay-as-You-Go Pension System

As was the case with most Latin American countries, Chile adopted a social security system in the 1920s. The original system was not, as it has often been argued, a pure pay-as-you-go one. During its early years, when contributions made by active workers exceeded pension payments, it was based on the collective capitalization of funds. As the system became more mature, it was expected that increasing obligations would be met both by drawing on these funds and by increasing active workers' contributions. Accumulated funds, however, were poorly managed, and benefits—especially for the more well-to-do—escalated quickly. As a result, the system ran into serious financial difficulties and, increasingly, relied on the government to meet its obligations. For all practical purposes, and in spite of the original intentions of its founders, by the 1970s the system had become an insolvent pay-as-you-go regime.

One of the most important characteristics of the old system was its lack of uniformity. There were more than one hundred different retirement regimes. While some workers could retire with a very high pension at forty-two years of age, blue-collar workers could retire only once they turned sixty-five, and yet others could retire at fifty-five with a full pension. Some pensions were not subject to an automatic cost-of-living adjustment. Senior bureaucrats, however, got a 100 percent–plus–inflation adjustment, as they maintained, through life, a pension equal to the salary paid to an active worker in a position similar to the last one they held. After fifty years of operation, and contrary to its architects' intentions, the system had become increasingly unfair. While upper- and middle-class workers were able to reap substantial benefits, poorer workers continued to face tough requirements to obtain a pension that was largely eroded by inflation. As a consequence of inflation and mismanagement, between 1962 and 1980 the average pension paid to a blue-collar worker had declined by 41 percent.

---

5. See, e.g., the Americas column in the 28 June 1996 issue of the *Wall Street Journal.*

Chile's traditional retirement system was characterized by very high contribution rates. In 1973, for example, total contributions—by employers and employees—varied between 16 and 26 percent of wages, depending on the type of job the individual held. By 1980, total contributions had been reduced to an average of 19 percent of (taxable) wages.[6] What made things worse was that there was almost no connection between retirement contributions and (perceived) benefits. In that regard, then, these contributions were largely seen as taxes on labor and contributed significantly to the poor performance of the country's labor market during the 1960s and 1970s (Cox-Edwards 1992).

Demographic trends worked steadily against Chile's traditional retirement system. While in 1955 there were twelve active contributors per retiree, this figure had declined to 2.5 by 1979. As a result of this and of highly inefficient management, the Chilean system became increasingly unfunded. By the early 1970s, the system as a whole was already running a dramatic deficit. The gap between revenues and outlays—administrative costs plus pensions—was made up by the public sector. By 1971, the central government's contributions to the system were already 4 percent of GDP, and the present valued of the system's contingent liabilities exceeded 100 percent of GDP.[7]

In 1981, the military government decided to introduce a sweeping reform of the retirement system. The decision to undertake the reform responded to four considerations: (a) the explosive fiscal consequences of the old regime; (b) the high degree of inequality of the old system; (c) its implied efficiency distortions; and (d) an ideological desire to reduce drastically the role of the public sector in economic affairs. Interestingly enough, in explaining the reform, the Chilean authorities barely referred to the (potential) effects of the new system on domestic savings.[8]

1.3   The Chilean Social Security Reform

On 4 November 1980, Chile's military government approved decrees 3,500 and 3,501, which drastically reformed the country's social security system.[9] In a speech delivered on 6 November 1980, Minister of Labor José Piñera explained that the goal of the reform was to create a retirement system based on

6. There has been some confusion as to the actual level of contributions in the old system. The reason for this is that these rates have traditionally been quoted as a social security aggregate, covering pensions, health, and disability. Total contributions were 54.4 percent in 1973 and were reduced to 37.6 percent in 1980 (Larraín A. 1995). The rates quoted above refer to pensions only.

7. For an analysis of the flow deficit of the system, see Myers (1988) and Cheyre (1988). I have used data reported by them and by Larraín A. (1995) to calculate the magnitude of the present value of the system's unfunded liabilities.

8. The father of the reform, then minister of labor José Piñera, has provided a fascinating account of the political economy of the reform (see Piñera 1991).

9. Paradoxically, 4 November 1980 was the tenth anniversary of President Salvador Allende's inauguration. President Allende had also promised to reform the country's social security system. His program, of course, was radically different from that of the military and called for an even greater role for the public sector.

"freedom, and solidarity; a fair and yet efficient retirement system; a retirement system for everyone." He went on to say that the reform was a "transcendental step that would benefit every Chilean, within the spirit of freedom, progress and justice" (Piñera 1988, 318).

From a political point of view, the launching of the reforms faced some difficulties. First, many interest groups—including public-sector workers, teachers, and workers in the health sector—firmly opposed any changes. Representatives of these groups realized early on that their best option was to line up the support of high-ranking military officers. They were partially successful, as for many months some key members of the (ruling) armed forces opposed the project. Second, the notion of a collectively funded, "solidarity-based" retirement system was deeply ingrained among intellectuals and the public. José Piñera, the father of the reforms, has pointed out that, owing to stiff opposition, the implementation of the reform had to be postponed for almost a full year. It was only in 1980 that Piñera and his team were able to persuade a reluctant General Pinochet of the merits of the project. The general himself, however, was not fully successful in convincing his military colleagues. The armed forces did not join the new system—an option not available to any other group in the country. As a way to increase the appeal of the new system and reduce political opposition, the architects of the plan determined the new contribution rates so as to increase net take-home pay for those joining the new system. On average, those who transferred to the privately run capitalization system experienced an 11 percent increase in after-tax pay (Iglesias and Vittas 1992). This increase in take-home earnings was engineered largely as a way of making the reforms popular and generating an incentive to encourage workers to shift voluntarily to the new system. At the same time, it was expected that, given the anticipated higher rates of return on the accumulated funds, the lower contributions would be enough to finance higher rates of replacement for pensions.

Despite some political difficulties, there is no doubt that, given the dictatorial nature of the Chilean government of the time, the authorities faced a significantly lower degree of political opposition than they would have encountered in a democratic regime. Some authors have, in fact, argued that, owing to the political considerations in most Latin American countries, it is not feasible to implement a Chilean-type reform (Mesa-Lago 1996).

1.3.1 Fundamental Aspects of the Reform

The reform of Chile's social security system replaced a basically insolvent pay-as-you-go regime with a capitalization system based on individual retirement accounts managed by private companies known as *administradoras de fondos de pensiones* (AFPs).[10] Each AFP can manage only one retirement fund,

---

10. In the reformed system, the state plays a fundamental role regulating and monitoring the operation of the management companies and guaranteeing "solidarity in the base" through a mini-

Table 1.2	Chile: Key Legal Requirements for AFPs
Initiating operations	*a)* Authorization by the Superintendency of AFPs *b)* Minimum capital requirement: UF5,000 (approx. U.S.$160,000)
Mandates	*a)* Manage *one* pension fund *b)* Provide and administer *only* the benefits permitted by law
Minimum capital and reserve requirements	*a)* Minimum capital requirements grow with the number of affiliates: UF10,000 for 5,000–7,499 affiliates, UF15,000 for 7,500–9,000 affiliates, and UF20,000 for 10,000 or more affiliates *b)* Reserve requirement: 1% of value of pension fund *c)* Minimum revenue rate: (1) the average, annual real revenue rate of all pension funds minus 2 percentage points, or (whichever is less); (2) 50% of the average, annual real revenue rate
Permitted investments	*a)* In firm's shares (stocks): (1) permitted in 1985, up to 5% of pension fund assets or of a firm's total shares, whichever was less; (2) since 1989, limit expanded to up to 7% of pension fund assets and maximum ownership of 1% of a firm's shares *b)* In foreign instrument: (1) permitted since 1990, but guidelines issued in mid-1992; (2) permitted to invest a small percentage of total assets in low-risk, fixed-return instruments issued by foreign banks or governments

and there is a strict separation between the retirement fund and the management firm's assets. This one-fund-per-AFP rule, in conjunction with a regulation that establishes a minimum rate of return on the funds, has resulted in a low degree of actual portfolio diversification across AFPs.

Workers have the freedom to choose the AFP with which they want to be affiliated and can transfer their funds freely among AFPs. When they retire, they can choose to buy an annuity or to withdraw their funds according to a predetermined (actuarially fair) plan.[11] The system also has survivors' benefits (term life insurance) and a disability program funded with an additional insurance premium. A detailed and modern regulatory framework—enforced by an institution especially created for this purpose, the Superintendency of AFPs—regulates investment portfolios and ensures free determination of fees and commissions and free entry into the industry. The Superintendency of AFPs established from the first day very precise norms to secure the diversification and transparency of AFP investments (for a list of key legal requirements for operating an AFP, see table 1.2).

Since its inception, the new Chilean retirement system has gone through a

mum pension. An important feature of the new social security system is that it is obligatory, requiring that all non-self-employed workers make contributions equal to 10 percent of their disposable income.

11. At this time, there are not enough (available) data to analyze the efficiency of the annuities market. There have been some claims, however, that these still have a very high price, one that exceeds the actuarially fair price (see Vittas 1995).

number of changes. Between November 1980 and August 1995, there have been thirty modifications made to the original legal texts. Of the ninety-seven permanent articles of decree 3,500, only twelve have not been modified during the first fifteen years of the reforms (Sequeira 1995). In this subsection, I describe in some detail the evolution of the system during its first fifteen years. In the subsections that follow, I deal with issues related to investment regulations, accumulated funds, and rates of return.

Coverage and Contribution Rates

Workers employed in the formal sector are required by law to participate in the retirement system. They must contribute, to the AFP of their choice, 10 percent of their wages. These funds are invested by the AFP and are accumulated in an individual retirement account. Participants can switch management funds up to four times a year.

There is an additional contribution of (approximately) 3 percent of wages as a premium for term life and disability insurance. Both these contributions are subject to a maximum wage base, which is currently equivalent to approximately U.S.$2,000 per month.[12] Self-employed workers are not required to participate in the system. They have the choice, however, to establish retirement accounts that are (basically) subject to the same regulations as those of formal-sector employees.

In analyzing the degree of coverage of the reformed Chilean system, it is important to distinguish between those workers who are *affiliated* to the system—that is workers who have, at one time or another, enrolled in an AFP—and those who are active *contributors* to the system. While the percentage of individuals affiliated to the system is very high—almost 99 percent of the labor force—the percentage of active contributors is significantly smaller, in 1995 standing at 58 percent of those employed. In addition, in 1994, those still affected by the old system represented 5.5 percent of total employment. The total coverage of the Chilean retirement system amounted, then, to 63.5 percent of the employed, approximately the same percentage as in the traditional system.

The relatively low percentage of active contributors is one of the most important weaknesses of the system and is explained by two basic factors: first, the self-employed are not required to participate in the system and, for a variety of reasons, including tax considerations, have no incentives to make voluntary contributions.[13] Second, the existence of a government-guaranteed (universal) minimum pension creates a moral hazard situation among low-income workers, many of whom are self-employed (for more details, see the discussion below). In their case, it pays to contribute only sporadically and only enough to obtain the minimum pension once they retire.

12. The amount of the maximum "pensionable" salary is set in UFs, Chile's indexed unit of account. The limit is sixty UFs per month. In October 1996, this was equivalent to U.S.$1,901.

13. Although, as explained below, voluntary contributions are (up to a limit) tax deductible, by contributing to an AFP a self-employed worker is revealing information to tax authorities.

Table 1.3   Chile: Evolution of the Pension Funds

Year	U.S.$Million[a]	% of GDP	Funds' Growth Rate (%)
1981	276.43	.86	
1982	871.00	3.36	215.12
1983	1,582.14	5.97	81.62
1984	2,062.68	7.88	30.38
1985	2,881.54	10.22	39.69
1986	3,775.84	12.48	31.04
1987	4,625.50	14.49	22.49
1988	5,640.05	15.39	21.94
1989	6,970.49	18.46	23.59
1990	9,243.57	24.73	32.61
1991	13,082.19	32.17	41.53
1992	14,587.29	32.24	11.50
1993	18,744.30	39.39	28.50
1994	22,663.69	41.18	20.91
March 1995	22,076.19		−2.59

Source: Bustamante Jeraldo (1995).
[a]March 1995 dollars.

Tax Treatment and Voluntary Contributions

In addition to the required contributions, employees can make voluntary contributions to the AFP that holds their retirement account.[14] Voluntary contributions have a limit of U.S.$2,000 per month. Required contributions are tax deductible, as is the income accrued to the accumulated fund during the contributor's active life. Voluntary contributions, on the other hand, are not tax deductible. Income accrued to voluntarily contributed funds is, however, free of taxes. Once workers retire, however, their pension becomes subject to income tax, as with any other source of income.

Despite tax incentives and the splendid financial result of the AFPs (for details, see below), the volume of voluntary funds has remained very small. Although by December 1994 there were more than 800,000 voluntary accounts, the total voluntary funds accumulated in the system amounted to only 1.4 percent of total funds (Fuentes Silva 1995).

1.3.2 Accumulated Funds, Investment Rules, and Rates of Return

The volume of pension funds privately managed by the AFPs has increased dramatically since 1981. As can be seen in table 1.3, between 1985 and 1995 they increased from 10 to almost 43 percent of GDP. Furthermore, recent simulations suggest that, by the year 2010, the accumulated funds will represent 110 percent of GDP and that, by 2020, they will have reached 134 percent of GDP (Fuentes Silva 1995).

From early on, the authorities tightly regulated the type of assets the funds

14. There is no special treatment for married couples.

could invest in. This regulation has taken the form of maximum limits on hold-ings of a particular type of financial instrument. The rationale for these limits has been safety. Initially, and especially given the opposition to the reform by influential members of the armed forces, the economic authorities decided that it was essential that the funds be invested mostly in high-grade securities. Dur-ing the early years, funds were largely restricted to government securities—with a limit of 100 percent of the fund—bank deposits, investment-grade cor-porate bonds, and mortgage bonds. In 1985, AFPs were allowed to invest in equities. Although the limit on equities was theoretically set at 5 percent of the funds, strict restrictions on the type of issuing firm seriously limited the AFPs' ability to invest in equities. In fact, during the second half of the 1980s, most funds invested exclusively in equities of firms that were being privatized. As a result of these restrictions, by the end of 1986 the AFPs had invested in only six stocks, representing less than 4 percent of the total fund.

By 1989, some of these restrictions were lifted, and most AFPs increased their equities positions significantly. At that time, equities from twenty-three firms were being held by the AFPs, adding up to 11 percent of the aggregate funds. However, more than 90 percent of the AFPs' equities portfolio was made up of only eight recently privatized firms. In 1989, AFPs were also al-lowed to invest in real estate, and, in 1992, they were permitted to invest up to 9 percent of the fund in foreign securities. Surprisingly, perhaps, there has been a very limited interest in investing in foreign instruments. By December 1995, less than 1 percent of the accumulated funds had been invested abroad.

As can be seen in table 1.4, rates of return on the accumulated funds have

Table 1.4   Chile: Annual Real Rates of Return of the Pension Fund System (%)[a]

Year	Weighted Avg.[b]	Range	Median
1982	28.8	23.2–30.2	27.6
1983	21.2	18.5–24.7	20.8
1984	3.6	2.2–5.1	3.5
1985	13.4	13.0–14.3	13.4
1986	12.3	10.6–15.5	12.4
1987	5.4	4.8–8.5	5.4
1988	6.5	5.9–8.7	7.1
1989	6.9	4.0–9.5	7.9
1990	15.6	13.3–19.4	17.0
1991	29.7	25.8–34.3	30.8
1992	3.0	.9–4.2	3.0
1993	16.2	14.6–16.9	16.1
1994	18.2	15.7–21.1	18.2
1995[c]	−4.7	−6.6−−3.5	−4.8

Source: Banco Central de Chile, *Boletín mensual* (various issues).

[a]Annual nominal change deflated by the indexed unit (UF) variation of the period.

[b]Weighted by the value of each AFP's assets.

[c]From December 1994 to November 1995.

been nothing short of spectacular. This has been largely the result of Chile's economic circumstances during this period. Between 1985 and 1995, Chile has experienced a period of tremendous growth, the value of assets, and in particular firms, increasing at a very fast rate. Additionally, between 1985 and 1991, real interest rates were very high, allowing funds that invested in fixed-income securities to experience very healthy returns. A recent study of the sources of AFPs' rates of return shows that the return on the stock of two electric utilities (Enersis and Endesa) explains almost 40 percent of the total return of the funds (Valck V. and Walker H. 1995). It is highly likely that, in the years to come, both interest rates and stock market returns will move closer in line with international levels, affecting the rate of return of pension funds. In fact, during 1995 and 1996, the AFPs have experienced, on average, a negative real return.

The Chilean system imposes a lower limit to the return that AFPs must pay their members. This minimum is either 50 percent of the average return across AFPs or 2 percentage points below the average—whichever is higher. Those AFPs that do not obtain this minimum return from their portfolio must make up the difference from funds withdrawn from an "investment reserve" especially set up for this purpose. This "reserve" must amount to at least 1 percent of the total value of the fund and is invested in a portfolio that exactly mimics that of the fund. If an AFP cannot meet a profitability shortfall out of its reserves, it is liquidated. The state makes up the difference between the actual and the minimum guaranteed return, and contributors transfer their funds to another AFP.

There is also a maximum allowable return, determined as 50 percent or 2 percentage points over the average across AFPs. Those companies that exceed the maximum have to deposit the excess funds in a "profitability reserve," which is part of the fund's (and not the management company's) assets. If in a subsequent year the AFP's portfolio underperforms, this reserve can be used to make up the difference between the actual and the minimum return.

The combination of the "one fund per AFP" and the minimum/maximum profitability rules has resulted in AFPs having extremely similar portfolios. In fact, as table 1.4 shows, the dispersion in returns has been very small. Although this homogeneity of results may have some political appeal—no group of participants will appear as being taken advantage of—it introduces nontrivial economic distortions. In particular, and as will be discussed in greater detail below, it increases the administrative costs of running funds and does not allow people with different tolerances for risk to have different portfolios.

1.3.3   Administrative Costs and Concentration

A number of critics of the Chilean social security reform have argued that a privately run system based on free choice is exceedingly costly. In particular, it has been argued that a system that allows—in fact, encourages—frequent transfers of funds across AFPs will tend to overspend in advertising and in sales. It has been proposed that a better solution would be either to have a public-sector institution manage the retirement funds or to restrict the participants' ability to transfer their funds across AFPs (Diamond 1994; Mesa-Lago 1996).

Fees and commissions are determined freely by the AFPs. Currently, they are allowed to charge the following fees: a proportional fee on contributions; a fee for opening a new account; a fee for managing programmed pension withdrawals; a fee for managing voluntary contributions; and a flat fee per period when contributions are made. In recent years, however, most AFPs have waived the flat fee (Vittas 1995). In addition to these fees, AFPs were allowed, until 1987, to charge a management fee on every account, including those of inactive workers. On the other hand, and in order to encourage competition, AFPs are not allowed to charge an exit fee.

Initially, administrative costs were extremely high. In 1984, for example, they amounted to 9 percent of wages, or 90 percent of contributions to the retirement system! By 1994, however, costs had declined significantly, amounting to 1 percent of wages or 10 percent of contributions. In spite of these high costs, the new capitalization system is significantly more efficient than the old pay-as-you-go regime. For example, Bustos (1995) has calculated that the total costs of the new regime are 42 percent lower than the average costs of the old system.

In terms of accumulated assets, administrative costs have declined from almost 15 percent in 1983 to 1.8 percent in 1993, including sales costs.[15] In spite of these relatively high administrative costs, the net return to participants for the system as a whole exceeded 10 percent in real terms during the first fifteen years of the system. Vittas (1995) has argued that, although Chilean administrative costs as a percentage of assets are not very different from those of U.S. and U.K. insurance companies, they are significantly higher than the costs incurred by government-run provident funds in Singapore and Malaysia—0.1–0.2 percent of accumulated assets.

Marketing and sales costs represent an important percentage of total administrative costs. Valdés-Prieto (1994), for example, has estimated that, in 1991, marketing and sales costs exceeded one-third of total costs. Margozzini Cahis (1995), on the other hand, has calculated that sales costs averaged 20 percent of total costs, with marketing costs representing an additional 3 percent. Moreover, there is evidence that, in the last few years, these costs have increased significantly. The total sales force for the system, for example, has increased from thirty-five hundred in 1990 to almost fifteen thousand in early 1995. All in all, sales costs as a percentage of total costs have more than doubled between 1988 and 1995.

Some critics of the Chilean reform have argued that limiting the frequency with which participants can switch funds provides an efficient way of reducing administrative costs and thus increasing the net return that accrues to contribu-

---

15. On the cost structure of AFPs, see, e.g., Margozzini Cahis (1995).

tors. However, since the cost of opening a new account represents a high percentage of the cost of transferring funds, a more effective solution—and one that would maintain individual's choice—would be to allow AFPs to manage more than one retirement fund. In this way, individuals could transfer their retirement savings to different funds, within the same AFP, at a reduced cost. Moreover, the elimination—or, at least, modification—of the minimum return requirement would increase the degree of competition among AFPs and would allow individuals with different attitudes towards risk to choose the type of fund that better suits their preferences.

When the new retirement system was launched in 1981, there were twelve pension management firms. By 1995, the total number had increased to twenty-one AFPs. In spite of relatively free entry, the industry has a nontrivial degree of concentration. In 1990–94, for example, 68 percent of all workers were affiliated to the three largest AFPs. The degree of concentration has declined considerably, however. According to a World Bank study, the Herfindahl concentration index fell from 2,200 in 1981 to 1,260 in 1994 (Vittas 1995).

During the first fifteen years of operation of the new system, AFPs have been, on average, highly profitable. Their average (real) return on equity has averaged 16.6 percent over a decade and a half, peaking in 1989–91, when it exceeded 35 percent per year. This high return, however, hides significant differences across AFPs. For example, in 1994, eleven of twenty-one AFPs incurred losses that in some cases bordered 50 percent of equity (see Margozzini Cahis 1995; and Vittas 1995).

1.3.4 Government Guarantees

Although the Chilean system is based on individually capitalized accounts managed by private firms, the government retains an important role that goes well beyond regulating and supervising the system. First, the government guarantees a minimum pension to poorer participants in the system. Those individuals who have contributed to the system for at least twenty years, and whose accumulated funds cannot cover a minimum pension, receive from the state a transfer that raises their pension to that minimum.

The value of the minimum pension is adjusted by inflation every time the accumulated change in the CPI reaches 15 percent. This means that, at the current level of inflation, minimum pensions get adjusted once every two years. Minimum pensions are currently equal to 25 percent of average wages and 75 percent of the minimum wage. In the past, they have been as low as 61 percent of minimum wages (in 1982) and as high as 91 percent of minimum wages (in 1987). The government also guarantees the minimum pension to those individuals who, having opted for a pension based on programmed withdrawals, outlive the program and exhaust their accumulated funds.

Second, and as explained in the preceding subsection, the government guarantees a minimum return on accumulated funds. If an AFP underperforms significantly and the funds in its reserves accounts—both the investment and the profitability reserves—are insufficient to bring the actual return to the minimum level, the government covers the difference. As pointed out, in this case the AFP is liquidated, and the participants transfer their funds to another institution. Third, the government also guarantees pension payments (up to a limit) in case an insurance company goes bankrupt.

In addition to its involvement in these areas, the Chilean government also makes pension payments to those individuals who, either by choice or because of their age, did not transfer to the new system. As is discussed in detail below, the cost of paying these pensions has been significant, exceeding, in some years, 4 percent of GDP.

From a policy point of view, the involvement of the government in providing and guaranteeing pensions means that, contrary to what has often been argued, the Chilean system relies on the "three pillars" recommended by the World Bank in its report *Averting the Old Age Crisis* (1994). There are, however, two main differences between the Chilean system and those in operation (or contemplated) in other countries: (*a*) in Chile, the "public pillar" plays the role of a provider of last resort; (*b*) in Chile, the obligatory capitalization pillar is privately managed. The government guarantees described above introduce a minimum sense of "solidarity" into the system. They do this, however, at the cost of introducing significant elements of moral hazard. In particular, there is an incentive for (lower-income) individuals to minimize their contributions and to obtain the minimum pension. An easy way to reduce this problem would be to establish some relation between guaranteed pension level and years of contributions. This means that, instead of a single guaranteed minimum pension, there would be a guaranteed pension "band," with those with, say, twenty years of contributions at the bottom of the band and those with thirty or more years of contributions at a higher level.

1.4   Pensions under the New System

One of the objectives of the Chilean pension reform was to increase the real value of pensions, especially for the poorer groups in the country (see Piñera 1988). Under the traditional system, retirement requirements and pension levels were determined in a discretionary fashion and, largely, responded to political influence. Under the new system, the value of pensions depends on the amount of funds accumulated. The new system established a retirement age of sixty-five years for men and of sixty years for women. As I discuss below, there is, however, the possibility of early retirement. When individuals retire, they can choose between two systems: they can use the accumulated funds to buy an annuity from an insurance company, or they can choose to enroll in a "programmed withdrawal" scheme, where the accumulated funds are drawn according to an actuarially determined schedule. Both these options have advantages and disadvantages. Under the programmed withdrawal alternative, any balance left when contributors die is inherited by their heirs. Also, under this program, retirees can continue to transfer their balance across AFPs, thus taking advantage of perceived (and expected) differentials in rates of return. Additionally, if individuals outlive the program and their fund is used up, they get the minimum pension for the rest of their life. Annuities, on the other hand, assure retirees a steady and known income stream for the rest of their life. In the case of annuities, however, there are no inheritance provisions, and fees have tended to be somewhat high.

Recent data based on a sample of 4,064 individuals who have retired under the new system suggest that the average replacement rate has amounted to 78 percent (Baeza Valdés and Burger Torres 1995).[16] Interestingly enough, the highest (relative) pensions have been obtained by those individuals who have opted for early retirement, with a replacement rate of 82 percent under programmed retirement. Baeza Valdés and Burger Torres (1995) attribute this result to the fact that only those that have had rapid accumulation of funds—mostly by making voluntary contributions—can in reality opt for early retirement. Disability pensions—which, as explained earlier, are financed with a 3 percent of wages insurance premium—have also had high replacement rates, reaching 67 percent. Finally, survivors' benefits have reached a 71 percent replacement rate. These replacement rates are significantly higher than the average for the old system—only 50 percent in 1980.

The system also allows for early retirement. However, this becomes an option only once the fund is high enough to produce a pension that covers at least 70 percent of the contributor's current salary. Those opting for early retirement can also choose between programmed withdrawals and annuities. By 1994, there were already 200,000 retirees receiving pensions under the new system. Of these, approximately half had opted for annuities and half for programmed withdrawal.

There is also the possibility of lump sum withdrawals. To qualify for this option, two requirements must be met: (a) the pension must have a replacement rate of at least 70 percent; and (b) the pension must be at least equal to 120 percent of the minimum pension. Although there are no exact figures on the percentage of individuals who have opted for lump sum payments, Baeza Valdés and Burger Torres (1995) discovered that 24 percent of the contributors in their sample had taken advantage of this option. They calculated that, when these payments are taken into account, the effective rate of replacement of the new system increases to 84 percent.

The coexistence of old- and new-system retirees allows for a direct comparison of pensions under the pay-as-you-go and capitalization systems. To December 1994, average old age pensions under the capitalization system were 42 percent higher than those under the pay-as-you-go regime. In the case of

---

16. These authors calculated the replacement rate on the basis of average real salary in the 120 months preceding retirement.

disability, pensions under the new system were 61 percent higher than under the old one.

Naturally, given the nature of Chile's capitalization system, it is not possible to know exactly how future pensions will compare with those currently being paid. One can expect, however, two forces that will operate in opposite directions in the future. On the one hand, a lower rate of return on the funds will reduce pension payments. On the other hand, if the steady-state rate of return is higher than 4 percent—the return of the recognition bond, which represented a large percentage of the current retirees' fund—we could expect a positive effect on pensions paid in the future.

The actual rate of replacement has differed slightly between annuities and programmed withdrawals. Baeza Valdés and Burger Torres (1995) found out that, for early retirement, the annuities scheme resulted in a replacement rate of 78 percent, while programmed withdrawal resulted in a replacement rate of 83 percent. For standard old age pensions, however, annuities yielded a replacement rate of 74 percent, while programmed withdrawal resulted in a replacement rate of 83 percent.

An important (indirect) effect of the reform is that it has encouraged the development of an active annuities market. Largely as a result of the pension reform, insurance companies' assets as a percentage of GDP have increased by more than four times between 1985 and 1995. Annuities, however, are currently very expensive, costing almost 4 percent of the value of the contract. This aspect of the system has generated important criticisms, including calls that, as a way of reducing cost, group purchases of annuities and greater regulation of the industry be allowed.

1.5   Transitional Issues

Dealing with the transition is one of the key policy questions in designing a pension reform program that replaces a pay-as-you-go system with a capitalization one. The transition poses three basic problems: (*a*) The first problem is determining the transfer rule for workers. Which workers will join the new system, and which ones will stay with the old one? Will workers have a choice? (*b*) The second is devising a method for crediting funds to those workers who transfer to the new system but who have already made contributions to the old system. (*c*) The third is financing pension payments to old-system retirees. Once contributions from active workers are pulled out of the old system and channeled to the individual capitalization accounts, the old system becomes completely unfunded.

The new Chilean pension law (title 15, article 1) established that workers who joined the labor force before 31 December 1982 had five years to decide whether to join the new system. Those joining the labor force after that date could not participate in the old system and had to become affiliated with an

AFP of their choice. Since those who joined an AFP experienced an immediate increase in net take-home pay of 11 percent, the number of people transferring to the new regime was very high. By the end of 1982, more than a million workers, representing 36 percent of total employment, had already transferred to the new system.

The government dealt with past contributions of transferees by issuing bonds that were deposited in their individual AFP accounts. The rationale for this was to "recognize" past contributions—the bonds therefore became known as *recognition bonds*—and to provide the basis for the new retirement fund. These bonds yielded a 4 percent return in real terms, significantly below the ex post market return, and, until 1995, could not be traded in the secondary market.

In order to be eligible to receive a recognition bond, an individual must have made at least twelve monthly contributions to the old system during the previous five years. The actual value of the recognition bond was calculated by using a rather complicated formula, consisting of the following steps: (*a*) The average annual base wage used to determine contributions made to the old system prior to 30 June 1979 was multiplied by 0.8. (*b*) This number was then multiplied by the ratio of total years of contributions to thirty-five (thirty-five years being the assumed number of working years for obtaining a "normal" pension). (*c*) The resulting number was multiplied by 10.35 for males and by 11.36 for females. (*d*) The number resulting from this calculation was then multiplied by a factor that varied according to the individual's age and gender. For males, the factor varied between 1 and 1.11; for females, it varied between 1 and 1.31.

At this point, it is illustrative to make some actual calculations using this formula. Assume first the case of a thirty-five-year-old male whose average pensionable salary was U.S.$6,000 per year and who had been contributing to the old system for fifteen years. In this case, the value of the recognition bond to be deposited in his new AFP account would be U.S.$20,292.[17] Consider now the case of a forty-five-year-old female with an average pensionable salary of U.S.$6,000 and twenty-five years of contributions. Her recognition bond would amount to U.S.$40,896. Recognition bonds yield 4 percent in real terms and can be redeemed when the individual retires, dies, or becomes disabled. In the case of our hypothetical male worker, at age sixty-five the value of the recognition bond would be U.S.$70,000; for our female participant, the recognition bond would have a value at retirement—recall that women retire at sixty—of almost U.S.$74,000. An interesting calculation refers to the hypothetical value of the recognition bond for a sixty-five-year-old individual who has contributed for thirty-five years to the old system. In a way, this number would reflect the authorities' implicit valuation of a lifetime of contributions to the system. In

17. Strictly speaking, this is only an approximation since the recognition bond was expressed in UFs, the Chilean indexed unit of account.

Table 1.5   **Chile: Fiscal Effect of Social Security Reform; Its Effect on the Deficit of the Old System (% of GDP)**

Year	Cash Deficit	Recognition Bonds	Total
1981	1.47	.01	1.48
1982	4.08	.11	4.19
1983	4.58	.22	4.80
1984	4.55	.25	4.80
1985	4.27	.30	4.57
1986	4.33	.41	4.74
1987	4.35	.49	4.84
1988	4.23	.50	4.73
1995	3.10	.80	3.91
2000	2.57	.94	3.51
2005	1.84	.99	2.83
2010	1.19	.80	1.99
2015	.80	.40	1.20

Sources: Ortúzar (1988) and IMF estimates.

the case of a male worker, this lifetime hypothetical recognition bond would be 9.198 times his average annual base salary. In the case of a woman, the hypothetical value of the lifetime recognition bond would be 11.905 times the base salary if she had worked thirty-five years and 10.205 times the base salary if she had worked thirty years (recall, once again, that women retire at age sixty).

From a fiscal point of view, the reform generated two major sources of public expenditures: (a) the servicing and payment of the recognition bonds and (b) the payment of retirees in the old system. Table 1.5 contains data on the fiscal costs of the transition. The first column contains information on the deficit (as percentage of GDP) stemming from the government's obligations toward "old" retirees. These include both those already retired when the reform was enacted and those who chose not to switch to the new system. Since most of the "cash" costs are related to pensions due to people who had already retired in 1981, these costs peaked rather early, in 1983, when they represented 4.58 percent of GDP. In fact, given life expectancy in Chile, these costs start declining rather rapidly after 1995. The second column in table 1.5 presents data on the cost of servicing and paying the recognition bonds (for details on the recognition bonds, see sec. 1.5 below) that were deposited in active workers' retirement accounts. The time path of the recognition bonds' costs is explained by the country's demographics. The pattern of projected retirements is such that the value of maturing bonds peaks in 2005.

Chile has opted to finance these costs directly out of general government revenues. In fact, one of the most attractive features of the Chilean reform is that it made the costs of old age security very transparent. The government had to recognize sizable unfunded liabilities and provide for their payment. Some authors have argued that, since these costs are, indeed, quite large, Chilean-style reforms cannot be replicated in other countries (Mesa-Lago 1996). This, however, is not clear a priori and will depend on a number of economic, financial, and especially political factors. Ultimately, the question is one of costs and benefits. Is it worthwhile maintaining a compulsory, and in most cases largely inefficient, government-run pay-as-you-go system alongside a privately managed one, in order to avoid the fiscal costs of the transition?[18]

1.6   Effects on Capital Markets, Saving, and Labor Markets

The Chilean pension reform has had important effects on the overall functioning of the economy. Perhaps one of the most important of these is that it has contributed to the phenomenal increase in the country's saving rate, from less than 10 percent in 1986 to almost 29 percent in 1996. This effect has taken place mostly through an increase in public-sector saving—public saving has increased from close to 0.1 percent of GDP in 1983 to more than 5 percent of GDP by 1993. A number of researchers have established that increasing public-sector saving represents the most effective way of increasing aggregate saving. In general, higher public saving unleashes a virtuous circle, where higher saving generates higher growth and higher growth (in turn) results in higher private saving (Edwards 1996). Whether the Chilean reform has actually increased private saving directly is still somewhat of an open question. Although cross-country regression analyses suggest that pension reform affects private saving, there still are no definitive studies of the Chilean case.[19] Haindl (1996), however, has recently attempted to estimate econometrically the effects of the reform on private-sector saving. Using an approach based on the inclusion of a series of dummy variables in a time-series analysis of the determinants of saving, he concludes that the reform indeed contributed to the increase in saving.[20] In a more ambitious attempt, Morande (1996) uses modern time-series analysis to estimate an error-correction model of saving for Chile. He concludes that there is preliminary evidence supporting the notion that the reform of the pension system encouraged private-sector saving. Finally, Bosworth and Marfan (1994) have argued that the contribution of the pension reform to the increase in saving bordered 3 percent of GDP.

Pension funds are the largest institutional investors in the Chilean capital market, with assets exceeding 40 percent of GDP, as compared to 0.9 percent in 1981. The asset composition of pension funds is described in table 1.6. As discussed above, the performance of AFP portfolios has been impressive in

18. This is the avenue chosen by some Latin American countries, such as Argentina.
19. On cross-country studies of saving and social security, see, e.g., Feldstein (1980) and Edwards (1996).
20. Haindl's (1996) analysis, however, is subject to a number of shortcomings, including the presence of a serious simultaneity bias.

Table 1.6   **Chile: Pension Fund Assets per Financial Instruments (% as of December of each year)**

Year	Securities	Time Deposits, Financial Institutions	Credit Notes, Financial Institutions	Corporate Bonds	Firms Shares	Investment Funds	Foreign Instruments[a]
1981	38.1	61.9	9.4	.6	.0	.0	.0
1982	26.0	26.6	46.8	.6	.0	.0	.0
1983	44.5	2.7	50.7	2.2	.0	.0	.0
1984	42.1	13.3	42.9	1.8	.0	.0	.0
1985	42.4	21.3	35.2	1.1	.0	.0	.0
1986	46.6	23.3	25.5	.8	3.8	.0	.0
1987	41.4	28.5	21.3	2.6	6.2	.0	.0
1988	35.4	29.5	20.6	6.4	8.1	.0	.0
1989	41.6	21.5	17.7	9.1	10.1	.0	.0
1990	44.1	17.5	16.1	11.1	11.3	.0	.0
1991	38.3	13.3	13.4	11.1	23.8	.0	.0
1992	40.9	11.1	14.2	9.6	24.0	.2	.0
1993	39.3	7.6	13.1	7.3	31.8	.3	.6
1994	39.7	6.3	13.7	6.3	32.2	.9	.9
1995[b]	40.7	6.0	16.0		36.9[c]	.4[d]	

Sources: Valck V. and Walker H. (1995) and Banco Central de Chile, *Boletín mensual,* January 1996.

[a]As of May 1993, AFPs began to invest in foreign instruments.
[b]November 1995.
[c]Corporate bonds plus firms' shares.
[d]Investment funds plus foreign instruments.

Table 1.7   **Chile: Annual Real Rates of Return on the Financial System and on Individual Pension Accounts, 1981–90 (%)**

Year	Financial System	Returns to Pension Account[a]
1981	13.2	5.3
1982	12.1	25.5
1983	7.8	19.4
1984	8.4	2.4
1985	8.2	11.6
1986	4.1	10.9
1987	4.3	4.5
1988	4.6	6.1
1989	6.8	6.7
1990	9.4	15.7
Average, 1981–90	7.8	10.4

Source: IMF, based on data provided by Chilean authorities.

[a]For the average assessable income. These returns are lower than the average for the AFPs (reported in table 1.1) owing to the existence of commissions for fees paid by asset holders.

terms of real rates of return, and, as shown in table 1.7, the returns to individual pension accounts have been higher (on average) than for the financial system as a whole. The massive amount of funds that AFPs control has helped create a dynamic and modern capital market. What is perhaps more important, however, is that it has allowed private firms to rely on long-term financing for their investment projects. This has been particularly important for the privatized utilities. Moreover, Chile's new and ambitious (privately funded) infrastructure program will be possible only if there is long-term financing available, of the type the AFPs are able of providing.

The pension reform has also had an important effect on the functioning of the labor market. First, by reducing the total rate of payroll taxes, it has reduced the cost of labor and, thus, has encouraged job creation. Second, by relying on a capitalization system, it has greatly reduced—if not eliminated—the labor tax component of the retirement system. Currently, (most) workers see their contributions as a deferred compensation rather than as a tax. A key question, however, is whether there is still an element of taxation involved in the system. This will depend on a number of factors, including the rate of return on the funds, the perceived future pension income, the magnitude of management fees, the degree of risk aversion, and the rate of discount of workers. Diamond and Valdés-Prieto (1994) have argued that, although it is likely that the new system still retains some implicit tax, this is substantially lower than in the old system.[21] Cox-Edwards (1992) has also argued that the Chilean pension reform

21. A modern and well-functioning labor market has been an important element of Chile's economic success. It has allowed for rapid job creation and has resulted in the reduction of a rate of unemployment that bordered 25 percent to one below 6 percent of the labor force.

system has resulted in a significant reduction in effective taxes on labor. She has argued that this has contributed to the surge in employment creation in Chile as well as to the rapid increase in (average) real wages since 1985.

1.7 Concluding Remarks

The Chilean pension reform program has been a pioneer in the world. It has successfully replaced an inefficient, unfair, insolvent pay-as-you-go system with a (reasonably) well-functioning privately managed system. Until now, the rates of return of the new system, as well as the pensions being paid out, have been very high. This trend, however, is likely to change in the years to come as Chile's rates of return begin to converge toward world levels. In fact, during the last eighteen months (1995 and the first half of 1996), the system as a whole has experienced negative returns. An interesting issue is how the system will react to this new state of affairs. The most likely scenario, in my opinion, is one where some of the current shortcomings of the system—including the limitation for multiple funds and the distortionary incentives generated by the government—will be addressed by the authorities. It is not unlikely, then, that the Chilean system will continue to evolve, providing fresh lessons in the future.

References

Baeza Valdés, Sergio, and Raúl Burger Torres. 1995. Calidad de las pensiones del sistema privado chileno. In *Quince años despues: Una mirada al sistema privado de pensiones,* ed. S. Baeza Valdés and F. Margozzini Cahis. Santiago: Centro de Estudios Públicos.

Bates, H. W. 1885. *Stanford's compendium of geography and travel: Central America, the West Indies and South America.* London: Edward Stanford.

Bosworth, Barry P., Rudiger Dornbusch, and Raúl Labán, eds. 1994. *The Chilean economy: Policy lessons and challenges.* Washington, D.C.: Brookings.

Bosworth, Barry P., and Manuel Marfán. 1994. Saving, investment and economic growth. In *The Chilean economy: Policy lessons and challenges,* ed. Barry P. Bosworth, Rudiger Dornbusch, and Raúl Labán. Washington, D.C.: Brookings.

Bustamante Jeraldo, Julio. 1995. Principales cambios legales al DL 3.500 en el período noviembre 1990–mayo 1995 y desafíos pendientes. In *Quince años despues: Una mirada al sistema privado de pensiones,* ed. S. Baeza Valdés and F. Margozzini Cahis. Santiago: Centro de Estudios Públicos.

Bustos, Raúl. 1995. Reforma a los sistemas de pensiones: Peligros de los programas opcionales en América Latina. In *Quince años despues: Una mirada al sistema de pensiones,* ed. Sergio Baeza y Francisco Margozzini. Santiago: Centro de Estudios Públicos.

Cheyre, Hernán. 1988. Análisis comparativo del antiguo régimen de pensiones y del nuevo sistema previsional. In *Sistema privado de pensiones en Chile,* ed. Sergio Baeza and Rodrigo Manubens. Santiago: Centro de Estudios Públicos.

Cox-Edwards, Alejandra. 1992. Economic reform and labor market legislation in Latin America. California State University. Mimeo.

Diamond, Peter. 1994. Privatization of social security: Lessons from Chile. *Revista de análisis económico* 9, no. 1 (June): 21–34.

Diamond, Peter, and Salvador Valdés-Prieto. 1994. Social security reforms. In *The Chilean economy: Policy lessons and challenges,* ed. B. Bosworth, R. Dornbusch, and R. Labán. Washington, D.C.: Brookings.

Edwards, Sebastian. 1996. Why are Latin America's savings rates so low? An international comparative analysis. *Journal of Development Economics* 51, no. 1:5–44.

Edwards, Sebastian, and Alejandra Edwards. 1991. *Monetarism and liberalization: The Chilean experiment.* 2d ed. Chicago: University of Chicago Press.

Feldstein, Martin. 1980. International differences in social security and saving. *Journal of Public Economics* 14 (October): 225–44.

Fuentes Silva, Roberto. 1995. Evolución y resultados del sistema. In *Quince años despues: Una mirada al sistema privado de pensiones,* ed. S. Baeza Valdés and F. Margozzini Cahis. Santiago: Centro de Estudios Públicos.

Haindl, Erik. 1996. Chilean pension fund reform and its impact on savings. Working paper. Universidad Gabriela Mistral, Santiago.

Harberger, Arnold. 1985. Observations on the Chilean economy, 1973–1983. *Economic Development and Cultural Change* 33 (April): 451–62.

Iglesias, A., and D. Vittas. 1992. The rationale and performance of personal pension plans in Chile. Working paper no. 867. Washington, D.C.: World Bank.

Larraín, Felipe, and Patricio Meller. 1991. The socialist-populist Chilean experience: 1970–1973. In *The macroeconomics of populism in Latin America,* ed. Rudiger Dornbusch and Sebastian Edwards. Chicago: University of Chicago Press.

Larraín A., Luis. 1995. El sistema privado de pensiones y el desarrollo económico. In *Quince años despues: Una mirada al sistema privado de pensiones,* ed. S. Baeza Valdés and F. Margozzini Cahis. Santiago: Centro de Estudios Públicos.

Lüders, Rolf. 1991. Massive divestiture and privatization: Lessons from Chile. *Contemporary Policy Issues* 9 (October): 1–19.

Margozzini Cahis, Francisco. 1995. La industria de las AFP. In *Quince años despues: Una mirada al sistema privado de pensiones,* ed. S. Baeza Valdés and F. Margozzini Cahis. Santiago: Centro de Estudios Públicos.

Mesa-Lago, Carmelo. 1996. Las reformas de las pensiones en América Latina y la posición de los organismos internacinales: Comentario a la propuesta de la CEPAL. Working Paper. Washington, D.C.: World Bank.

Morande, Felipe. 1996. Savings in Chile: What Went Right? Working Paper no. 322. Washington, D.C.: Inter-American Development Bank, Office of the Chief Economist.

Myers, Robert. 1988. Privatización en Chile del sistema de seguridad social. In *Sistema privado de pensiones en Chile,* ed. Sergio Baeza and Rodrigo Manubens. Santiago: Centro de Estudios Públicos.

Ortúzar, P. 1988. El déficit previsional: Recuento y proyecciones. In *Sistema privado de pensiones en Chile,* ed. S. Baeza Valdés and R. Manubens. Santiago: Centro de Estudios Públicos.

Piñera, José. 1988. Discurso del ministro del trabajo y previsión social con motivo de la aprobación de la reforma previsional. In *Sistema privado de pensiones en Chile,* ed. S. Baeza Valdés and R. Manubens. Santiago: Centro de Estudios Públicos.

———. 1991. *El cascabel al gato: La batalla por la reforma previsional.* Santiago: Zig-Zag.

Sequeira, Francisco. 1995. Una visión sobre el desarrollo legal. In *Quince años despues: Una mirada al sistema de pensiones,* ed. Sergio Baeza y Francisco Margozzini. Santiago: Centro de Estudios Públicos.

Valck V., Eugenio, and Eduardo Walker H. 1995. La inversión de los fondos de pensiones: Hitoria, normativa y resultados. In *Quince años despues: Una mirada al sistema privado de pensiones,* ed. S. Baeza Valdés and F. Margozzini Cahis. Santiago: Centro de Estudios Públicos.

Valdés-Prieto, Salvador. 1994. Cargos por administración en los systemas de pensiones de Chile, Los Estados Unidos, Malasia y Zambia. *Cuadernos de economía* 93 (August): 185–227.

Vittas, Dimitri. 1995. Strengths and weaknesses of the Chilean pension reform. Washington, D.C.: World Bank.

World Bank. 1994. *Averting the old age crisis: Policies to protect the old and promote growth.* New York: Oxford University Press.

Comment   Stephen P. Zeldes

Before the last presidential election, President Clinton was interviewed on television by Tom Brokaw. One of the topics discussed was social security reform, and Brokaw asked the president what he thought about the option of privatizing Social Security. Surprisingly, the president answered the question. He said that he was skeptical about mandatory privatization but thought that optional privatization merited study. He added, "But before we do something that totally changes something that's worked rather well, there ought to be a way to test it in kind of a laboratory sense. And I would favor looking at it very closely with some evidence before we made a big, sweeping decision" ("Transcript of Interview" 1996).

Sebastian Edwards provides an excellent description of the partial privatization of social security that was put into place in Chile in 1980 and continues today. In a very clear and careful way, the paper describes the economic environment prior to privatization, the transition plan, the mechanics of the current system, and the economic effects of changing systems. The focus of my discussion will be on what we can learn from the Chilean experience about privatizing social security elsewhere in the world and in particular in the United States. Specifically, does this provide us with what Clinton and many others want—"a way to test [privatization] in . . . a laboratory sense"?

There are a number of people, including José Piñera, the "father" of the Chilean reform, who claim that it does provide a test and that it has been wildly successful. The clear implication is that the United States should try to replicate the Chilean reforms.

This paper cries out for a sequel that examines whether this is true. In other words, now that we know what went on in Chile, what can we learn from Chile

Stephen P. Zeldes is the Benjamin Rosen Professor of Economics and Finance at the Graduate School of Business, Columbia University, and a research associate of the National Bureau of Economic Research.

Table 1C.1   **Comparing the Initial Situations in Chile and the United States**

Initial Feature/Situation	Present in Chile in 1980?	Present in the United States Now?
Government-controlled/administered defined-benefit plan?	Yes	Yes
Unfunded/pay-as-you-go system?	Yes (unfunded liability ≈ 100% of GDP)	Yes (unfunded liability ≈ 100%–200% of GDP)
Lack of uniformity of treatment?	Yes	Yes, but significantly less so
Falling ratio of workers to beneficiaries?	Yes	Yes
Benefits progressive? (higher rate of return for poorer individuals)	No (regressive)	Yes (probably)
Thin capital markets?	Yes	No
Large federal budget surplus?	Yes	No
Military regime in power?	Yes	No

about privatizing social security in the United States?[1] While I cannot answer that question, I do have some suggestions as to how it might be approached.

First, to draw implications about the United States from Chile, it is important that the structures of the economies and the initial conditions be similar. To what extent is this true? Second, if the economies and initial conditions are similar, then this suggests that what worked in Chile might very well work in the United States. Therefore, we need to ask what worked in Chile and what did not. This will help us determine whether privatization would be a good thing for the United States and, if so, which aspects of the Chilean program should be kept, which dropped, and which modified.

Table 1C.1 compares the initial situations in Chile in 1980 and in the United States today. The key similarities are the presence of an unfunded, pay-as-you-go government-administered defined-benefit plan and past and forecasted future declines in the ratio of workers to beneficiaries. There is some lack of uniformity in social security benefit formulas across households in the United States, but significantly less so than was the case in Chile. Major differences are that the Chilean system was regressive, with high-income households getting a better deal than low-income households, while the reverse is true in the United States.[2] Chile had very thin capital markets, while the United States has one of the best-developed capital markets in the world. Chile began with a large federal budget surplus, while the United States is running a budget deficit. Finally, the Chilean reform was instituted by a military government, a feature not present in the United States.

1. For work along these lines, see, e.g., Diamond (1994).
2. However, the tendency of high-income households to live longer than low-income households makes the system less progressive than it at first appears.

The key aspects of the new Chilean system are the following: (1) Recognition bonds were issued to cover the implicit liabilities, with interest and principal financed out of general revenues. (2) Mandatory contributions are set equal to 10 percent of wages. (3) Self-employed workers are not required to participate. (4) There are a small number of regulated AFPs with one fund each; portfolio choices available to households are very limited. (5) There is a regulated minimum and maximum rate of return (based on the average return across all AFPs), and there are restrictions on the assets held by the AFPs. (6) Unlimited switching between AFPs is allowed. (7) The government guarantees a minimum pension. (8) Individuals have a choice between annuitization and controlled withdrawals on retirement.

Privatization of the public pension system in Chile has been deemed a large success. Why is this? First, individuals have received high ex post returns on the system. Second, it has given people a greater sense of security, by reducing political risks about future benefits. Third, the system is more uniform and thus considered more progressive and more fair. Fourth, it has been followed by higher economic growth, higher government and national saving, and lower unemployment.

Which of these benefits are real ones for Chile?[3] Although I do not have all the answers, I raise the following questions. Regarding the first, how much of the high ex post return was due to the reform, how much to other economic changes, how much to luck, and how much to the fact that the transition costs were financed out of general revenue rather than from within social security (thus making returns appear higher than they were)? Regarding the fourth, how can we better estimate the quantitative effects of public pension reform? Although the paper describes the positive economic developments that occurred after 1980, it is unfortunately very difficult to disentangle the effects of social security reform from those of the other very large reforms that occurred simultaneously. For example, Edwards begins by describing the extensive privatization of government-owned businesses and the reduction of import tariffs and government controls that occurred at about the same time as the public pension reform. How are we to tell what the economic effects would have been if only the pension reform had been undertaken (or if the other changes had occurred without pension reform)?

What of the disadvantages of the Chilean reform (relative to the previous system)? The primary one seems to be high (but declining) administrative costs.

Which of these advantages and disadvantages would be relevant for the United States? Again, this is a topic that requires substantial additional work, but here is some speculation. As in Chile, the reduction in political risk would likely be substantial. It is likely that higher national saving would occur only if there were an increase in taxes (to pay interest and possibly repay principal

---

3. The following is based in part on Mitchell and Zeldes (1996).

on the "recognition bonds") or a cut in benefits or government spending. Labor supply distortions would be reduced (although less than in Chile because of the initial conditions), and, unlike in Chile, this would lead to a less progressive system with less earnings insurance. The high degree of success of the private annuity markets in Chile might very well carry over to the United States. Because stock and bond markets are already very extensive and deep, however, there would be minimal expansion or deepening of these markets. The high administrative costs would likely carry over to the United States, although it is unlikely that they would be as high as in Chile since in the United States markets are many times larger and mutual funds already have extensive experience.

Finally, there are some things that we cannot learn from Chile, including one of the questions most frequently raised about privatization in the United States. How would individuals, especially currently unsophisticated investors, respond to increased portfolio choice? Would they appreciate the added flexibility, and would they make "wise" choices? Having been denied genuine portfolio choice in their individual accounts, Chileans have not been given the opportunity to provide us with evidence on this crucial question. This is because all AFPs in Chile must invest in essentially the same portfolio or risk running afoul of rate-of-return restrictions and asset ceilings set by law.

Overall, this paper is very well done and will be a terrific resource for those working in the area of social security reform. I hope that there is a sequel that explores in detail what the Chilean experience can teach us about the effects of privatizing the U.S. social security system.

References

Diamond, Peter. 1994. Privatization of social security: Lessons from Chile. *Revista de Análisis Económico* 9, no. 1 (June): 21–34.

Mitchell, Olivia S., and Stephen P. Zeldes. 1996. "Social security privatization: A structure for analysis." *American Economic Review* 86, no. 2 (May 1996): 363–67.

"Transcript of Interview of President Clinton by Tom Brokaw of MSNBC." 1996. U.S. Newswire, 15/16 July.

Discussion Summary   Jeffrey Liebman and Andrew Samwick

The discussion began with one participant claiming that a country's budget position at the time of the privatization is not relevant to whether the privatization will increase national saving. He said that the benefits of the increased

Jeffrey Liebman is assistant professor of public policy at the John F. Kennedy School of Government, Harvard University, and a faculty research fellow of the National Bureau of Economic Research. Andrew Samwick is assistant professor of economics at Dartmouth College and a faculty research fellow of the National Bureau of Economic Research.

saving exist regardless of whether the budget is in surplus or deficit. It was further added that the saving response might be even *larger* if the budget was in deficit because politicians might be tempted to spend surpluses to achieve political rather than economic objectives. The author agreed with the claim that Chile's surpluses were political liabilities and described the way in which the government actually had to hide them from the military during Chile's transition. It was also pointed out that a budget surplus might facilitate the transition in a country like Chile, which was still in the process of a macroeconomic stabilization plan to reduce inflation. In addition to providing credibility, the budget surplus might allow the privatization to occur without a subsequent increase in taxes that might cause the privatization to be derailed once under way.

The discussion then turned to characteristics of the Chilean system of AFPs that manage the pension accounts. Many people remarked that the system of regulations that restricts participants to one account, AFPs to one fund, funds to a limited set of investment vehicles, and annual returns to lie within a very narrow band might encourage herding by AFP managers. Concern was then expressed regarding the effect of switching AFPs on administrative costs, especially since the AFPs all seem to invest in very similar portfolios yet devote substantial resources to marketing their funds. When asked why workers switch between AFPs given the similarity of returns, the author explained that the plans offer free toasters, green stamps, and sneakers to people who switch to their plan.

Another distinctive feature of the Chilean reform was the high returns achieved by the AFPs in the early years and the lower and even negative returns in recent years. The author acknowledged that much of the high return in the early years came from the holdings of two public utility companies that undertook the huge investment in infrastructure that occurred as part of Chile's overall stabilization policy. The high returns on these long-term bonds will not continue indefinitely. There has been no public outcry about the negative returns yet, but participants pointed out the risk of political pressure to "top off" returns in bad years. Proposals have been made to allow a broader range of investment options, including global funds that had previously been proscribed, to keep returns high.

The effects of Chile's history of high inflation were also acknowledged to have played a role in the privatization. High inflation eroded the value of the previous systems' funds. The low expectations that workers had for their future benefits may have made privatization an easier policy to accept. Chile is now a completely indexed country, and the new system was therefore able to provide real annuities and indexed benefit levels.

Concerns were also raised about potential leakages from the system leading to poverty in old age. For example, the self-employed are not required to participate in the system. Although some are wealthy, the welfare system provides minimal benefits, equal to approximately 40 percent of the minimum wage.

About 99 percent of the population has made at least one monthly contribution to an AFP. However, owing to the fact that some people are out of the labor force, unemployed, or self-employed, only 58 percent are actively contributing. The author noted that, because of this discrepancy, the rate of coverage is not much higher under the new system than it was under the old. Although poverty has been declining among the elderly lately, this likely has been due to high rates of overall economic growth.

The discussion ended by acknowledging the beneficial effect of the privatization on capital markets in Chile. Preliminary studies on the effect of the privatization on saving seem to suggest that private saving rose slightly while national saving increased substantially. Additionally, the market for long-term corporate securities has developed in large part to meet the demands of the AFPs.

2   Australia's Retirement Income System

Malcolm Edey and John Simon

2.1   Basic Features of the Australian System

Australia is currently in the early stages of introducing a system of self-provision for retirement through mandatory contributions to private superannuation funds. The system will take several decades to mature, but, when it does, it will substantially replace the government age pension, currently relied on by a large majority of retirees. Since the government pension is unfunded,[1] the overall transition represents a move from a predominantly unfunded to a predominantly funded basis for retirement incomes over the next few decades. In making this transition, Australia is one of relatively few countries moving toward a funded scheme, and it is almost unique in adopting a system that is government mandated but privately operated. The purpose of this paper is to outline the basic features of the Australian system and its historical background and to give some analysis of its possible effect on saving and capital markets.

The current policy has been put in place through a series of initiatives, to be elaborated on in section 2.2, that began in the mid-1980s. The various initiatives did not follow a preannounced plan but nonetheless have progressively established an overall timetable for phased increases in mandatory saving that now has bipartisan political support. The first main step was the introduction of a mandatory employer contribution to approved superannuation funds on behalf of each employee, set initially at 3 percent of salary. Subsequent policy decisions have provided for these to be increased to 9 percent of salary when

Malcolm Edey is head of economic analysis at the Reserve Bank of Australia. John Simon is a research economist at the Reserve Bank of Australia and a graduate student at the Massachusetts Institute of Technology.

The authors thank colleagues at the Reserve Bank of Australia for helpful comments and assistance in preparation of this paper.

1. That is, it is noncontributory and funded from general revenue.

the timetable is fully implemented in the 2002–3 financial year. Additional voluntary contributions are also possible. Although the maximum level of compulsory contributions is thus scheduled to be reached in only a few years from now, it will be some decades before the system matures in the sense of yielding maximum retirement incomes. Because final benefits for each individual will depend on the amount of savings they accumulate, the maximum level of benefits accruing from the compulsory contributions will not be attained until retirement of the first generation with an entire working life under the new system.

The superannuation funds that receive the compulsory contributions are, in contrast those to many countries, privately run and managed. They are also typically defined-contribution plans. In introducing the new scheme, the government has been able to take advantage of the existence of an already-large superannuation sector, which handled voluntary savings of predominantly high-income earners. This has meant that the compulsory scheme has been able to make use of a well-developed financial infrastructure already in place. In effect, the government has decided to expand a savings vehicle in use by a minority through the introduction of mandatory contributions for all employees.

Traditionally, the main source of government provision for retirement income in Australia has been a flat-rate age pension, which provides a means-tested payment generally indexed to 25 percent of average weekly earnings. This pension has existed for several decades and will remain in place as a safety net for those who do not accumulate sufficient private provision under the new system. The pension is funded from general government revenue and has never been contributory or related to an individual's previous income. Although the pension is means tested and, in that sense, regarded as a safety net, it is currently the main source of income for more than 60 percent of retirees.

To provide an international context for the Australian system, figure 2.1 gives a simple taxonomy of possible retirement schemes.

Many industrial countries have opted for various forms of unfunded but contributory defined-benefit schemes. A common characteristic of such schemes is that end benefits are related to an individual's contributions record but that those benefits are not funded from contributions in an actuarial sense. This gives rise to a quasi-contractual set of unfunded liabilities of the social security system for future pensions. For countries with this type of system, an important consideration in any transition to a funded scheme concerns the treatment of these existing unfunded liabilities.

In Australia, the transition envisaged is quite different since the existing government pension is flat rate and noncontributory and does not involve unfunded liabilities in the same way as social security schemes in other countries.[2] The

---

2. Governments do, however, have considerable unfunded superannuation liabilities to their own employees. The total unfunded liability to employees of all levels of government in Australia is estimated to be around $100 billion, or around 20 percent of GDP.

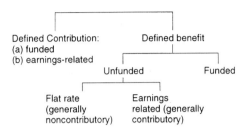

Fig. 2.1   Taxonomy of retirement schemes

transition to a substantially reduced reliance on the government pension will occur as a gradual consequence of the accumulation of private savings as the new defined-contribution scheme matures. Application of the existing means test will eventually ensure reduced eligibility for the government pension, as privately provided retirement incomes are raised.

The country that bears the closest similarity to the new Australian scheme would seem to be Chile, which also requires compulsory contributions to approved private funds. However, in contrast to Australia, Chile had a preexisting contributory pension with associated unfunded liabilities and has therefore had significantly different transitional issues to deal with. Another important difference has been that Chile allows individual choice of the fund, whereas in Australia the choice is typically made by employers or unions; however, this is to change as a result of recently announced measures to allow greater individual choice.

2.2   Background and Objectives

Australia first introduced an age pension in 1909. It was designed for poverty alleviation rather than as a comprehensive income support and was tightly means tested. Subsequently, however, the means tests were gradually relaxed, and the system took on more of the nature of a general entitlement. The take-up rate increased substantially, from around 30 percent when first introduced to a peak of around 85 percent in the mid-1980s; this has since fallen slightly, partly as a result of various measures to tighten eligibility since that time.[3] Although the pension provides a relatively low level of income support, its value is increased by a variety of health and public transport subsidies for which pensioners are also eligible, and there is some scope to earn supplementary private income. Also, in contrast to many countries, the large majority of elderly people own their own homes. The prominent role of the age pension across all but the highest income groups in the elderly population is illustrated by the summary of household characteristics presented in table 2.1.

---

3. For a discussion of this history, see Department of Social Security (1983) and Gruen (1985).

Table 2.1   **Households Where Head of Household Is over 65: Characteristics by Income Quintiles**

	1	2	3	4	5	Total
Average weekly household incomes ($)	129.16	196.73	273.21	351.19	790.81	348.68
Proportion of income from government benefits (%)	106.40	84.60	84.90	66.50	22.30	54.40
Average number of persons per household	1.11	1.08	1.83	1.89	2.32	1.65
Proportion of households in group that own house outright (%)	71.00	67.30	80.00	79.70	87.70	77.10

Source: Household Expenditure Survey, 1993–94, Australian Bureau of Statistics.

Voluntary superannuation has long been an important source of retirement income for a minority, mainly high-income earners and public-sector employees. As is common in many countries, voluntary superannuation savings benefited from generous tax treatment. Employer contributions and earnings on accumulated contributions were essentially tax free prior to 1983, subject only to a final tax on 5 percent of the accumulated lump sum at retirement. The tax benefit was particularly valuable for taxpayers on high marginal tax rates, but it was not necessarily attractive for low-income earners for whom a significant factor in savings decisions could be the potential effect on entitlement for the government pension. Tax concessions for superannuation were substantially curtailed in 1983 with the introduction of a 30 percent tax on lump sum benefits accrued after that date, and the system was further tightened by changes made in 1988 and subsequent years, including the introduction of a tax on fund earnings. Nonetheless, the tax treatment of superannuation remains concessional in a number of ways that are discussed further below.

The move to a system of compulsory superannuation had its origin in centralized wage negotiations that took place in 1985 and 1986. The federal government agreed to support a claim by the Australian Council of Trade Unions (ACTU) for a 3 percent employer-provided superannuation benefit to be incorporated in employment awards in lieu of a general wage increase. This was endorsed by the Industrial Relations Commission in June 1986. The move was advocated as a means of making superannuation more widely available, and it was also seen as furthering macroeconomic goals by promoting private saving. As a result of the decision, the 3 percent superannuation benefit was gradually incorporated in employment awards as they came up for renegotiation. These payments were directed either into existing funds or into union-created "industry" funds that in other respects were the same as those already in existence (i.e., managed by private funds management firms).

In 1991, the government announced a significant expansion of compulsory superannuation, along with the introduction of a new compliance mechanism

Table 2.2   **Superannuation Coverage**

	Public Sector		Private Sector		All Employers	
	% Covered	% of Labor Costs	% Covered	% of Labor Costs	% Covered	% of Labor Costs
1985–86			32.3	3.3		
1986–87	63.4		31.8	3.4	41.6	
1987–88	68.0		34.1	3.5	44.0	
1988–89	90.4		40.7	3.2	54.8	
1989–90	91.7		56.9	3.8	66.9	
1990–91	93.9	6.0	67.5	3.9	75.3	4.6
1991–92	94.6	6.4	70.7	4.2	77.6	4.9
1993–94	97.0	6.9	89.4	4.9	91.5	5.6

Source: Australian Bureau of Statistics.

known as the superannuation guarantee charge (SGC), which gave the system the basic shape it has today.[4] The SGC legislation established a timetable for employer contributions to be increased to 9 percent in most cases by the 2000–2001 financial year, with tax penalties for noncompliance.[5] Further measures were announced in 1995 to encourage additional contributions of 3 percent by employees, to be supplemented by a matching contribution from the federal government, thus bringing the total level of contributions eventually to 15 percent. (In the 1997 federal budget, this component of the scheme was replaced by a tax rebate on personal savings.) The move to a legislated system for employer contributions was partly a response to problems of administrative complexity and slow compliance under the award-based system. Award superannuation did not cover some significant parts of the workforce (e.g., the self-employed and part-time workers) and was taking longer than anticipated to implement because of negotiation delays.[6] As shown in table 2.2, superannuation coverage has widened substantially as a result of these measures.

The broad parameters of the compulsory superannuation policy have bipartisan political support, with the newly elected government in 1996 having endorsed the overall targets set by the previous government, although not necessarily the implementation method for employee contributions. The new government announced further changes in the 1996–97 budget, including the introduction of retirement savings accounts and a number of changes to the taxation of superannuation.

4. Full details are set out in "Superannuation Guarantee Levy" (Commonwealth Treasury 1991).
5. Vesting and preservation requirements were also standardized. Benefits were now required to be fully vested in the employee immediately and to be preserved in a superannuation fund until at least age fifty-five.
6. Seventy-five percent of employees had superannuation coverage by 1991, five years after the initial decision by the Industrial Relations Commission.

Introduction of the compulsory superannuation plan reflected a combination of policy concerns broadly related to the issue of raising aggregate saving. Like a number of other industrial countries, Australia has an aging population structure. However, the aged dependency ratio is still quite low and is not projected to rise as steeply as elsewhere (table 2.3), so it is ironic that Australia has moved comparatively early to establish the basis for a funded scheme. The timing of the initial move to award-based superannuation was in a sense accidental, reflecting the intricacies of the wage-bargaining process at the time. Nonetheless, the general policy thrust reflected underlying objectives of raising aggregate saving (an important macroeconomic objective in its own right) and of providing funded retirement incomes for the majority of employees. Once the principle of mandatory contributions was established, subsequent extensions to the scheme were aimed at increasing those contributions to a level high enough to ensure that these objectives could be adequately met.

The objective of increasing national saving in Australia has been on the policy agenda since at least the mid-1980s, when a chronically large current account deficit became apparent. The deficit reached 6 percent of GDP at that time and has since continued to fluctuate mainly in the 3–6 percent range, regarded by the government and many other observers as uncomfortably high. It is also the case that Australia is a relatively low-saving country, at both national and household levels, as discussed further in section 2.5. This combination of facts created a powerful prima facie argument for policies to promote aggregate saving. One important dimension of the policy debate has related to the role of fiscal policy, where there has been considerable emphasis on the need to improve cyclically adjusted budget balances.

There is also widespread agreement in Australia on the desirability of promoting private saving. It is argued that households undersave for a variety of reasons, including an inherent tendency to discount the future too heavily and disincentives to private saving created by the government pension system. Regarding the latter, it is argued that the system has created significant incentives

Table 2.3   International Comparison of Aged Dependency Ratios

	1960	1990	2000	2010	2020	2030
Australia	13.9	16.0	16.7	18.6	25.1	33.0
Canada	13.0	16.7	18.2	20.4	28.4	39.1
France	18.8	20.8	23.6	24.6	32.3	39.1
Germany	16.0	21.7	23.8	30.3	35.4	49.2
Italy	13.3	21.6	26.5	31.2	37.5	48.3
Japan	9.5	17.1	24.3	33.0	43.0	44.5
United Kingdom	17.9	24.0	24.4	25.8	31.2	38.7
United States	15.4	19.1	19.0	20.4	27.6	36.8

Source: World Bank (from Leibfritz et al. 1995).

for low- and middle-income earners to qualify for the age pension by not saving "too much."[7] The high take-up rate of government pensions, discussed earlier, is often cited as support of this view. Purely incentive-based approaches to promoting private saving, as existed under the pre-1983 taxation arrangements, appeared to have little effect on saving by low- and middle-income earners. Given this background and the objective of ensuring comprehensively available retirement support, the move to a compulsory saving system seems a logical outcome. The existence of a significant private superannuation system when the policy was introduced and a desire to achieve maximum returns were probably both important factors in ensuring that a privately run system was the preferred option.

2.3 Tax Treatment

The tax rules for superannuation are extremely complex and can be outlined here only briefly. Important changes to the tax rules were made in 1983, 1988, 1992, and 1996 that generally reduced the tax benefits to superannuation, although the treatment remained concessional. These changes and the current system are described in detail in the appendix. Changes were generally grandfathered at each stage, with the result that retirees would receive benefits taxed under a variety of rules depending on when contributions were made. The following description outlines basic features of the rules as they currently apply to new contributions.

The system distinguishes between contributions by employees (which are still largely voluntary) and those made by employers.[8]

Employee contributions are made from after-tax income. These contributions, in nominal terms and excluding the earnings they generate, are effectively available to be returned to the contributor after retirement without being further taxed. Earnings, however, are taxed in the same way as earnings from employer contributions, as outlined below.

Employer contributions and earnings on contributions from either source are taxed in the following way. Contributions are tax deductible to the employer but are subject to a 15 percent tax on entry to the fund. Following changes announced in the 1996–97 budget, this tax rate rises to 30 percent for high-income earners (for details, see the appendix). Fund earnings are then subject to a 15 percent tax each year as they accrue.[9] The taxation of final benefits

---

7. For a review of these arguments, see Freebairn, Porter, and Walsh (1989), Edey and Britten-Jones (1990), Robinson (1992), Bateman and Piggott (1993), and FitzGerald (1996).

8. Special rules apply to the self-employed, effectively allowing them "employer" tax treatment on part of their contributions, which is more favorable than "employee" treatment.

9. The actual tax paid is much less because funds are able to benefit from imputation credits for company tax already paid on their dividend receipts. These credits can be applied against taxable income from other sources, substantially reducing the overall tax liability.

financed by employer contributions and earnings depends on the form in which the benefits are taken. Annuities are subject to normal personal income tax as payments are made, less a 15 percent rebate, which is a form of compensation for the tax already paid on entry to the fund. Lump sum payouts are taxed at a standard rate of 15 percent (plus the Medicare levy) on amounts in excess of a tax-exempt minimum. The relative attractiveness of the two types of benefit will depend on a number of factors, including the size of the overall benefit and the retiree's income from other sources.[10]

All the concessional treatment implicit in these arrangements is subject to reasonable benefit limits (RBLs). These set the maximum amount of concessionally taxed benefits a person may receive in a lifetime, and benefits exceeding those limits are subject to standard marginal tax rates. The limits are higher for benefits taken in the form of annuities than for lump sums, a mechanism for discouraging the use of lump sum benefits. Changes introduced in 1992 substantially reduced the RBLs for high-income earners by expressing RBLs as flat rates rather than as multiples of income.

In its broad structure, the tax system for superannuation can be described as embodying a hybrid between expenditure tax and income tax principles.[11] Under a pure expenditure tax treatment, saved income (i.e., contributions and fund earnings) would be tax free, while postretirement expenditure (roughly equivalent to the annuity payment) would be taxed at standard rates. The various concessional elements in the tax treatment outlined above go some way toward approximating such an outcome. For employer contributions, if we do the mental exercise of offsetting the contributions tax against the postretirement rebate, then contributions would be viewed as tax free, with annuity benefits taxed at the standard marginal rate. Since fund earnings are only lightly taxed during the accumulation phase, the overall treatment of employer contributions could therefore be said to resemble that of an expenditure tax. Employee contributions are less favorably treated because they are made from after-tax income but still give rise to taxable earnings during the accumulation period and in retirement. Again, however, the taxation of earnings on these savings is considerably lower than would be the case outside the superannuation system.

The tax concessions for superannuation have a significant revenue cost, estimated in 1994–95 to be $7.3 billion, or around 1.6 percent of GDP. Most of this cost is accounted for, in roughly equal amounts, by the concessional tax rates applying to employer contributions and to fund earnings. These estimates are calculated relative to a baseline under which superannuation is taxed in the same way as other financial saving, which in Australia is essentially an income taxation system. Some commentators, such as Bateman and Piggott (1997) and FitzGerald (1996), argue that this is not the appropriate baseline and that the revenue costs are therefore overstated.

10. For an analysis, see Atkinson, Creedy, and Knox (1995).
11. A similar view is expressed by Covick and Lewis (1993).

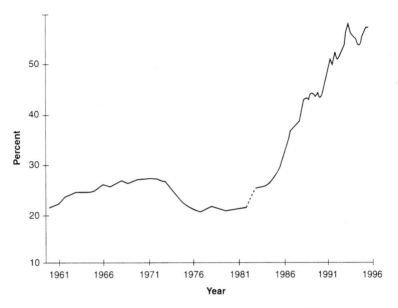

Fig. 2.2   Assets of life offices and superannuation funds (% of GDP)
Source: Australian Bureau of Statistics; Foster (1996).

2.4   Role of Superannuation in the Financial Sector

Assets of superannuation funds and life insurance offices have fluctuated mainly in a range of around 20–25 percent of the Australian financial system in recent decades.[12] They are currently around 26 percent, having risen strongly in recent years, and this share could be expected to increase further in future decades as compulsory contributions accumulate. The historical importance of these institutions reflected the significant use of superannuation as a voluntary savings vehicle, as has been discussed above, and was in part a result of their tax-favored status. There are currently over 100,000 superannuation funds in Australia, which range from the very large (the ten largest fund managers control around 60 percent of the assets) to the so-called do-it-yourself (DIY) funds with only a few members.[13]

Trends in the superannuation sector's overall size and its sources of funds are summarized in figures 2.2 and 2.3. Broadly, the historical growth of the superannuation sector can be divided into three phases. The first phase, which ended in the early 1970s, was one of moderate and fairly steady growth. In the

12. For statistical purposes, it is useful to treat life insurance and superannuation funds as a single aggregate because their activities are similar and much of the historical data do not distinguish between the two.

13. The situation is complicated by the fact that the major fund-management groups can run large numbers of separately constituted superannuation funds.

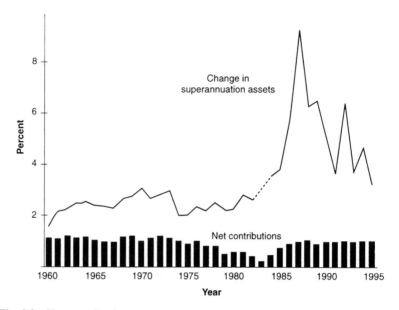

Fig. 2.3   Net contributions and growth in superannuation assets (% of GDP)
Source: Australian Bureau of Statistics.

second phase, which covered most of the 1970s, superannuation assets shrank relative to nominal GDP, largely reflecting poor earnings performance and high inflation. The third phase, from the early 1980s on, has been one of rapid expansion in which total assets more than doubled as a ratio to GDP, although this may have slowed down in the last few years. The data presented in figure 2.3 divide the sources of superannuation asset growth between net new contributions and a residual representing earnings on existing assets and capital gains. Although net contributions have fluctuated significantly in some periods, it is apparent that most of the variation in overall growth performance can be attributed to variation in the earnings and capital gain component rather than in contributions.[14] The three growth phases outlined above correspond broadly to periods of moderate, negative, and high real rates of return on financial assets, as summarized in table 2.4.

On the basis of currently available data, aggregate net contributions to superannuation funds do not yet show the upward trend expected to result from the compulsory plan.[15] A number of possible reasons can be given for this. First, there is likely to be a strong cyclic influence on net contributions. They

14. Capital gains are likely, however, to be understated in the 1960s and 1970s, and overstated in the early 1980s, as a consequence of the widespread use of historical cost valuations prior to the 1980s.

15. These data should be interpreted cautiously, however, as they have in the past been subject to substantial revision.

Table 2.4   **Superannuation Fund Earnings Rate**

	Average Earning Rate	Inflation Rate
1960s	5.2	2.5
1970s	6.8	9.8
1980s	14.9	8.4
Early 1990s	6.8	3.0

Source: Australian Bureau of Statistics.

fell substantially in the recession of the early 1980s, when withdrawals related to early retirements were likely to have been particularly important. This may again have been a factor in the early 1990s. In addition, many voluntary schemes contain a tranche of employee-contributed funds that do not have to be preserved to retirement but can be withdrawn on leaving a job.[16] There is also provision to allow early withdrawal of funds in cases of hardship. For all these reasons, recessions can be expected to result in significantly increased withdrawals from superannuation funds as jobs are lost. Second, many employers were already satisfying, at least partly, the requirements of the compulsory plan under preexisting voluntary arrangements. This has allowed some scope for absorption of the compulsory scheme into existing arrangements and has meant that the aggregate effect of the new compulsory schedule has so far been relatively small; but it can be expected to increase as the mandatory contributions rate increases significantly above levels currently prevailing. Third, an important factor in the second half of the 1980s was the phenomenon of overfunding of existing defined-benefit schemes. High rates of return meant that surpluses were accumulated in many of these schemes, enabling the employers who sponsored them either to withdraw funds or to finance their superannuation liabilities with reduced contributions. Finally, it is possible that increased tax rates on superannuation savings after 1983 have discouraged voluntary contributions.[17]

These factors provide a useful qualitative explanation for the behavior of aggregate contribution rates. However there is no direct way of measuring their quantitative effect and thus arriving at some measure of an "underlying" trend in contributions. This is an important issue for further investigation since, as discussed below in section 2.5, the capacity of the scheme to meet its objectives hinges critically on its compulsory nature and on the ability to discourage unintended leakages.

One important dimension of this issue is the growth of "rollover" funds,

16. Recent regulatory changes restrict this right of withdrawal, subject to grandfathering of existing withdrawable amounts.

17. There is also a serious longer-term policy concern: the potential for funds to leak from the compulsory scheme owing to incentives favoring early retirement and the dissipation of accumulated savings (see FitzGerald 1996).

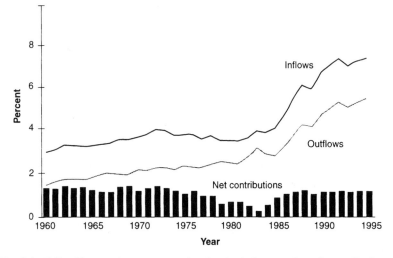

Fig. 2.4   Life offices and superannuation funds, inflows and outflows (% of GDP)
Source: Australian Bureau of Statistics.

created in 1983 as a vehicle for deferring tax liabilities by preserving with-drawn benefits within the tax-favored system.[18] Funds withdrawn as a result of leaving a job can be deposited in a rollover fund (until required to be drawn on) and continue to be treated for tax purposes like other superannuation funds. They can also be moved from one such fund to another at the discretion of the member. Rollover funds are a relatively small component of the superannuation system by assets (around 5 percent in 1995), but, because they are mobile at the member's discretion, they are responsible for a large part of the gross flows illustrated in figure 2.4. Part of the impetus for this increased turnover in the early 1990s probably came from increased redundancies and early retirements.

Assets of superannuation funds are invested across a wide spectrum of traditional investments, with no important portfolio restrictions other than a limit of 10 percent on the proportion of funds that can be invested with the sponsoring employer. Investments in the broad categories of equities, bonds, and property are shown in figure 2.5. The predominant trends have been a substantial reduction in the portfolio share of bonds and a rise in that of equities over the past three decades. Property investments had also been on an upward trend over much of the period but fell sharply at the end of the 1980s and in the early 1990s, largely reflecting valuation effects following the collapse of the property market. The long-term reduction in bond portfolios is likely to have been

18. Following rule changes in 1992, rollover-fund operations as described here can now be carried out within ordinary superannuation funds.

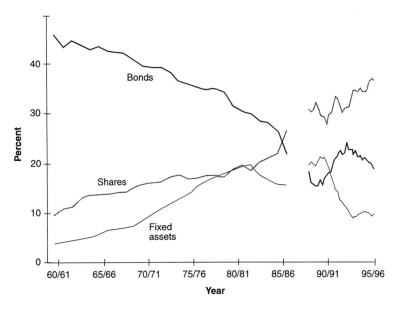

Fig. 2.5   Superannuation funds asset allocation, proportion of asset types in super funds
Sources: Australian Bureau of Statistics; Foster (1996).

a consequence of removal of earlier portfolio restrictions setting minimum holdings of government bonds,[19] along with a trend decline in public-sector debt ratios that reduced the available supply. Holdings of foreign assets are not separately shown in the figure as consistent data are unavailable for much of the period. However, their portfolio share has grown rapidly in recent years and is currently around 13 percent. A more detailed snapshot of the asset allocation at the end of 1995 is presented in table 2.5.

The superannuation sector is projected to expand considerably in future decades as the compulsory increases in contributions take effect. One estimate suggests an approximate doubling of the sector in relation to GDP, from 40 to 76 percent of GDP by the year 2020 (Knox 1995).[20] This policy-induced expansion raises a number of issues concerning the competitive position of superannuation within the financial system and the size of superannuation funds in the markets in which they operate. Some observers have argued that growth in the superannuation sector will in some degree occur at the expense of banks or will occur in a way that increases competitive pressure on banks (see, e.g., Thom 1992). Another issue is the possibility that the superannuation funds will "run out" of domestic assets to purchase as they expand or that their

19. Until 1981, funds were required to hold at least 30 percent of their assets as government bonds.
20. The estimates are for the superannuation sector excluding life-office business.

Table 2.5   Assets of Superannuation Funds (December 1995)

	$billion	%
Cash and short-term bank instruments	40.4	14.5
Loans	20.7	7.4
Fixed interest	53.7	19.2
Equities	99.2	35.6
Property	24.2	8.7
Foreign	37.2	13.3
Other	3.4	1.2
Total	279.0	

Source: Australian Bureau of Statistics.

holdings of such assets will grow to a point where they significantly change the characteristics of domestic asset markets. These issues are closely related to the question of how effective compulsory superannuation will be in generating additional saving rather than displacing existing forms of saving. To the extent that new saving is generated, it could be expected to lead to a general expansion of the financial system and of the supply of domestic assets, along with an accumulation of foreign assets, rather than drawing funds from other domestic financial institutions.

A good general case can be made that there has in the past been relatively little competitive overlap between banks and the superannuation sector, although in some respects this competitive separation seems to be breaking down, particularly on the liabilities side. On the asset side of these institutions' balance sheets, the competitive separation has been strong. Superannuation funds invest primarily in securities, while the traditional core business of banks is in nonsecuritized lending.[21] Banks' traditional lending activities now represent a declining proportion of their balance sheets and profits, but this is part of a worldwide phenomenon related to improvements in financial technology associated with securitization[22] and does not particularly seem to reflect competition arising from the growth of superannuation funds. While the trend of increasing securitization seems likely to continue, the potential erosion of banks' competitive position with respect to traditional lending can easily be overstated. As noted by Tease and Wilkinson (1993), banks continue to have a natural specialization in borrower risk assessment, and this is likely to remain important even when loans are increasingly in securitized form.

There is also a clear difference between the liability structures of these two classes of financial institutions. Superannuation fund liabilities are the long-term savings of their members, whereas bank liabilities are a combination of transaction balances, short-term savings, and marketable debt instruments. As is documented by Edey, Foster, and Macfarlane (1991), the banking system in

21. This distinction is discussed in the Australian context by Tease and Wilkinson (1993).
22. For a recent analysis of this global trend, see Bisignano (1995).

Australia has not traditionally been an important vehicle for longer-term saving, and the shorter-term balances held by households with banks bear a fairly stable relation with household income. These balances do not seem likely to be closely substitutable by compulsory superannuation balances. Nonetheless, the competitive separation between banks and superannuation funds on the liabilities side seems to be breaking down at the margin. One important aspect of this is the growth of rollover funds, which are tax-favored superannuation vehicles but which do have some of the characteristics of shorter-term savings since their funds are highly mobile and not necessarily locked in for long periods. Also important is that the superannuation sector is itself an important provider of funds to other parts of the financial system. From table 2.5, around $40 billion, or 15 percent of superannuation assets, is currently held as bank securities or deposits with financial institutions, a significant proportion of these institutions' liability base. Growth of these "wholesale" sources of funds to the banks represents a potential source of upward pressure on their average cost of funds. However, the role of superannuation in this process should not be overplayed because it is part of a trend that would be likely to occur anyway, through the growth of money market mutual funds and the increasing sophistication of retail depositors.

These competitive issues have led some banks to move into the superannuation area by establishing life-office subsidiaries or forming partnerships with existing major life offices. More recently, it has been announced that banks will be allowed to participate directly in some superannuation business by offering retirement savings accounts. Further issues concerning institutional distinctions between different parts of the financial sector, and their regulatory-policy implications, are the subject of a current government inquiry.

2.5   Effect on Saving

As has already been noted, Australia's gross national saving rate has historically been below OECD averages and has declined substantially in the past two decades. Much of this decline, illustrated in figure 2.6, can be attributed to reduced saving by the public sector. Gross private saving, as conventionally measured, has also been declining, although at a lesser rate, while household saving declined somewhat faster than the private-sector total. In interpreting private-sector saving trends, Edey and Britten-Jones (1990) argued for a focus on aggregate private saving rather than on the separate household and corporate-sector components since the exact boundary between them is somewhat arbitrary and there has historically been a high degree of offset between the two forms of saving. They also calculated an inflation adjustment of the private-saving aggregate that corrects for the wealth transfers between public and private sectors effected by inflation. The adjustment has the effect of lowering the peak in private saving recorded in the 1970s and produces an estimate of the gross private saving rate that has been fairly flat, at least until recently.

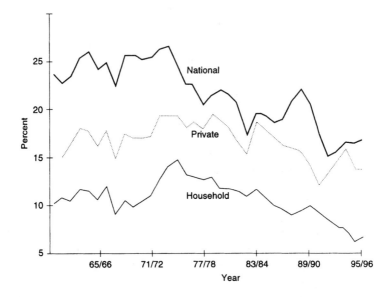

Fig. 2.6   Household, private, and national saving, gross savings measures (% of GDP)
Source: Australian Bureau of Statistics.

Net private saving, however, has still shown a trend decline, reflecting an upward trend in the ratio of depreciation to income.[23]

Since there has not yet been a sustained increase in superannuation contributions, for the reasons described in the previous section, the historical data do not provide any direct basis for inferring what is the likely effect of compulsory superannuation on aggregate saving. The answer to this question will depend critically on the extent to which superannuation displaces other forms of saving. A historical estimate of the degree of offset between the two categories of saving, reported by Morling and Subbaraman (1995), obtained the rather high figure 0.75, implying around three-quarters of a given change in superannuation saving would be offset elsewhere. But this estimate is derived from a historical sample dominated by the voluntary contributions of mainly high-income earners and is unlikely to have much bearing on behavior under the compulsory scheme, as the authors themselves acknowledge. The move to compulsory contributions and the expansion of coverage of the system among low-income earners, who are more likely to be liquidity constrained, can be expected to reduce substantially the degree of substitution between superannuation and nonsuperannuation saving in the future. Other studies have cited lower offset coefficients. FitzGerald (1993) uses a coefficient of 0.5, while

23. Edey and Britten-Jones (1990) also argue that the depreciation estimates may be unreliable, so they prefer a focus on the gross figures.

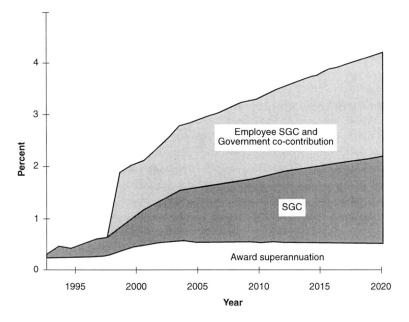

Fig. 2.7   RIM projections, addition to national savings (% of GDP)
Source: RIM Task Force.

Covick and Higgs (1995) estimate a figure of 0.37 and cite international evidence for figures of around one-third.

Projections of the effect of the compulsory scheme have been made by the Retirement Income Modelling (RIM) Task Force, using an assumed offset coefficient of one-third.[24] A summary of these projections is presented in figure 2.7, which shows the estimated additions to saving relative to a baseline scenario.[25] A sharp increase in aggregate saving is projected at the end of the current decade when the employee and government co-contributions come into effect. By the year 2003, when the schedule is fully implemented, saving is projected to have increased relative to the baseline by around 3 percent of GDP. The peak effect is reached much later, reflecting subsequent reinvestment of fund earnings and the fact that significant increases in retirement rates do not occur until sometime later. The projections take into account the fiscal revenue cost of superannuation tax concessions as applied to the increased contributions and also the beneficial effect of reduced government pension outlays; these are eventually projected to fall by around 1 percent of GDP when the system matures. However, a point of caution is that the funding for the govern-

24. The task force is jointly sponsored by the Treasury, the Department of Finance, and the Department of Social Security. Nonofficial estimates of the effect of employer contributions give broadly similar results (see Bateman and Piggot 1992; AMP Society 1995; Corcoran and Richardson 1995; and Covick and Higgs 1995).
25. The projections are discussed in Willis (1995).

ment co-contribution in these projections comes from *not* proceeding with tax cuts that were already announced, but not yet implemented, when this component of the scheme was adopted. These tax cuts are included in the baseline scenario. Also included in the baseline is the cost of tax concessions applied to the existing level of voluntary contributions.

An important dimension of the overall effect of compulsory superannuation concerns its likely effect on the behavior of those around retirement age. In Australia, there was a substantial increase in the rate of early (i.e., pre-sixty-five) retirement in the 1970s and 1980s, as illustrated by the declining male labor force participation rates for older age groups, shown in figure 2.8. Anecdotally, this trend is often argued to have been encouraged by the phenomenon of "double dipping." This is where individuals who have accumulated moderate amounts of superannuation savings retire early, consume the bulk of those savings, and then qualify for the government pension at age sixty-five. Such a strategy is thought to be attractive where individuals have accumulated enough savings to reduce entitlement to the government pension but not enough to generate a private income in retirement that would substantially exceed the pension. More generally, the interaction of the personal income tax system with the means testing of the government pension is argued to create very high effective marginal tax rates on saved income for some groups and therefore to encourage low rates of labor participation.

It is possible that this disincentive effect, acting in the years just prior to retirement, is a more important potential source of leakage of saving from the

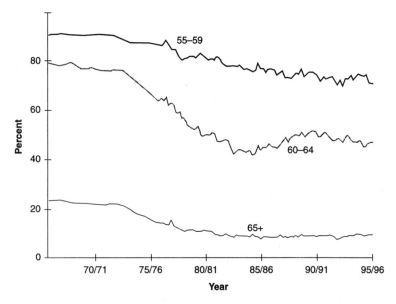

Fig. 2.8   Participation rate—males
Source: Australian Bureau of Statistics.

compulsory scheme than other actions to offset higher superannuation saving taken by individuals at earlier stages in their working lives. The size of the effect on saving and labor participation is not accurately known. However, the general observation that only a small minority of people currently receive their main retirement income from sources other than the government pension does seem to suggest important disincentives to save for retirement among low- and middle-income groups. This may well be a factor contributing to low labor force participation rates in the fifty-five to sixty-five age group, even though the strict "double-dipping" stereotype does not seem to be particularly common.[26]

Given the policy objective of maintaining a reasonable safety net through a government pension, two broad strategies are available to reduce the adverse effects on incentives to save for retirement. One is to make the government pension universal, as is the case in a number of countries, including New Zealand. This removes the adverse effect of the means test on effective marginal tax rates but raises problems of equity as well as increasing the cost to the government, possibly reducing the overall level of support that can be afforded. The other approach is to tighten the enforcement of compulsory self-provision for retirement. This is broadly what is happening in Australia through various measures to increase the attractiveness of annuity benefits relative to lump sums, along with a gradual increase in the compulsory preservation age for superannuation benefits.[27] These changes should reduce the potential for savings to leak from the system in the years immediately prior to retirement. But changes in these incentives are hard to bring about quickly because of a strong presumption that existing accumulated entitlements should be protected from significant rule changes.

2.6   Conclusions

The most important distinguishing features of the Australian system are that it is government mandated but privately run and that it has been able to make use of a well-developed financial infrastructure for superannuation saving, through which the new compulsory contributions could be channeled. This has meant that the financial system has adapted relatively smoothly to the new arrangements. However, the system has been criticized for being highly complex in its administrative rules and tax provisions. This complexity is a consequence of separate tax treatment of contributions from different sources, along with the cumulative effect of the various incremental changes that have been

26. Survey-based evidence on this issue is provided in Department of Social Security (1992). On the basis of this evidence, Kalisch and Patterson (1994) argue that stereotypical double dipping, in the form of holidays or other consumption expenditure financed by a lump sum, is rare. However, Bateman, Kingston, and Piggott (1994) argue that there is still a more broadly defined incentive problem associated with the age pension.

27. The preservation age is to be raised to sixty by the year 2025. Concerning tax incentives to encourage annuities, Bateman, Kingston, and Piggott (1992) argue that recently introduced incentives in this direction are not very strong.

made, with successive layers of changes often embodying special provisions to protect previously accrued rights.

The new system is projected to have a substantial effect on aggregate saving, increasing it by as much as 4 percent of GDP over the next three decades. However, it is still in an early part of the transitional stage, and there has not yet been a sustained increase in net contributions to superannuation funds, even though there has been a big expansion of membership. In part, this probably reflects significant withdrawals of funds from the superannuation system in recent years through increased redundancies and early retirements. These leakages might not be entirely a cyclic phenomenon and may also reflect underlying incentives that affect the attractiveness of early retirement. The longer-term success of the system in meeting its objectives will depend critically on whether these leakages can be contained, by discouraging the use of lump sum benefits to finance early retirement and by encouraging labor participation in the fifty-five to sixty-five age group.

Appendix
Further Details

This appendix gives additional details on some specific points relating to the operation of the previous and the new system in Australia.

The Previous System

Australia's previous system of official retirement income support consisted of two separate elements: the age pension, which provided a basic level of benefits for most people, and tax-advantaged voluntary savings for retirement.

The Age Pension

Benefits

Australia has an age pension that provides a flat-rate income for retirees. The level of the pension has varied between 20 and 25 percent of average weekly earnings (AWE) over the past forty years and is currently around 25 percent. The pension is indexed to the CPI, and the government has committed to making irregular ad hoc adjustments to maintain the level at around 25 percent of AWE. There are also various supplementary benefits available to age pensioners, such as cheap public transport, telephone services, and pharmaceutical benefits.

Eligibility

The age pension is available to men over sixty-five and women over sixty (although the eligibility age for women is being raised to sixty-five by 2014).

The benefit is asset and income tested. Over time, the stringency of the means testing has varied. Currently, the assets test reduces the value of the pension by $3.00 for every $1,000 of assets above a threshold level ($118,000 for single people and $167,500 for married couples). The family home is excluded from the assets test, although higher asset limits apply to nonowner occupiers (owner occupiers with homes worth more than $70,000 are better off under the test; the average house price is around $150,000). Income testing reduces the value of the pension by fifty cents for every dollar earned above a fairly low threshold ($94.00 per fortnight for singles and $164 per fortnight for couples). When this interacts with the income tax system, it can lead to quite high effective rates of marginal taxation.

Funding

The age pension is funded out of government consolidated revenue; there is no explicit tax for the provision of the pension. In 1994–95, the cost of the pension was $12.7 billion, or 2.8 percent of GDP. This proportion has been relatively stable over time, varying between 2 and 3 percent of GDP.

Voluntary Superannuation

The other form of officially sanctioned retirement provision was voluntary superannuation: that is, savings for retirement that are concessionally taxed and inaccessible until retirement. These schemes could be either accumulation funds, with the final payment related to contributions plus earnings, or defined-benefit schemes, where the final payment is related to final income. These funds invested in assets in much the same way as unit trusts and other professionally managed funds. Many of the funds were employer sponsored and structured as an employment incentive. Defined-benefit schemes tended to be weighted toward longer-term service with the one employer, thus encouraging loyalty. The private-sector schemes were all fully funded.

Public-sector schemes, in contrast to private-sector schemes, were predominantly unfunded. Voluntary employee contributions were paid into a fund and invested to earn income following a normal accumulation scheme. The government, however, did not pay anything into the schemes and met liabilities out of consolidated revenue as they arose. Current estimates of the net present value of these liabilities are around $100 billion for state and federal schemes, or around 20 percent of GDP.

Taxation Changes

Within this institutional framework, the taxation arrangements were the main area that changed prior to the introduction of the SGC legislation. New taxation arrangements introduced mainly in 1983 and 1988 continue to apply under the SGC. In the early 1980s, employer contributions to superannuation funds, employee contributions (up to a limit of $1,200, equivalent to around 9 percent of AWE), and income on superannuation assets were tax free. Pension payouts were taxed as normal income, while lump sum payouts had the first 5 percent added to income for taxation in the year of payout, with the remainder tax free.

In 1983, the status of employee contributions was changed to be no longer tax deductible, and they thus had to be paid out of after-tax income. Other changes at that time primarily involved the taxation of lump sum payments related to employer contributions and fund earnings. These were now taxed at 30 percent. If the recipient was over fifty-five, the first $55,000 was taxed at the concessional rate of 15 percent. While tougher, these changes still involved a concessional treatment as earnings remained tax free. There were also grand-fathering provisions that exempted pre-1983 contributions.

In 1988, the arrangements changed again. Employer contributions were now taxed at 15 percent on entry to super funds (although they remained fully tax deductible to the employer). Employee contributions were still paid out of after-tax income. Fund earnings were subject to a 15 percent tax. Pension pay-outs were subject to the normal income tax, with a 15 percent rebate, while lump sum payouts were subject to 20 percent taxation or, for recipients over fifty-five, were $60,000 tax free and 15 percent on the remainder. The lump sum component attributable to employee contributions was tax free. These pro-visions remain broadly in place subject to adjustment of the tax-free threshold.

Another change introduced in 1988 (and fully effective from 1994, after some transitional arrangements) was to revamp the reasonable benefit limits (RBLs). This was aimed at encouraging people to take benefits in the form of annuities and thereby provide for their retirement rather than relying on the government pension. The RBL rules stipulate a maximum amount of superan-nuation that can benefit from concessional taxation (initially $400,000, to be indexed by AWE). Beyond this limit, normal taxation (currently 48.5 percent) is applied; this limit doubles if more than half the payout is taken as an annuity. The limit is considered to be sufficiently high that it will affect only high-income earners, at least until the new SGC scheme matures in around forty years' time.

Further changes announced in the 1996–97 budget increase the tax on em-ployer contributions to 30 percent for employees earning more than $85,000. This higher tax rate is phased in for incomes between $70,000 and $85,000 and applies only to new contributions made after the announcement date.

Rules for the New System

The new system really begins with the introduction of the SGC legislation in 1991. However, the introduction of award superannuation in 1986 was an important precursor to this.

Award Superannuation

In 1985, the union movement argued for, and received, a commitment to establish a 3 percent employer-funded superannuation benefit, in lieu of a similar general wage rise. This was implemented by inserting a requirement into employment awards that employers pay 3 percent of wages into a nominated industry superannuation fund. Many different union-organized industry super-annuation funds were created to receive the contributions, which are beginning to attain a significant size. As awards were renegotiated, the coverage of super-annuation was increased to many more members of the workforce than had previously been the case. Nonetheless, the coverage of this scheme was not universal, and, owing to negotiation delays in some areas, not all union members received the benefits immediately.

SGC Legislation

In 1991, the government extended the coverage of superannuation to all employees by introducing the SGC legislation. The legislation mandated minimum levels of superannuation contributions by all employers on behalf of their employees. The levels were to start at 5 percent (or 3 percent for employers with a payroll of less than $500,000) and were scheduled to rise until they reached 9 percent in the 2000–2001 financial year. The government also flagged the possibility of raising contributions to 12 percent through employee contributions at some later date. The structure of the legislation was that employers were not technically mandated to contribute to employee superannuation but that, if they did not, the government would impose a superannuation guarantee charge of an equal amount through the tax system and then redistribute this to the employee. The SGC payments would not be tax deductible and would have an additional administration charge included. Thus, it would be cheaper for employers to make the superannuation contributions themselves.

Participation

Participation is mandatory in that employers are required to make contributions for all their employees, subject to some exemptions for part-time and casual workers who do not generate sufficient balances. These exemptions are made in order to reduce administrative problems associated with contributions of very small amounts. In all cases where people do not accumulate sufficient balances to fund their retirement, the age pension will continue to act as a safety net.

Contribution Rates

The required contributions are detailed in the table 2A.1.

Are Some Industries Subject to Different Rules?

Those industries that were subject to award superannuation continue to be bound by those rules. However, the levels of contributions required under the award are less than under the SGC legislation and, to that extent, subsumed. Nonetheless, the award provisions continue to govern the fund into which contributions have to be paid.

Table 2A.1   Mandated Employer Contributions

	Percent of Income
1993–94	5
1994–95	5
1995–96	6
1996–97	6
1997–98	6
1998–99	7
1999–2000	7
2000–01	8
2001–02	8
2002–03	9

Voluntary Contributions

Individuals may make additional voluntary contributions. These are typically in the range 2–10 percent of salary. However, the taxation treatment of additional contributions is different for employer-provided superannuation as those contributions must be paid out of posttax income. Contributions by the self-employed are essentially voluntary. Up to a threshold amount, they can benefit from employer treatment of their contributions for tax purposes. They can also qualify for the government co-contribution on any contributions as employees in line with the schedule.

Funds Management

The funds are generally managed by professional managers who are chosen by a board of trustees for each superannuation fund. The superannuation funds themselves are chosen by the employer or negotiated with the employer as part of the award process. This led to the establishment of union-created "industry funds" that cover many workplaces. It is also possible to appoint external trustees for a more "off the shelf" type of superannuation fund.

Investment Restrictions

There are practically no restrictions on where the funds can be invested. The only significant one is that no more than 10 percent of funds (at cost) can be invested in the business of the sponsoring employer. There are moves to reduce this to 5 percent (of market value). In the 1960s and 1970s, rules existed that required superannuation funds to invest a minimum of 30 percent of their assets in government securities, but these rules are no longer in place.

Payouts

Benefits must be "preserved," that is, made unavailable to the beneficiary, until age fifty-five, subject to exemption in cases of hardship and some voluntary contributions that can be withdrawn on change of employment. Legislation is proposed to raise this to sixty years by 2025. Traditionally, the most common form of benefit has been a lump sum. The more recent RBL provisions are aimed at encouraging people to take an annuity. The type of annuity purchased can be either a traditional annuity (which provides a given income for the rest of the person's life) or an allocated pension. An allocated pension pays an annual income based on investment earnings. The allocated pension is not guaranteed to last for the retiree's lifetime. The difference between these two products is that, with an annuity, the life assurance company bears the investment and mortality risk while, with the allocated pension, the retiree does. Thus, if a person with an allocated pension dies relatively early, there may be a lump sum to be distributed to his or her estate. If a superannuation fund member dies before payout, the accumulated contributions are paid to the estate and are tax free, regardless of the age of the beneficiary.

Life Insurance

Mandated life insurance or disability provisions do not exist. However, many funds offer these facilities, taking advantage of the fact that they can obtain cheaper life insurance without the necessity of everyone having a medical (i.e., pooled life insurance cover). Disability insurance is also offered by some on a similar basis. This usually involves the employer paying an extra contribution to cover the cost of the insurance. These policies can pay benefits as either lump sums or annuities, and the choice made will depend on individual circumstances. Some schemes also provide annuities on retirement that will revert to surviving spouses if the retiree dies relatively early, but this is not a mandated requirement.

References

AMP Society. 1995. *Supertrends,* no. 1. Sydney.

Atkinson, M. E., J. Creedy, and D. M. Knox. 1995. Planning retirement income in Australia: Routes through the maze. *Australian Economic Review* 112 (October–December): 15–28.

Bateman, H., G. Kingston, and J. Piggott. 1992. Taxes, retirement transfers and annuities. Superannuation Economics Research Group Paper no. 6. University of New South Wales.

———. 1994. Equity, efficiency and the superannuation guarantee. In *Superannuation contemporary issues,* ed. D. Knox. Melbourne: Longman Professional.

Bateman, H., and J. Piggott. 1992. The superannuation guarantee charge: What do we know about its aggregate impact. Superannuation Economics Research Group Paper no. 7. University of New South Wales.

———. 1993. Australia's mandated private retirement income scheme: An economic perspective. Superannuation Economics Research Group Paper no. 10. University of New South Wales.

————. 1997. Private pensions in OECD countries—Australia. Labour Market and Social Policy Occasional Paper no. 23. Paris: OECD.

Bisignano, J. 1995. Paradigms for understanding changes in financial structure: Instruments, institutions, markets and flows. Paper presented at the Conference on Structural Change and Turbulence in International Financial Markets, International Centre for Monetary and Banking Studies, Geneva, 9–10 November.

Commonwealth Treasury. 1991. Superannuation Guarantee Levy: Information Paper. Canberra: Australian Government Printing Service.

Corcoran, S., and C. Richardson. 1995. Superannuation and the macroeconomy. Paper presented at the twenty-fourth Conference of Economists, Adelaide.

Covick, O., and B. Higgs. 1995. Will the Australian government's superannuation initiatives increase national saving? Paper presented at the twenty-fourth Conference of Economists, Adelaide.

Covick, O. E., and M. K. Lewis. 1993. Insurance, superannuation and collective investments. In M. K. Lewis and R. H. Wallace, *The Australian financial system,* Melbourne: Longman Cheshire.

Department of Social Security. Development Division. 1983. Developments in social security: A compendium of legislative changes since 1908. Research Paper no. 20. Canberra.

————. Social Policy Division. 1992. Later life provision: A survey of older people's retirement income decisions. Policy Research Paper no. 63. Canberra.

Edey, M., and M. Britten-Jones. 1990. Saving and investment. In *The Australian macroeconomy in the 1980s,* ed. S. A. Grenville. Sydney: Reserve Bank of Australia.

Edey, M., R. Foster, and I. Macfarlane. 1991. The role of superannuation in the financial sector and in aggregate saving: A review of recent trends. Research Discussion Paper no. 9112. Sydney: Reserve Bank of Australia.

FitzGerald, V. 1993. National saving: A report to the treasurer. Canberra: Australian Government Printing Service.

————. 1996. An assessment of current superannuation arrangements. CEDA Information Paper no. 44. Melbourne: Committee for Economic Development of Australia, March.

Foster, R. A. 1996. Australian economic statistics: 1949–50 to 1994–95. Occasional Paper no. 8. Sydney: Reserve Bank of Australia.

Freebairn, J., M. Porter, and C. Walsh, eds. 1989. *Savings and productivity: Incentives for the 1990s.* Sydney: Allen & Unwin.

Gruen, F. H. 1985. Australian government policy on retirement incomes. *Economic Record* 61, no. 1 (September): 613–21.

Kalisch, D., and N. Patterson. 1994. Australia's retirement incomes system: "Double dipping" and consumer attitudes. In *Superannuation contemporary issues,* ed. D. Knox. Melbourne: Longman Professional.

Knox, D. 1995. Some financial consequences of the size of Australia's superannuation industry in the next three decades. Paper presented at the third annual Colloquium of Superannuation Researchers, Melbourne.

Leibfritz, W., D. Roseveare, D. Fore, and E. Wurzel. 1995. Ageing populations, pension systems and government budgets: How do they affect savings. OECD Economics Department Working Paper no. 156. August.

Morling, S., and R. Subbaraman. 1995. Superannuation and saving. Research Discussion Paper no. 9511. Sydney: Reserve Bank of Australia.

Robinson, I. 1992. Superannuation—a policy perspective. In *Superannuation and the Australian financial system,* ed. K. Davis and I. Harper. Sydney: Allen & Unwin.

Tease, W. J., and J. Wilkinson. 1993. The provision of financial services: Trends, prospects and implications. Research Discussion Paper no. 9315. Sydney: Reserve Bank of Australia.

Thom, J. 1992. Capital formation friction. In *Superannuation and the Australian financial system,* ed. K. Davis and I. Harper. Sydney: Allen & Unwin.

Willis, Ralph. 1995. Saving for our future [statement by the Honorable Ralph Willis, treasurer of the Commonwealth of Australia]. Canberra: Australian Government Printing Service.

Comment   John Piggott

Malcolm Edey and John Simon have written an excellent overview of Australian retirement income arrangements—clear and uncluttered with unnecessary detail, it emphasizes the main contours of the policies in place as well as those still maturing. Given the title of the conference, they have concentrated on the superannuation guarantee, as the mandatory element of Australian retirement provision is called. I have little to quarrel with in what they write. They focus on four key issues: (1) Australia's employment related retirement income policy, embodied in the superannuation guarantee, is government mandated but privately run. (2) The transition in Australia is different from that which might be contemplated in the United States or in other countries that have a pay-as-you-go type of employment-related social security system. (3) Taxation arrangements are very important, both in implementing the superannuation guarantee and in its operation; these are very complex. (4) The superannuation guarantee is projected to increase national saving substantially, but this outcome is threatened by leakages, particularly those associated with early retirement and the option, which still exists, to take retirement benefits as a lump sum.

I elaborate on each of these points and then add a list of policy issues that I think will need to be addressed as the superannuation guarantee develops further. In doing this, however, I do not want to suggest that this novel Australian policy is not working or that it faces insurmountable problems. In many ways, it is one of the most economically laudable retirement provision policies around. It is, however, a structure that is only half complete. The accumulation phase is well developed, if still a little fragile and prone to political risk; the benefits phase needs much more attention. Peter Diamond's remark, in the context of the paper on Chile, that it is important to examine the benefit design of these policies at the time they are first developed is germane here.

The Private Mandated Structure

Only three countries in the world, to my knowledge, have legislated retirement provision policies that are mandated by the government but privately operated and that are now well established—Australia, Chile, and Switzerland.

John Piggott is professor of economics at the University of New South Wales.

Each of these countries arrived at this policy posture from a different starting point, so the transition problems have been different, and the current state of the policy varies as well. Many pairwise comparisons can be made between Australia and each of the others that exemplify this. But comparing Australia with both the others as a combination, the three most important differences are the following: (1) Australia has no regulations concerning asset allocations or minimum rates of return, relying instead on the trustees in charge of each superannuation fund to act in the interests of their members. Australian law holds trustees personally liable for the competent discharge of this task. Chile and Switzerland both have maximum asset allocations for various types of asset and minimum rates of return. (2) The Australian government offers no minimum return guarantee on the mandated contributions, whereas both Chile and Switzerland offer such a guarantee. (3) In Australia, retirees can take their benefits as a lump sum—there is no annuity requirement. Both Chile and Switzerland, and, for that matter, almost all other developed countries, require compulsory retirement benefits to be taken as an income stream, usually for life (Chile is an outlier here). Lump sums from superannuation are prevalent in Australia; the life annuity market hardly exists. In 1992–93, Aus$4.7 billion was paid out in final benefits to private-sector retirees; only Aus$213 million was in the form of an annuity or pension (Bateman and Piggott 1997).

Transition Differences

Traditionally, most Australians have relied on the public age pension, along with the house they have bought and paid for throughout their working lives, to provide for their retirement. No employment-related pay-as-you-go national retirement scheme exists or ever existed, although at various stages such schemes have been proposed and, on one occasion, draft legislation was prepared, only to be postponed by the onset of World War II. The superannuation guarantee can thus be seen as Australia's version of retirement social security. It is an add on, and therefore no issue of compensation, recognition bonds, or anything else arises. This does not mean, however, that there is no transition problem in Australia.

The superannuation guarantee began with productivity award superannuation (PAS) in the mid-1980s. As the paper points out, this was a nationally negotiated arrangement, relying on Australia's (then) highly centralized wage determination system, and involved a 3 percent of wage payment into a designated superannuation fund in lieu of 3 percentage points of pay increase. The unions were therefore heavily involved in the early stages of the evolution of the superannuation guarantee. This had a number of implications: selling the idea to the Australian worker was made easy because the unions wanted it and supported it; coverage is restricted to employees; and many of the funds designated were "industry funds," coinciding in coverage with particular unions, and in which the 50 percent required employee trustee membership was effectively 50 percent union membership. This last consequence has meant that, even though the PAS has now become the superannuation guarantee, independent of wage negotiations, it is still hard to choose other funds because the 3 percent PAS must still be paid into the designated fund and to go elsewhere with superannuation guarantee contributions would simply double administration costs.

Second, as the authors correctly and pertinently observe, the superannuation guarantee used the administrative, legal, and financial structures under which the preexisting voluntary occupational superannuation worked. This meant that the design faults with occupational superannuation, which were not particularly serious because of the low voluntary private-sector (funded) coverage, applied also to the superannuation guarantee. In particular, lump sum withdrawals are permitted from the age of fifty-five, even though the means-tested public age pension is not available until at least sixty and until sixty-five for most men. This lack of coordination and integration between the publicly provided flat-rate pension and the private superannuation guarantee means that a gap exists where much leakage of retirement saving can occur. It probably encourages early retirement (Australia is in the top half of OECD countries in this regard) and also leads to early asset disposal so as to meet the means-test provisions for the age pension. This is the major structural problem in the development of the superannuation guarantee as an effective retirement income policy—I will return to it below when I get to my list of policy reforms.

Taxation Issues

The authors emphasize the complexity of the taxation of superannuation in Australia. But, in my view, they overemphasize grandfathering as its cause and play down the entirely avoidable complexity introduced by taxing contributions, earnings, and benefits. All are taxed concessionally, so it is less the burden of tax than its complexity that is the difficulty here. However, the flat-rate structure does introduce inequities, and the tax on earnings distorts net-of-tax returns, adversely affecting asset choice. In addition, earnings taxes probably further encourage early retirement since it is when retirement is a viable option that the earnings tax bites most severely, reducing the lifetime reward for working another year.

A further point about the separation of superannuation tax rates from the personal tax rate schedule is that political risk is increased—if, as in the United States, only benefits were taxed at the retiree's marginal rate, it would be much more difficult for any government to change superannuation taxation unless the personal schedule were also changed. (This observation was made before the 20 August 1996 budget statement, which increased the contributions tax on high-income earners from 15 to 30 percent.)

I also comment briefly on the allusion in the paper to tax expenditures. The authors quote the Aus$7.3 billion tax expenditure figure, the most recent annual estimate prepared by the Australian Treasury for the tax-expenditure statement. The most important of several objections that can be raised against the use of tax-expenditure estimates in the present context is that they are calculated using a single year. If a time dimension is introduced into the calculation, it is easy to show that, for many employees, the present value of the cost of the superannuation tax concession is negative, once reduced future age pension payouts are factored in. In fact, the Treasury has itself published a paper demonstrating exactly this proposition (Brown 1993). Tax expenditure estimates are important politically because they are used as a kind of weapon to fend off anyone who advocates tax-preferred status for saving—especially silly in a nation that publicly acknowledges its poor saving performance and that has a broad tax design tilted more toward capital taxes than in most comparable countries. Australia relies heavily on income taxation, including an indexed but full marginal rate–type capital gains tax, and there is neither a social security tax, nor state-based retail sales taxes, nor a general goods and services tax.

Saving

The superannuation guarantee must in the first instance be assessed as a mechanism for providing adequate retirement income. But, with looming demographic transition, the feasibility of such arrangements inevitably depends on their fundedness. An important by-product of the superannuation guarantee, which is by and large funded, is that the effect on private saving is likely to be positive. This has proved to be a major selling point for the policy; both government and industry regularly produce estimates of its positive effects on saving.

It is no doubt true that the superannuation guarantee will increase private and national saving. The quantum would be much larger if the integration and coordination of preservation age with the age pension were fixed up. The estimates quoted in the paper are based on the assumption that an indexed life annuity is bought by retirees to the value of 75 percent of their retirement benefit. While 25 percent lump sum dissipation is probably a reasonable assumption, very few retirees buy indexed annuities, and it is therefore probable that these estimates overstate the saving implied by controlled asset disposal *through* retirement. This affects both private saving (directly) and public saving: the consequent reduction in means-tested age pension outlays is probably overstated as well. Currently, the proportion of retirement cohorts drawing the age pension increases with age; in the absence of appropriately indexed annuity purchase, this pattern is likely to continue, even when the superannuation guarantee is fully mature.

A largely ignored effect of the superannuation guarantee is its effect on the composition of saving. Here, the benefits might be expected to be substantial. Housing is heavily tax preferred in Australia. Owner-occupier housing is omitted from the income tax base; it is exempt from the capital gains tax; and it has a negligible effect on access to the age pension. Residential real estate investment is particularly suitable for tax-minimizing negative-gearing arrangements because the debt service is more likely to be met evenly by rental returns than by returns on equity investment and real estate is an attractive form of collateral for lenders. Unlike most other OECD countries, there is no tax-preferred channel for financial saving that is not employment linked, such as an IRA. Nonworkers who inherit have the choice of paying a lot of tax, spending the inheritance, upgrading their owner-occupied home, or negatively gearing. It is not surprising that about 60 percent of private net wealth in Australia is in the form of residential real estate, owned or rented.

Under current policy, almost all superannuation guarantee saving is directed toward investments other than housing. This is likely to move the composition of saving in Australia in the right direction; although no quantitative research has been undertaken, I think it possible that the welfare gain from the reduction in this distortion is at least as important as the effect on aggregate saving rates.

A Partial Policy Agenda

It may be useful to lay out a list of outstanding policy deficiencies that will need to be addressed over the next period if Australia's mandatory retirement saving plan is to be a long-term success.

Retirement Income Streams

At the top of the list is the introduction of retirement income streams. Most analysts believe that this will eventually be achieved through compulsion in some form, although the design (a lump sum for the first $x, then compulsory annuity purchase, or compulsory annuity purchase to $y per year, then a lump sum option, to give two possibilities) remains unclear.

In the meantime, the market is drawing out some interesting products. One, which has emerged in the last few months, combines what in Australia are called *allocated pensions*, and in Chile are termed *phased withdrawals*, with a deferred life annuity that begins at age eighty, the expected exhaustion age of the allocated pension. The deferred life annuity, sold at age sixty-five, does not cost much, and the retiree retains considerable control over his or her capital through the fifteen-year deferral period. A second design, first suggested in the Australian context by Formica and Kingston (1991) and now being actively considered by annuity sellers, is an inflation-indexed annuity with a deductible. Indexation does not cut in until annuity purchasing power has been reduced through a cumulative price level increase of, say, 15 percent. In the version being considered commercially, the annuity payment then increases to 115 percent of its initial value and stays there until the price level has risen by a further 15 percentage points, at which time a compensating increase in the annuity payment is made once again. This design allows the initial annuity payment to be considerably larger than can be offered with a fully indexed instrument while at the same time providing inflation insurance against large and unexpected price-level movements.

A problem not so far addressed by either policy makers or researchers in Australia is that of annuity rate risk. If annuity purchase is to be mandatory, then variations in the price of the annuity close to the time of retirement can make a large difference to the rest of life income. One possibility is gradual deferred annuity purchase, along the lines proposed by Brugiavini (1993) (although his analysis is motivated by adverse selection considerations rather than annuity rate risk).

It is entirely possible that policy will converge with the market—eventually compelling an income product with longevity and inflation insurance properties that nevertheless does not cut into immediate consumption too deeply and that leaves the retiree with some capital discretion to cope with contingencies such as health expenses. Sooner rather than later, however, some policy initiative will be required on income streams.

Taxation

As I indicated earlier, the complexity of superannuation taxation in Australia stems from the multiple bases on which the tax is levied. To my knowledge, Australia is the only country to tax all three of these possible bases, and their consolidation would do everyone some good. The best option would be to abolish the taxes on contributions and earnings and to tax benefits at the retiree's marginal rate, as is done in the United States. The implications for the current budget balance probably render this infeasible. An alternative might be to tax contributions at a flat rate and tax benefits at the retiree's marginal rate less the flat-rate contributions tax. The earnings tax seems to have no virtue whatsoever and should be abolished without delay.

Coverage and Replacement

As the authors of the paper point out, superannuation guarantee coverage is confined to employees. It is likely to provide adequate retirement income only for those whose work histories have been more or less continuous. For those with broken work histories, the accumulations can be much less. In addition, coverage at any level remains voluntary for the self-employed, and, except for a recently introduced dependent-spouse provision, those not in the labor force enjoy no tax-preferred financial saving opportunities whatsoever.

It would appear desirable to extend superannuation guarantee coverage to these individuals. In part, their exclusion results from the union-based origins of the policy; in part, the accounting and compound interest properties of defined-contribution schemes tell against workers with broken work histories. The first of these is more easily overcome than the second. For those with broken work histories, the age pension acts as a form of social insurance, and the maintenance of its current support level then becomes a policy priority.

Member Choice

The present government has indicated that it will encourage greater choice for superannuation, both between funds and between portfolios within funds. While economic rhetoric clearly supports the idea that contributors should be able to change their fund if they wish, costs of administration, about which not nearly enough is known, may make this less desirable than it seems at first sight. Certainly, in some cases, the administrative costs of transfer between funds in Australia seem high, although this situation is being addressed through the agreement of a "transfer protocol." Additionally, choice of fund is seen by the industry as being associated with what in Australia is called *short termism* and what U.S. analysts succinctly term *myopic loss aversion.* This allegedly leads fund managers to invest more conservatively than might be appropriate for many of their members. The truth of this claim remains untested.

Of more interest is a move toward greater portfolio choice within a fund. A few years ago, I was involved in an informal survey of the hundred or so industry funds that receive a large proportion of the superannuation guarantee contributions. Only two offered members a choice of portfolios. Yet these funds have as members people of very different ages, for whom standard age-phasing arguments would seem to indicate very different optimal portfolios. Member investment choice is beginning to become more widely available and should, in my view, be actively encouraged by policy. One retarding factor thus far has been the nervousness of trustees, who have been unsure of their potential liability on advice to members as to which portfolio to choose. Appropriate guidance by the Insurance and Superannuation Commission, the Australian regulator, would appear to be all that is necessary to cope with this.

My comments have sought to elaborate on a paper that has met its objectives very well. In doing so, I have spent much time criticizing various aspects of current Australian arrangements. I would therefore like to conclude by reiterating that I think the Australian superannuation guarantee is a very good policy, one that in many respects other countries now seek to emulate. Because few countries have done anything similar, there are no really appropriate models from which Australia can work, and a number of difficulties, conceptual, ethical, and practical, still need to be addressed. It remains to be seen whether there is sufficient commitment to complete this task successfully.

References

Bateman, Hazel, and John Piggott. 1997. Private pensions in OECD countries—Australia. Labour Market and Social Policy Occasional Paper no. 23. Paris: OECD.
Brown, Colin. 1993. Tax expenditures and measuring the long term costs and benefits of retirement income policy. Retirement Income Modelling Task Force Conference Paper no. 93/1. Canberra, July.

Brugiavini, Agar. 1993. Uncertainty resolution and the timing of annuity purchases. *Journal of Public Economics* 50:31–62.

Formica, Andrew, and Geoffrey Kingston. 1991. Inflation insurance for Australian annuitants. *Australian Journal of Management* 16, no. 2:145–64.

Discussion Summary   Jeffrey Liebman and Andrew Samwick

The discussion began by noting some comparisons with the Chilean system. The employer mandate in the Australian system allowed for the selling costs to be priced on a group basis. Therefore, compared to Chile's system of individual selling, the administrative costs were hypothesized to be about two-thirds less. The authors quoted a figure of 1 percent of balances for administrative costs but acknowledged that the churning of accounts was expensive. The Chilean system is actually better designed to keep the number of accounts low, thereby contributing to administrative savings when jobs turn over. The authors responded that, in fact, much of the system in Australia is being organized on a group basis. For example, the current government has allowed for easier consolidation of accounts as long as they are held in banks.

The particular way that Australia means tests its retirement benefits required clarification. Benefits are reduced by 50 percent of income above a threshold and 3 percent of assets above a different threshold. The value of the family home is exempted from the means test. Married couples get approximately double the replacement rate of single persons, so it is unlikely that the means test is responsible for many "fiscal divorces." An example of the moral hazard that is permitted by the means test was to take early retirement at age fifty-five, receive a lump sum distribution, spend down assets, and then begin collecting the means-tested benefit in old age. It was noted that the replacement rate offered by the means-tested benefit is quite generous for workers below the top quintile of the income distribution. The authors suggested that reasonable benefit limits are likely within the next ten years to limit the amount of tax-preferred, nonannuity withdrawals.

Participants also inquired about the political economy of the transition. Low-income workers are thought to have lost out in the transition because they received roughly the same benefits as before but now make contributions. Union involvement was cited as being very important in the setup phase to gather support for a universal retirement scheme. Trade unions are also very involved in the details of the current system. Some of the idiosyncrasies of the government's plan were inherited from existing industrial relations agreements, and all revisions to the plan must still be ratified through the industrial relations system. The authors noted that the expectations of the unions were that the gains from privatization would come at the expense of wage increases. Several questions were asked regarding the response of employers to the transition. The authors admitted that there has been no solid evidence yet that retirement dates changed as a result of the transition, probably because such an effect would be difficult to identify against a backdrop of a secular trend toward earlier retirement, business-cycle effects, and a tendency for lay-offs in Australia to be concentrated among workers over age fifty-five.

Some participants wondered why the annuity option was not taken more frequently, given the apparent tax subsidy. Suggested reasons for the annuity option's unpopularity were the perceived low rates of return on annuities, possibly owing to adverse selection, and the feeling that investors lose control over their own money once it is annuitized. Still another possibility was the permissiveness of the lump sum option. In Chile, for example, the lump sum option is allowed only if it still leaves enough in the account to fund a benefit that is a 70 percent replacement rate and equals 120 percent or more of the guaranteed minimum pension. Only 24 percent of the eligible retirees in Chile have taken the lump sum option. Finally, under Australian tax rules, the principal of the annuity is taxed as income, so it was acknowledged that, in some instances, it might be better to take the lump sum distribution and pay the 15 percent tax rather than buying the annuity.

3   The Roles of the Public and Private Sectors in the U.K. Pension System

Alan Budd and Nigel Campbell

This paper describes the current arrangements for the provision of pensions in the United Kingdom. In particular, it describes the means by which the current and future public-sector cost of pensions has been controlled or reduced and private-sector provision has been encouraged.

The outstanding feature of the U.K. pension system is that, under current policies, public expenditure on pension provision will remain modest, compared with other industrial economies. For example, Chand and Jaeger (1996) estimate that the present value of the difference between the United Kingdom's public-pension expenditure and revenue up to 2050 is 4.6 percent of GDP, with existing policies and current contribution rates. This compares with a ratio of 26 percent for the United States and above 100 percent for Japan, Germany, and France. Current actuarial projections are that contribution rates will fall by 4 percentage points between now and the middle of the next century, in stark contrast with conditions elsewhere. The projected success in constraining public expenditure on pensions helps explain, in large part, why the United Kingdom avoids the longer-term fiscal crises forecast (under current policies) elsewhere. Shigehara (1995) estimates that the level of general government financial liabilities in the United Kingdom will be negative (i.e., there will be net assets) in 2030, compared with liabilities of 300 percent of GDP in Japan and 100 percent or more in the United States, Germany, France, and Italy.

This can partly be explained by more favorable (or less unfavorable) demo-

In 1996, Alan Budd and Nigel Campbell both worked for Her Majesty's Treasury. Alan Budd was H.M. Treasury's chief economic adviser and headed the Macroeconomic Policy and Prospects Directorate. He is a member of the Bank of England's monetary policy committee. Nigel Campbell is the economic adviser in the Treasury's social security team.

The views expressed in this paper are those of the authors and not necessarily those of Her Majesty's Treasury or the Bank of England. The authors are grateful to David Blake, Alexi Chan, Richard Disney, Marty Feldstein, Andrew Young, and participants at the NBER conference for valuable comments on earlier drafts.

graphic developments. (The "greying" of the U.K. population occurs later, and less dramatically, than elsewhere.) But the most important cause is the fixing of the value of the basic state pension in real terms. In addition, the future cost of the state's second-tier pension has been significantly cut by reducing the generosity of the benefits and by encouraging people to leave the scheme and move to private provision. Although the ratio of pensioners to the population of working age is forecast to rise from 30 percent in 1995 to 38 percent in 2030, the ratio of public expenditure on pensions to GDP is expected to fall over the same period, from 4.2 to 3.3 percent. One result of these changes is that the state pension (and other social security benefits) accounts for only about half the average pensioner income. This ratio will continue to fall in the future.

Another feature that distinguishes the United Kingdom from many other industrialized countries, particularly those in continental Europe, is that most of its occupational pension liabilities are already funded. U.K. private-sector pension funds have £600 billion worth of investments, more than the rest of the European Union put together.

However, current arrangements are not universally accepted as satisfactory. In particular, the current level of the basic state pension is slightly lower than the level of income support (a general means-tested benefit). The final sections of the paper describe some proposed reforms of the system.

Broadly, the U.K. system consists of a flat-rate basic state pension based on contributions.[1] There are also means-tested welfare benefits for those deemed to have inadequate income.[2] Second-tier pensions for employees are provided either by the State Earnings-Related Pension Scheme (SERPS) or by occupational or personal pension schemes. All employees (with incomes above a lower limit) must belong to either SERPS or an appropriate private scheme. (There are currently about 22 million employees in the United Kingdom.) The state system (flat rate and SERPS) is pay as you go. Private schemes are usually funded, although there are unfunded schemes for some public-sector employees. Approximately 73 percent of all employees are members of occupational pension schemes or have personal pensions. Twelve percent are only in SERPS. (About 5 percent of employees are in both occupational schemes and SERPS.) The 15 percent who are not covered consist mainly of those on low incomes. Over their lifetimes, such individuals are likely to accrue some entitlements.

---

1. Since we employ U.K. usage in this paper, American readers may find the following glossary helpful (the British term precedes the American): flat rate = lump sum; occupational = private; pensioner = retiree; pensions = social security; personal pensions = individual retirement accounts, 401(k) plans; preserved benefits = deferred benefits; social security = welfare plus social security; state = federal.

2. Welfare benefits available to U.K. pensioners include free medical treatment and medicines; free nursing care; means-tested long-term nursing or residential care; means-tested support to pay for housing and other living expenses; help with cleaning and other domestic duties for the frail infirm; and hot meals for the frail infirm living at home.

3.1   The State Pension System[3]

3.1.1   The Basic State Pension

The full basic state pension is currently (1996–97) £61.15 per week. This is about 15 percent of average full-time male earnings.[4] The pension is taxable. Current policy is to raise the pension annually in line with retail price inflation. Between 1975 and 1980, the policy was to uprate the pension in line with prices or average earnings, whichever was the greater. Before 1975, ad hoc increases had kept roughly in line with earnings increases since 1948.

Entitlement is based on a contributions record. Payment of the full level of benefit depends on the payment of contributions, or the receipt of credits, for about 90 percent of a working life (currently forty-nine years for a man and forty-four years for a woman). Contributions or credits of forty-four or more years for men and thirty-nine or more years for women entitle contributors to the full pension. Pensioners over eighty can receive the state pension (at a reduced rate) on a noncontributory basis.

Married women receive pensions on the basis of their own or their husband's contributions, whichever is more favorable. Almost all male pensioners receive the full pension, whereas only about 1.7 million of 6.1 million female pensioners receive the full pension on the basis of their own contributions. This position is steadily being changed by the introduction, in 1978, of home responsibilities protection (HRP), which provides credits for women who are out of work and caring for children or other dependents, and, in the same year, by the introduction of a requirement that married women must contribute to the National Insurance System and thus acquire entitlement to full pensions. An increasing proportion of women will thus become entitled to the full basic pension on the basis of their own contributions or credits.

The basic pension for single people is currently about 9 percent lower than the level of income support to which poor single pensioners are entitled. For couples the pension is about 6 percent lower. The gap is even larger for older pensioners because income support increases at ages seventy-five and eighty.

The cost in 1994–95 of the basic state pension was £27 billion (4 percent of GDP). Means-tested benefits to pensioners cost a further £8.5 billion.

The ratio of the state pension to average earnings has fallen from about 20 percent in 1977–78 to about 15 percent now. If real earnings grow by 1½ percent a year (which is a modest estimate relative to past trends), the ratio will

3. Much of the material in this paper is based on Johnson, Disney, and Stears (1996). Their comprehensive report on the U.K. pensions system formed volume 2 of the report of the Retirement Income Inquiry. Descriptions of the system and discussions of the main policy issues can be found in Blake (1995) and Dilnot et al. (1994).

4. Although the basic pension has declined relative to average earnings, it has stayed broadly constant at 20 percent of average manual male earnings throughout its ninety years of existence. In the United Kingdom, as in the United States, there has been a significant increase in the dispersion of incomes in recent years, with manual earnings falling relative to nonmanual earnings.

Table 3.1	Projected Cost of Basic Pension (£billion, 1994–95 prices)				
	1994–95	2000–2001	2010–11	2020–21	2030–31
Price indexed	26.9	29.8	33.6	35.2	41.9
Earnings indexed	26.9	32.6	42.6	51.8	71.6

Note: As a guide to the scale of these costs, GDP in 1994–95 was £680 billion.

fall to 9 percent by 2030. For the low paid, the basic state pension is likely to remain a substantial proportion of their retirement income.

The projected cost of the basic state pension is shown in table 3.1. For comparison, the table also shows the cost if the basic pension is uprated in line with earnings (at an assumed growth of 1½ percent a year).

3.1.2   The State Earnings-Related Pension Scheme

The State Earnings-Related Pension Scheme (SERPS) serves two functions in the U.K. system. It provides a second-tier pension for its members (about 17 percent of total employees), and it establishes the minimum (in terms of either benefits or contributions) for those who can be permitted to opt out of the state's second-tier system and to use occupational or personal pension schemes instead.

As subsequent sections will show, SERPS has changed significantly since it was first introduced. It is an earnings-related pay-as-you-go scheme. Benefits are based on earnings between the lower and upper earnings limits (described below). In the long term, under current rules, the pension received by members of SERPS with a full contribution record will be 20 percent of average reckonable[5] earnings over their working life, revalued in line with average earnings to retirement age.

The upper earnings limit is adjusted in line with prices rather than earnings. The value of the SERPS pension will therefore decline relative to average earnings through time.

As mentioned, about 17 percent of employees are contracted into SERPS, of which about 65 percent are women. About 70 percent of those in SERPS earn less than £10,000 a year. (Average full-time male earnings in the United Kingdom are £20,000 a year.) The self-employed do not qualify for SERPS.

The projected cost of SERPS is shown in table 3.2.

3.1.3   Contributions

Contribution rates are set at the time of the annual budget. There is a lower earnings limit (LEL) and an upper earnings limit (UEL), although employers pay contributions above the latter. These limits are adjusted annually in line with retail prices and in 1996–97 were £61.00 and £455 a week, respectively. The LEL is set at the rate of the single person's retirement pension rounded

---

5. *Reckonable earnings* are earnings between the lower and the upper earnings limits.

Table 3.2   **Projected Cost of SERPS (£billion, 1994–95 prices)**

1994–95	2000–2001	2010–11	2020–21	2030–31	2040–41	2050–51
1.9	4.2	8.4	10.9	12.0	10.2	9.9

down to the nearest pound per week. The UEL is approximately 7.5 times the LEL. No contributions are paid if earnings are below the LEL. The rates for 1996–97 are shown in table 3.3.

The contracted-in rate is paid by or on behalf of members of SERPS. Those contracted out of SERPS pay lower contributions. In 1996–97, this "contracted-out rebate" was 4.8 percent of earnings between the LEL and the UEL. It was reduced to 4.6 percent in April 1997, following the government actuary's regular five-year review of the rebate. Three percent is deducted from employers' contributions, and the rest (previously 1.8 percent, currently 1.6 percent) is deducted from employees' contributions.

It can be seen from table 3.3 that there is an "entry fee" of £1.22 for employees as soon as their income reaches £61.00 per week. The marginal contribution rate for employees falls to zero when weekly earnings exceed £455. Employers' contributions are paid on *all* earnings once they reach £61.00 per week; that is, an increase in earnings from £60.00 to £61.00 costs the employer £2.83. There are similar step increases as earnings move through the successive pay bands. An increase from £209 to £210 costs the employer £7.79.

National Insurance contributions (NICs) are also used to finance unemployment benefits and a number of other benefits, including incapacity benefit and statutory maternity pay. In addition, about 11 percent of NIC receipts are paid

Table 3.3   **National Insurance Contribution Rates, 1996–97 (% NIC rate)**

	Employees				Employers		
	Contracted In		Contracted Out				Contracted Out
	1st		1st		Contracted	1st	
Weekly Earnings	£61	Rest	£61	Rest	In	£61.00	Rest
Below £61.00 (LEL)	0	...	0	...	.0	.0	...
£61.00–£109.99	2	10	2	8.2	3.0	3.0	.0
£110–£154.99	2	10	2	8.2	5.0	5.0	2.0
£155–£209.99	2	10	2	8.2	7.0	7.0	4.0
£210–£455	2	10	2	8.2	10.2	10.2	7.2
Above £455 (UEL)	2	a	2	b	10.2	10.2	c

[a] 10 percent of earnings between £61 and £455; 0 percent on earnings over £455.

[b] 8.2 percent of earnings between £61 and £455; 0 percent on earnings over £455.

[c] The contracted-out rebate (described in the text) is available only with respect to earnings between the LEL and the UEL. Employers' NICs with respect to someone earning over the UEL are therefore 10.2 percent of their earnings minus 3 percent of the difference between the LEL and the UEL.

toward the financing of the National Health Service. The state pension scheme is contributory in the sense that entitlement to the basic state retirement pension depends on a contribution record. However, there need be no direct relation between the payments made by individuals (or their employer) and the basic pension received. This follows automatically from the fact that the pension is paid at a flat rate while contributions depend on earnings. Also, contributions are credited for those who are registered as unemployed or who receive certain social security benefits. As mentioned above, women can now receive credits for time spent caring for children. Employers' contributions do not gain any entitlement, and it is possible to make employee contributions in the course of a year that do not count. Finally, those without a full contributions record (who will largely consist of those who have earned below the LEL) can claim means-tested income support that is greater than the basic pension.

The rather tenuous link between contributions and benefits has led Johnson and Stears (1996) to suggest that the contributory requirements should be abolished and replaced by entitlement based on residence. Successive governments have chosen to retain the contributory principle partly on the ground that receipt of the basic pension does not carry the stigma that may be attached to income support and partly because they like to emphasize the link between contributions and benefits. In some cases, the contribution requirement saves public expenditure since there will be some pensioners who receive less than the full basic pension but who will not be eligible for income support (e.g., because they have too much capital). It is also true that the contributory principle means that increases in contribution rates have in the past not been subject to the same opprobrium as increases in income tax rates.

3.1.4   The National Insurance Fund

The National Insurance Fund (NIF) is one of eight funds and accounts used by the central government for its revenue and expenditure transactions.

National Insurance contributions are paid into the NIF, and contributory benefits are paid from it. The main contributory benefits are the basic retirement pension, SERPS, unemployment benefit, incapacity benefit, and widow's benefit. Entitlement to all these benefits is based to some extent on contributions made. In addition, some NICs are used to fund part of the National Health Service.

The fund operates on a pay-as-you-go basis, so contributions by current workers are used to pay current pensions. The NIF has been topped up with a supplementary payment from general taxation in most years since the NIF was set up in 1948–49.

Any pay-as-you-go scheme that pays benefits to all pensioners from the start would initially need significant financial support. This was true of the NIF, whose payments from general taxation averaged 34 percent of NIC revenue in its first three years. A lower proportion was needed thereafter, but the transfer from the general tax pool to the NIF was still part of the design of the system until 1989. This "Treasury supplement" was worth 18 percent of NIC revenue up to 1980–81, was reduced steadily to 5 percent in 1988–89, and then was abolished from 1989–90.

As the NIF did not have a huge surplus by 1989, it is clear that the previous forty years of Treasury supplements effectively subsidized the contribution rates (or allowed for more generous contributory benefits) over that period.

There were no payments to the NIF from general taxation in the four years from 1989–90. From 1993–94, however, it became possible for a "Treasury grant" to be payable to the NIF if it appeared that its balance by the end of the year would be below one-sixth of annual benefit expenditure. This Treasury grant was thus explicitly aimed at maintaining a working balance in the fund rather than (as with the Treasury supplement) implicitly subsidizing the contribution rate. The Treasury grant has been steadily reduced from 24 percent of NIC revenue in 1993–94 to under 5 percent in 1996–97.

The NIF ran deficits in three of the four years (from 1989–90 to 1992–93) in which no Treasury supplements or grants were paid. Only in 1988–89, when the NIF surplus exceeded the Treasury supplement by £1.4 billion, and 1990–91, when there was an NIF surplus of £1.5 billion and no supplement or grant, has NIC revenue exceeded NIF expenditure.

The overall picture, therefore, is of a pay-as-you-go scheme whose revenue has not fully covered its expenditure in all but two of the years since 1948. The transfer from general taxation needed has been significantly reduced over the years and is no longer built in as an implicit and permanent subsidy to the contribution rate.

3.1.5   The Self-Employed

In 1995, about 13 percent of those in work were self-employed. Unlike employees, the self-employed are not required to make compulsory second-tier pension provision, and self-employment income does not give entitlement to SERPS. The self-employed pay different (and generally lower) National Insurance contributions.

Self-employed people with earnings above £3,430 a year pay a flat-rate contribution of £6.05 a week. Those earning below £3,430 can opt to pay the charge. These contributions give entitlement to the basic state retirement pension. There is an additional contribution of 6 percent of profits between £6,860 and £23,660 a year (the latter equals the UEL for employees; the former is rather higher than the LEL).

Although there is no state second-tier provision for the self-employed, they are eligible for tax relief on their personal pension contributions up to a cap. They do not, however, receive tax relief for pension contributions that are invested in their own business.

3.1.6   Early Retirement

Labor force participation rates in the United Kingdom remain among the highest in Europe. But, since 1980, there has been a marked fall in the participation rates of men in the last ten years of their working life. In 1980, 90 percent of men aged fifty-five to fifty-nine and 71 percent aged sixty to sixty-four were either working or looking for work. By 1994, those proportions had fallen to 74 and 52 percent, respectively.

Many of those who retire early are eligible for occupational pensions. Those over fifty are able to use their personal pension fund to buy an annuity. They cannot, however, receive their basic state retirement pension or SERPS until they reach the state pension age (currently sixty-five for men and sixty for women).

The unemployed receive National Insurance credits, which count toward entitlement to the basic state pension. Early retirees may be eligible for these credits. People under sixty would have to show that they are available and looking for work to qualify for credits and (if applicable) unemployment benefits. Men over sixty receive automatic credits independently of availability for work, while women over sixty are already eligible for the state pension.

3.1.7   SERPS—a History

SERPS was introduced by a Labour government in the 1975 Social Security Pensions Act, which came into force in 1978.[6] It added an earnings-related pension to the existing basic pension.

As now, the scheme was based on contributions on reckonable earnings, that is, earnings between the LEL and the UEL. It originally provided a pension of a quarter of the individual's average revalued reckonable earnings (as defined at the end of this paragraph). Since one aim of the act was to make the new pension arrangements mature rapidly, a full earnings-related pension was based on the best twenty years of earnings since SERPS began. Thus, anyone who was earning for twenty years or more from 1978 could get a full pension if his or her earnings were high enough. (By contrast, full entitlement to the basic state pension required, for men, contributions of over 90 percent of a normal working life, although again, at its introduction, there was an accelerated accrual rate for those working at that time.) *Average revalued reckonable earnings,* for the relevant years, were calculated by revaluing each year's reckonable earnings in line with the change in average earnings for the whole economy between the original date and the retirement date. The pension was based on the average of the twenty best years. After retirement, the SERPS pension was to be indexed to prices.

Contracted-out occupational pension schemes had to provide a guaranteed minimum pension (GMP) broadly equivalent to the SERPS pension. They also had to meet a *requisite benefits test* and therefore had, in effect, to have a higher

---

6. An account of earlier earnings-related state schemes is provided in Blake (1995).

accrual rate than SERPS. Those retiring from contracted-out schemes also had additional pension rights under SERPS, but the GMP was deducted from their SERPS entitlement. Since SERPS was indexed to prices but the GMP was not, SERPS effectively provided some indexation for those in occupational schemes.

3.1.8   The 1985 Green Paper

In June 1985, the Conservative government published a green paper, *Reform of Social Security* (Secretary of State for Social Services 1985a). By that date, the bulk of spending on benefits for pensioners was still in the form of the basic pension. Less than 1 percent of expenditure resulted from the earnings-related additions, although this was due to rise significantly in later years. The single person's basic pension was worth one-third the average take-home pay for a manual worker, and the pension for a married couple was worth half the average take-home pay for a manual worker.

The green paper examined the implications of the basic state pension and SERPS over the following fifty years. It showed that, if the basic pension were indexed to prices, its cost would increase by 40 percent over the following fifty years. If it were linked to earnings, its cost would almost treble. Over the same period, the ratio of National Insurance contributors to pensioners was expected to fall from 2.3 to 1.6. The green paper pointed out that the increased cost of the basic pension would benefit all pensioners equally. However, the case was different for recipients of SERPS. Its earnings-related nature meant that the newly retired would benefit more than older pensioners. Also, half the extra cost would result from payments to members of contracted-out schemes (to provide indexation top-up to the GMP). The cost of SERPS (in 1985 prices) was expected to be about £24 billion in 2035, compared with a basic pension cost in 1985 of about £15 billion.

The green paper pointed out that the peak of occupational pension scheme membership had been reached in the mid-1960s. There had been growth in the public sector, but coverage of the total workforce was still only about half. The earlier decline in private schemes was thought to have been partly caused by uncertainty about the future of pensions policy. But the new system had produced little change. It was also believed that the complexities of contracting out discouraged companies from setting up their own schemes, partly because they had to match the standards of a defined-benefit scheme.

The government believed that occupational and personal pensions were the right way to provide second-tier pensions. It argued that it was preferable for individuals to make provision for such pensions rather than to leave responsibility wholly to the state and to require taxes to be levied on the next generation. It considered the following possibilities for change:

Abolition of SERPS without Replacement. This would restrict the role of the state to the provision of a basic pension. This option was rejected on the grounds that some employers and employees might take too short term a view. It would perpetuate "two nations" of those with and without additional pensions. Those with only the basic state pension would too often have to fall back on means-tested benefits.

A Restricted SERPS. This would restrict the scope and hence reduce the cost of the state scheme, without providing an alternative. Costs would be reduced by moves to change the period over which earnings were counted for entitlement; reduce the rate of accrual; make occupational schemes responsible for their own inflation proofing; reduce the widows' entitlement; increase the pension age for women; and reduce the maximum earnings on which entitlement would be calculated.

The green paper estimated that these latter changes could cut the eventual cost of the scheme by about half but that the changes would have essentially a negative effect: "It would make savings simply by reducing benefits. It would perpetuate the cumbersome structure of contracting out. It would do nothing to encourage employers to set up schemes or people to make extra provision through personal pensions" (Secretary of State for Social Services 1985a, par. 1.38). It therefore proposed "a new partnership" between state provision and occupational and personal provision. Its long-term goal was the position in which the state provided a basic pension for all and everybody also had an additional pension provided out of individual savings.

The main proposals for reform were to leave the basic state pension unchanged; to have men over fifty and women over forty-five continue under the existing system; to honor all existing pension entitlements under the state scheme (in the form of eventual pension payments rather than a "recognition bond"); and to phase out SERPS and replace it with occupational and personal pension schemes.

3.1.9   The 1985 Reforms

Ultimately, the government decided not to phase out SERPS. In the white paper *Reform of Social Security: Programme for Action* (Secretary of State for Social Services 1985b), published in December of the same year, it reported that a number of organizations, including in particular the Confederation of British Industry and the National Association of Pension Funds, had argued that the scheme should be modified rather than replaced. Opposition by employers partly reflected the perceived difficulties of matching the benefits offered by SERPS for the lower paid. That, in turn, was due to the fixed-cost element of pension arrangements and to the low real returns on pension funds being achieved at the time. The government accepted these arguments on the basis that it could meet two objectives: to reduce the emerging cost of SERPS and to ensure that conditions were created whereby individual pension provision could expand.

The changes to reduce the cost of SERPS followed those proposed in the green paper: Occupational pension schemes contracted out of the state scheme should be responsible for inflation-proofing GMPs up to 3 percent a year (previously full indexation of the GMP had been the responsibility of the state). SERPS pensions should be based on a lifetime's earnings, not on the best twenty years. SERPS pensions should be calculated on 20 percent of earnings rather than 25 percent. And widows and widowers over sixty-five should be allowed to inherit half their spouse's SERPS rights rather than the full amount. The net result of the changes was expected to nearly halve the cost of SERPS in 2033–34 from £25.5 billion to around £13 billion at 1985 prices.

At the same time, the government announced a strategy to extend individual pension provision, to widen the choice for the individual, and to increase competition among pension providers. Seven points of the strategy were emphasized: (1) Contracted-out occupational schemes could include defined-contribution schemes. The minimum contribution would be the contracted-out rebate. The government believed that this would encourage industry-wide schemes. (2) An additional incentive in the form of an additional NIC rebate of 2 percent would be granted for five years to encourage employers to set up new schemes and individuals to set up personal pensions. (3) Membership in occupational pension schemes would no longer be compulsory for eligible employees. (4) Personal pensions, which had hitherto been limited to the self-employed, would be a vehicle to allow employees to contract out. The full amount of the NIC rebate plus the 2 percent incentive could be devoted to these so-called appropriate personal pensions (APPs). Contributions would be given tax relief. (5) Banks, unit trusts, and building societies as well as insurance companies would be able to provide personal pension savings schemes. (6) All occupational scheme members would have the right to pay additional voluntary contributions to boost their pensions. (7) Steps would be taken to provide investor protection for members of occupational schemes and the holders of personal pensions.

These changes were in addition to reforms that had already been introduced in the 1985 Social Security Act. The reforms had included protection of the pension rights of early leavers from occupational pension schemes (by requiring them to be increased in line with prices up to 5 percent a year) and transfer rights (everyone leaving a scheme would have the right to a transfer value representing the value of deferred pension rights, which could be put in a new employer's scheme or a single premium annuity or, under the new proposals, into a personal pension).

It can be seen that the proposals were designed to encourage private provision of second-tier pensions and to increase the "portability" of pensions. The extension of personal pensions to employees would particularly favor those who expected to change jobs frequently and who tended to be penalized by defined-benefit schemes. (The origin of occupational pensions was of course expressly designed to encourage long-term job tenure in such industries as banking and insurance.)

The government actuary (Secretary of State for Social Services 1985b, app.) estimated that the National Insurance contribution rate to pay for National Insurance benefits would be 15 percent by 2033, assuming that the basic pension was uprated in line with prices, compared with 18 percent if SERPS had been left unchanged. He commented that the new rate was one that future generations should be able to afford. The changes to SERPS (along with other major reforms to the social security system) were introduced in the 1986 Social Security Act.

The contracted-out rebate and the additional 2 percent incentive made personal pensions a very good deal, particularly for the young, since the rebate was the same for all ages, whereas the value of the SERPS benefit given up increases with age. The Department of Social Security's working assumptions were that about 500,000 people would take out personal pensions and that the number might ultimately reach 1.75 million. In fact, take-up reached 4 million by the end of April 1990 and by 1993–94 had risen to 5.7 million, of whom about 4 million had rebates paid into their personal pensions.

The National Audit Office (1990) commissioned a survey of the cost to the NIF of the rebate and the additional incentive for the period to April 1993. The survey estimated that the gross cost could be £9.3 billion and that the present value of the savings in payments of pensions was about £3.4 billion. Hence, there was a net present value cost of £5.9 billion (in 1988 prices). However, this does not take account of the step change in personal pension take-up, which will have reduced state pensions yet further in the next century even after the end of the continuation of the 2 percent incentive.

A further shadow has been cast over this episode by the fact that some of those who joined personal pension schemes left occupational schemes that offered more favorable terms. Inquiries are still continuing into alleged cases of misselling of personal pensions during this period.

3.1.10   The 1995 Pensions Act

Further reforms to SERPS were introduced in the 1995 Pensions Act. The main purpose of the act was to provide additional safeguards for occupational pensions following the Maxwell affair[7] and to equalize the state retirement age (which mainly affects the basic state pension) by increasing women's retirement age from sixty to sixty-five. But, at the same time, changes were introduced to SERPS that further reduced its future cost.

The 1986 Social Security Act had, as described above, enabled people to contract out of SERPS and buy APPs or join a defined-contribution occupational scheme. The 1995 Pensions Act is expected to reduce further the cost of

---

7. The late Robert Maxwell allegedly diverted pension fund assets, including those of Mirror Group Newspapers, in an attempt to restore solvency and liquidity to other companies under his control, thereby undermining the solvency of the occupational pension schemes and thus threatening the pensions of current and former employees.

Table 3.4   **Reductions in SERPS Expenditure in 2030–31 as a Result of the 1995 Pensions Act (£billion, 1994–95 prices)**

Equalization of pension age for men and women	1.9
Annualization	2.5
Abolition of guaranteed minimum pension	2.4

SERPS in 2030–31 by £6.7 billion (in 1994–95 prices). Table 3.4 shows how the savings arise.

The raising of the state pension age for women to sixty-five will be phased in over a ten-year period from 2010. It follows the European Court of Justice ruling that men and women must receive equal pension treatment. Annualization will effectively introduce an annual calculation of entitlement to SERPS, rather than a calculation at the point of retirement. This change prevents earnings below the LEL, in any year, generating SERPS entitlement. Under the old arrangements, earnings in individual years were uprated by the growth in whole-economy average earnings until retirement. The LEL at the retirement date, which had since 1980 been uprated only in line with prices, was then subtracted from these revalued earnings. As a result, employees earning below the LEL were able to accumulate entitlement to SERPS. Even contracted-out employees (earning above the LEL) will have acquired around £2.80 a week worth of SERPS entitlement.

The abolition of the GMP breaks the links between SERPS and contracted-out pensions. The state will no longer guarantee price indexation for contracted-out pensions. (The act has, however, required private-sector schemes to index future pensions by inflation or by 5 percent a year, whichever is lower.)

The 1995 Pensions Act also required that age-related rebates for contracted-out defined-contribution schemes, including personal pensions, be introduced from April 1997. This was aimed at removing the excessive incentive for younger people to contract out and encouraging older people to do so.

Table 3.5 shows how the projected future costs of SERPS have changed since it was first introduced in 1975. The changes to the scheme in the 1986 Social Security Act and the 1995 Pensions Act are estimated to reduce the public-sector cost of SERPS in 2030 from £41 billion to £12 billion (at 1994–95 prices). These latest estimates imply that the original scheme would

Table 3.5   **Effect of Reforms to SERPS (£billion, 1994–95 prices)**

	1994–95	2000–01	2010–11	2020–21	2030–31
Original regime (1975–86)	1.8	4.2	12.0	25.0	41.0
After 1986 Social Security Act	1.8	4.2	9.2	14.5	18.7
After 1995 Pensions Act	1.8	4.2	8.4	10.9	12.0

Table 3.6   **Number of Employees in Occupational Pension Schemes, 1991 (millions)**

Type of Scheme	Private Sector Contracted Out	Private Sector Contracted In	Public Sector Contracted Out	Total
Defined benefit	5.04	.56	4.20	9.80
Defined contribution	.43	.47	.00	.90
Total	5.47	1.03	4.20	10.70

have been about £5 billion more expensive (in 1994–95 prices) than expected at the time of the 1986 act.

The lower public-sector cost of SERPS does not mean that large numbers of people now have only one-third their previous second-tier pension provision. Instead, much of the reduction comes from more contracting out, which yields public expenditure savings without necessarily affecting individuals' future pension entitlement.

3.2   Occupational and Personal Pensions

In 1991 (the last year for which figures are available), about 68 percent of employees belonged to non-SERPS pension schemes. About one-third of these belonged to personal pension schemes.

All personal pension schemes are defined-contribution schemes. Until the 1986 legislation, approved occupational schemes had to be of the defined-benefit form. Occupational pension schemes remain predominantly of this type. The position in 1991, as described in Disney (1995), is shown in table 3.6.

Some employers have expressed interest in shifting from defined-benefit to defined-contribution schemes now that they are permitted to do so and still be contracted out.[8] This interest may be partly based on the view that defined-contribution schemes are less risky for employers than defined-benefit schemes. However, as the table shows, 90 percent of employees in private-sector contracted-out occupational schemes were in defined-benefit schemes in 1991, and the following account is mainly based on schemes of this type.

Defined-benefit schemes are typically based on actual final salaries (or some average of final years' salaries). Employee contribution rates payable in 1991 are shown in table 3.7.

It can be seen that a contribution rate of 5–7 percent is typical, although a significant number of private-sector employees (typically in the financial sector) are in noncontributory schemes. Contributions by employers—for funded schemes—are based on actuarial estimates and can therefore vary from year to year according to the performance of the investment funds. The contracting-

---

8. Disney and Stears (1996) discuss the moves between defined-benefit and defined-contribution schemes.

Table 3.7 **Number of Members of Defined-Benefit Schemes Contributing Various Percentages of Salary (thousands)**

% of Salary	Private Sector Contracted Out	Public Sector
Under 2	20	650
2 and under 3	150	0
3 and under 4	275	0
4 and under 5	730	5
5 and under 6	1,690	240
6 and under 7	1,125	2,805
7 and over	105	210
Noncontributory	945	290

out arrangements impose minimum requirements on occupational schemes. The requirements correspond approximately to the benefits provided by SERPS, which can in turn be linked to the contracted-out rebate (currently 4.8 percent but to be reduced to 4.6 percent in 1997). Most occupational schemes are considerably more generous than this and provide combined contribution rates that are equivalent to up to 15 percent of total salary. It should be emphasized that, in the United Kingdom, unlike in some continental European countries, employers' contributions (as well as those made by employees) are explicit and placed in a separately identifiable fund. They are not simply recorded as a reserve.

Pensions are essentially subject to "expenditure tax" treatment. Contributions by employers and employees are tax free (subject to Inland Revenue limits), and returns on invested funds are also free of tax. Pensions in payment are taxable, but a tax-free lump sum may be withdrawn on retirement. The lump sum may be up to 1½ times final salary or 25 percent of the accumulated fund for a personal pension.[9]

Benefits vary from scheme to scheme. In the private sector, the normal retirement age for men, and now for women following the implementation of equal treatment, is predominantly sixty-five. In the public sector, more than 50 percent of employees have a normal retirement age of sixty or younger. In existing private-sector schemes, the normal retirement age for 50 percent of women is sixty. Following the 1995 Pensions Act, schemes must treat men and women equally. In private- and public-sector schemes, the accrual rate is typically one-eightieth per year for schemes that provide a pension and an additional lump sum and one-sixtieth for those that provide only a pension. (Since part of a pension-only scheme can be converted to a lump sum, the two systems of benefit are more or less equivalent.) Thus, after forty years' service in the same scheme, members of a typical defined-benefit scheme retire with a

9. The pension fund industry argues that lump sum treatment is not as generous as it seems since fund accruals are given tax relief only at the lower rate of income tax rather than members' marginal tax rate.

Table 3.8   **Defined-Benefit Schemes and Benefits Payable on Death in Service (thousands)**

Benefit Payable	Private Sector	Public Sector	Total
None	10	. . .	10
Lump sum	5,540	4,050	9,590
Refund of contributions	2,870	1,020	3,890
Pension to surviving spouse	5,450	4,200	9,650
Pension to surviving children	4,110	4,200	8,310
If unmarried, pension to a nominated person	1,870	750	2,620

Notes: Lump sum is subject to a maximum of four times annual salary if tax relief is to be provided. Schemes may appear under more than one category.

pension of two-thirds of their final salary (part of which may be converted to a lump sum).

Table 3.8 shows the benefits payable on death in service. Since there are 10.7 million members of pension schemes, it can be seen that almost all members are entitled to a lump sum and/or a pension for the surviving spouse on death in service.

Since the 1986 Social Security Act, members of occupational pension schemes have been able to transfer their accrued pension rights to another occupational scheme or to a personal pension.

Large schemes (i.e., those with more than five thousand members) are usually self-administered, with the funds invested by their own investment managers or an insurance company. Smaller schemes are usually insured schemes.

By international standards, there are few restrictions on the types of investment allowed funded occupational schemes. There are, for example, no limits on the proportions devoted to investment in equities or in overseas securities. There are limits on self-investment, and schemes cannot provide loans to members or on residential property. As table 3.9 shows, the United Kingdom has a high proportion of private-sector pension funds invested in overseas equities.

3.2.1 Personal Pensions

Information on personal pensions is difficult to extract and analyze (see Johnson, Disney, and Stears 1996, chap. 5). It is estimated that, in 1991, 24 percent of employees had contracted-out personal pensions. The only investment in about three-fifths of these personal pensions was the rebate, equal to the contracted-out rebate together with any related incentives, which is paid

Table 3.9   **Percentage of Pension Funds Held in Foreign Assets, 1993**

Belgium	29	Japan	14
Canada	9	New Zealand	34
France	5	United Kingdom	27
Germany	3	United States	4

into the scheme by the Department of Social Security. For young individuals in particular, a rebate-only pension should provide a better pension than SERPS.

Personal pensions are available from a number of providers. These providers are mainly insurance companies, although building societies, unit trusts, and other financial organizations are permitted to administer pensions (at least up to retirement). As with occupational schemes, there are relatively few restrictions on investments.

Protected rights from appropriate personal pensions are now available from age fifty for both men and women. In general, proceeds from personal pension funds must be used to purchase an annuity. Recent changes in legislation have increased the individual's freedom of choice between alternative annuity suppliers. They have also allowed the purchase of an annuity to be deferred until age seventy-five (with upper and lower limits on the sums that can be withdrawn up to that point).

Personal pensions receive the same tax privileges as occupational pensions.

3.2.2 Annuities

In the United Kingdom, people "annuitizing" any individual pension savings will normally stay with the insurance provider or, on occasion, take advantage of any "open market option" to withdraw their accumulated fund and purchase the annuity from a different insurer. Any penalty is usually relatively small (and, where there is a change of insurer, is presumably more than offset by the better terms offered by the annuity provider). This market is at present unaffected by contracted-out appropriate personal pensions as these have been concentrated at younger ages. The effect of these on the annuity market will not be evident for about twenty years.

Income withdrawals from a personal pension fund prior to purchasing an annuity has generally been limited to those with relatively large pension savings. One reason for this is that such people are in a better position to understand and accept the risks involved in betting against the investment market and their individual mortality. But it is also true that the expense charges appear to be relatively high and would be an onerous burden on smaller pensions savings.

One particular aspect of the uncertainty over the date of annuity purchase is selection, that is, individuals and/or the insurance companies trying to opt for arrangements that prove to be (or at least seem likely to be) most beneficial to them. This can reduce the validity of detailed historical analysis looking solely at what has happened in the annuity market before, although, as relevant data become available, proper allowance can be made for such options.

Insurance companies could aim to select people in the hope that they would die quickly. In a perfect market, another company would offer higher pensions at retirement to such "poorer lives." It is worth noting that some insurance companies in the United Kingdom offer enhanced pensions to such "impaired" lives. One company—Stalwart Insurance—has recently extended this approach beyond the very ill. They intend to offer annuities that pay more to those with medical conditions that are more likely to cause an early death (obesity, high cholesterol levels, high blood pressure, and diabetes) but whose conditions are not life threatening.

Indexed annuities are widely available in the U.K. market.

In summary, the U.K. pension annuity market is well developed and on a sound actuarial basis, with the result that the scope for selection is very restricted. It is only in newer aspects, such as perhaps income withdrawal, where statistical experience is lacking, although it is possible to use the data available to make reasonable assumptions about the potential effect on both those taking up such options and, equally important, those not doing so.

3.3   Distribution of Pensioner Incomes

Average pensioner incomes have risen by about 50 percent in real terms since 1979. Higher incomes from occupational pensions and from investments, both of which have more than doubled, account for most of this increase. Pensioners' earnings from employment have fallen somewhat, while state pensions plus benefits have gone up. Table 3.10 shows how the mean income from each source, adjusted for the falling proportion of pensioners who are single, has changed since 1979.[10] (The raw figures show even higher average real increases in incomes.)

The increases in occupational pension and investment income reflect both higher real amounts on average and a bigger proportion of pensioners receiving these types of income. Seventy-three percent of pensioners had some investment income in 1993, up from 62 percent in 1979. The average amount increased by 88 percent over the same period. The proportion receiving occupational pensions rose by nearly half (from 43 to 62 percent), and the average occupational pension paid increased by 63 percent.

This increase in average incomes has been accompanied by a widening of the distribution of pensioners' incomes, as it has for the population of working age. However, table 3.11 shows that real incomes have increased significantly for all quintiles of the distribution.

Fewer pensioners are now at the bottom of the distribution of all household incomes. The bottom quintile of the income distribution contained 25 percent of all pensioners in 1992–93, compared to 47 percent in 1979.

3.4   Notes toward an Assessment

The main focus of this paper is on description rather than evaluation. As already discussed, the main features of the U.K. system are the modest level

10. The material on the distribution of pensioner incomes comes from Department of Social Security (1995).

Table 3.10   **Average Pensioner Incomes**

	1979[a]	1993[a]	% Real Increase, 1979–93
Gross income	113.40	166.70	47
Of which:			
State pension plus benefits	69.20	89.40	29
Occupational pension	18.20	40.90	125
Investment income	12.30	26.70	117
Earnings	13.10	9.20	−30
Other income	.70	.50	−25

[a]£ per week, July 1993 prices.

of the basic state pension, the encouragement of private-sector schemes for the provision of second-tier pensions, and reduced entitlements under the state earnings-related second-tier system. This section discusses some aspects of the economic consequences of the U.K. system. Typically, the relevant consequences are effects on savings, including public finances, and effects on labor supply, in terms of retirement and work/leisure choices during employment.

A common element in assessing these consequences is the rate of return on pension contributions. For example, Feldstein (1996) argues that contributions to the federal system are in effect a tax since the implied returns are lower than those available in private schemes. The following subsection discusses some calculations with respect to the U.K. system. We do not discuss labor supply effects, a discussion of which can be found in Dilnot et al. (1994).

3.4.1 Rates of Return

As Samuelson (1958) has shown, the return on a pay-as-you-go earnings-related scheme depends on the growth of the working population and of average earnings. In the United Kingdom, under current policy the basic state pension is fixed in real terms, whereas contributions are related to earnings. It follows that the return on contributions will be different for different cohorts. In addition, since benefits are flat rate, whereas contributions are earnings re-

Table 3.11   **Distribution of Pensioners' Incomes**

	1979[a]	1993[a]	% Real Increase, 1979–93
Mean	98.20	148.55	51
10th percentile	54.40	67.30	24
30th percentile	63.40	86.10	36
Median	69.40	98.50	42
70th percentile	86.30	142.40	65
90th percentile	165.30	262.40	59

[a]£ per week, July 1993 prices.

lated, there is a redistributional element in the basic state scheme. (However, as Dilnot et al. [1994] point out, the effect is offset by the greater longevity of the higher paid.)

Disney and Whitehouse (1993a) estimated rates of return for the state pension scheme as a whole. Their results—reproduced in table 3.12—show that the real rate of return on state pensions will be negative for men retiring after 2020. (The returns will be higher for women than for men.)

These results precede the 1995 Pensions Act, which reduced both future benefits and contributions, and whose net effect on the rate of return was therefore unclear.

Disney and Whitehouse (1993b) also attempted to estimate the effect of contracting out of SERPS on the above analysis. They believe that those contracted out may have an intergenerational rate of return 0.5–1 percent higher than those who remain contracted in.

The reason for these low estimated rates of return is that the basic state pension is assumed to be fixed in real terms. Current employees are paying for pensions that are higher (relative to average real earnings) than those that they will receive when they in turn retire. This effect adds to the normal effect whereby rates of return for successive cohorts fall as state pension schemes mature.

Blake (1994) has estimated the rate of return from SERPS and from a typical contracted-out defined-benefit occupational scheme. For the first twenty years, the real rate of return from SERPS was 6.7 percent a year, about twice the 3.3 percent from the occupational scheme. This reflected the generosity of SERPS when it was initially set up, not because SERPS paid a very high pension—it paid 25 percent of the best twenty years' earnings, usually well below the occupational equivalent—but because contributions into SERPS were comparatively low and particularly benefited those close to retirement.

After the 1985 reforms, the real rate of return on SERPS fell from 6.7 percent per annum to 1.7 percent. The 1995 Pensions Act reduced it yet further, to 1.2 percent per annum. Thus, the real return on SERPS varies between 6.7 percent (for those who retire before 1999) and 1.2 percent (for those who will retire after 2030).

The rate of return on SERPS will affect not just savings (for those who remain members). It will also affect the decision on whether to join the

Table 3.12   **Intergenerational Real Rates of Return (% per annum)**

Cohort Retiring In	Mean	2nd Decile	Median	8th Decile
2000	1.0	.5	.0	2.2
2010	.2	−.1	.1	.5
2020	−.9	−.1	−1.2	−.5
2025	−.7	−.5	−.9	−.8

scheme. As described earlier, the choice was complicated by the special temporary incentives to leave the scheme and by the fact that the contracted-out rebate was the same for all ages. That particularly encouraged the younger employees to leave. Optimal strategies that involve leaving and then rejoining SERPS are described in Dilnot et al. (1994). The contracted-out rebate is, as of April 1997, age related, drastically reducing this incentive to switch into and out of SERPS.

It is clear that contributions to the basic state pension, particularly for the higher paid, are in effect a form of taxation and can therefore give rise to deadweight costs of the type described in Feldstein (1996). The position on SERPS is rather more complicated since employees are able to contract out into a private scheme, including personal pensions. If those who remain members are acting rationally, they must believe that the returns on contributions to SERPS are at least as good as those in a private pension scheme (for an equal contribution). Since most of those who have remained in SERPS are among the lower paid, it is reasonable to believe that they are indeed acting rationally. It is, however, possible that the element of compulsion causes them to contribute more to pension schemes than they would choose freely.

3.4.2   Macroeconomic Effects

This section provides a preliminary assessment of the extent to which the current system and changes to it over the past twenty years have affected private and public savings.

The introduction of SERPS in 1978 extended earnings-related pensions, on a generous basis for older employees, to a wider section of the population than had previously had access to them. Since it was a pay-as-you-go system and was additional to the basic state pension, one might have expected it to replace, at least at the margin, individual savings for retirement and thereby to have reduced personal-sector savings. As Feldstein (1996) has pointed out, the extent of displacement will depend, among other things, on the relative returns on the state scheme and on private-sector schemes. As already described, Blake's calculations suggest that the return on SERPS, particularly for those approaching retirement, was significantly higher than the return available on occupational pension schemes. This reinforces the view that personal savings are likely to have fallen as a result of the introduction of SERPS.

The same arguments would suggest that the subsequent reductions in the benefits available from SERPS would have raised personal-sector savings for those who remained members of the scheme. This effect should have been reinforced by those who left SERPS and moved to personal pensions, which are funded defined-contribution schemes.

Blake (forthcoming) has made a preliminary study of whether changes in pension wealth can explain movements in the personal-sector savings ratio. Using data from 1949 to 1994, he finds a significant negative relation between SERPS wealth and the savings ratio. In other words, the introduction of SERPS seems to have lowered the personal-sector savings ratio, and the subsequent reforms seem to have raised it. He finds no significant effects on savings from changes in basic state pension wealth but a significant effect from the real rate of return on the basic state pension. The freezing of the real value of pensions—which was a change from the previous policy and which reduced the real rate of return—thus raised the personal sector's savings ratio.

In addition to the effect on discretionary private savings, we can ask whether the changes in policy had any effect on public-sector savings. At the time of the introduction of SERPS, the total National Insurance contribution rate for contracted-in employees was raised from 14½ percent to 16½ percent. There was also a 2 percent surcharge, introduced as a fiscal measure. Thus, the increased flow of revenue could have been used to raise public-sector savings. However, there are reasons for believing that this is unlikely to be the case, although it is difficult to define the counterfactual. The United Kingdom sets its fiscal policy in relation to the public-sector borrowing requirement (PSBR), which is a cash-flow measure. Its policy does not take explicit account of contingent liabilities such as future pension payments. Thus, it will not have reduced its budget deficit (or increased its surplus) to allow for higher future payments under SERPS. In practice, the increased current revenue from higher National Insurance contributions will have been used to finance higher public spending or cuts in other taxes.

Since 1988, the government's fiscal objective has been a zero PSBR when the economy is at its trend level. Thus, the SERPS reforms, which reduced revenue flows, will not have led to a fall in public savings.

Blake does, however, find positive effects on savings from both occupational and personal pension wealth. Thus, it appears that the favorable tax treatment provided to these schemes has raised private savings and, given the exogenous nature of public-sector savings, will have raised total savings.

The fact that income support, which is a means-tested benefit, is higher than the basic state pension is likely to cause some discouragement of savings for the lower paid. There is in effect a 100 percent marginal tax rate on income from savings between the basic state pension and income support. Since the gap between the two is between 6 and 9 percent, the disincentive effects could be significant (see Hubbard, Skinner, and Zeldes 1995), although this will be offset by the requirement for all employees earning over £61.00 a week to make second-tier provision. Approximately 17 percent of pensioners receive income support.

3.5   Proposals for Reform

If the present system is maintained, the real value of the basic state pension will remain constant and hence fall relative to average earnings. At the same time, the value of the SERPS pension and of the compulsory element of contracted-out pensions will also fall relative to average earnings. If the real value of income support is also held constant, the increased level of entitlement to earnings-related schemes should reduce the need for payments of income support to pensioners. However, those pensioners with no or only a small amount of earnings-related pension will have a low level of entitlement relative to average earnings in the longer term.

This expected outcome is consistent with the then Conservative government's approach to public expenditure and to individual choice and is consistent with the Beveridge approach to pensions. An adequate level of income (but low relative to earnings) will be available to pensioners, mainly through the contributory basic state pension. Compulsory second-tier provision provided either by the state or by the private sector will provide a fairly modest earnings-related pension. Beyond that, the choice will be up to individuals and employers, assisted by tax incentives. The public-sector cost of pensions will fall relative to GDP, and, for given demographics, National Insurance contribution rates will be reduced.

A more radical application of this approach might raise questions as to why there is any compulsory second-tier provision at all and why such provision should still involve, at least to some extent, the public sector. However, most comment on pensions focuses on rather different questions. In particular, it draws attention to the continued reliance on income support of a significant proportion of pensioners and argues that the compulsory element of the second-tier pension is inadequate.

Suggested changes to the basic state pension include restoring the basic state pension to 20 percent of average male earnings and uprating it thereafter in line with average earnings. Such a move would be costly and would bring little benefit to the poorest pensioners, who are already entitled to income support. An alternative proposal is to concentrate the benefit of the basic pension on the least well off by increasing the benefit earned by lower-paid contributors and reducing the benefit earned by higher-paid contributors. Schemes of this type would achieve a significant effect only after many years. They have been criticized on the grounds that they would be highly complex, would undermine the contributory principle, and could have unfavorable effects on incentives.

3.5.1   An Assured Pension

The Retirement Income Inquiry (RII)[11] proposed a new minimum pension guarantee, provided to all people over state pension age as of right. It would be specifically designed to provide an adequate level of income for those who do not have sufficient income from other sources. It proposed the name *Assured Pension.*

The assessed income would disregard all assets but would take into account

11. The Retirement Income Inquiry, under the chairmanship of Sir John Anson, was set up by the National Association of Pension Funds. The inquiry was completely independent, and members served in an individual capacity. Their proposals are set out in Retirement Income Inquiry (1996).

other pension income and other income from savings (with a small disregard). The withdrawal of the assured pension would be tapered. The RII did not propose a specific rate at which withdrawal would be tapered but argued that some degree was essential. All those receiving an income-related pension under the assured pension would qualify automatically for means-tested benefits, such as the housing benefit.

The RII did not make a specific proposal about the level of the assured pension although that would be critical in determining both the cost and the fundamental nature of the overall scheme. It illustrated the costs of schemes that, at age sixty-five, would provide a weekly pension for a single person of £65.00 (approximately the current level of income support), £73.50 (20 percent of average male earnings), £80.00, and £120 (approximately one-third of average male earnings). The costs are shown in table 3.13.

In its least costly form, the assured pension (with no taper) is much the same as the present system except for increasing the take-up of income support and allowing extra disregards. If (as the RII proposes) there are changes to the second-tier system that improve private provision of pensions, the introduction of an assured pension should not involve any increase in costs beyond those outlined in table 3.13.

The RII proposed that the assured pension should be financed from general taxation, apart from the basic pension, which would continue to be met from the National Insurance Fund. If the basic pension continues to be indexed to prices rather than earnings, it will provide a decreasing proportion of the assured pension (and of pensioners' incomes in general).

The RII argues that the assured pension is a more effective way of using money to provide an adequate minimum retirement income than proposals to increase the value of all pensions. This is part of the general debate about means testing versus universal provision.

3.5.2 Second-Tier Provision

Compulsory second-tier provision for employees is currently either provided through SERPS or requires, in effect, contributions of 4.8 percent of earnings between the LEL and UEL to be paid into an approved occupational or personal pension scheme.

Table 3.13   **Additional Costs of an Assured Pension (£billion per year)**

	Amount per Week, Single Person (Couple)			
Withdrawal Rate	£65.00 (£104)	£73.50 (£117.60)	£80.00 (£128)	£120 (£192)
100 percent (no taper)	1.0	2.6	4.6	17.2
75 percent	1.2	3.0	5.4	19.7
50 percent	1.8	4.0	6.8	22.9

The argument for compulsory second-tier provision may rest partly on the view that individuals are not the best judges of their own savings decisions. A more compelling argument may be that it reduces the need for individuals to rely on (noncontributory) state support. Frank Field M.P. in particular has argued for the extension of compulsory earnings-related schemes (see Field 1995; and Field and Owen 1994). He is strongly opposed to means-tested benefits, which, he argues, "penalise all those values which make strong, vibrant communities" (Field 1995, 10). He proposes a two-part social security system. Public welfare provision would be administered by an independent stakeholders' insurance corporation that would, in due course, set contribution and benefit rates subject to a veto by the chancellor of the Exchequer. Contributions would be earnings related for all employees, including part-time workers and others below the LEL. The government would make contributions for the lowest-paid workers, but there would be a clear distinction between the redistributive function of the scheme (based on taxation) and its savings function (based on graduated contributions).

There would also be a compulsory second-tier system operating through a stakeholders' private pension corporation. All employees and self-employed persons would be compelled to become members of a private pension scheme. The board of the corporation would set the rate of contributions for employee and employer. Contributions would start at a modest level and would be progressively raised.

Many of Field's proposals were incorporated in the report of the Commission on Wealth Creation and Social Cohesion in a Free Society (Dahrendorf et al. 1995).

The RII concluded that a compulsory second tier is needed in order to avoid excessive costs to the taxpayer of providing an adequate minimum retirement income. It proposed that the minimum level of contributions to the second tier should be sufficient and its coverage wide enough to ensure that, in the future, almost all the retired population will have adequate incomes and will not require additional state support to achieve the minimum level of income guaranteed by the assured pension. If the assured pension is related to average earnings, and if the basic state pension remains fixed in real terms, the level of contributions to the second tier will need to rise through time.

Beyond that, the RII argued that the level of contributions to pensions should be a matter of personal choice. It proposes that SERPS should be phased out and replaced by a funded national pension scheme. It would be a defined-contribution scheme, with funds invested in a well-balanced portfolio of investments. The scheme would be compulsory for those not in a scheme meeting minimum requirements, but it would be open for anyone to join, and members could contribute above the minimum required level. Tax relief would be given to contributions and to income earned within the scheme, as is currently the case with occupational and personal pensions. On retirement, the proceeds will be used to purchase annuities. The committee argues that the national pension scheme would be particularly suitable for low-paid and mobile workers and those in small firms. It also believes that it would keep administrative costs low. It assumes that the national pension scheme would not be identified as part of public expenditure.

Employers and employees would be required to provide between them at least a minimum contribution to an approved scheme or to the national pension scheme. The employee would exercise the choice. The committee proposes that the minimum combined contribution should be set at the current contracted-out rebate of 4.8 percent. Compulsory contributions would be subject to an upper earnings limit, set at about the same level as the current UEL. There would also be a lower limit, which could be fixed at about the current LEL.

The committee proposes that rights already accrued under SERPS would be preserved and the eventual SERPS pensions financed on a pay-as-you-go basis from the National Insurance Fund. It also recommends that anyone within fifteen years of pension age should be allowed to remain in SERPS if they wish. Their compulsory contributions would be paid into the National Insurance Fund. Contracted-out rebates would cease. The new NIC rate would be set 0.5–0.7 percent higher than the current contracted-out rate, 4.3–4.1 percent lower than the contracted-in rate.

If the minimum contribution remains at 4.8 percent, the effect on contributions for employees and employers would be that those already contracted out would pay a higher NIC rate and existing contributions to an occupational or personal pension; that those leaving SERPS would pay a lower NIC rate and a minimum of 4.8 percent to their new funded scheme; and that those remaining in SERPS would pay a lower NIC rate but would pay 4.8 percent toward their SERPS pensions.

Compulsory contributions to the second tier should be increased through time to constrain the public-sector cost of paying the assured pension. This could presumably be done through increases in the compulsory contribution rate. The committee recommends that pensions should be required to provide at least limited price indexation and should include survivors' benefits. They also recommend that men and women should get equal pension rates for equal contributions within the compulsory element.

3.6   Privatization and the U.K. Experience

In this final section, we consider briefly, in the context of this collection of papers, the extent to which privatization has played a part in the development of the U.K. pensions system.

It is clear, from the other studies, that the key elements in the reforms elsewhere are privatization and funding, with the funds being invested in productive capital. Although the United Kingdom played a leading part in the privatization of activities formerly run by the public sector, it has not generally counted its changes to the pension system as part of this process. Richard Disney has commented that the first major change in the U.K. pensions system in the postwar period went in the opposite direction. The introduction of SERPS, and its predecessors, was an attempt to supplement the private sector's occupational pension schemes by extending second-tier pensions to a wider range of employees. It did not involve nationalization of the existing private schemes, but, at the time of its introduction, it provided a generous alternative, particularly for those close to retirement. In addition, it provided a potential supplement to all private-sector schemes by providing postretirement indexation at a time when most private schemes did not do so.

One can say that SERPS added an unfunded earnings-related public scheme to the funded private-sector pension schemes.

The reforms since 1985 certainly qualify as a move to privatization and funding. Those who have left SERPS have moved from public-sector to private-sector schemes. They have also moved from unfunded to funded schemes that are largely invested in equities. About half the employees who were members of SERPS in 1985 have left the scheme. In addition, new entrants to the labor force may join occupational pension schemes, if they are available, or can start personal pension schemes, using the contracted-out rebate plus possible supplements from employers or employees. These schemes are funded.

It remains true that all employees and the self-employed (with earnings above a lower limit) must belong to the basic state contributory pension scheme, which is pay as you go. However, under current policy, the value of the basic pension is fixed in real terms. The public-sector component of pension incomes is therefore withering away relative to private, funded provision. There is clearly an issue of whether this system too should be privatized and funded. That would, in turn, raise questions about whether it should become earnings related or whether there should continue to be at least a flat-rate element.

There is also the question of whether SERPS should be privatized and funded. That would be a rather simpler matter than privatizing and funding the basic pension scheme. That was, in effect, the original proposal in 1985, but, at that time, the private sector was reluctant to accept responsibility for providing earnings-related pensions for the low paid and workers who moved often into and out of employment.

Like other moves toward funded schemes, the United Kingdom's reforms have had a transitional cost. Disney estimates that the switch to personal pensions may currently be reducing National Insurance Fund revenue by about £3 billion a year (about 0.5 percent of GDP) and that to offset this an increase in contribution rates of up to 2 percentage points would be required. It is clear that current pensioners are not bearing this cost, nor are those who have contracted out of SERPS (except insofar as they share the general burden through higher National Insurance contributions or taxes). The £3 billion is being met by National Insurance contributors and/or taxpayers.

In general, one can say that the modest public-sector cost of pension provision in the United Kingdom does reflect a policy of privatization. Under current policies, funded private-sector schemes will provide an increasing proportion of retirement income. In the United Kingdom, by contrast with some other cases, this private provision—assisted by favorable tax treatment—will be largely voluntary rather than compulsory. Although employees are compelled to make pension provision (either in the state scheme or by investing in private pensions), there is less compulsion than there was before the reforms and significantly less than in many other industrial and developing countries.

References

Blake, D. 1994. Pension choices and pensions policy in the United Kingdom. Paper presented at the conference "Pensions: Funding, Privatisation and Macroeconomic Policy," Santiago, Chile, January.

———. 1995. *Pension schemes and pension funds in the United Kingdom.* Oxford: Clarendon.

———. Forthcoming. The effect of different wealth components on consumption in the United Kingdom. Pensions Institute Discussion Paper. Birkbeck College.

Chand, S. K., and A. Jaeger. 1996. Aging populations and public pension schemes. Occasional Paper no. 147. Washington, D.C.: International Monetary Fund.

Dahrendorf, R., F. Field, C. Hayman, W. Hutton, I. Hutcheson, D. Marquand, A. Sentance, and I. Wrigglesworth. 1995. *Report on wealth creation and social cohesion.* London: Commission on Wealth Creation and Social Cohesion.

Department of Social Security. 1995. *The pensioners' income series, 1993.* London.

Dilnot A., R. Disney, P. Johnson, and E. Whitehouse. 1994. *Pensions policy in the UK: An economic analysis.* London: Institute for Fiscal Studies.

Disney, R. 1995. Occupational pension schemes: Prospects and reforms in the UK. *Fiscal Studies* 16, no. 3: 19–39.

Disney, R., and G. Stears. 1996. Why is there a decline in defined benefit pension plan membership in Britain? Institute for Fiscal Studies Working Paper no. W96/4. London.

Disney, R., and E. Whitehouse. 1993a. Will the younger cohorts obtain a worse return on their pension contributions? In *Industrial concentration and economic inequality: Essays in honour of P. E. Hart,* ed. J. Creedy and M. Casson. Aldershot: Edward Elgar.

———. 1993b. Contracting out and lifetime redistribution in the UK state pension system. *Oxford Bulletin of Economics and Statistics* 55, No. 1:25–42.

Feldstein, M. 1996. The missing piece in policy analysis: Social security reform. Working Paper no. 5413. Cambridge, Mass.: National Bureau of Economic Research.

Field, F. 1995. *Making welfare work.* London: Institute of Community Studies.

Field, F., and M. Owen. 1994. *National pensions savings plan.* London: Fabian Society.

Hubbard, R. G., J. Skinner, and S. Zeldes. 1995. Precautionary saving and social insurance. *Journal of Political Economy* 103, no. 2:360–99.

Johnson, P., R. Disney, and G. Stears. 1996. *Pensions: 2000 and beyond.* Vol. 2, *Analysis of trends and options.* London: Retirement Income Inquiry.

Johnson, P., and G. Stears. 1996. Should the basic state pension be a contributory benefit? *Fiscal Studies* 17, no. 1:105–12.

National Audit Office. 1990. *The elderly: Information requirements for supporting the elderly and implications of personal pensions for the national insurance fund.* London: H.M. Stationery Office.

Retirement Income Inquiry. 1996. *Pensions 2000 and beyond.* Vol. 1, *The report of the Retirement Income Inquiry.* London.

Samuelson, P. 1958. An exact consumption loan model of interest with or without the social contrivance of money. *Journal of Political Economy* 66:467–82.

Secretary of State for Social Services. 1985a. *Reform of social security.* Cmnd. 9517 and Cmnd. 9518, vols. 1, 2. London: H.M. Stationery Office.

———. 1985b. *Reform of social security: Programme for action.* Cmnd. 9691. London: H.M. Stationery Office.

Shigehara, K. 1995. Commentary on "Long-term tendencies in budget deficits and debt" by P. Masson and M. Mussa. In *Budget deficits and debt: Issues and options: Proceedings of a symposium sponsored by the Federal Reserve Bank of Kansas City.* Kansas City, Mo.: Federal Reserve Bank of Kansas City.

Comment   Richard Disney

Discussion

Alan Budd and Nigel Campbell are to be congratulated on providing a clear and succinct account of the pension system in the United Kingdom, in particular concerning its historical reform process as well as reform proposals now on the table. Unlike in Chile, there was no "clean" privatization of social security in the United Kingdom: just over two decades ago, the U.K. system was characterized by a flat social security pension augmented by welfare benefits, coupled to private pension plans covering 50 percent of the workforce. The 1975 legislation saw the introduction of an additional social security pension scheme, the State Earnings-Related Pension Scheme (SERPS), for most workers not covered by private pensions. Existing private pensions were brought into the social security system by the means of "contracting out": company pension schemes paid lower rates of contribution to the National Insurance Fund on behalf of their members and in turn took on responsibility for paying a guaranteed minimum pension (GMP) to their members in retirement in lieu of SERPS.

This framework of contracting out was used as the basis for the partial privatization of the U.K. social security system after the 1986 legislation, which had stemmed from a projection that the long-run costs of SERPS were unaffordable. Now, in exchange for sacrificing their SERPS entitlement, individu-

Richard Disney is professor of economics at Queen Mary and Westfield College, University of London, and a research fellow of the Institute for Fiscal Studies, London.

als could have their contracted-out rebate paid into an individual savings account known as a personal pension. Such approved personal pension accounts (APPs) could be augmented by additional voluntary tax-relieved contributions. Around 25 percent of the workforce availed themselves of the opportunity of establishing APP accounts between 1987–88 and 1994–95, with a few choosing to leave company pension plans in order to do so. With the decline in the value of the flat basic pension charted by Alan Budd and Nigel Campbell and around 75 percent of the workforce in some form of pension plan or APP account, pensioners in the United Kingdom in the future will largely rely on private pensions for their income.

Projections

The effect of this reform process, described by Budd and Campbell, is summarized in table 3C.1, which gives official projections of the future costs of providing social security in the United Kingdom. The table shows that, despite the decline in the support ratio of workers to pensioners from 2.1 at the turn of the century to just over 1.5 in 2050–51, the required National Insurance contribution rate of the pay-as-you-go social security program actually falls by over 4 percentage points. The authors describe how this "financing miracle" is achieved by the decline in the value of the basic pension, relative to earnings, the equalization of state pensionable age for men and women at sixty-five after 2010–11, the projected cutbacks in the generosity of SERPS, and the increase in contracting out of the social security program. They do not perhaps give sufficient emphasis to this last point. Tax expenditures of lower National Insur-

Table 3C.1	**Future Trends in United Kingdom Support Ratio, Social Security Expenditure, and Contribution Rates**				
	1994–95	2000–2001	2010–11	2030–31	2050–51
Basic pension[a]	26.9	29.8	33.6	41.9	42.3
SERPS[a]	1.8	4.2	8.4	12.0	9.9
Incapacity benefits[a]	6.3	5.7	6.3	6.9	6.5
Other benefits[a,b]	2.5	2.6	2.4	3.0	2.9
Total	39.9	42.2	50.8	63.8	61.7
Contribution rate (%)[c]	18.3	17.9[d]	17.5	17.4	14.1
No. of pensioners[e]	10.6	11.0	12.4	14.7	14.9
No. of contributors[e]	22.0	22.7	24.0	23.9	22.9
Support ratio	2.06	2.06	1.94	1.63	1.54

Source: National Insurance Fund (1995).
[a]£billion at 1994–95 prices.
[b]Including widow's benefits and other benefits.
[c]Joint contribution for contracted-in employees.
[d]Assumed contracted-out rebate for the period from 1997–98 to 2001–2002 is 4.95 percent.
[e]In millions.

ance contributions to APP members are currently running at some £3 billion a year, and these rebates were a major reason for the rise in contribution rates and the deficit financing of the National Insurance Fund in the early 1990s. I calculate that the contribution rate required to finance social security is up to 2 percentage points higher currently as a result and some 2 percentage points lower in the future also. In other words, the contribution rate would have remained roughly constant, at 16 percent of eligible earnings, from 1994–95 to 2050–51 rather than falling by 4 percentage points, as indicated in table 3C.1, had APPs not been introduced.

Rates of Return

Feldstein (1996) has pointed to the implicit deadweight loss arising from pay-as-you-go (PAYGO) financing of pensions when capital market returns exceed the growth of the earnings base. Such a discrepancy might also provide a rationale for the shift from SERPS to APPs in the 1980s and 1990s in the United Kingdom. Table 3C.2 shows that the United Kingdom does indeed obtain an excess return on full funding over PAYGO funding of around 6½ percentage points annual return. Indeed, my calculations in Disney and Whitehouse (1993) suggest that returns for men remaining in SERPS will actually be negative in the future, providing a rationale for why so many young men not covered by company pension plans have purchased APPs.

However, the "premium" of funded schemes should be qualified by considerations of risk and transactions costs. Figure 3C.1 shows clearly that the performance of real returns of pension funds tends to fluctuate much more widely than the Samuelsonian "return" on PAYGO funding. Table 3C.3 compares transactions costs on different types of pension plans and social security using

Table 3C.2   **U.K. Real Rates of Return**

Pension fund investment performance, 1979–94, median fund's real return[a]	8.5 percent per annum
Growth of PAYGO earnings base, 1979–94, annual growth of earnings bill[b]	1.8 percent per annum
Memo items:[c]	
Growth of retail prices, 1979–94	6 percent per annum
Growth of real earnings, 1979–94	2 percent per annum
SERPS + BSP,[d] men retiring 2000 (mean return)	1.0 percent per annum
SERPS + BSP, men retiring 2020 (mean return)	−.9 percent per annum

[a]The median return obtained by all the pension funds participating in the Combined Actuarial Performance Services Ltd. sample. A "typical" fund will invest as follows: domestic equity, 60 percent; foreign equity, 20 percent; other, 20 percent. *Source:* Bacon & Woodrow (1996).

[b]*Source: Economic Trends.*

[c]For contracted-out men, rates of return on BSP + GMP are some 0.5–1.0 percent higher. For women, rates of return on SERPS + BSP may be considerably higher. *Source:* For social security returns, see the text of Budd and Campbell.

[d]Basic state pension.

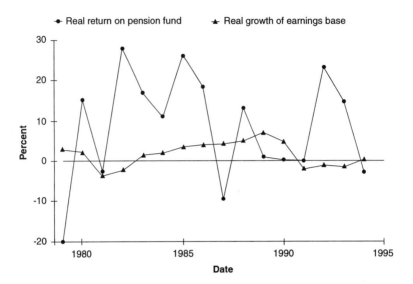

Fig. 3C.1   Annual real growth of funding and social security bases

Table 3C.3   U.K. Pension Transactions Costs

Social security pension: Administrative costs as % of expenditure[a]	1.2
Occupational (company) pensions: "Expenses and miscellaneous expenditures" as% of expenditure[b]	5.1
Personal pensions:[c] Average charges attached to a five-year monthly premium APP as % of fund value	
£200 per month, taken out 1 January 1993, retire at sixty-five (highest, 24.0 percent; lowest, 3.3 percent)	13.0
One stand-alone premium (of £10,000) (highest, 14.7 percent; lowest, 4.3 percent)	10.2

[a]*Source: The Government's Expenditure Plans.*

[b]*Source: Eighth Survey of Occupational Schemes, 1987* (1991).

[c]These are based on plan charge structures (reported in Walford 1995), applied to a projected APP given the above assumptions plus an assumed rate of return (10 percent per annum gross). Actual payouts (which may incorporate differences in plan performance) are also reported in Walford (1995).

a comparable measure across plan types (for a discussion of the appropriateness of this measure and other measures, see Mitchell, chap. 10 in this volume). Social security pensions are by far the cheapest to operate, and the costs attached to company pension plan management and to APPs should be regarded as reducing returns by up to 50 and 150 basis points, respectively. Note, too, the extent of idiosyncratic plan risk as indicated by the spread of returns within APP plans and the fact that APP charging structures typically contain a lump sum element that should discourage purchasers with the very lowest incomes.

Who Are Approved Personal Pension Members?

In any discussion of the privatization of U.K. social security, it is APP members who are of most interest. Unlike in Chile, individuals in the United Kingdom can opt to remain in social security or to buy an APP, or to participate in a group plan, whether of the defined-benefit or the defined-contribution type, if covered. The choice structure is a more complex version of the structure modeled by Gustman and Steinmeier (chap. 8 in this volume). Although it would be possible to construct scenarios where individuals differed in their degree of risk aversion and where utility maximization decisions "sorted" individuals into different sectors (as in Brugiavini and Disney 1995), the choice between SERPS and an APP has been driven by the differential accrual structures and the financial nexus (Disney and Whitehouse 1992). Thus, APP members are typically young (people aged under thirty constituted 66 percent of optants in 1987–88, although that figure fell to 49 percent of the total in 1992–93) and male (68 percent of members in 1987–88, 63 percent in 1992–93). The median contribution of contracted-out rebate into an APP account was £9.00 per week in 1992–93 for a man (roughly £11.00, or U.S.$17.00, in current prices) and £6.00 per week in 1992–93 for a woman. These financial amounts are not large.

For individuals who lose or leave their job, no statutory contribution is made. The proportion of APP members reporting zero earnings, and therefore zero statutory contributions, rose from 11 percent in 1987–88 to 21 percent in 1992–93. And, according to official statistics from the Department of Social Security, only half of those with APPs in 1992–93 who started their accounts before 1990–91 reported having positive earnings in every year. This low proportion is not surprising given the age profile of APP members, but it raises some concern as to whether all individuals with APP accounts will obtain reasonable incomes on retirement. This concern has permeated some of the reform proposals described by Budd and Campbell, in particular the idea of having higher mandatory minimum contributions into these individual savings accounts. But it should be borne in mind that, given the differences in expected returns, APP members should be no worse off than were they to have remained in SERPS.

Of some interest given these low "basic" contributions, and the recent debate in the United States concerning the effect of IRAs and 401(k) plans on savings, is the scope for making additional voluntary contributions into APP accounts. For various reasons, official data have been very poor on this question in the United Kingdom. However, waves 2–4 of the British Household Panel Survey (BHPS) of incomes provide some interesting data on this issue. Official figures suggest that roughly 50 percent of APP members make additional contributions, and, according to BHPS data, mean weekly contributions (of those who contributed) were £11.60 in 1992, £12.50 in 1993, and £14.70 in 1994. These figures gross up to total additional contributions (savings) of some £2.2 billion in 1994, consistent with Inland Revenue data.

Preliminary tabulation of the data suggest some degree of persistence in savings behavior. For example, there is no tendency for the probability of contributing to decline with the duration since the APP contract was taken out. Furthermore, individuals who contributed at $t-1$ are disproportionately more likely to contribute a larger amount at t, when controlling for background characteristics. But the evidence of variability in savings (and probably in job holding) is also strong: only 40 percent of the sample contributed in *every* year from 1992 to 1994. Of those who *did not* contribute in 1994, 43 percent had made an additional contribution in 1993 and 59 percent in 1992. Conversely, of those who did not contribute in 1993, 40 percent did contribute in 1994.

Overall, the picture is of a minority of APP members who are engaged in a persistent lifetime savings strategy. Others, whether owing to myopia, youth, or searching the labor market for better jobs, have a more erratic record of contribution to their APPs. This instability, plus complaints over high selling charges and misselling of some APPs, has cast a cloud over the APP "privatization" in the United Kingdom. Nevertheless, the underlying fundamentals and the maturation of contributors give hope that this sector will become a central component of future pension provision in the United Kingdom.

References

Bacon & Woodrow. 1996. *Pensions pocket book, 1996.* London: NTC.
Brugiavini, A., and R. Disney. 1995. The choice of private pension plan under uncertainty. Working Paper no. 95/5. London: Institute for Fiscal Studies, May.
Disney, R., and E. Whitehouse. 1992. *The personal pension stampede.* London: Institute for Fiscal Studies. Report Series.
———. 1993. Will the younger cohorts obtain a worse return on their pension contributions? In Industrial concentration and economic inequality: Essays in honor of P. E. Hart, ed. J. Creedy and M. Casson. Aldershot: Edward Elgar.
Economic Trends. Various years. London: Her Majesty's Stationery Office.
Eighth Survey of Occupational Pension Schemes, 1987. 1991. Government Actuary's Department. London: Her Majesty's Stationery Office.
Feldstein, M. 1996. The missing piece in policy analysis: Social security reform (Richard T. Ely lecture). *American Economic Association Papers and Proceedings* 86 (May): 1–14.
The government's expenditure plans: Social security. Various years. London: Her Majesty's Stationery Office.
National Insurance Fund: Long term financial estimates: Third quinquennial review by the government actuary. 1995. House of Commons Paper no. 160. London: Her Majesty's Stationery Office.

Walford, J. 1995. *Personal pensions, 1994.* London: Financial Times Business Enterprises.

Discussion Summary   Jeffrey Liebman and Andrew Samwick

Many of the questions in the discussion focused on the unique "contracting-out" features of the British system. The contracting-out rebate is currently 4.8 percent, falling to 4.6 out of a total 20.2 percent maximum tax rate on all social insurance contributions. The option to contract out partially does not exist. Many participants asked whether it was optimal to contract out or to switch back and forth between SERPS and being contracted out. The authors replied that it was clearly optimal for younger workers to be contracted out and that the government has lost money owing to the switching back into SERPS later in life (any revenue shortfalls are simply made up out of general tax revenues). Recently enacted measures may have ameliorated the problem of gaming the system by capping the contracted-out rebates and having them increase with age.

The discussion then turned to the issues of annuitization and inflation for contracted-out workers. The market for annuities is organized on an individual basis and is composed of all workers who have contracted out with personal pensions. The market is only lightly regulated, and it does not appear that there is much screening of individuals by companies. For example, much to the surprise of the conference participants, premiums are typically not made conditional on gender or health status. Approximately 50 percent of the funds are annuitized, and there is protection for spouses of those who have contracted out. The state benefits are indexed against inflation up to a limit. In the period since SERPS was enacted, most occupational pensions have implemented at least a limited cost-of-living adjustment in order to satisfy the contracting-out requirement. There was some speculation as to why indexation was not full given the availability of indexed bonds.

Other questions pertained to the way workers who had used personal pensions to contract out were investing their accounts. It was pointed out that, in the Australian system, there was great concern that workers would invest too conservatively. The authors replied that workers in the United Kingdom did have control over their accounts and that most of the funds are in equities. Furthermore, the personal pensions are virtually unregulated, with only "trustee law" and a few small safeguards to prevent disasters like the Maxwell affair.

Another question concerned the labor market consequences of the introduction and subsequent reforms of SERPS. The authors responded that there were simply too many other changes taking place during this time period to identify the effects of the privatization on labor outcomes.

The discussion concluded with questions about the political resistance to the recent reforms, given the large reduction in SERPS that they seem to have made. The authors replied that the contracting-out rebate helped reduce opposition. They also suggested that the fact that many people do not know that they are covered by SERPS may have led to the muted opposition. The government was also fortunate enough to have acted very early in the program so that there were few groups that had accumulated large entitlements at the time. The value of the basic pension is a more hotly contested political topic.

4   Pension System Reform: The Mexican Case

Carlos Sales-Sarrapy, Fernando Solís-Soberón, and
Alejandro Villagómez-Amezcua

This paper analyzes the 1995 reform of Mexico's pension system. The reform substituted for the pay-as-you-go (PAYGO) system a fully funded system with individual accounts and a minimum pension guarantee. Section 4.1 reviews the basic characteristics of the old social security system in Mexico as well as the reasons to reform it. Section 4.2 discusses the main features of the pension reform approved in December 1995. We include an analysis of some specific features related to the design of the new system that are different from recent pension reforms in other Latin American countries. Section 4.3 discusses the costs of the reform on the basis of simulation results from an actuarial model. In section 4.4, we comment on some of the likely effects of the reform on saving and on the development of the financial system. The last section presents final comments.

Recent changes in life expectancy, population growth, and health-care costs, as well as an increased level of benefits without the corresponding adjustment in contributions, made the Mexican PAYGO pension system financially unsustainable. Mexico has joined the group of countries that chose to substitute for the state-run PAYGO system a defined-contribution fully funded scheme with individual accounts. As in most countries, the reform of the pension system in Mexico has important economic, social, and political consequences. Therefore, a better understanding of this process in Mexico requires that it be put in a broad perspective. The implementation of the pension reform should be

Carlos Sales-Sarrapy works at Protego Investment Associates and teaches public finance at the Instituto Technológico Autónomo de México (ITAM). Fernando Solís-Soberón is president at the Comisión Nacional del Sistema de Ahorro para el Retiro (CONSAR) and teaches macroeconomics at ITAM. Alejandro Villagómez-Amezcua is professor of economics at the Center for Research and Education in Economics (CIDE) in Mexico City.

The views presented in this paper are those of the authors and do not necessarily represent the opinions of the institutions with which they are affiliated. The authors are grateful to Cristina Rohde, Francisco Pérez, and Juan Manuel Valle for very efficient research assistance.

viewed as part of a major transformation of the Mexican economy that started in 1988 and that has included profound structural and macroeconomic reforms.[1] It should be stressed that the restructuring of the financial sector undertaken in the last few years has produced a radical change in the Mexican financial system. Measures such as financial deregulation, the strengthening of preventive regulations, and the modernization of supervisory bodies will be an important complement to the pension reform.

4.1   Background to the Reform

Social security in Mexico is provided by two major groups of institutions. IMSS (Instituto Mexicano del Seguro Social) and INFONAVIT (Instituto del Fondo Nacional de la Vivienda para los Trabajadores) provide services to workers in the private sector, ISSSTE (Instituto de Seguridad y Servicios Sociales de los Trabajadores del Estado) and FOVISSSTE (Fondo de la Vivienda del Instituto de Seguridad y Servicios Sociales de los Trabajadores del Estado) to the labor force employed by the public sector.[2] In 1992, SAR (Sistema de Ahorro para el Retiro), a fully funded system complementary to the existing PAYGO programs, was created on the basis of individual retirement accounts for every worker affiliated with IMSS or ISSSTE.

IMSS provides insurance for health and maternity, old age retirement, severance at old age, disability, life, child-care services, and workers' compensation. INFONAVIT is a housing agency managed by the government and representatives of labor and business organizations. It was created in 1972 with the purpose of providing affordable housing to workers employed in the formal sector and affiliated with IMSS. ISSSTE and FOVISSSTE provide similar services and insurance for workers in the public sector.

Contributions to the social security system have become a heavy burden on private companies and workers and, given its current structure, a major source of distortion in the labor market. Table 4.1 summarizes current social security contributions for workers in the private sector.

Health and maternity insurance has accounted for an average of 63 percent of total expenditures of the system during the last thirty years but only 52 percent of its revenues. During its fifty-one years of existence, the system has had only six years with a positive balance and has therefore placed significant financial pressure on other programs. Although, by law, every branch of insurance at IMSS should be self-financing, it has been a common practice to subsidize programs running a deficit. In particular, surplus funds from the pension

---

1. For example, a major privatization program, trade liberalization, deregulation of financial markets, legal changes to allow private investment in several infrastructure-related sectors, tax reform, and a significant reduction in government expenditures.
2. There are several other public social security systems directed to the armed forces and workers at the public oil company as well as private retirement programs. These programs are small compared to those described in the text.

Table 4.1   **Social Security Contributions in Mexico as Percentage of Payroll**

	Total	Employer	Employee	Government
IMSS:				
IVCM[a]	8.5	70	25	5
Health and maternity	12.5	70	25	5
Workers' compensation	2.5	100	0	0
Child care	1.0	100	0	0
SAR system:				
INFONAVIT (housing)	5	100	0	0
Retirement	2	100	0	0
Total	31.5	25.2	5.25	1.05

[a]IVCM = Invalidez, vejez, cesantía y muerte (disability, old age, severance at old age, and life insurance). The base salary on which contributions apply has an upper limit equivalent to ten times the minimum wage, except for the retirement SAR account and the health and maternity insurance, which are limited to the equivalent of twenty-five times the minimum wage. The base wage for INFONAVIT contributions is lower than for IMSS contributions.

system have been used to cover expenses related to health and maternity insurance (IMSS 1995).

Workers' compensation provides insurance against accidents that occur on the job, including disability and death, and pays medical costs and compensation while workers are out of work. Child-care services were introduced in 1973 as women's participation in the labor force increased. IVCM[3] is a defined-benefit PAYGO system that provides insurance for old age retirement, severance at old age, and disability and death.[4] Historically, a significant portion of IVCM surpluses has been used to maintain the viability of the health branch.

During the last ten years, social security expenditures have increased over 60 percent in real terms, growing from less than 2.5 to 3.9 percent of GDP in 1994.[5] Pension expenditures have also grown very rapidly in real terms: IMSS pensions alone grew 150 percent during the period, increasing from 0.22 to 0.56 percent of GDP, while IMSS and ISSSTE total pension expenditures increased 98 percent, reaching 0.8 percent of GDP in 1994.

4.1.1 The Old Pension System

Mexico's old pension system consists of a defined-benefit PAYGO public pension scheme. As mentioned above, most of this system is operated by IMSS for private-sector employees and by ISSSTE for federal government employees. The majority of the working population in the formal sector is covered by IMSS. The IMSS system is the one that was reformed in December 1995. Therefore, we will explain the old pension system by referring to the main

3. See the first paragraph of sec. 4.1.1 below.

4. This insurance applies only if the worker dies or becomes disable as a result of an accident or sickness not due to his or her job.

5. This section includes only figures for IMSS and ISSSTE.

features of the IMSS program, known as the disability, old age, severance at old age, and life insurance program (IVCM).[6]

Evolution of the IVCM-IMSS Pension System

The IVCM-IMSS program was implemented in 1944 as a collective fund. The original IVCM-IMSS can be characterized as a partially funded defined-benefit scheme. The surpluses of the program were used to pay for investment or current expenditures of other branches of IMSS. Its main features are as follows:

Coverage. The program covers registered employees participating in the formal private sector and self-employed workers (and their families) who voluntarily choose to contribute to the system. In November 1995, 10.9 million people were affiliated with IMSS. Although this amount represented only 29.6 percent of the economically active population (EAP), it is estimated that it was almost 80 percent of the labor force in the formal sector.[7] The ratio of contributing workers to IMSS pensioners has fallen from around sixty-seven workers per pensioner in 1950 to around eight in 1994.

Contributions. This program is financed by contributions from the employer (70 percent), the employee (25 percent), and the government (5 percent). The total contribution for 1996 amounts to 8.5 percent of the base salary. This base salary, used to compute contributions and benefits, is the worker's contractual wage plus other payments (such as bonuses).[8] The total contribution is distributed as follows: disability and life, 3.0 percent; old age and severance at old age, 3.0 percent; medical services for the retired, 1.5 percent; administrative expenses, 0.6 percent; and social assistance, 0.4 percent. In the case of workers earning the minimum wage, the worker's contribution is paid by the employer.[9]

Eligibility. In order to qualify for a disability pension, disability must be formally certified by IMSS. To be eligible, the worker must have contributed for at least 150 weeks. To receive an old age pension, the insured must be at least sixty-five years old (sixty for severance at old age) and have contributed for a minimum of 500 weeks. At a worker's death, a survivor's pension is paid to the widow and/or descendants or to surviving parents. In any case, the insured must have contributed for at least 150 weeks.

---

6. *Severance at old age* refers to the case when a worker loses his or her job and is over sixty years old, regardless of whether he or she resigns or is dismissed.

7. The number of IVCM pensioners at that time was around 1.2 million, of which 65 percent were receiving old age pensions and 35 percent pensions for widows, orphans, and other relatives.

8. The base salary on which the contribution applies has a limit of ten times the minimum wage.

9. In Mexico, the minimum wage is set by law, and employers are required to comply with it. This variable is used as a reference of the wage structure of IMSS affiliates. The monthly minimum wage in July 1996 was equivalent to U.S.$90.00. The average wage for workers affiliated with IMSS is 2.8 times the minimum wage.

Benefits. Benefits for the disabled depend on the degree of disability determined by IMSS. The pension for an individual classified as totally disabled is 70 percent of the last wage; for partial disabilities, adjustments are made according to the labor law. Benefits for old age and severance at old age depend on the contributing period exceeding the required 500 weeks. Benefits are based on the average of the base salary of the last five years divided by the current minimum wage. Additionally, all retired workers have the right to receive medical assistance for themselves and their families. All pensions are indexed to changes in the minimum wage. In 1995, the replacement rate for the worker with the average wage path, after contributing twenty years, would be 50 percent.[10] This percentage could reach 100 percent if the individual contributes for forty-five years.[11] The government guarantees that the minimum pension will not be smaller than the minimum wage. Figure 4.1 shows the replacement rates under different assumptions about wage levels and contributing periods.

Reserves and Investment. Reserves should be invested in federal government bonds or in other assets of highly rated issuers as approved by the National Banking and Securities Commission. The income and spending of each branch of insurance should be registered in separate accounts. These resources should be used to cover only the services corresponding to each branch of insurance. As explained below, reserves were not constituted or invested according to the regulations.

Tax Treatment. Employers can deduct as expenses their contributions to IMSS. Workers pay taxes at the moment of retirement when they receive the benefits, but taxes apply only to the amount in excess of nine times the minimum wage.

The Fully Funded Retirement Saving System (SAR)

The Retirement Saving System (SAR) was established in 1992 as a mandatory fully funded savings scheme to complement the public PAYGO system. The SAR program is a fully funded defined-contribution system based on individual accounts. Some of the main characteristics of the SAR system are the following:[12]

Coverage. All workers who are affiliated with IMSS or ISSSTE must contribute to the SAR system.

Contributions. Each worker has an individual bank account integrated by two subaccounts: one for retirement and one for housing. Employers pay 2 percent

10. The *replacement rate* is defined as the ratio of the worker's pension divided by his or her last salary.

11. In 1995, the wage for the average worker was 2.8 times the minimum wage, and the average contributing period was almost twenty years.

12. A more comprehensive discussion of the SAR is presented by Solís-Soberón (1995).

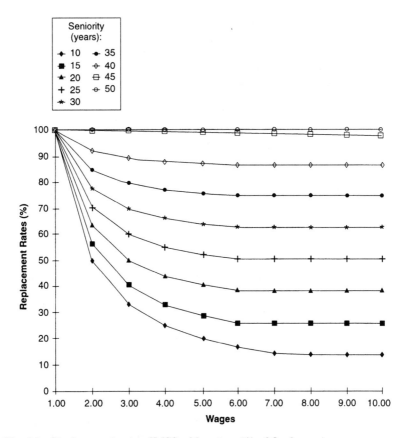

Fig. 4.1   Replacement rates, IMSS, old system (% of final wage)

of the base salary to the retirement subaccount and 5 percent to the housing subaccount.[13] The funds in the retirement subaccount are invested in direct loans to the federal government, while the funds of the housing subaccount are channeled to INFONAVIT. These contributions are in addition to the contributions paid to the IMSS public pension system. Worker can make additional voluntary deposits in their individual accounts.

Benefits. Workers are entitled to receive the total capitalized funds from their individual subaccounts in one payment or to purchase an annuity either at retirement or when they are entitled to receive a pension from IMSS because of partial or permanent disability. In the case of death, the funds are given to the beneficiaries chosen by the insured.

13. The base salary to which this contribution applies has an upper limit of twenty-five times the minimum wage.

Other Benefit Provisions. The insured has the right to withdraw as much as 10 percent of the total balance of the retirement subaccount if partial disability lasts longer than the period established by the social security law or in case of unemployment. The latter can be claimed only by workers whose balance in the retirement subaccount is no less than eighteen times their last contribution and only if there have been no withdrawals during the previous five years. With respect to the housing subaccount, if the worker receives a loan for housing from INFONAVIT, the funds accumulated in the subaccount must be used as a down payment, and the employer's contributions plus a worker's contribution equal to 25 percent of his or her wage are used to pay the loan.

Administration. Contributions are deposited in individual accounts managed by commercial banks. Banks are responsible for record keeping, generating financial statements, and making various required filings. They can hold the SAR funds for up to four days, after which time they must send them to the central bank (Banco de Mexico), in the case of the retirement subaccount, or to INFONAVIT, in the case of the housing subaccount. Commercial banks charge 0.8 percent per year of the retirement subaccount balances for operating expenses.[14]

Investment. Funds in the retirement subaccount are channeled to the government as a direct loan. The government pays an interest rate for the use of these funds that must be no less than 2 percent per year, on a monthly basis, over the inflation-adjusted balance using the inflation rate of the previous month. Funds in the housing subaccount earn interest according to the remaining operation surplus for the corresponding year. Actual returns on the retirement subaccount have been more than 5 percent in real terms. However, returns on the housing subaccount have been negative. In 1995, the real return was −9 percent.

Regulation. The regulatory agency is the Comisión Nacional del Sistema de Ahorro para el Retiro (CONSAR), established in July 1994. Its main function is to determine the rules and procedures that will ensure the correct functioning of the system. This supervisory body is responsible for overseeing all the financial intermediaries that participate in the SAR system, except INFONAVIT.

Tax Treatment. SAR contributions by the employer are deductible. Voluntary contributions by the workers are tax deductible up to a limit. Interest accumulation is tax free. Withdrawals are tax free to the limit of nine times the minimum wage in the case of the annuity option for the retirement subaccount. There is a higher limit for tax exemption if the employee chooses to withdraw all the funds at once. For the housing subaccount, withdrawals are not taxed at all.

---

14. This fee is divided between 0.5 percent for the bank and 0.3 percent for a clearinghouse that operates a centralized data bank for the SAR system.

4.1.2   The Case for Reform

The most important reason behind the reform was the increasing financial problems being faced by the old IVCM-IMSS pension program, which rendered it financially unsustainable. Another important reason was the need to foster domestic saving. Finally, there were other significant distortions derived from the old pension system, in particular, distortions generated in the labor market owing to the fact that contributions paid did not necessarily reflect benefits received.

Current Pension System Diagnosis

Since the end of the 1980s, it was evident that the public pension system was facing severe financial problems as a result of its actuarial imbalance. Recent estimates of the actuarial imbalance of the IVCM system show that it represents at least 80 percent of the Mexican GDP.[15] Therefore, it became evident that a complete restructuring of the pension system was needed. We stress the main causes of the IVCM financial problems below.

Demographic Trends. The IVCM-IMSS program was being pressured by demographic trends, in particular, the changing population structure and an increase in life expectancy. Mexico's population grew at high rates, 3.7 percent per year on average from 1970 to 1990. Recent estimates yield 1.9 percent for 1990–95. In 1930, the total population was 16.5 million, rising to 90 million in 1994. Despite the fact that the population pyramid shows a significant proportion of young people, 35.8 percent of the population 14 years old and younger, the population measured as contributors to the social security system is aging very rapidly. Mexico's total population is expected to be over 142 million by 2030, and those over sixty-five years of age will represent around 10 percent of that total. These trends imply that the ratio of retirees to workers would drive up the cost of the current pension system and generate major long-term financing problems. The elderly dependency ratio is expected to increase from 7.0 percent in 1995 to 14.8 percent in 2030.

According to IMSS (1995), the expected average annual rate of growth of retirees for the next twenty years will be 5.7 percent, compared with a rate of 2.6 percent for contributors. Moreover, this problem is being accentuated by an increase in life expectancy at birth, which has risen from 49.6 years in 1950 to 70.8 years in 1995. Finally, there is a reduction in the fertility rate, which has gone down from 6.45 children per woman at the end of the fertility period in 1950 to 2.84 in 1995.

The system has also been negatively affected by increased informality in the labor market and lower real wages. In particular, real wages in the manufacturing sector declined 44 percent between 1978 and 1995.

---

15. This result is highly sensitive to the real interest rate assumed.

Insufficient Contributions. Current contributions will be insufficient in the medium and long terms to finance the increasingly generous benefits of the old system that were extended to all the worker's family. Originally, the system covered only the worker, not dependents. The minimum pension has been increased from 35 percent of the minimum wage before 1989 to 100 percent in 1995, while contributions were gradually raised beginning in 1992 from 6 percent of the base salary to 8.5 percent in 1996 (it is important to remember that, from this contribution, 3 percent corresponds to life and disability insurance and 3 percent to retirement, severance at old age, and old age insurance). According to IMSS (1996), contributions would have to be increased to 23.3 percent of the base salary in 2020 to avoid a cash-flow deficit in the system in that year.

Weak Relation between Contributions and Benefits. There is almost no relation between benefits received and lifetime contributions paid, which encourages evasion, underreporting of wages, and informality in the labor market. For example, on average, IMSS pays each insured worker a pension for a period of eighteen years and the corresponding widow's pension for twelve years more. Together, this amounts to a thirty-year pension toward which the worker can have contributed for as few as ten years, the required vesting period. (Workers who contributed for fewer than ten years receive no benefits at all.) Finally, the reference base salary used to calculate the pension is based on the average of the wages earned during the last five years divided by the current minimum wage, not on earnings during all years of service.

High Payroll Taxes. The marginal payroll tax rate is very high even for low-income workers. For example, for a worker earning between one and two times the minimum wage, the marginal tax rate is over 25 percent. For workers earning more than five times the minimum wage, the marginal tax rate is close to 40 percent. This raises labor costs, favors evasion, and induces informality.

Growing Informal Sector and Low Coverage. Another problem that pressures the financial position of the system has been the increasing size of the informal sector of the economy. It is estimated that about 35 percent of the EAP was affiliated with the social security system (including IMSS and ISSSTE) in November 1995.

Portability Losses.[16] Given the IMSS-IVCM and the ISSSTE pension system defined-benefit formulas, there are portability loses between different pension systems in Mexico. Employees with only one employer might receive higher benefits at retirement than employees with more than one employer. Moreover,

---

16. Portability of benefits among different pension systems requires that benefits not be lost or diminished by shifting jobs in the formal sector.

some workers might lose all benefits if they change from a job covered by IMSS insurance to one covered by another program.

Inadequate Use of Reserves. Another important problem with the IVCM-IMSS program is the inappropriate use of reserves, which has affected its financial position. From its creation, the surplus generated by the pension program has been used to finance infrastructure requirements of IMSS and (partially) health and maternity insurance, which traditionally operated showing a deficit. These transfers of resources have strongly decapitalized the reserves of the pension system. A conservative estimate of expected IMSS reserves can be obtained by accumulating the annual net flows (contributions minus payments) of IVCM. Accumulated flows in each period were assumed to earn a real interest rate equivalent to 3.5 percent per year. Under these estimates, reserves for 1994 should have been around 11 percent of GDP. However, reserves in 1995 were close to 0.4 percent of GDP (IMSS 1995). It is worth mentioning that the level of reserves presented in the exercise is a conservative estimate of the actual reserves needed to make the system financially viable because, in actuarial terms, the contributions were not high enough to cover future benefits.

4.1.3   The Savings Problem[17]

The Mexican economy still faces a serious shortage of short-term savings and a severe scarcity of long-term savings. During the last seven years, the domestic saving rate declined.[18] According to Banco de Mexico (1996) estimates, gross domestic saving reached an average of 20 percent of GDP during the 1980s, dropping to slightly less than 16 percent of GDP by 1994. The main contributing factor was a reduction in private saving, which declined continuously from a level of around 18 percent of GDP in 1988 to around 11 percent during the first part of the 1990s, showing a recovery since 1995. On the other hand, public saving has shown major fluctuations since the beginning of the 1980s.[19] In any case, Mexico's moderate level of domestic saving has constituted a constraint for investment and has made the country more vulnerable to foreign capital flows. It is now widely accepted that, although foreign savings will continue to play an important role in the medium and long terms, it is crucial to increase domestic saving as the main source for financing growth.

The National Development Plan 1995–2000 stated as one of its main eco-

---

17. A broader discussion of this issue can be found in Solís-Soberón and Villagómez (1996).

18. As is well known, it is difficult to quantify the precise magnitude of this variable because of several measurement problems. Most of the existing estimates are drawn directly from national income accounts as a residual after deducting the balance of payments deficit on the current account from estimates of gross domestic capital formation. There are other serious problems when breaking down gross domestic savings into its components, private and public savings. These problems arise from different quantitative estimations, although in general these estimations offer similar trends. For a discussion of this issue, see Gil-Díaz and Carstens (1996).

19. For a discussion of this issue, see Villagómez (1993).

nomic objectives the urgent need to foster domestic saving. The goal is to increase domestic saving 6 percentage points of GDP by the turn of the century. This requires an increase in both public and private saving. The creation of a fully funded retirement savings program is one of the elements of this strategy. In this sense, one of the objectives of the recent pension reform has been the creation of a system that could generate domestic saving to support economic development.[20]

4.2   The Pension Reform

Since the early 1990s, there was a generalized consensus that the social security system, and in particular the IVCM-IMSS pension system, needed to be reformed. There was a long debate about the main elements of the reform and about the depth of the measures to be taken. The president submitted to Congress a proposal for a new social security law, which was approved in mid-December 1995, while the regulations regarding the operation of the financial aspects of the system were approved at the end of April 1996.

4.2.1   Main Features of the Pension Reform

The reform substitutes for the old PAYGO system a mandatory defined-contribution fully funded system with individual accounts, complemented with a minimum pension guarantee. Basically, this requires the improvement and strengthening of the individual capitalization fully funded scheme under the SAR system. This includes the development of transparent mechanisms for pension funds management that generate the right incentives for all participants, the development of clear regulations and supervision processes for the management and investment of funds, a clear separation from other social security benefits, a close relation between contributions paid and benefits received, and the design of an adequate transition mechanism.[21] The main features of the new system are summarized below.

Basic Operating Characteristics

Coverage. The new system is mandatory for all workers in the labor force who are affiliated with IMSS. This includes all workers participating in the formal private sector and self-employed workers (and their families) who voluntarily choose to contribute to the system.

Contributions. Contributions will continue to be made by employers, employees, and the government, as shown in table 4.2. The former 8.5 percent of base wage contribution for IVCM will be divided into two parts: 4.5 percent will be

20. In a recent paper, Feldstein (1995) put forward several suggested tax reforms to stimulate saving in Mexico. He also discusses the transition to a fully funded social security system.
21. An interesting discussion about alternative possible reform proposals can be found in Feldstein (1995) and Bosworth, Dornbusch, and Poterba (1995).

Table 4.2   Contributions to the Pension System (%)

	Before the Reform	With the Reform	
Insurance	DOSL (IVCM)	RDO	LDA
IMSS contributions	8.5	4.5	4
SAR retirement	2	2	
SAR housing	5	5	
Social contribution	0	2[a]	
(Total)		(13.5)	(4)
Total contributions	15.5	17.5	
Total employer	12.95	12.95	
Total employee	2.125	2.125	
Total government	.425	2.425	

Source: IMSS and CONSAR.

Note: DOSL = disability, old age, severance at old age, and life insurance; RDO = retirement, severance at old age, and old age; LDA = life and disability.

[a]The social contribution is equivalent to 2 percent of the average wage of workers affiliated with IMSS. It was established at 5.5 percent of the minimum wage.

accumulated in individual accounts, and 4 percent will go directly to IMSS for the provision of life and disability insurance (2.5 percent) and of health services for pensioners (1.5 percent). Additionally, contributions to individual accounts will include the former 7 percent contributions to SAR (2 percent for retirement and 5 percent for housing). There is a new "social contribution" by the government that is a fixed amount equivalent to 5.5 percent of the minimum wage in January 1997. This amount will be indexed to the CPI. For workers earning the minimum wage, total contributions to their individual account will represent 17 percent of their salary. For workers earning the average wage, total contributions will represent 13.5 percent.[22] Funds in individual accounts (except the 5 percent that corresponds to housing) will be managed by specialized pension fund management firms, AFOREs (Administradora de Fondos para el Retiro). In the case of workers' compensation, the employer will pay a premium determined by a formula that includes the base wage and the loss ratio for each firm's activity.[23] The new law considers the possibility of voluntary contributions from workers and employers to the individual accounts.

Benefits for Retirement or Severance at Old Age. To be eligible for a retirement pension, the worker must be at least sixty-five years old. In the case of sever-

22. It should be noted that the social contribution in terms of the wage will tend to diminish as real wages increase.

23. The premium paid by each firm is obtained by multiplying the loss ratio of the firm (based on the percentage of permanent, partial and total disabilities, the number of deaths, and the average active life of a worker without an accident considered by this insurance) by a premium factor (equal to 2.9) and adding to this amount 0.0025, the estimated minimum risk premium. The estimated premium will be revised on an annual basis.

ance at old age, the age requirement is reduced to sixty years. Benefits depend on the contributions accumulated during the affiliate's working life, plus the returns minus the commissions paid. Workers who have contributed for 1,250 weeks can chose between two options: (*a*) to purchase an annuity from a private insurance company that guarantees a fixed monthly pension for the insured and their survivors and (*b*) to receive programmed withdrawals from AFORE, calculated by dividing the balance (including interests) from the affiliates' individual account by the number of years that they are still expected to live.[24] In the first case, an annual payment of at least the same amount of the minimum pension guaranteed by the government is required. Otherwise, affiliates should take option *b*, where the government minimum pension guarantee is applied. If workers contributed for fewer than 1,250 weeks, they are not entitled to the minimum pension. However, they are allowed to withdraw the balance of their account all at once if they prefer not to buy an annuity or take programmed withdrawals. Early retirement is possible if workers accumulate in their account the balance necessary to purchase an annuity at least 30 percent higher than the minimum pension.

Figure 4.2 shows the replacement rates under the new fully funded scheme for workers with the average wage path. These rates assume that the worker used neither the retirement funds for marriage expenses or when unemployed nor the housing funds for mortgage loans. Note that the discontinuity at 0 percent real interest rate in the graph is explained by the fact that, for a contributing period under twenty-five years, workers have no right to receive the guaranteed minimum pension. For workers who have contributed for twenty years, a 7 percent real interest rate would be required to guarantee a pension equal to the one they could have obtained under the old system. It must be said, however, that, under the old system, contributions would have been insufficient to finance such a pension.

The replacement rates are highly sensitive to the contribution period and the interest rate. For example, given a 6 percent real interest rate for the retirement subaccount and 0 percent for the housing subaccount, an increase in the contributing period from twenty-five to thirty years raises the replacement rate from 52.5 to 74.5 percent.[25] Regarding the interest rate, workers with a twenty-five-year contributing period will have their replacement rate increased from 68 to 78 percent when the real interest rate in the retirement subaccount increases from 8 to 9 percent.

Benefits Due to Disability or Death. The risk of disability and death is covered by two types of insurance: workers' compensation and life and disability insur-

---

24. Programmed withdrawals are calculated taking into consideration the age of the worker and his or her dependents.

25. This is due to an increase in the numerator (the result of higher accumulated balances in the worker's individual account) and a decrease in the denominator (the result of the reduction in wages that the average worker faces after forty-one years of age).

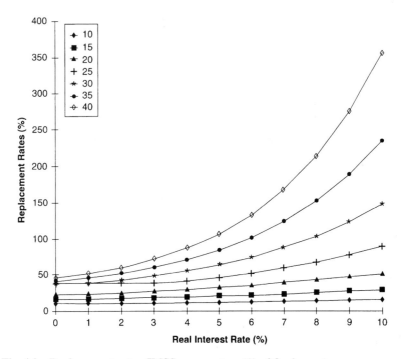

Fig. 4.2   Replacement rates, IMSS, new system (% of final wage)
Source: Authors' calculations.
Note: It is assumed that the IMSS housing subaccount is accumulated with a zero real interest rate.

ance. Both are provided solely by IMSS. When a covered accident occurs at the workplace, workers' compensation applies. Workers who become disabled under such circumstances will receive 100 percent of their current wage for a period of time not to exceed one year, during which IMSS will determine whether the disability is permanent or temporary. If the disability is determined to be permanent, IMSS will decide whether it is total or partial. Workers declared totally disabled will receive 70 percent of their current wage.[26] Workers declared partially disabled will receive a pension adjusted according to the degree of disability. Death benefits for the typical family with three children are 70 percent of the last wage received by the deceased.[27]

In the case of disability or death that is not job related, life and disability insurance applies. Eligibility requires a minimum contributing period of 250

26. If a disability is due to a work-related disease, the pension will be 70 percent of the average base wage of the last fifty-two contributing weeks.

27. The widow will receive an amount equivalent to 40 percent of the insured's corresponding disability pension, and the pension of each child younger than sixteen (or twenty-five if still a student) represents 20 percent of this disability pension. If the deceased leaves neither a widow nor any children, the remaining dependents will receive a pension equivalent to 20 percent of the disability pension.

weeks. However, this requirement is reduced to 150 weeks if the disability is greater than 75 percent. Total disability is declared when a worker cannot be employed at a wage greater than 50 percent of previous earnings. The amount of the pension is equal to 35 percent of the average wage, adjusted by the CPI, of the last 500 weeks of contributions. This pension also includes additional payments for relatives, with the result that, for an average family with three children, the total pension is equivalent to 51 percent of the average wage.[28] For pension benefits in the case of death, the worker must have at least 150 weeks of contributions. For the typical family described above, the pension would be 53 percent of the average wage used to calculate the disability pension.[29]

In the case of both workers' compensation and disability and life, IMSS must pay workers or their beneficiaries a sum insured equal to the difference between the cost of an annuity, based on the benefits mentioned above, and the accumulated balance in the individual account (excluding voluntary contributions). With the accumulated balances and the sum insured paid by IMSS, workers or their beneficiaries must purchase the corresponding annuity from an insurance company chosen by the workers. If the accumulated balance is higher than the cost of the annuity, workers or their beneficiaries can withdraw the excess funds or increase the benefits of the annuity. In any case, if the benefits are lower than the minimum pension, the government will make up the difference, allowing workers to purchase with the income flow an annuity equal to the minimum pension. These pensions are adjusted annually according to changes in the CPI.

Guaranteed Minimum Pension. The government guarantees a minimum pension equal to the general minimum wage at the time of the reform. This pension will be adjusted for inflation according to the CPI. Table 4.3 shows the average yearly returns needed for workers to accumulate sufficient resources to finance a minimum pension, for different wage levels, in the cases of retirement at old age and severance at old age.

Partial Withdrawals from the Individual Accounts. After an unemployment spell of forty-five days, workers are allowed to withdraw at most 10 percent of

28. These additional payments include 15 percent of the pension for the wife and 10 percent of the pension for each child younger than sixteen years or 10 percent of the pension for the insured's parents (if there are no other beneficiaries). Workers who have no beneficiaries will receive an additional 15 percent of their pension, or 10 percent if there is only one beneficiary. In all cases, there is an additional payment equivalent to 20 percent of the pension if the insured requires permanent assistance. Finally, it is required that the total pension should not exceed 100 percent of the average wage used to calculate the pension.

29. The widow will receive an amount equivalent to 90 percent of the insured's corresponding disability pension, and the pension for each child younger than sixteen years (or twenty-five if still a student) will be equivalent to 20 percent of this disability pension. If the deceased leaves neither a widow nor children, any remaining dependents will receive a pension equivalent to 20 percent of the disability pension.

Table 4.3   Minimum Pension Yearly Implicit Return (%)

	Base Wage[a]	Implicit Real Return
	1	9.81
	2	6.59
	3	4.37
	4	2.65
	5	1.23

Source: Authors' calculations.
Note: Contributing period = 1,250 weeks. Real wage annual growth equal to 2.5 percent a year.
[a]Number of times the minimum wage.

the accumulated balance in their retirement subaccount if they have at least 250 weeks of contributions and made no other withdrawals during the previous five years. On getting married, workers with 150 weeks of contributions may withdraw from their retirement subaccount an amount equivalent to their monthly wage; this benefit is granted only once. The benefits and operation of the housing funds remain unchanged.

Tax Treatment. Contributions by the employer will be tax deductible, and compulsory contributions will not be taxable income for the worker. Voluntary contributions by the workers will be subject to favorable tax treatment, and interest accumulation will be tax free. Withdrawals will not be taxed up to a limit of nine times the minimum wage, and there is a higher limit for tax exemption when employees withdraw all their funds at one time.

Administration

Management. The management of pension funds will be entrusted to private pension fund administrators (AFOREs), which will be regulated and supervised by CONSAR. These institutions should have as their only activity the management of pension funds. AFOREs will inform workers about the accumulated balances from their retirement, voluntary, and housing subaccounts but will manage the resources only of the retirement and voluntary subaccounts.

Individual Accounts. Participants must choose one AFORE. Affiliates have the right to transfer their accounts to another AFORE once per year. However, workers are free to transfer their accounts whenever the AFORE changes its commissions or its investment policies.

Housing Subaccount. The 5 percent contributions to the housing subaccount will continue to operate as before. These funds will be channeled to INFONAVIT. There will be a return on these funds according to the operating surplus of the institute.

The Role of the AFOREs. Each AFORE is allowed to operate several pension funds for its affiliates. Workers are allowed to invest their resources in one or several of the pension funds managed by their AFORE. In addition, the AFOREs' main functions include record keeping, issuing valuation reports and financial statements, making various required filings, and paying benefits if the affiliate chooses the scheduled withdrawals option. Each pension fund, known as a SIEFORE (Sociedad de Inversión Especializada en Fondos para el Retiro), will have a committee that will make the investment decisions.

The Role of IMSS. IMSS will be responsible for the collection of contributions. It also has auditing and enforcement powers to ensure that employers and workers comply with their obligations. Also, the approved law allows IMSS to own an AFORE as long as it complies with all the regulatory provisions.

Central Account. Contributions will be deposited in an account at the Banco de Mexico while the individualization process takes place and the resources then transferred to the AFOREs and INFONAVIT. All information about contributions will be managed by a centralized entity created for that purpose, supervised by CONSAR. If workers have not chosen an AFORE, the resources from their retirement subaccount will be deposited in this central account for a maximum period of four years, starting 1 July 1997. After this period, CONSAR will assign an AFORE to those workers according to criteria as yet to be determined.

Commissions. AFOREs will be allowed to charge management fees as a percentage of contributions or of the outstanding individual account balance, or some combination of the two. AFOREs will not be allowed to discriminate against any of their affiliates. Individuals will receive differential treatment only in order to encourage permanence in the AFORE and to promote voluntary savings.

4.2.2   Regulation and Supervision

CONSAR

The regulatory and supervisory tasks will be performed by CONSAR. Its main functions are to determine the criteria and procedures that will ensure the correct functioning of the pension system. This supervisory body will have the power to grant and revoke AFOREs' licenses, to monitor the pension funds, and to enforce its regulations. CONSAR is also responsible for supervising the operations and investment policies of the pension funds.

Investment of Funds

The authorities have stated that the basic operating principles that will guide investment will be safety and profitability. Therefore, pension funds will be invested only in approved and diversified assets. These assets include government securities, the securities of state-owned companies, equity, private debt instruments, shares of other pension funds, and other debt instruments issued or endorsed by credit institutions. Investment in foreign instruments is allowed only in the case of Mexican issuers. CONSAR will establish limits on the amount of investment in specific securities as a share of the value of the fund, but it can at its discretion impose limits expressed as a share of each issuer in the total liabilities of all issuers from the same sector. These limits are maximum limits, and AFOREs are free to seek the highest returns under these rules. There are disclosure requirements with respect to the structure of the investment portfolio and the returns obtained. Finally, it is important to emphasize that the AFOREs are allowed to operate several pension funds but that at least one of those funds should contain only fixed-income securities, including indexed bonds. The law specifies no minimum guaranteed return, in either absolute or relative terms.

AFOREs

Minimum Capital and Fixed Capital. AFOREs should always have fixed capital at least equal to the minimum capital required that is not subject to withdrawal, an amount to be determined by CONSAR. Foreign investors are allowed to own up to 49 percent of an AFORE's capital. But, in the case of affiliates of countries that have signed an international agreement with Mexico that includes financial services provisions, such as NAFTA, foreign investment can rise to 100 percent.

Investment Reserve. AFOREs are required to maintain an investment reserve known as a *special reserve* as a percentage of the total assets under their management. This amount will be determined by CONSAR. The investment reserve must be invested in the same assets as the resources of the pension funds.

Market Share Limits. Starting in 1997, and continuing for the next four years, the law has established a maximum market share limit of 17 percent for each AFORE. After this period, the limit will rise to 20 percent of the market. However, CONSAR can approve larger limits. The law does not specify how the limits are to be determined; however, it is most likely that they will be based on the number of workers affiliated with IMSS registered at each AFORE.

Other. AFOREs must meet rigorous information disclosure requirements. There will be regulations regarding marketing and advertising. In addition, AFOREs are not allowed to issue liabilities, provide guarantees, obtain loans, or control companies.

4.2.3   The Transition

As mentioned above, the new pension system began functioning on 1 July 1997. There are currently around 1.5 million pensioners, of whom 780,000 receive disability and death benefits, 475,000 retirement pensions, and 265,000 workers' compensation. Since the new system is mandatory, all workers are required to switch to the new individual capitalization scheme and stop contributing to the old system as of 1997. In the following discussion, we distinguish between *current pensioners*, or those already receiving a pension when the reform was enacted, and *transition pensioners*, or all active workers who have contributed to the IMSS-IVCM program before 1 July 1997 and therefore have acquired rights under the old system.

IMSS will continue to pay benefits to current pensioners, but those benefits will be financed out of existing IVCM reserves and resources obtained directly from the general revenues of the federal government. In the case of transition pensioners, the reform established the following procedure. Workers already contributing to the old system will now make contributions to the new system. When they reach retirement age, they will be able to choose the higher of the two pensions determined under the rules of the old system (using the IVCM benefit system [see sec. 4.1], including the SAR funds accumulated as of June 1997 plus the returns from that date until retirement) and the new system (the funds accumulated in their individual account). If they choose the latter, the new rules apply. If they choose the former, the pension will be calculated as if they had contributed to the old system during the time that they were actually contributing to the new one, and the pension will be financed with funds from their individual account complemented by government resources.

4.2.4 Analysis of the New Pension System Design

It is clear that successful pension system reform depends crucially on the design of the regulatory and supervisory framework. Obviously, there is no evidence yet with which to evaluate the Mexican reform, but, given the extensive documentation of design problems discovered in recent, similar reforms in other Latin American countries, discussion of relevant issues can usefully highlight the advantages and disadvantages of the new Mexican pension system.

The main advantages of the new pension scheme are that the new system respects acquired as well as expected rights of current workers and pensioners; that the new system completely replaces the old, facilitating the move to a more unified pension system; that transfers between AFOREs are limited to one per year, reducing administrative costs; that AFOREs are allowed to operate several funds; that the law does not establish a minimum guaranteed rate of return for the funds managed by AFOREs; and that there exist a centralized collection agency and a centralized data bank, potentially reducing administrative costs.[30]

In particular, regarding the centralized collection of contributions by IMSS,

---

30. There is some evidence that there are economies of scale that result from such centralization. For a discussion of this issue, see Diamond (1994), who characterizes the provision of such services as the collection of monthly payments and record keeping as a natural monopoly.

there is a potential gain to be derived from the reduction of administrative costs (e.g., with respect to Chile) since there is some evidence that there are economies of scale involved in the provision of this service. In order for this gain to be realized, adequate supervision—limiting potential political risks and possible excessive administrative costs—is required. Alternatively, a state-run agency (one closely supervised by CONSAR) or, as suggested by Diamond (1994), a clearinghouse collectively owned by the AFOREs and barred from making a profit (to prevent its use in a collusion to raise industry profits) could provide this service exclusively.

Another important feature of the new system is the ability of workers to chose an AFORE, which introduces the element of competition. While the potential long-term benefits resulting from competition are great, they might (as discussed by Arrau, Valdés-Prieto, and Schmidt-Hebbel 1993) be limited in the short run—in particular during the transition period—as a consequence of the amount of information required by the decision to purchase a new and unknown product. Therefore, at the beginning, the costs implied by the learning process will be relatively high. According to Arrau et al., under the new system there will be initially a low elasticity of individual consumer demand, favoring a monopolistic competition structure and resulting in high individual contracting costs and high marketing costs.

The new system also incorporates what we consider to be problematic features: in particular, the prohibition against including foreign securities in the pension funds' investment portfolios; the operation of the housing subaccount; the minimum pension guarantee; the disability and life insurance monopoly; the market share limits; portability problems; and the IMSS AFORE. We elaborate on these issues below.

Foreign Securities. The prohibition against including foreign securities in the pension funds' investment portfolios is based on the argument that channeling long-term savings abroad is not desirable when those savings are urgently required by the domestic economy. However, the possibility of diversifying the investment portfolio and minimizing risk is thereby inhibited. A more diversified portfolio will work in favor of future pensioners.

Housing Subaccount. The housing subaccount, which receives a contribution of 5 percent of the base salary, represents more than 30 percent of total contributions to the new system. These resources are not part of the pension funds managed and invested by the AFOREs and are channeled to INFONAVIT. The institute is structured in such a way that most of the risks are born by the savers. Returns on their savings depend on the operating surplus of the institute, which is the difference between interest payments actually collected by the institute and operating expenses and reserve creation. The interest payments received by INFONAVIT depend on the interest rate charged to the borrower, which is between 4 and 8 percent on the outstanding balance of the loan adjusted according to increases in the minimum wage.[31] Total payments to INFONAVIT also depend on the employment situation of the worker. It is difficult for the institute to collect payments from unemployed workers, and it rarely forecloses on homes. The institute is also not always able to keep track of workers who change jobs, and, in many cases, it does not continue to collect payments. These factors, as well as the labor market conditions and real wage behavior during recent years, have affected the operating surplus of INFONAVIT and help explain the negative real returns on individual accounts.

Minimum Pension Guarantee. It has been argued that a PAYGO system plays an important redistributive role by providing retirement income for the elderly poor. This implicit redistributive function could be lost under a fully funded system. As Valdés-Prieto (1994) shows, the introduction of a fully funded system can raise long-run income and welfare. However, a redistributive instrument might still be needed, and a government-guaranteed minimum pension can perform this function. While it can be argued that a guaranteed minimum pension can raise moral hazard issues by increasing the fiscal deficit, it can also be argued that the government has the responsibility to assist the elderly poor. In this case, means-tested criteria might be in order. A positive feature of the minimum pension in Mexico is that it is indexed to the consumer price index, not to the evolution of real wages. Since, in the medium term, real wages should rise, the indexing of the minimum pension to the CPI reduces its rate of increase.

Disability and Life Insurance. Under the new system, disability and life insurance will be provided only by IMSS, which will charge a fixed premium equal to 2.5 percent of the base salary. There are several problems with this arrangement. The cost is high compared to that observed for this type of insurance in other Latin American countries where the pension fund managers compete among themselves and purchase the insurance for their affiliates from an insurance company. In these countries, workers can choose the pension fund manager that offers the best conditions. For example, in 1995, the cost of this type of insurance in Chile and Argentina was, on average, 0.67 and 1.17 percent of the base salary, respectively.[32] In Mexico, IMSS will have insufficient incentive to reduce the loss ratio and its administrative costs beyond what is needed to maintain the financial viability of the system, and therefore it is not likely that there will be a reduction in this premium over time.

Market Share Limits. This provision may entail some negative effects to the functioning of the system. Although the conventional wisdom is that more con-

---

31. Changes in the minimum wage are determined yearly by a government commission that includes representatives of labor and business organizations.
32. The range is 0.4–1.73 percent of the base salary in Chile and 0.32–2.18 percent in Argentina.

centration implies less competition, a well-known result in the industrial organization literature is that this is unambiguously true only for an industry composed of firms producing homogeneous products for which the strategic variable of competition is quantity produced. For AFOREs, competition will be over commissions, returns, and services provided. Therefore, it is possible that, in the market equilibrium, the market share limits may imply that some workers will not be able to open an account in the AFORE of their choice. A higher social cost for the provision of services may also result if the cost structure of the firms is not the same.

Portability. The new system still generates portability losses because the reform affects only the IVCM-IMSS program, leaving unaltered other pension programs. In particular, it is important to emphasize that, as long as other pension systems, like ISSSTE, remain unreformed, workers changing from a job covered by IMSS to a job covered by other programs might lose pension benefits.

The IMSS AFORE. The new pension law allows IMSS to manage its own AFORE, as long as it complies with the corresponding regulations. However, since IMSS also conducts the collection of all pension contributions and has audit and enforcement powers, there is a real risk of unfair competition, favoring the IMSS AFORE, if the authorities do not enforce the regulations meant to prevent this situation.

An interesting feature of the new system is that transition workers will be able to choose the higher of the old- and new-system pensions when they retire. In other countries, such a situation has been managed through the issuance of recognition bonds. The Mexican scheme does not require the calculation of the present value of past contributions or of future expected benefits, as do systems utilizing transition bonds. This design recognizes that workers have acquired rights, and that recognition helps make the reform politically viable. However, one important problem with the Mexican scheme is that it creates some moral hazard problems. Workers could pursue riskier investment strategies knowing that they can always fall back on the benefits of the old system. Also, because of the distortions of the previous system, workers could have fewer incentives to participate in the formal sector of the economy since they are eligible to obtain a pension under the old system after contributing to it for only ten years.

4.3   Costs of the Current and the New Systems

One crucial issue that shapes the long-term effects and determines the success or failure of a pension system reform that entails a shift from a PAYGO to a fully funded system is the transition. This process has important fiscal and income redistribution effects that may have long-term implications, affecting the achievement of the reform's goals.[33]

As a consequence of substituting a fully funded for a PAYGO system, the government faces the problem of paying the pensions of current pensioners and of honoring the claims of workers who have contributed to the old public pension system. This situation implies that government expenditures should be financed by higher taxes, a reduction of other government expenditures, or the issuance of new debt because contributions are now directed toward the new individual accounts. The size of these obligations may have an important fiscal effect on the government's budget, while the way this deficit is financed has important effects on intergenerational (between current and future generations) and intragenerational (between rich and poor) income redistribution.

Basically, we can distinguish two ways of financing this deficit. On the one hand, the government may issue new debt, trading the old, implicit PAYGO debt for new, explicit debt. Debt financing implies that, in the short run, national saving, the capital stock, and the intergenerational distribution of welfare are only marginally affected, by magnitudes that depend on the net efficiency gains of the reform. On the other hand, the deficit can be financed by raising taxes or cutting government expenditures. A completely tax-financed transition is equivalent to combining a pension reform with a contractionary fiscal policy, and therefore there is a transfer of resources from current to future generations, encouraging higher saving rates and capital formation and raising future per capita income and wage levels. It is possible to have any combination of both options. The net result will depend on the particular mix of instruments used to finance the transition.[34]

The size of the pension debt and the fiscal effect differ among pension reforms depending on the degree of maturity of the old pension system, the size of the formal and informal sectors, the amount of benefits and its relation to contributions, and the performance of such macroeconomic variables as interest rates, output, and wage growth.

33. Arrau (1990), Arrau and Schmidt-Hebbel (1993), Arrau, Valdés-Prieto, and Schmidt-Hebbel (1993), Schmidt-Hebbel (1994), and Corsetti and Schmidt-Hebbel (1996) analyze these effects in the case of a representative economy and in the Chilean and Colombian reform experiences. These papers are based on a framework developed by Auerbach and Kotlikoff (1987). The main features of the representative economy model used are that households maximize lifetime utility, there is no intergenerational altruism, there are no borrowing constraints, and voluntary savings are higher than mandated savings. Households of a given cohort are identical to each other. There is no uncertainty, and the economy is closed. Labor is supplied inelastically, and market clearing allows continuous full employment.

34. As explained by Arrau and Schmidt-Hebbel (1993), the intermediate case was chosen by Chile. The government distinguished among two components of its pension debt: the part due to current PAYGO pensioners (operational deficit) and the part due to past contributions made by currently active workers to the old system (honored with recognition bonds). Debt was used to pay for maturing recognition bonds, and taxes were used to pay the operational deficit.

4.3.1   The Fiscal Cost of the Reform

In this section, we perform a numerical simulation of an actuarial model that estimates the annual pension revenues, expenditures, and liabilities of the IVCM-IMSS pension program as affected by the reform under various circumstances. This model is a partial equilibrium framework that treats relevant macroeconomic variables as given. Nevertheless, for our purposes, it is a useful instrument, one that allows us to deal with more disaggregation in a simple way, compared with a general equilibrium simulation model à la Auerbach and Kotlikoff (1987).

The model is estimated for the two components of the transition fiscal cost: current and transition pensioners. We call the sum of these two components *total transition deficit.* In both cases, we consider pensions paid for old age, severance at old age, and disability and life insurance. The simulations include the case of reform and the case of no reform. The estimates are performed assuming different performances of the main macroeconomic variables. We present a case that we call *full fiscal cost,* which includes both the transition and the permanent cost of the reform. As explained below, the permanent cost of the reform is a consequence of the particular features of the new system. The basic macroeconomic variables that shape the results are the real interest rate and the rates of growth of output, wages, and number of affiliates.

Case 1: The Cost of the Transition

We estimate the fiscal deficit derived from honoring the rights of current and transition pensioners, including pensions paid to widows, children, and other relatives.[35] We perform the simulations for the period 1997–2047 for two scenarios: one assuming low economic growth and the other assuming better economic conditions (see table 4.4). For each case, we also assume three different interest rates. Remember that, in the reformed system, transition workers have the option at the time of retirement to choose between the pension granted under the old system or that granted under the new one. The decision will be determined by accumulated individual savings, which depend on the contributing period, the real interest rate, and the real growth of wages. Throughout the simulations, it is assumed that the labor force covered by the new system will grow according to IMSS (1995) demographic projections.[36] Our assumptions about these variables satisfy the steady-state condition that real output growth

---

35. We constructed these simulations using publicly available information; they may vary from those constructed by others, depending on the demographic and macroeconomic assumptions made. In particular, we do not consider changes in the age distribution; also, our fiscal cost estimates do not include workers' compensation pensions, commissions paid by the workers, or the SAR's accumulated balances before the reform.

36. IMSS assumes that the number of affiliates will grow by 2.3 percent in 1997, 2.9 percent in 1998, and 2.2 percent thereafter.

Table 4.4   **Actuarial Model Basic Assumptions (%)**

Scenario	Real Output Growth	Real Wages Growth	Real Interest Rate, Retirement	Real Interest Rate, Housing
High growth	5	2.8	$\left\{\begin{array}{c} 3.5 \\ 6 \\ 8 \end{array}\right\}$	0
Low growth	3	.8	$\left\{\begin{array}{c} 3.5 \\ 6 \\ 8 \end{array}\right\}$	0

is equal to real wage growth plus labor force growth (Harrod-neutral rate of technical progress).[37] In all simulations, it is also assumed that the balance from the housing subaccount is accumulated with a zero real interest rate and that there are no withdrawals from the individual account during the contributing period.

High-Growth Scenario. Table 4.5 reports the estimated total transition deficit, as a percentage of GDP, derived from the pension reform under the high-growth scenario. We report only the first year, the last year, and the year in which the deficit reaches its maximum in our simulation period. The appendix figures show the evolution of this variable for the whole period.

Assuming an interest rate of 3.5 percent, the total transition deficit rises from 0.48 percent of GDP in 1997 to a maximum of 2.59 percent of GDP in 2035, falling to 1.87 percent of GDP in 2047. If the interest rate is 6 percent, the maximum transition cost is 2.29 percent of GDP in 2035, falling to 1.76 percent of GDP in 2047. Finally, if the interest rate is equivalent to 8 percent, the maximum transition cost is 1.99 percent of GDP in 2031, falling to 1.47 percent of GDP in 2047.

Current pensioners' deficit represents most of the total deficit in 1997, decreasing continuously after that year. This deficit is not affected by the interest rate, but it does depend on the number of current pensioners, including their widows and other relatives, as well as the increase in the minimum wage. The presence of widows and other relatives explains why the operational deficit lasts for a long period of time. The deficit derived from the transition workers depends on the interest rate because, the higher the interest rate, the higher will be the funds accumulated in the individual accounts, and the lower the number of workers choosing the old system. Finally, both components of this

37. It should be noted that, if the rate of technical progress is not neutral, our results will change. In particular, if wL (where w is the wage rate and L is labor) grows at a higher rate than output, the cost will be higher because the pensions under the old system, which are an option for transition workers, are indexed by the minimum wage.

Table 4.5   Total Transition Deficit, High-Growth Scenario (% GDP)

Real Interest Rate and Year	Current Pensioners	Transition Workers	Total
3.5%:			
1997	.45	.03	.48
Maximum (2035)	.03	2.56	2.59
2047	.01	1.86	1.87
6.0%:			
1997	.45	.03	.48
Maximum (2035)	.03	2.26	2.29
2047	.01	1.75	1.76
8.0%:			
1997	.45	.03	.48
Maximum (2031)	.04	1.95	1.99
2047	.01	1.46	1.47

Source: Authors' calculations.

total transition deficit are affected by real wage growth since benefits depend on this variable.

Low-Growth Scenario. Assuming an interest rate of 3.5 percent, the total transition deficit rises from 0.48 percent of GDP in 1997 to a maximum of 2.30 percent of GDP in 2033, falling to 1.79 percent of GDP in 2047. If the interest rate is 6 percent, the maximum transition cost is 1.96 percent of GDP in 2030, falling to 1.41 percent of GDP in 2047. Finally, if the interest rate is equivalent to 8 percent, the maximum transition cost is 1.68 percent of GDP in 2027, falling to 1.04 percent of GDP in 2047 (see table 4.6).

Transition Cost Comparison

To get an idea of the importance of the accumulated total transition cost in terms of GDP at present value with respect to other Latin American countries that have carried out similar reforms, we estimate the cumulative transition fiscal cost relative to GDP for the complete simulated period. To make our estimate comparable to other studies, we use an interest rate of 5 percent, equal to output growth. The total transition pension cost for the next fifty years is estimated at 82.6 percent of GDP for this scenario. If we compare this amount with the Chilean and Colombian cases, it turns out that the Mexican cumulative transition cost is lower. Using similar assumptions for these two countries, Schmidt-Hebbel (1994) estimates a cumulative cost relative to GDP of 86.5 percent for Colombia and 126 percent for Chile. The difference in these amounts can be explained, in particular with respect to the Chilean case, by the lower maturity of the Mexican pension system, its younger population structure, and the lower population coverage of the system.

Table 4.6   **Total Transition Deficit, Low-Growth Scenario (% GDP)**

Real Interest Rate and Year	Current Pensioners	Transition Workers	Total
3.5%:			
1997	.45	.03	.48
Maximum (2033)	.03	2.27	2.30
2047	.01	1.78	1.79
6.0%:			
1997	.45	.03	.48
Maximum (2030)	.05	1.91	1.96
2047	.01	1.40	1.41
8.0%:			
1997	.45	.03	.48
Maximum (2027)	.06	1.62	1.68
2047	.01	1.03	1.04

Source: Authors' calculations.

Case 2: Full Cost

This simulation includes transition costs plus fiscal costs that are permanent as long as the new scheme is in place. The new pension system implies three additional government expenditures: the minimum pension guarantee, the "social contribution," and the government's share of the global contribution for retirement, disability, and life insurance.

As is shown in table 4.7, in the high-growth case, the total cost rises from 0.77 percent of GDP in 1997 to 2.53 percent of GDP in 2031, falling to 2.02 percent of GDP when an 8 percent real interest rate is considered. For medium and low interest rates, the maximum total cost relative to GDP is equivalent to 2.96 and 3.39 in 2035 and 2036, respectively. The full cost declines to 2.46 and 2.72 percent of GDP in 2047, respectively.

In the low-growth scenario, as is shown in table 4.8, the total cost rises from 0.77 percent of GDP in 1997 to 2.16 percent of GDP in 2026, falling to 1.46 percent of GDP with the high interest rate. For medium and low interest rates, the maximum total cost relative to GDP is equivalent to 2.54 and 3.05 in 2030 and 2035, respectively. The full cost declines to 1.98 and 2.62 percent of GDP in 2047, respectively.

Case 3: No Reform

This case assumes that there is no reform and that the IVCM-IMSS program will continue indefinitely. Table 4.9 reports the simulation results for the high- and low-growth scenarios and the same demographic assumptions as the previous exercises in this section. We do not report the simulations for each interest rate because results are not directly affected by this variable. Given the current low level of IVCM-IMSS reserves, the effect of the interest rate on the simulation results is negligible.

Table 4.7   Reform Full Cost, High-Growth Scenario (% GDP)

Real Interest Rate and Year	Total Transition Deficit	New Pensions[a]	Other[b]	Total
3.5%:				
1997	.48	.00	.29	.77
Maximum (2036)	2.57	.67	.15	3.39
2047	1.87	.75	.11	2.72
6.0%:				
1997	.48	.00	.29	.77
Maximum (2035)	2.29	.54	.13	2.96
2047	1.76	.59	.11	2.46
8.0%:				
1997	.48	.00	.29	.77
Maximum (2031)	1.99	.40	.14	2.53
2047	1.47	.44	.11	2.02

Source: Authors' calculations.

[a]Includes payments of benefits due to disability and life insurance.

[b]Includes social contribution and government contributions for retirement and disability and life insurance.

Table 4.8   Reform Full Cost, Low-Growth Scenario (% GDP)

Real Interest Rate and Year	Total Transition Deficit	New Pensions[a]	Other[b]	Total
3.5%:				
1997	.48	.00	.29	.77
Maximum (2035)	2.29	.65	.11	3.05
2047	1.79	.75	.08	2.62
6.0%:				
1997	.48	.00	.29	.77
Maximum (2030)	1.96	.46	.12	2.54
2047	1.41	.49	.08	1.98
8.0%:				
1997	.48	.00	.29	.77
Maximum (2026)	1.67	.35	.14	2.16
2047	1.04	.34	.08	1.46

Source: Authors' calculations.

[a]Includes payments of benefits due to disability and life insurance.

[b]Includes social contribution and government contributions for retirement and disability and life insurance.

Table 4.9   **No Reform Fiscal Cost (% GDP)**

Year	High Growth	Low Growth
1997	1.55	1.61
2022	3.58	5.43
2047	6.29	14.01

Source: Authors' calculations.

The fiscal cost without reform, assuming high growth, rises from 1.55 percent of GDP in 1997 to 3.58 percent of GDP in 2022 and to 6.29 percent of GDP in 2047. If we assume low growth, these values are much higher; 5.43 percent and 14.01 percent of GDP, respectively. Comparing these results with the values obtained for the full fiscal cost in the case of reform, it is clear that the cost of not reforming the current pension system would be much higher in the future.

4.4   Macroeconomic Implications of the Reform

Pension reform in Mexico can have important effects on labor market dynamics, domestic saving rates, capital market development, investment, and output growth. These elements will lead to improved overall economic efficiency, making it likely that the Mexican economy can enter a period of sustainable growth.

4.4.1   Labor Market Efficiency

Even though the new pension reform does not involve a reduction in the ratio of pretax and after-tax wages, it does imply a substantial gain compared to the current PAYGO system. The pension reform makes the system work more as a mandated benefit scheme than as a pure tax, as benefits become more closely related to contributions. Therefore, it reduces distortions in the labor market (see Summers 1989).

On the other hand, the minimum pension guarantee can have negative effects on labor market efficiency. As interest rates and output grow, the number of low-income individuals will decline, reducing government exposure to the fiscal cost generated by pension guarantees. Nevertheless, at the margin, the minimum pension deters workers from productive activities in the formal sector: because future contributions will not imply more income at retirement, workers entitled to receive the minimum pension will have fewer incentives to offer additional labor.

4.4.2   Savings

Several studies have analyzed the transition from a PAYGO to a fully funded system and the effect on saving, both for a representative economy and for specific countries, on the basis of the Auerbach and Kotlikoff framework (1987).[38] The majority of these papers analyze the transition cost and the alternatives for financing it, which, as discussed in section 4.3, can be reduced to two: tax and debt financed.

Theoretical simulations for tax-financed reforms yield increases in stationary saving rates of 3–5 percent of GDP (Arrau and Schmidt-Hebbel 1993; Cifuentes and Valdés-Prieto 1994). For the case of Colombia, it has been estimated that a tax-financed reform can increase stationary saving rates by 2.4 percent of GDP. For debt-financed transitions, the representative economy obtains a reduction in long-term output of around 1–4 percentage points of GDP (Arrau and Schmidt-Hebbel 1993),[39] while steady-state saving is slightly lowered. Partially debt-financed transition exercises yield intermediate results.

These authors have also explored the possibility of liquidity-constrained consumers in the transition to a fully funded system.[40] In this case, the new scheme forces individuals to a corner solution where their personal savings are increased to a higher level than originally desired. These exercises yield long-term GDP growth estimates as high as 16 percent for a closed representative economy and 4–14 percent for the Colombian case (Cifuentes and Valdés-Prieto 1994; Schmidt-Hebbel 1994). Mexican reform limits individual total indebtedness capacity since workers cannot use their accumulated balances as guarantees in other financial operations.

Mexico's transition is expected to be partially debt financed, but, at the time of this writing, the government has not announced the way in which it will be financed. To assess the effect of Mexican pension reform on savings, we undertook a simple and conservative estimation of the possible evolution of accumulated balances in the individual accounts.

The exercise assumes real GDP growth of 3 percent per year, a real interest rate of 6 percent, and a real wage increase of 0.8 percent a year. It also assumes that the total fiscal cost is partially (50 percent) tax financed and that there is no reduction in voluntary private saving.[41] The increase in contributing workers behaves like IMSS projections.[42] It is assumed that balances in the housing subaccount keep their real value over time and that there are no withdrawals from any subaccount prior to retirement.

Table 4.10 shows the accumulated balance in the individual accounts (including contributions and interest earned minus withdrawals from future pensioners), the fiscal cost per year as estimated in section 4.3, an implied reduction in public-sector savings as the transition is partially tax financed, and the

---

38. The specific characteristics of the Kotlikoff and Auerbach framework are explained in n. 33 above.

39. This result is driven by the future tax changes assumed by Arrau and Schmidt-Hebbel.

40. Villagómez (1993) found significant empirical evidence to support the liquidity-constrained consumers hypothesis in the case of Mexico.

41. Workers are supposed to have no voluntary savings. This strong assumption is possible in the Mexican case considering current real wages and saving patterns.

42. For projections, see n. 36 above.

Table 4.10   **Effects of the Reform on Savings (% GDP)**

Years	Accumulated Balances (A = Sum Bs)	Flows to Individual Accounts (B)	Total Fiscal Cost (C)	Public-Sector Savings Reduction (D = ½ C)	Net Savings Annual Increase (E = B − D)	Accumulated Savings Increase (G = Sum Es)
1	3.98	2.21	.48	.24	1.97	3.74
5	13.16	2.44	.52	.26	2.18	12.15
10	25.95	2.72	.72	.36	2.36	23.66
15	40.07	2.97	1.08	.54	2.43	35.7
20	55.31	3.16	1.45	.72	2.44	47.88
30	88.2	3.43	1.91	.95	2.47	72.35
40	123.75	3.74	1.87	.94	2.81	98.57

Source: Authors' calculations.

estimated net financial savings increase, defined as the difference between annual flows into the individual accounts plus interest minus withdrawals and the public-sector savings reduction. Finally, it includes an estimation of the accumulated savings increase associated with the pension reform.

As can be seen, net saving can be increased by around 2.18 percentage points of GDP in five years to around 2.81 percentage points after forty years of the introduction of the pension reform. This is a conservative estimate since it assumes low growth conditions and does not consider a positive real rate of return on the housing subaccount.

4.4.3 Capital Markets

Pension reform will produce a significant long-term increase in the availability of financial resources to the economy. This will promote further financial specialization and the creation of new instruments, especially those related to long-term investments. As can be seen in figure 4.3, total financial savings are highly concentrated in short-term instruments. Long-term instruments account for only 21.7 percent of total financial savings and 11.9 percent of GDP. With the pension reform, long-term instruments could reach 21.9 percent of GDP in 2000 and around 45 percent of GDP in 2010.

The capitalization value of the Mexican Stock Exchange in 1995 was equivalent to 44 percent of GDP. If we consider the accumulated balances of the individual retirement accounts estimated in the savings section and assume that AFOREs invest their resources as does a typical pension fund in the United States (60 percent equity and 40 percent debt), we could expect that total pension fund participation in the stock exchange will be around 1.9 percent of the total during the first year and that after fifteen years it could reach around 15 percent of GDP.

The availability of these resources will promote financial deepening and

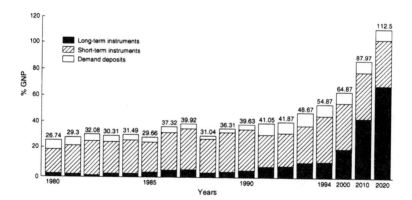

Fig. 4.3 Financial savings (M4N currency)
Source: Banco de Mexico.

long-term investment. These gains could have a significant effect on investment decisions and growth.

4.4.4   Investment and Growth

The National Development Plan 1995–2000 estimates that, in order for the Mexican economy to grow at the rate of 5 percent annually, Mexico requires an investment rate equivalent to 24 percent of GDP. The plan projects that this investment rate will be financed by domestic savings, representing 22 percent of GDP, and foreign savings, equivalent to 2 percent of GDP. The domestic savings goal requires an increase in this variable of about 6 percentage points of GDP.

From the results of the savings projections, and assuming that all new savings are channeled to finance investment and not to reduce the current account deficit, the pension reform will directly generate savings that could finance close to 25 percent of the additional required investment by the year 2000. As the system matures, the effect of the reform on savings will be higher, and therefore its contribution to investment and growth will be more significant.

4.5   Concluding Remarks

Pension reform is now a worldwide phenomenon forced by changing economic, demographic, and social structures. In general, these processes have been part of major economic transformations. Social security reforms involve many different aspects in a complicated manner. There is no one way to proceed, and each country has developed its own model. However, it is clear that any solution chosen should meet at least two requirements: financial and social viability.

This paper analyzed the Mexican pension reform and made some preliminary assessments about its future effects on the Mexican economy. We presented and compared the most important characteristics of the old and the new pension systems. There were several factors that caused the reform. First, the old IVCM-IMSS system was financially unsustainable; second, the Mexican economy needs to increase its domestic saving rate.

The reform basically consists of establishing a fully funded defined-contribution system based on individual accounts with a minimum pension guarantee provided by the government. Total contributions amount to 13.5 percent of the salary of the average worker for accumulation in the individual accounts plus 2.5 percent for disability and life insurance, which is still managed by IMSS.

The new Mexican system shares many common elements with other Latin American reforms. However, it also has its own advantages and disadvantages. The advantages are that the new system respects the acquired rights of current workers, that the old system is completely replaced by the new system, that administrative costs are reduced by limiting the number of transfers between pension fund managers to one per year, that pension managers are allowed to operate several funds, that the law does not establish a minimum guaranteed rate of return for pension funds, and that there is a centralized collection agency and a centralized data bank. The disadvantages include that the funds are prohibited from investing in foreign securities, that the IMSS is the sole provider of disability and life insurance, and that the minimum pension is guaranteed. Other disadvantages are the IMSS AFORE, the operation of the housing subaccount, portability problems, and the market share restrictions. These situations should be modified in the future to further improve the new system.

The fiscal cost of the transition to the new system is relatively low compared to similar reforms in other Latin American countries. The present value of the transition cost represents about 82.6 percent of GDP, lower, for example, than in Chile and Colombia. This mainly reflects the fact that the reform was undertaken when Mexico's population was still relatively young.

The reform will have a significant effect on financial savings. Accumulated balances in the individual accounts could reach 24 percent of GDP after ten years, around 48 percent after twenty years, and 72 percent after thirty years. This will increase the possibility of financing long-term investment projects in Mexico and will also promote more efficiency in the financial sector.

Appendix

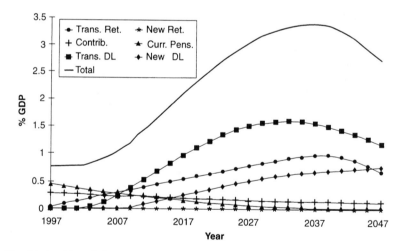

Fig. 4A.1   Cost of the reform, high-growth scenario (interest rate 3.5%)
Source: Authors' calculations.
Note: Trans. Ret. = old age and severance at old age pensions paid to transition pensioners. New Ret. = expenses in old age and severance at old age pensions for new pensioners. Trans. DL = disability and life pensions paid to transition pensioners. New DL = expenses in disability and life pensions for new pensioners. Contrib. = contributions. Curr. Pens. = pensions of current pensioners.

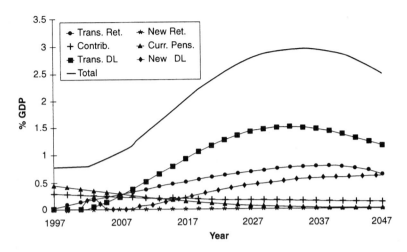

Fig. 4A.2   Cost of the reform, high-growth scenario (interest rate 6%)
Source: Authors' calculations.
Note: For abbreviations, see fig. 4A.1.

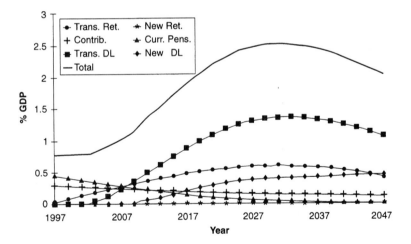

Fig. 4A.3   Cost of the reform, high-growth scenario (interest rate 8%)
Source: Authors' calculations.
Note: For abbreviations, see fig. 4A.1.

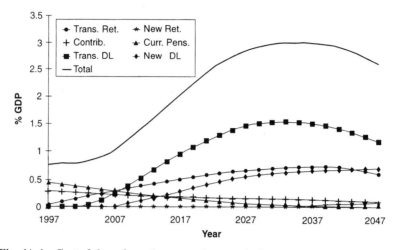

Fig. 4A.4   Cost of the reform, low-growth scenario (interest rate 3.5%)
Source: Authors' calculations.
Note: For abbreviations, see fig. 4A.1.

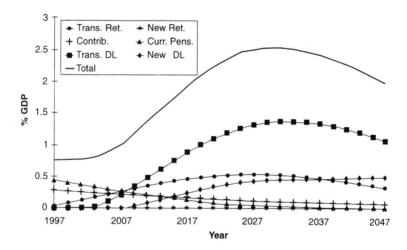

Fig. 4A.5   Cost of the reform, low-growth scenario (interest rate 6%)
Source: Authors' calculations.
Note: For abbreviations, see fig. 4A.1.

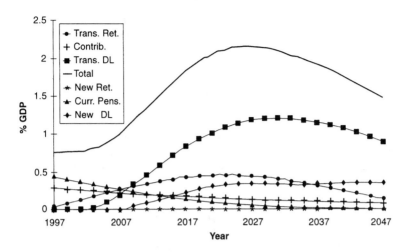

Fig. 4A.6   Cost of the reform, low-growth scenario (interest rate 8%)
Source: Authors' calculations.
Note: For abbreviations, see fig. 4A.1.

References

Arrau, Patricio. 1990. Social security reform: The capital accumulation and intergenerational distribution effect. Working Paper no. WPS 512. Washington, D.C.: World Bank, Policy, Research and External Affairs, October.

Arrau, Patricio, and Klaus Schmidt-Hebbel. 1993. Macroeconomic and intergenerational welfare effects of a transition from pay-as-you-go to fully-funded pension system. Paper presented at the twelfth Latin American meeting of the Econometric Society, Tucumán, Argentina.

Arrau, Patricio, Salvador Valdés-Prieto, and Klaus Schmidt-Hebbel. 1993. Privately managed pension systems design issues and the Chilean experience. Background paper for the Old Age Security Project. World Bank: Washington, D.C.

Auerbach, A., and L. Kotlikoff. 1987. *Dynamic fiscal policy.* Cambridge: Cambridge University Press.

Banco de México. 1996. *Informe anual, 1995.*

Bosworth, B., R. Dornbusch, and J. Poterba. 1995. Public policies to support saving and investment in Mexico. Mimeo.

Cifuentes, R., and S. Valdés-Prieto. 1994. Transition from PAYGO to funding in the case of credit constraints. Paper presented at the conference Pensions: Funding, Privatization, and Macroeconomic Policy, Catholic University of Chile.

Corsetti, Giancarlo, and Klaus Schmidt-Hebbel. 1996. Pension reform and growth. In *Pensions: Privatization, funding and macroeconomic policy,* ed. Salvador Valdés-Prieto. Cambridge: Cambridge University Press.

Diamond, Peter. 1994. Privatization of social security: Lessons from Chile. *Revista de análisis económico* 9, no. 1 (June): 21–33.

Feldstein, Martin. 1995. Public policies to increase the saving rate in Mexico. Mexico D.F.: Asociación Mexicana de Bancos. Mimeo.

Gil-Díaz, Francisco, and Agustín Carstens. 1996. Some hypotheses related to the Mexican 1994–95 crisis. Documento no. 9601. Mexico D.F.: Banco de México.
Instituto Mexicano del Seguro Social (IMSS). 1995. *Diagnóstico IMSS*. Mexico D.F.
———. 1996. Aportaciones al debate. Mexico D.F.
Schmidt-Hebbel, Klaus. 1994. *Colombia's pension reform: Fiscal and macroeconomic implications*. Washington, D.C.: World Bank, Policy and Research Department, October.
Solís-Soberón, Fernando. 1995. Descripción del sistema de ahorro para el retiro. Documento de Trabajo no. 3. Mexico D.F.: CONSAR, September.
Solís-Soberón, Fernando, and Alejandro Villagómez. 1996. Domestic savings in Mexico and pension system reform. Paper presented at the Conference on Mexico sponsored by the Institute of Latin American Studies at the University of London.
Summers, Lawrence. 1989. Some simple economics of mandated benefits. *American Economic Review* 49 (May): 177–82.
Valdés-Prieto, Salvador. 1994. Distributive concerns when substituting a pay-as-you-go by a fully funded pension system. *Revista de análisis económico* 9, no. 1 (June): 77–104.
Villagómez, Alejandro. 1993. Los determinantes del ahorro en México: Una reseña de la investigación empírica. *Economía mexicana* 2, no. 2:305–28.

Comment   Aaron Tornell

This paper analyzes the transition of the Mexican pension system from a pay-as-you-go to a fully funded system. It gives a diagnostic of the old system, describes the institutions under the new system, and evaluates the macroeconomic consequences of the reform. The paper is very informative and provides a well-rounded evaluation of the reform's implementation. My comments concentrate on the possible macroeconomic consequences of the reform. They should be considered as simply speculative and complementary to the paper.

The authors give two reasons why pension reform has been implemented in Mexico. First, the old system became insolvent. Second, pension reform will increase national saving, and this in turn will induce a higher growth rate, as occurred in Chile.

Two issues determine whether pension reform leads to higher growth. One involves fiscal redistribution. The other has to do with the proper functioning of the regulatory framework. I consider each in turn.

The first point I want to make is that pension reform is not a sufficient condition for a higher saving rate. If pension reform is not accompanied by judicial reform, it is unlikely that the saving rate will increase.

During the last quarter century, Mexico has enjoyed several episodes of oil windfalls, which were not permanent with perfect certainty. A puzzling aspect of these episodes is that the windfalls did not increase the saving rate in Mex-

Aaron Tornell is associate professor of economics at Harvard University and a faculty research fellow of the National Bureau of Economic Research.

ico. Moreover, they induced significant deteriorations of the current account. Mexico is not alone in this: Nigeria and Venezuela are prime examples of other countries that had similar experiences. One explanation for this response is that shocks were considered 100 percent permanent, but this is difficult to believe since other countries experiencing similar shocks did not have such deteriorations in their current accounts. Another explanation is that there was an institutional problem, that there were some groups within society with the power to appropriate fiscal resources and no countervailing institutions to check this power. Thus, when the windfall occurred, groups simply became more voracious and appropriated more, and national saving and higher growth failed to materialize. Of course, these mechanisms might not exist in developed countries, but Mexico is not yet in that situation.

Suppose, then, that pension reform is a success and increases workers' savings. This creates a windfall for the country relative to the status quo ex ante. If the same mechanism that operated with the oil windfalls operates now, appropriation in other areas of the economy may increase. As a result, the net effect of pension reform on the national saving rate might be nil. This does not mean that pension reform should not be implemented. Rather, it implies that policy makers should not be content with the implementation of pension reform alone as the way to increase productive investment. Policymakers should also implement judicial reforms to create countervailing institutions that will limit or eliminate the power of special groups to engage in discretionary redistribution.

The previous discussion suggests that simplistic extrapolations of the Chilean experience, in which pension reform led to an increase in savings, might be misleading. The reason is that the political economies of Mexico and Chile are quite different. Pension reform in Chile was undertaken in the aftermath of a civil struggle and a military coup, in which several powerful groups lost the power to appropriate fiscal resources that they enjoyed in the 1960s. One could say that, in the Chilean case, the government was relatively autonomous. This is not the case in Mexico today.

Let me shift now to the second issue, which is the proper functioning of the regulatory framework. The guaranteeing of the pensions' real return by the government might generate incentive compatibility problems with pension funds' managers. Thus, strict regulation is extremely important. Given the recent banking history of Mexico, this should not be taken for granted. During the early 1990s, after the privatization of the banks, there was a lending boom in which bank credit to the private sector increased 116 percent from 1990 to 1994. This lending boom led to a quick deterioration of the quality of banks' portfolios for two reasons. First, consumer credit increased exponentially. Second, banks engaged in risky off–balance sheet investments. In the end, the government absorbed a big share of the costs associated with these risks. The problem cannot be traced back to a lack of regulatory law or the absence of a regulatory body. In fact, at the time of the banks' privatization, a law to regulate the privatization was drafted, and the National Banking Commission had the power to oversee banks. The problem was that the commission was not sufficiently equipped to monitor the exponential increase in bank lending and investment activities.

Extrapolating from the experience with the banks in Mexico, one should emphasize the need for a very strict regulatory framework for pension managers during pension reform, at least during the transition period.

Discussion Summary   Jeffrey Liebman and Andrew Samwick

The discussion began with comments about Aaron Tornell's suggestion that increased corruption might negate the gains of social security privatization. One participant said that Tornell's arguments were not arguments against market incentives such as privatizing social security; rather, they were an argument for liberalization of both the political and the economic spheres. Another participant questioned whether it was generally the case in representative agent models of rent-seeking behavior that investment would decline in response to a positive terms-of-trade shock. He suggested that there were not clear implications from such a model. He also argued that there would be fewer possibilities for theft of the surplus from social security reform than from a terms-of-trade shock. A third participant argued that the effects of reforms on investment were likely to be the opposite of what Tornell claimed. Since the reforms were likely to boost private and national saving, they would increase the confidence of foreign lenders, and this would lead to a greater inflow of capital from abroad.

However, another member of the group said that Tornell was right about graft and corruption and said that the Mexican reforms are going to be a disaster. He said that, while it makes sense to have a single collection agency, Mexico has chosen IMSS, the most inefficient and corrupt agency in the government, for this role. Another participant questioned whether it was wise for IMSS simultaneously to be administering the program and to be competing as a fund manager. He thought that it might be possible for IMSS to subsidize itself out of general collections of payroll taxes and therefore gain an unfair competitive advantage. Sales responded that he thought that IMSS was capable of doing a good job of collecting the revenues, but he agreed that it was problematic for IMSS to be a fund manager at the same time that it has enforcement powers and the authority to sanction employers who do not comply with the social security law.

It was pointed out that the housing funds run by INFONAVIT have been yielding −5 percent a year. Thus, if a rate of return of 9.6 percent is expected for the entire social insurance contribution and 30 percent is invested in the housing fund, the other 70 percent will have to yield an unlikely 15 percent for the typical worker to avoid relying on the minimum pension.

The discussion turned to annuitization, and one participant asked whether Mexico had any previous experience with annuities. Sales reported that, under the old SAR system, all workers took a lump sum payment, with the result that there is currently no annuity market in Mexico. People who outlive their lump sum receive the minimum pension from the old IMSS system.

Another participant expressed concern that Mexico was going to give people the option at retirement of choosing the maximum of the old system benefits and the new system benefits. He said that this would create a serious moral hazard problem and that people would buy extremely risky portfolios that contained a small probability of a very high return. Sales agreed that there was indeed a risk that investors would gamble with risky investments since they could always fall back on the minimum pension. Indeed, he reported that he had spoken with a future pension fund administrator who was planning to offer a portfolio with exactly such a strategy.

A member of the group questioned whether it was wise to turn implicit debt into explicit debt in a country like Mexico that often suffered from difficult macroeconomic conditions. Explicit debt can lead to exploding interest payments and an economic crisis.

In wrapping up the discussion, Sales described three troubling trends in Mexican public finance. First, he said tax evasion is increasing. Between the first quarter of 1995 and the first quarter of 1996, the VAT increased from 10 to 15 percent. GDP and consumption fell by 1 percent over this interval. However, tax revenues increased by only 15 percent in response to this 50 percent increase in tax rates. Second, he said that health care expenditures are consuming an increasing fraction of the government budget and that it would be important to keep an eye on the results of the recent reforms of health care financing. Third, he said that privatization of state-owned firms is proceeding very slowly.

5   The Shift to a Funded Social Security System: The Case of Argentina

Joaquín Cottani and Gustavo Demarco

The Argentine social security system has been modified a number of times since its creation in 1904. The pay-as-you-go system was adopted in 1954. The reform of 1969 established the system's definitive structure, which remained substantially unchanged for more than twenty years. However, the system's underlying financial problems led the government to undertake an integral reform of its social security program in 1993. The government adopted a mixed system by introducing private pensions into the program. In this report, *former system* or *old system* will refer to the retirement program that existed between 1969 and 1993.

The former pay-as-you-go system included a single regime for public- and private-sector employees and a separate regime for the self-employed (whose affiliation to the social security program is mandatory in Argentina). In theory, more than 90 percent of the labor force was insured under these two systems, with exclusions made only for state and local government employees, armed and security forces, and certain professionals with independent retirement systems. However, owing to pervasive evasion, especially among the self-employed, many workers were not eligible for benefits on reaching retirement age.

The former system was funded with payroll taxes and, when necessary, with other forms of taxation. The government was exclusively responsible for its administration. Future benefits were predefined, but the actual link between

Joaquín Cottani was undersecretary of macroeconomic programming of Argentina (1991–93) and undersecretary of finance (1994–96). He is currently the financial representative of Argentina in the United States and Canada. Gustavo Demarco was consultant to the secretary of social security of Argentina (1991–94) and is currently operations manager of the Superintendencia de Administradoras de Fondos de Jubilaciones y Pensiones (AFJP).

The authors acknowledge able assistance and helpful comments from Diane Cashman, Rafael Rofman, Hugo Bertin, and Marcelo De Biase. Paola Comparatore and Marcela Lopez Mendez provided efficient secretarial aid.

the amounts of contributions and benefits was very weak. This was especially true when the system's financial problems became particularly serious and beneficiaries had to accept lower than anticipated pensions.

To receive an old age pension, public and private employees had to attain a specified retirement age (sixty for men and fifty-five for women) and make contributions for a minimum period. In practice, however, excessive permissiveness in the system allowed some workers to obtain pensions without accumulating the required contributions. Conditions of eligibility for disability and survivorship pensions were also lax.

In theory, the pension formulas for dependent workers were extremely generous by international standards and were linked to wages received during the last years of service. However, the methodology used to index pension benefits allowed distortion of the relation, and this happened for decades of high inflation.[1]

Typically, there was little connection between workers' past wages and their pension entitlements under the old system. There was also very little connection between their years of covered employment and their pension entitlements. These factors contributed to the creation of undesirable labor market incentives and significant redistribution effects that were generally capricious.

The cost of the pay-as-you-go system increased dramatically over time as a result of demographic and other factors. To cope with this problem, the government raised payroll taxes and earmarked other tax revenues for the system. In 1993, the year of the reform that introduced private pension funds, the payroll tax rate was 26 percent. In addition, the system received 10 percent of total VAT collection, 20 percent of income tax collection, 100 percent of the personal tax on wealth, 30 percent of all capital revenues obtained by the federal government from the sale of public enterprises, and the entire surplus of the family allowances program funded by an additional payroll tax. Currently, social security expenditures represent 6 percent of GDP, almost as much as the consolidated expenditure of the central government and its decentralized agencies, including transfers to public enterprises and to the private sector.

The financial position of the social security system began to deteriorate in the 1980s. The crisis became so severe that the government declared a state of emergency and rescheduled the debt of the system to avoid a total collapse of the system. In 1993, the Argentine Congress sanctioned new legislation to create a mixed system based on the coexistence of private pensions and individual retirement accounts and the pay-as-you-go institutional arrangement (Schulthess and Demarco 1994).

The purpose of this report is to analyze the factors that led to the 1993 reform (sec. 5.1) and describe the principal characteristics of the new system (sec. 5.2). In section 5.3, we examine some results of the new social security

---

1. The Social Security Department developed its own wage index for the purpose of adjusting base pensions.

system by observing the evolution of a group of global indicators. Finally, in section 5.4, we make inferences about the macroeconomic effects of the pension funds on variables such as the public budget and the savings rate.

5.1 Factors Leading Up to the Reform of the Social Security System

The social security system's reform was the response of the government to the financial crisis that had been building for many years. One clear manifestation of the deteriorating financial position of the system was the extremely low level of benefits paid (as compared to the legal targets) and the growing indebtedness with beneficiaries. The financial problems were not merely the result of inefficient administration but reflected, to a large extent, fundamental institutional weaknesses that ultimately threatened the solvency of the system. The growing number of lawsuits brought against the system throughout the 1980s revealed its vulnerability to legal challenges regarding benefit levels and undermined the ability of the government to administer the system with available resources.

The situation was complicated by increasing evidence of the inequities of the system, which were as much the result of general pension legislation as of special laws introduced to benefit some segments of the labor force. In short, when the government submitted legislation to initiate a profound reform of the social security retirement program, it was clear that the financial problems of the system were just one of many factors contributing to the crisis. We will address each of these factors in turn.

5.1.1 Chronic Financial Disequilibria

The financial problems of the system resulted from trends in labor market demographics, payroll tax evasion, and structural problems inherent in the pay-as-you-go system. To better understand the financial implications of the pay-as-you-go system, it is useful to analyze the following condition for financial equilibrium:

$$(1) \qquad\qquad Aaw(1 - e) + T = Bbw',$$

where A = number of contributors, a = payroll tax rate, w = average wage, e = rate of evasion, T = resources from the national Treasury (including earmarked taxes), B = number of beneficiaries, b = replacement rate, and w' = pensionable wage (i.e., reference wage to determine pensions).

The left-hand side of equation (1) corresponds to the revenues of the system, and the right-hand side represents its outlays. If we express T as a proportion of payroll taxes,

$$(2) \qquad\qquad T = \tau aAw(1 - e),$$

equation (1) may be rewritten as follows:

(3) $ad(1 - e)(1 + \tau)(w/w') = b.$

Equation (3) indicates that the replacement rate (b) increases with the payroll tax rate (a), the dependency ratio ($d = A/B$), defined as the potential number of contributors to pensioners, the amount of earmarked taxes, and the ratio between the current average wage and the pensionable wage and decreases with the rate of evasion. Variable e measures evasion as a proportion of potential payroll tax collection.[2]

Parameters involved in (3) are consistent if the equation is verified. For the values for d, a, (w/w'), and e approximate to those in Argentina before the reform, consistency would require an enormous increase in resources from the national Treasury, which should be 2.2 times the payroll taxes to guarantee the level of b promised by the law ($b = .70$). Alternatively, with the amount of resources from the Treasury actually available ($\tau = .33$), b should shrink to .29, a level rejected by Argentine society.

Changes in other parameters could certainly have helped, but, as we shall see, tendencies appeared to worsen these results.

Dependency Rate (d)

There has been a steady decline in the dependency ratio in Argentina before the social security reform as labor market demographics changed, conditions governing the extension of benefits became lax, and evasion increased.

Population aging is a well-known phenomenon that occurs as a consequence of economic development. During the first phases, it derives from a decline in birth rates parallel to an increase in life expectancy. Figure 5.1 illustrates that this phenomenon has occurred in Argentina. It is important to state that population aging is not a mere "transition problem": developed economies increasingly improve health and life conditions, thus increasing the proportion of old persons in total population. This is a leading reason why pay-as-you-go social security systems' financial problems are so generalized all over the world.

The primary effect of population aging on these systems is realized through a decline in the dependency ratio. Table 5.1 illustrates the projected dependency rate by extrapolating from actual demographic trends observed in the period preceding the 1993 reform. As illustrated, this rate was insufficient to meet the requirement for financial equilibrium even in the initial period. Moreover, the parameter declines throughout time, exacerbating the financial problems of the system even further.

In addition to demographic tendencies, excess permissiveness in the administration of benefits contributed to lowering the dependency rate. This was particularly clear in the case of disability and survivorship pensions (table 5.2),

---

2. Parameter e reflects just part of total evasion. In fact, evasion can affect revenues by lowering the number of contributors (A) or the amount contributed (aw). This has been a common form of payroll tax evasion in Argentina, where workers and firms have typically underdeclared wage incomes.

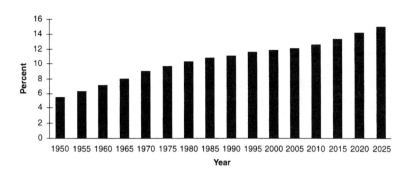

Fig. 5.1   Percentage of elderly population
Source: Superintendencia de AFJP, Unidad de Estudios Económicos y Estadísticas.

Table 5.1   **Projected Dependency Ratio (thousands of persons)**

Years	Contributors	Total Equivalent Pensions[a]	Dependency Ratio
1990	1,890	2,944	1.66
1995	5,260	3,447	1.53
2000	5,663	3,765	1.50
2010	6,654	4,339	1.53
2020	7,723	4,964	1.56

Source: Lo Vuolo (1994).
[a]Each survivorship pension is equivalent to 0.70 of a retirement pension.

Table 5.2   **Survivorship and Disability Pensions (thousands of persons)**

Year	Survivorship (1)	Disability (2)	Total (3)	$\{[(1) + (2)]/(3)\} \times 100$
1980	780	187	2,342	41.3
1985	951	302	2,743	45.7
1990	1,124	523	3,110	53.0
1991	1,141	525	3,204	52.0

Source: Schulthess and Demarco (1993).

noncontributory pensions (*pensiones graciables*), and special regimes for privileged sectors (characterized by higher benefits and less strict conditions for eligibility), which rose from 51 percent of total cases in 1975 to 56 percent in 1992 and from 39 percent of total expenditures to 49 percent.

Average Salary/Best Salary Proportion (w/w′)

In many countries, this variable is higher than one due to increases in labor productivity. In Argentina, however, annual productivity growth was negative between 1974 and 1990. Moreover, pay-as-you-go benefits were based on the individual's highest remuneration, not on average wages during the active years.[3] As a result, w/w' was typically lower than one, thus affecting the equilibrium equation. In addition, benefits defined as a proportion of best last salaries (and not to average) favored a form of evasion consisting in underdeclaring salaries during an important part of active life.

Evasion (e)

Since contributions made in years other than the last ten had no effect on benefit levels, young workers were particularly averse to complying with legal contribution levels. These factors, combined with the extremely high payroll tax that finances social security programs, explain the observed tendency toward evasion that is realized in the form of total or partial omission of contributions.[4] According to available data presented in table 5.3, evasion exceeded 40 percent of potential collections, on average, during the period 1980–92.

Evasion is partially a consequence of underdeclaration of wages and also one of illegal employment. One can infer the magnitude of the last by examining the evolution of informal employment. There is clear evidence that informal employment became more important in Argentina in the period preceding the 1993 reform since the share of employment in the personal and social services sector increased from 20 to 33 percent between 1960 and 1990. The increase in the share of the labor force employed in low-productivity activities had a negative effect on the financial position of the system since evasion is more pervasive among self-employed workers.

In summary, the factors analyzed in this section explain why Argentina's social security system developed financial problems in the years leading up to the reform. The tendencies observed during the period demonstrate clearly that the necessary conditions for financial equilibrium were already absent in the 1980s.

The data contained in table 5.4 reflect the financial structure of the social security system. As illustrated, the system relied increasingly on external sources of financing and transferred its financial difficulties to the national budget. Table 5.5 illustrates the evolution of social security revenues and expenditures prior to the reform. As observed, even the addition of Treasury resources was insufficient to reverse the basic trend toward financial disequilibria.

---

3. For salaried workers, the former legislation defined *highest remuneration* as the highest three-year average remuneration received during the last ten-year period in the worker's active work life.

4. In addition to pensions, payroll taxes fund four other social insurance programs: health insurance for active workers, health insurance for pensioners, family allowances, and unemployment insurance. Total contributions under the former regime were 33 percent for employers and 16 percent for workers, raising the overall payroll tax to 49 percent of wages.

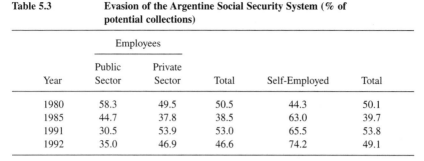

Table 5.3   **Evasion of the Argentine Social Security System (% of potential collections)**

| | Employees | | | | |
Year	Public Sector	Private Sector	Total	Self-Employed	Total
1980	58.3	49.5	50.5	44.3	50.1
1985	44.7	37.8	38.5	63.0	39.7
1991	30.5	53.9	53.0	65.5	53.8
1992	35.0	46.9	46.6	74.2	49.1

Source: Durán (1993).

Table 5.4   **Financing the Social Security System (%)**

Years	Own Resources	Earmarked Taxes	National Treasury and Central Bank	Total
1975	79.6	.3	20.1	100
1980	85.1	10.6	4.3	100
1985	74.3	15.9	9.8	100
1990	65.8	21.8	12.4	100
1991	74.2	15.9	9.9	100

Source: Schulthess and Demarco (1993).

Table 5.5   **Revenues and Expenditures of the Social Security System (million pesos)**

	1975	1980	1985	1990	1991
Revenues	8,016	11,694	10,737	9,241	10,384
Own revenues	7,984	9,955	6,715	7,366	8,302
Other	32	1,739	4,022	1,875	2,082
Expenditures	10,130	11,674	9,940	9,963	9,668
Net (revenues minus expenditures)	−2,114	20	797	−722	716

Source: Schulthess and Demarco (1993).

5.1.2   Debt with Pensioners

Growing financial difficulties and natural limitations on the extent to which the deficits of the system could be financed with tax revenues prompted the government to lower the pensions paid to beneficiaries through an "adequate" manipulation of benefit adjustment indexes. The result was that the replacement rate promised by law (70–82 percent of the best wage) was systematically violated. The subsequent legal challenges to the constitutionality of the practice ended in the system's "indebtedness crisis."

Between 1991 and 1992, the government consolidated all the system's debts with pensioners. The government canceled its debts with pensioners partially with cash and partially with bonds (BOCON). The total amount of debt recognized by the system through the consolidation process reached U.S.$12.5 billion. The government also used resources it received from the privatization of the national oil company, YPF, to cancel part of the bonds it had issued to cancel the system's debts.

Notwithstanding the special factors that contributed to restoring equilibrium to the system during the period 1991–93, the continuing inconsistency among the pay-as-you-go arrangements' basic parameters threatened to destabilize the system again. The traumatic consequences of managing such an enormous debt burden strengthened other arguments in favor of an integral reform of the social security system.

5.1.3   Inequities

Apart from its financial weaknesses, the pay-as-you-go system exhibited extreme inequities in the allocation of benefits. As mentioned earlier, special regimes proliferated and introduced marked differences in the criteria used to extend benefits to particular workers. For example, public-sector employees generally received more generous pensions than private-sector employees. The practice of applying different adjustment procedures to different pensions produced inequities and also led to settlements in favor of workers that brought lawsuits against the system. The settlements typically included provisions to apply adjustment procedures that were even more generous than those provided for in the general legislation. In some cases, maximum legal pensions were exceeded.

The general pension legislation itself was a source of inequity since an individual's benefit rate was completely divorced from the effort he or she made to contribute to the system. As a result, two similarly paid workers who contributed to the system during a different number of years could receive similar benefits in retirement.

The inequity effects of the pay-as-you-go system can be quantified by comparing the internal rate of return of the social security system of the general and special regimes. We estimated the corresponding IRR.[5] In spite of the additional contributions of 2 percent of the salary, special regimes yielded benefits that exceeded those of the general regime by 66 percent in the case of men (5.8

---

5. The IRR were calculated on the basis of estimated contributions during the active working life and projected benefits during retirement. Greater detail on the methodology used can be found in Schulthess (1991) and in Demarco and Posadas (1992).

percent per year vs. 3.5 percent in the general case) and by 30 percent in the case of women (8.0 vs. 6.1 percent).

5.1.4   Effect on Saving

The effects of private pensions on saving constitute an additional argument for the reform of social security. Owing to its low internal saving rate, Argentina's growth is crucially dependent on foreign savings, its economy being thus exposed to great instability as a consequence of fluctuations in variables affecting financial markets. Long-run reduction in social security's public deficit and the development of an institutional capital market would certainly contribute to self-sustainable economic growth.

The poor growth performance of Argentina in the 1980s was closely associated with a decline in gross domestic investment relative to GDP, from 25.3 percent in 1980 to 14 percent in 1990. During the same period, the national saving rate decreased from 23.3 to 18.6 percent. Although the investment rate picked up in 1991 and 1992, reaching 16.7 percent in 1992, this was entirely due to an increase in foreign saving since the saving rate decreased to 14.3 percent in 1992. Thus, net capital inflows financed not only an increase in investment but also an increase in consumption, raising doubts about the capacity of the economy to generate foreign exchange to maintain external solvency in the long run.

The debate over the current account deficit, which reached 2.4 percent of GDP in 1992, helped the government push the reform of the social security system by arguing that such a reform would have a positive effect on the national saving rate, thereby reducing dependency on foreign saving. To substantiate this argument, the government committed itself to maintaining in 1993, 1994, and 1995 the same consolidated primary budget surplus that had been attained in 1992 (i.e., 1.5 percent of GDP), in spite of the shift of funds that would materialize once the social security reform was implemented. The government was confident that this result was possible because of the reduction in payroll tax evasion that would follow the reform.

The three-year (1993–95) fiscal program was supported by the IMF under the Special Drawing Rights (SDRs) $4.0 billion Extended Fund Facility. However, owing to the complexity of the reform and the extensive discussions that followed, Congress did not approve the law until October 1993. Moreover, the reform was not implemented until July 1994.

5.2   The Rules of the New System

The system, called the integrated system of retirement and pensions (SIJP), is a mixed program consisting of a public pay-as-you-go institutional arrangement and an individual retirement account program known as the capitalization regime (CR). All workers eighteen years of age or older are required to participate in the system. Employees of the armed and security forces, state and local governments, and certain professionals with independent retirement systems are not obligated to participate.[6]

Individuals are free to choose whether they affiliate with the CR or the pay-as-you-go regime. The so-called private pension regime is not purely private since the government intervenes in some aspects of its administration.

The SIJP is financed through statutory contributions paid by employees and their employers. The employee contribution is 11 percent and the employer contribution 16 percent.[7] In the case of self-employed workers, a 27 percent contribution rate is applied to a schedule of reference incomes to calculate the individual's statutory contribution. The reference for these workers is not their actual income but rather an estimated income level.

The pay-as-you-go regime is financed with (a) the payroll tax paid by employers, (b) the contributions of employees who are affiliated with the system, and (c) earmarked taxes and funds provided by the public budget. The capitalization regime is funded by the individual's statutory contributions, any voluntary contributions made by the affiliates or by persons or firms to the affiliate's account based on a prior agreement with the affiliate, and indemnifications paid by life insurance companies in the event of disability or death.[8]

The public pay-as-you-go regime extends benefits to pensioners under the old system and also to affiliates of the two regimes under the new system. The benefits for the new system are (a) the basic universal pension (PBU), (b) the compensatory pension (PC), (c) additional pension for permanence (PAP), and (d) survivorship and disability pensions. The basic universal pension (PBU) is a redistributive (minimum) elderly pension; affiliates of any regime who have contributed to the system for thirty years or more are eligible at sixty-five years of age.[9] The compensatory pension (PC) is also a pension for those elderly individuals who meet the criteria for the PBU and who have also contributed to the old previsional system. The additional pension for permanence (PAP) is a pension for individuals who are eligible to receive a PBU and who chose to remain in the pay-as-you-go system after the new system was established.

Under the capitalization regime, affiliates may be eligible for a PBU and also for a PC, but the PAP is replaced by an ordinary retirement pension (JO) based on the accumulation of personal contributions made to individual accounts managed by private pension fund managers called AFJPs. After com-

6. State and local governments may participate in the SIJP if they choose to. To date, six of twenty-three state governments and the municipal government of Buenos Aires have subscribed to the system. Subscription by these governments to the SIJP involves the transference of the local pension regimes to the national regime and the obligatory participation by all personnel employed in these governments in the SIJP.
7. The employers' contribution was recently reduced in variable proportions according to different geographic regions.
8. Although not the only way, employers' voluntary contributions represent one way to channel bonuses or profit sharing to the employees.
9. Women can retire five years earlier than men.

missions have been deducted, the contributions to individuals' accounts are invested in assets and capitalized together with the profits that are obtained by investing the funds. The individual retirement account can be increased through voluntary contributions.

Affiliates with the capitalization regime may begin to draw on their assets at the age of sixty-five (men) or sixty (women). Individuals may choose to purchase annuities with their accounts or to receive programmed periodic payments ("programmed withdrawals") until the account is exhausted. In the event of disability or death, the AFJP must draw on a collective life and disability insurance policy to add to the capital accumulated in the individual's retirement account until there are sufficient funds to generate a defined-benefit pension.

5.2.1 Pension Fund Managers (AFJP)

The AFJPs are private or public companies created for the exclusive purpose of investing affiliates' contributions to their individual retirement accounts and administering payments to affiliates who choose to draw down their accounts through scheduled withdrawals in retirement. Current legislation sets minimum requirements for the volume of capital and minimum reserve requirements that must be held.

The AFJP is the primary institution with which current workers affiliate. The AFJP remains the primary institution during the worker's retirement years if the individual retirement account is drawn down through programmed withdrawals. The AFJP is responsible for investing its affiliates' retirement funds, for guaranteeing the statutory minimum return on these investments, and for providing supplementary capital when necessary for affiliates who are disabled or die before retirement. Individuals cannot be affiliated with more than one AFJP, but they may change AFJPs up to two times per year after making four consecutive monthly contributions to a single AFJP.

5.2.2 Pension Funds

The pension fund is composed of the affiliates' statutory and voluntary contributions plus preconvened deposits, less commissions, plus profits earned by investing the funds. The fund is the property of the affiliates and is legally separated from the capital constituted by the AFJP. The legal separation is necessary to isolate the AFJP's financial position from the pension fund and to protect the fund if the AFJP goes into bankruptcy. Each AFJP manages just one pension fund, which consists of investing the funds accumulated through individual contributions and capital contributed by life insurance companies.

The fund may be invested in a number of alternative financial instruments, such as government bonds, corporate bonds, time deposits, corporate stocks, shares in mutual funds, and mortgage-backed securities. There are legal limits on the percentage of the fund's total resources that may be invested in any one kind of instrument or in any single issuer. The supervisory body may also issue regulations to lower percentages below those set in the law. Table 5.6 illustrates

Table 5.6   Pension Fund Investment Rules

Assets	Asset Ceiling (% of Portfolio)
Securities issued by the national government	50
Securities issued by provincial and local governments	15
Long-term securities issued by domestic private corporations	28
Short-term securities issued by domestic private corporations	14
Certificates of deposit in local banks	28
Domestic corporate shares	35
Shares of recently privatized domestic public enterprises	35
Domestic mutual investment funds	14
Foreign corporate securities	10
Foreign government securities	7

the structure of investments permitted together with the accompanying regulations.

The profitability of a particular fund is measured as the percentage change in the value of one share between two consecutive periods. Returns are not guaranteed in absolute terms, but each fund manager is required to produce a minimum investment return equivalent to 70 percent of the system's average return or 2 percentage points lower than the system's average, whichever is lower. Each AFJP must guarantee that affiliates earn at least the minimum return by using funds, when necessary, from (a) the special fluctuation fund, (b) minimum reserves required by law to be held by the AFJPs, and (c) the AFJP's own capital.

The special fluctuation fund is constituted by setting aside all profits that exceed by 30 percent the system-wide average return or 2 percentage points higher than the system average whenever the system average is positive, whichever is greater. The minimum reserve requirement represents 2 percent of the fund's assets and cannot be less than 3 million pesos (equivalent to U.S.$3 million).

5.2.3   Benefits

The SIJP covers contingencies for retirement, disability, and death. Retirement benefits vary depending on whether the worker has participated in the pay-as-you-go regime or in the capitalization regime. In either case, the total retirement pension has three components, two of which are common to both regimes and administered by the government.

As mentioned previously, affiliates of the pay-as-you-go regime are eligible to receive the PBU, the PC, and the PAP. The PBU is a uniform and universal retirement benefit, approximately equivalent to 20 percent of the average salary economy-wide. It is not linked to individual wages.

For a transition period, the government will pay the PC to workers affiliated with either regime when they demonstrate that they made contributions to the former pension system. In order to qualify for the PC, the worker must first qualify for the PBU. The PC is calculated as a percentage of the average income received by the worker during the last ten years of active employment. The percentage is equivalent to 1.5 percent for each year that the worker contributed to the former pension system.

The PAP is a benefit that the government extends to all workers who choose to be affiliated with the pay-as-you-go regime after the social security reform. The requirements to receive the PAP are the same as those needed to receive the PBU. The PAP is calculated as a percentage of the average income the worker received during the last ten years of active employment. The percentage is equal to 0.85 percent for each year that the worker contributes to the pay-as-you-go regime under the new system.

Affiliates of the private pension regime are eligible to receive the PBU, the PC, and the ordinary retirement pension (JO). Affiliates who have reached sixty-five years of age in the case of men or sixty years of age in the case of women may receive a JO, which is related to the amount they have available in their individual retirement accounts. The total amount available may be used to purchase an annuity, or the total may be depleted gradually through a program of scheduled withdrawals. Figure 5.2 illustrates the relation between the various components of retirement benefits.

The PC was extended to smooth the transition between the former and the current retirement system while recognizing the contributions made under the former system. Once it disappears, retirement benefits will be consolidated into the PBU, which is the redistributive component of the system, and the JO. The PAP should also disappear over time since its implicit rate of return is relatively low.

The dependents of a worker who dies during his or her productive years are entitled to receive a survivorship pension, which is equivalent to a percentage of the worker's average income received in the five years prior to death. Depen-

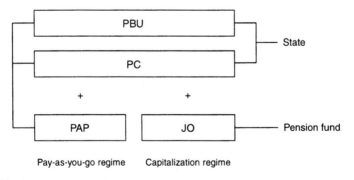

Fig. 5.2   Retirement pensions

dents include the worker's wife, husband, or partner, incapacitated children, or children who are minors.

SIJP benefits are also extended to workers who become completely disabled at some time during their active working lives. The technical definition of *complete incapacitation* is 66 percent or greater. The disability benefit is equivalent to 70 percent of the average income earned during the five years prior to being declared incapacitated.

During the two years' transition period until the definitive disability is declared, the AFJP must pay the monthly disability benefit with funds provided by a life insurance company. Once the disability becomes definitive, the life insurance company must supply complementary funds to the individual retirement account until it is possible to purchase an annuity that generates the defined-benefit pension.

5.2.4 Institutional Organization of the SIJP

One significant difference between the new and the former social security system is the number of institutions involved in their administration. Under the former system, the government had a complete monopoly on the collection of funds, on the allocation and administration of benefits, and on the regulation of a single social security system. Currently, different institutions are responsible for different functions.

The Dirección General Impositiva (DGI), tax collection agency, is responsible for collecting contributions to the pay-as-you-go as well as to the capitalization regime. Once the funds are collected, the DGI transfers them to the appropriate AFJP and to the government's social security administration agency, the Administración Nacional de la Seguridad Social (ANSES). Employers' contributions are also collected by the DGI, and the funds go to ANSES, independent of the worker's affiliation. ANSES is a decentralized agency operating under the authority of the Social Security Department. It is responsible for administering the benefits of individuals affiliated with the pay-as-you-go system. ANSES also administers other benefits extended by the social security system, such as unemployment payments, welfare pensions, and family allowances.

As mentioned previously, the new system is a mixed one, so, even in the case of workers who have chosen to affiliate with the capitalization regime, ANSES is responsible for the administration of their PBU and PC. Finally, ANSES shares with the private pension funds the cost of disability or death insurance for workers who are affiliated with the capitalization regime and who were at least thirty years of age when the new system was adopted.

By contrast, the capitalization regime is managed by a number of public and private institutions. To start, the AFJPs are responsible for investing individuals' contributions to the system. The Superintendency of the AFJP is the regulatory body authorized to supervise the activities of the AFJP. The superintendency is a decentralized agency that operates under the authority of the

Ministry of Labor and Social Security. It is responsible for the authorization of AFJPs, the supervision of their activities, the imposition of legal sanctions, and the liquidation of an AFJP when necessary. The superintendency is also authorized to issue resolutions in areas that affect the functioning of the system, and it monitors the performance of the individual AFJP and the system by controlling for the quality and accuracy of indicators of contributions, investments, profitability, required reserves, and fluctuation funds, to name a few.

There are other institutions that are not specifically part of the private pension regime but are necessary for the development of the capital market, which is itself a necessary element of the regime. A couple of examples are the risk-rating agencies and such regulatory bodies as the National Securities Commission. Insurance companies that offer life and retirement insurance are becoming very active as a consequence of the new regime, and they will grow in the future. Figure 5.3 summarizes the various institutions involved in the public pay-as-you-go regime as well as their specific functions. Figure 5.4 summarizes the institutional structure of the private pension regime.

5.3   Evolution of the New Pension System

The new pension system was established in July 1994 and has been functioning for three years. It would be difficult to undertake a complete evaluation of the system after such a short period. In the following sections, we focus on the recent evolution of some of its components.

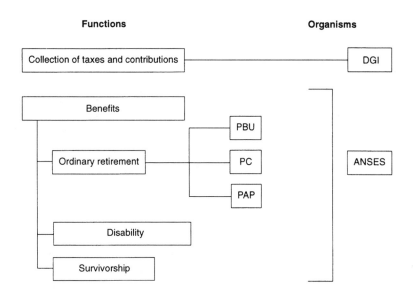

Fig. 5.3   Institutional structure of the pay-as-you-go regime

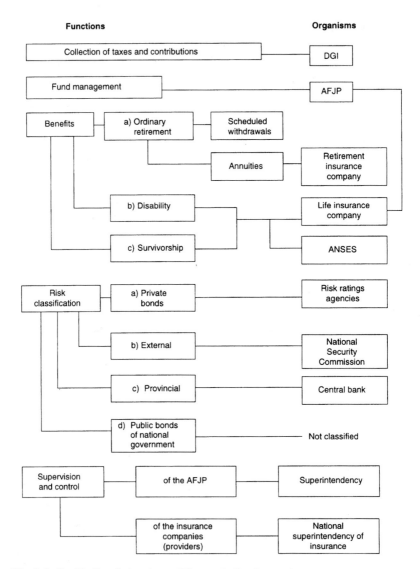

Fig. 5.4   Institutional structure of the capitalization regime

5.3.1   Affiliation

Table 5.7 provides information on the number of workers who chose to affiliate with the capitalization regime and with the pay-as-you-go regime. As illustrated, between August 1994 and June 1997, there has been continuous growth in the number of affiliations and in the share of the private pension affiliations in total affiliations.

Table 5.7   **Affiliates of the Capitalization and Pay-as-You-Go Regimes**

	Affiliates (thousands)			Affiliates (%)		
Date as of	Pay as You Go	Capitalization	Total SIJP	Pay as You Go	Capitalization	Total
September 1994	2,674	3,034	5,708	46.9	53.1	100.0
December 1994	2,901	3,679	6,580	44.1	55.9	100.0
June 1995	2,840	4,137	6,977	40.7	59.3	100.0
December 1995	2,709	4,921	7,630	35.5	64.5	100.0
June 1996	2,598	5,476	8,074	32.2	67.8	100.0
December 1996	2,544	5,633	8,177	31.1	68.9	100.0
June 1997	2,396	5,997	8,393	28.6	71.4	100.0

Source: Superintendencia de AFJP, *Memoria trimestral* (1994–97).
Note: "Capitalization" includes the National Fund of Employment and the undecided.

The growth trend is weakened if the rate of effective contributors to affiliates is analyzed during the same period. This variable tends to decline for both regimes during the period, and the decline is particularly pronounced in the case of the private pension regime. This phenomenon may be explained by the increase in unemployment observed during the period, the effect of the 1995 recession on delaying contributions to the system, and the problem of irregular affiliations. Both unemployment and irregular forms of affiliation tend to affect the capitalization regime more markedly than the pay-as-you-go regime since affiliates in the capitalization regime are on average younger.

Participation in the capitalization regime has been more important among formally employed workers than among the self employed, and this trend has increased through time. Even though the new legislation requires the self-employed to participate, the AFJPs have been less aggressive in affiliating them since their contributions to the system are generally low and there is a greater tendency among the self-employed to evade contributions.

Another interesting characteristic to consider is the composition of affiliates on the basis of their age and sex. There is a clear preference for the capitalization regime among young men, which is illustrated in figure 5.5.

The concentration of young male affiliates to the capitalization regime is explained by the greater benefits it offers this segment of the labor force. For younger workers, more time available to contribute to the system means that there will be greater expected benefit levels in retirement. Moreover, men, with lower life expectancy, have greater expected benefits for a given amount of capital than do women.

5.3.2   Pension Fund Managers (AFJPs)

Although eighteen AFJPs are actually operating, just four of them represent more than 60 percent of total affiliates in the capitalization regime, with collections amounting to 63 percent of the total in June 1997 (fig. 5.6).

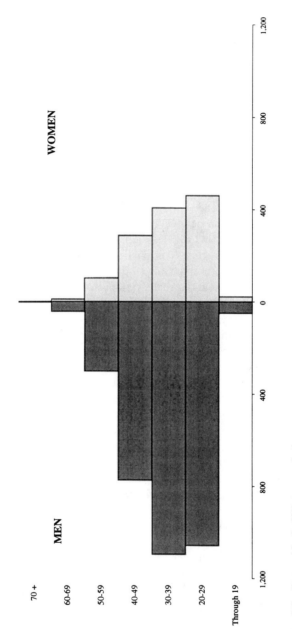

Fig. 5.5　Pyramid of affiliate population
Source: Superintendencia de AFJP, *Memoria trimestral* (1997).

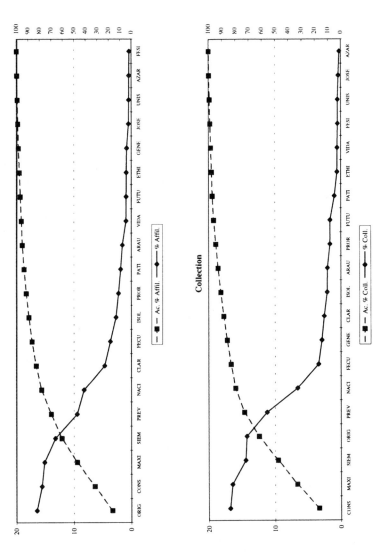

Affiliates

Collection

Fig. 5.6   Affiliates and contributions collection (June 1997)
Source: Superintendencia de AFJP, *Memoria trimestral* (1997).

Another important characteristic of the market for AFJPs is the composition of shareholder capital. Table 5.8 and figure 5.7 illustrate the composition of AFJP shareholder capital, dividing shareholders into banks, insurance companies, unions, nonfinancial companies, and others. As illustrated, banks and insurance companies represent almost 90 percent of total capital invested in the AFJPs. The union associations, which are eligible to form their own AFJP directly, have invested only 5.2 percent of the total amount invested in the AFJPs. Nonfinancial institutions have invested just 3.2 percent of the total.

5.3.3   Pension Funds' Investments and Profitability

Since their creation, the private pension funds have been growing by more than 200 million pesos per month on average. By the end of June 1997, the total value of the retirement and pension funds represented more than 7.3 billion pesos.

The notable growth in the monthly fund totals is the result of the growth in the number of affiliates, which was discussed previously, and of the high rate of return realized on investments during the period analyzed. As illustrated in table 5.9 and figure 5.8, the funds accrued very favorable real returns on their investments throughout 1995. In fact, the extremely high annual returns recorded at the end of 1995 and 1996 are explained by the comparison with low asset prices quoted after the 1994 Mexican crisis. Nonetheless, even the lowest rates earned in the months preceding the crisis were very high.

Such high rates of return on fund assets are a consequence of the structure of fund portfolios. This information is illustrated in table 5.10. A striking feature that emerges from the data is that changes in the structure of the portfolios had a very limited effect on returns. During the first two years of the period analyzed, investments were concentrated in fixed-income instruments such as government bonds and time deposits, while investments in variable-income instruments such as stocks were well below the legal limits permitted. Since

Table 5.8   **Capital Structure of the AFJP (June 1997)**

	Millions of Pesos	%
Banks	5,857.4	79.8
Insurance companies	715.9	9.7
Labor associations	380.6	5.2
Nonfinancial companies	229.5	3.1
Foreign pension funds	.0	. . .
Other	161.1	2.2
Total	7,344.6	100.0

Source: Superintendencia de AFJP, *Memoria trimestral* (1997).

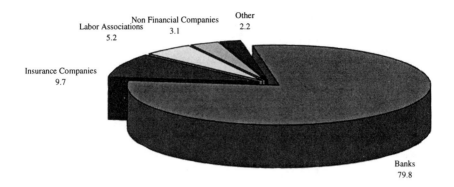

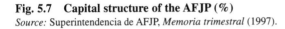

Fig. 5.7   Capital structure of the AFJP (%)
Source: Superintendencia de AFJP, *Memoria trimestral* (1997).

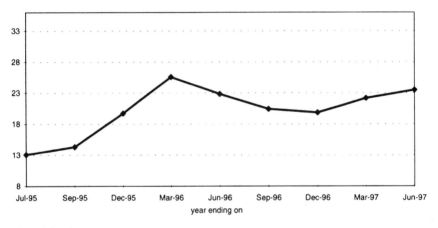

Fig. 5.8   Average system return
Source: Superintendencia de AFJP, *Memoria trimestral* (1994–97).

Table 5.9   Average System Return (%)

12-Month Period Ending	Average Annual Return
July 1995	13.1
September 1995	14.3
December 1995	19.7
March 1996	25.6
June 1996	22.8
September 1996	20.4
December 1996	19.8
March 1997	22.1
June 1997	23.5

Source: Superintendencia de AFJP, *Memoria trimestral* (1994–97).

Table 5.10   Percentage Distribution of Investment Portfolio by Type of Instrument

Instrument	Dec. 1994	June 1995	Dec. 1995	June 1996	Dec. 1996	June 1997
Cash reserves	6.3	2.3	1.7	2.2	1.8	1.4
Bonds	49.8	51.5	52.7	51.8	52.7	49.3
Time deposits	27.6	27.1	24.8	17.6	14.2	16.4
Stocks	1.5	2.0	5.9	13.5	18.7	21.8
Corporate bonds	5.8	6.8	8.7	10.7	7.8	4.8
Mutual funds	5.0	4.2	1.7	1.5	2.3	4.1
Foreign bonds	.1	2.8	.7	.5	.2	.4
Other	3.8	3.4	3.9	2.4	2.3	1.8
Total	100.0	100.0	100.0	100.0	100.0	100.0

Source: Superintendencia de AFJP, *Memoria trimestral* (1994–97).

June 1996, however, an important substitution took place from time deposits to stocks (fig. 5.9).

5.3.4   Commissions

The commissions that the fund managers charge their affiliates are determined freely. They include a charge for the collective life and disability insurance policy that each fund manager must maintain to confront the eventual contingencies discussed in previous sections.

The level of commissions charged by various AFJPs is one indicator of their efficiency. If we observe the evolution of the system-wide average commission, separating out the portion of the fee charged for the life insurance premium and the administration cost, the most significant observation is the sharp reduction in the average cost of collective life and disability insurance. With the improvement in information on mortality rates, which were lower than expected, insurance companies and the AFJPs were able to adjust the cost.

The significant reduction in the insurance premium (from an average of 2.2 percent of wages in July 1994 to 1.0 percent in June 1997) was not passed on to affiliates in the form of lower overall commissions. To the contrary, average commissions remained at a constant level of 3.3 percent of salaries between July 1994 and June 1997.

This means that a significant increase in the part of the commission was used to finance the administration of the fund managers. It may be the case that the low mortality rates produced a source of financing to cover the high start-up costs of the AFJPs' activities, which in many cases resulted from an overestimation of the size of the market. The mergers between companies that are taking place and the more austere commercial policies being adopted by the fund managers will be key to determining whether commissions will decline (Rofman 1996).

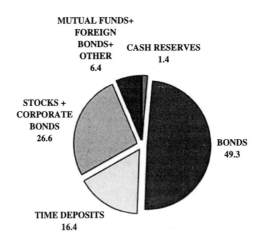

Fig. 5.9   Percentage distribution of investment portfolio by type of instrument (as of 30 June 1997)
Source: Superintendencia de AFJP, *Boletín mensual* (1997).

5.3.5   Benefits

It is difficult to evaluate the administration of benefits under the new system since its number is still quite low. Since most affiliates under the new private regime consist of young workers, most of the benefits that have been extended correspond to disability or survivorship pensions.

The only remarkable fact in this regard is the important decrease in the ratio of disability pensions to total pensions as compared with the levels before the reform. This is important in explaining the low level of life and disability insurance.

5.3.6   Summary

It is still difficult to evaluate the results of the new previsional system adopted by Argentina in 1993. The indicators analyzed in this section show, however, that Argentine society is increasingly accepting this alternative organization of social security. An important growth in the number of affiliations confirms this. AFJPs are proving that they can administer pension funds efficiently, and insurance costs are surprisingly low. However, commissions still remain high.

One can expect commissions to be reduced as the number of affiliates (or the size of the fund administered) grows, increasing the return on investment. Mergers will certainly help, as will the government's efforts to reduce evasion.

In spite of the insufficiency of evidence, one can conclude that many of the chronic problems with the old previsional system are apparently disappearing.

Time will confirm whether the new system provides better service to affiliates and beneficiaries.

In the next section, we focus on some macroeconomic effects of pension funds. The most important for the Argentine economy are the effects on the public budget and on the national saving rate.

5.4   The Effect of the New System on Saving

Macroeconomic effects of social security reforms have become part of the discussion as relevant aspects to consider when introducing capitalization regimes (Uthoff 1995). One of the most discussed questions in this respect is the effect of pension funds on national saving. This has been an important concern in Argentina, a country characterized by a structurally low national saving rate and a strong macroeconomic exposure to fluctuations in international financial markets. It is our purpose, not to test theoretical hypotheses, but to examine probable empirical results from projections for the economy as a whole.

The initial effect of social security reform is to increase the government's deficit since public social security expenditures will be reduced much more slowly than the payroll taxes collected by the state. The effect of the reform on saving will thus depend on the relative size of the government's deficit vis-à-vis the annual growth of the pension funds. We examine separately projections of the public deficit and of pension funds for the period 1995–2020 before concluding with a consideration of the expected net effect on private saving.

5.4.1   Public Social Security Deficit

When a pay-as-you-go system is replaced by a capitalization regime, there will exist a period of time in which the new system coexists with benefits defined under the former regime. As a result, the government will have to finance expenditures generated under the former regime with a smaller amount of resources, the result of the partial or total transfer of workers' contributions to the capitalization regime.

The *transition period* is defined as the period of time it takes until the former regime disappears. During the transition period, the financial pressures generated by the shift in resources away from the pay-as-you-go regime will become even more pronounced. Even though the transition is temporary, it is important to have an estimate of the size and probable evolution of the deficit and to adopt necessary corrective measures (Posadas 1994).

It is necessary to analyze the evolution of the transition period correctly in order to quantify the effect of the reform on national savings. As we have stated, the reduction in government savings that takes place during the transition could completely offset the increase in private-sector savings channeled through pension funds. Prior to continuing the analysis of the transition period, it is helpful to review the expenditures and revenues of the state-run social security system before the reform and the projections for the transition period and for the long run (after the former system ceases to exist).

a) Prior to the reform, the government was exclusively responsible for all pension benefits extended to public- and private-sector employees as well as self-employed workers. The government financed these expenditures with payroll taxes: a 10 percent personal contribution and a 16 percent employer contribution. Since these revenues were insufficient to fund the system's obligations, the government began to use part of the tax revenues collected from income taxes, the value-added tax, the asset tax, etc.

b) Once the new regime becomes fully operational (i.e., in the long run), the government will be responsible only for the payment of the PBUs. To finance these expenditures, the government will draw on the employers' contribution, which has been reduced in variable percentages depending on the employer's geographic location.[10] Given that the government will pay only the minimum pensions, the public system will generate a surplus if the current level of taxes used to finance the system is applied identically in the future. This would allow the government to reduce payroll taxes even further in the future, thereby reducing the distortion that this tax has produced in labor markets.

c) During the transition, the government must continue to pay the benefits generated under the former system. In addition, the government must contribute to the financing of benefits that the capitalization regime extends to workers who would have received benefits before the reform. Finally, the government will be responsible for the pensions of those affiliates who choose to remain in the state-run system.[11] To finance the transition period, the government can draw on employer payroll taxes and personal contributions of workers who opt to remain in the pay-as-you-go system.

Table 5.11 summarizes the expenditures and revenues of the state-run system. Since, in Argentina, workers are free to choose between the pay-as-you-go and the capitalization regimes, the projections on financing the state social security system are based on alternative assumptions regarding individual preferences for the alternative systems.

Table 5.12 contains the financing projections for the state social security system realized by Schulthess and Demarco (1996).

10. The government reduced the employer contribution in October 1995 in response to the growth in unemployment observed since 1993. The minimum reduction of 30 percent (equivalent to a rate of 11.2 percent of wages) is applied in the most-developed regions of the country, where the unemployment problem is less severe. The maximum reduction of 80 percent (equivalent to a rate of 3.2 percent) is applied in the least-developed regions.

11. As we have already argued, even though workers will be free to choose between regimes in the future, it is expected that new workers will on the whole find the capitalization regime more attractive since it offers comparatively higher benefits than the pay-as-you-go regime for active affiliation throughout total years of employment.

Table 5.11   **Benefits and Revenues of the Public Pension Program**

	Benefits	Revenues
Before the reform	Retirement and pensions of public- and private-sector employees and self-employed workers	Personal contributions: 10% of wages Employer contributions: 16% of wages Other tax revenues (part of value-added and income taxes, wealth, etc.)
During the transition	Benefits already extended under the former system Part of the benefits under capitalization regime for workers who contributed to the former system Benefits to affiliates of the pay-as-you-go regime PBU	Personal contributions of workers who opt for the pay-as-you-go regime (11% of wages) Employers contribution (16% of wages reduced in most regions of the country) Other tax revenues
Under one unique regime	PBU	Employer contribution Other earmarked revenues

The employer's contribution reflects the reduction that was implemented during 1995 when the amount was 16 percent.[12] These projections allow us to draw the following conclusions. First, there is a significant disequilibrium in the years immediately following the reform that tends to correct itself over time. In the long term, the deficit becomes a surplus since, under the new system, the government is responsible only for the minimum pensions.

It is important to point out that a high proportion of the difference is the direct result of reduction in employer contributions from 16 to 12 percent, not the consequence of the pension reform per se. This reduction is part of a plan to lower labor costs by reducing the proportion of public social security financed through payroll taxes. It obviously requires an important reduction in public expenditure and a redistribution of public resources from other uses, a process that is now taking place but that is still incomplete.

In essence, the only truly significant issue that emerges from projections of a considerable deficit in the social security system is how it is going to be financed. Since, in the long term, the deficit becomes a surplus, there is the possibility of financing it through issuing debt. In other words, since the long-term solvency of the system does not deteriorate (to the contrary), it is possible to think of an intergenerational transfer that offsets a large part of the reform's effect on saving.

12. This assumes that, at some point during the transition, contribution rates will be increased to yield an average of 12 percent, which is higher than current levels.

Table 5.12   **Projections of Revenues, Expenditures, and the Deficit of the Public Pension Regimen (millions of pesos)**

Year	Total Revenues	Total Expenditure	Deficit	Accumulated
1995	10,489	14,239	3,750	3,750
1996	10,677	14,436	3,760	7,510
1997	10,918	14,621	3,703	11,213
1998	11,176	14,725	3,550	14,762
1999	11,406	14,799	3,392	18,155
2000	11,586	14,865	3,279	21,434
2001	11,772	14,827	3,055	24,488
2002	11,962	14,825	2,863	27,351
2003	12,155	14,775	2,620	29,971
2004	12,350	14,751	2,401	32,371
2005	12,546	14,661	2,115	34,486
2006	12,740	14,625	1,885	36,371
2007	12,931	14,547	1,616	37,987
2008	13,118	14,489	1,372	39,359
2009	13,296	14,391	1,096	40,454
2010	13,463	14,334	872	41,326
2011	13,617	14,233	616	41,942
2012	13,761	14,175	414	42,356
2013	13,895	14,077	182	42,539
2014	14,017	13,981	−36	42,503
2015	14,126	13,879	−247	42,256
2016	14,221	13,777	−444	41,812
2017	14,304	13,691	−613	41,199
2018	14,377	13,574	−804	40,395
2019	14,439	13,468	−971	39,424
2020	14,490	13,373	−1,117	38,308

Source: Schulthess and Demarco (1996).

Alternatively, the government could reduce public expenditure, or increase tax collections (contributions, transfers, and others), by fighting tax evasion or increasing tax rates. The possibility of achieving an increase in total national savings (public and private) with this approach is considerably greater. In view of the difficulties observed in reducing evasion, an important redistribution of public resources to public social security from other uses results in the crucial issue of financing transition without (or with a low level of) public indebtedness.

These alternative instruments could be complemented by some redefinition (reduction) in the level of certain public pensions. In fact, some critics oppose the high level of basic redistributive pensions (such as the PBU). Since public pensions do not adjust automatically, the system does contemplate reductions in real terms without the need of a legal amendment if Congress authorizes adjustments at a rate lower than the inflation rate.

5.4.2 Pension Funds' Projection and the Net Effect on Saving

Table 5.13 contains projections of retirement savings under assumptions consistent with those used for the projections presented in table 5.12 above and assuming that the rate of return on the capitalization fund is 4 percent. By comparing the two tables, it is possible to conclude that, during the years immediately following the reform (from 1995 to 1998), private savings channeled through the pension funds are less than the dissaving by the public sector that is necessary to finance the pay-as-you-go system during the transition.

We can conclude from the information presented in table 5.13 that, once the negative effect of the public deficit has passed (from 1998 on), the social security system will increasingly add to national saving. Projections for 2020 reflect an increase of the savings rate induced by social security reform of about 2.5 percent of GDP (almost 15 percent of the saving rate previous to social

Table 5.13   **Estimate of Total Effect of Pension Funds on Saving**

Year	Millions of Pesos			% of GDP		
	Public	Private	Total	Public	Private	Total
1995	−3,750	1,973	−1,777	−1.33	.70	−.63
1996	−3,760	2,290	−1,470	−1.33	.81	−.52
1997	−3,703	2,887	−816	−1.26	.98	−.28
1998	−3,550	3,376	−174	−1.16	1.10	−.06
1999	−3,392	3,918	526	−1.07	1.23	.17
2000	−3,279	4,392	1,113	−.99	1.33	.34
2001	−3,055	5,017	1,962	−.89	1.46	.57
2002	−2,863	5,398	2,535	−.80	1.51	.71
2003	−2,620	6,037	3,417	−.70	1.62	.92
2004	−2,402	6,299	3,897	−.62	1.63	1.01
2005	−2,115	6,908	4,793	−.53	1.72	1.19
2006	−1,885	7,548	5,663	−.45	1.80	1.35
2007	−1,616	8,213	6,597	−.37	1.89	1.51
2008	−1,372	8,895	7,523	−.30	1.96	1.66
2009	−1,096	9,605	8,509	−.23	2.04	1.81
2010	−872	10,307	9,435	−.18	2.10	1.93
2011	−616	10,980	10,364	−.12	2.15	2.03
2012	−414	11,677	11,263	−.08	2.20	2.12
2013	−182	12,396	12,214	−.03	2.25	2.22
2014	36	13,062	13,098	.01	2.28	2.28
2015	247	13,740	13,987	.04	2.30	2.35
2016	444	14,432	14,876	.07	2.33	2.40
2017	613	15,137	15,750	.10	2.35	2.44
2018	804	15,853	16,657	.12	2.36	2.48
2019	971	16,565	17,536	.14	2.37	2.51
2020	1,117	17,266	18,383	.15	2.38	2.53

Sources: Schulthess and Demarco (1996) and Rofman and Stirparo (1996).

security reform). This proportion would be greater if we introduce more optimistic assumptions about the evolution of earmarked taxes.[13]

Apart from the magnitude of the effect on saving, a qualitative effect on capital market development is expected as a result of the reform. Whereas the effect of private pension plans on the saving rate is a subject of discussion, there is practically no doubt regarding its importance in strengthening capital markets through the development of long-run investments and the introduction of institutional investors.

In summary, expected long-run effects on saving and the development of capital markets appear optimistic if the government can solve the financial problems of the transition. It is difficult to anticipate how the government will deal with the transitional period on the basis of its behavior in 1995 when the new pension system had been in effect for one full year. The year was exceptional to the extent that the increase in the global fiscal deficit substantially exceeded the loss in personal contributions to the pay-as-you-go system. It is important to keep in mind that the Argentine economy suffered a tremendous confidence shock at the beginning of the year as a result of the Mexican peso devaluation, which precipitated a 20 percent reduction in deposits. The external shock produced a sharp recession (GDP fell by 4.4 percent), which led to a sharp reduction in fiscal revenues. In the social security system, in spite of the increased affiliations that resulted from the reform, the lack of credit and the decline in the level of economic activity reduced the system's revenues significantly. At the same time, there was an alarming increase in the expenditures of the social security system during 1994, which demonstrated clearly that the problems inherent in the former system persisted even after the reform.

To offset these effects, the Argentine government implemented very important measures to demonstrate its commitment to increasing national saving through the social security reform. First, it proposed the Ley de Solidaridad Previsional, which was approved at the beginning of 1995. The law established maximum benefits and limits on the growth in the system's expenditures, eliminated definitively the practice of indexation, and established that any increase in benefits extended under the pay-as-you-go system would be decided by the national Congress, through the approval of the Annual Budget Law, on the basis of the system's available resources. This signified the guarantee of a true pay-as-you-go system. The government also implemented a far-reaching tax and pension moratorium, which resulted in nearly $5 billion in debts declared by contributors. The moratorium allowed affiliates of the SIJP and other contributors to regularize their pension situation after they had postponed contributions following the tequila effect (Schulthess 1994).

13. With an annual 4 percent growth rate in GDP, tax collection should increase by more than the proportion assumed in our projections in table 5.12. In addition, a redistribution of public resources is taking place at present between social security and non–social security public expenditure, and one could expect this tendency to continue.

The Argentine government anticipates that its operational deficit (without including privatization revenues) will be $2.5 billion. This figure is similar to the projected flows of contributions to the capitalization regime. Nonetheless, in view of the prevailing standby agreement with the IMF, the deficit must disappear in 1997. In order to comply with this target and maintain it in successive years, the pension reform will have a very positive effect on savings resulting from the government's commitment to refrain from using debt to finance the pension reform.

References

Demarco, Gustavo, and Laura Posadas. 1992. Las inequidades en el régimen nacional de previsión social. *Estudios* (Fundación Mediterránea) 15, no. 62:61–75.

Durán, Viviana. 1993. La evasión en el sistema de seguridad social de Argentina. In *Serie política fiscal,* no. 50. Santiago de Chile: Economic Commission for Latin America and the Caribbean.

Lo Vuolo, Rubén. 1994. *Análisis de la actual situación del mercado de trabajo y su probable proyección futura.* Buenos Aires: Ministerio de Trabajo y Seguridad Social.

Posadas, Laura. 1994. El nuevo sistema de jubilaciones y pensiones y el déficit previsional público. In *Estudios,* vol. 17, no. 68 (January–March). Córdoba: IEERAL.

Rofman, Rafael. 1996. Evolución, componentes y efectos de las comisiones del régimen de capitalización. In *Serie estudios especiales,* no. 2. Buenos Aires: Superintendencia de AFJP.

Rofman, Rafael, and Gustavo Stirparo. 1996. Proyección del tamaño de los fondos de jubilaciones y pensiones. In *Serie estudios especiales,* no. 4. Buenos Aires: Superintendencia de AFJP.

Schulthess, Walter. 1991. Costos y beneficios financieros en el régimen nacional de jubilaciones para personas en relación de dependencia. *Económica* (Universidad Nacional de La Plata) 27, nos. 1–2:115–29.

———. 1994. Antecedentes y fundamentos del anteproyecto de ley de solidaridad previsional. *Previsión social,* vol. 5, no. 16 (October–September). Buenos Aires: ANSES.

Schulthess, Walter, and Gustavo Demarco. 1993. *Argentina: Evolución del sistema nacional de previsión social y propuesta de reforma.* Santiago: Economic Commission for Latin America and the Caribbean.

———. 1994. *Reforma previsional en Argentina.* Buenos Aires: Abeledo-Perrot.

———. 1996. El financiamiento del régimen previsional público en Argentina después de la reforma. Santiago de Chile: CEPAL. Mimeo.

Superintendencia de AFJP. Various numbers, 1994–97. *Boletín estadístico mensual.* Buenos Aires.

———. Various numbers, 1995–97. *Memoria trimestral.* Buenos Aires.

Uthoff, Andras. 1995. Promoción del ahorro y los sistemas de pensiones. Santiago: Economic Commission for Latin America and the Caribbean. Mimeo.

Comment   Anita M. Schwarz

Had I been asked to comment on this paper a year ago, I would have concentrated on some of the technical flaws in the Argentine reform. None of these flaws are fatal, but they nonetheless exist and will need to be addressed at some time by the government. Over the last year, watching the reform unfold, I have become an admirer of the political strategy used in reforming the social security system in Argentina and am convinced that the political economy dimensions of the reform may be applicable to other countries as well. I devote the first part of my comments to the technical flaws and the last part to explaining my still favorable view of the reform.

Technical Flaws

There are three main technical problems with the newly reformed Argentine system. These include issues of long-run sustainability, the parallel operation of multiple systems, and, last but not least, evasion.

Long-Run Sustainability

In the long run, the employer contribution to the social security system, which is currently averaging around 12 percent of wage today, is meant to finance the basic universal pension to all individuals of retirement age who have contributed for thirty or more years. This basic pension is flat, currently set at 27.5 percent of the economy-wide average covered wage. In many respects, this system is quite similar to the British system, but recall that the British flat pension is currently only 15 percent and is expected to fall to 9 percent in the future, as a result of the decision to fix benefits in real terms.

The question is whether this level of basic pension can be sustained in the future. A simple back-of-the-envelope calculation, assuming two contributors per retiree in the future, suggests that 12 percent of wage can support a pension worth only 24 percent of wage, not 27.5 percent of wage, even if there are no administrative costs or disability payments to finance. If the fiscal projections shown in table 5.2 were extended for another fifteen to twenty years, they themselves would show the system once again running deficits. In fact, longer-run projections done by a group at the University of Buenos Aires do show deficits in the system beyond 2020, with the surpluses being generated in the medium term, peaking around 2013. This is quite different from the cases of Mexico or Chile.

In both Mexico and Chile, the government faces liabilities during the transition to a new pension system. Current pensioners and those with accrued rights to pensions under the old system have to be paid, while the contributions from

Anita M. Schwarz is an economist in the Social Protection Division in the Human Development Department at the World Bank.

current workers are invested in their own individual accounts. However, the life spans of those with accrued rights to the old system are finite. Subsequently, the only liabilities faced by the governments are contingent liabilities, arising from minimum pension guarantees, limited to those who are extremely poor or to those with extremely erratic work histories.

Argentina faces transition liabilities like these other countries, but it also has to finance this public flat pension. There is no question that this flat pension allows the system to provide more redistribution and more poverty alleviation than the Chilean and Mexican systems, although one could argue that the expenditures in Argentina are less targeted toward the poor. The critical question is whether this level of redistribution is optimal and affordable in the long run. In pension systems, there is always a trade-off between redistribution and providing individuals a reasonable return on their mandated savings. The more you redistribute, the lower the rate of return some individuals will receive relative to what the market would have provided. This low rate of return increases the incentive to evade.

Reducing the size of this public flat pension and thus the contribution necessary to finance it relative to the defined-contribution pillar would improve incentives to contribute, provide individuals with a better return on their overall contribution, and be more affordable, but still allow positive redistribution.

Parallel Systems

A second problem is the parallel operation of a new public pay-as-you-go, defined-benefit scheme that operates as an option to the fully funded, defined-contribution scheme and is financed by the employee contribution. The parallel operation of two schemes is especially troubling because currently individuals can go back and forth between the schemes. Eventually, on entry to the labor force individuals will choose which scheme is preferred, and, subsequently, they can opt for the fully funded scheme, but no one who opts for the fully funded scheme can go the other way.

From a fiscal standpoint, not only does the Argentine system continue to accrue liabilities in its flat, redistributive pillar, but it is also generating new liabilities in this pay-as-you-go, defined-benefit system. Pay-as-you-go systems are fiscally sustainable as long as the benefits are defined with regard to future declines in the number of contributors. This system is particularly vulnerable since, of the overall number of contributors under the age of thirty, more than 90 percent have chosen the private system. Since individuals cannot change back in the future, the contributor base will dwindle quite rapidly, leaving the government to cover the remaining liabilities.

The operation of this parallel system has effectively increased the costs of transition and increased the duration of the transition period in Argentina. Argentina not only has the normal problem of financing the transition away from a pay-as-you-go system toward a funded system but also has the additional problem of financing the transition from its new public pay-as-you-go second pillar to a funded system. And the acquired rights prior to the reform were rewarded generously, making the transition in both cases quite costly.

Evasion

Evasion is probably the most pressing problem in the Argentine pension system and one that not only plagued the previous system but continues virtually unchanged in today's system. The extent of this evasion can be seen by comparing the demographic support ratio, the number of working age individuals divided by the number of elderly, with the beneficiary-contributor ratio in the system. While the demography suggests a support ratio of 5.86, the system shows a support ratio of only 1.55 contributors per retiree. There are either enormous numbers of unreported workers, enormous numbers of excess retirees, or some combination of the two. By contrast, in countries like the United States, the demographic ratio is virtually identical to the system support ratio. In fact, on a graph showing the relation between the two for a group of forty-two countries for which data are available, Argentina is a clear outlier (World Bank 1994, 146).

Moving from a public pay-as-you-go system to a funded private system should reduce evasion. Individuals in the funded private system cannot receive substantial benefits without contributing. The penalty for not contributing is a sizably reduced pension.

Although Argentina has adopted a funded private pillar, there has not yet been a change in evasion. This judgment is not entirely fair in that, six months after the reform, a severe recession began and the unemployment rate began to skyrocket, which reduced both contributions and contributors, making it difficult to measure changes in evasion. But I would argue that some of this lack of progress in combating evasion can also be attributed to the system design.

For starters, the overall payroll tax rate in Argentina is 49 percent. Including income taxes and value-added taxes, the tax burden is enormous. Under the reform, only 11 percentage points of that 49 percent tax go toward the funded system for the people opting for the private system. The remainder is in varying degrees a tax, particularly for higher-income people because of the heavy redistributive element involved. As a result, despite the social security reform, there is still a powerful incentive to evade, particularly since payroll taxes are collected together with income taxes. The government is aware of this problem and is trying to reduce payroll taxes, but, in the short run, cutting tax rates reduces the contribution revenue, exacerbating fiscal problems. The increased fiscal problems make the policy less credible in the long run. As a result, employers and employees are not responding to the tax cut, which is perceived as transitory.

Second, the benefit structure is such that the flat, first-tier pension is received for only thirty years of contributions, with no benefits at all for anything less than thirty years. Take the example of a woman who works from age twenty to age twenty-five, drops out of the labor force for fifteen years to raise children, reenters at age forty, and retires at the statutory age of sixty-two. She will not complete thirty years of contributions, so, even if she contributes, she receives nothing in return. In most cases, a spouse's income may provide the family with eligibility for health benefits and family allowances. The only benefit she may receive for her 49 percent payroll tax is unemployment insurance. She could self-insure much cheaper than that.

Similarly, the individual who was in the informal sector when the reform began and had already reached the age of forty without formal contributions would never have the opportunity to complete thirty years of contributions and would thus find that most of the payroll tax would be exactly that, a tax. It is no wonder, then, that evasion has not dropped significantly. One way of dealing with this problem is to prorate the flat benefit on the basis of the number of years of contributions.

Finally, in Argentina, unlike in Chile, both employers and employees contribute to most benefit plans. Both have an incentive to collude by underreporting the number of employees, the number of hours worked by each employee, and the wages paid because such collusion results in lower taxes for both employer and employee. In Chile, by contrast, only the employees pay. The wages of contributors to the new system were increased to compensate for the former split payment, but the payment responsibility lies strictly with the employee today. Now, employers have no incentive to collude. In fact, given that employee wages are tax-reducing costs, employers have every incentive to report accurately, which makes it much easier for tax authorities to catch evading employees.

Lessons from the Argentine Reform

Despite these technical problems, the political economy of the Argentine reform holds lessons for other reforming countries. Take as an example the case of the new parallel system. The architects of the reform did not want a parallel system. They wanted a new system with a flat pillar and a private funded pillar. But, politically, it was not possible to force individuals, even new employees, into a private pension system. Insisting on this provision would have derailed the entire reform effort. However, now, only two years after the reform was initiated, almost 90 percent of new employees are choosing the private system. Within a year, it will be possible to pass a law mandating that all new employees join the private system, without causing political uproar. The compromise was costly, but it was a price that had to be paid in order to develop public confidence in private pensions and to change a mind-set accustomed to public pension rights.

In too many countries, public social security programs have become the third rail. Touch them, and you die. Incremental reform, such as what happened in Argentina, may be more feasible than a big-bang one-shot reform, particularly where the political obstacles to reform outweigh the technical obstacles. Subsequent minor adjustments can now take place in an environment where public opinion is no longer hostile to private participation in pension provision. These minor adjustments will always be necessary as technical problems arise and circumstances change.

However, the first reform, the introduction of the private funded accounts in a substantive way, paves the way for all future reform. In this context, we should regard the Argentine reform as a second-best solution that serves as a conduit to the first-best solution rather than evaluating it strictly as a final solution in its own right.

Reference

World Bank. *Averting the old age crisis.* Oxford: Oxford University Press, 1994.

Discussion Summary   Jeffrey Liebman and Andrew Samwick

The discussion began by considering differences between the Argentine and the Chilean plans. It was noted that the minimum guarantees are quite different in the two countries. In Argentina, all workers who have contributed to the system for thirty years or more receive the basic universal pension (PBU), which is equal to about 20 percent of the average wage level in the economy. This basic benefit amount is not linked to the individual worker's earnings history and is not reduced if the workers are entitled to additional pensions. Thus, there is no distortion from phasing out the pension. However, since all retirees receive it, it is not very well targeted. The Chilean plan, in contrast, contains a guaranteed minimum that results in a 100 percent tax rate on savings in the relevant range. The participant suggested that some combination of the two approaches to the minimum guarantees was likely to be better than either of the simple schemes and that it would be helpful to see some simulations on this issue.

Another participant noted that, in Chile, there was no intention of including redistribution in the privatized retirement system. He said that, while figuring out how to achieve a more equal income distribution was a very important problem in Latin America, he doubts that transferring income through retirement programs is an efficient way to help the poor.

It was also noted that, while the administrative fees charged by the plans in Chile come from additional contributions above the mandatory savings, in Argentina they are subtracted from the mandatory contributions. The authors explained that having the administrative costs deducted from the mandatory payments makes it easier to observe whether the funds are transferred to the management firm. This observability reduces tax evasion.

The discussion turned to more general evasion issues, and one participant reported that a former cabinet minister in Argentina had said that evading taxes was Argentina's national sport. The participant questioned whether it made sense to have the DGI (Argentina's IRS) collect the funds for the retirement system since it has been shown to be incapable of collecting other tax revenue. In response, the author noted that it is hard to tell whether tax evasion has diminished in recent years. Argentina has had a reasonably good measure of evasion only since the new retirement system was put into place. Before that, it was impossible to determine what was in each individual's accounts. Moreover, unemployment has been very high recently, making comparisons with earlier periods difficult.

A participant questioned the wisdom of forbidding workers from moving back and forth between the old and the new systems. He said that economists generally prefer to influence people by altering the incentives they face rather than by mandating particular behavior. He recommended that Argentina should arrange the incentives to discourage workers from gaming the system by moving back and forth between the old and the new systems (as the United Kingdom recently has done), rather than forbidding switches.

Members of the conference expressed surprise at some of the numbers presented in the paper. One participant remarked that the rates of returns achieved by the plans were very high and wondered whether the rates of return were real or nominal. The author explained that the returns are real but that it is very difficult to measure the returns achieved by the plans (they are calculated as yield to maturity). In addition, interest rates have been very high in Argentina, in large part owing to the tequila effect (the Mexican crisis), and that fact partially explains the high rates of return. A second participant inquired whether it was really true that 42 percent of workers had retirement accounts but were not contributing to them. He also expressed surprise that few workers took advantage of the opportunity to make additional voluntary contributions to their accounts. The author confirmed the numbers and said that there were policies under consideration to encourage additional contributions by adding an insurance component to the plan. A third participant noted that the 49 percent payroll tax rate in Argentina is very high, especially for low-wage workers and workers with intermittent attachment to the labor force who would receive no marginal retirement benefits from their payments. The author explained that the payroll tax funds health insurance and family allowances in addition to retirement benefits, so all workers get something for their contributions. In addition, the high marginal tax rates are falling since the employer contribution rate is declining. Health reform might make it possible to reduce this tax rate further.

II Privatization Issues for the United States

6 The Transition Path in Privatizing Social Security

Martin Feldstein and Andrew Samwick

6.1 Background and Overview

There is now substantial experience around the world with partial or complete shifts from government pension systems to private funded plans. Although there are important common features of all such transitions, each country that makes such a transition faces a unique problem, reflecting the demographic and economic situation of that country and the promises and expectations embedded in existing law.[1]

In the United States, the actuarial projection that the social security trust fund will be depleted by the year 2030 has fostered interest in options to shift from the pay-as-you-go system to a funded or privatized system.[2] The very low implicit rate of return earned on contributions in the existing pay-as-you-go system and the adverse effect of the unfunded program on national saving have also encouraged consideration of the possibility of shifting to a partially or fully funded system and, in particular, to a system with individual funded accounts (see, e.g., Feldstein 1996; Kotlikoff 1996).

This paper shows that shifting to a funded system would permit the existing 12.4 percent payroll tax to be replaced in the long run by a payroll tax of about 2 percent because a funded system has so much higher a rate of return than the implicit rate of return in a pay-as-you-go unfunded social security program.

Martin Feldstein is the George F. Baker Professor of Economics at Harvard University and president of the National Bureau of Economic Research. Andrew Samwick is assistant professor of economics at Dartmouth College and a faculty research fellow of the National Bureau of Economic Research.

The authors are grateful to the participants in the preconference and conference meetings for their comments and suggestions. They have extended the analysis of this paper in several ways in Feldstein and Samwick (1997).

1. See, e.g., World Bank (1994) and the papers in this volume describing the experiences in Argentina, Australia, Chile, Great Britain, and Mexico.

2. See the alternative proposals in Advisory Council on Social Security (1997).

This reduction in the payroll tax results in a reduction in the deadweight loss that is itself equal to about 2 percent of payroll. Thus, the long-run gain from shifting to a funded system is almost as large as the entire 12 percent payroll tax. This is equivalent to a permanent increase in real income of about 5 percent of GDP.

A major concern in all discussions of privatizing social security is the transition path. Critics of privatization argue that current and projected conditions in the United States—a population that is growing slowly and aging rapidly, a low rate of economic growth, and a very generous level of promised benefits—make the transition from the existing unfunded system to individual funded accounts too costly to be politically acceptable. Current employees now pay a 12 percent payroll tax to finance the benefits of current retirees. In the transition to a funded system, these employees would have to pay this plus the contributions to fund their own future benefits. Critics argue that this combination would be too onerous to be acceptable, and even those who favor a funded system in principle may fear that they are correct.

The purpose of this paper is to examine the basic issues involved in a transition and to explore alternative feasible transition paths from the existing U.S. pay-as-you-go social security system to a program of funded mandatory individual retirement accounts (MIRAs). The transition plans that we study are constrained to provide the same level of benefits in each future year as retirees would receive from the existing social security system. In addition, the financing leaves the projected path of the social security trust fund unchanged, thus guaranteeing that any additional private saving that results from the mandatory individual retirement accounts is a net addition to the nation's capital stock.

An important finding in our analysis is that the additional payments that are required in the early years of the transition are small relative to the existing payroll tax and to the long-run gains from privatization. These additional payments during the early part of the transition can be anywhere from 1 to 3 percent of payroll. Younger workers at the time of the transition are net beneficiaries over their own lifetimes. Although the gains of the older workers are not large enough to compensate them for the higher costs in the early years of the transition, when we look at nuclear families of parents and their children, we see that a substantial majority of two-generation pairs are likely to be net gainers. More generally, the gains occur quickly enough and are large enough that the present value of the annual net changes over the first fifty years are positive for any reasonable discount rate.

A basic problem in analyzing alternatives to the current system is that the benefits "promised" in current law are inconsistent with the current level of taxes. The social security actuaries predict that the existing trust fund will be exhausted by about the year 2030, a date that has been advanced repeatedly during the past decade. We therefore cannot sensibly compare alternative transition paths to the tax and benefit schedules in current law but must make some assumption about how the system would be kept solvent if it were not privatized. Most of our simulations make the simple assumption that the current system would keep the existing 12.4 percent tax rate for the old age, survivors, and disability insurance (OASDI) program but would cut benefits when the trust fund is exhausted. We refer to all these feasible benefit paths as the *baseline benefit paths* to distinguish them from the *current law benefit path*. We also simulate a proposal to maintain the benefit rules embodied in current law by raising the tax rate after 2030 to the level required to meet the resulting benefit obligations.

One final introductory comment is needed about our use of the term *privatize*. We are analyzing the transition to a system of mandatory individual retirement accounts, similar to current IRAs and 401(k)s, to which employers and/ or employees would be required to make contributions that would then be invested in stocks and bonds. There are two aspects of this that should be emphasized. First, participation is not voluntary. Everyone must participate and thus provide for his or her retirement.[3] Second, while the funds could in principle be collected and invested by the government, we believe that there are many reasons for preferring a decentralized system in which individuals and/or employers choose private fund managers. For this reason, we refer to the proposed alternatives as *privatizing* social security.

To motivate interest in the problem of transition, this paper begins in section 6.2 by indicating in more detail the potential steady-state benefit of substituting a funded mandatory individual retirement account program for the existing U.S. pay-as-you-go social security system. The remaining sections of the paper present our simulations and analyses of a variety of feasible transition paths for the U.S. social security system.

Section 6.3 provides some simple calculations to show the order of magnitude of the extra taxes required during the transition to a funded system that maintains a feasible baseline benefit path. Section 6.4 then describes our social security simulation model (SS-SIM) and discusses the parameter values that we have used. Section 6.5 presents results for the simulation of a gradual transition to a privatized system for all employees. Section 6.6 deals with the distributional issue of the benefits for lower-income individuals in a privatized system. Section 6.7 discusses the problem that the returns on privately invested funds are uncertain and that actuarially fair annuities based on debt and equity returns are not available.

In section 6.8, we analyze an alternative baseline in which the annual infla-

---

3. The individual's decision to shift from the existing pay-as-you-go social security system to the system of individual investment accounts could be made voluntary. Since our analysis assumes that individuals receive full credit against their payroll tax liability for contributions to the funded retirement accounts, the incentive for individuals to shift voluntarily would be extremely strong. But, although the choice between the current system and the funded alternative could be made voluntary, individuals are required to participate in one of the two.

There are two obvious alternatives to a mandatory system: a voluntary system coupled with either a means-tested benefit or a uniform flat-rate benefit. A means-tested system runs the risk of discouraging savings if the level of benefits is set high enough or of leaving undesirable poverty if it is set too low (see Feldstein 1987). A flat-rate benefit may also discourage private saving and may require a high tax rate with a correspondingly high deadweight loss.

tion adjustment to social security benefits would be reduced by 1 percentage point. In section 6.9, we turn in the opposite direction and consider a transition to a privatized system that maintains the *current law benefit path.* Instead of requiring a rise in the payroll tax from 12.4 to more than 19 percent, the fully funded system can maintain benefits with a long-run contribution rate of only slightly more than 3 percent. We present the corresponding transition path.

A final section summarizes our findings and comments on some issues that remain to be analyzed.

6.2   The Steady-State Advantage of a Funded Retirement Program[4]

In a growing economy with an unchanging age structure, an unfunded pay-as-you-go (PAYGO) social security retirement system that is financed by a constant payroll tax rate provides each cohort of participants with an implicit real rate of return on their tax contributions equal to the aggregate rate of growth of the economy (Samuelson 1958). For the current illustrative calculation, we take this rate of return to be 2.5 percent, the rate of growth of real wage and salary payments between 1960 and 1995 (*Economic Report of the President* 1996).[5]

In contrast, funds that are saved and invested in the nation's capital stock earn a real rate of return for the nation that is equal to the pretax marginal product of capital. For the past thirty-five years, this has averaged slightly more than 9.0 percent.[6] We now assume that the individual can in principle receive the entire 9 percent in a funded account; we defend the reasonableness of this assumption below.

To see the importance of the difference between the 2.5 and the 9 percent rates of return for the required amount of retirement saving, consider the very simple example of an individual who saves at one point during the middle of his working life for consumption during the middle of his retirement years. More specifically, consider an individual who is age forty-five and who "saves" $2,600 (approximately the current average payroll tax payment) to finance retirement consumption at age seventy-five. With the PAYGO real return of 2.5 percent, this $2,600 increases over the thirty-year period to $5,454. If the individual had instead earned a real 9 percent return on his retirement saving, this

---

4. The steady-state gain of a funded program must be balanced against the costs of transition. Realistic estimates of these costs are the primary focus of this paper. We present calculations that show that the present value of the gains exceeds these costs for any reasonable discount rate, even when the horizon is limited to forty years. For a theoretical discussion of the conditions under which shifting from an unfunded to a funded program has a positive present value, see Feldstein (1995c).

5. Because of the reduced rate of growth during the past two decades, Board of Trustees (1995) assumes that the rate of growth in the future will be only 2 percent.

6. Rippe (1995), following the method described in Feldstein, Dicks-Mireaux, and Poterba (1983), found that the real pretax marginal rate of return on capital in the nonfinancial corporate sector averaged 9.3 percent between 1960 and 1994.

$5,454 retirement amount could have been "purchased" at age forty-five for only $411 instead of $2,600.

If the $2,600 PAYGO contribution is obtained by a 12.4 percent payroll tax, this implies that the tax could be reduced to ($[411/2600] \times 12.4$ percent $=$) 1.96 percent.

The individual benefits in two quite distinct ways from being in the high-yield funded program rather than the low-yield PAYGO program. First, the individual saves $2,190 in taxes at age forty-five while maintaining the original benefits in retirement. Second, the distortionary payroll tax is reduced from 12.4 to 1.96 percent. Each of these deserves more comment, as does the assumption that the entire 9 percent pretax return is available to the mandatory individual retirement account.

First, the individual's gain at age forty-five is not a "future" gain in the form of higher benefits (which might be discounted by the individual at a high personal discount rate) but a tax reduction available immediately for additional consumption. Moreover, valuing this as $2,190 of additional consumption at age forty-five may understate its value to the individual, who may be able to obtain a higher level of utility by saving some of that additional disposable income.

Second, the existing 12.4 percent payroll tax distorts employment and compensation decisions. While 1.96 percentage points can be thought of as the amount needed to purchase a retirement benefit, the remaining 10.44 percentage points represent a pure tax. A deadweight loss results from this tax because of the compensated change in individual labor supply broadly defined (to include not only participation and hours but also choice of job, degree of effort, location, etc.) and in the consumption of such things as fringe benefits and better working conditions that are not part of taxable payroll income. The magnitude of the deadweight loss depends on the combined marginal tax rate that results from the income and payroll taxes. Taking the combined federal and state marginal income and sales tax rates to be 25 percent implies that the net payroll tax of 10.44 percent raises the marginal tax rate from approximately 25 percent to approximately 35.5 percent. The deadweight loss rises from being proportional to the square of 0.25 (i.e., to 0.0625) to being proportional to the square of 0.355 (i.e., 0.126, about twice as large).

Since the deadweight loss reflects changes in both labor supply and the form of compensation, the relevant elasticity is the compensated elasticity of the taxable income with respect to the net-of-tax share of income (Feldstein 1995b). If we write that elasticity as ε, the increased deadweight loss due to the 10.4 percent net payroll tax can be written (following Harberger 1964; and Browning 1987) as $0.5\varepsilon(0.126 - 0.0625)(wL)/(1 - 0.355)$, where wL is the taxable payroll, and the division by $1 - 0.355$ reflects the fact that the elasticity is evaluated empirically at the net-of-tax wage rate (Browning 1987). In the current example, since the 12.4 percent payroll tax produced revenue of $2,600, the value of wL is $20,967. The increased deadweight loss is therefore

$1,032\varepsilon$. Although estimates of ε for changes in the income tax for high-income individuals suggested values of ε between 1.0 and 1.5 (Feldstein 1995a; Auten and Carroll 1994), we will be conservative and assume $\varepsilon = 0.5$. With this value, the increased deadweight loss associated with a PAYGO tax of 12.4 percent is $516, or 2.5 percent of payroll earnings.

Note that this point is fundamentally different from the reduced payroll tax distortion discussed in Kotlikoff (1996) and in Auerbach and Kotlikoff (1987). Their analyses emphasized the fact that, in the current social security system, some individuals receive substantially higher implicit rates of return on their contributions than others. They note that, because of these differences and the great complexity of the benefit rules, individuals may disregard the link between contributions and benefits completely, treating the entire payroll tax as a pure tax for which nothing is received in return. They then assume that shifting to individualized accounts in which all individuals are treated equally can be used to eliminate the deadweight loss that results from the payroll tax distortions even if the individual accounts remain on a pay-as-you-go basis. They arrive at this conclusion by assuming that the benefits could be paid in a way that eliminates the net tax *at the margin* even though the average benefit represents a very low rate of return on the taxes paid. This is possible in their simulation model because all individuals have the same income. In effect, Auerbach and Kotlikoff require each individual to pay both a proportional payroll tax at a relatively low rate and a large lump sum tax. The revenue from the lump sum tax is used to subsidize the benefits so that the implied return on the payroll tax is equal to a market rate of return, eliminating the distorting effect of the payroll tax. As a practical matter, however, a lump sum tax equal to at least two-thirds of the average social security payroll tax would not be feasible. Although some reductions in deadweight loss could no doubt be achieved within the pay-as-you-go unfunded system by reducing the anomalies in the links between taxes and benefits,[7] those gains would be small in comparison to the gains that would be achieved by shifting from a pay-as-you-go system to a funded system. All the welfare gain from reduced distortion in our current analysis comes about because individuals are investing in higher-yielding assets.

In summary, by being in a funded program rather than the PAYGO system, our forty-five-year-old individual saves 10.4 percent of payroll in contribution and an additional 2.5 percent of payroll in reduced deadweight loss. For the individual, the gain is equivalent to 12.9 percent of payroll. Note that this gain is more than the entire initial level of the payroll tax.

The relative size of the gain depends of course on the age of the individual. For someone at age thirty, the gain is substantially larger, while, for someone on the verge of retirement, it is significantly smaller. A thirty-year-old who now pays a tax of $2,600 to buy benefits at age seventy-five could buy those

---

7. On the extent of these differences in effective tax rates, see Feldstein and Samwick (1992).

benefits in a funded program (with a 9 percent return) with a payment of only $55.00. A sixty-five-year-old who is buying benefits at age seventy-five can reduce his cost only from $2,600 to $1,406.

To get a very rough sense of the overall aggregate effect, consider a work-force of individuals between age thirty and age sixty-five with each year's co-hort 1 percent larger than the cohort born a year earlier. If all individuals earn the same average income and save to receive benefits at age seventy-five, a PAYGO system with a 12.4 percent tax would provide the same benefit as a funded system with a 9 percent rate of return and a contribution rate of 2.2 percent. This is surprisingly close to the example of the forty-five-year-old examined above. The combination of the reduced contribution and the reduced deadweight loss due to the distorting payroll tax is equivalent to about 12.5 percent of payroll up to the social security maximum. Since the payroll covered by social security is about 40 percent of GDP (Board of Trustees 1995, 190), the gain from having a funded system rather than a PAYGO system is equal to about 5 percent of GDP.

This calculation assumes that it is appropriate to attribute the entire real pretax return of 9 percent to the mandatory individual retirement accounts. About 40 percent of the 9 percent pretax return on capital (i.e., an amount equal to a 3.6 percent return on the private capital investment) is now collected by the government in corporate taxes and property taxes. It would be reason-able and fair for this return to be given back to the capital that earned it by crediting the mandatory individual retirement accounts with a government matching contribution that supplements the income earned in the account (just as the Treasury now rebates the tax collected on social security benefits to the social security trust fund). This "government contribution" would not represent a net cost to the government since it would simply be the extra corporate tax collected because of the new funded retirement accounts.[8]

6.3   The Strategy of Privatization

The strategy of privatization that we pursue in this study does not deal with the normative issue of the proper level of social security benefits. Instead, we assume that benefits in each future year will be maintained at the same levels that would prevail in the absence of privatization. We also assume that, by investing the MIRA accounts in the market mixture of debt and equity and receiving rebates of the tax revenues collected from the corporations on the

8. It would clearly be wrong to ignore the approximately 3.6 percent return captured in taxes and credit the mandatory retirement accounts with just the net 5.4 percent. It could, however, be assumed as a matter of political economy that the government would not credit this 3.6 percent of MIRA assets back to the MIRAs but would spend it on current consumption or tax cuts. If so, it would be necessary to recalculate the mandatory retirement contributions on the basis of the lower return and to consider a way to treat the corporate tax collections as an offset to the resulting higher payroll taxes. We present such a calculation based on a 5.4 percent return on MIRA assets in sec. 6.5.5 below.

incremental MIRA capital, the MIRA funds can earn the real pretax return of 9 percent. If these funds are used to purchase annuities (so that there are no bequests to children from MIRA accounts), the full 9 percent can be used to fund retirement and survivor benefits.[9]

As noted above, the future benefits in our baseline case are not at the level implied by the formula in current law since that is not feasible without substantially raising the existing 12.4 percent payroll tax rate. The social security actuaries now project that, under current law, the real value of the trust fund begins declining in 2015 and reaches zero in 2030. Our simulations essentially reproduce this projection. To assume a feasible baseline benefit path, we assume that benefits in each year after 2030 are adjusted to the level that can be financed in that year with a 12.4 percent payroll tax. Thus, the trust fund is zero in each year after 2030.[10]

After the privatization begins, individuals (or their employers or both) are required to contribute to a mandatory individual retirement account. The amount that is contributed for each individual depends on that individual's age and is calculated to be such that, when the privatization process is fully phased in,[11] the contribution would grow at 9 percent to equal the same benefit stream in retirement that the individual would have obtained under the existing unfunded system (as modified to maintain solvency) by contributing 12.4 percent of his or her covered earnings.[12] Each individual's MIRA contribution is credited against that individual's payroll tax obligation. A temporary uniform payroll tax surcharge must therefore be levied on all employees and employers to maintain the social security trust fund on its currently projected path.[13]

In the first year of privatization, individuals and their employers in the aggregate thus pay an amount equal to the full 12.4 percent social security payroll tax plus a surcharge that in the aggregate has the value of the specified MIRA contributions.

It is tempting to say that the MIRA surcharge is unnecessary since the credit given for the MIRA contributions could instead be offset by reducing the ex-

9. We are not explicit in the current analysis about survivors or the treatment of spouses. Similarly, the 12.4 percent tax rate includes social security disability benefits, and these are implicitly incorporated in our system.

10. Section 6.9 presents an alternative analysis in which taxes are raised after 2029 to maintain the level of benefits implied by current law.

11. We discuss a phase-in method of gradually shifting from the current system to the MIRA system in sec. 6.5.

12. If all individuals make MIRA contributions in this way, the transition is similar in spirit to the system of recognition bonds used for social security privatization by Chile and other countries. It differs in defining the value of the individual's claim to be based on the benefits to which he or she is entitled rather than the taxes that he or she paid. The current strategy also has the feature that the existing payroll tax is used to pay principal and interest on the implicit "recognition bonds" and that those "bonds" are completely paid off at the death of the youngest covered worker at the time of privatization.

13. There are of course many alternative transition paths with different distributional consequences for employees of different ages. For example, if MIRA contributions are not credited against payroll tax obligations, the transition is much more favorable to younger employees and less favorable to those nearer to retirement. In principle, payroll tax rates could vary by age.

isting social security trust fund. But reducing the trust fund in this way would defeat the purpose of the MIRA contributions. The reduction in the trust fund would exactly offset the increase in capital formation in the MIRAs that provides the higher return than the current unfunded system.

To assure that the nation's aggregate capital stock increases by the amount of the MIRA contributions, we assume that the payroll tax plus the surcharge is set in each year to maintain the trust fund at the level that would have prevailed in the absence of privatization. (This is not necessary, but any decision to reduce the trust fund must be reflected in a lower capital stock and a reduction in national income calculated as the product of the reduced capital stock and the marginal product of capital, not the government bond rate.)

The pure pay-as-you-go payroll tax that is required to keep the current trust fund path unchanged declines gradually as more and more of the retirement benefits come to be funded out of the MIRAs. Eventually, the traditional payroll tax is unnecessary, and the only contribution that individuals are required to make is to the mandatory individual retirement account.[14]

Under the current law, social security benefits are based only on the taxes that individuals pay when they are thirty years old or older (technically, on the thirty-five years of highest income). If full privatization began now for all employees between the ages of thirty and sixty-five (we assume that everyone retires at age sixty-five),[15] when the current thirty-year-olds retire, they would not receive any PAYGO benefits but would receive benefits wholly on the basis of their MIRA contributions. Those who are now over the age of thirty would continue to have some vestige of PAYGO benefits as long as they live. The payroll tax could therefore continue for as long as seventy years, but at a very much reduced rate. At some point in the future, long before seventy years from now, the reduction in the PAYGO benefits to retirees would exceed the MIRA contributions. At that point and ever after that, the combination of the payroll tax and the MIRA contribution would be less than the 12.4 percent payroll tax.

The specific timing of this crossover from mandatory contributions (the payroll tax plus the MIRA contributions) that are greater than 12.4 percent to mandatory contributions that are lower than 12.4 percent will depend on such things as (1) whether participation is initially universal or phased in over time and (2) whether the MIRA contributions are immediately set to substitute completely for the 12.4 percent funding of future benefits or for just a fraction of those benefits. We focus on the case in which everyone over age twenty-nine is covered immediately but in which the MIRA contributions begin at a level equal to just one-fourth of the full amount required to fund future benefits and rise gradually until they reach the full amount after twenty-five years.

Before turning to our detailed analysis of the transition options for the U.S.

14. At some point, when the traditional payroll tax is small enough, the system of crediting MIRA contributions would be eliminated. By then, all individuals would be paying a combined MIRA contribution plus payroll tax that is substantially less than the current 12.4 percent.

15. To the extent that those who retire before (after) age sixty-five have an actuarially fair reduction (increase) in their benefits, the age of retirement does not matter for our calculations.

economy, it may be helpful to consider briefly the way that our basic transition would operate in a simple stylized economy. For this purpose, we assume that the economy experiences steady-state growth at 2.5 percent and currently has an unfunded social security program in which benefits rise at 2.5 percent a year at a level that is compatible with a constant 12.4 percent payroll tax rate. We assume also that additions to the capital stock earn a real return of 9 percent. (The key difference from the actual situation in the United States is that the U.S. combination of benefit promises, changing demography, and initial trust fund is not consistent with a 2.5 percent implicit return and is not financially viable.)

The required MIRA contributions in this steady-state economy have already been derived in section 6.2 above. We saw there that a forty-five-year-old who earned 9 percent instead of 2.5 percent could replace a 12.4 percent tax with a 1.96 percent MIRA contribution. More generally, we saw that, if the labor force is growing at 1 percent a year, the real wage rate is rising at 1.5 percent a year and, if all workers earn the same wage, the 12.4 percent tax could be replaced by a 2.2 percent MIRA contribution.

The 2.2 percent is therefore an estimate of the level of MIRA contributions that would be possible in steady state after the last PAYGO retiree had died. It is also a rough estimate of the payment that workers (and/or their employers) would have to make in the first year of the transition (before there is any benefit replacement) in addition to the 12.4 percent PAYGO tax if there is an immediate shift to full MIRA contributions.[16] Thus, the tax rises in the first year to 14.6 percent. In the second year, however, the new retirees receive some of their retirement income from the MIRA saving that they did in the previous year and therefore receive less in PAYGO benefits. Thus, 14.6 percent would be the maximum tax during the privatization period and would fall rapidly over the transition period as the amount of the future PAYGO retiree benefits is replaced by MIRA benefits.

Rather than explore the time path for this hypothetical economy, we return to the simulation analysis of the actual U.S. economy and its current and future demographic structure.

6.4   The SS-SIM Model

This section describes the micro simulation model that we use to analyze alternative privatization paths. The model has four basic components: (1) demographic projections; (2) basic economic assumptions; (3) social security rules; and (4) the response of taxpayers to changes in tax rates and the associated changes in deadweight losses. The model is calibrated so that, with the current social security rules, it reproduces the basic time series of benefits, revenues, and trust fund assets predicted in Board of Trustees (1995).

16. With a 25 percent phase-in in the first year, the corresponding incremental payment would be one-fourth of the 2.2 percent, or 0.55 percent.

6.4.1 Demographics

The unit of analysis in the simulation is the individual. We simplify the social security rules by making no specific adjustments for married couples or survivor benefits. The values of these benefits as well as of the disability benefits are all subsumed in the projected individual retirement benefits.

Our analysis incorporates the actual current age structure of the population and the Census Bureau projections of future births through 2050 and the cohort-specific life tables for individuals born through 2050.[17] To reflect the net inflow of immigrants, we scale up the projected population uniformly at every age to coincide with the aggregate projections of the Social Security Administration.

6.4.2 Economic Assumptions

The simulations assume that individuals enter the labor force at age twenty-one and work until age sixty-five (or death if that occurs sooner). Since not everyone in the population actually works during these years, and since there are workers in covered employment at younger and older ages, we select a labor force participation rate among twenty-one- to sixty-four-year-olds that gives the correct number of covered workers in 1995 (Board of Trustees 1995, 122). This is a 94 percent participation rate among individuals aged twenty-one through sixty-four. The number of workers in future years is also calibrated to the social security projections, implying small fluctuations in future labor force participation rates.

The assumed wage in 1995 is the average earnings in covered employment ($24,825). This reflects the ceiling on taxable wages ($61,200 in 1995) but overstates the taxable payroll because some employees with multiple jobs exceed the maximum taxable wage. Taxable payroll per employee has averaged about 83.5 percent of the average wage in covered employment, a ratio that we assume holds in the future as well.

We use the historic data for average earnings in covered employment in previous years and follow the intermediate assumption in Board of Trustees (1995) that, after 1995, the average real wage rises at 1.0 percent per year. The movements in the average real wage are assumed to reflect changes in the age structure of the labor force and differences among age groups in the rate of increase of wages. More specifically, on the basis of the pattern of covered earnings by age as reported in Social Security Administration (1995), we assume that annual earnings rise at $g + 3$ percent for individuals under age thirty-five, at $g + 1$ percent for individuals between thirty-five and forty-five, and at $g - 1.5$ percent for those above forty-five years old, where the value of g for each year is chosen to make the overall rise in wages equal to the historic record before 1995 and to the projected 1 percent rise after 1995.

---

17. Our source for the initial population numbers is Bureau of the Census (1996b). The census source of both births and mortality projections is Bureau of the Census (1996a).

The social security trustees assume that the assets in the trust fund will earn a 2.3 percent real interest rate in the future. Since the basic policies that we study leave the path of benefits and taxes (and therefore of the trust fund) unchanged, this rate of interest is not relevant for the analysis of these options.

The real marginal product of capital is assumed to be 9 percent. As noted above, the average pretax rate of return on capital in the nonfinancial corporate sector from 1960 through 1994 has been slightly above 9 percent (Rippe 1995). This figure is derived, following Feldstein, Dicks-Mireaux, and Poterba (1983), by adding corporate profits, net interest payments, and all taxes paid to measure the pretax product of capital and then dividing that by the estimate of the capital stock at replacement cost.[18] Our estimate makes no allowance for the lower return that is earned on capital outside the corporate sector or on the net effect of increased capital accumulation on the marginal product of capital and on the net international capital flow.

6.4.3   Social Security Rules

Each individual is subject to an initial social security payroll tax of 12.4 percent. Since average real wages are projected to rise at 1.0 percent a year, we increase taxable wages at that same rate.

Because we use the individual as the unit of analysis, we do not have separate survivors' benefits. The "return" on contributions to social security (and to the MIRAs) is calculated as if it is all paid in the form of annuities to the retired individuals. We also do not make separate provision for disability benefits. We include the disability tax by using the 12.4 percent tax rate but include the disability benefits with the retirement annuity.

Individuals become eligible for benefits at age sixty-five in the simulation and receive benefits until they die. In actual practice, some individuals retire earlier than sixty-five, and some wait until later to retire. To the extent that social security benefits are adjusted for the retirement age in an actuarially fair way, these differences in retirement age do not change the costs of providing benefits.

Because we do not distinguish income levels or family structures, we cannot apply the actual social security benefit rules. We therefore calculate benefits by attributing a rate of return on the taxes that each individual has paid. We follow current social security rules and assume that only those taxes paid between age thirty and age sixty-five—the highest thirty-five years of earnings— are used in calculating benefits. The cohort-specific real rates of return that we use are modifications of earlier estimates by Boskin et al. (1987); their estimates, which were for single-earner couples, have been adjusted to produce aggregate benefit amounts that coincide with the trustees' projections of the benefits implied by the current law for future years: 7.0 percent for those born before 1915, 4.21 percent for those born in 1915, 2.52 percent for those born in 1930, 1.67 percent for those born in 1945, 1.39 percent for those born in

---

18. These figures relate profits and interest earned in the United States to the value of the domestic capital stock.

1960, 1.39 percent for those born in 1975, and 1.43 percent for those born in 1990 or after.

Even with the lower rates of return for younger workers implied by this procedure, the projected benefits cannot be financed by the existing 12.4 percent OASDI tax rate because of the changing age structure of the population. The changing demographics cause the trust fund to be exhausted in the year 2030. Our basic simulations assume that, at that point, benefits under the existing system would be reduced to the level that can be financed on a current basis by the taxes collected with a 12.4 percent payroll tax. The calculations presented in the next section show that this requires a benefit reduction that begins at 18 percent and rises to 35 percent. Two alternatives are also examined: the analysis in section 6.8 modifies the existing inflation indexing rule, and the analysis of section 6.9 maintains the current law benefits by increasing the tax or MIRA contributions.

6.4.4 Taxpayers' Responses, Tax Rates, and Deadweight Losses

The projections of taxable earnings described in section 6.4.2 must be modified to incorporate the changes in taxpayer behavior that would result from changes in the payroll tax rates. This is important to estimate both the required payroll tax rates and the associated changes in deadweight losses. Traditional estimates of the effects of tax rates on labor supply indicate that participation rates and average hours are quite insensitive to net-of-tax wages among prime-age males and single women but much more sensitive among married women. However, this is too narrow a measure of taxpayers' responses for the current purpose. The change in revenue and therefore the required revenue neutral change in tax rates reflects not only changes in working hours but also a broader definition of *labor supply* (one that includes choice of job, degree of effort, location, etc.) as well as any shift between cash compensation and fringe benefits, improved working conditions, and other things that are not subject to the payroll tax. Feldstein (1995b) showed that the deadweight loss associated with the tax rate depends on the compensated elasticity of taxable income with respect to the net-of-tax share.

There is, unfortunately, no good evidence on this elasticity for changes in the payroll tax rate. The estimated elasticities of between 1.0 and 1.5 for the income tax (Feldstein 1995a; Auten and Carroll, 1994) are not directly relevant because they include changes in deductibles and are for higher-income individuals. In what follows, we assume that the uncompensated elasticity of labor earnings with respect to the relevant net-of-tax rate is only 0.5. Although the compensated elasticity would be larger, we also use an elasticity of 0.5 for the deadweight loss calculations. The calculation of the earnings response and the associated adjustment in the tax rate, as well as the implications for the deadweight losses, are developed in section 6.5.3.

Our analysis does not take into account the broader general equilibrium effects of the shift to a funded system. The primary general equilibrium effect is the effect of the increased national capital stock on the rate of return and on real wages. Although the higher real wages reinforce the effect of lower tax rates to increase labor supply, the effect is smaller than the tax effect because the higher marginal product of labor does not affect the choice between taxable wages and other forms of compensation.[19]

6.5   Simulation Results for Gradual Privatization

This section begins by presenting the values of key variables under current law and then shows the "solvency adjustment" to benefits needed to avoid a tax increase when the trust fund is exhausted. It then goes on to consider the effect of a gradual privatization on tax rates and on the deadweight loss of the tax system.

6.5.1   Current Law and Baseline Simulations

Table 6.1 shows the projected values of the numbers of covered workers and of beneficiaries in each year from 1995 through 2071. (The number of beneficiaries is the number of persons who are supported by social security. For a married couple, this is two persons regardless of whether each would claim benefits as a retired worker or one would claim as a dependent spouse.)

The ratio of covered workers per beneficiary declines from the current value of 3.27 to 2.03 in the year 2031 and then continues to decline to 1.80 at the end of the period.

Table 6.2 shows our simulation of the projected values of payroll tax receipts and of retirement benefits under current law. The payroll tax revenue is the result of a constant 12.4 percent rate applied to the projected labor force with real wages per employee growing at 1.0 percent per year. The initial payroll tax per worker is $2,570. All dollar amounts are reported in constant 1995 dollars.

The retirement benefits reflect the projected numbers of retirees and the assumption that benefits are calculated by giving a return to each cohort as described above.

Table 6.3 shows how the trust fund evolves under current law. The fund is increased by the payroll taxes received, receipts from the Treasury, and interest on the fund balance, and it is reduced by the benefits paid and administrative expenses.[20] In addition, the trust fund is assumed to spend 0.8 percent of benefits on administrative costs.[21]

---

19. For examples of the general equilibrium analysis of the effects of social security reforms, see Auerbach and Kotlikoff (1987) and Kotlikoff (1996, chap. 7 in this volume).

20. Under current law, the Treasury adds to the social security trust fund the income tax that it collects on benefits. This starts with a very small amount ($5.13 billion in 1995) but grows rapidly because the income tax is applied to 85 percent of benefits above an *unindexed* amount of $32,000 per couple and $25,000 per single individual. The calculations of the cohort-specific rates of return are based on benefits net of the income tax so that this is already taken into account.

21. The administrative cost of the funded program is assumed to come from the difference between the assumed 9 percent rate of return and the total return of 9.30 percent that Rippe (1995) actually reported.

Table 6.1   **Demographic Projections**

A. Covered Workers (millions)						
1995	141.21	142.49	143.77	145.04	146.32	147.60	148.77
2002	149.95	151.12	152.29	153.47	154.47	155.47	156.48
2009	157.48	158.49	159.06	159.63	160.20	160.78	161.35
2016	161.60	161.84	162.09	162.34	162.59	162.79	162.99
2023	163.19	163.39	163.59	163.87	164.15	164.43	164.71
2030	164.99	165.38	165.77	166.16	166.55	166.94	167.32
2037	167.70	168.09	168.47	168.85	169.11	169.38	169.65
2044	169.91	170.18	170.37	170.55	170.74	170.92	171.11
2051	171.25	171.39	171.53	171.67	171.81	171.95	172.09
2058	172.23	172.37	172.52	172.67	172.83	172.98	173.14
2065	173.30	173.44	173.58	173.72	173.87	174.01	174.15

B. Beneficiaries (millions)						
1995	43.22	43.86	44.50	45.15	45.79	46.43	47.11
2002	47.79	48.47	49.15	49.83	50.73	51.64	52.55
2009	53.46	54.37	55.62	56.88	58.14	59.40	60.65
2016	62.15	63.65	65.14	66.64	68.14	69.59	71.04
2023	72.50	73.95	75.41	76.49	77.58	78.67	79.76
2030	80.85	81.50	82.15	82.80	83.44	84.09	84.32
2037	84.56	84.79	85.02	85.25	85.48	85.70	85.93
2044	86.16	86.38	86.70	87.01	87.32	87.63	87.94
2051	88.42	88.90	89.38	89.86	90.34	90.82	91.30
2058	91.78	92.26	92.73	93.13	93.52	93.92	94.31
2065	94.70	95.05	95.39	95.73	96.08	96.42	96.76

C. Support Ratio						
1995	3.27	3.25	3.23	3.21	3.20	3.18	3.16
2002	3.14	3.12	3.10	3.08	3.04	3.01	2.98
2009	2.95	2.92	2.86	2.81	2.76	2.71	2.66
2016	2.60	2.54	2.49	2.44	2.39	2.34	2.29
2023	2.25	2.21	2.17	2.14	2.12	2.09	2.06
2030	2.04	2.03	2.02	2.01	2.00	1.99	1.98
2037	1.98	1.98	1.98	1.98	1.98	1.98	1.97
2044	1.97	1.97	1.97	1.96	1.96	1.95	1.95
2051	1.94	1.93	1.92	1.91	1.90	1.89	1.88
2058	1.88	1.87	1.86	1.85	1.85	1.84	1.84
2065	1.83	1.82	1.82	1.81	1.81	1.80	1.80

The simulations show that the net additions to the trust fund continue to be positive until 2012 and then turn negative. Even after net additions to the trust fund (from taxes and Treasury transfers minus benefits and administrative costs) become negative, the trust fund continues to grow because of the interest earned on the government bonds in which the funds are invested and the Treasury tax collections on benefits that are transferred to the trust fund. At its peak in the year 2015, the trust fund has $1,482 billion (at the 1995 price level). The

Table 6.2   **Current Law: Taxes and Benefits**

A. Payroll Taxes ($billions)

1995	362.96	369.91	376.96	384.12	391.38	398.75	405.93
2002	413.23	420.63	428.13	435.75	442.98	450.32	457.76
2009	465.30	472.95	479.40	485.94	492.56	499.26	506.05
2016	511.90	517.81	523.79	529.84	535.95	541.98	548.07
2023	554.23	560.47	566.76	573.41	580.13	586.93	593.81
2030	600.76	608.21	615.74	623.37	631.08	638.89	646.75
2037	654.70	662.75	670.89	679.13	687.01	694.97	703.03
2044	711.17	719.41	727.40	735.48	743.64	751.90	760.24
2051	768.47	776.79	785.19	793.69	802.27	810.97	819.75
2058	828.63	837.61	846.68	855.92	865.26	874.70	884.25
2065	893.90	903.58	913.37	923.26	933.26	943.37	953.59

B. Payroll Taxes per Worker ($thousands)

1995	2.57	2.60	2.62	2.65	2.67	2.70	2.73
2002	2.76	2.78	2.81	2.84	2.87	2.90	2.93
2009	2.95	2.98	3.01	3.04	3.07	3.11	3.14
2016	3.17	3.20	3.23	3.26	3.30	3.33	3.36
2023	3.40	3.43	3.46	3.50	3.53	3.57	3.61
2030	3.64	3.68	3.71	3.75	3.79	3.83	3.87
2037	3.90	3.94	3.98	4.02	4.06	4.10	4.14
2044	4.19	4.23	4.27	4.31	4.36	4.40	4.44
2051	4.49	4.53	4.58	4.62	4.67	4.72	4.76
2058	4.81	4.86	4.91	4.96	5.01	5.06	5.11
2065	5.16	5.21	5.26	5.31	5.37	5.42	5.48

C. Retirement Benefits ($billions)

1995	324.72	331.44	338.02	344.77	351.65	358.83	366.48
2002	374.17	382.29	390.56	398.92	409.38	420.00	430.97
2009	441.79	452.67	466.87	482.00	497.25	512.61	528.26
2016	546.18	564.51	582.85	601.17	619.56	637.58	655.33
2023	673.18	690.91	708.69	723.30	738.02	752.92	767.96
2030	783.16	794.17	804.99	816.10	827.44	839.10	846.86
2037	854.47	862.13	870.04	878.36	887.20	896.59	906.75
2044	917.61	929.38	942.67	956.75	971.47	986.70	1,002.99
2051	1,021.89	1,040.90	1,061.14	1,082.29	1,104.54	1,127.39	1,150.55
2058	1,174.02	1,197.94	1,222.39	1,245.46	1,268.22	1,290.68	1,312.88
2065	1,334.81	1,355.78	1,376.50	1,396.95	1,417.22	1,437.30	1,457.25

D. Benefits per Retiree ($thousands)

1995	7.51	7.56	7.60	7.64	7.68	7.73	7.78
2002	7.83	7.89	7.95	8.01	8.07	8.13	8.20
2009	8.26	8.33	8.39	8.47	8.55	8.63	8.71
2016	8.79	8.87	8.95	9.02	9.09	9.16	9.22
2023	9.29	9.34	9.40	9.46	9.51	9.57	9.63
2030	9.69	9.74	9.80	9.86	9.92	9.98	10.04
2037	10.11	10.17	10.23	10.30	10.38	10.46	10.55
2044	10.65	10.76	10.87	11.00	11.13	11.26	11.41
2051	11.56	11.71	11.87	12.04	12.23	12.41	12.60
2058	12.79	12.99	13.18	13.37	13.56	13.74	13.92
2065	14.09	14.26	14.43	14.59	14.75	14.91	15.06

Table 6.3   Current Law: Trust Fund

A. Net Addition to Trust Fund ($billions)

1995	35.65	35.82	36.24	36.59	36.92	37.05	36.53
2002	36.06	35.28	34.45	33.63	30.33	26.95	23.34
2009	19.97	16.65	8.79	.08	−8.67	−17.44	−26.43
2016	−38.65	−51.22	−63.72	−76.14	−88.57	−100.71	−112.50
2023	−124.33	−135.97	−147.60	−155.68	−163.79	−172.01	−180.29
2030	−188.66	−192.32	−195.69	−199.26	−202.97	−206.92	−206.88
2037	−206.60	−206.27	−206.11	−206.26	−207.29	−208.79	−210.98
2044	−213.77	−217.41	−222.81	−228.92	−235.60	−242.70	−250.77
2051	−261.60	−272.44	−284.43	−297.26	−311.10	−325.44	−340.00
2058	−354.78	−369.92	−385.49	−399.50	−413.10	−426.30	−439.13
2065	−451.60	−463.05	−474.15	−484.86	−495.29	−505.43	−515.32

B. Total Amount in Trust Fund ($billions)

1995	501.70	559.60	619.90	681.29	743.41	805.73	867.24
2002	928.45	988.80	1,047.97	1,105.71	1,161.47	1,215.13	1,266.42
2009	1,315.52	1,362.43	1,402.56	1,434.90	1,459.23	1,475.34	1,482.84
2016	1,478.30	1,461.08	1,430.97	1,387.74	1,331.09	1,261.00	1,177.50
2023	1,080.26	969.14	843.83	707.56	560.05	400.91	229.84
2030	46.46	−144.79	−343.81	−550.98	−766.62	−991.17	−1,220.85
2037	−1,455.54	−1,695.29	−1,940.39	−2,191.27	−2,448.96	−2,714.08	−2,987.48
2044	−3,269.97	−3,562.58	−3,867.33	−4,185.20	−4,517.06	−4,863.65	−5,226.28
2051	−5,608.09	−6,009.51	−6,432.17	−6,877.36	−7,346.64	−7,841.05	−8,361.40
2058	−8,908.49	−9,483.30	−10,086.91	−10,718.41	−11,378.03	−12,066.03	−12,782.68
2065	−13,528.28	−14,302.48	−15,105.58	−15,937.88	−16,799.74	−17,691.56	−18,613.79

decline in the trust fund after that date causes the fund to be exhausted in the year 2030, a date that also coincides with the social security actuaries' projection.

Since a negative trust fund is not feasible, for the rest of our calculations in this section we assume that the current system shifts to a pay-as-you-go basis after 2030, with benefits reduced to keep outlays equal to the funds raised by a combination of the 12.4 percent payroll tax and the Treasury tax collections on existing benefits, all net of the small administrative charge. Table 6.4 shows the percentage by which benefits must be reduced beginning in 2031. The reduction goes from about 18 percent in that year to 24 percent in the next and then rises steadily. These simulation results provide the basis for the alternative privatization paths that we now consider.

6.5.2   Phase-In from Partial to Total Privatization

Table 6.5 shows the effect of starting with a partial privatization for everyone and then expanding the privatized share until it completely substitutes for the unfunded program. More specifically, in the first year individuals are required to contribute to the MIRA an amount that at a 9 percent rate of return will accumulate enough by age sixty-five to replace one-fourth of the correspond-

Table 6.4   **Current Law: Solvency Adjustment**

	A. Fraction by Which Benefits Must Be Reduced (%)						
1995	.00	.00	.00	.00	.00	.00	.00
2002	.00	.00	.00	.00	.00	.00	.00
2009	.00	.00	.00	.00	.00	.00	.00
2016	.00	.00	.00	.00	.00	.00	.00
2023	.00	.00	.00	.00	.00	.00	.00
2030	.00	18.09	24.12	24.22	24.34	24.46	24.24
2037	23.99	23.74	23.50	23.30	23.18	23.10	23.08
2044	23.11	23.21	23.45	23.74	24.06	24.40	24.80
2051	25.40	25.97	26.59	27.25	27.94	28.64	29.32
2058	29.98	30.63	31.29	31.82	32.32	32.77	33.18
2065	33.56	33.88	34.17	34.43	34.67	34.89	35.08

	B. New Path of Retirement Benefits ($billions)						
1995	324.72	331.44	338.02	344.77	351.65	358.83	366.48
2002	374.17	382.29	390.56	398.92	409.38	420.00	430.97
2009	441.79	452.67	466.87	482.00	497.25	512.61	528.26
2016	546.18	564.51	582.85	601.17	619.56	637.58	655.33
2023	673.18	690.91	708.69	723.30	738.02	752.92	767.96
2030	783.16	650.54	610.86	618.42	626.08	633.82	641.62
2037	649.51	657.49	665.57	673.74	681.55	689.46	697.45
2044	705.53	713.70	721.63	729.64	737.74	745.93	754.21
2051	762.37	770.62	778.96	787.39	795.91	804.53	813.25
2058	822.06	830.96	839.96	849.13	858.40	867.76	877.23
2065	886.80	896.41	906.12	915.93	925.85	935.88	946.02

Table 6.5   **Phase-In from Partial to Total Privatization**

	A. Mandatory Individual Contributions ($billions)						
1995	20.25	23.12	26.18	29.44	32.88	36.43	40.11
2002	44.07	48.04	52.22	56.67	61.11	65.70	70.25
2009	75.07	79.99	84.82	88.94	93.25	97.70	102.05
2016	106.10	110.13	114.06	117.82	121.27	120.74	120.64
2023	120.09	119.59	118.81	118.04	117.53	117.14	116.90
2030	116.82	117.11	118.10	118.88	119.58	120.03	120.34
2037	121.17	122.29	123.42	124.33	125.21	126.20	127.08
2044	127.96	128.60	129.28	129.89	130.58	131.44	132.06
2051	132.69	133.78	134.61	135.35	135.87	136.38	137.07
2058	137.91	138.89	139.94	141.10	142.35	143.70	145.14
2065	146.67	148.27	149.94	151.68	153.49	155.35	157.25

	B. Mandatory Individual Contributions (% of Payroll)						
1995	.69	.78	.86	.95	1.04	1.13	1.23
2002	1.32	1.42	1.51	1.61	1.71	1.81	1.90
2009	2.00	2.10	2.19	2.27	2.35	2.43	2.50
2016	2.57	2.64	2.70	2.76	2.81	2.76	2.73
2023	2.69	2.65	2.60	2.55	2.51	2.47	2.44
2030	2.41	2.39	2.38	2.36	2.35	2.33	2.31
2037	2.29	2.29	2.28	2.27	2.26	2.25	2.24
2044	2.23	2.22	2.20	2.19	2.18	2.17	2.15
2051	2.14	2.14	2.13	2.11	2.10	2.09	2.07
2058	2.06	2.06	2.05	2.04	2.04	2.04	2.04
2065	2.03	2.03	2.04	2.04	2.04	2.04	2.04

	C. Benefits Replaced Owing to Privatization ($billions)						
1995	.00	.13	.38	.78	1.35	2.18	3.25
2002	4.52	6.22	8.25	10.62	13.57	17.03	21.32
2009	25.93	31.17	37.29	45.26	53.82	63.07	73.44
2016	85.18	97.86	111.70	126.74	143.23	160.99	178.93
2023	198.55	218.93	240.74	262.44	284.59	307.56	331.29
2030	355.89	310.24	303.98	320.95	338.42	356.61	375.26
2037	393.42	411.53	430.08	449.32	468.52	487.90	507.68
2044	527.69	548.06	568.03	587.98	607.72	627.03	646.30
2051	664.97	682.81	700.46	717.66	734.44	750.59	766.05
2058	780.86	795.15	808.95	822.37	835.40	848.07	860.44
2065	872.55	884.37	896.00	907.47	918.83	930.10	941.30

	D. Payroll Tax Needed to Maintain Trust Fund Trajectory (% of Payroll)						
1995	12.40	12.40	12.39	12.37	12.36	12.33	12.30
2002	12.26	12.22	12.16	12.10	12.02	11.93	11.82
2009	11.70	11.58	11.43	11.24	11.03	10.82	10.59
2016	10.32	10.04	9.73	9.41	9.06	8.69	8.32
2023	7.92	7.52	7.09	6.68	6.27	5.85	5.43
2030	5.00	6.02	6.23	5.96	5.70	5.42	5.15
2037	4.89	4.64	4.39	4.13	3.88	3.63	3.37
2044	3.13	2.88	2.64	2.41	2.19	1.98	1.77

(*continued*)

Table 6.5   (continued)

	D. Payroll Tax Needed to Maintain Trust Fund Trajectory (% of Payroll)						
2051	1.58	1.41	1.25	1.10	.96	.83	.72
2058	.62	.53	.46	.39	.33	.28	.24
2065	.20	.17	.14	.11	.09	.08	.06

	E. Total Payroll Tax Plus Mandatory Contribution (% of Payroll)						
1995	13.09	13.17	13.25	13.32	13.40	13.46	13.53
2002	13.59	13.63	13.67	13.71	13.73	13.74	13.72
2009	13.70	13.67	13.62	13.51	13.38	13.25	13.09
2016	12.89	12.68	12.43	12.17	11.87	11.45	11.05
2023	10.61	10.16	9.69	9.23	8.78	8.32	7.87
2030	7.41	8.41	8.61	8.33	8.05	7.75	7.45
2037	7.18	6.93	6.67	6.40	6.14	5.88	5.62
2044	5.36	5.09	4.84	4.60	4.36	4.14	3.93
2051	3.73	3.55	3.38	3.21	3.06	2.92	2.79
2058	2.69	2.59	2.51	2.43	2.37	2.32	2.27
2065	2.23	2.20	2.17	2.15	2.13	2.12	2.11

ing unfunded social security benefits. In the second year, the share of retirement benefits that is to be prefunded (by that year's contributions) rises from 25 to 28 percent. The privatized share increases in this way by 3 percentage points a year for twenty-five years until MIRA contributions are enough to prefund 100 percent of the benefits associated with that year's contributions. (These figures ignore the effect of changes in tax rates on pretax earnings, a restriction that we correct in sec. 6.5.3.)

The contribution to the mandatory individual retirement account is $20.3 billion in 1995. This implies that the MIRA contributions are equivalent to 0.69 percent of taxable payroll, an amount shown in panel B of table 6.5. This measures the extent to which the existing generation of employees is required in the first year of the transition to pay for their own retirement as well as for the existing retiree benefits. It is clearly very much less than having to pay twice the existing payroll tax (i.e., an additional 12.4 percent), as some critics of privatization imply will happen.

Since there are no MIRA benefits paid in 1995, panel C of table 6.5 shows no benefits replaced owing to privatization for 1995. The basic payroll tax needed to meet the existing benefit requirements and to keep the trust fund on its original trajectory therefore remains 12.40 percent of payroll, the amount shown for 1995 in panel D of the table.

Combining the 0.69 percent of payroll MIRA contribution with the 12.4 percent payroll tax needed to maintain the trust fund trajectory implies total contributions of 13.09 percent of payroll, the amount shown in panel E of the table.[22]

---

22. It would of course be possible to keep the combined MIRA contributions and payroll tax unchanged while meeting existing benefit obligations by reducing the trust fund or by explicit

As the privatization program moves forward through time, two major changes occur. First, the amount of MIRA contributions rises (1) as the privatization share rises from 25 to 100 percent over a twenty-five-year phase-in period and (2) as the labor force grows and wages increase. This increase in MIRA contributions is shown in panel A of table 6.5. The changing age structure of the workforce and the changes in relative benefit levels projected for the future also cause the mandatory individual contributions as a percentage of payroll to vary in a moderate way; panel B of table 6.5 shows that the contribution per dollar of payroll reaches a high of 2.81 percent of payroll in 2011 and then declines to a long-run level of 2.04 percent.

The second major change is the gradual replacement of the unfunded social security benefits with the MIRA benefits. In 1996, those who were sixty-four years old in 1995 retire and receive some benefits on the basis of their MIRA contributions in the previous year. These benefits are just $0.13 billion (as shown in panel C of table 6.5). By the year 2000, these benefits are $1.35 billion; this reduces the pay-as-you-go tax rate required to maintain the trust fund trajectory from 12.40 to 12.36 percent.

Over time, this benefit replacement becomes much more important. After twenty years (in 2014), MIRA benefits reach $63.07 billion and therefore permit the payroll tax needed to maintain the trust fund trajectory to decline from the initial 12.40 percent to 10.82 percent, as shown in panel D of table 6.5. Seven years later, in 2021, the required pay-as-you-go tax is down to 8.69 percent.

Those individuals who are thirty years old or younger in 2020 (when the MIRA system is fully phased in) eventually finance their retirement solely with MIRA withdrawals. Unlike earlier cohorts, they receive no PAYGO benefits. Since we assume that no one lives beyond age one hundred, this means that the PAYGO system is completely finished by the seventieth year after privatization begins (i.e., in 2090). The results in panel D of table 6.5 show that, as a practical matter, the required pay-as-you-go payroll tax is essentially zero (i.e., less than 0.5 percent) in 2059 and beyond.

Combining the MIRA contribution (panel B) and the required payroll tax (panel D) produces the combined payroll tax and MIRA contribution shown in panel E of table 6.5. This combination remains higher than the existing 12.4 percent payroll tax for twenty-four years. After that, the combined cost falls rapidly. In the thirtieth year, the combined ratio is down to 10.16 percent, and by the fortieth year it is down to only 8.02 percent, less than two-thirds of the original 12.4 percent payroll tax that would otherwise be required to finance

---

borrowing from the public by the social security program. Either of these would increase the unified budget deficit and reduce national saving by an amount that offsets the increased national saving in the MIRAs. Of course, if additional actions were taken to keep the budget deficit unchanged, the national saving rate would still increase by the amount of the MIRA accumulations. The possibility of these additional changes in government spending or taxes lies beyond the scope of the current paper.

the same benefits. These figures imply that an individual who is a young employee at the start of privatization pays slightly higher taxes plus contributions in the early years but then sharply lower total taxes and contributions during later years. Before looking at the implication of such individual time paths for the present value of such payments, we consider the effect of the plan on taxpayers' behavior and the implications of that response for tax rates and deadweight losses.

6.5.3   Behavioral Response, Required Tax Rates, and Deadweight Losses

The existing payroll tax causes employees to reduce their labor supply (broadly defined to include effort, occupational choice, and location as well as the number of hours worked) and to substitute untaxed fringe benefits and nicer working conditions for taxable cash compensation. We model the reduction in taxable payroll earnings as the product of an elasticity and the change in the marginal net-of-tax share of wages, that is, as the product of an elasticity and "one minus the effective marginal tax rate." The effective marginal tax rate includes the federal and state personal income tax rate, the effective state and local sales tax rates, and the *net* payroll tax rate. We assume (quite conservatively) a rate of 20 percent for the taxes other than the payroll tax. The *net* payroll tax rate is the difference between the payroll tax payment (12.4 percent of payroll) and the amount that the individual would have to pay to purchase the same benefit at the higher rate of return available in the market.

The cost of purchasing that benefit is calculated in the following way. If the implicit rate of return that the individual earns on social security payroll taxes[23] is denoted γ, a dollar of payroll tax paid at age a could provide a cash benefit of $(1 + \gamma)^{65-a}$ at age sixty-five. If ANN65(γ) is the actuarial present value of a dollar a year from age sixty-five to death based on a return of γ, the dollar of payroll tax paid at age a earns an annuity starting at age sixty-five of $(1 + \gamma)^{65-a}/\text{ANN65}(\gamma)$. To purchase that same annuity in a private pension plan, an employer would have to spend only $[(1 + \mu)^{65-a}/\text{ANN65}(\mu)]^{-1}$, where μ is the rate of return earned in the private pension alternative. Because pension funds do not pay tax on their income, a plausible value for μ is the return on capital net of corporate and property taxes but before all personal income taxes. A pretax real return of 9 percent and a corporate tax rate (including state taxes and property taxes) of 40 percent imply $\mu = 5.4$ percent. Since μ is substantially greater than γ, there is a substantial effective tax implied by the payroll tax. For example, since someone born in 1960 would receive a return on social security taxes of only ($\gamma =$) 1.39 percent, each dollar of payroll tax could be replaced by only 9.7 cents of contribution to a private pension fund at age thirty. This implies that 90.3 percent of the 12.4 percent payroll tax is a pure tax since the same benefits could be bought for a private pension contribu-

---

23. Recall that this implicit return has declined from 7.0 percent among individuals born before 1915 to less than 1.5 percent among individuals born after 1960.

tion of only 1.2 percent of the individual's payroll. More generally, we define the effective payroll tax rate as

$$\{1 - [(1 + \gamma)/(1 + \mu)]^{65-a}[\text{ANN65}(\mu)/\text{ANN65}(\gamma)]\}\tau_p$$

where τ_p is the payroll tax rate (currently 0.124). Alternatively, we can write the individual's effective payroll tax rate as $\tau_p - \beta$, where

$$\beta = [(1 + \gamma)/(1 + \mu)]^{65-a}[\text{ANN65}(\mu)/\text{ANN65}(\gamma)]\tau_p$$

is the value of the benefit that the individual receives per dollar of incremental earnings.[24]

Combining this with the marginal personal income tax rate (θ) implies a net-of-tax share under existing social security rules of $1 - \theta - \tau_p + \beta$. We denote this net-of-tax share by N_0. For example, with $\theta = 0.20$, $\gamma = 0.0139$, and $\mu = 0.054$, the net-of-tax share for a current thirty-five-year-old is $N_0 = 0.688$.

In the MIRA system, the individual would continue to pay a payroll tax to meet the remaining pay-as-you-go benefit obligations plus a surcharge to offset the revenue lost because individuals reduce their regular payroll tax obligations by the amount of their MIRA contributions. If we denote this combined tax plus surcharge (shown in panel E of table 6.5 as "total payroll tax plus mandatory contribution") by τ_p^*, we can write the individual's net-of-tax share under the MIRA system as $N_1 = 1 - \theta - \tau_p^* + \beta$ (where β is the same as in the current system since the value of the benefits is unchanged by switching to the MIRA system).

At first, the net-of-tax share declines because τ_p^* is greater than the τ_p under the existing system. After a while, however, the net-of-tax rate rises, and the corresponding effective marginal tax rate falls.

Our assumed elasticity of 0.5 implies that taxable income rises by a factor of $[N_1/N_0]^{0.5}$. This in turn means that the payroll tax revenue collected by tax rate τ_p with the initial labor supply can be collected at a lower tax rate $\tau_p' = \tau_p[N_1/N_0]^{-0.5}$. Similarly, the personal income tax rate that collects the same revenue falls to $\theta' = \theta[N_1/N_0]^{-0.5}$.

The path of the adjusted tax rates is shown in panels B and C of table 6.6. In the first year, the combination of the MIRA surcharge and the unchanged payroll tax causes the net-of-tax share to fall and therefore the aggregate labor supply to decline. The effect is small and is offset by raising the payroll tax rate from 12.40 to 12.46 percent. Similarly, the personal income tax rate must be raised only from 20 to 20.10 percent. But, by the eighth year, the payroll tax rate is lower than the initial 12.4 percent, and, by year 25, the increased taxable labor income causes the payroll tax rate to be lower than it would be with no allowance for the change in labor income (i.e., by year 25, the payroll

24. Our analysis does not classify individuals by income level and therefore does not distinguish between the average and the marginal benefits per dollar of earnings.

Table 6.6   **Effect of Phase-In Partial Privatization on Tax Base and DWL**

	A. Payroll Tax Needed to Maintain Trust Fund with No Behavioral Response[a]						
1995	12.40	12.40	12.39	12.37	12.36	12.33	12.30
2002	12.26	12.22	12.16	12.10	12.02	11.93	11.82
2009	11.70	11.58	11.43	11.24	11.03	10.82	10.59
2016	10.32	10.04	9.73	9.41	9.06	8.69	8.32
2023	7.92	7.52	7.09	6.68	6.27	5.85	5.43
2030	5.00	6.02	6.23	5.96	5.70	5.42	5.15
2037	4.89	4.64	4.39	4.13	3.88	3.63	3.37
2044	3.13	2.88	2.64	2.41	2.19	1.98	1.77
2051	1.58	1.41	1.25	1.10	.96	.83	.72
2058	.62	.53	.46	.39	.33	.28	.24
2065	.20	.17	.14	.11	.09	.08	.06

	B. New Payroll Tax Rate Allowing for Labor Supply Response						
1995	12.46	12.46	12.46	12.46	12.44	12.43	12.40
2002	12.37	12.32	12.27	12.21	12.13	12.04	11.93
2009	11.81	11.68	11.53	11.32	11.11	10.89	10.64
2016	10.36	10.06	9.74	9.39	9.03	8.63	8.24
2023	7.82	7.40	6.96	6.53	6.11	5.69	5.26
2030	4.83	5.86	6.07	5.80	5.53	5.25	4.98
2037	4.72	4.47	4.22	3.96	3.71	3.47	3.22
2044	2.98	2.74	2.51	2.28	2.07	1.87	1.67
2051	1.49	1.33	1.17	1.03	.90	.78	.67
2958	.58	.50	.43	.36	.31	.26	.22
2065	.18	.15	.13	.10	.08	.07	.05

	C. New Personal Income Tax Allowing for Labor Supply Response						
1995	20.10	20.11	20.12	20.13	20.14	20.15	20.16
2002	20.17	20.18	20.18	20.19	20.19	20.19	20.19
2009	20.19	20.18	20.17	20.16	20.14	20.12	20.10
2016	20.07	20.04	20.00	19.97	19.93	19.87	19.81
2023	19.75	19.69	19.63	19.57	19.51	19.45	19.39
2030	19.33	19.46	19.49	19.45	19.42	19.38	19.34
2037	19.31	19.27	19.24	19.21	19.17	19.14	19.11
2044	19.08	19.05	19.02	18.99	18.96	18.93	18.91
2051	18.88	18.86	18.84	18.82	18.80	18.79	18.77
2058	18.76	18.75	18.74	18.73	18.72	18.72	18.71
2065	18.71	18.70	18.70	18.70	18.70	18.69	18.69

	D. Change in Deadweight Loss Owing to Privatization ($billions)						
1995	3.78	4.49	5.22	6.00	6.77	7.50	8.18
2002	8.87	9.39	9.87	10.36	10.64	10.80	10.72
2009	10.60	10.32	9.75	8.37	6.90	5.29	3.36
2016	1.00	−1.63	−4.56	−7.81	−11.46	−16.30	−20.96
2023	−26.07	−31.24	−36.69	−42.04	−47.31	−52.60	−57.90
2030	−63.22	−56.17	−55.84	−59.86	−63.99	−68.30	−71.35
2037	−74.04	−76.53	−79.01	−81.58	−84.04	−86.41	−88.79
2044	−91.12	−93.53	−95.78	−97.96	−100.01	−101.88	−103.77

Table 6.6   (continued)

	D. Change in Deadweight Loss Owing to Privatization ($billions)						
2051	−105.52	−107.00	−108.49	−109.92	−111.31	−112.59	−113.69
2058	−114.63	−115.43	−116.16	−116.82	−117.40	−117.91	−118.37
2065	−118.77	−119.12	−119.42	−119.68	−119.92	−120.13	−120.32

	E. Change in Deadweight Loss as % of Covered Wages						
1995	.13	.15	.17	.19	.21	.23	.25
2002	.27	.28	.29	.29	.30	.30	.29
2009	.28	.27	.25	.21	.17	.13	.08
2016	.02	−.04	−.11	−.18	−.27	−.37	−.47
2023	−.58	−.69	−.80	−.91	−1.01	−1.11	−1.21
2030	−1.30	−1.15	−1.12	−1.19	−1.26	−1.33	−1.37
2037	−1.40	−1.43	−1.46	−1.49	−1.52	−1.54	−1.57
2044	−1.59	−1.61	−1.63	−1.65	−1.67	−1.68	−1.69
2051	−1.70	−1.71	−1.71	−1.72	−1.72	−1.72	−1.72
2058	−1.72	−1.71	−1.70	−1.69	−1.68	−1.67	−1.66
2065	−1.65	−1.63	−1.62	−1.61	−1.59	−1.58	−1.56

[a]Panel D of table 6.5.

tax rate in panel B of table 6.6 is less than the payroll tax rate in panel D of table 6.5). The personal income tax rate in that year is also lower than its no-behavioral-response value.

By year 52, the personal income tax rate is reduced from 20 to 19 percent. The payroll tax rate is also reduced by one-twentieth, from 2.61 to 2.48 percent.

The changes in the rates of payroll tax and income tax cause corresponding changes in the deadweight loss of the tax system. Using the traditional Harberger-Browning approximation for the deadweight loss, the change in the deadweight loss can be written

$$\Delta \text{DWL} = 0.5\varepsilon[t_1^2 - t_0^2](1 - t_0)^{-1}wL,$$

where wL is the current payroll tax base, $t_0 = 1 - N_0$, and $t_1 = 1 - N_1$.

Panel D of table 6.6 shows the annual changes in the deadweight loss that result from the changes in net-of-tax shares. The annual deadweight loss of the tax system initially rises by about $3.8 billion, an amount equivalent to 0.13 percent of covered wages (as shown in panel E of table 6.6). At its maximum, the increased deadweight loss is 0.30 percent of payroll (in years 11 and 12). By year 23 (2017), the shift to an MIRA system is reducing the deadweight. The decline in the overall deadweight loss of the tax system rises rapidly to $53 billion in 2028, $100 billion in 2048, etc. In the final year of the simulations, the reduced deadweight loss is 1.56 percent of covered wages.

Putting the pieces together, the analysis in table 6.5 and 6.6 shows that, in the long run, privatization reduces the burden on employees from a 12.4 percent payroll tax in the current pay-as-you-go system to a mandatory MIRA contribution of 2.04 percent of payroll (panel B of table 6.5)[25] and reduces the deadweight loss of the income and payroll taxes by 1.57 percent of payroll (panel E of table 6.6). The combined gain to individuals is the sum of the reduction in the cash contributions (12.4 percent − 2.04 percent = 10.36 percent of payroll) and the reduction in the deadweight loss of the tax system (1.56 percent of payroll) for a combined gain of 11.92 percent of payroll. The long-run gain is thus equal to almost the entire current tax paid by employers and employees and is achieved without any reduction in the retirement benefits below what could be purchased with the current 12.4 percent payroll tax.

In the earlier years of the transition, the net effect on real disposable income (adjusted for the change in the deadweight loss) is at first negative and then becomes a positive gain. Thus, in the first year, there is (1) no effect on the payroll tax rate,[26] (2) an MIRA surcharge of 0.69 percent, and (3) an increased deadweight loss of 0.13 percent of payroll. The total burden rises by 0.82 percent of payroll to 13.22 percent. By year 15, (1) the payroll tax rate is down to 11.7 percent, a decline of 0.7 percent of payroll, (2) the MIRA surcharge is 2.00 percent of payroll, and (3) the deadweight loss of the tax system is increased by 0.28 percent of payroll. The total burden rises by only 1.58 percent of payroll. But, by year 25, the real disposable income is higher under the MIRA system: the payroll tax is only 9.41 percent, the MIRA surcharge 2.76 percent; the combined 12.17 percent rate implies that the deadweight loss is reduced (a reduction of 0.18 percent of payroll), implying a net burden of 11.99 percent of payroll. After that, the net burden falls rapidly. By year 35, the combination of the payroll tax and the MIRA surcharge is only 7.87 percent of payroll, and the deadweight loss reduction is 1.21 percent of payroll, implying a net burden of 6.66 percent of payroll and therefore a net gain of 5.74 percent of payroll.

Looking at the aggregate gains and losses (i.e., multiplying these percentage of payroll changes by the aggregate payroll) shows that the present value of the changes during the first forty-one years is positive at any real discount rate of 5 percent or less. As the horizon extends beyond forty-one years, the present value of the changes becomes increasingly positive. Even with a very high real discount rate of 7 percent, the present value of the changes is positive for any horizon of fifty-one years or more. The shift to a privatized plan with MIRA accounts using the transition path analyzed in this section thus has a positive aggregate present value for all plausible discount rates and does so even if the horizon is limited to only fifty-one years.

25. The actual long-run MIRA contribution is reduced from 2.04 to 1.94 percent of payroll because the lower marginal tax rates cause an increase in payroll income. The correct way to compare the reduced cash tax burden (i.e., the effect on net income) is, however, to use the payroll tax rate on the initial base.

26. To calculate the change in real disposable income, it is appropriate to use the tax rate that would be applied to the original tax base (12.40 percent) rather than the tax rate that would be applied to the slightly reduced tax base (12.46 percent). Of course, the deadweight loss calculation does use the higher tax rate.

The next section discusses what happens to the individual initial age cohorts during this transition.

6.5.4   The Effects of the Transition on Different Age Cohorts

The transition option that we have been analyzing is more favorable to younger employees (and, of course, to future generations) than to those who are currently in middle age or near retirement. An analysis of the distribution of gains by the current age cohorts is interesting in itself and shows that the gains and losses cannot be redistributed among the initial generation of employees in a way that makes everyone better off. It also shows that the present value of the losses to those in the initial generation of employees who do lose are relatively very small.

To study this, we calculate the lifetime path of the payroll taxes, MIRA surcharges, and deadweight loss changes for a representative individual in each age cohort from age five to age sixty.[27] For each individual, the net gain in each year is the difference between the payroll tax (in constant 1995 dollars) that the individual would pay at the 12.4 percent rate in the current pay-as-you-go system and the sum of the payroll tax, the MIRA surcharge, and the deadweight loss change under the MIRA system.

Table 6.7 shows the resulting paths of net gains for individuals who are twenty-five, forty, and fifty-five years old in 1995, the assumed first year of the program. Note that the twenty-five-year-olds are affected for forty years while the forty- and fifty-five-year-olds are affected for shorter periods until they retire at age sixty-five.

During the first two decades, each of these representative individuals incurs a small loss, exceeding 2 percent of payroll only for the oldest age group. When the current twenty-five-year-olds reach age fifty, they begin to have positive annual benefits.

Table 6.8 summarizes the actuarial present values of these annual effects of privatization on representative individuals in each initial age cohort from five through sixty years old. Estimates are presented for three different real discount rates. The common feature among all these figures is that they are quite small for existing employees (aged twenty through sixty), indicating that the transition generations do not pay a large price for the benefits that will accrue to future generations.

With a real discount rate of 3 percent, the initial cohort of fifty-year-olds incurs lifetime losses with an actuarial present value of $4,680. The lifetime gains to those who are twenty years old when privatization begins are worth

---

27. The representative individual is someone with mean earnings for that age cohort. The issues associated with income distribution and the redistribution of the current social security program to individuals with low lifetime covered earnings are discussed in sec. 6.6.

The changes in the deadweight losses involve the approximating assumption that all the change in the deadweight loss that results from the changes in the marginal tax rates faced by the individual accrues to that individual. While this is true when there is no preexisting tax rate, part of the gain that results from a change in an existing tax rate accrues to the government in the form of additional revenue. Our calculation implicitly assumes that this is returned to the individual.

Table 6.7   Net Gains (% of payroll) from Phase-In Partial Privatization (by cohort)

			Age in 1995 = 25			
1995	−.08	−.18	−.28	−.37	−.47	−1.06	−1.15
2002	−1.25	−1.33	−1.40	−1.47	−1.51	−1.55	−1.55
2009	−1.55	−1.54	−1.50	−1.38	−1.25	−1.11	−.94
2016	−.72	−.48	−.21	.08	.42	.90	1.35
2023	1.85	2.34	2.87	3.38	3.87	4.36	4.86
2030	5.35	4.12	3.83	4.11	4.39	.00	.00

			Age in 1995 = 40			
1995	−.82	−.94	−1.07	−1.19	−1.31	−1.42	−1.53
2002	−1.64	−1.73	−1.81	−1.89	−1.95	−1.99	−2.01
2009	−2.02	−2.02	−1.99	−1.89	−1.77	−1.65	−1.49
2016	−1.29	−1.07	−.82	−.54	.00	.00	.00

			Age in 1995 = 55			
1995	−1.39	−1.53	−1.66	−1.79	−1.92	−2.04	−2.16
2002	−2.27	−2.36	−2.45	−.00	−.00	−.00	−.00

Table 6.8   Actuarial Present Values of Net Gains from Phase-In Partial Privatization

	Thousands of Dollars per Worker			% of Future Wages		
Age (1995)	$r = 3\%$	$r = 5\%$	$r = 8\%$	$r = 3\%$	$r = 5\%$	$r = 8\%$
5	19.24	8.61	2.81	4.52	3.84	2.96
10	14.39	6.55	2.10	3.06	2.41	1.58
15	9.34	4.11	1.08	1.81	1.25	.58
20	4.39	1.44	−.20	.77	.36	−.08
25	.20	−.99	−1.48	.04	−.24	−.51
30	−3.14	−3.11	−2.74	−.59	−.75	−.92
35	−5.40	−4.50	−3.50	−1.12	−1.17	−1.20
40	−6.24	−5.12	−3.93	−1.50	−1.49	−1.45
45	−5.84	−4.91	−3.88	−1.74	−1.70	−1.64
50	−4.68	−4.09	−3.40	−1.86	−1.83	−1.78
55	−3.24	−2.96	−2.62	−1.91	−1.90	−1.87
60	−1.63	−1.57	−1.48	−1.89	−1.88	−1.87

$4,420 in present value. But those who have not yet joined the labor force can look forward to substantially larger gains: $9,380 for fifteen-year-olds and $14,440 for ten-year-olds.

Although different phase-in schedules or age-related payroll taxes could change this pattern, there is no way in which all age cohorts in the labor force at the time of privatization can be made better off. The cumulative present value for all those age twenty to sixty-five at the time of privatization is clearly negative.[28]

The result would, however, look quite different if we took the nuclear family as the unit of observation for our analysis. Consider a couple of which the husband and wife are both aged forty-five with two children aged ten and fifteen. Although the forty-five-year-olds have a combined net present value loss of $11,680 (at a 3 percent discount rate), this is outweighed by the children's gains of more than $23,000. Younger families would tend to be even bigger gainers.

6.5.5   Effect of a Lower Return on MIRA Contributions

Throughout this section, the analysis has assumed that MIRA contributions earn a real return equal to the full 9 percent pretax marginal product of capital. To achieve this, the federal and state governments would have to contribute to each MIRA account an amount estimated to be the corporate taxes collected on the incremental capital represented by that account. In the current analysis, which has ignored fluctuations in stock and bond prices, this would be about 3.6 percent of the assets in each account.

Although a proper accounting of the effects of the MIRA contributions does require attributing the additional corporate tax collections to the MIRA accounts, in practice the government may not be willing to make such a transfer and may use the increased corporate tax revenue to fund other government spending or tax reductions. It is worthwhile therefore to ask what the MIRA contributions would have to be if the real return earned by the MIRA accounts is limited to the 5.4 percent that is net of corporate tax payments (and therefore that could be earned directly by investing in the market mixture of equity and debt).

The long-run effect is to raise the required MIRA contribution from 2.04 percent of payroll to 3.31 percent of payroll, that is, slightly less than in inverse proportion to the decline in the rate of return. Panel B of table 6.9 shows that this same almost exact inverse proportion relation holds for each year in the transition. Thus, even with this much-reduced return, the long-run mandatory contribution is reduced by almost three-fourths of the current 12.4 percent tax rate. Moreover, during the transition, the combination of the payroll tax plus mandatory contribution rises only from the current 12.4 percent to a maximum of 14.8 percent after fourteen years (panel E of table 6.9) and is permanently down below 12.4 percent after twenty-eight years.

We reiterate, however, that this is looking at the pension contributions in

28. It would of course be possible to create what appears to be a Pareto-improving privatization by combining social security privatization with another fundamental reform (e.g., the shift from an income tax to a consumption tax) and distributing the gains from that reform in a way that causes the combination of the two reforms to make everyone better off. Since the tax reform could be done separately, the Pareto improvement cannot properly be attributed to the privatization of social security.

Table 6.9   **Phase-In from Partial to Total Privatization at $\rho = 5.4\%$**

	A. Mandatory Individual Contributions ($billions)						
1995	34.10	38.88	43.85	49.05	54.47	60.05	65.76
2002	71.71	77.67	83.84	90.30	96.70	103.21	109.78
2009	116.57	123.46	130.07	136.09	142.28	148.59	154.89
2016	160.81	166.64	172.45	178.19	183.76	183.56	183.72
2023	183.52	183.38	183.06	182.83	182.85	183.00	183.33
2030	183.80	184.68	186.13	187.38	188.55	189.52	190.38
2037	191.67	193.21	194.76	196.16	197.49	198.93	200.31
2044	201.72	202.97	204.24	205.49	206.86	208.39	209.76
2051	211.15	212.94	214.55	216.11	217.52	218.97	220.59
2058	222.37	224.28	226.28	228.39	230.61	232.93	235.34
2065	237.84	240.41	243.06	245.78	248.58	251.44	254.34

	B. Mandatory Individual Contributions (% of Payroll)						
1995	1.17	1.30	1.44	1.58	1.73	1.87	2.01
2002	2.15	2.29	2.43	2.57	2.71	2.84	2.97
2009	3.11	3.24	3.36	3.47	3.58	3.69	3.80
2016	3.90	3.99	4.08	4.17	4.25	4.20	4.16
2023	4.11	4.06	4.01	3.95	3.91	3.87	3.83
2030	3.79	3.77	3.75	3.73	3.70	3.68	3.65
2037	3.63	3.61	3.60	3.58	3.56	3.55	3.53
2044	3.52	3.50	3.48	3.46	3.45	3.44	3.42
2051	3.41	3.40	3.39	3.38	3.36	3.35	3.34
2058	3.33	3.32	3.31	3.31	3.30	3.30	3.30
2065	3.30	3.30	3.30	3.30	3.30	3.30	3.31

	C. Benefits Replaced Owing to Privatization ($billions)						
1995	.00	.13	.38	.78	1.35	2.18	3.25
2002	4.52	6.22	8.25	10.62	13.57	17.03	21.32
2009	25.93	31.17	37.29	45.26	53.82	63.07	73.44
2016	85.18	97.86	111.70	126.74	143.23	160.99	178.93
2023	198.55	218.93	240.74	262.44	284.59	307.56	331.29
2030	355.89	310.24	303.98	320.95	338.42	356.61	375.26
2037	393.42	411.53	430.08	449.32	468.52	487.90	507.68
2044	527.69	548.06	568.03	587.98	607.72	627.03	646.30
2051	664.97	682.81	700.46	717.66	734.44	750.59	766.05
2058	780.86	795.15	808.95	822.37	835.40	848.07	860.44
2065	872.55	884.37	896.00	907.47	918.83	930.10	941.30

	D. Payroll Tax Needed to Maintain Trust Fund Trajectory (% of Payroll)						
1995	12.40	12.40	12.39	12.37	12.36	12.33	12.30
2002	12.26	12.22	12.16	12.10	12.02	11.93	11.82
2009	11.70	11.58	11.43	11.24	11.03	10.82	10.59
2016	10.32	10.04	9.73	9.41	9.06	8.69	8.32
2023	7.92	7.52	7.09	6.68	6.27	5.85	5.43
2030	5.00	6.02	6.23	5.96	5.70	5.42	5.15
2037	4.89	4.64	4.39	4.13	3.88	3.63	3.37
2044	3.13	2.88	2.64	2.41	2.19	1.98	1.77

Table 6.9 (continued)

	D. Payroll Tax Needed to Maintain Trust Fund Trajectory (% of Payroll)						
2051	1.58	1.41	1.25	1.10	.96	.83	.72
2058	.62	.53	.46	.39	.33	.28	.24
2065	.20	.17	.14	.11	.09	.08	.06

	E. Total Payroll Tax Plus Mandatory Contribution (% of Payroll)						
1995	13.57	13.70	13.83	13.96	14.08	14.20	14.31
2002	14.42	14.50	14.59	14.67	14.72	14.77	14.79
2009	14.81	14.81	14.79	14.71	14.62	14.51	14.38
2016	14.22	14.03	13.82	13.58	13.31	12.89	12.48
2023	12.03	11.57	11.10	10.63	10.18	9.72	9.25
2030	8.79	9.79	9.98	9.69	9.40	9.10	8.80
2037	8.52	8.25	7.99	7.71	7.44	7.17	6.91
2044	6.64	6.38	6.12	5.87	5.63	5.41	5.20
2051	4.99	4.81	4.64	4.47	4.32	4.18	4.06
2058	3.95	3.85	3.77	3.70	3.64	3.58	3.54
2065	3.50	3.47	3.44	3.42	3.40	3.38	3.37

isolation and ignores the favorable effect on revenue elsewhere in the system. A complete accounting requires crediting the additional corporate tax revenue.

6.6 Distributional Considerations: Protecting the Poor

The method of calculating social security benefits in the current unfunded system is designed to provide some redistribution from individuals with high lifetime earnings to those with low lifetime earnings. In practice, this redistribution is attenuated and in some cases reversed because of a variety of ways in which low- and high-income individuals differ. Low-wage workers generally enter the full-time labor force at an earlier age, have higher mortality rates, and are more likely to be in two-earner families. Each of these characteristics reduces the implicit rate of return on the household's social security taxes.[29] In order to prevent poverty in old age, the regular social security program is currently augmented by the means-tested supplemental security income (SSI) program. The SSI program could of course be continued in parallel to a privatized social security system, a subject that we will not pursue further here.[30]

A privatized system of individual funded accounts is explicitly nonredistrib-

29. On the relation between social security net transfers and income distribution, see Hurd and Shoven (1985).

30. The combination in the SSI program of an age test in addition to a means test reduces the problem of the work disincentive associated with means-tested welfare programs for younger workers. The SSI means test still creates incentives to reduce saving during working years. It also encourages low-wage workers to work in the underground economy to avoid social security payroll taxes since any resulting increase in social security benefits would be fully offset by lower SSI payments.

utive. Each individual receives income after age sixty-five on the basis of that individual's MIRA contributions. It is worth stressing, however, that the MIRA system would make low-income workers much better off after the transition than they would be with the current unfunded system. The reason for this is that, instead of a payroll tax of 12.4 percent, they would pay an MIRA contribution of only about 2 percent of payroll. They would receive the benefit of a tax cut equal to 10 percent of income.

A modification of the basic MIRA system might permit individuals with below-average earnings to make voluntary contributions, perhaps limited by the level that would provide the same benefits that they would have received under the existing social security system. A lower-income individual who earns the equivalent of a 4 percent rate of return under the unfunded system (because of its redistributive features) could make MIRA contributions that achieved that level of benefits and still enjoy a substantial net tax reduction.[31]

Although we do not pursue this possibility, we do want to address the question of how the system of individual accounts could be modified in a simple way so that no individual is left with an unacceptably low annuity. For this purpose, we define *unacceptably low* to mean less than half the average annuity. The calculations that we report in this section show that a very small tax transfer at retirement would be sufficient to provide all retirees with at least this level of retirement annuity.[32]

Since the size of each individual's accumulated MIRA funds at age sixty-five depends on the entire annual pattern of earnings from age thirty to age sixty-five, the frequency and extent to which the MIRA accounts at age sixty-five fall below half the mean account cannot be inferred from single cross sections of earnings. We therefore use the Social Security New Beneficiaries Survey, a unique data set that provides the necessary lifetime earnings histories. More specifically, the data are a sample of all persons who began receiving social security retirement benefits between June 1980 and May 1981. For each person in the sample, social security earnings histories are available beginning with 1951. Since most people in the sample were between thirty-two and thirty-six in 1951 (88 percent of the sample were born between 1915 and 1919), we assumed that the real earnings between age thirty and the age in 1951 were the same as the actual earnings in 1951. All nominal dollar amounts are restated to 1996 dollars using the CPI. Since the rate of MIRA contributions varies over time during the transition, we calculate the long-run value of the annual MIRA contributions as shown in panel D of table 6.5, that is, 2.04

---

31. Workers born in 1945 who have a dependent spouse and who earn half the median income would receive an actuarial return of about 3.5 percent on the taxes that they and their employer pay.

32. We are grateful to Jeffrey Liebman for making the calculations that we report in this section. The current analysis does not deal with differences in rates of return that different individuals in the same age cohort would earn on their savings. To the extent that this reflects voluntary decisions to hold different types of portfolios because of differences in risk preferences, it may not be appropriate to compensate individuals with low outcomes (other than through the means-tested SSI program). We return to the subject of return uncertainty in the next section.

percent of the amount of earnings up to the annual social security maximum covered earnings.

Among men who retired in 1980–81, MIRA contributions of 2.04 percent of their earnings from age thirty would have accumulated (at a 9 percent real rate of return) to a mean value of $82,985 in 1981 at the 1996 price level.[33] Approximately 19 percent of such accumulated MIRA accounts had less than half this amount. The average shortfall among these accounts, that is, the amount that must be added to these accounts to bring them up to half the mean account, was $3,889.[34] The aggregate amount of this shortfall is thus equivalent to only 4.7 percent of the total of all MIRA accounts at age sixty-five. This implies that increasing each MIRA contribution by 4.7 percent, that is, from the 2.04 percent of covered earnings reported as the long-run value in panel E of table 6.5 to 2.14 percent of covered earnings, and then levying a "tax" of 4.7 percent on all accounts at age sixty-five would provide the funds to preclude any account from having less than half the mean account while keeping the mean net-of-tax annuity equal to the level of social security benefits projected in current law (with the solvency correction described above).[35]

This calculation of an additional 0.10 percent of payroll MIRA contribution and the associated tax on the accumulated accounts assumes that levying the tax and providing the transfer would not alter individuals' incentives to earn. Even if this had to be adjusted because of incentive effects, the implication is clear that "unacceptably low" accumulations can be avoided with a relatively small tax and transfer. The distributional issue, judged in this way, need not be an impediment to privatized individual MIRA accounts.

6.7   Risks: Uncertain Returns and Imperfect Annuity Markets

Until now we have ignored the problem that funded MIRA accounts involve risky investments. Of course, the current unfunded pay-as-you-go system is also risky, although in a very different way. Despite the reforms of 1983, it is clear that the existing system cannot pay the "promised" benefits. Many

33. To put this number in perspective, note that, with a 9 percent real return, such an accumulated amount would produce an annuity of about $9,950 a year. For comparison, the average annual social security benefit in 1980 (in 1996 dollars) of a retired worker was $7,795, that of a retired worker and wife $12,928.

34. There are two reasons why this overstates the cost of assuring that everyone has a fund equal to at least half the mean fund. First, many of the low social security individuals would now be eligible for SSI benefits, which would help defray the cost of increasing the fund. Second, many of those with low social security earnings are individuals who had spent most of their careers in the federal government or in state governments that provide pensions and remain outside the social security system.

35. This calculation is based on the earnings of men only, even in two-earner couples. Applying the same method of accumulation to the earnings of husbands and wives in a pooled account leads to similar conclusions. The mean accumulated MIRA account based on 2.04 percent of husbands' and wives' earnings was $104,511 in 1986 dollars. Only 19.2 percent of MIRA accounts had less than half this total, with a mean shortfall of $4,204, corresponding to a 4.2 percent tax on accumulated accounts.

younger persons say that they believe that social security benefits will not be there when they retire. Legislative proposals involve reducing all benefits, taxing the benefits of higher-income recipients, and other changes that would reduce the real value of the benefits for some individuals very substantially. This section focuses on the risks of the funded MIRA accounts and asks how individuals could be protected from such risks.

Although the real pretax return on the nonfinancial corporate capital stock has averaged somewhat more than 9 percent since 1960, there are substantial year-to-year fluctuations in the return earned by portfolio investors. If MIRA contributions are based on the expected 9 percent return (as in the calculations of sec. 6.5 above), an individual who is fortunate enough to save and contribute to an MIRA account during years when the stock and bond markets are relatively low and to retire and dissave when those markets are relatively high will enjoy a level of benefits greater than those provided by the pay-as-you-go social security system (as well as having paid a much lower cost of financing that benefit). Conversely, an individual who retires when the level of stock prices is relatively low will receive annuity payments that are less than those provided by the pay-as-you-go system if the MIRA contributions are based on an assumed 9 percent return.

The lifetime return in an MIRA account that is invested in the market's debt-equity mixture is almost certain to exceed the return in the pay-as-you-go unfunded social security system.[36] Nevertheless, the existing variability of returns does mean that an individual who contributes on the basis of an expected 9 percent return could have very much lower retirement income if the ex post return is substantially lower.

This market fluctuation risk is compounded by the inability to purchase actuarially fair variable annuities based on the return earned by the market's debt-equity mixture. Without such an annuity, individuals must save enough to finance more than the total benefits that they expect to receive or must accept the risk of a much-reduced level of consumption if they live longer than the normal life expectancy. Although the life expectancy for men at age sixty-five is now nearly sixteen years, 33 percent of sixty-five-year-old men live more than an additional twenty years, and 5 percent live more than thirty years.

Although the introduction of a universal system of MIRA accounts might lead to market innovations that ameliorate the market risk (e.g., the availability of long-term put options) and the annuity risk (e.g., the availability of actuarially fair variable annuities), we have explored how the MIRA program might

---

36. This is similar to MaCurdy and Shoven's (1992) conclusion that individuals who invested in equities are almost certain to receive a higher rate of return than those who invested in bonds or money market instruments. They show that lifetime equity returns have been better than debt return for individuals who began their life-cycle saving in every year for more than three quarters of a century. MacCurdy and Shoven's analysis takes the amount of saving as given and shows that the equity returns have dominated in the past. That is, of course, separate from the question of how much an individual should save.

be adjusted in the current institutional context in which such products are not available. Our approach does not seek an optimal adjustment of the MIRA program to the risks that we have identified. Instead, we have imposed a very demanding requirement on the MIRA accounts by asking the following question:

> In the absence of any annuity, and given the historic market uncertainty of returns on debt and equity, how much would individuals have to contribute to MIRA accounts to be able to receive the baseline level of social security benefits with probability 0.95 even if they might live to age one hundred?

Individuals who will receive some pay-as-you-go social security benefits during the transition are partially protected from these risks. In the long run, however, individuals will be wholly dependent on MIRA accounts for their retirement income.[37] We believe that the right strategy for individuals in this situation would be to "oversave," that is, to contribute more to their MIRA accounts than would be necessary to fund the target level of benefits if they knew that they would obtain a 9 percent rate of return with certainty. We have done some preliminary calculations that suggest that the contributions required achieve a probability of 95 percent of obtaining retirement income equal to the social security benefits would be very much less than the pay-as-you-go rate.[38]

Raising the average MIRA contributions in this way implies that individuals will generally die with substantial balances in their MIRA accounts. These extra MIRA contributions are returned to the next generation as either private bequests or tax revenues (if bequests from the MIRA accounts are not permitted and are taxed at death). In exchange for the resulting bequests, the subsequent generation might agree to reinsure the individuals against the "5 percent" risk that the combination of poor average stock and bond market performance for their age cohort and above-average longevity of the individual causes funds to be exhausted. This might be formalized by a government reinsurance arrangement. Such possibilities will not be explored further here.

In future work we will present simulations of the time path of the MIRA asset for someone who starts contributing to the MIRA at age thirty, works until age sixty-five, and then dissaves the social security baseline benefits from age sixty-five until death. We repeat the simulation one thousand times and note the fraction of times that the individual still has positive MIRA assets at death. We will identify that rate of MIRA calculations that implies that 95 percent of individuals die with positive assets.

In concluding this discussion of risk, we reiterate that this calculation is not

---

37. Individuals could of course continue to have private pensions, voluntary IRAs, and voluntary 401(k) accounts. By being *wholly dependent* on the MIRA account, we mean only that they will not receive any unfunded social security benefits.

38. Some calculations presented at the conference and in NBER Working Paper no. 5761, on which this chapter is based, contained an error that caused the required contributions to be understated. Subsequent work indicates that the correct calculation will still imply contributions that are still very much less than the pay-as-you-go tax rates.

presented as an optimal response to the market risk and annuity risk; rather, it is intended to provide a framework for calculating the contribution rate necessary to maintain the full baseline benefits and to show that this can be achieved with a relatively small increase in the MIRA contributions, one that still leaves the MIRA contributions less than the existing payroll tax.[39]

6.8   An Alternative Baseline for Social Security: Modifying the Inflation Indexing

For the simulation in sections 6.5–6.7, the benefits correspond to the formula in the existing social security law until the trust fund is exhausted in 2030 and then drop sharply to the level of benefits that can be financed with the 12.4 percent payroll tax. This sharp drop in benefits in the year 2030 is the simplest case to analyze, but it is not the most realistic. A more plausible assumption is that, whether or not social security is privatized, the growth of benefits will be reduced gradually by reducing the annual inflation indexing of benefits.[40]

Reducing the annual indexing of benefits by 1 percentage point causes the aggregate level of social security benefits to decline eventually by about 9 percent. The decline does not continue beyond this level because the modification of indexing only affects postretirement benefits, not the level of benefits of new retirees.

The effect of this temporarily lower rate of growth of social security benefits depends on how the resulting funds are used. We assume that the path of the trust fund is kept unchanged and therefore that the payroll tax is reduced. This makes the transition to the MIRA system more attractive to the initial generation of employees as well as reducing the relative magnitude of the benefit reduction in 2030 when the trust fund is exhausted.

Panel A of table 6.10 shows the percentage reduction in benefits that results from the 1 percentage point adjustment to the indexing. At the end of seven years, aggregate benefits are 4.64 percent lower, and, at the end of twenty-one years, they are 7.97 percent lower. After 2030, the benefit reduction is the same relative to existing law as we showed in table 6.4.[41]

Table 6.11 presents our standard analysis of the time path of payroll taxes and MIRA surcharges for the policy of adjusting retiree benefits by 1 percent less than the increase in the consumer price index. Since future benefits (before 2030) will be lower than they would be with full CPI indexing, the required

---

39. One plausible modification would reduce benefits in any year in which the accumulated assets are less than some threshold fraction (e.g., 70 percent) of the predicted MIRA account value for that year.

40. The Senate Finance Committee has appointed an expert committee to consider how the indexing of social security benefits should be modified to be consistent with the true increase in the cost of living (see Boskin et al. 1996). For an earlier advocacy of such an inflation adjustment, see Feldstein and Feldstein (1984).

41. We discontinue the indexing adjustment after the benefit reduction in 2030.

Table 6.10   **Partial Indexation: Trust Fund and Solvency Adjustment**

A. Reduction in Benefits Owing to Partial Indexation and Solvency Adjustment (%)

1995	.00	.93	1.79	2.60	3.35	4.02	4.64
2002	5.23	5.72	6.17	6.57	6.91	7.20	7.40
2009	7.61	7.78	7.93	7.92	7.94	7.97	7.97
2016	7.97	7.99	8.00	8.01	8.01	8.00	8.05
2023	8.08	8.13	8.18	8.23	8.31	8.41	8.51
2030	8.62	18.09	24.12	24.22	24.34	24.46	24.24
2037	23.99	23.74	23.50	23.30	23.18	23.10	23.08
2044	23.11	23.21	23.45	23.74	24.06	24.40	24.80
2051	25.40	25.97	26.59	27.25	27.94	28.64	29.32
2058	29.98	30.63	31.29	31.82	32.32	32.77	33.18
2065	33.56	33.88	34.17	34.43	34.67	34.89	35.08

B. Retirement Benefits under Partial Indexation and Solvency Adjustment ($billions)

1995	324.72	328.37	331.96	335.80	339.86	344.38	349.46
2002	354.62	360.42	366.48	372.70	381.08	389.75	399.07
2009	408.17	417.45	429.85	443.82	457.78	471.76	486.14
2016	502.64	519.41	536.21	553.01	569.96	586.60	602.57
2023	618.79	634.72	650.75	663.78	676.68	689.63	702.59
2030	715.62	650.54	610.86	618.42	626.08	633.82	641.62
2037	649.51	657.49	665.57	673.74	681.55	689.46	697.45
2044	705.53	713.70	721.63	729.64	737.74	745.93	754.21
2051	762.37	770.62	778.96	787.39	795.91	804.53	813.25
2058	822.06	830.96	839.96	849.13	858.40	867.76	877.23
2065	886.80	896.41	906.12	915.93	925.85	935.88	946.02

MIRA contributions and required payroll tax are smaller than they would otherwise be. Since this affects only the transition before 2030, in the very long run the tax and MIRA contributions are essentially unchanged from the case of full indexing. Table 6.12 shows the analogous calculations of the resulting shift in labor supply and the change in the deadweight loss of the payroll tax.

Perhaps most interesting are the disaggregated analyses for representative individuals that are presented in tables 6.13 and 6.14. With this CPI-minus-one adjustment of benefits, the actuarial present value of the change in real disposable income is positive for all current individuals who are younger than thirty years of age. The present value losses for those who are older are substantially less than they are with no benefit adjustment before 2030.[42] The maximum loss occurs for forty-five-year-olds, and, at a 3 percent real discount rate, the loss for a couple is $6,560. If the couple has two children aged ten and fifteen, the net gain for the nuclear family would be more than $25,000.

42. Of course, these individuals will receive lower benefits at retirement than under current law. But that is common to the pay-as-you-go and privatized systems if the CPI adjustment will be adopted in either case.

Table 6.11   **Phase-In Partial Privatization (Partial Indexation)**

	A. Mandatory Individual Contributions ($billions)						
1995	19.01	21.76	24.69	27.82	31.14	34.58	38.16
2002	42.02	45.92	50.03	54.41	58.81	63.37	67.93
2009	72.76	77.72	82.59	86.83	91.26	95.84	100.34
2016	104.57	108.77	112.87	116.81	120.44	120.11	120.17
2023	119.75	119.37	118.68	117.98	117.50	117.13	116.90
2030	116.82	117.11	118.10	118.88	119.58	120.03	120.34
2037	121.17	122.29	123.42	124.33	125.21	126.20	127.08
2044	127.96	128.60	129.28	129.89	130.58	131.44	132.06
2051	132.69	133.78	134.61	135.35	135.87	136.38	137.07
2058	137.91	138.89	139.94	141.10	142.35	143.70	145.14
2065	146.67	148.27	149.94	151.68	153.49	155.35	157.25

	B. Mandatory Individual Contributions (% of Payroll)						
1995	.65	.73	.81	.90	.99	1.08	1.17
2002	1.26	1.35	1.45	1.55	1.65	1.74	1.84
2009	1.94	2.04	2.14	2.22	2.30	2.38	2.46
2016	2.53	2.60	2.67	2.73	2.79	2.75	2.72
2023	2.68	2.64	2.60	2.55	2.51	2.47	2.44
2030	2.41	2.39	2.38	2.36	2.35	2.33	2.31
2037	2.29	2.29	2.28	2.27	2.26	2.25	2.24
2051	2.14	2.14	2.13	2.11	2.10	2.09	2.07
2058	2.06	2.06	2.05	2.04	2.04	2.04	2.04
2065	2.03	2.03	2.04	2.04	2.04	2.04	2.04

	C. Benefits Replaced Owing to Privatization ($billions)						
1995	.00	.13	.38	.78	1.34	2.16	3.20
2002	4.44	6.10	8.08	10.37	13.21	16.55	20.70
2009	25.12	30.15	35.99	43.66	51.86	60.68	70.56
2016	81.72	93.74	106.84	121.06	136.64	153.40	170.19
2023	188.59	207.61	227.96	248.15	268.62	289.78	311.54
2030	334.04	310.24	303.98	320.95	338.42	356.61	375.26
2037	393.42	411.53	430.08	449.32	468.52	487.90	507.68
2044	527.69	548.06	568.03	587.98	607.72	627.03	646.30
2051	664.97	682.81	700.46	717.66	734.44	750.59	766.05
2058	780.86	795.15	808.95	822.37	835.40	848.07	860.44
2065	872.55	884.37	896.00	907.47	918.83	930.10	941.30

	D. Payroll Tax Needed to Maintain Trust Fund Trajectory (% of Payroll)						
1995	12.40	12.29	12.19	12.09	11.98	11.88	11.78
2002	11.68	11.57	11.47	11.36	11.24	11.11	10.97
2009	10.83	10.68	10.50	10.30	10.09	9.87	9.63
2016	9.35	9.06	8.75	8.42	8.07	7.70	7.32
2023	6.93	6.53	6.10	5.70	5.30	4.89	4.48
2030	4.06	6.02	6.23	5.96	5.70	5.42	5.15
2037	4.89	4.64	4.39	4.13	3.88	3.63	3.37
2044	3.13	2.88	2.64	2.41	2.19	1.98	1.77
2051	1.58	1.41	1.25	1.10	.96	.83	.72

Table 6.11   (continued)

	D. Payroll Tax Needed to Maintain Trust Fund Trajectory (% of Payroll)						
2058	.62	.53	.46	.39	.33	.28	.24
2065	.20	.17	.14	.11	.09	.08	.06

	E. Total Payroll Tax Plus Mandatory Contribution (% of Payroll)						
1995	13.05	13.02	13.00	12.98	12.97	12.96	12.95
2002	12.94	12.93	12.92	12.90	12.88	12.85	12.81
2009	12.77	12.72	12.64	12.52	12.39	12.25	12.08
2016	11.88	11.66	11.42	11.15	10.85	10.44	10.04
2023	9.61	9.17	8.70	8.26	7.81	7.37	6.92
2030	6.47	8.41	8.61	8.33	8.05	7.75	7.45
2037	7.18	6.93	6.67	6.40	6.14	5.88	5.62
2044	5.36	5.09	4.84	4.60	4.36	4.14	3.93
2051	3.73	3.55	3.38	3.21	3.06	2.92	2.79
2058	2.69	2.59	2.51	2.43	2.37	2.32	2.27
2065	2.23	2.20	2.17	2.15	2.13	2.12	2.11

6.9   Maintaining Current Law Benefits

Our final analysis deals with the possibility of maintaining the level of bene-fits specified by current law. The future insolvency of the existing social secu-rity system will force a reduction in benefits unless taxes are raised dramati-cally or a much higher return is earned on individual contributions. Unlike the previous sections of this paper, we now explore the role of the MIRA system if the level of benefits implied by current law is to be maintained.

Tables 6.3 and 6.4 showed that, with the current pay-as-you-go system, the trust fund is projected to be exhausted in 2030 (panel B of table 6.3) and that benefits must be reduced by 24 percent in 2032 if they are to be financed by the revenue produced by a 12.4 percent tax. The benefit reduction consistent with a 12.4 percent tax rises to 35 percent by the last year of the projections (2071). These numbers imply that maintaining the level of benefits implied by current law would require raising the tax by 31 percent in 2032 (from 12.4 to 16.3 percent) and then continuing to raise the tax rate, reaching 19.1 percent in 2071.[43]

The MIRA system would permit benefits to be maintained at the level pro-vided by current law with a long-run MIRA contribution rate of only 3.15 percent (instead of the 2.04 percent required to finance the level of benefits that would result from maintaining the 12.4 percent payroll tax). Thus, the MIRA contributions rise in approximately the same proportion as the payroll

43. This calculation ignores the effect of the higher tax rate on labor supply and taxable income. Because the shift from a 12.4 to a 19.1 percent tax rate would reduce taxable income, a higher rate would be necessary to offset the resulting reduction in payroll and income tax revenue.

Table 6.12   **Effect of Phase-In Partial Privatization on Tax Base and DWL Partial Indexation and Solvency Adjustment**

A. Payroll Tax Needed to Maintain Trust Fund with No Behavioral Response[a]

1995	12.40	12.29	12.19	12.09	11.98	11.88	11.78
2002	11.68	11.57	11.47	11.36	11.24	11.11	10.97
2009	10.83	10.68	10.50	10.30	10.09	9.87	9.63
2016	9.35	9.06	8.75	8.42	8.07	7.70	7.32
2023	6.93	6.53	6.10	5.70	5.30	4.89	4.48
2030	4.06	6.02	6.23	5.96	5.70	5.42	5.15
2037	4.89	4.64	4.39	4.13	3.88	3.63	3.37
2044	3.13	2.88	2.64	2.41	2.19	1.98	1.77
2051	1.58	1.41	1.25	1.10	.96	.83	.72
2058	.62	.53	.46	.39	.33	.28	.24
2065	.20	.17	.14	.11	.09	.08	.06

B. New Payroll Tax Rate Allowing for Labor Supply Response

1995	12.46	12.35	12.24	12.14	12.03	11.93	11.83
2002	11.72	11.62	11.51	11.40	11.27	11.14	11.00
2009	10.86	10.70	10.52	10.31	10.09	9.86	9.60
2016	9.32	9.01	8.69	8.34	7.98	7.59	7.21
2023	6.80	6.38	5.95	5.54	5.14	4.73	4.31
2030	3.89	5.86	6.07	5.80	5.53	5.25	4.98
2037	4.72	4.47	4.22	3.96	3.71	3.47	3.22
2044	2.98	2.74	2.51	2.28	2.07	1.87	1.67
2051	1.49	1.33	1.17	1.03	.90	.78	.67
2058	.58	.50	.43	.36	.31	.26	.22
2065	.18	.15	.13	.10	.08	.07	.05

C. New Personal Income Tax Allowing for Labor Supply Response

1995	20.09	20.09	20.08	20.08	20.08	20.08	20.08
2002	20.08	20.07	20.07	20.07	20.07	20.06	20.06
2009	20.05	20.04	20.03	20.02	20.00	19.98	19.96
2016	19.93	19.90	19.86	19.83	19.79	19.73	19.68
2023	19.62	19.56	19.50	19.44	19.39	19.33	19.27
2030	19.22	19.46	19.49	19.45	19.42	19.38	19.34
2037	19.31	19.27	19.24	19.21	19.17	19.14	19.11
2044	19.08	19.05	19.02	18.99	18.96	18.93	18.91
2051	18.88	18.86	18.84	18.82	18.80	18.79	18.77
2058	18.76	18.75	18.74	18.73	18.72	18.72	18.71
2065	18.71	18.70	18.70	18.70	18.70	18.69	18.69

D. Change in Deadweight Loss Owing to Privatization ($billions)

1995	3.46	3.35	3.28	3.27	3.29	3.30	3.29
2002	3.31	3.22	3.13	3.08	2.86	2.55	2.11
2009	1.64	1.05	.15	−1.33	−2.91	−4.62	−6.60
2016	−8.99	−11.64	−14.55	−17.73	−21.27	−25.89	−30.39
2023	−35.29	−40.25	−45.46	−50.53	−55.55	−60.59	−65.64
2030	−70.71	−56.17	−55.84	−59.86	−63.99	−63.30	−71.35
2037	−74.04	−76.53	−79.01	−81.58	−84.04	−86.41	−88.79
2044	−91.12	−93.53	−95.78	−97.96	−100.01	−101.88	−103.77

Table 6.12   (continued)

	D. Change in Deadweight Loss Owing to Privatization ($billions)						
2051	−105.52	−107.00	−108.49	−109.92	−111.31	−112.59	−113.69
2058	−114.63	−115.43	−116.16	−116.82	−117.40	−117.91	−118.37
2065	−118.77	−119.12	−119.42	−119.68	−119.92	−120.13	−120.32

	E. Change in Deadweight Loss as % of Covered Wages						
1995	.12	.11	.11	.11	.10	.10	.10
2002	.10	.09	.09	.09	.08	.07	.06
2009	.04	.03	.00	−.03	−.07	−.11	−.16
2016	−.22	−.28	−.34	−.42	−.49	−.59	−.69
2023	−.79	−.89	−.99	−1.09	−1.19	−1.28	−1.37
2030	−1.46	−1.15	−1.12	−1.19	−1.26	−1.33	−1.37
2037	−1.40	−1.43	−1.46	−1.49	−1.52	−1.54	−1.57
2044	−1.59	−1.61	−1.63	−1.65	−1.67	−1.68	−1.69
2051	−1.70	−1.71	−1.71	−1.72	−1.72	−1.72	−1.72
2058	−1.72	−1.71	−1.70	−1.69	−1.68	−1.67	−1.66
2065	−1.65	−1.63	−1.62	−1.61	−1.59	−1.58	−1.56

[a]Panel D of table 6.11.

Table 6.13   **Net Gains (% of payroll) from Phase-In Partial Privatization (by cohort) Partial Indexation and Solvency Adjustment**

	Age in 1995 = 25						
1995	−.02	.01	.04	.06	.08	−.42	−.42
2002	−.43	−.44	−.44	−.45	−.44	−.43	−.40
2009	−.37	−.33	−.26	−.14	−.00	.14	.32
2016	.53	.77	1.04	1.33	1.66	2.12	2.57
2023	3.05	3.54	4.05	4.54	5.02	5.49	5.97
2030	6.44	4.12	3.83	4.11	4.39	.00	.00

	Age in 1995 = 40						
1995	−.76	−.76	−.76	−.76	−.77	−.79	−.81
2002	−.83	−.84	−.86	−.88	−.89	−.89	−.87
2009	−.86	−.83	−.77	−.66	−.54	−.41	−.26
2016	−.06	.16	.41	.69	.00	.00	.00

	Age in 1995 = 55						
1995	−1.34	−1.34	−1.35	−1.37	−1.39	−1.42	−1.44
2002	−1.47	−1.50	−1.52	−.00	−.00	−.00	−.00

tax would have to rise (from 12.4 to 19.1 percent), but the level is dramatically lower.

Table 6.15 presents our usual analysis of the transition path. The analysis assumes that benefits are maintained at the levels implied by current law after the trust fund is exhausted. Thus, instead of cutting the benefits at that time to

Table 6.14   **Actuarial Present Value of Net Gains from Phase-In Partial Privatization Partial Indexation and Solvency Adjustment**

Age (1995)	Thousands of Dollars per Worker			% of Future Wages		
	$r = 3\%$	$r = 5\%$	$r = 8\%$	$r = 3\%$	$r = 5\%$	$r = 8\%$
5	22.06	10.36	3.69	5.18	4.62	3.89
10	18.20	9.03	3.46	3.88	3.32	2.61
15	14.02	7.30	2.97	2.71	2.21	1.60
20	9.61	5.12	2.11	1.68	1.28	.81
25	5.50	2.80	.95	.97	.67	.33
30	1.95	.60	−.30	.37	.15	−.10
35	−1.04	−1.21	−1.24	−.22	−.31	−.43
40	−2.75	−2.38	−1.96	−.66	−.69	−.72
45	−3.28	2.81	−2.30	−.98	−.98	−.97
50	−3.02	−2.67	−2.26	−1.20	−1.19	−1.18
55	−2.38	−2.20	−1.96	−1.41	−1.40	−1.40
60	−1.38	−1.33	−1.27	−1.60	−1.60	−1.60

the level that can be financed with the 12.4 percent payroll tax, the tax rate is raised to keep the trust fund at zero. In table 6.5, the payroll tax rate rises from 5.00 percent in 2030 (when the trust fund was exhausted), to 6.02 percent in the next year, and 6.23 percent in 2032, before resuming its gradual decline. In contrast, in table 6.15, the payroll tax rate rises from 5.00 percent in 2030, to 7.57 percent in 2031, and 8.21 percent in 2032, before resuming a gradual decline. Panel E of table 6.15 shows that the maximum combined amount of payroll tax and MIRA contribution rises from 8.30 percent in 2030 to 11.50 percent in 2032 and then declines. Thus, maintaining the original level of benefits after the trust fund is exhausted does not require a tax rate that is as high as the current 12.4 percent, which would not be capable of financing the existing benefit formula in a pay-as-you-go system. Note also that, in the earlier years, there is little difference in the combined payroll tax and MIRA contribution. For example, in 2005, the combined payment is 13.87 percent versus the 13.71 percent in the baseline case. That is not surprising since, in these early years, most employees need make little provision for the benefits to be received after 2030.

6.10   Summary and Questions for Future Research

The analysis in this paper has convinced us that the transition to a fully privatized system of individual retirement accounts can be conducted in a way that conveys a very substantial long-run benefit and that has relatively modest transition costs. The longer-term benefits would exceed 5 percent of GDP every year. Younger employees at the time of the transition would be net gainers in their own working lives. The net extra costs incurred by older employees during the transition would be very small and would generally be more than

Table 6.15   **Phase-In from Partial to Total Privatization with Current Law Benefits**

	A. Mandatory Individual Contributions ($billions)						
1995	21.09	24.19	27.52	31.09	34.91	38.88	43.05
2002	47.55	52.14	57.01	62.24	67.55	73.09	78.73
2009	84.74	90.97	97.18	102.82	108.77	115.00	121.26
2016	127.32	133.46	139.63	145.75	151.66	152.71	154.18
2023	155.13	156.10	156.69	157.20	157.91	158.63	159.41
2030	160.20	161.29	163.28	165.02	166.68	168.00	169.30
2037	171.25	173.61	176.00	178.13	180.24	182.49	184.61
2044	186.72	188.51	190.33	192.04	193.85	195.87	197.53
2051	199.16	201.40	203.24	204.91	206.23	207.48	208.95
2058	210.62	212.44	214.34	216.37	218.52	220.78	223.15
2065	225.63	228.19	230.85	233.59	236.41	239.30	242.23

	B. Mandatory Individual Contributions (% of Payroll)						
1995	.72	.81	.91	1.00	1.11	1.21	1.32
2002	1.43	1.54	1.65	1.77	1.89	2.01	2.13
2009	2.26	2.39	2.51	2.62	2.74	2.86	2.97
2016	3.08	3.20	3.31	3.41	3.51	3.49	3.49
2023	3.47	3.45	3.43	3.40	3.38	3.35	3.33
2030	3.31	3.29	3.29	3.28	3.28	3.26	3.25
2037	3.24	3.25	3.25	3.25	3.25	3.26	3.26
2044	3.26	3.25	3.24	3.24	3.23	3.23	3.22
2051	3.21	3.22	3.21	3.20	3.19	3.17	3.16
2058	3.15	3.14	3.14	3.13	3.13	3.13	3.13
2065	3.13	3.13	3.13	3.14	3.14	3.15	3.15

	C. Benefits Replaced Owing to Privatization ($billions)						
1995	.00	.13	.38	.78	1.35	2.28	3.25
2002	4.52	6.22	8.25	10.62	13.57	17.03	21.32
2009	25.93	31.17	37.29	45.26	53.82	63.07	73.44
2016	85.18	97.86	111.70	126.74	143.23	160.99	178.93
2023	198.55	218.93	240.74	262.44	284.59	307.56	331.29
2030	355.89	378.74	400.58	423.54	447.27	472.11	495.30
2037	517.57	539.62	562.21	585.79	609.89	634.48	660.04
2044	686.31	713.69	742.02	770.99	800.25	829.43	859.48
2051	891.33	922.29	954.19	986.44	1,019.23	1,051.81	1,083.78
2058	1,115.19	1,146.31	1,177.25	1,206.22	1,234.25	1,261.40	1,287.75
2065	1,313.36	1,337.57	1,361.13	1,384.04	1,406.46	1,428.41	1,449.99

	D. Payroll Tax Needed to Maintain Trust Fund Trajectory (% of Payroll)						
1995	12.40	12.40	12.39	12.37	12.36	12.33	12.30
2002	12.26	12.22	12.16	12.10	12.02	11.93	11.82
2009	11.70	11.58	11.43	11.24	11.03	10.82	10.59
2016	10.32	10.04	9.73	9.41	9.06	8.69	8.32
2023	7.92	7.52	7.09	6.68	6.27	5.85	5.43
2030	5.00	7.57	8.21	7.87	7.53	7.18	6.79
2037	6.43	6.08	5.74	5.38	5.05	4.71	4.39

(*continued*)

Table 6.15 (continued)

	D. Payroll Tax Needed to Maintain Trust Fund Trajectory (% of Payroll)						
2044	4.07	3.75	3.45	3.16	2.88	2.61	2.36
2051	2.12	1.91	1.70	1.51	1.33	1.16	1.02
2058	.89	.77	.67	.57	.49	.42	.36
2065	.30	.25	.21	.17	.14	.12	.10
	E. Total Payroll Tax Plus Mandatory Contribution (% of Payroll)						
1995	13.12	13.21	13.29	13.38	13.46	13.54	13.61
2002	13.69	13.75	13.81	13.87	13.91	13.94	13.95
2009	13.96	13.96	13.94	13.86	13.77	13.68	13.56
2016	13.40	13.23	13.04	12.82	12.57	12.18	11.81
2023	11.39	10.97	10.52	10.08	9.64	9.20	8.76
2030	8.30	10.86	11.50	11.15	10.80	10.44	10.04
2037	9.68	9.33	8.99	8.64	8.30	7.97	7.64
2044	7.32	7.00	6.69	6.39	6.11	5.84	5.58
2051	5.34	5.12	4.91	4.71	4.52	4.34	4.18
2058	4.04	3.92	3.81	3.71	3.62	3.55	3.48
2065	3.43	3.38	3.34	3.31	3.29	3.26	3.25

offset by the positive net benefits that their own children would receive. For the first fifty years of the transition taken as a whole, the present value of net gains would be positive for any reasonable rate of interest.

Our research has suggested a variety of issues that deserve further attention. One important issue is the ability to protect individuals from the risk of market volatility. Another significant issue is the treatment of couples, including the special problems caused by divorce and remarriage. In principle, this should be easier to deal with in a system of individual accounts, but this deserves detailed analysis.

The role of survivor benefits and disability benefits should also be considered more explicitly. How can these be provided in a way that captures the potential real return on the market mix of equity and debt? How would permitting bequests affect the economics of the program?

Although our calculations indicate that a small tax-based redistribution of MIRA assets at age sixty-five can prevent poverty in old age, it would be good to examine this and other distributional issues in more detail.

The potential long-run gain from privatizing social security implies that further research on these issues deserves a very high priority.

References

Advisory Council on Social Security. 1997. *Quadrennial report.* Washington, D.C.: U.S. Government Printing Office.

Auerbach, Alan, and Laurence Kotlikoff. 1987. *Dynamic fiscal policy.* Cambridge: Cambridge University Press.

Auten, Gerald, and R. Carroll. 1994. Taxpayer behavior and the 1986 Tax Reform Act. Washington, D.C.: Treasury Department, Office of Tax Analysis, July.

Board of Trustees. Federal Old Age and Survivors Insurance and Disability Trust Funds. 1995. *Annual report.* Washington: U.S. Government Printing Office.

Boskin, Michael, Laurence Kotlikoff, Douglas Puffert, and John Shoven. 1987. Social security: A financial appraisal across and within generations. *National Tax Journal* 40:19–34.

Boskin, Michael, et al. 1996. *Preliminary report to Senate Finance Committee.* Washington, D.C.: U.S. Government Printing Office.

Browning, Edgar. 1987. On the marginal welfare cost of taxation. *American Economic Review* 77, no. 1 (March): 11–23.

Bureau of the Census. 1996a. Population projections of the United States by age, sex, race and Hispanic origin: 1995 to 2050 (vital rate inputs). Washington, D.C. Machine-readable data file.

———. 1996b. U.S. population estimates by age, sex, race and Hispanic origin: 1990 to 1995. Washington, D.C.: Machine-readable data file.

Economic report of the president. 1996. Washington, D.C.: U.S. Government Printing Office.

Feldstein, Martin. 1987. Should social security be means tested? *Journal of Political Economy* 95, no. 3 (June): 468–84.

———. 1995a. The effect of marginal tax rates on taxable income: A panel study of the 1986 Tax Reform Act. *Journal of Political Economy* 103, no. 3 (June): 551–72.

———. 1995b. Tax avoidance and the deadweight loss of the income tax. Working Paper no. 5055. Cambridge, Mass.: National Bureau of Economic Research, March.

———. 1995c. Would privatizing social security raise economic welfare? Working Paper no. 5281. Cambridge, Mass.: National Bureau of Economic Research.

———. 1996. The missing piece in policy analysis: Social security reform (Richard T. Ely Lecture). *American Economic Review* 86, no. 2 (May): 1–14.

Feldstein, Martin, Louis Dicks-Mireaux, and James Poterba. 1983. The effective tax rate and the pretax rate of return. *Journal of Public Economics* 21, no. 2 (July): 129–58.

Feldstein, Martin, and Kathleen Feldstein. 1984. Time for a threshold. *Boston Globe,* 27 November 1984.

Feldstein, Martin, and Andrew Samwick. 1992. Social security rules and marginal tax rates. *National Tax Journal* 45, no. 1 (March): 1–22.

———. 1996. The transition path in privatizing social security. NBER Working Paper no. 5761. Cambridge, Mass.: National Bureau of Economic Research.

———. 1997. The economics of prefunding social security and medicare benefits. In *NBER macroeconomics annual 1997,* ed. B. Bernanke and J. Rotemberg. Cambridge, Mass.: MIT Press.

Harberger, Arnold. 1964. Taxation, resource allocation, and welfare. In *The role of direct and indirect taxes in the Federal Revenue System,* ed. J. Due. Princeton, N.J.: Princeton University Press.

Hurd, Michael, and John Shoven. 1985. The distributional impact of social security. In *Pensions, labor and individual choice,* ed. D. Wise. Chicago: University of Chicago Press.

Kotlikoff, Laurence. 1996. Privatization of social security: How it works and why it matters. In *Tax policy and the economy,* ed. James Poterba. Cambridge, Mass.: MIT Press.

MaCurdy, Thomas, and John Shoven. 1992. Stocks, bonds and pension wealth. In *Topics in the economics of aging,* ed. David Wise. Chicago: University of Chicago Press.

Poterba, James, and Andrew Samwick. 1995. Stock ownership patterns, stock market fluctuations, and consumption. *Brookings Papers on Economic Activity*, no. 2:295–357.

Rippe, Richard. 1995. Further gains in corporate profitability. *Economic Outlook Monthly*, August. New York: Prudential Securities.

Samuelson, Paul. 1958. An exact consumption loan model of interest with or without the social contrivance of money. *Journal of Political Economy* 66:467–82.

Social Security Administration. 1995. *Social Security Bulletin, Annual Statistical Supplement*. Washington, D.C.: U.S. Government Printing Office.

World Bank. 1994. *Averting the old age crisis: Policies to protect the old and promote growth*. Policy Research Report Series. Oxford: Oxford University Press for the World Bank.

Comment   John B. Shoven

This is a "must read" paper for anyone interested in privatizing social security. The reason is that it addresses the most difficult aspect of social security reform—the transition. It is a fundamentally honest paper in that it shows that, even though a mature MIRA (mandatory individual retirement account) system could be funded with approximately a 2 percent contribution rate, there would be a transitionary period where the total contributions for social security retirement would have to be increased from the existing 12.4 percent of covered payroll. The startling aspect of the paper, however, is how small and temporary the necessary contribution increase is. The authors phase in the MIRA plan in such a way that total payroll deductions for social security and the MIRA accounts peak at 13.74 percent in 2007. The total deductions and contributions fall below 12.4 percent by 2019 and eventually decline to about 2.1 percent. Often it is stated that stopping a pay-as-you-go retirement system would of necessity cause one generation to pay for two retirements. Feldstein and Samwick show that there is some merit to that logic but that the losses to those working during the transition can be kept quite modest. The long-run gains are extremely impressive in this analysis, approximating 12 percent of covered payroll, or 5 percent of GDP.

There are a number of features of the Feldstein-Samwick study that are worth noting. First, they credit the additional saving in the MIRA accounts with the full pretax return (estimated at a real 9 percent) on the incremental capital. As the authors argue, some accounting of the tax proceeds generated by the additional capital is necessary for a complete economic analysis of the plan. They credit the tax proceeds (primarily the corporate income tax) back to the MIRA accounts. As political economy, this is more questionable. Again,

John B. Shoven is the Charles R. Schwab Professor of Economics and dean of the School of Humanities and Sciences, Stanford University, and a research associate of the National Bureau of Economic Research.

the authors realize this and provide some analysis crediting the accounts with only the 5.4 percent net of corporate tax rate of return. With the 5.4 percent return, the long-run MIRA contribution rate rises to roughly 3.3 percent. The authors also do not deduct a management fee for those handling the MIRA accounts. There is room for disagreement about the necessary magnitude of such fees, but a deduction of between 0.2 and 1.0 percent a year would seem reasonable. To offset such a reduction in net rates of return, the required contribution rate would have to be slightly increased.

A second feature of the Feldstein-Samwick paper that represents good economic analysis is that they have recognized that the existing social security system is unsustainable. Before you can compare the outcomes with the MIRA system with the existing structure, you have to make assumptions about how the existing system will be changed to regain financial sustainability. Their base-case adjustment to the present system is to assume that it will switch to a pure pay-as-you-go basis once the trust fund is exhausted and that benefits will be reduced to live within the proceeds of the 12.4 percent payroll tax. The benefit reductions begin in 2031 and are approximately 24 percent initially, rising to 35 percent by 2070. These reductions could be partially achieved by raising the retirement age more than currently scheduled. As a matter of political economy, once again, the adjustments to restore long-run solvency to the existing system might well involve tax increases as well as benefit reductions. While this would slightly raise the required MIRA contribution rate, it would presumably only increase the efficiency gain of the privatized plan over the pay-as-you-go social security system.

The authors discuss the issue of risk. One of their initial points is that even the current social security system with its set of defined benefit promises is risky. Certainly, the system as it stands today cannot be sustained, and its participants bear the risk of how it will be changed. Still, once fully implemented, the MIRA system would be risky in that the rate of return in financial markets is highly variable, more so than reflected in the accounting returns and the tax proceeds on corporate capital. One potential stabilizing force offered by Feldstein and Samwick is the rebate of the corporate tax attributable to the MIRA capital. Perhaps the best measure of the riskiness of financial investments is captured by Tobin's Q, the ratio of the paper value of the nation's capital stock (i.e., the value of the stocks and bonds) to the accounting or book value of the replacement cost of the capital. The graph of Tobin's Q, as taken from Poterba and Samwick (1995), is shown in figure 6C.1.

The decline between 1968 and 1974 is truly staggering, with Q falling by more than 70 percent. The climb from 1984 to 1995 is equally dramatic, with Q more than tripling. This gives some idea of the variability in the value of the MIRA accounts through time owing to market fluctuations. Feldstein and Samwick address this by suggesting that the MIRA contribution rate could be increased by about one-third over what would be necessary on the basis of the average or expected outcome. This "oversaving" would reduce the probability

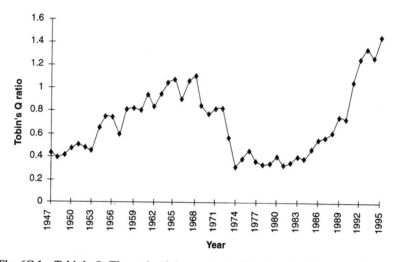

Fig. 6C.1   Tobin's *Q*: The ratio of the market value of equity dividend by the replacement cost of net assets

of faring worse than with the existing social security system to less than 5 percent even if an individual lived to the age of one hundred. Another possibility mentioned by the authors would be to leave the means-tested supplementary security income program in place to protect those who fare particularly poorly.

My own guess is that there will be a large debate between those who favor a plan such as that described by Feldstein and Samwick and those who favor a "double-decker" plan that retains a certain level of defined-benefit promises. One such plan is described by the 1994–96 Social Security Advisory Commission as personal security accounts and involves flat benefits of $410 per month for singles, $600 per month for married elderly couples, plus the proceeds of a 5 percent individual account. The first tier of defined-benefit money provides a floor of support and somewhat stabilizes retirement income, particularly for lower-income individuals. The difference between the first-tier benefits for singles and marrieds retains the transfer to couples in the current law, again particularly for low-income individuals. The benefits of the two-tier approach come at a cost, of course. The flat benefits must be tax financed, and thus the two-tier program would offer much smaller efficiency benefits for the economy than the MIRA plan described by Feldstein and Samwick.

My conclusion is that Feldstein and Samwick have provided the analysis that makes considering the privatization of social security in the United States feasible. They are not advocating the particular features of the plan that they present; rather, they are simply showing that the transition costs can be manageable and that the potential for efficiency gains for the economy is enormous. They have raised a number of issues that need to be studied further, including accounting for the total return of incremental saving and dealing with the riskiness of both pay-as-you-go plans and privatized plans. To end where I began, this paper is a "must read."

Reference

Poterba, James M., and Andrew A. Samwick. 1995. Stock ownership patterns, stock market fluctuations, and consumption. *Brookings Papers on Economic Activity,* no. 2:295–357.

Discussion Summary   Jeffrey Liebman and Andrew Samwick

The discussion began by focusing on whether the gains achieved by the Feldstein-Samwick plan were unique to social security privatization. One participant argued that any other method of reducing the national debt would do the same thing by taking advantage of the tax wedge in the rates of return to capital. He noted that, in a simple lifetime utility model, we do not want to tax the rate of return. Another participant said that it was not necessary for the plan to include a payroll tax increase and that reduced government spending could achieve the same ends. A third participant said that the Feldstein-Samwick proposal was not really about social security reform but was instead really just a way to raise taxes that will reduce the national debt and therefore increase the capital stock. In response, a member of the Social Security Advisory Council said that the paper did an important service by making it explicit that either benefits need to be cut or taxes raised in the transition to a new system. He said that cutting benefits is as much a cost as raising taxes.

Discussion turned to the authors' assumptions about the rate of return that could be earned under their plan. One participant said that the key to the paper is the difference between the rate of return paid on equities and the rate of return paid by social security. He said that, if there were no other distortions and full access to capital markets, the higher rate of return on stocks results because there is more risk with stocks. Since some people will get hurt by this risk, it is a mistake to use the high average rates of return without adjusting for risk. One member of the Social Security Advisory Council questioned the authors' assumptions about rates of return on the accounts. The council member explained that the council's plan assumed that people hold 50 percent bonds and 50 percent equities and that there is a 4 percent spread between the returns on bonds and the returns on equities. Then 1 percent was subtracted for administrative costs. This produced a rate of return of 3.65, which is quite different from the 9 percent rate used by Feldstein and Samwick. Another participant concurred that the 9 percent rate of return was too high and asked how all the additional saving would affect the economy and interest rates. He also argued that the Latin American experience demonstrates that the administrative costs of a privatized system are at least 1 percent.

In response, Feldstein defended the rate-of-return assumptions in the paper. He said that the paper assumes that people hold 60 percent equities and 40 percent debt. This is the same blend as in the economy as a whole. If equities currently receive a 7 percent return and debt around 3 percent, the average is 5.4 percent. However, it is necessary to add back the corporate tax payments. Thus, $5.4 + 3.6 = 9$ percent. In fact, the historical average is 9.3 percent. Even accounting for administrative costs, this number is likely to be at least 8.5 percent.

The discussion turned to general equilibrium effects. One member of the group suggested that investors would reduce their holding of equities in other accounts since their MIRA accounts would be riskier than their current social security wealth. It was also pointed out that the paper assumed that MIRA contributions are net new savings because the dollars are assumed to come out of consumption. But, if there are other offsetting changes in savings, this is incorrect, and the paper overstates the benefits of this plan.

Feldstein responded that it is unlikely that many people would decrease other savings by much since most people are saving so little currently. Moreover, average retirement benefits would not increase in this plan, so it is hard to see why other retirement savings would decline.

7

Simulating the Privatization of Social Security in General Equilibrium

Laurence J. Kotlikoff

The privatization of social security is one of the hottest policy issues currently under discussion in the United States. Much of this interest seems motivated by a desire to find a way out of the U.S. social security system's long-run financing problem. But there is also a growing awareness among Americans of Chile's success in privatizing social security and the fact that countries all over the world are trying to replicate it. Chile's privatization coincided with the spectacular takeoff of its economy and has led some observers to suggest that privatizing social security was the key to Chile's economic growth. The truth here is hard to know. The Chilean economy benefited from a number of concomitant economic reforms. It also benefited from a stable government and from improvements in external economic conditions. Given the potential for exaggerating the effect on Chile of privatizing social security, it is important to take a hard-nosed look at what economic analysis tells us privatization can and cannot do.

This paper does this. It draws and builds on Kotlikoff (1996a, 1996b, 1996c) in trying to identify the economic arguments for and against privatization. One of the main, although certainly not novel, points in these papers is that, absent

Laurence J. Kotlikoff is professor of economics at Boston University and a research associate of the National Bureau of Economic Research.

The author thanks Martin Feldstein and Jan Walliser and other members of the NBER project on privatizing social security for very helpful comments. He also thanks Andrew Samwick for providing data and Jan Walliser for excellent research assistance. Part of this study relies on Kent Smetters's, Jan Walliser's, and my modification of the Auerbach-Kotlikoff dynamic life-cycle model to incorporate multiple income groups. Support for Walliser's work on this modification was provided by the National Bureau of Economic Research. Support for Smetters's work on the modification was provided by the Congressional Budget Office. The author is very grateful to both organizations for providing this assistance.

efficiency improvements, welfare improvements accruing to particular generations as the result of privatization come at the expense of welfare losses to
other generations. Moreover, absent efficiency gains or intergenerational redistribution, making some members of a generation better off requires making
other members worse off. Policy makers should, presumably, be interested in
identifying and immediately enacting any reforms that constitute Pareto improvements. Hence, understanding the potential pure efficiency gains from privatization is important. But policy makers also routinely trade off the welfare
of one generation against that of another. Consequently, they also need to understand the potential role of privatization in redistributing resources across
and within generations.

This paper uses the Auerbach-Kotlikoff (1987) dynamic fiscal policy model
(the AK model) to simulate the macroeconomic and efficiency effects of privatization. Most of the results reported are based on the single-agent version of
the model in which all cohort members are identical. But the final section of
the paper reports some preliminary results based on a multiagent version of the
model in which cohort members differ with respect to their earnings abilities.
This new version of the AK model builds on the important work of Fullerton
and Rogers (1993), which appears to represent the first serious attempt to incorporate intragenerational heterogeneity in a life-cycle simulation model.

This paper adds to a growing literature on the economics of privatizing social security. Feldstein (1995) uses a partial equilibrium framework, and Arrau
(1990) and Arrau and Schmidt-Hebbel (1993) use a version of the AK model
to make a number of the points argued here. The AK model used by Arrau and
Arrau and Schmidt Hebbel takes labor supply as exogenous. This is a significant shortcoming since the efficiency gains from privatizing social security
arise, in large part, from eliminating social security's distortion of labor supply
decisions. Raffelhueschen (1993) does include variable labor supply in his
simulation analysis of privatizing social security, and his qualitative conclusions are quite similar to those reached here. But Raffelhueschen's model
contains only two periods, which limits the applicability of his quantitative
findings. Like this study, Imrohoroglu, Huang, and Sargent (1995) use a
multiperiod life-cycle model to simulate the effects of privatizing social security. Although their model is more elaborate than the one used here, it does not
include variable labor supply, which precludes separating efficiency gains from
intergenerational redistribution. Nonetheless, their general findings concerning
noncompensated social security privatization transitions accord with those presented here.

The paper proceeds in section 7.1 by discussing the potential macroeconomic and efficiency effects of pay-as-you-go social security. Section 7.2 describes the AK model and its parameterization for this study. Sections 7.3 and
7.4 report results for a one-income-class and multi-income-class versions of
the AK model. The final section summarizes and concludes the paper.

7.1 Social Security's Privatization and the Macro Economy

7.1.1 Social Security and Saving

Most industrialized economies and a good many developing countries have spent the postwar period dramatically expanding their pay-as-you-go social security programs. Although this expansion has reduced poverty rates among the elderly, it has also redistributed tremendous sums from young and future generations, as a group, to contemporaneous older generations, as a group.

The mechanism underlying the redistribution to the initial elderly is clear. Generations that are retired or close to retirement at the time pay-as-you-go social security benefits are increased receive windfalls. Initial young as well as all future generations are then left contributing to a retirement system whose rate of return is dictated by the total earnings of subsequent contributors and, thus, the economy's rate of growth of labor earnings. In the United States, this growth rate appears to be about one-third the rate of return available from investing in the market.[1]

This intergenerational redistribution, which produces a very big windfall for the initial elderly and imposes a smaller, but still substantial, loss on all subsequent generations, has a major macroeconomic fallout. It raises the current consumption of the elderly by more than it reduces the current consumption of the current young as well as that of future generations, whose current consumption is obviously zero. Consequently, the policy lowers national saving. The consumption of the elderly rises by more than that of the young for two reasons. First, the elderly have higher propensities to consume out of remaining lifetime resources than do the young.[2] Why? Because the elderly are closer to the ends of their lives and have, therefore, fewer years over which to spend each dollar of remaining lifetime resources. Second, as mentioned, the windfalls to the current elderly are paid for, not only by the current young, but also by future generations. So the resource loss to the initial young is smaller than the resource gain to the initial elderly.

Figure 7.1, based on data developed in Gokhale, Kotlikoff, and Sabelhaus (1996), documents the difference by age in propensities to consume. It shows that propensities to consume of American cohorts are roughly constant through age sixty and then rise dramatically. Figures 7.2 and 7.3 use the same data to show how relative age-consumption and age-resource profiles for American cohorts have changed since the early 1960s. Note that the very substantial in-

---

1. In a setting in which the growth rate of earnings as well as the market return on capital are risky, the comparison between the return paid by social security and that paid by the market requires appropriately adjusting for risk. It seems unlikely, however, that such an adjustment would make pay-as-you-go social security a better investment than investing in the market.

2. The term *resources* refers to the present value of all remaining lifetime nonasset income (net of taxes and gross of transfer payments received) plus current net wealth.

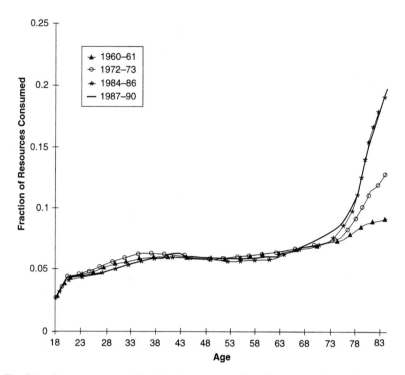

Fig. 7.1 **Average propensities to consume out of total resources ($r = 6$ percent)**
Source: Authors' calculations.

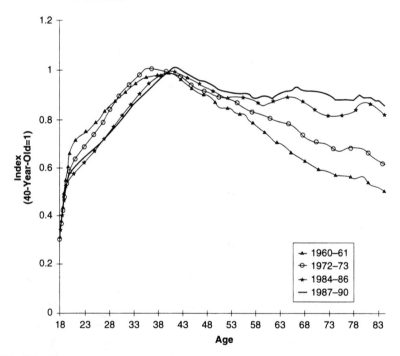

Fig. 7.2 **Relative consumption profiles**
Source: Authors' calculations based on the Consumer Expenditure Survey.

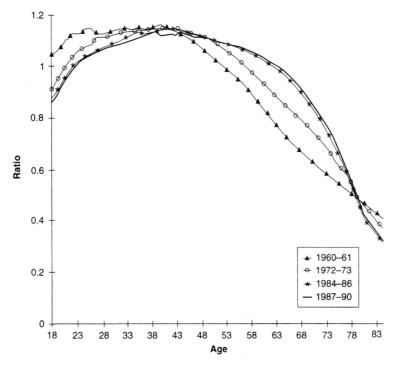

Fig. 7.3   Cohort resources per capita/per capita resources
Source: Authors' calculations.

crease in the resources of the elderly relative to the young has coincided with an equally substantial increase in their relative consumption. The secular increase in the relative resources of the elderly reflects many factors. But the predominant factor is direct government redistribution to the elderly through social security, Medicare, and Medicaid.

As figure 7.4 shows, U.S. intergenerational redistribution has led to precisely what the life-cycle model predicts—a decline in the rate of U.S. saving. The greater than two-thirds decline in the rate of U.S. saving since the 1950s and 1960s has meant a much lower rate of U.S. domestic investment. This, in turn, has raised real interest rates and reduced labor productivity and real wage growth substantially below what would otherwise have been the case (see fig. 7.5). Thus, these general equilibrium feedback effects have exacerbated the direct redistribution from young and future generations to the initial old through pay-as-you-go social security.[3]

The fiscal burdening of young and future generations through pay-as-you-go social security can occur just as well in settings with stable as well as unstable

---

3. For a simulation analysis showing how alternative government policies affect the welfare of current and future generations, see Auerbach and Kotlikoff (1987).

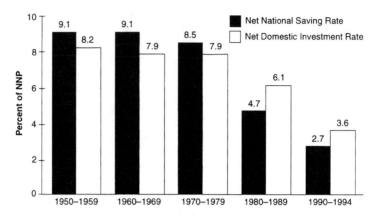

Fig. 7.4   The postwar decline in U.S. saving and investment

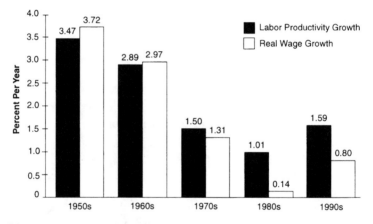

Fig. 7.5   Labor productivity and real wage growth

demographics. But a baby boom followed by a baby bust of the kind being experienced by most developed economies places greater stress on the social security chain letter. Indeed, the United States, Japan, Germany, Italy, France, and a host of other countries now face the unpleasant prospect of either dramatically raising their payroll tax rates over the next few decades or dramatically reducing their social security benefits. It is this impending demographic/social security crunch, rather than a real appreciation of the intrinsic problem with running unfunded social security programs, that seems to be leading politicians to consider privatizing social security.

7.1.2   The Saving, Investment, and Growth Effects of Privatization

If privatization ends up placing a larger fiscal burden on initial older generations, it will lower the fiscal burden not only of the initial young but also of all future generations. In this case, the initial elderly, with their high propensities to consume, will reduce their consumption by more than the initial young will raise their consumption. Thus, the net effect will be a rise in national saving, investment, and, at least in the short run, real wage growth.

The personal security system described in Kotlikoff (1996b) provides an example of how privatization may produce *income effects* that are conducive to more national saving. In this scheme, social security benefits are phased out over a forty-five-year period. Since payroll contributions to social security are immediately privatized (i.e., the contributions are made to and invested within private accounts), an alternative fiscal instrument is needed to finance social security benefits during the transition. The personal security system uses a consumption tax, specifically a federal retail sales tax, to pay for transitional benefits. Since the elderly account for a larger share of consumption than they do of social security payroll contributions, this policy imposes a larger fiscal burden on them.

In addition to altering national saving via income effects, privatization may also change saving incentives in a way that either encourages or discourages current consumption. Suppose, for example, that income tax financing is used to pay for interest on debt issued in the course of privatizing social security. The higher effective rate of capital income taxation that results from higher income tax rates raises the price of consuming in the future relative to the present and provides the young and old alike an incentive to substitute current for future consumption, that is, to save less.[4] Indeed, such positive *substitution effects* on current consumption could outweigh the negative income effects on current consumption arising under particular privatization schemes, producing, on balance, a decline in national saving.

Since the saving, investment, and growth effects of privatizing social security are theoretically ambiguous, depending on how privatization is achieved, simulation analysis is needed to understand the net macroeconomic effect of privatization. Before turning to such analysis, let us consider other issues involved in privatizing social security.

7.1.3 Are There Efficiency Gains from Privatizing Social Security?

Economic efficiency concerns the structure of economic incentives, such as the incentive to consume now rather than later or the incentive to work rather than enjoy leisure. Since privatization of social security will generally alter economic incentives, the possibility arises that privatization could make the economy more efficient—that it could improve the structure of incentives and, in the process, make some generations better off without making others worse off.

The most important incentive affected by social security is the incentive to

---

4. Changes in the relative of price of current and future consumption may also produce income effects, unless households are compensated for such relative price changes.

work. By financing social security benefits via payroll taxation, social security reduces this incentive, although the degree to which it does so depends on the nature of its marginal linkage between social security benefits and contributions. This linkage can be positive, negative, or zero. Zero linkage occurs when social security benefits are determined, at the margin, independent of contributions or when workers incorrectly perceive that contributing more to social security will not raise their future social security benefits. In the United States, misconception of the true nature of benefit-tax linkage seems plausible given the complex nature of the U.S. social security benefit formula.

In a "pay-as-you-go" system with zero actual or perceived linkage, workers will consider 100 percent of their payroll tax contribution to be a tax on their labor supply. Nonetheless, in a pay-as-you-go program with stable growth, workers will, on average, receive some return on their contributions to social security—a return that is governed by the rate of growth of the economy. So, on average, social security contributions are not just a tax.

This point notwithstanding, there is no necessary relation between the average and marginal returns to social security contributions. To see this, suppose the social security payroll tax rate is 15 percent. If benefits are provided as a lump sum independent of past contributions, the marginal return from an extra dollar of contributions is zero, and social security adds 15 percentage points to the total effective marginal tax rate on labor supply. If, on the other hand, the government were to provide, in present value, two dollars for every dollar contributed to social security above some contribution level, social security would represent a marginal subsidy to labor supply for all those contributing above that level. Such a subsidy would reduce the total effective marginal tax rate on labor supply by 15 percentage points.

Although providing 100 percent or greater marginal benefit-tax linkage to some contributors is certainly feasible, providing such linkage to all contributors may be politically impossible because of equity considerations. Ignoring other fiscal instruments, providing such high marginal benefit-tax linkage on each dollar contributed to social security requires imposing a large inframarginal tax. Since this large inframarginal tax would be independent of labor earnings, low-wage earners would face a higher average tax from social security than would high-wage earners, making the system regressive.

7.1.4   The Potential Efficiency Gain from Eliminating the U.S. Social Security Payroll Tax

The smaller is a social security system's marginal benefit-tax linkage, the larger are the chances that privatizing social security can support an efficiency gain. To see this, consider a preprivatization situation in which social security benefits are provided to workers independent of their past contributions; marginal linkage is therefore zero, and workers view all their payroll tax contributions as a marginal tax on their labor supply. Also assume that privatization is accomplished by paying only those social security benefits owed to existing retirees as well as those benefits that current workers have accrued as of the date of the privatization. In this case, the payroll tax will, over time, disappear as a smaller and smaller number of original retirees and workers with accrued benefits remain alive. As the payroll tax rate falls, the total effective tax on labor supply will fall as well. Since the government's distortion of labor supply is reduced over time, this method of privatizing social security has the potential of improving economic efficiency.

Distortions of economic decisions rise with the square of the total effective marginal tax on the decision, so the contribution of the payroll tax to distorting labor supply depends on the size of marginal income taxes as well as other effective marginal labor taxes. In the United States, workers who earn less than social security's covered earnings ceiling (currently \$62,500) are subject to the full 15.3 percent marginal social security payroll tax.[5] Most of these workers are likely to be in the 15 percent federal marginal income tax bracket. They are also likely to face a 5 percent state marginal income tax and state sales taxes as well as federal excise taxes, which together effectively tax their labor earnings at about 5 percent.

In combination, these non–social security marginal taxes total 25 percent. The 15.3 percent U.S. social security payroll tax rate raises the total effective marginal tax rate on labor supply from 25 to 39 percent once one takes into account the fact that half the payroll tax contribution (the employer's contribution) can be deducted from the federal income tax. Now, .25 squared equals .0625, and .39 squared equals .1521. Since the distortion of labor supply is proportional to the square of the total effective marginal labor tax rate, the U.S. social security payroll tax may be raising labor supply distortions of low-income workers by 143 ($[(.1521/.0621) - 1] \times 100$) percent even though it raises the total effective marginal labor tax rate by only 56 ($[(.39/.25) - 1] \times 100$) percent.[6]

7.1.5 The Linkage at the Margin of Benefits to Earnings[7]

This analysis may overstate social security's actual distortion of labor supply and the efficiency gains from privatization because of marginal benefit-tax linkage under the current system. In the United States, marginal benefit-tax linkage varies enormously across the population. Many secondary earners in two-earner couples and all nonworking spouses in single-earner couples col-

---

5. The 15.3 payroll tax rate includes the Medicare (hospital insurance) tax.

6. For low-income workers covered by the earned income tax credit, the payroll tax's marginal distortion is even larger. Such workers lose twenty cents of their earned income tax credit for every dollar that they earn. Hence, their total effective marginal labor tax rate is 45 percent absent the social security payroll tax and 59 percent with the payroll tax. For such workers, the payroll tax raises their total effective marginal tax rate by 31 percent, but their labor supply distortion by 72 percent. Compared to workers who face the earned income tax credit, the incremental distortion from the payroll tax (which is proportional to the difference between .3481 and .2025) is 62.5 percent larger than the incremental distortion for workers who do not face the earned income tax credit (which is proportional to the difference between .1521 and .0625).

7. This section draws on Kotlikoff (1996c).

lect dependent retirement and survivor benefits based solely on their spouse's earnings histories. Consequently, they receive zero additional benefits in exchange for their marginal payroll tax contributions to social security.[8] The same is true for workers under age twenty-two since their earnings are not included in the calculation of average indexed monthly earnings for purposes of determining retirement benefits. On the other hand, benefit-tax linkage for many primary earners in two-earner couples is significant.

Table 7.1 presents net marginal tax rates on social security contributions for six different household types taking into account benefit-tax linkage. These data were provided by Andrew Samwick and are based on a benefit-calculating program developed in Feldstein and Samwick (1992).[9] The calculations assume a 6 percent real rate of discount, a 1.2 percent rate of real wage growth, and a 3.5 percent rate of inflation and consider the net rate of social security benefit taxation arising from a permanent increase in monthly earnings by $1.00. The table considers only the old age and survivors (OASI) components of social security, and its net tax rates should be compared with the 11.2 percent OASI payroll tax. Negative values refer to subsidies.

The table shows three things. First, it confirms that marginal OASI net tax rates differ greatly across different Americans. For example, at age fifty, the table's low-earner, single-earner husband faces a 12 percent social security subsidy, whereas a high-earner (in the 15 percent benefit bracket), single male age fifty faces a 10 percent marginal tax. Second, OASI net tax rates decline, often substantially, over the life cycle. Consider again the low-earner, single-earner husband. His net tax rate falls from 2 to −23 percent between ages twenty-five and sixty. The reason for the decline in net tax rates with age is that, the closer one gets to collecting marginal benefits arising from additional labor earnings, the less severe is the discounting of those benefits.

Third, as one goes from low- to high-earner households who are earning less than social security's covered earnings ceiling, net marginal tax rates rise substantially. For example, there is a 15 percentage point spread between the 5 percent subsidy facing fifty-year-old, low-earning, single males and the 10 percent tax facing fifty-year-old, high-earning, single males. On the other hand, once one passes the covered earnings ceiling, the marginal OASI net tax drops to zero. Workers earning more than social security's covered earnings ceiling face zero marginal OASI payroll taxation and also receive no marginal social security benefits.[10]

Do workers whose benefits are linked at the margin to additional earnings

8. This discussion abstracts from disability benefits.

9. Boskin et al. (1987) is an earlier study of the marginal net rate of social security taxation that reaches similar conclusions.

10. For this large group of workers, social security does, however, represent a substantial inframarginal tax. Indeed, it is this large inframarginal tax on high earners that is used to provide low earners, as a group, with low or negative marginal OASI net tax rates and average rates of return on their contributions that exceed the economy's growth rate.

Table 7.1   **Net Marginal OASI Tax Rate on $1.00 Rise in Monthly Wages (%)**

Age in 1995	Case					
	A	B	C	D	E	F
25	5	10	2	10	11	0
30	3	10	−0	10	11	0
35	1	10	−2	9	11	0
40	−1	10	−6	9	11	0
45	−3	10	−9	9	11	0
50	−5	10	−12	9	11	0
55	−8	9	−16	8	11	0
60	−12	9	−23	8	11	0

Source: Calculations by Andrew Samwick.

Note: The cases are defined as follows: A = single female, 90 percent benefit bracket, faces no federal income tax. B = single male, 15 percent benefit bracket, faces 85 percent benefit taxation at a 33 percent rate. C = husband in single-earner couple, 90 percent social security benefit bracket, faces no federal income tax. D = husband in single-earner couple, 15 percent social security benefit bracket, faces federal income taxation of 85 percent of benefits at a 33 percent rate. E = secondary earner collecting benefits based solely on spouse's earnings record. F = very high earner (earnings above social security's earnings ceiling).

understand the linkage? We do not know. However, we do know that correctly assessing the linkage is very difficult. Doing so requires knowledge of intricate OASI benefit provisions and the ability to make sophisticated actuarial calculations. Since very few workers have such knowledge or an actuarial background, the vast majority are, presumably, guessing about the degree to which their benefits are linked at the margin to their additional earnings. If they are overassessing the degree of linkage, the present social security system may be less distortionary than it appears. On the other hand, if they are underassessing the degree of linkage, the opposite will be true. In this case, privatizing social security can be beneficial by simply making clear that the true rate of marginal taxation of labor supply is less than the perceived rate.

7.1.6 Other Efficiency Issues Raised by Social Security's Privatization

In addition to its effect on effective marginal tax rates on labor supply, privatization may also alter other effective marginal tax rates. For example, if privatization is accomplished by using income tax financing to pay, over time, the accrued benefits owed to current retirees and workers, there will be a temporary increase in effective marginal capital income taxation. If effective marginal capital income taxation is already quite high owing to, say, a high corporate income tax, privatization could well reduce economic efficiency. Thus, there is no guarantee that privatizing social security will improve economic efficiency. It all depends on the type of social security system being privatized, the nature of other fiscal distortions, and the manner in which privatization takes place.

An entirely different efficiency issue raised by social security's privatization is its effect on the availability to the elderly of longevity insurance (insurance against outliving one's resources). Social security provides this insurance by paying retirees benefits for as long as they live. Social security overcomes the adverse selection problem faced by private insurers in trying to sell annuities by simply forcing everyone into its insurance pool; that is, it effectively forces everyone to buy its annuities. The government has a second important advantage vis-à-vis private insurers, namely, the ability to provide inflation-indexed benefits. The U.S. government appears poised to assist private insurers in selling indexed annuities by following the example of England and several other countries in issuing indexed debt. Insurance companies will be able to purchase this debt to hedge their exposure in selling indexed annuities to the public.

Research is now under way to assess the potential efficiency costs of eliminating the compulsory purchase of annuities through social security, which would potentially leave the elderly with much less longevity insurance. These costs may be substantial because, as demonstrated in Kotlikoff and Spivak (1981), the value of longevity insurance can be very high even for households with moderate degrees of risk aversion. On the other hand, Kotlikoff and Spivak also show that extended families, for whom information problems are surely less severe, can insure their members against longevity risk to a surprising degree. The fact, recently documented by Hayashi, Altonji, and Kotlikoff (1996), that extended families do not self-insure does not preclude their choosing to do so in response to the privatization of social security. Anecdotal as well as hard evidence on extended family living arrangements suggests that self-insurance by extended families was much greater in the United States prior to the expansion of social security. In any case, until this important issue is resolved, it will be impossible to assess the net efficiency gains from privatizing social security.[11]

7.2   Using the Auerbach-Kotlikoff Model to Study Social Security's Privatization

7.2.1   The Auerbach-Kotlikoff Model

The Auerbach-Kotlikoff model (the AK model) can provide some sense of the potential saving, investment, and growth effects of privatizing social security.[12] The AK model calculates the time path of all economic variables in its economy over a 150-year period. The model has fifty-five overlapping genera-

11. Note that, in a privatized system, the government could limit the degree of adverse selection by (a) compelling each cohort to annuitize all its accumulated privatized account balances, say, at age sixty-five and (b) prohibiting insurance companies from restricting the sale of its annuities to individuals with particular characteristics.

12. For a detailed description of the AK model, see Auerbach and Kotlikoff (1987).

tions. Each adult agent in the model lives for fifty-five years (from age twenty to age seventy-five).

There are three sectors: households, firms, and the government. Households (adult agents) decide how much to work and how much to save based on the after-tax wages and after-tax rates of return they can earn in the present and the future on their labor supply and saving, respectively. The work decision involves not only deciding how much to work in those years that one is working but also when to retire. The AK model's time-separable, CES consumption and leisure preferences that underlie these decisions were chosen in light of evidence on actual labor supply and saving behavior.

As agents age in the model, they experience a realistic profile of increases in wages. This age-wage profile is separate from the general level of wages, the time path of which determined in solving the model. Fiscal policies affect households by altering their after-tax wages, their after-tax rates of return, and, in the case of consumption taxes, their after-tax prices of goods and services. The model is equipped to deal with income taxes, wage taxes, capital income taxes, and consumption taxes. It is also able to handle progressive as well as proportional tax rates. Finally, and most important for this study, the model includes a pay-as-you-go social security system in which the perceived linkage between taxes and benefits can be set at any desired value.

The model's base-case population growth rate is set at a constant 1 percent rate, with the population of each new cohort being 1 percent larger than that of the previous cohort. All agents are assumed to have the same preferences, so differences in behavior across agents arise solely from differences in economic opportunities. Until section 7.4, all agents within an age cohort are assumed to be identical; that is, differences in economic opportunities are present only across cohorts. Section 7.4 considers a heterogeneous-agent version of the model, developed by Kent Smetters, Jan Walliser, and myself. This modified model considers twelve earnings groups within each cohort. Each earnings group experiences the same longitudinal growth in earnings but has a different level of earnings. This modified model facilitates the study of the effect of privatization on the intragenerational distribution of economic resources and welfare.

The AK model's output is produced by perfectly competitive firms that hire labor and capital to maximize their profits. These firms produce subject to a CES production function, which, for purposes of this study, is restricted to the Cobb-Douglas form. The government sector consists of a treasury that collects resources from the private sector to finance government consumption and an unfunded, "pay-as-you-go" social security system that levies payroll taxes to pay for contemporaneous retiree benefit payments. There is no money in the model and, thus, no monetary policy. There is, however, government debt, and the model can handle deficit-financed reductions in payroll and other taxes. It can also handle gradual phase-ins of one tax for the other. Finally, the model contains a lump sum redistribution authority (LSRA)—a hypothetical government agency that can use lump sum taxes and transfers to redistribute among generations alive at a point in time as well as those who will be born in the future. The LSRA can be used (switched on) to study the pure economic efficiency effects of particular policy changes.

Although the model handles a great number of complex processes, it leaves out certain portions of reality, some small and some large. For one thing, there are no liquidity constraints. Leaving out liquidity constraints greatly facilitates the simulation of social security's privatization. The reason is that one can model the act of privatizing social security contributions as equivalent to simply eliminating the payroll tax. This reflects the fact that agents in the model cannot be forced to save. Any attempt to do so simply leads them to borrow against their future wealth. This applies to forcing agents to invest their social security contributions in private accounts. Doing so would produce the same net saving as not doing so. This said, it is worth pointing out that, in the particular economies simulated here, agents do not actually seek to borrow. So, even if a liquidity constraint (specifically, a constraint against negative net wealth) were added to the model, it would not be binding.

The version of the model used here ignores saving for purposes other than retirement, such as bequests. The model also ignores uncertainty with respect to either individual or macroeconomic outcomes. These and other omissions suggest viewing the model's results cautiously.

7.2.2   Modeling Social Security's Privatization

As just mentioned, in the AK model, privatizing social security contributions just requires setting the model's social security payroll tax rate to zero.[13] Hence, there is no need to add a formal private pension system to the model. Beyond eliminating the payroll tax, privatizing social security benefits within the model involves three key decisions: how fast to phase out benefits, whether to issue explicit government debt for a period of time to make up for some or all of the loss in payroll tax revenue, and what tax instrument to use, during the benefit phase-out period, to pay for benefits that are not financed by explicit borrowing and to meet, during and after the benefit phase-out period, interest on new debt issued as part of the privatization.[14]

13. Again, this can be thought of as forcing agents to make their contributions to private pension accounts but permitting them to reduce their other saving and, indeed, borrow against these accounts if they so desire.

14. These three decisions are illustrated in Chile's privatization of social security. Chile's privatization honored benefit commitments to existing retirees. It also provided existing workers *recognition bonds*—explicit IOUs that would come due when workers reached retirement age. These recognition bonds compensated workers for the elimination of their claims to future social security benefits—claims that they had accrued as the result of past contributions. Because the timing of the payment of principal and interest on the recognition bonds is similar to the timing of the payment of the accrued social security benefits that these workers would otherwise have received, the Chilean reform can be viewed as paying off all accrued benefits under the old system but disallowing any further accrual of social security benefits. Consequently, it amounts to a particular benefit-phase-out policy. Chile used deficit finance to cover some of the losses in revenue arising from the discontinuation of the payroll tax. This deficit finance took the form of running smaller

Table 7.2   **Baseline Parameter Values and Spending and Tax Rates**

Parameter	Value
Intratemporal elasticity of substitution	.800
Intertemporal elasticity of substitution	.250
Weight of leisure	1.500
Pure rate of time preference	.015
Elasticity of substitution between labor and capital	1.000
Population growth rate	.010
Output share of government consumption	.224
Average income tax rate	.224
Average marginal income tax rate	.328
Payroll tax rate	.122

7.2.3   The AK Model Used to Study Social Security's Privatization

As reported in table 7.2, the preprivatization economy features a progressive income tax (with an average marginal tax rate of 33 percent) that finances government consumption equal to 22 percent of output, a 12 percent social security payroll tax, zero linkage between social security benefits and taxes, zero initial official government debt, a 1 percent population growth rate, zero technological change, a Cobb-Douglas production function, a CES utility function in consumption and leisure with intertemporal and intratemporal elasticities of substitution of .25 and .8, respectively, and a time preference rate of 1.5 percent.

Our baseline economy has a 2.5 percent rate of national saving and a ratio of social security outlays to output of .089.[15] The pretax interest rate (the marginal product of capital) is 10.3 percent. At the micro level, consumption more than doubles between ages twenty-one and seventy-five, which is consistent with the findings in figure 7.2 above. Social security benefits constitute between 55 and 60 percent of consumption for agents over sixty-five. Labor supply at age sixty-five is about 70 percent lower than labor supply at age twenty-one; it is virtually zero after age seventy-one.

The simulation phases out social security benefits in a linear manner over a forty-five-year period. This phase-out period starts eleven years after the payroll tax is eliminated, thus permitting all beneficiaries at the time of the reform to collect all their benefits. Social security benefits during the transition are financed by either a proportional consumption tax, a progressive income tax, a

surpluses than would otherwise have been the case. Finally, Chile used its income tax to make up the rest of the lost payroll tax revenue and, implicitly, to meet interest payments on its additional borrowing.

15. Note that this is higher than the 1994 5.2 percent NNP share of social security spending. It also exceeds the respective 7.5 percent for combined spending on Medicare and social security. This difference arises from the stylized assumption of constant 1 percent population growth. The current U.S. population, in contrast, reflects high birth rates in the 1950s and 1960s, and payroll taxes are levied on a relatively larger working population.

payroll tax, or initial deficit financing coupled with subsequent increases in either proportional consumption tax rates or progressive income tax rates. For each case, I present results in which the welfare (utility) of initial generations is allowed to change in response to the privatization as well as results in which the welfare of initial generations is held constant. In the latter simulations, the LSRA redistributes in a lump sum manner so as (*a*) to leave all generations alive at the time of the transition with precisely the same utility they would have enjoyed absent privatization and (*b*) to equalize the utility of all generations born after the policy is initiated. Finally, I consider alternative degrees of benefit-tax linkage.

7.3   Simulation Findings

7.3.1   Simulating a Cold-Turkey Privatization

To place subsequent privatization results in perspective, I first simulate the macroeconomic and efficiency effects of an immediate and complete elimination of social security benefits and taxes. Although such a privatization is unlikely ever to be undertaken, simulating it clarifies the maximum damage that could be done to initial older generations from privatization as well as the maximum efficiency gains available from privatization after initial older generations are fully compensated for their loss of benefits.

Figure 7.6 shows that this policy would have a major effect on the macro economy as well as the intergenerational distribution of welfare. The top panel in the figure provides an index of the policy's induced changes (relative to initial steady-state values) in the capital stock (K), output (Y), labor supply (L), the real wage (w), and the real interest rate (r). The first rows of tables 7.3–7.8 (run 1) record the values graphed in the figures.

As indicated, the "cold-turkey" elimination of social security leads to a 57 percent long-run increase in the economy's capital stock relative to its initial steady-state value. The long-run increases in labor supply, output, and the real wage are 6, 17, and 10 percent, respectively. The long-run reduction in the real interest rate is 25 percent, and the long-run increase in welfare (the increase in utility of those alive in the long run) is 10.79 percent. This percentage change in remaining lifetime utility is measured as the percentage increase in remaining lifetime consumption and leisure at each age needed in the initial steady state to produce the same level of utility for the generation in question as it enjoys under privatization.

Although figure 7.6 and the tables point to a very major long-run gain to the economy and its future inhabitants from a "cold-turkey" transition, they also show that these gains come at the cost of major utility losses to initial older generations. For example, the oldest members of society—those born fifty-four years before the reform—suffer a 26 percent reduction in remaining lifetime welfare.

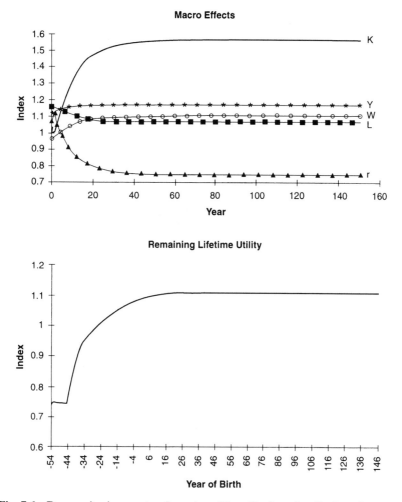

Fig. 7.6   Progressive income tax financing of benefits, benefits eliminated immediately

To investigate how much of the improvement in the welfare of future genera-tions reflects efficiency improvements as opposed to simply redistribution away from initial generations, I repeated the "cold-turkey" simulation but in-structed the LSRA to compensate all initial generations to prevent any loss in their utility levels. The results are shown in figure 7.7 and reported as run 2 in the tables. The long-run increase in the capital stock in this case is lower—36 rather than 57 percent—but still remarkably large. It is large enough to raise long-run output by 14 percent, raise the long-run real wage by 6 percent, lower the long-run real interest rate by 16 percent, and raise the utility levels of all

Table 7.3 Percentage Change in Capital Stock Relative to Steady State

Run	Tax Financing Soc. Sec. Benefits	Years Benefits Phased Out	LSRA	BTL	Years of Deficit Financing	Year of Transition 5	10	25	150
1	Yprog	0	No	0	0	16.11	31.68	50.28	56.67
2	Yprog	0	Yes	0	0	5.71	11.85	25.16	35.24
3	Yprog[a]	0	No	0	0	10.04	19.30	30.20	33.60
4	Yprog[a]	0	Yes	0	0	2.84	5.56	10.62	13.64
5	Yprog	0	No	.1	0	15.75	30.96	49.03	55.19
6	Yprog	0	Yes	.1	0	5.01	10.35	21.89	31.75
7	Yprog	0	No	.3	0	15.07	29.60	46.74	52.49
8	Yprog	0	Yes	.3	0	3.72	7.63	16.09	24.19
9	Yprog	55	No	0	0	-.52	-.57	4.96	56.67
10	Yprog	55	Yes	0	0	-1.72	-3.54	-4.90	8.82
11	W	55	No	0	0	.79	1.68	7.52	56.67
12	W	55	Yes	0	0	.01	-.45	-1.56	7.01
13	C	55	No	0	0	5.54	11.54	25.60	56.67
14	C	55	Yes	0	0	2.98	6.27	13.64	20.28
15	Yprog	55	No	0	5	4.32	1.43	-4.16	40.43
16	Yprog	55	Yes	0	5	3.98	0.70	-7.81	4.15
17	C	55	No	0	5	2.02	4.25	12.04	39.31
18	C	55	Yes	0	5	1.27	2.21	5.64	10.70
19	Yprog	55	No	.1	0	-.92	-1.34	3.74	55.19
20	Yprog	55	Yes	.1	0	-2.38	-4.92	-7.56	5.41
21	Yprog	55	No	.3	0	-1.68	-2.82	1.47	52.49
22	Yprog	55	Yes	.3	0	-3.60	-7.45	-12.45	-1.59
23	C	55	No	.1	0	5.17	10.82	24.41	55.19
24	C	55	Yes	.1	0	2.31	4.84	10.67	16.20
25	C	55	No	.3	0	4.48	9.49	22.22	52.49
26	C	55	Yes	.3	0	1.05	2.24	5.33	8.90

Note: LSRA = Lump sum redistribution authority. BTL = Benefit-tax linkage. Yprog = Progressive income tax. C = Proportional consumption tax. W = Payroll tax.

[a]Three percent population growth.

Table 7.4   Percentage Change in Aggregate Labor Supply Relative to Steady State

Run	Tax Financing Soc. Sec. Benefits	Years Benefits Phased Out	LSRA	BTL	Years of Deficit Financing	Year of Transition			
						5	10	25	150
1	Yprog	0	No	0	0	13.89	11.08	7.26	6.28
2	Yprog	0	Yes	0	0	10.74	10.08	8.63	7.36
3	Yprog[a]	0	No	0	0	7.68	6.15	4.05	3.58
4	Yprog[a]	0	Yes	0	0	5.37	5.07	4.46	4.14
5	Yprog	0	No	.1	0	12.69	9.94	6.22	5.28
6	Yprog	0	Yes	.1	0	9.42	8.85	7.56	6.56
7	Yprog	0	No	.3	0	10.42	7.80	4.25	3.37
8	Yprog	0	Yes	.3	0	6.97	6.54	5.55	5.00
9	Yprog	55	No	0	0	1.64	1.67	5.00	6.28
10	Yprog	55	Yes	0	0	1.05	1.22	4.83	8.28
11	W	55	No	0	0	.43	.14	3.87	6.28
12	W	55	Yes	0	0	-.13	-.49	3.35	8.49
13	C	55	No	0	0	5.13	4.48	4.97	6.28
14	C	55	Yes	0	0	4.38	4.06	4.91	7.61
15	Yprog	55	No	0	5	8.58	-2.53	2.11	5.18
16	Yprog	55	Yes	0	5	8.19	-2.73	1.82	6.42
17	C	55	No	0	5	7.15	1.51	2.98	6.05
18	C	55	Yes	0	5	6.67	1.18	2.72	6.04
19	Yprog	55	No	.1	0	.43	.53	4.00	5.88
20	Yprog	55	Yes	.1	0	-.20	.06	3.90	7.59
21	Yprog	55	No	.3	0	-1.83	-1.61	2.09	3.37
22	Yprog	55	Yes	.3	0	-2.59	-2.16	2.15	6.04
23	C	55	No	.1	0	3.95	3.36	3.96	5.28
24	C	55	Yes	.1	0	3.14	2.89	3.93	6.80
25	C	55	No	.3	0	1.73	1.26	2.02	3.37
26	C	55	Yes	.3	0	.77	.68	2.07	5.21

Note: For abbreviations, see table 7.3.

[a]Three percent population growth.

Table 7.5   Percentage Change in Output Stock Relative to Steady State

Run	Tax Financing Soc. Sec. Benefits	Years Benefits Phased Out	LSRA	BTL	Years of Deficit Financing	Year of Transition			
						5	10	25	150
1	Yprog	0	No	0	0	14.44	15.91	16.70	17.11
2	Yprog	0	Yes	0	0	9.46	10.52	12.54	13.95
3	Yprog[a]	0	No	0	0	8.27	9.29	10.05	10.39
4	Yprog[a]	0	Yes	0	0	4.73	5.19	5.96	6.44
5	Yprog	0	No	.1	0	13.45	14.86	15.47	16.00
6	Yprog	0	Yes	.1	0	8.30	9.22	10.97	12.36
7	Yprog	0	No	.3	0	11.56	12.88	13.55	13.92
8	Yprog	0	Yes	.3	0	6.15	6.81	8.09	9.58
9	Yprog	55	No	0	0	1.10	1.11	5.00	17.11
10	Yprog	55	Yes	0	0	.35	.01	2.31	8.42
11	W	55	No	0	0	.52	.53	4.78	17.11
12	W	55	Yes	0	0	-.09	-.48	2.10	8.11
13	C	55	No	0	0	5.23	6.20	9.79	17.11
14	C	55	Yes	0	0	4.03	4.61	7.03	10.65
15	Yprog	55	No	0	5	7.50	-1.55	.50	13.06
16	Yprog	55	Yes	0	5	7.12	-1.89	-.68	5.84
17	C	55	No	0	5	5.85	2.18	5.18	12.77
18	C	55	Yes	0	5	5.30	1.44	3.44	7.06
19	Yprog	55	No	.1	0	.09	.06	3.93	16.00
20	Yprog	55	Yes	.1	0	-.75	-1.21	.91	7.04
21	Yprog	55	No	.3	0	-1.79	-1.92	1.93	13.92
22	Yprog	55	Yes	.3	0	-2.84	-3.51	-1.71	4.08
23	C	55	No	.1	0	4.25	5.18	8.73	16.00
24	C	55	Yes	.1	0	2.93	3.38	5.57	9.08
25	C	55	No	.3	0	2.41	3.26	6.73	13.92
26	C	55	Yes	.3	0	.84	1.07	2.88	6.13

Note: For abbreviations, see table 7.3.

[a]Three percent population growth.

Table 7.6   **Percentage Change in Wage Relative to Steady State**

Run	Tax Financing Soc. Sec. Benefits	Years Benefits Phased Out	LSRA	BTL	Years of Deficit Financing	Year of Transition 5	Year of Transition 10	Year of Transition 25	Year of Transition 150
1	Yprog	0	No	0	0	.48	4.35	8.80	10.19
2	Yprog	0	Yes	0	0	−1.16	.40	3.60	6.14
3	Yprog[a]	0	No	0	0	.54	2.96	5.77	6.57
4	Yprog[a]	0	Yes	0	0	−.61	.11	1.44	2.21
5	Yprog	0	No	0	0	−.54	−.56	.00	10.19
6	Yprog	0	Yes	0	0	−.70	−1.20	−2.41	.11
7	Yprog	0	No	0	0	−.34	−.47	−.06	10.19
8	Yprog	0	Yes	0	0	−.56	−1.27	−2.88	−.51
9	Yprog	55	No	0	0	1.04	4.71	8.92	10.21
10	Yprog	55	Yes	0	0	−.76	.25	2.41	4.26
11	W	55	No	0	0	.09	.38	.87	10.19
12	W	55	Yes	0	0	.03	.01	−1.21	−.34
13	C	55	No	0	0	−.25	1.65	4.59	10.19
14	C	55	Yes	0	0	−.34	.52	2.02	2.81
15	Yprog	55	No	0	5	−1.00	1.00	−1.57	7.49
16	Yprog	55	Yes	0	5	−.99	.87	−2.46	−.54
17	C	55	No	0	5	−1.22	.67	2.13	7.30
18	C	55	Yes	0	5	−1.29	.25	.70	1.11
19	Yprog	55	No	.1	0	−.34	−.47	−.06	10.19
20	Yprog	55	Yes	.1	0	−.56	−1.27	−2.88	.51
21	Yprog	55	No	.3	0	.03	−.31	−.15	10.21
22	Yprog	55	Yes	.3	0	−.26	−1.38	−3.79	−1.85
23	C	55	No	.1	0	.29	1.76	4.59	10.19
24	C	55	Yes	.1	0	−.20	.47	1.58	2.12
25	C	55	No	.3	0	.66	1.97	4.62	10.21
26	C	55	Yes	.3	0	.07	.38	.78	.85

Note: For abbreviations, see table 7.3.

[a]Three percent population growth.

Table 7.7 Percentage Change in Interest Rate Relative to Steady State

Run	Tax Financing Soc. Sec. Benefits	Years Benefits Phased Out	LSRA	BTL	Years of Deficit Financing	Year of Transition 5	10	25	150
1	Yprog	0	No	0	0	-1.44	-11.98	-22.35	-25.25
2	Yprog	0	Yes	0	0	3.55	-1.19	-10.08	-16.36
3	Yprog[a]	0	No	0	0	-1.61	-8.39	-15.48	-17.38
4	Yprog[a]	0	Yes	0	0	1.85	-.35	-4.21	-6.34
5	Yprog	0	No	.1	0	-1.99	-12.30	-22.43	-25.26
6	Yprog	0	Yes	.1	0	3.14	-1.02	-8.95	-14.71
7	Yprog	0	No	.3	0	-3.04	-12.90	-22.61	-25.30
8	Yprog	0	Yes	.3	0	2.34	-.77	-6.88	-11.77
9	Yprog	55	No	0	0	1.62	1.69	.00	-25.25
10	Yprog	55	Yes	0	0	2.12	3.69	7.59	-.33
11	W	55	No	0	0	-.60	-1.13	-2.55	-25.25
12	W	55	Yes	0	0	-.09	-.02	3.73	1.03
13	C	55	No	0	0	-2.22	-4.78	-12.59	-25.25
14	C	55	Yes	0	0	1.03	-1.55	-5.81	-7.98
15	Yprog	55	No	0	5	3.05	-2.40	-4.87	-19.49
16	Yprog	55	Yes	0	5	3.03	-2.56	7.75	1.65
17	C	55	No	0	5	3.75	-1.98	-6.13	-19.06
18	C	55	Yes	0	5	4.00	-.75	-2.07	-3.27
19	Yprog	55	No	.1	0	1.02	1.43	.19	-25.26
20	Yprog	55	Yes	.1	0	1.68	3.92	9.17	1.55
21	Yprog	55	No	.3	0	-.11	.93	.45	-25.30
22	Yprog	55	Yes	.3	0	.80	4.27	12.28	5.75
23	C	55	No	.1	0	-.87	-5.10	-12.60	-25.26
24	C	55	Yes	.1	0	.62	-1.39	-4.59	-6.11
25	C	55	No	.3	0	-1.98	-5.69	-12.67	-25.30
26	C	55	Yes	.3	0	-.20	-1.13	-2.32	-2.59

Note: For abbreviations, see table 7.3.

[a]Three percent population growth.

Table 7.8   Percentage Change in Remaining Lifetime Utility

Run	Tax Financing Soc. Sec. Benefits	Years Benefits Phased Out	LSRA	BTL	Years of Deficit Financing	Year of Birth						
						−54	−25	−10	0	10	25	150
1	Yprog	0	No	0	0	−25.60	.43	6.09	8.70	10.04	10.59	10.79
2	Yprog	0	Yes	0	0	.00	.00	.00	7.23	7.23	7.23	7.23
3	Yprog[a]	0	No	0	0	−23.54	−1.83	2.27	4.07	4.92	5.27	5.39
4	Yprog[a]	0	Yes	0	0	.00	.00	.00	2.45	2.45	2.45	2.45
5	Yprog	0	No	.1	0	−25.70	.18	5.85	8.48	9.79	10.32	10.79
6	Yprog	0	Yes	.1	0	.00	.00	.00	6.32	6.32	6.32	6.32
7	Yprog	0	No	.3	0	−25.8	−.27	5.41	8.08	9.33	9.84	10.79
8	Yprog	0	Yes	.3	0	.00	.00	.00	4.65	4.65	4.65	4.65
9	Yprog	55	No	0	0	−.14	−1.67	.04	1.52	2.78	5.82	10.79
10	Yprog	55	Yes	0	0	.00	.00	.00	1.65	1.65	1.65	1.65
11	W	55	No	0	0	.00	−1.18	−.44	.33	1.86	5.35	10.79
12	W	55	Yes	0	0	.00	.00	.00	1.08	1.08	1.08	1.08
13	C	55	No	0	0	−4.71	−1.19	1.81	3.55	5.07	7.57	10.79
14	C	55	Yes	0	0	.00	.00	.00	4.33	4.33	4.33	4.33
15	Yprog	55	No	0	5	.10	−.91	.18	1.26	.55	3.18	8.67
16	Yprog	55	Yes	0	5	.00	.00	.00	1.27	1.27	1.27	1.27
17	C	55	No	0	5	.10	−1.01	1.26	2.66	2.63	5.03	8.52
18	C	55	Yes	0	5	.00	.00	.00	2.98	2.98	2.98	2.98
19	Yprog	55	No	.1	0	−.17	−1.95	−.23	1.24	2.48	5.53	10.79
20	Yprog	55	Yes	.1	0	.00	.00	.00	.66	.66	.66	.66
21	Yprog	55	No	.3	0	−.22	−2.46	−.77	.73	1.95	5.02	10.79
22	Yprog	55	Yes	.3	0	.00	.00	.00	−1.22	−1.22	−1.22	−1.22
23	C	55	No	.1	0	−4.76	−1.46	1.55	3.30	4.80	7.30	10.79
24	C	55	Yes	.1	0	.00	.00	.00	3.40	3.40	3.40	3.40
25	C	55	No	.3	0	−4.37	−1.94	1.06	2.85	4.30	6.80	10.79
26	C	55	Yes	.3	0	.00	.00	.00	1.64	1.64	1.64	1.64

Note: For abbreviations, see table 7.3.

[a]Three percent population growth.

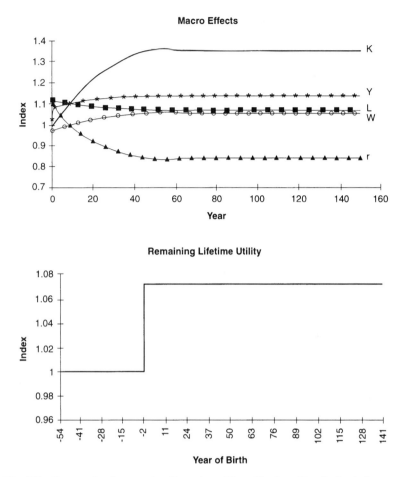

Fig. 7.7   Progressive income tax financing of benefits, benefits eliminated immediately, welfare of living generations constant
Note: K = capital stock; Y = output; W = the real wage; L = the labor supply; and r = the real interest rate.

those born after the reform by 7.23 percent. As excess burden calculations go, this is a very large efficiency gain.

The efficiency gains are measured here as the percentage increase in full lifetime income (the present value of expenditures on consumption and leisure). Since every generation born after the reform begins enjoys this efficiency gain, it represents an ongoing flow to the economy. This flow can readily be expressed as a percentage of initial GDP by simply multiplying the reported efficiency gain by the ratio of the steady-state present value of full income to GDP. The latter turns out to be .53 for all runs except the high-growth economy. In other words, the welfare gains expressed as a percentage of GDP are about half as large as the welfare gains expressed as a percentage of discounted lifetime full income.

To check the sensitivity of the results to the assumed growth rate, I next repeated (in runs 3 and 4) both simulations assuming a 3 percent population growth rate. The payroll tax is held constant in this analysis. Consequently, the replacement rate is twice as high as with 1 percent population growth. Accordingly, income and consumption levels are much smaller in the initial steady state. "Cold turkey" privatization of social security without LSRA leads to a larger percentage increase in capital stock, income, and wages than with 1 percent population growth. The long-run welfare gain is 10.7 percent. With LSRA turned on, the high benefit level requires large transfers to the old, who would otherwise lose up to 41 percent of their lifetime utility. Therefore, the capital stock grows more slowly. Overall, the efficiency gain is 5.64 percent in the high-growth case compared to the 7.23 percent with 1 percent growth.

Runs 5–8 let us consider the extent to which the results in runs 1 and 2 depend on the degree of marginal benefit-tax linkage in the initial social security system. Runs 5 and 6 consider 10 percent marginal linkage, whereas runs 7 and 8 consider 30 percent marginal linkage. Thus, in these sets of simulations, the total effective marginal tax rate on labor supply includes either 90 or 70 percent of the social security payroll tax rate. As a comparison of runs 5 and 7 with run 1 indicates, macroeconomic effects of the no LSRA simulations are fairly similar to those without benefit-tax linkage. For example, with 30 percent benefit-tax linkage, there is a 52 percent long-run increase in the capital stock compared with 57 percent with zero linkage. The LSRA runs (runs 6 and 8) are more interesting. As shown in table 7.6, the efficiency gain from social security's privatization is 6.32 percent with 10 percent linkage and 4.65 percent with 30 percent linkage. These figures are smaller than the 7.23 percent efficiency gain found in run 2 when the economy features zero initial linkage. They indicate that even a small degree of benefit-tax linkage can have a substantial effect on social security's distortion of labor supply.

7.3.2   Progressive Income Tax or Wage Tax Financing of Transition Benefits

The next simulations, shown in figures 7.8 and 7.9, consider privatizing social security but raising progressive income tax rates to pay for transitional benefits. In the uncompensated (no LSRA) transition (run 9), the long-run position of the economy is exactly the same as in the corresponding cold-turkey transition. But the economy's short-term transition is quite different. The induced capital accumulation occurs much more slowly, and initial older generations suffer much smaller reductions in their levels of remaining lifetime utility. In the compensated transition (run 10), the efficiency gain is 1.65 percent compared with 7.23 percent in the cold-turkey run. Although this is a very big difference, a 1.65 percent efficiency gain is nontrivial.

The fact that the efficiency gain is positive may, itself, be surprising. Intuitively, raising progressive income tax rates to pay for social security benefits

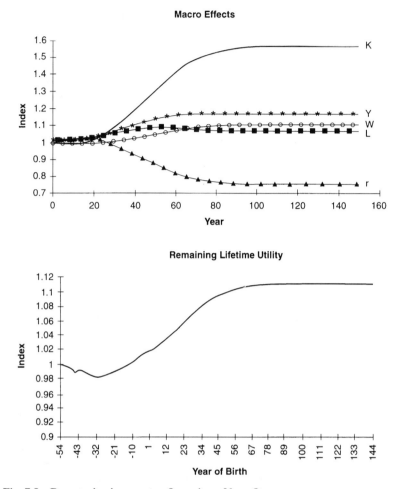

Fig. 7.8   Progressive income tax financing of benefits
Note: K = capital stock; Y = output; W = the real wage; L = the labor supply; and r = the real interest rate.

during the transition temporarily adds extra distortions to the fiscal structure at the same time it eliminates a permanent distortion from payroll taxation. These extra distortions involve both the labor-leisure decisions and intertemporal consumption decisions. Now, one might think that a tax structure with permanently low tax rates would be more efficient than one that collects, in present value, the same amount of revenue but does so with higher marginal tax rates in the short run than in the long run. This intuition follows from the fact that tax distortions rise with the square of the tax rate, with the result that smoothing tax rates over time provides a way of mitigating deadweight loss.

This intuition is correct as far as it goes. But switching from payroll tax to

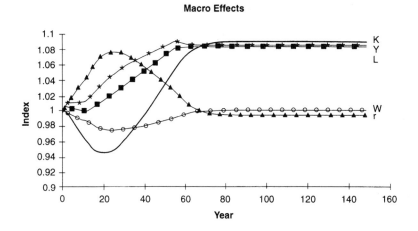

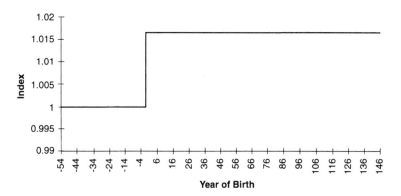

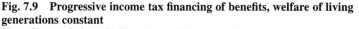

**Fig. 7.9   Progressive income tax financing of benefits, welfare of living
generations constant**
Note: K = capital stock; Y = output; W = the real wage; L = the labor supply; and
r = the real interest rate.

income tax financing of social security benefits in the short run has four additional features that need to be considered. First, the switch equalizes the marginal tax rates affecting labor-leisure and intertemporal consumption choices, so it smooths tax rates over economic choices.[16] Second, the capital income tax component of the progressive income tax has a lump sum tax element to it. In the short run, capital income is given, so taxing it via a higher rate of capital income taxation represents an implicit lump sum tax. Third, the decline over

16. In the initial steady state, the tax rate on the labor-leisure margin exceeds that on the intertemporal consumption margin because the payroll tax taxes only labor income.

time in progressive income tax rates as social security benefits are phased out acts like a negative capital income tax rate, which offsets the distortion caused by the capital income tax component of the progressive income tax that is financing government purchases. Fourth, if, as assumed in these simulations, social security benefits are provided independent of tax contributions, one could reduce the distortion of labor supply by linking benefits to marginal contributions. For example, one could provide a rate of return equal to the economy's growth rate on each dollar paid to social security. This marginal benefit-tax linkage would lower the effective rate of marginal payroll taxation. Although the current social security privatization simulations eliminate social security benefits over time rather than marginally linking them to contributions, the result, in the long run, is quite similar because this needless additional distortion is eliminated.

Runs 11 and 12 phase out benefits in the same manner as runs 9 and 10 but pay for them with a payroll tax rather than a progressive income tax. As table 7.3 shows, compared to income tax financing, payroll tax (wage tax) financing of transition benefits speeds up capital accumulation in the early phase of the transition. This reflects the greater saving disincentives associated with temporarily high capital income taxes.

The pattern of welfare gains and losses also differs. With income tax financing, there are bigger welfare losses to initial elderly cohorts in the non-LSRA runs (runs 9 and 11) but also bigger gains to initial younger cohorts as well as those born shortly after the reform. Given these differences, which financing mechanism is more efficient? The answer, given in LSRA runs 10 and 12, is progressive income tax financing. There is a 1.65 percent efficiency gain with progressive tax financing compared with a 1.08 percent gain with payroll tax financing.

7.3.3 Consumption Tax Financing of Transition Benefits

The next two simulations use a proportional consumption tax to finance transitional benefits. As figures 7.10 and 7.11 and runs 13 and 14 indicate, consumption tax financing produces much more favorable short-run macroeconomic effects in both the compensated and the uncompensated runs. For example, in the uncompensated run, the capital stock is 12 percent bigger in the tenth year of the reform than when the reform begins. With progressive income tax financing, the tenth-year capital stock is actually smaller, by .6 percent. After twenty-five years, the capital stock is 26 percent larger in the uncompensated consumption tax transition but only 5 percent larger in the uncompensated income tax transition. Since in both the uncompensated consumption and income tax runs the capital stock ultimately ends up 57 percent higher than its initial value, virtually all the crowding in of capital in the income tax financing run occurs more than a quarter century from the time the social security reform is initiated.

The better short-run macroeconomic performance in the no-LSRA con-

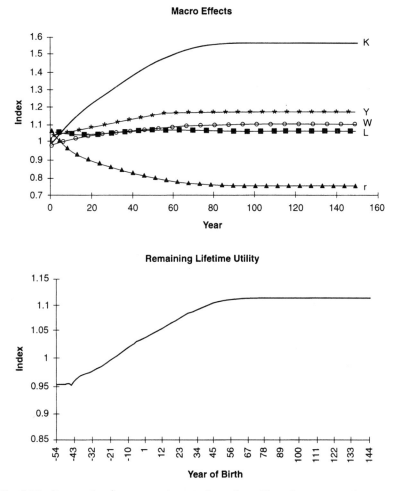

Fig. 7.10   Proportional consumption tax financing of benefits, progressive income tax finance of general revenues
Note: K = capital stock; Y = output; W = the real wage; L = the labor supply; and r = the real interest rate.

sumption tax run comes at the price of larger welfare losses to initial older generations. For example, the oldest generation at the time of the reform suffers a 4.7 percent welfare loss with consumption tax financing but only a -0.4 percent loss under income tax financing. The question begged by this result, of course, is whether consumption tax financing is more efficient than income tax financing; that is, whether there is still an advantage to consumption tax financing once initial generations have been fully compensated for the additional fiscal burden arising under consumption taxation.

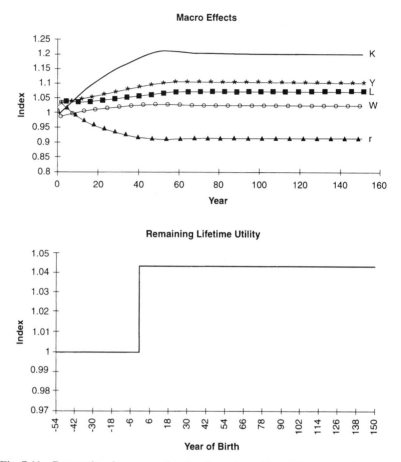

Fig. 7.11   Proportional consumption tax financing of benefits, progressive income tax finance of general revenues, welfare of living generations constant
Note: K = capital stock; Y = output; W = the real wage; L = the labor supply; and r = the real interest rate.

The answer is a strong yes. The efficiency gain available with consumption tax financing is a quite substantial 4.33 percent. This is almost two-thirds of the maximum efficiency gain achievable from privatizing social security and 2.5 times the efficiency gain available under income tax financing! As discussed in Chamley (1981) and Auerbach and Kotlikoff (1987), consumption taxation is more efficient than income or wage taxation because it incorporates a lump sum tax on existing wealth.

How much of this efficiency gain could be achieved by just financing existing social security benefits through a consumption tax? A run that substitutes for the payroll tax a consumption tax and keeps benefits in place while compensating living generations gives the answer: the efficiency gain is 3.44 percent compared to 4.33 percent if benefits are phased out over time. Note, however, that, in the absence of compensation, the long-run gains from simply switching to consumption tax financing of social security are much smaller than those arising when one also phases out social security benefits over time. For example, the capital stock increases by only 17.5 percent, compared to 56.7 percent when benefits are phased out. And the long-run welfare gain is only 4.05 percent, compared to 10.79 percent.

7.3.4   Sensitivity Analysis

To what extend does the choice of parameter values influence the findings outlined above? Table 7.9 addresses this question. It shows efficiency gains from privatizing social security with income or consumption tax financing for combinations of intratemporal substitution elasticities ranging from 0.50 to 1.20 and intertemporal elasticities of substitution ranging from 0.15 to 0.50. The qualitative results are the same for all the combinations indicted. Future generations' welfare increases between 0.7 and 2.7 percent with income tax financing and between 3.5 and 5.1 percent with consumption tax financing. Since—as discussed before—efficiency gains largely arise from eliminating the payroll tax's distortion of labor supply decisions, the intratemporal elasticity of substitution between leisure and consumption has a larger influence on the magnitude of efficiency gains than does the intertemporal elasticity of substitution.

7.3.5   The Importance of the Initial Debt Position

Thus far, I have assumed no government debt in the initial steady state. To check whether this matters, I repeated runs 9 and 10 as well as 13 and 14 with

Table 7.9   **Sensitivity Analysis**

Intratemporal Elasticity of Substitution	Intertemporal Elasticity of Substitution		
	.15	.25	.50
	Efficiency Gains with Income-Tax Finance (%)		
.50	Not converged	.65	1.08
.80	1.65	1.67	1.96
1.20	2.46	2.44	2.70
	Efficiency Gains with Consumption-Tax Finance (%)		
.50	Not converged	3.67	3.53
.80	4.78	4.33	4.22
1.20	5.05	4.75	4.72

an initial 50 percent debt-to-GDP ratio. Recall that runs 9 and 10 incorporate progressive income tax financing of social security benefits, whereas runs 13 and 14 incorporate consumption tax financing. Runs 9 and 13 are non-LSRA, and runs 10 and 14 are LSRA. In all cases, the welfare gains are larger with initial debt than without. Welfare increases by 11.5 percent compared to 10.8 percent in runs 9 and 13. Efficiency gains from privatization are 1.91 percent in the income tax financing case and 4.72 in the consumption tax financing case, an increase of .15 and .29 percentage points, respectively.

The reason for these differences in straightforward. During the transition, capital accumulation reduces interest rates, which also reduces the fiscal burden of debt service. This permits a reduction in tax rates. This, again, induces more capital accumulation and labor supply. In fact, repeating run 9 with initial debt leads to a 61.7 percent higher long-run capital stock and a 7.21 percent higher long-run labor supply. The concomitant numbers without debt are 56.7 and 6.28 percent, respectively. Similar results apply to the other runs. Thus, the calculations presented so far can be understood as lower bounds for an economy with initial debt.

7.3.6   Using Debt Financing in the Short Run

An alternative to immediately raising either income or consumption tax rates to pay for transition benefits is to borrow for a while. The next set of simulations considers a postreform period of borrowing that lasts for five years. Figures 7.12 and 7.13 and runs 15 and 16 consider raising progressive income tax rates after the five-year issuance of debt to pay both interest on the accumulated debt and social security benefits during the remainder of the transition. Figures 7.14 and 7.15 and runs 17 and 18 repeat this analysis but use a proportional consumption tax to pay for social security benefits after the five-year period of deficit financing is completed.

Consider first the uncompensated runs. With income tax financing, capital is first crowded in, then crowded out, then crowded in. As discussed in Auerbach and Kotlikoff (1987), short-run crowding in can arise in the presence of deficit financing as workers take advantage of temporarily low marginal tax rates to increase their labor supply. This leads them to both earn and save more. Once income taxes are raised (indeed, raised above their initial values) to pay interest on past accumulated debt as well as to pay for ongoing spending, workers reduce their labor supply below their initial values. In run 17, the crowding-in/crowding-out/crowding-in effects of deficit financing alter the basic short-run pattern of capital accumulation observed in no-deficit, income tax financing (run 9). The deficit financing also reduces the amount of long-run crowding in of capital, with the long-run capital stock now only 40 percent, rather than 57 percent, larger than in the initial steady state.

In contrast to the income tax cum temporary deficit results, the consumption tax cum temporary deficit displays smaller crowding in in the very short run. The principal reason is that the prospect of a near-term (after year 5) increase

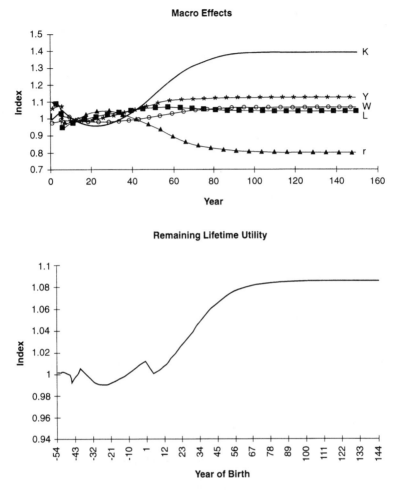

Fig. 7.12   Progressive income tax financing of benefits, 5 year debt finance
Note: K = capital stock; Y = output; W = the real wage; L = the labor supply; and r = the real interest rate.

in consumption tax rates acts just like a temporarily high rate of capital income taxation, leading households to substitute current for future consumption. The smaller short-run crowding in under consumption tax financing necessitates more debt accumulation in the consumption tax run than in the income tax run. This higher debt-to-output ratio explains why long-run capital formation is slightly smaller under consumption tax financing than income tax financing.

The use of short-term deficit financing during the transition leaves the economy with permanently higher marginal tax rates. It also particularly distorts the choices of how much to work and how much to save right before and right after the period of deficit financing. Hence, it is not surprising that the LSRA

Macro Effects

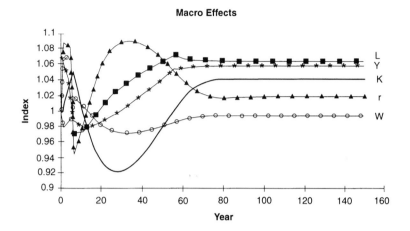

Remaining Lifetime Utility

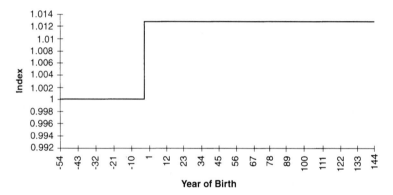

Fig. 7.13   Progressive income tax financing of benefits, 5 year debt finance welfare of living generations constant

Note: K = capital stock; *Y* = output; *W* = the real wage; *L* = the labor supply; and *r* = the real interest rate.

runs produce smaller efficiency gains from privatization with deficit financing than without it. In the income tax runs, the efficiency gain is 1.27 percent with deficit financing, compared to 1.65 percent without. In the consumption tax runs, the efficiency gain is 2.98 percent with deficit financing, compared to 4.33 percent without it.

7.3.7   Privatizing from a Position of Partial Benefit-Tax Linkage

The remaining eight sets of simulations, runs 19–26, also phase out social security benefits over a fifty-five-year period but do so assuming either 10 or

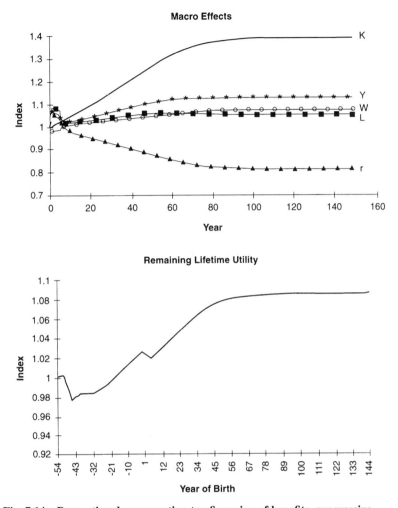

Fig. 7.14   Proportional consumption tax financing of benefits, progressive income tax finance of general revenues, 5 year debt finance
Note: K = capital stock; Y = output; W = the real wage; L = the labor supply; and r = the real interest rate.

30 percent marginal benefit-tax linkage. As tables 7.3–7.8 indicate, the crowding in associated with privatization is smaller the higher the degree of benefit-tax linkage. For example, with 30 percent linkage, the long-run increase in capital in the no-LSRA income and consumption tax runs is 52 percent, compared with 57 percent with no linkage. These differences and those of other macro variables are not large. But the differences in efficiency gains with and

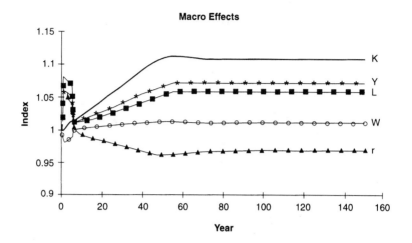

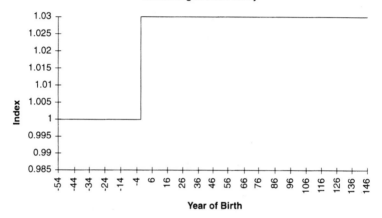

Fig. 7.15   Proportional consumption tax financing of benefits, progressive income tax finance of general revenues, 5 year debt finance, welfare of living generations constant

Note: K = capital stock; Y = output; W = the real wage; L = the labor supply; and r = the real interest rate.

without partial linkage are substantial. Run 20 in table 7.8 indicates only a 0.66 percent gain under income tax financing when linkage is 10 percent compared to a 1.65 percent gain with zero linkage. And run 22, which features income tax financing with 30 percent linkage, actually shows a 1.22 percent efficiency loss. In the case of consumption tax financing, the efficiency gain is 4.33 percent with zero linkage, 3.4 percent with 10 percent linkage, and 1.64 percent with 30 percent linkage. These efficiency gains are 61, 55, and 37 percent, respectively, of the corresponding maximum efficiency gains reported in runs 2, 6, and 8 of table 7.6 from replacing social security with lump sum net taxes.

7.4 Incorporating Intracohort Heterogeneity

The multi-income version of the AK model developed by Kent Smetters, Jan Walliser, and me follows Fullerton and Rogers (1993) in positing twelve earnings classes within each cohort. Each of these earnings classes experiences the same longitudinal age-earnings profile as described in Auerbach and Kotlikoff (1987), but each has its own wage level. Thus, the classes can be thought of as differing in their endowments of human capital. Following Fullerton and Rogers (1993), the bottom decile of wage earners is divided into classes 1 and 2. Class 1 contains 2 percent of the distribution, and class 2 contains 8 percent of the distribution. Classes 3–10 contain 10 percent each of the distribution, and classes 11 and 12 contain the highest decile, with class 12 containing 2 percent of the distribution and class 11 containing 8 percent. The initial steady-state wage rates for the twelve classes are also taken from Fullerton and Rogers (1993) and are 1, 1.7, 2.2, 2.7, 3.1, 3.5, 3.8, 4.2, 4.7, 5.5, 7.2, and 10.2, respectively.

Tables 7.10–7.15 use the multi-income model to consider two alternative privatization policies. One uses a consumption tax to finance transition benefits, the other a progressive income tax. Both simulations are uncompensated.

Table 7.10   **Percentage Change in Capital Stock Relative to Steady State with Multiple Income Classes**

Run	Tax Financing Soc. Sec. Benefits	Years Benefits Phased Out	LSRA	BTL	Years of Deficit Financing	5	10	25	150
27	C	55	No	0	0	5.75	11.85	26.06	55.64
28	Yprog	55	No	0	0	−.50	−.56	5.09	55.64

Note: For abbreviations, see table 7.3.

Table 7.11   **Percentage Change in Labor Supply Relative to Steady State with Multiple Income Classes**

Run	Tax Financing Soc. Sec. Benefits	Years Benefits Phased Out	LSRA	BTL	Years of Deficit Financing	5	10	25	150
27	C	55	No	0	0	5.64	4.86	5.34	6.55
28	Yprog	55	No	0	0	1.82	1.84	5.49	6.55

Note: For abbreviations, see table 7.3.

Table 7.12 Percentage Change in Output Relative to Steady State with Multiple Income Classes

	Tax Financing Soc. Sec.	Years Benefits Phased			Years of Deficit	Year of Transition			
Run	Benefits	Out	LSRA	BTL	Financing	5	10	25	150
27	C	55	No	0	0	5.67	6.57	10.17	17.14
28	Yprog	55	No	0	0	1.23	1.24	5.39	17.14

Note: For abbreviations, see table 7.3.

Table 7.13 Percentage Change in Wages Relative to Steady State with Multiple Income Classes

	Tax Financing Soc. Sec.	Years Benefits Phased			Years of Deficit	Year of Transition			
Run	Benefits	Out	LSRA	BTL	Financing	5	10	25	150
27	C	0	No	0	0	.03	1.63	4.59	9.93
28	Yprog	55	No	0	0	−.57	−.60	−.09	9.93

Note: For abbreviations, see table 7.3.

Table 7.14 Percentage Change in Interest Rates Relative to Steady State with Multiple Income Classes

	Tax Financing Soc. Sec.	Years Benefits Phased			Years of Deficit	Year of Transition			
Run	Benefits	Out	LSRA	BTL	Financing	5	10	25	150
27	C	55	No	0	0	−.08	−4.72	−12.60	−24.73
28	Yprog	55	No	0	0	1.73	1.81	1.00	−24.73

Note: For abbreviations, see table 7.3.

Table 7.15 Percentage Change in Remaining Lifetime Utilities for Selected Income Classes

	Year of Birth						
Run and Class	−54	−25	−10	0	10	25	150
27:							
1	−4.58	−1.79	1.17	2.91	4.29	6.78	10.13
3	−4.17	−1.61	1.17	2.81	4.03	6.27	9.22
6	−4.01	−1.39	1.27	2.83	3.97	6.08	8.82
9	−3.89	−1.16	1.38	2.87	3.96	6.00	8.59
12	−3.67	−.23	1.88	3.10	4.03	5.89	8.12
28:							
1	−.14	−1.70	.00	1.32	2.29	5.08	10.13
3	−.11	−1.64	−.10	1.18	2.10	4.70	9.22
6	−.13	−1.52	.00	1.13	2.04	4.57	8.82
9	−.09	−1.50	−.11	1.11	2.02	4.53	8.59
12	−.19	−1.19	.00	1.10	2.04	4.52	8.12

The corresponding one-income-class runs with which to compare these results are listed in tables 7.3–7.8 as runs 13 and 9. (Table 7.16 shows the share of tax revenue paid by the different income classes, and table 7.17 shows the percentage changes in labor supply and consumption.)

Such comparisons indicate that changes in macroeconomic variables in the multi-income-class model are very close to those in the one-income-class model. Take, for example, year 5 and year 150 increases in the capital stock under consumption tax financing. They are 5.75 and 55.64 percent, respectively, in the multi-income-class run and 5.54 and 56.67 percent, respectively, in the one-income-class model. Or consider the year 5 and year 150 increases in output in the progressive tax run. They are 1.23 and 17.14 percent, respectively, in the multi-income-class run and 1.10 and 17.11 percent, respectively, in the one-income-class model. Intracohort earnings heterogeneity does not, then, alter this paper's central finding that privatizing social security can produce very major long-run improvements in the state of the economy.

Table 7.15 indicates that the welfare gains and losses associated with uncompensated transitions to privatized social security can differ significantly across members of a cohort and that these differences can flip signs over time. Take run 27, which incorporates consumption tax financing. In this run, all members of the oldest cohort at the time of the reform, those age fifty-four, end up worse off. But the poorer elderly suffer a relatively larger welfare loss. For example, class 1 fifty-four-year-olds suffer a 4.58 percent reduction in re-

Table 7.16   **Share of Tax Revenues by Class in Steady States (%)**

1	2	3	4	5	6	7	8	9	10	11	12
.48	3.33	5.54	6.77	7.91	8.88	9.65	10.77	12.17	14.33	14.95	5.22
.40	2.94	5.05	6.32	7.52	8.57	9.42	10.67	12.27	14.80	16.08	5.96

Table 7.17   **Percentage Change in Labor Supply and Consumption**

			Class		
Age	1	3	6	9	12
Labor supply:					
15	.46	.97	1.44	1.86	3.60
35	21.70	23.76	22.56	20.39	9.96
45	167.60	168.50	108.49	69.61	11.78
55	.00	.00	.00	.00	7.55
Consumption:					
15	27.50	28.60	29.65	30.59	33.35
35	18.00	18.86	19.47	19.87	19.73
45	12.51	12.44	12.26	11.97	9.58
55	−1.66	−1.76	−1.56	−1.38	2.65

maining lifetime utility, whereas the class 12 fifty-four-year-olds experience only a 3.67 percent utility loss.

These differences reflect two factors. First, the reform induces a significant and immediate increase in labor supply (see table 7.11), which raises the year 1 interest rate from 9.4 to 9.8 percent. This benefits the rich elderly more than the poor elderly because a bigger share of their old age consumption is financed by their assets (as opposed to their social security benefits). Second, the increase in labor supply means more income, which means a larger income tax base. This permits the government to cut its income tax rates, which is relatively more important to the rich elderly, who start out in quite high marginal tax brackets.

Interestingly, the distribution of long-run utility gains in run 27 is quite different from the distribution of the short-run gains. As table 7.15 points out, all income groups benefit in the long run, but the welfare gains to poorer income groups exceed those to richer ones. For example, members of the class 1 cohort alive in the long run enjoy a 10.13 percent increase in lifetime utility, compared to an 8.12 percent increase for members of the class 12 cohort alive in the long run. What explains this? The answer is that, for lower income classes, social security's implicit tax associated with its pay-as-you-go financing represents a larger share of its lifetime resources than it does for the higher income classes. Hence, eliminating pay-as-you-go social security provides lower income classes with a larger percentage welfare gain than it provides higher income classes.

Comparing the top and bottom halves of table 7.15 shows that the short-run distribution of welfare gains from privatizing social security is critically dependent on the method used to finance the transition. The bottom half of the table, run 28, considers progressive income tax financing of transition benefits. Since this is disadvantageous to the richer agents as well as less efficient overall compared to consumption tax financing, it is not surprising that initial elderly and young members of income class 12 are worse off in this run compared to run 27. It is also not surprising that, for example, the richest fifty-four-year-olds suffer a bigger welfare loss than do the poorest fifty-four-year-olds.

7.5 Conclusion

The privatizing of social security is spreading from South America. It could well spread to the United States as politicians grapple with ways of addressing the fiscal/demographic debacle facing the country. This paper's simulations of the AK model show that privatizing social security is likely to generate major long-run increases in output and living standards. But, unless privatization includes compensation to initial generations, these long-run gains will come, in large part, at their expense. This said, the pure efficiency gains from privatization can be substantial. Their precise size depends on the existing tax structure, the linkage between benefits and taxes under the existing social security system, and the choice of the tax instrument used to finance benefits during the transition. When the initial tax structure features a progressive income tax, when benefit-tax linkage is low, when consumption taxation is used to finance social security benefits during the transition, and when existing generations are fully compensated for their privatization losses, there is a 4.3 percent welfare gain to future generations. But, if these circumstances do not hold, the efficiency gains from privatization are likely to be smaller, possibly even negative. Indeed, with income tax financing of transitional benefits, 30 percent linkage, and full compensation paid to initial generations, future generations suffer a 1.2 percent welfare decline.

There are two lessons to be drawn from this multi-income-class analysis. First, policies that equalize the intracohort distribution of utility in the long run may fail to do so in the short run. Second, in the long run, since the privatization of social security eliminates an implicit tax that places a relatively high proportional burden on the lifetime poor, it is likely to improve the well-being of the lifetime poor relative to the lifetime rich; that is, as a long-run proposition, privatizing social security is progressive.

References

Arrau, Patricio. 1990. Social security reform: The capital accumulation and intergenerational distribution effect. Washington, D.C.: World Bank. Mimeo.

Arrau, Patricio, and Klaus Schmidt-Hebbel. 1993. Macroeconomic and intergenerational welfare effects of a transition from pay-as-you-go to fully funded pensions. Washington, D.C.: World Bank, Macroeconomics and Growth Division, Policy Research Department. Mimeo.

Auerbach, Alan J., and Laurence J. Kotlikoff. 1987. *Dynamic fiscal policy.* Cambridge: Cambridge University Press.

Boskin, Michael J., Laurence J. Kotlikoff, Douglas J. Puffert, and John B. Shoven. 1987. Social security: A financial appraisal across and within generations. *National Tax Journal* 40, 1:19–34.

Chamley, Christophe. 1981. The welfare costs of capital income taxation in a growing economy. *Journal of Political Economy,* vol. 89, no. 3.

Feldstein, Martin. 1995. Would privatizing social security raise economic welfare? Harvard University. Mimeo.

Feldstein, Martin, and Andrew Samwick. 1992. Social security rules and marginal tax rates. *National Tax Journal* 45, no. 1:1–22.

Fullerton, Don, and Diane Lim Rogers. 1993. *Who bears the lifetime tax burden?* Washington, D.C.: Brookings.

Gokhale, Jagadeesh, Laurence J. Kotlikoff, and John Sabelhaus. 1996. Understanding the postwar decline in U.S. saving: A cohort analysis. *Brookings Papers on Economic Activity,* no. 1:315–90.

Hayashi, Fumio, Joseph Altonji, and Laurence J. Kotlikoff. 1996. Risk-sharing between and within families. *Econometrica* 64, no. 2:261–94.

Imrohoroglu, Selahattin, He Huang, and Thomas J. Sargent. 1995. Two computational experiments to privatize social security. University of Southern California. Mimeo.

Kotlikoff, Laurence J. 1996a. Privatizing social security: How it works and why it matters. In *Tax policy and the economy,* ed. James Poterba. Cambridge, Mass.: MIT Press.

———. 1996b. Privatizing social security at home and abroad. *American Economic Review* 86, no. 2:368–72.

———. 1996c. Privatizing social security in the United States: Why and how. In *Fiscal policy: Lessons from economic research,* ed. Alan Auerbach. Cambridge, Mass.: MIT Press.

Kotlikoff, Laurence J., and Avia Spivak. 1981. The family as an incomplete annuities market. *Journal of Political Economy* 89, no. 2 (April): 372–91.

Raffelhueschen, Bernd. 1993. Funding social security through Pareto-optimal conversion policies. In *Public pension economics,* ed. Bernhard Felderer. *Journal of Economics/Zeitschrift fur Nationalokonomie,* suppl. 7.

Comment   Thomas J. Sargent

The U.S. social security system was conceived during the 1930s, when many academic economists believed that excessive saving and overaccumulation of capital were fundamental macroeconomic problems. Because it depressed the prospective returns to new physical investments, a large capital stock promoted unemployment. This was the stagnation thesis. An unfunded social retirement system could "cure" the problem of capital overaccumulation by diminishing incentives to save: taxes from young workers were to be transferred to retirees. The promise that they too should expect to receive transfers when they were old would dissuade the young from saving. This cure for too much capital was later formalized by the analysis of Paul Samuelson's (1956) overlapping generations model (see, e.g., Diamond 1996; and Gale 1973). In that model, capital overaccumulation threatens when the rate of return on capital falls short of the rate of growth of the labor force. Low rates of return on bonds prevailed in the United States during the 1930s.

With the passage of years, concerns about capital overaccumulation and stagnation have receded into memory, to be replaced by public concern over a low U.S. saving rate. But we continue to live with a social retirement system that was designed to arrest saving. This dissonance is the origin of calls to reform the social retirement system to make it match what are *now* thought to be the economic rewards to national saving, not those feared in the 1930s.

The political difficulties of reforming social security are inherited from the economic transition dynamics associated first with installing, then with reforming, an unfunded social retirement system. Installing the system *ab novo* is easier because many of those who might be harmed by the proposal cannot vote. A brand new system helps early retirees at the expense of future generations, who cannot vote until much later, after the system is already in place. Reforming an ongoing system is more difficult because the beneficiaries of the old system *do* vote. This makes it necessary somehow not to undo the old

Thomas J. Sargent is a professor at the Hoover Institution of Stanford University.

system too rapidly and to honor the government's promises to retirees who live through the transition. It seems easier to vote an unfunded social retirement system in than to vote one out.

Laurence Kotlikoff is the coauthor of the Auerbach-Kotlikoff (1987) model (the AK model), our most important practical tool for quantitatively studying alternative proposals to reform social retirement arrangements. The present paper by Kotlikoff consists of two broad parts, each of which is informed by Kotlikoff's work with the AK model. The first is a wide-ranging informal discussion of a host of financing and incentive issues. The second part is a battery of numerical simulations of a calibrated version of the AK model. These simulations add weight to the opinions Kotlikoff expresses in the first, less formal section.

The Model

The AK model is the correct tool for this job. It consists of overlapping generations of long-lived people. The equilibrium is competitive, with an exogenous government policy. A government policy is a specification of rules for setting tax rates and transfers and for managing the government's debt. An equilibrium is a price system, a consumption allocation (to each person of each cohort at each age), and a government policy at which households are optimizing and the government is satisfying its sequence of budget constraints. There is no uncertainty in the environment and therefore no demand for insurance. Thus, for Kotlikoff, an equilibrium is a collection of sequences of real numbers. Were there uncertainty facing households, an equilibrium would be a sequence of probability distributions of wealth and consumption.

Kotlikoff at first assumes a single type within each cohort and then, in order to study within-cohort distribution effects, a version in which there are twelve earning classes within each cohort. A good feature of the model is that Kotlikoff's specification of a household's preferences induces endogenous work reductions at the end of life (i.e., retirements).

The AK model is a machine for studying how tax and transfer policies affect distributions of consumption and welfare when households are free to rearrange their own affairs in reaction to government policies. A general equilibrium imposes two kinds of discipline. First, the government must respect its budget constraint—deficit financing limits the government's opportunities in the future. Second, households respond purposefully, not arbitrarily, to government policies.

Issues

Kotlikoff analyses alternative tax and transfer policies that can eventually lead to a fully funded system. Many policies can do the job. Kotlikoff's paper compares a number of them with an eye toward their political sustainability. Attaining political sustainability requires transferring enough of the long-term gains from posterity to those entitled under the initial unfunded systems. When the eventual gains from full funding are large enough—as they are with Kotlikoff's parameter settings—there is plenty of room to redistribute some of the gains toward these entitled people.

Kotlikoff's paper contains a valuable discussion of benefit-tax linkages. Whether the social security tax acts entirely as a payroll tax or partly as a saving plan depends on workers' perception of how their prospective receipts vary with their contributions. This perception interacts with their labor supply elasticities to influence the distortions associated with the social security payroll tax.

Kotlikoff also compares consequences of alternative means of financing a scheme to compensate those who would be hurt by a sudden transition to a fully funded system. I commend his welfare analysis of the use of a consumption tax to finance the transition. His discussion well balances the efficiency and redistribution consequences of using a consumption tax. This work continues Auerbach and Kotlikoff's focus on the intergenerational redistributional consequences of moving, say, from a tax on capital to a consumption tax.

Extensions

Kotlikoff's formal model excludes aspects that his informal discussion mentions, the social insurance provided by the social security system. How and whether this exclusion affects the case for fully funding social security depends on how one models markets for insurance. Settings with incomplete markets augment forces for capital accumulation and make more room for using a tax-transfer mechanism to correct the problem. In addition, with incomplete markets, uncertainty activates mechanisms that cause aggregate randomness to affect income distributions.

It is possible and natural to extend the basic AK model to uncertain environments with incomplete markets. The cheapest extension covers settings with no aggregate uncertainty but uninsurable uncertainty at the individual level, which averages out in the aggregate. In recent work, two sorts of individual uncertainty have been included: life-span risk and household-specific endowment or labor-income risk (see Imrohoroglu, Imrohoroglu, and Joines 1995). Even with one type of household ex ante, market incompleteness causes the distribution of consumption across individuals within a cohort to spread. Deaton and Paxson (1994) discuss the fanning-out mechanism, an implication of the permanent income theory with incomplete markets. An equilibrium of such a model induces a probability distribution of consumption across households for each cohort for each time period. Figures 7C.1 and 7C.2 display the mean and standard deviation of consumption distributions for such a model, during a funding experiment similar to one of Kotlikoff's (these figures are taken from Huang, Imrohoroglu, and Sargent [1996]). The experiment is a transition from an unfunded to a fully funded retirement system in which the initially entitled people are fully compensated. The compensation to the old—which is over 2.5 times GDP—is financed by issuing bonds, then raising the tax rate on labor income until the extra bonds are retired. Notice how this transition eventually

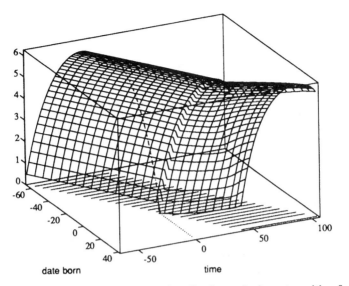

Fig. 7C.1   Mean consumption profiles for all cohorts during a transition for experiment 1 of Huang, Imrohoroglu, and Sargent (1996), a bond-compensated, tax-financed removal of social security. The shadow on the floor depicts when a cohort is alive.

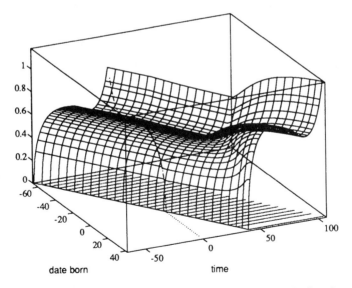

Fig. 7C.2   Standard deviations of consumption for all cohorts during the transition for experiment 1 of Huang, Imrohoroglu, and Sargent (1996).

raises both the mean and the standard deviation of the age-consumption profiles. The point of these pictures is to extend the analysis of Kotlikoff's section 7.4. Government policy affects not only the mean but also the standard deviation of these distributions. The details of the transition financing scheme affect how much the distribution of consumption across households will spread or compress in response to the reform. This point reinforces Auerbach and Kotlikoff's long-standing emphasis on the distributional consequences of alternative fiscal policies. It warns us not to oversell the benefits of a transition: not everyone is likely to be a winner. The current system provides some social insurance that is not likely to be fully replaced.

More challenging aspects of uncertainty to include are aggregate risk about two features of the environment: returns on capital and demography. These are technically difficult to incorporate because they cause the aggregate state for the economy to include distributions of wealth across people, a feature that makes the dimension of the state unmanageably large. Progress is being made with studying such models (see Krusell and Smith 1995), and it is important to bring that progress to bear on AK types of models. Our estimates about the benefits of funded versus unfunded social security and retirement arrangements will hinge on our calibrations of the riskiness of returns to capital and demography.

References

Auerbach, Alan J., and Laurence J. Kotlikoff. 1987. *Dynamic fiscal policy.* Cambridge, Mass.: Cambridge University Press.
Deaton, Angus, and Christina Paxson. 1994. Intertemporal choice and inequality. *Journal of Political Economy* 102:437–67.
Diamond, Peter. 1965. National debt in a neoclassical growth model. *American Economic Review* 55:1126–50.
Gale, David. 1973. Pure exchange equilibrium of dynamic economic models. *Journal of Economic Theroy* 6:12–36.
Huang, He, Selahattin Imrohoroglu, and Thomas Sargent. 1996. Two computations to fund social security. *Macroeconomic Dynamics.*
Imrohoroglu, Ayse, Selahattin Imrohoroglu, and Douglas Joines. 1995. A life cycle analysis of social security. *Economic Theory* 6:83–114.
Krusell, P., and A. Smith. 1995. Income and wealth heterogeneity in the macroeconomy. Mimeo. no. 399. Rochester Center for Economic Research.
Samuelson, Paul A. 1958. An exact consumption-loan model of interest with or without the social contrivance of money. *Journal of Political Economy* 66, no. 6:467–82.

Discussion Summary   Jeffrey Liebman and Andrew Samwick

The first comments of the general discussion focused on some of the simplifications used in the model used to simulate privatization. Some caution was suggested in allowing for the labor supply response to an improved benefit-tax linkage because not all people behave according to the model presented in this paper. In particular, some people might be myopic or simply have high discount rates and face liquidity constraints. The private returns or welfare gains to these people may be very low. Another participant responded that, since the gains came in the form of lower taxes, discounting was not a main concern for evaluating this proposal. The author added that the reduction in payroll taxes might help ease the liquidity constraints on the young workers. Another simplification that was brought to light is that, in a model with income uncertainty, the social security system provides insurance to the extent that it is progressive. Because the author's model eliminates the current system completely, it loses the benefit of this insurance. When evaluating the author's model without uncertainty, the paper's focus on achieving "no distortion" would no longer be appropriate, as the concerns of insurance and redistribution would have to be balanced against efficiency.

The discussion then turned to the role of the consumption tax in the proposed privatization. In particular, given the heavy reliance on the consumption tax for the efficiency gains, the question was raised as to the extent to which this proposal should be considered a privatization rather than simply a change in fiscal policy. In this model, the privatization of social security is simply the elimination of the payroll tax. Because the payroll tax and the consumption tax have identical steady states, the efficiency gains arise from the substitution of the latter for the former in a way that taxes the current elderly disproportionately. One participant noted that the author's claim that implementing a retail sales tax would increase the burden on the elderly owing to higher prices was not necessarily true. If the Fed used monetary policy to keep the price level constant, then more of the burden would be borne by working generations in the form of lower real earnings. The author later responded that the basic proposition here is to make current generations better off by raising the burden on the elderly and that all privatizations are essentially just alternative ways of financing retirement obligations.

The author concluded the discussion by addressing two of the improvements to the overall setup of the simulation model that he has been working on. The first is the more realistic modeling of the demographic changes that will arise as the population ages. These demographics have been included in the original Auerbach-Kotlikoff model and could be incorporated in the privatization model as well. The second is to allow for at least some forms of heterogeneity within each age cohort. In particular, there are preliminary versions of the model that have twelve different income brackets, the results of which are that low-income workers can be taxed less because high-income workers choose to work more and therefore pay more taxes.

8 Privatizing Social Security: First-Round Effects of a Generic, Voluntary, Privatized U.S. Social Security System

Alan L. Gustman and Thomas L. Steinmeier

Increasing financial pressures on the U.S. social security system are likely to foster further changes in the system.[1] A wide variety of potential changes have been discussed. The Technical Panel on Trends and Issues in Retirement Savings of the 1994–95 Advisory Council on Social Security has considered the implications of a number of incremental changes, including reducing social security benefits further and raising social security taxes.[2] The Bipartisan Commission on Entitlements and Tax Reform has proposed means testing social security benefits. Others are proposing to privatize the social security system or some portion of it.[3]

Alan L. Gustman is the Loren M. Berry Professor of Economics at Dartmouth College and a research associate of the National Bureau of Economic Research. Thomas L. Steinmeier is professor of economics at Texas Tech University.

The authors acknowledge support from the National Institute on Aging and support for Gustman from a Rockefeller Center Reiss Family Fellowship at Dartmouth College. They also thank Richard Disney, Martin Feldstein, Richard Ippolito, Olivia Mitchell, participants in the NBER project on privatizing social security, and participants in a seminar held at RAND for helpful comments. The authors are grateful to Stan Panis and Lee Lillard for correspondence about estimates of returns to social security with projected life tables and to Michael Leonesio for providing tabulations from social security data matched to SIPP.

1. The financial outlook for the social security system is less favorable than was projected at the time of the 1983 reforms, which were designed to bring about a balance in the system's finances (see, e.g., Board of Trustees 1995). Among other things, the pressures for changing the system are created by adverse financial projections for social security, reflecting demographic and other trends, and the perception that, in the United States, saving is too low.

2. Benefits might be reduced by speeding up the changes called for under the 1983 reforms, by further increasing the retirement age, by reducing cost-of-living adjustments, or by making other changes. It is also possible to raise income taxes on social security benefits by counting a larger fraction of the benefits as income.

3. Senators Kerrey and Simpson have introduced legislation based on the options discussed by the Bipartisan Commission on Entitlements and Tax Reform to privatize a portion of social security using 2 percent of the payroll tax. The Technical Panel on Trends and Issues in Retirement Savings of the 1994–95 Advisory Council on Social Security also discussed the possibility of partial privatization through converting part of the social security trust funds into individual ac-

Along with the other papers in this volume, this paper is concerned with the effects of privatizing social security. Consistent with the privatization schemes adopted in Great Britain (Budd and Campbell, chap. 3 in this volume), Argentina (Cottani and Demarco, chap. 5 in this volume), and elsewhere, under the privatization proposal analyzed here, the individual remains free to choose between a traditional social security system, perhaps modified where necessary, and a privatized alternative. Specifically, the individual is assumed to be free to choose whether to allocate the 10.6 percent payroll tax contribution, currently earmarked for old age and survivors benefits, to a private IRA or to use it to qualify for benefits under the traditional social security system. Moreover, the analysis assumes that the social security system and the privatized system will exist side by side, not just in a transition, but also in the new steady state. In that sense, the privatized system analyzed here differs from a privatization system where participation in the IRA is mandatory and vestiges of the social security system are left to a grandfathered benefit system or to recognition bonds. These differences make the choice of which program to participate in a central focus of our analysis.

The paper begins by exploring the incentive structure to opt out of social security that is created by this privatization proposal. Simulations then analyze the differences in central outcomes under our current system and the privatized alternative. Outcomes examined include program participation, the path of benefits and taxes, and retirement behavior.

The sensitivity of the simulations to behavioral assumptions is examined, including the sensitivity to how respondents value spouse and survivor benefits and to their expected mortality. Economic assumptions are varied, including the real discount rate and the effect of social security reforms on pensions in the economy. Alternative assumptions are made about reductions in benefits. Program parameters are changed by imposing different gaps between the return to the IRA and the economy-wide discount rate. Also, one run assumes that participation in the privatized IRA is mandatory. Most of the analysis focuses on the transition from the current system to the privatized alternative, but we also simulate the program in the steady state.

Econometric estimates of a structural retirement model are used to simulate outcomes under the rules that apply under present law and then under the assumption that, in 1996, a mixed privatized system is established.[4] The simulation maximizes a utility function, with parameters estimated from behavior observed for cohorts who have already retired. The opportunity set includes

counts. The advisory council has been locked in a debate about the merits of privatizing social security, but two minority reports favor partial privatization. Many authors have proposed fully privatizing the system. For a recent discussion, see Feldstein (1996).

4. The population base for the simulation analysis is from the 1989 Survey of Consumer Finances (SCF). The preference functions have been estimated from data for males in the Retirement History Survey in Gustman and Steinmeier (1994a), modified to reflect trends toward earlier retirement, and involve a modification of our earlier work (Gustman and Steinmeier 1986b).

earnings in full-time and part-time work, pension incentives, and the appropriate social security or privatized alternative. In these simulations, households with single female earners are not considered. Men in households make all the behavioral decisions.[5] The simulation analysis for the transition period focuses on cohorts who would first become eligible to opt out to a privatized system in 1996. The cohorts have already generated a coverage history under the current social security system and must choose whether to opt out for a portion of their remaining work life. In contrast, the steady-state analysis assumes coverage under the privatized alternative for the individual's full working life.

The mixed privatization scheme is outlined and the incentives for participation analyzed in section 8.1. Section 8.2 discusses the simulation methodology. The simulation analysis is presented in section 8.3. Section 8.4 extends the analysis to consider the participation decision in two-earner households. Section 8.5 concludes the paper.

8.1   Incentives for Participation in a Privatized System

8.1.1   Basic Features of the Privatization Scheme

The analysis assumes a simple, choice-based scheme to privatize social security in the United States. Under this scheme, for each year an individual explicitly chooses to opt out of social security, the individual and the employer pay no payroll taxes; but one-thirty-fifth of future benefits are lost to the individual. Specifically, if the individual opts out for one or more years, electing to have the employer transfer the payroll tax payment to the worker's private IRA, we assume that the primary insurance amount (PIA), on which benefits are based, is reduced proportionately. That is, if the individual opts out for twenty years, the PIA would be only 43 percent (fifteen years of the thirty-five years currently used in the PIA calculations) of the PIA he would receive if he had not opted out, and, as a consequence, benefits are 43 percent of the level they would otherwise be.[6]

---

5. There are a number of reasons for adopting these simplifications, in which the men in the household make all the behavioral decisions. The work history in the SCF is inadequate for projecting a covered earnings history of wives under social security. Moreover, although we have an estimate of a joint utility function for husbands and wives (Gustman and Steinmeier 1994b), that utility function cannot simulate partial retirement. Thus, we have estimates of utility function parameters based on past retirement behavior only for men. In addition, there are complex issues that must be faced in deciding how spouse and survivor benefits for couples are to be determined under the social security alternative to a privatization option. These issues are discussed in sec. 8.5, where we consider the effects of simplifying the analysis by ignoring the decisions of wives in two-earner families and outline an approach to broadening the analysis. To bracket the sensitivity of the findings to the work history of the wife, we conduct a set of runs in which the husband values only his own benefits and puts no value on spouse or survivor benefits.

6. There is no special penalty reducing the PIA for any year the worker chooses not to work. In that case, as described below, the average indexed monthly earnings (AIME) are computed using zero earnings for the year in question. The PIA is reduced by one-thirty-fifth only for each year the individual works and chooses explicitly to transfer the payroll tax to an IRA account.

The taxes that would have been paid are instead invested in a mandatory individual retirement account (IRA) on behalf of the worker. The scheme is generic in that the IRA alternative to social security has no special design features or requirements, such as requirements for additional savings.[7] Nor does the IRA provide a basic benefit. Moreover, in any year, the entire payroll tax may be deposited in an IRA. That is, in contrast to some of the proposals emerging in the discussions of the Advisory Council on Social Security, where an addition to the payroll tax is used to finance an IRA and the rest is used to finance social security, in the privatization scheme analyzed here an individual is free to participate fully in a privatized alternative, in that the full payroll tax paid by the employee and employer is invested in the IRA.

Consider how the years opted out affect the AIME calculations. It is probably not feasible to include all years, whether in or out of the system, in these calculations. Otherwise, individuals could concentrate earnings in years they opt out of the system, which would reduce taxes without affecting AIME amounts. However, it would be unfair simply to exclude years that the individual opts out from the calculations while still using the high thirty-five of forty years of earnings. This approach would impose a double penalty for the years out: first, the AIME would be proportionately reduced because of the years out of the system since zeros would effectively replace years with earnings; and, second, the PIA would be proportionately reduced.

A plausible way around this problem would be to exclude, from both the numerator and the denominator of the AIME calculations, years in which the individual opts out. For instance, if the individual opts out for twenty years, the AIME would be the average of the highest fifteen years of indexed earnings during the period that the individual was in the traditional system rather than the highest thirty-five, as would otherwise be the case.[8]

8.1.2   Benefits for Those Who Are Covered by the Privatization Option for Their Entire Worklife

To illustrate the fundamentals of the participation decision, we make a number of simplifying assumptions. These are relaxed in the course of the empirical analysis. For purposes of introducing the basic incentives, assume that an-

7. An alternative proposal, in which the privatization scheme requires all workers to make a basic contribution to social security to fund its redistributive portion, is analyzed later in the paper. In that scheme, when a person opts out of social security, only a portion of the payroll tax is deposited in an IRA.

8. This penalty, of proportionately reducing the fraction of the AIME that is reflected in benefits for each year the individual has the payroll tax deposited in an IRA, may be compared with another approach, entering zero earnings in the AIME for any year the individual opts out. The former approach exacts a larger penalty for opting out on those in the transition generation who have already accumulated many years under the social security system. Indeed, under the latter approach of counting opt-out years as years of zero earnings, members of the transition generation who had accumulated thirty-five years under the current scheme would experience little or no reduction in benefits from opting out of social security for their remaining working life.

nual earnings w_t increase proportionately to the average wage index.[9] This implies that the indexed wage used in the AIME calculations is a constant w.[10] Further, let us make the following definitions: g = the real growth rate of wages; r = the real interest rate (i.e., the discount rate); x = the total number of years of work; x_s = the number of years that the individual remains in the social security system; and x_o = the number of years that the individual opts out of the system ($= x - x_s$). For this calculation, we also assume that the total number of years of work, x, is fixed at $x = \bar{x}$. In the simulation analysis to follow, we allow the individual to choose the optimal length of work, x, but, for this simple illustration of the factors governing the length of stay in the social security system, x_s is the only variable under the individual's control.

The modified AIME discussed above is given in equation (1):

$$\text{AIME} = \frac{xw - x_0w}{35 - x_0} = \frac{x_s w}{35 - (x - x_s)} \quad \text{if } x < 35,$$

(1)

$$= \frac{35w - x_0 w}{35 - x_0} = w \quad \text{if } x \geq 35.$$

In both instances, the numerator is the wages that would normally go into the AIME calculation, the thirty-five highest years of wages less the wages associated with the years the individual opts out of the system by transferring the payroll tax to the privatized IRA. Similarly, the denominator is reduced by the number of years the individual is out of the system.

The PIA is a quasi-concave function of the AIME where the function f is 90 percent of the first \$437 of AIME, 32 percent of AIME between \$437 and \$2,635, and 15 percent of AIME over \$2,635.[11] The PIA is given in equation (2):

$$\text{PIA} = \left(1 - \frac{x_0}{35}\right) f(\text{AIME}) \quad \text{if } x_0 < 35,$$

(2)

$$= 0 \quad \text{if } x_0 \geq 35.$$

The first factor on the right-hand side of equation (2) simply reflects that the PIA is reduced proportionately for years out of the system and in a privatized IRA.

The value of the stream of social security benefits at age sixty-two, less the value of the contributions, is given by

9. For an analysis of analogous choices made within the British system, see, e.g., Disney and Whitehouse (1992) and Brugiavini, Disney, and Whitehouse (1993).

10. This assumption is only approximate. The actual rules state that wages before age sixty are indexed up to age sixty for the AIME formula and that wages after age sixty enter the formula unindexed.

11. These are the 1996 bend points.

(3) $$V = g(a_0 + x)\text{PIA} - \int_{(a_0+x)-x_s}^{a_0+x} \beta we^{-(r-g)(t-62)}dt.$$

In the first term, $g(a_o + x)$ is the annuitized value of the social security benefits for each \$1.00 of PIA, adjusted for the early retirement penalty or late retirement credit and discounted to age sixty-two. The individual starts work at age a_o and retires at age $a_o + x$. For example, if the individual retires at age sixty-three, the value of a \$1.00 annuity starting at age sixty-three and discounted to age sixty-two would be \$13.61.[12] The individual would be eligible for 86.7 percent of the PIA (because he retired two years before the normal retirement age), so the value of the function g would be \$13.61 times 86.7 percent, or \$11.80.[13]

In the second term, β is the social security contribution rate, currently 10.6 percent. The expression $\beta we^{-(r-g)(t-62)}$ represents the value of the contributions paid at age t, discounted to age sixty-two. The discounted value of these contributions decreases over time since the discount rate exceeds the growth rate of wages. This means that, if the individual plans to spend any years in the privatized alternative, he or she will want to choose those years as early as possible since the discounted value of the contributions that would otherwise be paid will have to be maximized if the individual spends the early rather than the later years in the privatized alternative. This means that, if the individual begins work at age a_o and will work for x_s years in the traditional system out of a total of x years of work, he or she will spend the years between $(a_o + x) - x_s$ and $(a_o + x)$ in the traditional system. The second term in the equation above thus reflects the discounted value of contributions during the years the individual remains in the traditional system.

We are now in a position to characterize how the value of traditional social security varies with the number of years the individual spends in the traditional system. The analysis is somewhat different depending on whether the individual plans to work more or less than thirty-five years in total. Let us examine the case where the individual plans to work $x \geq 35$ years first. Substituting the AIME and PIA formulas into the value formula yields

$$V = -\int_{(a_0+x)-x_s}^{a_0+x} \beta we^{-(r-g)(t-62)}dt \quad \text{if } x_s < x - 35,$$

(4)
$$= g(a_0 + x)\left(1 - \frac{x - x_s}{35}\right)f(w)$$

$$- \int_{(a_0+x)-x_s}^{a_0+x} \beta we^{-(r-g)(t-62)}dt \quad \text{if } x_s \geq x - 35.$$

12. This calculation uses a 2.3 percent real interest rate, consistent with the assumptions of the social security trustees.

13. In this analysis, and in the subsequent empirical analysis, we ignore the effects of the individual's private information, i.e., known differences among individuals about their life expectancy that may make social security more attractive to individuals with a long life expectancy and less attractive to those who expect to live for fewer years.

The upper part of equation (4) refers to the situation where the individual has participated in the privatized system for more than thirty-five years and hence has lost all benefits in the traditional system. Thus, the contributions for any years the individual is in the traditional system buy no benefits.

Differentiating this expression by x_s yields

(5)
$$\frac{\partial V}{\partial x_s} = -\beta w e^{-(r-g)(a_0+x-x_s-62)} \quad \text{if } x_s < x - 35,$$

$$= \frac{1}{35} g(\cdot) f(w) - \beta w e^{-(r-g)(a_0+x-x_s-62)} \quad \text{if } x_s \geq x - 35.$$

The first few years in the traditional system, between 0 and $x - 35$ additional years, clearly have a negative effect on the value of the traditional benefits net of contributions. Contributions are paid, but there are still no benefits because the individual is still participating in the privatized system for more than thirty-five years. For additional years in the traditional system beyond $x - 35$, the marginal effect on the value is ambiguous. The situation is illustrated in figure 8.1. The relation between years in the traditional system and the value of the traditional benefits net of contributions is negative at first, but, at $x - 35$, the slope increases by the amount $(1/35)g(\cdot)f(w)$. Remember that, in figure 8.1, the length of the work life is fixed. Work years spent out of the social security system reduce the PIA only if the individual requests that payroll taxes earned be transferred to a private IRA.

The relation is further clarified by looking at the curvature, obtained by differentiating again by x_s:

(6)
$$\frac{\partial^2 V}{\partial x_s^2} = -(r - g)\beta w e^{-(r-g)(a_0+x-x_s-62)} < 0.$$

Since this is always negative, the relation between x_s and V is concave except at the point B. There are several possibilities for the optimal value of x_s in this problem. The curve is clearly negative between A and B, but between B and C the situation is ambiguous. If the curve slopes uniformly upward and the point C_1 is above the horizontal axis, the optimal solution is to remain in the traditional system the entire time. If the curve rises to a peak between B and C_2 and the peak is above the horizontal axis, the individual will spend a few years in the privatized alternative at the beginning of the work life and then switch to the traditional system.[14] If the peak is below the horizontal axis, as occurs between B and C_3, the individual will never choose the traditional system.

Equations (4) and (5) suggest the kinds of factors that make it more likely that the individual will stay in the traditional system and increase the number of years in the system. If the maximal value given in equation (4) is positive,

---

14. We assume that the IRA would be made available in installments starting at age sixty-two, with the result that the decision is not driven by liquidity constraint considerations.

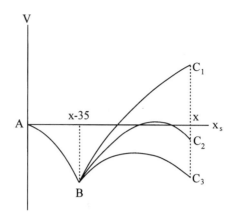

Fig. 8.1   Value function for a fixed work life ≥ 35 years

the individual will choose to remain at least partly in the traditional system. And the greater the first term of equation (5) is relative to the second, the greater will be the optimal value of x_s that equates these two terms. The maximal value of equation (4) is more likely to be positive, and the optimal value of x_s in equation (5) will be higher, if (i) the contribution rate is lower, (ii) the generosity (i.e., the value of $f[w]$) is higher, (iii) the mortality rate is lower (which increases $g[\cdot]$), and (iv) the interest rate is lower (which lowers the value of discounted contributions relative to benefits).

Now turn to the case where the individual plans to work for fewer than thirty-five years. There are two main differences between this and the previous case. First, the value function does not have a segment corresponding to AB in figure 8.1. Second, the expression for AIME is no longer simply w. Substituting the expression for the AIME, as given in equation (1), into the value function given in equation (3) yields

$$V = g(a_0 + x)\left(1 - \frac{x - x_s}{35}\right) f\left(\frac{x_s w}{35 - (x - x_s)}\right)$$

(7)

$$- \int_{(a_0 + x) - x_s}^{a_0 + x} \beta w e^{-(r-g)(t-62)} dt.$$

Differentiating this with respect to x_s yields (after some algebraic manipulation)

(8) $$\frac{\partial V}{\partial x_s} = \frac{1}{35} g(\cdot)\left\{ f(\cdot) + f'(\cdot)\frac{(35 - x)w}{35 - (x - x_s)}\right\} - \beta w e^{-(r-g)(a_0 + x - x_s - 62)}.$$

Differentiating again by x_s yields (after some additional manipulation)

(9)
$$\frac{\partial^2 V}{\partial x_s^2} = \frac{1}{35} g(\cdot) \frac{(35 - x)^2 w^2}{[35 - (x - x_s)]^3} f''(\cdot)$$
$$- \beta w(r - g) e^{-(r-g)(a_0 + x - x_s - 62)} < 0.$$

The sign of equation (8) is indeterminate, but, since f is quasi concave, f'' is nonpositive, and the second derivative is negative. This implies that the value function must take a form such as those illustrated in figure 8.2. If the first derivative is positive throughout the range (as occurs if the value function is BC_1), the optimal solution is always to remain in the traditional system. If the function rises to a peak and then declines (BC_2), the optimal solution is to spend the first few years in the privatized alternative, then to join the traditional system for the last x_s years. Finally, if the first derivative is negative throughout the range (as in BC_3), the optimal choice would be to switch to the privatized alternative and remain there.

Factors that make the first term of equation (8) large relative to the second term will tend to increase the number of years that a worker will remain in the traditional system. These factors include all the things listed in the previous case, such as higher generosity and lower contribution rates, lower mortality, and lower interest rates. In addition, a higher value for the marginal generosity, which is $f'(w)$, increases the first term and increases the number of years an individual would wish to remain in the traditional system.

8.1.3 Analysis for Workers during the Transition

A steady-state worker who chooses to spend part of his or her time in the privatized system and part in the traditional system will want to choose the privatized system early in his or her career and the traditional system later. For a worker during the transition period, however, this is not possible since such

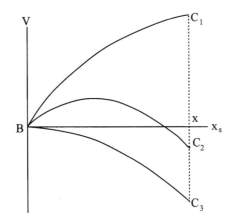

Fig. 8.2 **Value function for a fixed work life < 35 years**

a worker will have already spent a number of years in the traditional system before the privatized system is made available. To continue the analysis for transition workers, we introduce a new definition: x_i = the number of years the worker has spent in the traditional system before the privatized system is introduced. In the analysis for transition workers, we will assume that the total number of years in the work life is greater than thirty five but that the number of years left in the work life after the privatization option is introduced is less than thirty-five. This will simplify the presentation, and the extension to cases where the work life is greater than thirty-five is straightforward.

The choices of x_s are now limited to lie between $x_i \leq x_s \leq x$, where $x_i \geq x - 35$. The benefit side of the value function remains the same as in the previous case, but the contribution term is somewhat different. The individual will still want to bunch the years of participation in the traditional system as late as possible since the discounted value of the contributions is lowest in those years. The individual has already spent the first x_i years in the traditional system, and he or she will want to bunch the remaining $x_s - x_i$ years at the end of the work life. This means that the integral in the value function representing the discounted contributions will be split into two integrals, as follows:

$$
V = g(a_0 + x)\left(1 - \frac{x - x_s}{35}\right) f\left[\frac{x_s w}{35 - (x - x_s)}\right]
$$

(10)

$$
- \int_{a_0}^{a_0 + x_i} \beta w e^{-(r-g)(t-62)} dt - \int_{(a_0+x)-(x_s-x_i)}^{a_0+x} \beta w e^{-(r-g)(t-62)} dt .
$$

The first integral is the discounted value of the contributions before the privatized alternative is made available, and the second integral is the discounted value of the contributions for the $x_i - x_s$ years that the individual chooses to be in the traditional system after the introduction of the privatized alternative. Note that the years in the traditional system after the alternative is offered will be concentrated at the end of the work life since the discounted value of the contributions is least then.

To get an idea of the nature of the relation between the decision to remain in the traditional system and the value of the traditional benefits less contributions, we again differentiate the value function as given above:

(11)
$$
\frac{\partial V}{\partial x_s} = \frac{1}{35} g(\cdot) f(w) - \beta w e^{-(r-g)[(a_0+x)-(x_s-x_i)-62]} .
$$

As before, it is relatively simple to evaluate $\partial^2 V / \partial x_s^2$ and show that it is negative.

The value function is illustrated in figure 8.3. As compared to the steady-state situation, the value function for transition workers is lower for a given number of years in the traditional system. The reason is that, while the benefits are the same, some of the contributions will have been made in the preprivatization years, when the discounted value of those benefits is higher. Thus, each of the curves in figure 8.3 is a little lower than the corresponding curve in figure

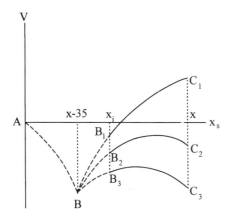

Fig. 8.3   Value function for transition workers

8.1 above. However, the slope of the value function for transition workers is higher in the relevant range of x_s than it is for steady-state workers. This is because the exponential term in equation (11) is smaller than the corresponding term in equation (5).

The decision to participate in the traditional system is as follows. Recall that the individual has already spent x_i years in the traditional system, so the optimal choice of values for x_s is constrained to lie between x_i and x, that is, along the solid parts of the curves. If the value function is the curve B_1C_1 in figure 8.3, the individual will always choose to be in the traditional system. If the curve is B_2C_2 in figure 8.3, the individual will maximize his or her traditional benefits less contributions by being at the peak of the curve. Note that this peak is to the right of the peak of the corresponding curve in figure 8.1 since the slope of the value function is more in figure 8.3 than it is in figure 8.1. This implies that the transition worker will spend longer in the traditional system than would a steady-state worker in similar circumstances. Finally, if the value function is represented by the curve B_3C_3 in figure 8.3, the individual will choose enough additional years of traditional coverage to reach the peak in the curve. Note that the corresponding individual in figure 8.1 would have opted out of traditional coverage altogether. However, the transition individual has already been forced to absorb the loss of paying social security contributions in years for which there will be no effective benefits, and, given that situation, it will pay him or her to be in the system a few more years in order to minimize those losses. The worker will still want to bunch the remaining years of traditional coverage at the end of the work career. As a result, such a worker will opt out of traditional coverage as soon as the privatized alternative is made available but will eventually return to the traditional system as he or she approaches retirement.

The net result is that some transition workers will spend more years in the traditional system than they otherwise would have in a steady-state situation and that others will voluntarily choose to be in the system after the privatization alternative is introduced even though they would not have chosen to be in the traditional system at all had they had the option from the beginning of their working careers. For both reasons, the participation in the traditional system will be higher among transition workers than among steady-state workers, even in years after the privatized alternative is available.

8.1.4   From the Simple Example to More Complex Specifications

The preceding analysis has been highly simplified to illustrate some of the basic considerations governing the choice between the IRA and the social security alternative. In the example, length of work life is fixed, wage growth is constant and equal to the rate of increase in the economy-wide wage index, spouse and survivor benefits are not considered, the return to the mandatory IRA is assumed to be equal to the economy-wide discount rate, and effects on private pensions are ignored, to name a few. The simulation analysis will relax all these simplifications and introduce a number of other complexities.

8.2   The Simulation Methodology

In order to investigate the likely effects of privatization in a more concrete setting, we begin with simulations for a transition cohort of individuals who are midstream in their careers when the privatization is made available. The scheme that is to be simulated is the generic program described above, to be made available beginning in 1996. There are many outcomes of potential interest, but we focus on the fraction of the workforce participating in a privatized social security system, labor force participation patterns, and benefit payouts and payroll tax payments under the remaining federal system.

Labor supply is assumed to be determined in the context of a life-cycle model with a perfectly operating capital market.[15] The opportunity set for the simulations comes from thirty- to fifty-five-year-old males in the 1989 Survey of Consumer Finances. These cohorts of males have already spent many years under the current system. Nevertheless, if privatization were introduced in 1996, they would still have a considerable period of time under the privatized system. The life-cycle preferences come from a model we have previously estimated. We simulate the choices that individuals with these preferences would make, given the opportunity set both with and without privatization, and compare the outcomes.

---

15. Although it is convenient for this type of initial analysis, a bare-bones life-cycle model is much too simple for understanding the central behavioral features characterizing savings, labor supply, and pensions. These behaviors have not yet been successfully integrated into a single empirical analysis. For a discussion of the shortcomings of present models, see Gustman and Juster (1996).

8.2.1 The Opportunity Set

The opportunity set for the simulation model is estimated for males in the 1989 Survey of Consumer Finances who were working full-time and who were neither self-employed nor government employees.[16] Wages in full-time jobs and in partial retirement are calculated, with wages being assumed to be a quadratic function of experience.[17] Pension plan features for covered individuals are reported by their employers and are used to calculate the pension accrual rates associated with alternative retirement dates.[18] The current social security law is coded and applied to each individual in the sample, including rules governing the earnings test, the delayed retirement credit, and benefit recomputation, as they separately apply to each individual according to year of birth. In our basic set of runs, benefits are then reduced by 20 percent on the assumption that individuals are adjusting benefits down by that amount to reflect expected adjustments to the financial problems of the system.[19] The interest rate used in the initial simulations and the overall wage growth rate correspond to the long-term intermediate social security projections.[20] In the basic set of runs, the IRA in a privatized system is assumed to earn this interest rate. The chance of falling into poor health is modeled as a hazard and is built into the opportunity set.

The simulation algorithm does not assume that the opportunity set is continuous. There is a discontinuity created by the minimum hours constraint on the main job. If the individual leaves the main job for part-time work, the wage declines, and this decline is assumed to be irreversible. In addition, the incentives to postpone retirement that are created by the pension plan are frequently discontinuous. Large returns are often gained if the covered worker waits until he meets the plan's eligibility requirement for early or normal retirement. These discontinuities are taken into account in calculating the worker's optimal date of retirement.

16. These simulations focus on the transition cohorts of these groups. Since social security contains workers from the excluded groups, there is no obvious reconciliation if one were to try to derive implications for the finances of the entire social security system.

17. The coefficients of experience and experience squared are 0.0138 and -0.000283, respectively, and the coefficient of experience interacted with education is 0.000996. This calculation of benefits is based on an earnings profile that ignores year-to-year variation in wages around the earnings function. For a model where wages follow a random walk process, see Samwick (1993). For analysis of the participation decision in the British system when earnings vary from year to year, see Brugiavini, Disney, and Whitehouse (1993).

18. Where the individual's own pension is unavailable, pensions from other individuals with the same personal and job characteristics (union status, employer size, wage level, etc.) are used.

19. According to data recently collected in the Health and Retirement Survey, future recipients place the odds that social security benefits will be decreased in the future at six of ten (see Gustman, Mitchell, and Steinmeier 1995).

20. These assumptions are 6.3 percent for the interest rate, 5.0 percent for wages, and 4.0 percent for prices (Board of Trustees 1995, 12).

8.2.2   Preferences

The preference function used in the simulations has been estimated with data from the 1969–79 Retirement History Study using the opportunity sets covering workers in that study. The lifetime utility function for the model is given by

$$(12) \qquad U = \sum \left[\frac{1}{\alpha} C_t^\alpha + e^{X_t \beta + \varepsilon} f(L_t, \delta) \right],$$

where C_t is consumption at time t, and L_t is leisure at time t; $f(L_t, \delta)$ is 0 at full-time work, 1 in retirement, and an intermediate value, related to δ (with $\delta < 1$), for partial retirement work.[21] If δ is close to 1, $f(L_t, \delta)$ is approximately proportional to leisure for partial retirement work, while, if δ is large and negative, $f(L_t, \delta)$ is almost 1. This means that, the closer δ is to unity, the greater is the relative disutility of partial retirement work, and the shorter and less frequent are periods of partial retirement. ε determines the relative utility of leisure as opposed to consumption. In the utility function, both ε and δ are taken to be individual fixed effects coming from the distributions $f(\varepsilon) = N(0, \sigma_\varepsilon)$ and $f(\delta) = \gamma e^{\gamma(1-\delta)}, \gamma > 0$.

The parameters of the utility function, which are α, γ, σ_ε, and the elements of β, are estimated using data from the Retirement History Survey (RHS) and reported in table 8.1. These results use a likelihood function developed and estimated in our previous work (Gustman and Steinmeier 1985, 1986a, 1986b, 1994a). Since the time period of the RHS, however, there has been a sharp trend toward earlier retirement by the younger cohorts. Only a quarter to a third of this trend can be accounted for by changes in pensions and social security (Anderson, Gustman, and Steinmeier 1996). Because the simulations with the SCF sample would otherwise understate retirement, with individuals working approximately three years too long, we have adjusted the constant in the linear term, β_0, to reduce the retirement age by about three years on average.[22] This should not affect the differences in outcomes between runs with the current and privatized social security system, but it will affect the levels of benefits.

---

21. Specifically, for partial retirement work, $f(L_t, \delta) = (L_t^\delta - L_f^\delta)/(1 - L_f^\delta)$, where L_f is the leisure associated with full-time work.

22. In the simulations, we fix the vintage coefficient at the average value of the RHS. If we use the SCF vintages in the simulations, they very substantially overpredict retirement. This overprediction probably occurs because the coefficient of this variable, which is estimated using the 1906–11 cohorts in the RHS, is being extrapolated far outside the estimation range to the SCF cohorts. In particular, the retirement trends in the 1970s were much stronger than the trends observed in the 1980s. Indeed, in the mid-1980s through the early 1990s, the trend toward earlier retirement had stopped. For related data and analysis, see Anderson, Gustman, and Steinmeier (1996). Although it would have been possible to mimic the trend toward earlier retirement by changing other parameters of the utility function beside the constant, it would have made little difference to the ultimate estimates of the effect of privatization. These estimates are based on the differences in outcomes under the current and privatized systems, and the differences are not very sensitive to the parameters of the utility function.

Table 8.1   **Parameters of the Utility Function**

Variables	Coefficient	t-Statistic
α, exponent of consumption	.09	2.42
γ, parameter for δ	.27	56.65
σ_ε, standard deviation of ε	1.11	65.85
β_0, constant in linear term	.07	2.40
β_1, coefficient of age[a]	.26	65.34
β_2, coefficient of health	.67	19.97
β_3, coefficient of vintage[b]	.12	9.81
Number of observations	3,283	
Log likelihood	$-9,750.97$	

Source: Gustman and Steinmeier (1994a).
[a]The actual variable is (age $-$ 62).
[b]The actual variable is (vintage $-$ 9).

8.3   Simulation Results

Simulations have been conducted for private-sector, non-self-employed males in the 1989 Survey of Consumer Finances (SCF) who were between the ages of thirty and fifty-five in 1989.[23] Thus, the analysis pertains only to males in the labor force who have been continuously covered in their employment by social security, although it takes into account relevant spouse and survivor benefits. The sample includes 186 men without a pension and 692 with a pension. One thousand simulations were run for each of these individuals.

Each set of simulations was run under current law and under a privatization program. The key simplification here is the assumption that, for purposes of calculating social security benefits arising from participation in the program by these men, only primary benefits based on the earnings of the man in the household, and associated spouse and survivor benefits, matter.[24] For each set of simulations, results are calculated for the fraction of time spent in the social security program as opposed to the privatization program, the labor force participation rate, and the amounts of social security taxes and benefits. To keep track of benefits paid on behalf of and contributions made by those who did not survive, the present-value figures for benefits and taxes pertain to the original cohort population, not just to survivors.

The simulations focus on transition cohorts who are old enough to have already spent several years under the current system. If the privatized system were introduced in 1996, their ages would range from thirty-seven to sixty-two. At younger ages, many individuals in this sample would not be able to opt

23. Thus, the typical person in the sample is about halfway through with his or her work life in 1989, which is the base year to which all discounted values are taken. By the time the privatization is realized in 1996, the average person in the sample is almost fifty years old.
24. The consequences of making this simplifying assumption are explored in sec. 8.4.

out because they reached the specified age before 1996, while, at older ages, some workers will have already retired. Although these results cannot be viewed as an indication of the eventual steady state but are best viewed as the likely experience of the transition cohorts, we do explore outcomes under steady-state assumptions, where we assume that each individual spent his entire career under the revised system.

The basic simulations assume a time trend in mortality and, in addition, differential mortality rates according to family income and initial marital status. First, the 1990 *Vital Statistics* mortality rates are adjusted to reflect a reduction in mortality of 1.22 percent per year.[25] Then, for whites and nonwhites separately, the mortality rates for married and unmarried individuals are adjusted by fractions so that overall mortality rates are the same as the projected rates.[26] The mortality rates in various income brackets are also adjusted down for high-income individuals and up for low-income individuals in such a manner that the overall mortality rates are the same as the projected rates.[27] In addition, as noted above, these basic results assume that individuals all discount the value of social security by 20 percent.

Following the basic results, but still using the Social Security Administration's assumptions about interest rates, additional findings are presented using alternative assumptions about the life expectancies that govern the economic decisions of individuals, about how the workers in the sample value the spouse and survivor benefits offered by social security, and about whether workers anticipate the possibility of reduced benefits in the future. Next, we consider the effects of varying the interest rate and allowing the returns to differ between the privatized IRA and other market investments. Finally, we consider the effects of the privatized alternative in a steady state rather than in the transition period from the current system.

8.3.1   Effects on Participation in Social Security Using SSA Assumptions

Using the basic Social Security Administration (SSA) assumptions of 4 percent inflation, a 6.3 percent interest rate, and 5 percent wage growth, with the result that the real interest rate is 2.3 percent, figure 8.4 shows the reduction in social security participation (the number opting for the private IRA) between a regime where the privatized system is available from 1996 on for those who

25. This trend is based on results reported in Panis and Lillard (1995, table 1).

26. Panis and Lillard (1995) estimated the ratio of mortality rates between married and unmarried white males to be 0.781. Applying this result to our study, we multiply the overall mortality by 0.987 for married white males and by 1.264 for unmarried white males.

27. Duleep (1989, table 1) found the following ratios of mortality by income class (1972 income in 1959 prices): 1.59 (under $2,000), 1.79 ($2,000–$4,000), 1.04 ($4,000–$6,000), 0.90 ($6,000–$8,000), 0.87 ($8,000–$10,000), and 0.71 (over $10,000). For blacks and whites separately, the widths of these intervals were adjusted so that the total mortality rate of the group was the same as the overall projected rate. For whites, this means that the *Vital Statistics* mortality is multiplied by 1.59 for family income levels of $11,268 and below, by 1.79 for family income levels of $11,368–$22,736, by 1.04 for family income levels of $22,736–$34,104, and so on. For blacks, the width of the income intervals is $6,641.

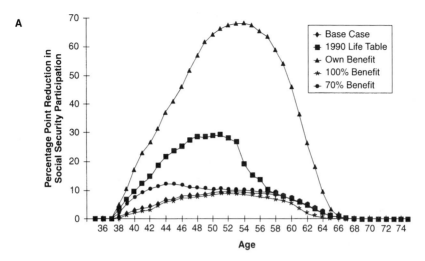

Fig. 8.4A   Decline in social security participation with privatization (figure assumes 2.3% real interest rate)

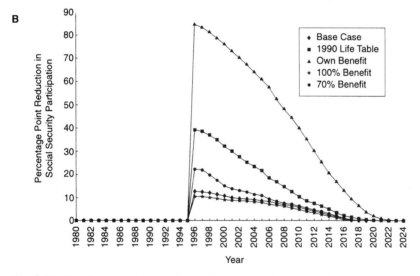

Fig. 8.4B   Decline in social security participation with privatization (figure assumes 2.3% real interest)

choose it and the current system.[28] By *social security participation,* we mean that the individual both has earnings at a particular age or during a particular

---

28. We measure the participation rate in the social security program as a fraction of the original cohort population, not as a fraction of survivors, with the result that the changes in participation rates shown are the differences in percentages computed with the original cohort population as the base.

year and chooses to pay taxes into the social security system rather than opting out and paying an equivalent amount into a qualifying IRA. Figure 8.4a shows the absolute value of the reduction in social security participation by age, while figure 8.4b shows the corresponding absolute value of the reduction by year.

Consider first the results for the "base case," demarcated by diamonds in figure 8.4, which indicate the reduction in social security participation on the assumptions (a) that individuals value fully the potential spouse and survivor benefits and that the full potential value for spouse and survivor benefits is realized, (b) that they anticipate the effects of trends in mortality, and (c) that they expect that, because of current financial problems, benefits will be reduced by 20 percent from current promised levels. The relevant curve is the second from the bottom in each figure.

In figure 8.4a, which indicates the decline in social security participation by age, the inverted U shape of the curve results from different factors at younger and older ages. At the younger ages indicated, relatively few individuals in the cohort of thirty- to fifty-five-year-olds in 1989 would be able to change their participation. For example, almost all are out of their thirties when privatization is introduced in 1996, so there is little indicated participation in a privatized system at those ages. At older ages, much of the sample is retired and cannot participate in the privatized system.

As seen in figure 8.4b, consistent with the analysis in section 8.1 above, the largest number opt out of social security in the initial year, 1996. As labor force participation falls, fewer people are left to opt out, so, in later years, the difference in social security participation brought about by the privatization program is lower. At its peak effect in 1996, if cohort members evaluate social security taxes and benefits as suggested by the base-case simulation, the privatization would reduce social security participation by about 13 percentage points.[29]

The next set of results, demarcated by squares and labeled *1990 life table* in figure 8.4, assumes that individuals use the 1990 life tables, uncorrected for mortality trends, and further that they ignore differential mortality rates according to family income and initial marital status in predicting life expectancy. If potential participants ignored trends in mortality, we see that many more individuals would leave the social security system for a privatized system than if they factored in the effects of the extended life expectancy on their social security benefits. Specifically, in figure 8.4b, just under 40 percent of covered individuals would opt to participate in a privatized system. The infer-

---

29. Specifically, in 1996, according to our runs, 91 percent of the original cohort of private-sector, non-self-employed workers would otherwise be covered by the current social security system. (The rest would have been retired or deceased.) Note that, because we have no firsthand knowledge of the learning process, the time paths in fig. 8.4 ignore any lag in adjustment that would accompany the implementation of such a plan. In fact, the adjustment is likely to be slower than that shown in the figure, perhaps substantially so.

ence is that the social security annuity is much more valuable when the lengthening of life expectancy is taken into account, and, if individuals understand this, it will greatly reduce the attractiveness of a privatized retirement system.

The third set of results, labeled *own benefit* and demarcated by triangles in figure 8.4*a–b*, uses the projected life tables but assumes that, for married workers, the individual places zero value on spouse or survivor benefits.[30] That is, under this assumption, individuals value only their own benefits and do not value benefits that will be available to their spouse either when the earner retires or as a survivor benefit. When only own benefits are valued, in 1996 almost everyone in these cohorts drops out of the social security system. Clearly, the effect of the introduction of a privatized system on participation in social security will very much depend on how spouse and survivor benefits are valued.

The fourth set of results shown in figures 8.4*a–b*, demarcated by an *x*, uses the projected life tables and assumes that spouse and survivor benefits are valued on a par with the basic benefit. However, these simulations assume that individuals believe that all benefits will be fully valued as projected under current law. For example, the individual may be unaware of the current financial problems with the system and their significance, or the individual may expect that subsidies will come from general revenue. Results under this scenario are very similar to the results under the base case. In 1996, 10.8 percent of those still covered by the social security system would opt out, only 2 percent fewer than opted out under the base case when benefits are valued at 80 percent of the promised amount.

Finally, the fifth set of results, demarcated by a star, varies the base-case result by assuming that all individuals in the sample expect only 70 percent of the promised benefits to be paid under social security. Here, 22 percent choose the private alternative when given the choice in 1996.

Because any social security reform may treat low earners differently from high earners, the actual program may involve a mix of the scenarios examined in figure 8.4. For example, rather than adopting a uniform set of rules, one can visualize a privatization reform in which low earners who continued in social security would not have their benefits altered but high earners might experience a substantial reduction should they continue under social security. Variations of means testing of benefits might be tried, with different potential effects on incentives.[31]

30. Since many spouses will be entitled to at least some benefits on the basis of their own work, the marginal values of spouse and survivor benefits are overstated in the previous calculations. For further discussion, see sec. 8.4.

31. Edey and Simon (chap. 2 in this volume) describe the Australian system, where extensive income testing may encourage the spending down of accumulated assets in the years before acceptance of social security benefits.

8.3.2   Effects of Privatizing Social Security on Labor Supply

Essentially, the changes in social security participation rates pictured in figure 8.4 have two components: changes in labor supply and changes in participation conditional on labor supply. Figure 8.5 indicates the effects of privatizing on labor force participation rates, computed by summing full-time and part-time participants.[32] The curve demarcated in diamonds indicates the change in labor force participation under the base case. Examining the scale on the y axis suggests that the change in labor supply is entirely insignificant and that the change in social security participation conditional on labor supply is the only decision that matters. This result is consistent with earlier findings (Gustman and Steinmeier 1985, 1991). The social security system is approximately actuarially fair for many of those in the cohorts we analyze, and so is the privatized system.[33]

The generic system analyzed here does not impose any special eligibility requirements for participants in the social security system to opt into the privatized system. One possibility is that participation in the privatized system will require the individual to save more than the payroll tax contribution.[34] Any requirement for additional savings might encourage firms that offer defined-benefit plans to change them to qualifying types of defined-contribution plans so that their employees could meet the savings requirements of a privatized system with little further reduction in consumption.[35] We have conducted a number of runs on the assumption that defined-benefit plans are converted to defined-contribution plans, altering retirement incentives. Figure 8.5 shows the results of one such set of runs. The findings suggest that, if defined-benefit plans were abolished as a result of privatization, labor force participation by those in their sixties might increase slightly as a result of privatization, with a

32. Labor force participation rates are calculated here as a fraction of the surviving population and thus are not strictly comparable to the social security participation rates presented in fig. 8.4. Comparable patterns to the labor force participation rates are obtained when the figures for earnings changes are plotted.

33. Available evidence suggests that labor force participation responds to differences in the reward for marginal effort around the age of retirement, such as the discontinuities created by bonuses or declines in benefit accrual often brought about by provisions of pension plans. But the evidence also suggests that retirement is not very responsive to differences in wages, as wealth and substitution effects are roughly offsetting (Gustman and Steinmeier 1986b).

34. The effects of such a requirement would depend in part on the savings that the individual already had. Under such a system, with a higher propensity to save, higher-income individuals are more likely to meet any savings requirement. They are also more likely to opt out not only because of the progressivity of the benefit structure but also because those with high incomes will meet any minimum savings rates more easily since such required minimum savings levels are likely to bear a relation to the maximum social security benefit. For those who would not otherwise accumulate the required level of savings to meet any eligibility requirements, the extent of participation in a privatized system would depend on the disutility of additional required savings. This is an issue that our model does not address.

35. In the British system, one may opt out of the equivalent of our social security system by participating in the equivalent of a defined-benefit pension. For further discussion, see Disney and Whitehouse (1992).

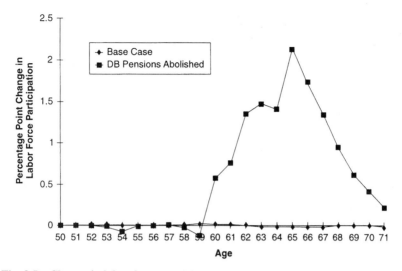

Fig. 8.5 **Change in labor force participation with privatization (figure assumes 2.3% real interest)**

maximum increase in participation at age sixty-five amounting to 2 percentage points.

8.3.3 Effects on Present Values of Taxes and Benefits

Table 8.2 reports, under alternative scenarios, the present value of total earnings, the present value of total payroll taxes paid into the social security system by the cohort members, the present value of all benefits paid to the cohort members including own, spouse, and survivor benefits, and the present value of own benefits. These values are averages per member of the simulated cohorts. For instance, the entry of $110,812 in the first row of the column labeled *taxes* means that, on average, under the current system, over his lifetime each member of the simulation group would pay that amount in social security taxes, discounted to 1989. As previously noted, to keep track of benefits paid on behalf of and contributions made by those who did not survive, these present values pertain to the original cohort population, not just to survivors.

Reflecting the findings of no effect of privatization on labor force participation, changes in the present value of earnings with privatization are minuscule. Earnings are predicted to rise very slightly if a privatized system were instituted and there were no changes in pensions. Even if pensions did change, the effect on earnings would be very small.

The fall in social security participation with privatization is mirrored in the declines in taxes paid. Because these figures refer to the entire lifetime of the individual, not just to the time since the system is privatized, the declines in benefits and taxes are measured on average over only a third of the working

Table 8.2   **Present Values of Earnings, Social Security Payroll Taxes, and Benefits for Cohorts Born from 1934 to 1959, Transition Results at 2.3 Percent Real Interest (thousands of 1989 dollars)**

	Earnings	Taxes	Total Benefits	Own Benefits
Projected life tables (base case):				
Current system	1,382,597	110,812	121,248	66,831
Privatized system	1,382,687	105,530	117,822	63,591
Privatized—current	90	−5,282	−3,426	−3,240
Only own benefits valued:				
Current system	1,383,745	110,916	120,234	67,587
Privatized system	1,383,593	74,382	73,073	40,816
Privatized—current	−152	−36,534	−47,161	−26,771
Benefits valued at 100%:				
Current system	1,381,897	110,747	151,549	83,530
Privatized system	1,381,936	106,252	148,152	80,147
Privatized—current	39	−4,495	−3,397	−3,383
Benefits discounted 30%:				
Current system	1,382,952	110,845	106,096	58,479
Privatized system	1,383,085	103,268	100,927	54,448
Privatized—current	133	−7,577	−5,169	−4,031
1990 life tables:				
Current system	1,368,296	109,830	96,036	48,597
Privatized system	1,369,105	94,440	83,901	41,357
Privatized—current	809	−15,390	−12,135	−7,240
Defined-benefit converted to defined-contribution plans:				
Current system	1,382,597	110,812	121,248	66,831
Privatized system	1,389,766	106,011	118,059	63,700
Privatized-current	7,169	−4,801	−3,189	−3,131
IRA returns 3% above real interest:				
Current system	1,382,597	110,812	121,248	66,831
Privatized system	1,383,742	79,104	81,995	44,449
Privatized—current	1,145	−31,708	−39,253	−22,382
IRA deposits 3% below payroll tax:				
Current system	1,382,597	110,812	121,248	66,831
Privatized system	1,382,618	107,979	118,941	64,524
Privatized—current	21	−2,833	−2,307	−2,307
Mandatory schemes:				
Current system	1,382,597	110,812	121,248	66,831
Privatized system	1,386,033	69,134	68,494	37,528
Privatized—current	3,436	−41,678	−52,754	−29,303

life. As expected in a system with voluntary choice, where individuals will choose a privatized system only if there is a net benefit associated with the choice, the decline in taxes exceeds the decline in benefits. In the base case, where spouse and survivor benefits are fully valued, taxes and benefits fall with privatization by 5 and 3 percent, respectively. The differences are very small, with the excess in the decline of taxes over benefits amounting to about 2 percent of the basic lifetime tax payment. A somewhat larger change is found when 1990 life tables are used. The present values of lifetime social security taxes and benefits fall about 14 percent and 12.5 percent, respectively.

When social security potential beneficiaries do not value spouse or survivor benefits, then privatization has a very large effect on taxes and benefits, with total but not own benefits falling much more than taxes do. Table 8.2 also indicates the decline in benefits and taxes if participation in the private IRA were made mandatory and thus indicates the maximum decline in benefits and taxes per individual that could be realized for these cohorts in the transition period. Comparing the tax and benefit declines when only own benefits are valued with the results for mandatory privatization, 88 percent of the maximum decline in tax receipts and 89 percent of the maximum decline in benefit payments would be realized if individuals do not value spouse and survivor benefits and are given the chance to opt out of social security.

The differences in the present values of taxes and benefits associated with voluntary privatization indicate one dimension of the financial costs of privatization. But the major concern is not with the present values but with the time paths of taxes and benefits. These are illustrated in figure 8.6a–b and indicate the problem privatization will create. As seen in figure 8.6a, under all scenarios, the decline in taxes is immediate. From figure 8.6b, it can be seen that the decline in benefits does not become substantial until well into the next century. This difference is a source of the immediate cash-flow problem for the system that analysts are well aware of, a cash-flow problem that is going to be made significantly worse when those outside these transition generations are included in the analysis.

8.3.4   Effects of a Higher Return to Capital

Feldstein and Samwick (chap. 6 in this volume) argue that a higher discount rate should be used than the 2.3 percent real return projected by the Social Security Administration. In particular, they argue for the use of a 9 percent real return on physical capital in the United States. That 9 percent real rate has two components, one a roughly 6 percent return to investors after taxes, the other a rebate on corporate income and property taxes raising the real return to the IRA by 3 percent. The real rate of return to equities from the Ibbotson data cited by Poterba and Wise (chap. 9 in this volume) is also around 6 percent.

Clearly, the costs of privatizing will be substantially reduced if individuals can be persuaded to invest entirely in equities, and it is prudent to ask how a voluntary privatized system will function over a range of interest rates.[36] At the

36. There is substantial disagreement about what an appropriate adjustment is for the additional risk associated with equity investments. If the entire difference between the returns to equities and bonds reflects risk, even when investments are pooled at the level of the economy, then there is no advantage to an all-equity portfolio. The appropriate rates of return to use in discounting also depend on the level of risk that is attached to the receipt of social security benefits relative to equities and bonds.

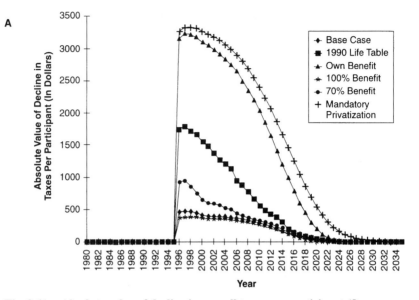

Fig. 8.6A   Absolute value of decline in payroll taxes per participant (figure assumes 2.3% real interest)

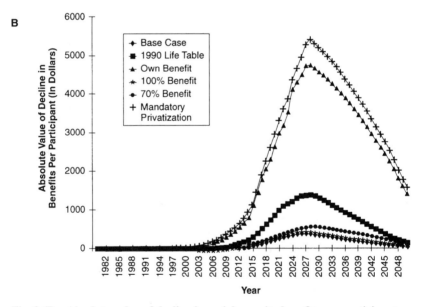

Fig. 8.6B   Absolute value of decline in social security benefits per participant (figure assumes 2.3% real interest)

top of the range, we will conduct a set of simulations with a 6 percent real discount rate. As will be seen, that rate is high enough that the vast majority of covered workers will choose the privatized alternative. Therefore, at least from the perspective of choice, it is not necessary to ask what the effect of a 9 percent real interest rate will be—it will have the same effect as a 6 percent real rate. An additional set of simulations will use a real rate of 4.2 percent, halfway between 6 percent and the 2.3 percent used by the Social Security Administration.[37]

Figure 8.7 presents a number of runs that indicate the sensitivity of the decline in social security participation with privatization to the interest rate in the economy. All use the demographic assumptions of the base case and assume that primary earners fully value all spouse and survivor benefits. As a point of reference, the run demarcated by diamonds assumes that there is a 2.3 percent real discount rate in the economy and comparable interest on the IRA. As noted before, in 1996 social security participation declines with privatization about 13 percentage points of a maximum possible decline of about 90 percent. Once the interest rate reaches 4.2 percent real, participation in social security falls to 14 percentage points in 1996 and slowly rises to a peak participation under privatization of 27 percentage points in 2010. At a real return of 6 percent, participation in social security falls with privatization to 3.6 percentage points in 1996, rising to 10.6 percentage points in 2014. These increases in social security participation over time reflect the higher present value of tax costs at younger ages, where individuals consequently are more likely to opt out.

Table 8.3 reports the effects of privatizing on the present values (in 1989 dollars) of earnings, social security taxes paid, and total and own benefits. The results are reported at the three different assumed real interest rates.[38] At 2.3 percent real interest, as a result of privatization, taxes per initial sample member decline in value by $5,282. Examining the second row, labeled *mandatory schemes,* it can be seen that, over the transition period, the maximum decline in taxes per initial participant as a result of privatization is $41,678. Thus, the decline due to privatization is about 13 percent of the discretionary taxes that remain to be paid after 1996 by these transition cohorts. Looking at the third row of table 8.3, with a 4.2 percent real interest rate payroll tax contributions are seen to fall by $20,815. This may be compared to a maximum decline of $29,642 that would be observed with a mandatory privatization program under a 4.2 percent real interest rate. At a real interest rate of 6 percent, over the transition period the present value of tax contributions per initial participant

37. More generally, individuals with heterogeneous preferences for risk may buy portfolios ranging from fully invested in stocks to mostly invested in bonds.

38. Present values of earnings and taxes under the current system are higher the higher the interest rate. The reason is that all discounting is taken to 1989 and that earnings and taxes paid in years before 1989 are indexed upward by the interest rate. Thus, the accrual of interest raises the value of these earlier earnings by more than the discounting of earnings and taxes paid after 1989 reduces them.

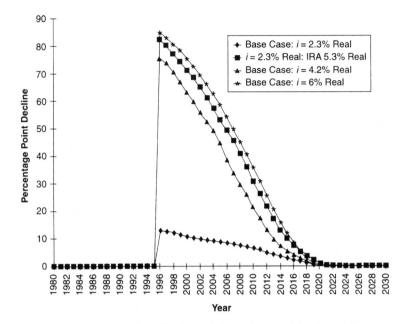

Fig. 8.7   Absolute value of decline in social security participation with privatization at different interest rates

Table 8.3   Present Values of Differences in Social Security Payroll Taxes and Benefits with Privatization under Voluntary and Mandatory Systems Estimated for the Transition Period (thousands of 1989 dollars)

	Taxes	Benefits
2.3% real interest:		
Voluntary	−5,282	−3,426
Mandatory	−41,678	−52,754
4.2% real interest:		
Voluntary	−20,815	−14,704
Mandatory	−29,642	−24,524
6.0% real interest:		
Voluntary	−20,099	−10,384
Mandatory	−21,802	−12,494

falls by $20,099, where a mandatory program would result in a decline in payroll taxes of $21,802. Thus, at a 4.2 percent real interest rate, the participation in social security as measured by tax receipts falls by about two-thirds, while, at a 6 percent real interest rate, the decline in payroll taxes is over 90 percent. Analogous results are seen for the decline in benefits at higher interest rates.

Finally, consider why the labor supply effects of privatizing are so small, even at different interest rates, especially in the transition period. The transition individuals do not have the possibility of opting out for their entire working life, which would generally be much preferable to opting out in their later years, for two reasons. The tax payments are more valuable in the early years. In addition, if the individuals work more than thirty-five years, the tax payments for the extra years buy essentially nothing in the way of benefits.

As a result, the transition individuals are faced with the decision of whether to buy out a few years toward the end of the working life. Consider an individual who currently is sixty years old. If he stays in social security that year, he loses 10.6 percent of salary because that is the tax. If he opts out, he loses one-thirty-fifth of his benefits. Suppose that the replacement rate is 35 percent. In the high–interest rate setting, the total value of the benefits is around nine times the annual benefit: in the low–interest setting, the ratio may be fifteen or higher. Consider the high–interest rate setting, which means that the total value of the benefits is 35 percent of nine, or 3.15 times the current wage. If the individual loses one-thirty-fifth of the benefits, he will lose $(3.15/35 =)$ 9.0 percent of the wage. Thus, he loses around 10 percent of his wage whether he stays in the program or not. If the lost benefits are higher than the taxes, he will stay in; otherwise, he will drop out. Even if he drops out, however, the benefit is never more than a percentage or so; the assumptions generating the 9.0 percent are about as far as you can go to make the benefit loss seem small compared to the wage.

If he does drop out rather than stay in, his effective wage is higher by at most a percentage or so. This translates into a critical value percentage of the term epsilon in the utility function that is higher by about 0.01 or so. The percentage of the normal distribution that lies within a 0.01 interval, and that is subject to working in one regime and not working in the other, is around 0.35 percent (a fractional equivalent of 0.0035). And this is in the high–discount rate case. With lower discounts, the ratio of the value of the benefits to the annual benefit is considerably higher, and the labor supply effect is correspondingly lower.

This explains another phenomenon. The aggregate reduction in taxes must always be lower than the reduction in benefits since people drop out only if the reduction in taxes is bigger. However, the aggregate drop in benefits is never very much more than the drop in taxes. The fact that even among the individuals who drop out the balance between taxes and lost benefits is about equal would help explain this fact.

8.3.5   Differences between the Discount Rate and the Return to the Private IRA

If there are no special returns to the IRA, then the discount rate and the IRA will exhibit similar returns. But a difference may be created if there is a special rebate of corporate taxes only to IRA participants, as suggested by Feldstein and Samwick. On the other hand, the generic system analyzed here does not impose any special fee or additional requirements for those who wish to opt out of the social security system to participate in the privatized IRA. Thus, it might be possible to find less than the full payroll tax refunded to those choosing the IRA.[39]

Figure 8.7 also reports results, indicated in squares, for a case with a 2.3 percent real interest rate in the economy but with a real return on the private IRA of 5.3 percent. This is the expected relation if there is a refund of corporate income and property taxes to holders of privatized IRAs. Here, in 1996, all but 8 percent of the relevant population opts out of the social security system and chooses the privatized IRA. In 2010, 22 percent of participants remain in the privatized system, compared with 53 percent in the base case presented in table 8.2 above. When we did a comparable run (not shown in fig. 8.7) in which 3 percent of the payroll tax is not refunded, the decline in social security participation in 1996 is only about 10 percentage points.

8.3.6   Voluntary versus Mandatory Privatization

Other papers in this volume consider mandatory privatization schemes rather than the voluntary privatization scheme considered here. To put the issue of mandatory versus voluntary participation into perspective, focus again on table 8.3.

Consider how differences in taxes and benefits collected under social security change when mandatory and voluntary privatization schemes are introduced and how these differences vary with the interest rate. Under the voluntary schemes, the decline in benefits is always less than the decline in taxes. Under mandatory schemes, the decline in benefits exceeds the decline in taxes with privatization when interest rates are low. However, because benefits are realized at the end of the life cycle, benefits are discounted more heavily than taxes. As a result, when interest rates are higher, the decline in the value of taxes exceeds the decline in the value of benefits, even under the mandatory schemes. More generally, at higher interest rates, the values of both taxes and benefits are lower, the key relation underlying the modest costs of privatizing estimated by Feldstein and Samwick.

Most important, we can see that, if the real interest rates are low, there is a dramatic difference in the effects of adopting a voluntary as opposed to a mandatory scheme. At low interest rates, there will be a much smaller effect of the voluntary than of the mandatory scheme. But, at higher interest rates, there is almost no difference since most participants will opt out. It appears that most of the effects of privatization will be realized if privatization is voluntary and the appropriate real interest rate is 4.2 percent.

---

39. To be sure, if there is a fee charged to cover the cost of the redistributive portion of social security while at the same time there is a rebate of the corporate income and property tax, the result may roughly be a wash.

8.3.7   Steady-State Analysis

The data used in the simulations presented to this point pertain to cohorts who already have spent a considerable amount of time under the current social security system. Accordingly, the analysis we have conducted pertains to differences under the social security system and the generic, privatized system, but only for a transition period.

It is of interest to ask what behavior will look like in the steady state. To gain some insight, we restart the simulation model at the beginning of the work life for each sample member and assume that, from the first day in the labor market, the individual is operating under the privatized system. Thus, the results that we label *steady state* still pertain to the same cohorts we have examined above and to the same time period. The differences are that incentives from privatization are assumed to have existed from day 1 of the individual's work life, not to have begun in 1996, and that the contribution rate is assumed always to have been 10.6 percent, rather than the historical contribution rate that was used in the simulations for transitions.

Table 8.4 shows the effects of privatizing in the steady state, comparing the current system with a privatized system. A major difference from the results for the transition is that, in the steady state, even at a real interest rate of 4.2 percent, there is virtually no participation in the social security alternative. As seen in column 2, at 4.2 and 6.0 percent real interest, almost no taxes are paid to the social security alternative to the private IRA. The voluntary IRA totally dominates social security. In contrast, at a 2.3 real interest rate, about 60 percent of social security taxes realized under the current system would continue

Table 8.4   **Present Values of Earnings, Social Security Payroll Taxes, and Benefits for Cohorts Born from 1934 to 1959, Steady-State Results at Different Interest Rates (thousands of 1989 dollars)**

	Earnings	Taxes	Total Benefits	Own Benefits
2.3% real interest:				
Current system	1,383,042	119,078	121,268	66,842
Privatized system	1,383,812	73,139	85,217	44,585
Privatized—current	770	−45,939	−36,051	−22,257
4.2% real interest:				
Current system	1,411,386	120,044	60,459	33,996
Privatized system	1,411,928	936	1,059	566
Privatized—current	542	−119,108	−59,400	−33,430
6.0% real interest:				
Current system	1,552,167	129,461	33,191	19,676
Privatized system	1,551,936	227	224	128
Privatized—current	−231	−129,234	−32,967	−19,548

to be paid under the privatized system, and 70 percent of benefits would continue to be realized.

In figures 8.8*a–c*, social security participation, labor force participation, and taxes and benefits are plotted by age under a steady-state simulation. However, these figures pertain only to the interest rate where social security participation will be substantial, a 2.3 percent real interest rate. Figure 8.8*a* indicates that the number opting out of social security is largest at the early ages, reaching a peak of about one-third. The reason again is that the real value of social security tax payments is highest at younger ages. Over time, the number opting out declines steadily, even throughout the age ranges when individuals are too young to retire. The effect of privatization on labor force participation at different ages in the steady state is modest. The maximum increase in labor force participation occurs at age sixty-five and is less than 1 percentage point. As before, the financing problem for privatization (as illustrated in fig. 8.8*c*) is reflected in the fact that the decline in taxes precedes the decline in benefits for each individual.

8.4   Further Analysis

8.4.1   Joint Decision Making

Earnings and Benefits of Husbands and Wives

Among the important simplifying assumptions made in the preceding analysis, behavioral decisions are made only by men. Limitations in the data forced

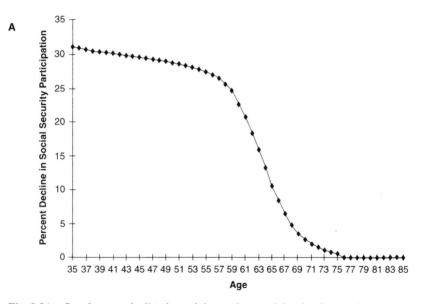

Fig. 8.8A   Steady-state decline in social security participation by age due to privatization (figure assumes 2.3% real interest)

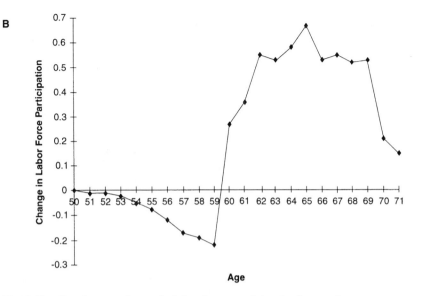

Fig. 8.8B   Steady-state change in labor force participation by age due to privatization (figure assumes 2.3% real interest)

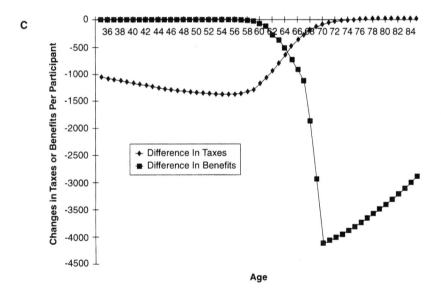

Fig. 8.8C   Steady-state decline in taxes and benefits per participant due to privatization (figure assumes 2.3% real interest)

us to ignore the labor market behavior and participation decisions of wives and their consequences for social security evaluations made by each spouse and to exclude single women from the analysis.[40] Not only does ignoring the labor market behavior of married women make our analysis relevant to only a part of the population, but it also causes some distortion in the behavioral estimates we make for married men. In addition, we oversimplify the determination of spouse and survivor benefits, not allowing appropriately for households in which there are dual earners who nevertheless partially benefit from spouse and survivor social security benefits. Once we recognize the role of labor market participation by the spouse, however, there are additional consequences for the estimated effects of privatizing social security. Specifically, we must confront the question of how the social security rules are going to be modified when either spouse may choose not to participate in the social security system.

Thus, the assumptions that we made in our earlier discussion greatly simplified matters by allowing us to focus on basic aspects of behavior rather than on the details of the alternative policies. In particular, under the assumption that wives claim spouse or survivor benefits only, but not benefits based on own earnings, one can analyze the effects of privatization on the social security system by comparing outcomes in the presence and absence of a privatized alternative. Whether or not there is a privatized alternative, the social security system is assumed to operate under current rules.

In contrast, when wives also earn social security benefits based on own earnings, a new set of rules must be drawn up to address the question of how spouse and survivor benefits are handled when either spouse is free to opt out. Thus, when the privatized system is introduced, it comes with an alternative set of rules for social security. Consequently, there are two social security systems to consider in estimating the effects of privatization. One is the present system operating in the absence of a privatized alternative. The other is a social security system with modified rules operating in the presence of a privatized alternative. As will be seen below, not only will the responses to privatization depend on the fact that a privatized alternative to social security is made avail-

---

40. Two key limitations in the data have narrowed the focus of our analysis to the decisions made by men. The parameters of the utility function we use are estimated in the context of a structural retirement model, with estimation based on data from the Retirement History Study, which is a representative sample of men. The budget constraint is estimated from more recent data, the 1989 Survey of Consumer Finances. At the time of writing, the SCF was the only data set available that included employer-supplied descriptions of pension plans, from which we obtain our data on pension incentives. But the SCF does not provide detailed information on work history. Considering the limitations in the SCF data, it is not too distortionary to use the information the SCF reports on the number of years of full-time and part-time participation to impute the covered earnings history and AIME of men in the sample. Since most of the sample worked full-time, we probably will not be too far off in our calculation of the incentives for continued coverage by social security. But the information on years of full-time and part-time work is inadequate to impute the covered earnings history of the women in the SCF. We would have a great deal of difficulty imputing the covered wage in years when employment was reported and in deciding whether employment was in a covered job.

able, but they will also depend on exactly how the social security system is modified under the privatization scheme.

Because the simplifications that we have adopted cause us to ignore the behavior of the woman in the household and to oversimplify the behavior of the man, it is useful to discuss the next steps required to generalize this line of research.[41] Ideally, we would like to expand this work using a survey that provides updated information on labor supply, provides information on covered earnings history, and also includes employer-provided pension plan descriptions for calculating retirement incentives created by pensions. The new Health and Retirement Survey (HRS) is designed to provide this information, and the required data will be available in a year or so.[42]

It is also useful to discuss the nature of the bias that has resulted from the simplified treatment of spouse and survivor benefits. In the discussion that follows, we consider, first, how the work histories of spouses, which we have ignored, may affect the valuation of spouse and survivor benefits under the current social security system. We then consider how the determination of spouse and survivor benefits under the social security alternative to the privatized system may be modified to take account of the earnings of spouses and the incentives that will be created, affecting the decisions of husbands and wives to participate in a privatized system.

41. The present analysis is also limited because we do not have parameters from a model of joint retirement decisions by husbands and wives. In other work, we have estimated parameters of a utility function for husbands and wives in the context of a preliminary model of joint retirement (Gustman and Steinmeier 1994b). But that model has two limitations for the purposes of the current analysis. First, there is no partial retirement in that model. Second, the parameters were estimated on the basis of pension plan descriptions provided by the respondent, who is the woman covered by the survey, the National Longitudinal Survey of Mature Women (NLS-MW). Plan descriptions obtained from covered workers are typically imperfect (Mitchell 1988; Gustman and Steinmeier 1989). Descriptions of plan features provided by the spouse of a covered worker are likely to be even less reliable.

Employer-provided pension plan descriptions have just become available for the NLS-MW. We are now estimating a family retirement model using NLS-MW data together with matched employer-provided pension plan descriptions.

Note that labor supply is less responsive to market incentives when the utility function in Gustman and Steinmeier (1994b) is used as the basis for simulations than when the utility function from table 8.1 is used to examine sensitivity to market incentives. That is, whichever utility function is used, the findings will suggest that labor supply response to privatization will not be of major importance.

42. After entering the field in the spring of 1996, the third wave of the HRS will be cleaned. It will be ready for analysis in 1997. Information from the third wave of the HRS is necessary to fit a structural model of the type required to analyze privatization issues. Matched data from the social security earnings histories are being released in a restricted data file. These will be invaluable for classifying families according to the way that privatization will affect incentives for each spouse to participate in a privatized system. The HRS also is making available a restricted data file with detailed information on pensions. Currently, the restricted pension and social security earnings files cannot be merged. It is not clear when a restricted file containing both social security earnings histories and detailed pension data will be made available, but a file with aggregate pension data and detailed social security records could conceivably be forthcoming shortly.

A limitation of the HRS data is that, currently, they pertain to a cohort born from 1931 to 1941. Younger cohorts will be added to the survey every five years.

In the current social security system, there are specific rules for determining spouse and survivor benefits. When an individual is entitled both to old age benefits based on own earnings and to spouse or survivor benefits, the procedure is to pay benefits based on own earnings first. If spouse or survivor benefits are below benefits based on own earnings, no spouse or survivor benefits are paid. If spouse or survivor benefits exceed benefits based on own earnings, then the difference is paid on top of the payment based on own earnings, and the recipients are called *dual beneficiaries.* In the end, the individual receives the highest of the benefits he or she is entitled to.

Social security benefits are structured so as to increase the likelihood of a spouse collecting benefits based on own earnings rather than on the record of the primary earner. For example, the progressivity of the benefit formula makes it easier for the secondary earner in a household to earn at least half the benefits of the primary earner. To be entitled to half the benefits of the primary earner, the spouse of a primary earner whose indexed yearly earnings fall at the second bracket amount or beyond, that is, whose average indexed monthly earnings multiplied by twelve are $31,620 or more in 1996, must earn one-third the amount earned by the primary earner.[43]

The progressivity of the benefit formula reduces the effect of additional earnings by the primary earner on benefits paid to the spouse or survivor. To the extent that the secondary earner's labor supply over the life cycle is substantial and largely predetermined as far as the social security participation decision is concerned, the simulations made under the assumption that the primary earner largely ignores spouse benefits will be closer to the mark than the simulations in which spouse benefits are positively valued.

From the perspective of the secondary earner, benefits accrued as a result of own earnings are much smaller than the nominal benefits called for under the system. Indeed, the availability of a privatization scheme provides a mechanism for two-earner couples to avoid a system that is notoriously unfair to them relative to one-earner couples. Accordingly, not only will the husbands in two-earner families come closer to the scenario in which spouse benefits are not valued and be more likely to opt out of the system, but, to the extent that the

43. Using 1996 bend points, each dollar of the first $5,244 of average indexed earnings per year results in almost three times the benefit, as does each dollar of earnings between $5,244 and $31,620, and six times the benefit from average indexed earnings between $31,620 and the maximum covered earnings. For a family whose primary earner has earnings at the second bracket point, i.e., who has indexed earnings of $31,620 per year, the primary earner will receive $13,160 per year. To earn half those benefits, $6,580, the secondary earner must have average indexed yearly earnings of $11,058. Thus, the secondary earner requires just over a third of the earnings of the primary earner to be eligible for half the benefits of the primary earner. For a family with a primary earner who has $50,000 in average indexed yearly earnings, the yearly social security benefit of the primary earner is $15,917. For the spouse to earn half that benefit based on own earnings, $7,958, the spouse needs average indexed yearly earnings of $14,840. So it takes about 30 percent of the primary earner's income for a spouse to be entitled to half the benefit to be received by a primary earner with $50,000 in average indexed earnings a year.

rules force a joint decision to participate, wives in families with substantial earnings are also likely to opt out.

To provide some insight into the relative size of the different groups among the currently retired, it is useful to distinguish three groups of spouses.[44] We do so in the context of current data on beneficiaries. In 1994, there were 20.8 million women beneficiaries age sixty-two or over. The three groups are as follows: *group 1* is the 8 million women sixty-two or older in 1994 entitled to benefits as a wife or widow, not having worked enough to qualify for any benefits based on own earnings history; *group 2* is the 5.3 million who were dual beneficiaries, receiving spouse or survivor benefits; *group 3* is the 7.5 million entitled to workers' benefits only (Social Security Administration 1996, 214).

The husbands and wives in these three groups face different incentives and would react differently to a privatized system. The 8 million households in group 1, with women who did not become covered on the basis of their own work history, fit the single-earner model that we analyzed above. Only the earnings of the primary earner are relevant to the participation decision. And the outcome will depend primarily on the value that husbands place on spouse and survivor benefits, as we have simulated.

Those in groups 2 and 3 are entitled to benefits from own work even in the absence of benefits from their husband's work. Accordingly, they would place a lower value on spouse and survivor benefits, which are of value only to the extent that they exceed the benefits the spouse is entitled to from own work. The 5.3 million women in group 2 who qualified for benefits on the basis of their own work history, but effectively received no increment in their benefits due to their own work, would value spouse and survivor benefits more strongly than the 7.5 million in group 3, whose benefits from own earnings exceed the benefits due to their husband's earnings.[45] We can expect the husbands of those in group 2 to place a stronger value on spouse and survivor benefits than do the husbands of women in group 3.

The women in group 3 find their benefits increased from own earnings when their husbands are alive, but, with few exceptions, their benefits will be no higher as a result of own earnings should their husbands have died.

We have also obtained data that provide a rough indication of the relative size of each group for cohorts between the ages of forty-five and sixty and

44. The discussion takes the husband as the primary earner. Although that may change in the future toward a situation where more husbands earn less than their wives, the assumption is consistent with the data to date. For example, in 1994, there were 2.4 million women who were dual beneficiaries receiving spouse benefits, while there were 27,000 men who were dual beneficiaries receiving spouse benefits (Board of Trustees 1995, table 5.G2). Similarly, 3.0 million wives were entitled to spouse benefits solely because of age, along with 30,000 husbands (Board of Trustees 1995, table 5.F1). There were 5.0 million women receiving nondisabled widows' benefits and 37,000 nondisabled men receiving widowers' benefits in 1994 (Board of Trustees 1995, table 5.F8), with 38 percent of those dual beneficiaries (Board of Trustees 1995, table 5.G2).

45. Some of the women in group 2 may have been in group 3 before their husbands died.

those sixty to seventy.[46] These summary data have been obtained for couples in the Survey of Income and Program Participation (SIPP). Researchers at the SSA have matched restricted social security earnings records to the survey data provided by SIPP participants and have run the earnings records through the Social Security Administration's ANYPIA program to estimate the benefits to which each individual would be entitled on the basis of covered earnings through 1 January 1990.

Table 8.5 shows the relative valuation of spouse and survivor benefits for those families with a husband over and under age sixty. Evaluating these benefit outcomes is a bit tricky because earnings until retirement are not projected by the SSA; instead, benefit amounts are computed by assuming that there are zero earnings between 1990 and retirement. The failure to project earnings may be quite important because the benefit formula is progressive. A related complication is that, in these projections, there are different numbers of years of zero earnings counted for those who survive until the social security retirement age and those who do not.[47] The last column of table 8.5 shows the ratio of a to b, where a is the sum of spouse and survivor benefits plus the husband's own benefits and b is his own benefits. The first panel uses the SCF sample analyzed above, under the assumption that the wife has no earnings. Under this assumption, spouse and survivor benefits are worth 70 or 80 percent of the husband's own benefits, depending on the interest rate. For the SIPP group under age sixty, the spouse and survivor benefits are worth between 34 and 42 percent of the husband's benefits. For those over age sixty, a group that is less subject to bias from assuming that future earnings are zero but that is more likely to be subject to mortality bias, spouse and survivor benefits are worth 32–38 percent of the husband's benefits.

This finding does not mean that one could correct our earlier analysis simply by dividing spouse and survivor benefits by 2. In addition to the appropriate corrections for the biases mentioned above, one would still need to know the distribution of earnings histories among husbands and wives, that is, how the earnings history for each wife matched up to the earnings history for each husband.

Table 8.6 provides another measure from the SIPP sample, this time the number of people in each family type. In about a third of the families with a

46. Michael Leonesio of the Social Security Administration has kindly provided these data, which are still preliminary and subject to revision.

47. Expected survivor benefits are calculated by multiplying the value of survivor benefits for each year of death by the probability of the covered worker dying. For example, because death benefits are paid on a shorter work history according to date of death rather than on the high thirty-five years of earnings, the portion of survivor benefits that assumes death in 1990 is calculated with no zero earnings appearing in the husband's AIME formula. However, the wife's benefits from her own work are calculated on the assumption that she earns zero from 1990 until retirement. Thus, the failure to project earnings until retirement may differentially affect the value of own and spouse benefits. Similarly, there is an effect due to the progressivity of the PIA formula of counting many years of zero earnings in the PIA, and there is also the possibility that a spouse who will eventually qualify for own benefits has not done so yet.

Table 8.5   **Value of Spouse and Survivor Benefits in SCF under Base-Case Assumptions and Computed with SIPP Matched Social Security Earnings Histories ($)**

	Husband's Total Benefit	Husband's Own Benefit	Ratio Total to Own
SCF base-case assumptions:			
2.3% real interest	121,248	66,831	1.81
4.2% real interest	60,445	33,989	1.78
6.0% real interest	29,289	16,974	1.73
SIPP sample under age 60:			
2.3% real interest	107,357.86	75,527.56	1.42
4.2% real interest	70,578.07	51,426.48	1.37
6.0% real interest	48,999.47	36,661.71	1.34
SIPP sample over age 60:			
2.3% real interest	140,921.55	101,788.74	1.38
4.2% real interest	114,963.56	85,441.15	1.35
6.0% real interest	96,847	73,559.50	1.32

Source: Preliminary data provided by Michael Leonesio of the Social Security Administration, matching the 1990 SIPP Full Panel Longitudinal Research File, limited to couples in which the husband or wife was at least forty-five years old. This produced a file with 5,975 couples, reduced to 4,770 after restricting ages to less than seventy, and to 3,580 after eliminating cases with unmatched social security data or uninsured husband.

Table 8.6   **Distribution of Couples by Wife's Eligibility Status for Social Security Benefits**

	Husband Younger than 60		Husband Aged 61–70	
	Number	Percent	Number	Percent
Wife is not eligible for benefit based on her own work	767	32.2	365	30.5
Wife is dual beneficiary when husband is alive	312	13.1	209	17.5
Wife is dual beneficiary only when husband is dead	1,206	50.6	516	43.1
All of wife's benefits are due to her own earnings	99	4.2	106	8.9
Total	2,384	100.1	1,196	100.0

Source: SIPP and matched social security records.

husband under age sixty in 1990, the wife is not eligible for benefits based on her own work. In about a seventh of those families, the wife is a dual beneficiary when the husband is alive and thus will also be a dual beneficiary should the husband die. In about half the families with a husband under age sixty in 1990, the wife will be a dual beneficiary only when the husband is dead. When he is alive, she will receive benefits based on her own earnings. And, in 4 percent of these families, all the wife's benefits are due to her own earnings, even when the husband dies. By and large, the results are consistent for those families with a husband who was sixty-one to seventy in 1990.[48]

Our simulations in the base case pertained only to the primary earner. These simulations had nothing to say about tax receipts from the wife or benefits paid to the wife based on her own earnings. The behavior observed for the base case continues to apply to those one-earner families where the sole earner fully values spouse and survivor benefits. For the few cases in which both spouses have similar earnings histories, with the result that neither spouse nor survivor benefits are of any value, the simulations under the situation where spouse and survivor benefits are not valued at all apply not only to the husband but also to the wife. Other families fall between these cases, meaning not only that spouse and survivor benefits are not fully valued by the primary earner but also that the spouse does not fully value own benefits. This sets up a situation in which participation by each spouse will be sensitive to the precise set of rules established for determining spouse and survivor benefits under the social security system that will function side by side with a privatized IRA.

Potential Changes in Social Security Rules Affecting Spouse and Survivor Benefits

For any alternative set of rules for the social security alternative to the privatized system, it seems reasonable to assume that, when an individual opts out, social security benefits are prorated depending on the fraction of time spent in the privatized alternative, as in the analysis outlined above. A few approaches are considered, but many more combinations of these policies are possible.[49] The policies differ in their treatment of own benefits and of spouse and survivor benefits when one spouse or the other opts out of the social security system.

Own Benefits and Benefits Payable to the Individual's Spouse or Survivor Are Lost. One option is that offered under the current system where spouse and survivor benefits are payable to the degree that the worker stays in and pays social security taxes. For most families with two earners, under a requirement in which spouse and survivor benefits depend only on the participation of the primary earner, at least one partner will drop out of the system. Consider families with a high and a low earner. If the higher earner stays in, then the taxes paid by the lower earner are buying almost no additional benefits, and that earner will surely drop out. If the higher earner drops out, the lower earner will benefit from the progressivity of the PIA formula and may well stay in. To be

48. The fact that the proportion of those families with a wife who will receive benefits based only on own earnings is higher for those families with a husband over age sixty than for families with a husband under age sixty is suspicious; it may or may not be a result of truncation of the earnings histories, especially for those families with a head between forty-five and sixty in 1990.

49. For a discussion of these and related issues, see General Accounting Office (1996).

sure, there may be some exceptions. But, most commonly, the social security alternative to the privatized system will lose the taxes from at least one individual, with probably only a minimal reduction in benefit obligation.

Own Benefits, Entitlement to Benefits as a Spouse or Survivor, and Benefits Payable to the Individual's Spouse or Survivor Are Lost. There is already a precedent for adjusting spouse benefits on the basis of the spouse's own participation in an uncovered system. In particular, there is a special provision that reduces spouse and survivor benefits for a spouse who works in uncovered employment, which up until now involved work in exempt government employment. Two-thirds of the outside pension, or imputed pension if there is a lump sum pension settlement from the government employer, are subtracted from the spouse or survivor benefit under social security.[50]

What would adjusting spouse and survivor benefits based on both the worker's and the spouse's participation do to participation in the social security alternative to the privatized system by members of the three groups analyzed above? The answer is that the husbands of those in group 1, those whose spouse did not work, would stay in or leave independently of such a scheme and their wives would remain out of the labor force. Members of group 3, those families with wives whose current benefits are based only on own earnings, are likely to behave according to the simulations for single earners. Thus, in the case of those in group 3, the behavior of husbands will be similar to the behavior of males who do not value spouse benefits as simulated above, and many of their wives will behave in a similar fashion. This suggests that many will choose the privatized system. This response depends, however, on the extent to which survivor benefits are adjusted for nonparticipation of the spouse. Similarly, members of group 2, dual beneficiaries, will divide in accordance with own and spouse earnings and the specific set of offset rules that is adopted.

All Spouse and Survivor Benefits Are Provided through Actuarially Fair Adjustments in the Primary Earner's Benefits. The logical conclusion to an argument that two-earner couples should not be placed at a disadvantage relative to single-earner couples is to eliminate spouse and survivor benefits as additional benefits, providing them only as part of an actuarially fair joint and survivor benefit. Thus, members of two-earner families might receive both benefits from own covered earnings and benefits as a spouse or survivor, rather than the highest of the benefits to which the individual is entitled. The terms for the

---

50. To reduce the primary benefits of those who were in exempt employment until 1983, there is an ad hoc reduction in the calculation of the PIA. After a transition phase, those who were in exempt employment have their benefits computed as 40 percent of the AIME up to the first bracket amount, rather than the 90 percent figure called for when computing the benefits of those continually in covered employment.

joint and survivor benefits might vary under different proposals. Here, primary earners from couples would receive a lower basic benefit than a single earner with the same earnings history, but the expected total payment to the single and to the couple would be the same. There would be no need to eliminate spouse or survivor benefits of those spouses who opted out of the system because the total benefit they and the primary earner received would depend only on the participation of the primary earner.[51]

Given the earnings distribution, the progressivity of the benefit structure (which, however, would be more difficult to maintain), and the possible use of unisex life tables, we would expect, in accordance with the incentives for participation in a privatized alternative analyzed above, that many more husbands than working wives would opt out of the system.

Joint Accounts Are Set Up in Which Both Spouses Share Credit for Working. Given the redistributive aim of the social security benefit formula, to take account of full family income and avoid distortions due to unequal allocation of market and nonmarket time within the family and unequal wage offers, a modified system might include some form of income averaging for the couple. That is, instead of a scheme in which the contribution of each spouse to total family benefits is determined independently by own earnings, as in the preceding proposal, the earnings of both spouses may be aggregated into a single account, with half the earnings attributed to each. Outcomes under such a scheme will again depend on the specific rules adopted for determining benefits from these individual accounts, with the progressivity of benefits determining the reactions of couples according to the earnings of each spouse.

8.4.2   Further Caveats

The present analysis indicates the sensitivity of choice of program under a privatized social security system to a set of behavioral, market, and program parameters. But it is highly simplified and leaves many questions unresolved.

Because the actual values of many of the key parameters driving the simulation outcomes are not known to us, a wide range of outcomes is possible. Moreover, the analytic framework has simplified various dimensions of economic behavior and is only a partial equilibrium analysis. It includes first-round responses by individuals, but it does not include the consequences of whatever redesign of the revenue system or borrowing alternative is adopted to ensure financial solvency. For example, depending on how a privatized pro-

---

51. To be sure, moving to a system in which all those covered workers with the same earnings received a social security package, for them and their families, that had the same expected benefit, irrespective of marital status, is not likely to be feasible for the transition generation. Many families with only one earner will have planned their life-cycle participation with the idea that they will be eligible for the higher amounts that the current system now provides in the form of spouse and survivor benefits. Nevertheless, it is still useful to consider this alternative.

gram is financed, there may be a wide range of changes in income taxes, and these changes may differentially affect families with different social security entitlements. Nor does the analysis consider the macroeconomic implications of privatization.[52]

To recognize the implications of the financial imbalance in the current system for social security benefits, the base-case analysis assumes that benefits under the current social security regime, and under the social security alternative to a private IRA, would be reduced by 20 percent. We also examine an alternative where the benefit reduction is 30 percent, which is about the size of the projected shortfall in the financing of the current system. Additional costs of a voluntary program are not explicitly considered but may be treated as incorporated within the 20 or 30 percent benefit reduction from current levels and whatever tax increases are imposed. To incorporate a range of outcomes, we have also run the simulations with no benefit reduction. To allow for special charges for opting out, we have run simulations in which some of the payroll tax is retained in social security. Other simulations have raised the return to the privatized IRA above the market discount rate. Each of these is only a crude adjustment. Future analysts will have to do a better job of including the consequences of financial adjustments to privatization.

In the present analysis, no special value is placed on the full annuitization of the benefits provided under social security. Although it is possible that a significant number of people are overannuitized, this simplification will most likely lead to an understatement of the value of the conventional social security option.[53] To be sure, provisions may be adopted to foster a well-functioning annuity market, for example, by requiring annuitization of the IRA alternative.[54]

With the advent of indexed bonds in the United States, the full indexation of benefits under social security will be less of a novelty. Nevertheless, the analysis does not include the inflation insurance from having indexed benefits under social security.

The present model, with its perfect capital market assumption, oversimplifies the savings decision. Available evidence suggests that savings behavior is

52. For discussions that do take macroeconomic effects into account, see Feldstein and Samwick (chap. 6 in this volume) and Kotlikoff (chap. 7 in this volume).

53. If participation in an annuity is not required of those who choose the IRA, adverse selection will raise the costs to those who wish to use the proceeds from their IRA to obtain the kind of annuity at retirement age that social security now provides. Other things the same, those who expect to live for a long time will favor the indexed annuity and, thus, the social security program. To the extent that the population does not fully understand the advantages of an annuity, these effects are weakened.

54. Some of those who choose a lump sum benefit or limited payment period under a privatized alternative may outlive their assets. It is hard to reconcile a retirement savings program with mandatory participation, on the one hand, with an option that allows the individual to spend down retirement assets, perhaps having to resort to some other form of public support, on the other. Thus, it would not be surprising to see the IRA adopted with some form of mandatory annuity provision.

governed by a mix of precautionary and life-cycle motives, leaving some workers liquidity constrained.[55] For constrained workers, heterogeneity in time preference will generate additional heterogeneity in social security participation and labor market choices. Further, although a privatization program may present a choice between social security and a privatized IRA, the program may come with additional restrictions, such as requiring additional savings beyond the payroll tax. These restrictions will create additional behavioral responses that can be analyzed only in the context of a model that is correctly parameterized to reflect observed savings behavior.

The analysis clearly shows the sensitivity of program choice to the interest rate. But we still need to determine exactly what the appropriate interest rate is. Moreover, the return on each asset should be adjusted to reflect some proper risk factor. This requires a better idea of what the proper premium is to attach to social security owing to political and other risks. It also requires a better understanding of the behavior governing choice of investments that will be made in the privatized IRA.[56]

Nor has anything been said about investment costs or losses from inefficient churning by some ill-informed investors.[57] Moreover, the present analysis has ignored the value of the life insurance component of social security for those with small children. This feature should be explicitly valued.

Any policy analyst is going to want information on winners and losers and where they lie in the income distribution. If the assumption is correct that there is a single earner in each household and spouse and survivor benefits are fully valued, with the result that AIME reflects lifetime earnings, then the answer is clear. People leave the system voluntarily only if there is a gain to their expected incomes, and the gains accrue first to those with the highest incomes. In those runs in which only a small fraction of the individuals leave the system, in particular the runs with low real interest rates, the gains accrue to those with the very highest covered earnings. If the real interest rate is higher and most therefore choose to opt out, then the gains accrue throughout the income distribution. But the largest gains still accrue to those with the highest incomes since they are not the beneficiaries of redistribution via the social security benefit structure. What clouds this discussion is the failure to incorporate good information on the role of spouse earnings. Those two-earner couples who are heavily disadvantaged by the treatment of spouse earnings under social security are not necessarily high-income couples, allowing the benefits from privatization to spread more evenly throughout the income distribution. A further problem is that we have not included the effects of unearned incomes in the analysis. Given the preliminary nature of this analysis, the sense of false precision that

---

55. For a related discussion of savings and retirement behavior, see Gustman and Juster (1996).

56. For a discussion of the range of investments in IRA and 401(k) accounts, see Poterba and Wise (chap. 9 in this volume). For a discussion of the range of risks associated with defined-contribution and related pension plans, see Bodie (1990).

57. Mitchell (chap. 10 in this volume) discusses the investment costs of privatized systems.

would accompany inclusion of data on nonwage income and wealth is not warranted.

One could take a very different approach to the analysis of privatization, at least for the scenarios in which the real interest rate is above 2.3 percent. The present analysis essentially links the idea of funding and privatization together. If the real interest rate were 4.2 or 6 percent, one could break the changes analyzed here into two parts, asking first what the cost is of fully funding social security and then how a voluntary, privatized system compares to a fully funded social security system. The work by Feldstein and Samwick (chap. 6 in this volume) suggests that fully funding social security will first increase the payroll tax but in the long term reduce it. In that case, a voluntary, privatized system might be even more attractive compared to a fully funded social security system in the short run, but it might be less attractive in the long run.

8.5   Conclusions

This analysis has provided a framework for analyzing choice within the context of a voluntary privatized social security system, has provided some initial estimates of the participation that might be observed under different circumstances, and has highlighted the sensitivity of choice between programs to key behavioral and economic parameters. We have been able to determine which economic measures and taste parameters are central to the decision to opt out of social security and which are not. By adopting alternative assumptions about key parameters, we have a first indication about the range of outcomes that might result from such a program.

The choice between a private IRA and a traditional social security alternative is very sensitive to the real interest rate. At the higher interest rate examined, a real return of 6 percent, it becomes less important to offer a choice between a traditional social security alternative and a private IRA because most will choose the private IRA. At the lower interest rate, a real return of 2.3 percent, a wide range of outcomes is possible. A private IRA will be chosen by most in the transition group if spouse and survivor benefits are not very important or are not highly valued by the primary earner. A private IRA is also more likely to be chosen if life expectancy is not projected by most individuals. At the 2.3 percent real interest rate, if spouse and survivor benefits are highly valued, and if individuals are aware of trends in life expectancy, most would remain with the traditional social security alternative, and first-year participation in a privatized system could therefore be below 10 percent. A common problem for all alternatives is that, with privatization, taxes decline earlier than benefits, creating the potential of a substantial cash-flow problem for social security.

Our findings also suggest that, in judging the effects of privatization, labor supply adjustments will not be very important. This is true even if major changes in the pension system are induced to allow more workers to qualify for the privatized scheme. The findings about changes in labor force participation suggest that simulation models of the effects of privatization may, as a first approximation, ignore labor supply responses.

An analysis of the type presented here, modified to incorporate a more sophisticated model of two-earner decision making, savings behavior and differential risk, and budget and tax consequences at the level of the economy, could provide the basis for a model of public choice, which in turn will provide an indication of whether such a privatization program would generate a majority in favor of its adoption.

References

Anderson, Patricia, Alan L. Gustman, and Thomas L. Steinmeier. 1996. Trends in male labor force participation and retirement: Some evidence on the role of pensions and social security in the 1970's and 1980's. Working paper. Dartmouth College, Department of Economics.

Board of Trustees. Federal Old Age and Survivors Insurance and Disability Insurance Trust Fund. Various years. *The annual report of the Federal Old-Age and Survivors Insurance and Disability Insurance Trust Fund.* Washington, D.C.: U.S. Government Printing Office.

Bodie, Zvi. 1990. Pensions as retirement income insurance. *Journal of Economic Literature* 28, no. 1: 28–49.

Brugiavini, Agar, Richard Disney, and Edward Whitehouse. 1993. Choice of pension arrangements under uncertainty in the U.K. Paper presented at the Royal Economic Society conference, 15 April. (Reprint available from the Institute for Fiscal Studies, London.)

Disney, Richard, and Edward Whitehouse. 1992. The personal pensions stampede. Report series. London: Institute for Fiscal Studies.

Duleep, Harriet. 1989. Measuring socioeconomic mortality differentials over time. *Demography* 26 (May): 345–51.

Feldstein, Martin. 1996. The missing piece in policy analysis: Social security reform. *American Economic Review, Papers and Proceedings* 86, no. 2:1–14.

General Accounting Office. 1996. *Social security: Issues involving benefit equity for working women.* GAO/HEHS-96-55. Washington, D.C., April.

Gustman, Alan L., and F. Thomas Juster. 1996. Income and wealth of older American households: Modeling issues for public policy analysis. In *Assessing knowledge of retirement behavior,* ed. Eric A. Hanushek and Nancy A. Maritato. Washington, D.C.: National Academy Press.

Gustman, Alan L., Olivia S. Mitchell, and Thomas L. Steinmeier. 1995. Retirement research using the health and retirement survey. *Journal of Human Resources* 30:S57–S83.

Gustman, Alan L., and Thomas L. Steinmeier. 1985. The 1983 social security reforms and labor supply adjustments of older individuals in the long run. *Journal of Labor Economics* 3, no. 2:237–53.

———. 1986a. A disaggregated structural analysis of retirement by race, difficulty of work and health. *Review of Economics and Statistics* 67, no. 3:509–13.

———. 1986b. A structural retirement model. *Econometrica* 54, no. 3:555–84.

————. 1989. An analysis of pension benefit formulas, pension wealth and incentives from pensions. *Research in Labor Economics* 10:53–106.

————. 1991. Changing social security rules for workers over 65: Proposed policies and their effects. *Industrial and Labor Relations Review* 44, no. 4: 733–45.

————. 1994a. Employer provided health insurance and retirement behavior. *Industrial and Labor Relations Review* 48, no. 1:124–40.

————. 1994b. Retirement in a family context: A structural model for husbands and wives. Working Paper no. 4629. Cambridge, Mass.: National Bureau of Economic Research, January.

Mitchell, Olivia S. 1988. Worker knowledge of pension provisions. *Journal of Labor Economics* 6, no. 1 (January): 28–39.

Panis, Constantijn W. A., and Lee A. Lillard. 1995. Socioeconomic differentials in the returns to social security. Santa Monica, Calif.: Rand, January.

Samwick, Andrew. 1993. Wage risk compensation through employer-provided pensions. Dartmouth College. Typescript.

U.S. Department of Health and Human Services. Social Security Administration. 1996. *Social Security Bulletin, Annual Statistical Supplement, 1995.* Washington, D.C.: U.S. Government Printing Office.

Comment   David M. Cutler

In many analyses, privatizing social security is envisioned as a mandatory change in retirement programs. A common scenario, for example, is to redirect some share of individual contributions to a private account rather than the current social security system, regardless of whether people want to make this substitution.

But, if we actually do privatize social security, participation in the new system is likely to be voluntary rather than mandatory. Because so many people like social security so much, it will be hard to deny people the ability to remain in that system. Most likely, contributions will be made to private accounts only if people direct them to be so.[1]

Recognizing this political imperative, Gustman and Steinmeier make a valuable contribution to the privatization debate. They analyze the "first-round" effects of a voluntary privatization system. The "first round" on which they focus principally comprises the share of people who would opt out of the system, ignoring "feedback" effects such as changes in real interest rates or wage rates. They conclude that the most important factor affecting individual choice is the real interest rates: at high interest rates, essentially everyone would opt out of the traditional system; fewer people opt out as interest rates fall.

At its basic level, Gustman and Steinmeier's analysis is straightforward. The

David M. Cutler is professor of economics at Harvard University and a research associate of the National Bureau of Economic Research.

1. For example, in the Republican proposals to "privatize" Medicare in 1994–95, individuals were given the option to remain in the traditional Medicare system at no additional cost. This option was guaranteed because the current system was so popular.

return to social security has two parts. The first is the return in a pay-as-you-go system. As Samuelson (1958) showed, pay-as-you-go social security has an implicit return equal to the rate of real wage growth—the sum of labor force growth and the growth of real wages per worker. Generally, labor force growth is about 1 percent per year, and real wage growth is about 1 percent per year, so the average social security return is about 2 percent per year.

There are then additions and subtractions to this for particular families because of the redistribution in social security. Social security redistributes from rich to poor, by lowering the replacement rate for high-income workers. Social security also redistributes from families with working spouses to families without working spouses, through its spousal and survivorship rules.

The return to individuals saving on their own, in contrast, is the real interest rate. Gustman and Steinmeier consider real interest rates around 2–4 percent. In light of this, it is easy to understand Gustman and Steinmeier's results. When the return to private saving is very high (4 percent or more), the private return dominates social security for just about everyone. As a result, essentially everyone opts out of the system. When the private return is only 2 percent, however, the benefits to opting out vary across families. This is particularly true because of the redistributional component in social security. As a result, higher-income families and two-income families will be particularly likely to opt out of Social Security.

I want to stress one point about this analysis. We typically think that giving people choice is optimal since people can decide what is best for them. Thus, the economic bias is to believe that, if people want to opt out of social security, they should be allowed to do so. In the context of social security privatization, however, this analysis is *not* right. Allowing people to opt out of social security to avoid adverse redistribution is not efficient; it just destroys what society was trying to accomplish. If rich people and two-worker families opt out of social security, for example, we will no longer be able to redistribute from rich to poor or from dual earners to single earners. One of the purposes of social security will have been defeated. This is a cost of privatization of which we must be aware.

An analogy may be helpful. Suppose that contributions to national defense are made voluntary. Probably, few people would choose to contribute; why pay when you can get the public good for free? Realizing this, we make payments for national defense mandatory. The same is true of redistribution. Redistribution is a public good just as much as national defense; no one wants to do it, but everyone benefits from it. As a result, making contributions to redistribution voluntary will be just as bad as making contributions to national defense voluntary. We need to make redistribution mandatory, or no one will pay for it.

One may not like all the forms of redistribution in social security. For example, most people would agree that the rules subsidizing nonworking spouses are a relic of a bygone era. But, if that is true, we should change those rules in the current social security system, not allow that system to fall apart by letting people opt out of that transfer.

This principle leads to some interesting design issues for social security privatization. There may be ways to allow people to opt out of social security while still paying the amount they would have contributed to redistribution. Perhaps the employee contribution to social security, but not the employer contribution, should be refundable. Or individuals might forfeit a one-time amount if they opt out of social security, which would offset the losses from redistribution.

I would like to have seen more analysis in Gustman and Steinmeier's paper about when voluntary privatization is good and when it is harmful and what to do in the latter case. The importance of this issue depends on the assumed real interest rate. When the real interest rate is 4 percent or higher, the gains to privatization can be large, and the harmful effects are smaller. At lower real interest rates, the harmful effects increase in proportion. By leaving aside the issue of the social costs and benefits of choice, Gustman and Steinmeier implicitly use a framework where choice is automatically good. That is not the right starting point.

I want to highlight one other issue in Gustman and Steinmeier's analysis—the rules regarding choice will matter a great deal for how many people will opt in or out of the current system. Consider one seemingly innocuous assumption of the analysis: for every year the person opts out of social security, one-thirty-fifth of future benefits are lost. Suppose that an individual has already worked for thirty-five years and is thinking of working an additional year. If she remains in the current system, her benefits are unaffected. If she opts out, her social security benefits fall. In both cases, contributions are the same. Now suppose that we change the rules slightly. Rather than subtracting one-thirty-fifth of benefits if the individual opts out for a year, we count up the number of years the individual is in the social security system, with a maximum of thirty-five. In this case, opting out after thirty-five years in the system results in no loss in benefits.

The decision to be in or out of social security will be very different in these two cases. In the case as Gustman and Steinmeier have analyzed it, the individual is likely to remain in the current system because the loss in benefits from opting out may be large. In the alternative scenario, the individual will likely opt out of the current system since traditional social security benefits are unaffected by the decision to be out for a year. As the population ages and people are capable of working longer, this type of choice will become a very important issue.

The point is not that Gustman and Steinmeier's assumptions are wrong. It may be that their system is the one that we will enact. The point is that the effects of choice on participation in social security may depend critically on a large number of seemingly innocuous rules. I could add to the list substantially: the rules on opting out for all or part of a year; the rules on individual versus family choice; the rules of integration of spousal coverage with the opt-out decision; etc.

My guess is that variations in these rules could have dramatic effects on participation in the social security system. And, unlike the "good scenario," where people opt out of social security because the rate of return is so much higher outside than in the current system, these choices would be for the "bad scenario" because there are games people can play to maximize their return.

For people who are serious about social security privatization, it is time to worry about these issues. We need less emphasis on estimating the real interest rate and more emphasis on determining how we can achieve the gains of privatization without the costs of unraveling social ties or gaming the system. Gustman and Steinmeier have made a nice start on this issue. It is time for others to follow.

Reference

Samuelson, Paul. 1958. An exact consumption-loan model of interest with or without the social contrivance of money. *Journal of Political Economy* 467–82.

Discussion Summary   Jeffrey Liebman and Andrew Samwick

The discussion quickly focused on the voluntary aspects of the privatization plan examined in the paper. The first consideration was that offering workers a choice to opt in or out may be costly owing to adverse selection on the annuity margin, as noted by the authors. A suggestion was later made that offering multiple tax and benefit schedules to those who opt out might help alleviate the potential adverse selection problem. The authors were then cautioned that it is a mistake to infer from the finding that many people opt out of the old system that privatization is a successful policy. Privatization might just be offering windfalls to some groups of workers. In fact, there did not seem to be anything in the model that made choice beneficial. The authors responded that this was explicitly a behavioral, not a normative, analysis of a particular privatization plan.

Some participants were curious as to why the analysis did not seem to generate large effects of privatization on the timing of retirement given the careful structural modeling of the retirement decision. The authors replied that the parameters of the simulation model, together with the changes in pensions and social security over the past two decades, are able to explain about one-third of the contemporaneous reduction in the labor force participation of older workers. A participant then noted that the absence of retirement effects in this case was itself an important result. The date of retirement in such a model is determined by the relative incentives to retire at one date versus another, and the privatization scheme examined here does not substantially alter the lifetime budget constraint in a way that provides marginal incentives to retire at particular dates.

Another suggestion was made that the uncertain rates of return under a privatized system might allow for a larger effect on the timing of retirement if they were incorporated into the model. Presumably, those workers whose funds appreciated substantially would consume the added wealth in part as a longer retirement, while those whose funds did poorly would work longer and retire later. The authors agreed that incorporating uncertainty in this manner would be an interesting extension and cited other work in progress as the first stages of such an analysis.

9   Individual Financial Decisions in Retirement Saving Plans and the Provision of Resources for Retirement

James M. Poterba and David A. Wise

Two important design features in proposals to supplement or replace the current social security system with a system of individual saving accounts are the degree of individual autonomy that would be allowed with respect to the investment of accumulating assets and with respect to the distribution of accumulated assets. At one extreme are proposals that would mandate the allocation of assets between stocks, bonds, and other investment categories during the accumulation phase and require the purchase of a government-provided annuity at retirement. At the other extreme are plans that would allow substantial individual choice in the investment of assets and in the time profile and method of distributing accumulated assets.[1]

Asset-allocation decisions can have important implications for the rate of return on retirement assets and hence on the degree of retirement security that a given stream of individual contributions during the working life can provide. The standard source of data on long-term returns, Ibbotson Associates (1995), reports that, since 1926, the distribution of returns on a diversified portfolio of corporate stocks has a mean of 9.9 percent per year, compared with a mean of 4.8 percent for a portfolio of long-term bonds and 3.8 percent, barely more than the inflation rate, for a portfolio of short-term Treasury bills. Siegel (1994)

James M. Poterba is the Mitsui Professor of Economics at the Massachusetts Institute of Technology and director of the public economics research program at the National Bureau of Economic Research. David A. Wise is the John F. Stambaugh Professor of Political Economy at the John F. Kennedy School of Government, Harvard University, and director of aging studies at the National Bureau of Economic Research.

The authors are grateful to Jeff Brown, Jeff Close, Peter Diamond, Matthew Eichner, Martin Feldstein, Brett Hammond, Thomas Hungerford, Thomas Juster, John Rea, Andrew Samwick, and Jack VanDerhei for helpful comments or assistance with data analysis and to the National Institute of Aging, the National Science Foundation (Poterba), the James Phillips Fund (Poterba), and the Hoover Institution (Wise) for research support.

1. Diamond and Valdés-Prieto (1994) and Feldstein (1996) discuss a range of issues that arise in considering social security reform proposals.

presents similar findings using data from 1802–1992: the mean equity return is 8.1 percent, the mean bond return is 4.7 percent, and the mean inflation rate is 1.3 percent. The expected value at retirement of an accumulated retirement fund invested in equities is greater than the expected value of one invested in less risky fixed-income assets, although there is also a greater chance of having sustained losses on such a portfolio.

Mandatory saving plans that provide substantial investment discretion to individual participants have led to discussion of two conflicting concerns regarding individual asset-management choices. One is the possibility that some individuals will invest conservatively, thereby earning low rates of return on their account balances and thus not accumulating sufficient resources to finance retirement consumption. The other concern is that some individuals will invest their accounts recklessly, bearing substantial risk and incurring substantial probability of reaching retirement with a very small account accumulation. It is in principle possible that each of these investment patterns might apply to some part of the population, with the result that the group reaching retirement with low levels of resources would consist of some conservative investors and some plungers.[2] Restricting asset-allocation options provides one way to avoid either of these outcomes.

It is difficult to evaluate the importance of restricting individual investment choice since there has never been a universal system of retirement saving accounts in the United States. A substantial fraction of U.S. households accumulates very little financial wealth (see Poterba, Venti, and Wise 1994b), instead relying primarily on social security and to a lesser extent corporate pensions to sustain retirement consumption. Another group, which does accumulate some financial wealth, tends to hold only fixed-income instruments in their portfolio. It is difficult to gauge how such households would invest their retirement saving assets if they were provided with the chance to do so. A particularly difficult issue is how a potential reduction in the current level of social security benefits, which provide a real annuity "floor" under retirement consumption, would affect asset-allocation choices earlier in the lifetime.

A related set of issues arises with respect to payouts from mandatory saving accounts. One of the risks that is partially insured against by current defined-benefit pension plans (through annuity contracts purchased with the accumulation in defined-contribution pension plans) and by social security is that of outliving one's resources. Mandatory saving plans that require annuitization of accumulated balances at retirement or at a particular age, such as sixty-five, also provide a guarantee that resources will be spread over an individual's remaining lifetime. Such plans also entail tighter restrictions on individual choice than plans that would allow more discretion in asset withdrawal, and

---

2. The average return to all investors in a cohort might not be affected by the presence of some very conservative, and some risk-loving, investors, but the distribution of wealth at retirement would be affected.

they may involve additional government involvement in the provision of annuities or the oversight of the private annuity market.

At the center of the discussions of both accumulation and withdrawal options are questions of how individuals and couples would behave in a system of mandatory saving accounts. One potential source of information on these issues is the behavior of participants in various targeted retirement saving plans, such as individual retirement accounts (IRAs), salary-reduction arrangements (SRAs), 401(k) plans, and other self-directed defined-contribution pension plans. The growth of such targeted retirement saving plans has expanded the set of individuals with substantial financial asset holdings and some discretion regarding their investment. The participants in these plans tend to have higher incomes than nonparticipants, so there are immediate questions about the degree to which findings based on such groups can be generalized to the population as a whole. Nevertheless, it seems appropriate to examine the behavior of participants in these plans and to extract what information is available about accumulation and distribution behavior.

This paper considers a range of different saving vehicles that provide individuals with some discretion in investment and some opportunity to choose the nature of their payouts, including IRAs, SRAs, 401(k) plans, the TIAA/CREF retirement system for college and university employees, and the federal government's thrift saving plan. It provides evidence on individual financial decisions in these plans.

The paper is divided into five sections. Section 9.1 presents summary information on participation in various retirement saving programs, drawing on data from the 1992 Survey of Consumer Finances and the recently released Health and Retirement Survey. Section 9.2 summarizes asset-allocation decisions in a variety of the existing saving plans. We note that available evidence from 401(k) plan providers suggests that the equity allocation of new contributions to 401(k) plans is greater than that for the existing stock of assets and that there are differences by age and income in the asset-allocation pattern in 401(k) plans. Section 9.3 focuses on both accumulation and withdrawal decisions of TIAA-CREF participants and summarizes the allocation of retirement saving contributions between stocks and fixed-income assets. Section 9.4 considers the demand for annuities among TIAA-CREF participants, relying in particular on a 1988 survey of TIAA-CREF retirees to explore how individual characteristics affect annuity demand. A brief conclusion suggests several issues for further investigation.

9.1 The Growth of Participation in Targeted Retirement Saving Plans

In the last decade and a half, the structure of the private pension system has shifted substantially from defined-benefit to defined-contribution plans, and many individuals have taken advantage of opportunities for tax-deferred saving in targeted retirement saving accounts. The result of these changes has been a shift, small for those already retired but potentially much greater for those who will retire in the future, toward retirement saving accounts that rely in some way on individual investment decisions.

The first substantial targeted retirement saving plan was the individual retirement account (IRA). IRAs were introduced for most households in 1981 and rose to substantial popularity, with nearly 16 million contributors, before the 1986 Tax Reform Act curtailed the tax benefits for IRA participation by higher-income households. Since 1986, the flow of new contributions to IRAs has been substantially reduced, but total assets in IRAs have continued to grow as a result of rollover contributions from other retirement plans and the increase in value of previously invested assets. By the end of 1995, Bernstein Research (1995) estimates that nearly $1 trillion was held in IRAs.

In contrast to IRAs, a second targeted saving plan, the 401(k) plan (named after the section of the Internal Revenue Code that created it), has expanded rapidly since the early 1980s. Although formally created in 1978, 401(k)s did not gain popularity until after 1981, when the Treasury Department issued clarifying regulations that made it possible for employers to establish such plans. These plans have diffused rapidly through the workplace, first at large employers, then at smaller firms. Participants in 401(k) plans can defer income tax liability on their contributions. Assets in 401(k) accounts accumulate tax free, and income from these plans is taxed when the funds are withdrawn. Prior to 1987, employees could contribute up to $30,000 each year to a 401(k) plan. The Tax Reform Act of 1986 reduced the limit to $7,000 beginning in 1987 and instituted indexation for inflation in subsequent years. The contribution limit was $9,235 for the 1995 tax year. Many employers match employee contributions to 401(k) plans, often at rates between 50 and 100 percent (see Poterba, Venti, and Wise 1994a). The number of participants in 401(k) plans has increased from 7.5 million in 1984, to 15.2 million in 1988, to 22.4 million in 1992, the most recent year for which the U.S. Department of Labor (1996) has released detailed information from IRS form 5500 filings. Bernstein Research (1995) estimates that the market value of assets in 401(k) plans was approximately $650 billion at the end of 1995 and that these assets will increase rapidly in the future. Contributions to IRAs and 401(k) plans now exceed contributions to traditional employer-provided defined-benefit pension plans.

Both IRAs and 401(k)s provide individuals with opportunities to make financial decisions about the investment of retirement plan assets and about the distribution of these assets after retirement age. Individuals have substantially the greatest discretion in investing IRA assets. Although some assets, such as gold and silver coins and hedge funds, could not be held in IRAs until recently, these restrictions are unlikely to constrain the investment choices of many IRA participants. IRA assets can be withdrawn in various ways, including lump sum payouts at any age (although such payouts before age 59½ incur a 10 percent penalty tax on withdrawal), according to a schedule of participant age-specific minimum distributions determined by the IRS, or by purchasing an annuity.

Participants in 401(k) plans face less discretion than IRA investors with respect to asset allocation. The available investment options are plan specific and as such are determined by the employer's arrangement with the 401(k) provider. Since 1993, however, Department of Labor guidelines have required that most 401(k) plans offer at least three investment options, including a broadly based equity fund, a bond fund, and a money market fund. Many 401(k) plans offer a more diverse range of investment options. Assets can be withdrawn from 401(k) plans at any time, although lump sum withdrawals before age 59½ that are not rolled over into other tax-deferred retirement saving plans incur the same 10 percent penalty tax as withdrawals from IRAs. Some 401(k) plans offer annuitization options, while others can be annuitized only if the individual participant purchases an annuity in the private insurance market.

To provide some information on the characteristics of current participants in IRAs and 401(k) plans, table 9.1 presents information on the age-specific prevalence of IRA ownership and the rate of 401(k) participation in 1991. These patterns are important background information given the data that will be presented below on the asset allocation of IRA and 401(k) participants. The data in the upper panel show that IRA participation rises with income and also with age. More than 40 percent of those between the ages of fifty-five and sixty-five have individual retirement accounts, while only one-quarter of those in a cohort twenty years younger have such accounts. The prevalence of IRAs is also sharply rising with income. The data on IRAs indicate only that a respondent has an account, not that contributions to such accounts were made in the survey year (1991). Thus, it is possible that many of the participants opened these accounts before 1986 and have continued to hold the accounts without making contributions.[3] Between 1986 and 1989, IRA contributions fell by roughly 75 percent. Some IRA holders are also likely to have created these accounts as vehicles into which to roll over distributions from other tax-qualified retirement saving plans.

The center panel of table 9.1 shows the probability of participating in a 401(k) plan. These probabilities vary relatively little by age but once again rise substantially as income increases. As the data in the lower panel of table 9.1 show, most of the income dependence in 401(k) participation rates arises from varying rates of 401(k) eligibility, not from variation in participation rates conditional on eligibility. The 401(k) take-up rate for all eligibles was 70.8 percent in 1991, substantially higher than the IRA participation rate for all but the highest income categories. It is possible that some of the participation in 401(k)s at lower income levels reflects employer "helper" contributions that are made to include these employees in the plan and thereby to satisfy nondiscrimination rules for plan qualification.

We have also explored the prevalence of IRAs and various salary reduction

---

3. Some individuals may have multiple individual retirement accounts and make contributions in a given year to only one of these accounts.

Table 9.1   **IRA and 401(k) Participation, by Age and Income, 1991 (%)**

Income (thousands)	Age Category				
	25–35	35–45	45–55	55–65	All
	IRA Participation				
< 10	3.8	10.1	6.0	14.8	7.9
10–20	4.8	6.8	12.9	24.1	9.7
20–30	9.3	15.4	24.9	37.6	18.6
30–40	14.8	20.0	31.3	45.7	24.7
40–50	17.9	33.0	47.3	59.5	35.6
50–75	23.6	38.7	50.2	63.4	41.1
> 75	43.2	59.9	66.3	75.5	61.6
All	13.2	26.3	35.3	43.8	27.1
	401(k) Participation				
< 10	4.1	6.6	1.5	6.7	4.5
10–20	9.4	13.6	8.5	9.8	10.5
20–30	21.2	20.7	15.9	10.2	18.4
30–40	29.7	27.3	19.2	26.5	26.2
40–50	28.7	31.6	39.8	25.6	31.8
50–75	39.1	36.3	42.3	43.6	39.4
> 75	44.2	39.5	46.3	31.7	41.3
All	23.0	26.5	25.9	20.9	24.6
	401(k) Participation Given Eligibility				
< 10	79.8	58.4	72.5	85.2	70.8
10–20	63.2	67.7	51.5	68.3	63.0
20–30	70.3	59.8	57.6	49.0	61.7
30–40	74.1	63.7	58.5	72.5	67.3
40–50	73.8	68.7	81.6	67.8	72.9
50–75	76.1	67.2	75.1	84.0	73.3
> 75	86.2	83.8	88.1	85.7	85.8
All	73.5	67.7	72.3	72.3	70.8

Source: Poterba, Venti, and Wise (1995). Tabulations are based on 1991 SIPP.

plans in the Health and Retirement Survey (HRS), an ongoing survey of 12,600 individuals between the ages of fifty-one and sixty-one in 1992.[4] The HRS questionnaire does not ask the same questions as the SIPP (Survey of Income and Program Participation) survey instrument, but it is nevertheless possible to estimate the prevalence of IRAs, defined-contribution plans at the respondent's current job and from former jobs, and other tax-deferred saving vehicles such as 401(k)s and 403(b)s. The results are shown in table 9.2.

The HRS findings are broadly consistent with those from the SIPP. For

---

4. Poterba, Venti, and Wise (1998) analyzed the HRS data in studying the utilization of lump sum distributions from defined-contribution plans.

Table 9.2   **Prevalence of Retirement Saving Arrangements in HRS Population (%)**

Income (thousands)	IRA Only	401(k) Only	DC Only	IRA and 401(k)	Other Multiple	None
< 10	23.6	2.0	3.9	2.7	3.2	64.7
10–20	19.3	5.3	6.4	2.4	2.6	63.1
20–30	24.2	5.3	7.2	5.9	6.0	51.4
30–40	28.4	6.6	7.2	7.4	6.6	43.9
40–50	31.3	8.0	7.2	7.3	9.1	37.0
50–75	33.6	6.6	6.1	11.4	12.8	29.6
> 75	42.7	4.1	4.4	15.8	19.0	14.0
All categories	28.7	5.3	6.0	7.4	8.4	44.4

Note: Authors' calculations using Health and Retirement Survey database. Income is defined as the sum of wage income, professional practice income, and income from a second job; it is essentially a labor income concept. The unit of measurement is the household. DC = defined contribution.

IRAs, the HRS data suggest that 36.1 percent of respondents have an IRA or an IRA and a 401(k) plan. Of the 8.4 percent of the respondents who are shown as *other multiple* in table 9.2, 7.7 percent report having an IRA, so the total IRA participation is 43.8 percent for the HRS respondents. This compares with 35.3 percent for the forty-five to fifty-four age group and 43.8 percent for the fifty-five to sixty-four age group in the SIPP data shown in table 9.1 above. With respect to 401(k) plans, the HRS data suggest that 14.8 percent of respondents participate; this percentage is somewhat lower than in the SIPP sample.

The SIPP and HRS data suggest that IRA and 401(k) participation is not randomly distributed across the income distribution but tends to increase with age and income.[5] The sample of participants in these plans will therefore provide more information on the investment decisions of older, higher-income groups that are more likely to participate in these plans than on younger, low-income workers who are not. We address these issues in our subsequent analysis by stratifying households by age and income where possible.

9.2   Asset-Allocation Patterns in Retirement Saving Plans

This section presents information on the asset allocation of retirement saving plans. We begin by presenting survey-based information from the 1992 Survey of Consumer Finances, which asked respondents about investment patterns in IRAs, salary-reduction arrangements (SRAs) such as employer thrift plans, and 401(k) and traditional defined-contribution pension plans. We then present information from other sources, such as industry association tabulations on asset-allocation decisions in IRAs and 401(k) plans or specialized

---

5. This is why studies of the saving effects of these retirement saving plans, such as Poterba, Venti, and Wise (1995), stratify households by income level in carrying out saving comparisons.

tabulations on asset allocation in the federal government's Thrift Savings Plan. Each of these different methods of obtaining information provides some evidence on current patterns of household asset allocation.

9.2.1 Summary Information from the Survey of Consumer Finances

The Survey of Consumer Finances (SCF) is a stratified random sample of U.S. households administered by the Federal Reserve Board. It is designed to gather detailed information on assets, liabilities, and demographic characteristics. To collect useful information on asset holdings, in light of the skewed distributions of many types of financial and real assets, each survey oversamples high-income households. Each SCF contains an area-probability sample, which is a stratified random sample of households chosen from the population at large, and a stratified random sample of households drawn from a set of high-income tax returns. Both samples are surveyed using the same questionnaire, but missing value imputations in the public release versions are typically done separately. We use the most recent publicly available survey, the 1992 SCF, to provide some information on asset-allocation patterns in IRAs, 401(k) and 403(b) plans and other supplemental retirement accounts, and traditional defined-contribution pension plans. The latter category in the SCF includes profit-sharing or thrift plans and employee stock ownership plans (ESOPs).[6]

Table 9.3 presents data on the fraction of assets in each of these retirement saving vehicles that are held in the form of corporate stock or mutual funds that invest primarily in corporate equities.[7] The data are stratified by age in each case. The results show that approximately half the assets in each of these accounts are held in corporate equities. At least for the individuals who are currently participating in these plans, it therefore appears that equity investment is viewed as an important aspect of accumulating assets for retirement. There are apparent differences in age-specific rates of equity ownership, with those over the age of sixty-five showing a lower equity fraction of IRA and SRA assets than comparable, but younger, individuals.

One difficulty in evaluating results such as those in table 9.3 is that it is not clear what it is that "theory" suggests we should find. There is no presumption that households of different ages should allocate the same fraction of their portfolio to equities. Bodie, Merton, and Samuelson (1992) develop an argument for reducing equity exposure as households age, and Samuelson (1989, 1990) discusses arguments for age-related variation in equity holding.[8] Simi-

---

6. The critical limitation of the SCF for studying this question, and a limitation of most survey data on retirement saving plan asset allocation, is that we do not know whether the retirement plan is self-directed. In some plans, the plan sponsor may restrict asset-allocation choices, e.g., by allocating all employer contributions to a pension plan to an account that holds only company stock.

7. Related discussion and data summary may be found in U.S. General Accounting Office (1996).

8. Even if households reduce equity exposure as they age, they may still want to hold equities after retirement because of the long life expectancy of many couples at retirement age.

Table 9.3   **Share of IRA, SRA, or Defined-Contribution Pension Assets in Equities, 1992 (%)**

	IRAs	401(k)s and 403(b)s	Traditional DC Plans
Age group:			
< 35	50.5	44.7	47.9
35–44	50.4	44.5	46.4
45–54	51.7	49.3	50.8
55–64	51.7	45.4	49.1
> 65	33.0	39.8	49.6
Income group (thousands):			
< 30	32.4	37.5	45.4
30–50	41.4	41.8	47.7
50–100	47.2	38.1	49.2
> 100	52.2	56.0	50.0
Total	46.5	46.8	49.1

Source: Authors' tabulations from 1992 Survey of Consumer Finances. SCF respondents with IRAs are asked whether their assets are held in various asset categories, such as "bank accounts, CDs, and money market funds," "stocks," "bonds," "a combination of stocks and bonds," etc. The fraction holding stocks is computed by adding together all holdings of those who report that they hold stocks and $1/N$ times the holdings of those who report investing in combinations of N assets, one of which is stocks. For example, half the assets of individuals reporting "a combination of stocks and bonds" is added to the equity total. For 401(k), 403(b), and other defined-contribution (DC) pension fund investments, the options are "mostly in stocks," "mostly in bonds," and "split between." We add those assets that are held mostly in stocks to half the assets that are "split between" to compute the total equity investment in these accounts. The 401(k) and 403(b) category also includes assets in supplemental retirement accounts; the traditional defined-contribution pension plan entries include ESOPs and profit-sharing plans.

larly, if households view their retirement accounts as part of a broader portfolio selection problem, one must analyze their overall investment decisions rather than allocation choices in these accounts alone. For individuals who face high marginal tax rates on interest income, for example, holding bonds rather than equities in their tax-favored retirement accounts may provide higher after-tax portfolio returns than alternative portfolio profiles.

9.2.2   Other Sources of Information on IRA and 401(k) Asset-Allocation Patterns

In addition to survey information like that contained in the SCF, it is also possible to obtain data on asset allocation in IRAs and some other categories of retirement saving accounts from financial industry sources that monitor aggregate trends. Information of this type is presented for IRAs in table 9.4, which shows data for 1989 and 1994. These data are disaggregated by the type of financial institution holding the IRA, but this provides a reasonable guide as to the assets held in the account. In 1989, commercial banks, credit unions, and thrift institutions accounted for 49.1 percent of all IRA assets. IRAs with these institutions were presumably invested in various fixed-income securities.

Table 9.4   Distribution of IRA Assets, 1989 and 1994 (%)

Intermediary or Asset	1989	1994
Commercial bank	21.8	14.5
Thrifts	21.5	8.0
Life insurance companies	8.3	8.2
Credit unions	5.8	3.5
Mutual funds	24.6	31.1
Equity funds	11.5	16.7
Money market funds	5.6	8.7
Bond and income funds	7.5	5.6
Other self-directed	18.1	34.6

Source: Investment Company Institute (1995).

Adding money market mutual funds and bond and income funds to these assets brings the total of fixed-income assets to 62.2 percent. By 1994, the share of assets in these fixed-income categories had declined to 40.3 percent. Equity mutual funds increased from 11.5 to 16.7 percent of IRA assets during this period, but the sharpest increase (from 18.1 to 34.6 percent) was in "other self-directed" assets. The data from the Survey of Consumer Finance suggest that various types of equity investment are likely to account for a substantial share of this category.

The best source of aggregate information on 401(k) plan asset allocation is the annual set of IRS form 5500 filings, most recently published for 1992 data in U.S. Department of Labor (1996). These show 401(k) plan assets of $510.2 billion, with employer securities (presumably company stock) worth $88.2 billion, or 17.3 percent of the total. Identifiable interest-bearing assets, which include interest-bearing cash, CDs, corporate and government debt, and various loans, totaled $60 billion, or 11.2 percent of the total. Common and preferred stock direct holdings totaled $45.7 billion, or 9 percent of all assets. "Indirect investments," which are not identified by the nature of the underlying securities on form 5500, are an important and unallocated category, including $101.9 billion in "interests in master trusts," $47.2 billion in registered investment companies, $75.6 billion in insurance company general accounts, and $26.9 billion in unspecified general investments.

The coarse information on form 5500 has led to a number of private-sector surveys of 401(k) plan asset allocation. Such surveys are based on a subset of existing 401(k) plans, and whether the plans included in each survey are representative of the broader population of plans is difficult to evaluate. Nevertheless, these surveys provide an important source of evidence on the evolving pattern of 401(k) asset allocation. Table 9.5 presents this type of data from two different surveys over the period 1988–95. These surveys, by Access Research and IOMA, have been conducted periodically since the late 1980s or early 1990s. The survey findings suggest that there are some differences in results

Table 9.5   **Asset Allocation in 401(k) Plans (%)**

	Access Research (1995)		
Asset Category	1991	1993	1995
Corporate equities	11	16	21
Company stock	26	24	22
GICs	31	27	23
Balanced funds	13	13	14
Bonds	5	7	8
Money market funds	9	7	6
Other	6	6	6
	RogersCasey and Institute of Management and Administration (1995)		
	1988	1992	1995
Corporate equities	43	47	55
GICs	44	38	28
Balanced, bonds and cash	13	15	17

Source: Various reports as indicated in references.

across the two surveys, even in a given year, but the trends in the two surveys over time are similar.

There are several noteworthy findings in table 9.5. First, consistent with the Survey of Consumer Finance evidence, approximately half of 401(k) assets are currently invested in equities. However, the data presented here suggest that a higher fraction of 401(k) assets than of other equity assets is invested in shares of the company where an individual works. There is a correspondingly lower investment fraction in diversified national or international equity portfolios. The Access Research findings suggest 43 percent in corporate equities or company stock, with another 14 percent in balanced funds that would include some equity holdings. The IOMA findings suggest 55 percent in corporate equities, without further detail as to breakdown. The data from the form 5500s and the Access Research results suggest that one important feature of 401(k) plans is their substantial holdings of company stock. One reason for the significant level of such holdings is that employers sometimes channel their matching funds into accounts that are limited to holding corporate stock. In such cases, employees may have some discretion in the investment of their own contributions but no control over the investment of employer contributions.[9]

9. How individuals adjust their portfolio holdings to the existence of corporate defined-contribution plan accounts held in company stock is an important unresolved issue. If individuals do recognize the employer's contribution and pursue the imperfect hedging strategy of reducing their holdings of equity in general to offset the holding of employer shares, then the data suggest

The second significant finding in table 9.5 is that the share of 401(k) assets held in equity securities has increased substantially during the last half decade. Both the Access Research and the IOMA data suggest a sharp increase, with an 8 percent increase between 1992 and 1995 in the latter. This trend toward equity investment coincides with a decline in the share of guaranteed investment contracts (GICs). The trend toward greater equity holdings may be the result of several factors: high equity returns raising the relative asset share of these securities, even if 401(k) investors hold fixed their contribution allocation between equities and fixed-income assets; declining nominal long-term interest rates, which have made GICs less attractive in the eyes of some investors; and rising expectations of future equity returns, driven in part by extrapolative expectations and the recent period of strong equity returns.

The 401(k) asset-allocation choice reflects two decisions: one by employers with regard to which investment options to offer and a second by employees with respect to which investments to choose, given the available menu. Broad choice is now the rule, rather than the exception, in 401(k) plans. A recent RogersCasey (1995) survey found that only 1 percent of 401(k) participants worked at firms with only a single investment option; 2 percent had two options, 6 percent three options, 9 percent four options, 18 percent five options, and 74 percent six or more investment options. More than three-quarters of 401(k)s offer an actively managed domestic equity investment vehicle, compared with 62 percent offering a money market fund, 61 percent offering a stable value fund, and 60 percent offering a U.S. balanced fund.

Table 9.6 presents information from the 1994 Access Research (1995) survey that shows both the availability of various investment options and the use of these options given their availability. The data show that roughly 60 percent of individuals make at least some use of equity mutual funds when they are included in the opportunity set. Index funds and international equity funds are somewhat less popular, conditional on availability, than various types of growth funds. The data in table 9.6 shed some light on the role of company stock (shares in the firm that employs the workers who participate in the plan) in 401(k) plans and suggest that some individuals purchase company stock even though they are not required to do so by plan regulations.[10] While less than half the 401(k) participants surveyed had a company stock investment option in their 401(k) plan, nearly 60 percent invested in company stock if this option was available. Company stock, GICs, and various growth-oriented equity mutual funds have the three highest take-up rates conditional on availability.

---

that individuals seek to hold roughly half their assets in equities. If they do not consider the employer contributions, however, then it becomes appropriate to subtract this 20 percent of the value of 401(k) assets from both the equity holdings and the total value of these accounts. This suggests an equity share of slightly less than 40 percent.

10. Whether employers exert tacit pressure for purchasing company stock in retirement accounts is an open issue.

Table 9.6   **Investment in 401(k) Asset Categories, by Investment
                     Availability (%)**

Investment Option	Availability	Use Given Available
Equity funds:		
Long-term growth	59.6	60.5
Growth and income	52.1	64.0
Aggressive growth	45.1	59.9
International	27.1	50.1
Index fund	33.7	41.2
Company stock	41.6	59.4
Balanced funds	23.9	58.7
Bond funds:		
High-yield bond	13.6	25.8
Long-term bond	19.0	32.7
Corporate bond	9.2	34.1
U.S. government bond	23.7	29.6
Short-term bond	9.8	22.1
Guaranteed investment contract	42.0	55.4
Money market fund	35.9	36.4
Asset-allocation funds:		
High risk	15.4	44.9
Moderate risk	18.7	43.4
Low risk	14.1	38.6

Source: Access Research (1995).

All the foregoing data focused on aggregate allocation patterns in 401(k) assets, with no information on how individuals in different circumstances choose to allocate their assets. Table 9.7 presents information drawn from Goodfellow and Schieber's (1996) analysis of almost thirty-six thousand participants in twenty-four 401(k) plans.[11] The table shows the fraction of 401(k) plan assets held in each asset category, by age of plan participant.[12] The data show clear asset-allocation differences across age groups. Younger plan participants are more likely to invest their 401(k) assets in stock funds or company stock than are older workers. The fraction of assets in the three equity categories, domestic and international stock funds and company stock, declines from 52.9 percent for those aged twenty-one to thirty to 30.3 percent for those in their fifties and 13.4 percent for those over the age of sixty.[13]

11. The Employee Benefit Research Institute (1996b) presents a related analysis of the asset-allocation choices of investors in three large 401(k) plans. The results are broadly consistent with those from the large sample of plans analyzed by Goodfellow and Schieber (1996).

12. The entries in the total column raise some questions about the comparability of this sample with the 401(k) universe. The share of assets held in company stock is substantially less than that for all 401(k) plans, with a correspondingly greater share of fixed-income investments.

13. Goodfellow and Schieber (1996) also present data on the fraction of 401(k) participants who allocate none of their contributions to equity investments (31.2 percent of the total sample, with some age variation, as suggested by 29.2 percent for those aged twenty-one to thirty, 30.6

Table 9.7   Allocation of Funds in 401(k) Investment Plans, by Participant
                   Age (%)

| | Age Group | | | | | |
Investment Category	21–30	31–40	41–50	51–60	> 60	Total
Stock funds	39.1	36.4	29.7	22.0	9.5	25.3
Company stock	11.0	8.9	6.1	5.8	2.7	6.1
International stock funds	2.8	3.1	3.8	2.5	1.2	2.8
Fixed-income funds	41.4	43.4	49.4	61.5	85.2	58.1
Balanced funds	5.7	8.2	11.0	8.3	1.3	7.8

Source: Goodfellow and Schieber (1996).

Table 9.8 presents analogous information with participants disaggregated by income level. Since the analysis is based on 401(k) plan records, income in this context represents wage and salary income from the plan-sponsoring firm, not total family income. As with age, there is a clear pattern in asset allocation by income category. Higher-income earners allocate substantially larger shares of their 401(k) assets to equity securities. For participants with incomes between \$15,000 and \$25,000, for example, 29.9 percent of 401(k) assets are held in equities, compared with 59.4 percent for those with incomes between \$75,000 and \$100,000 and 64.5 percent for those with incomes above \$100,000. The fraction of assets held in balanced funds also increases with income, while the allocation to fixed-income funds falls roughly in half between the lowest and the highest income categories.

The relation between income and the share of contributions allocated to equities in the Goodfellow and Schieber (1996) data parallels our earlier finding from the Survey of Consumer Finances, but the link between participant age and contribution mix (table 9.6 above) is much stronger than in the Survey of Consumer Finances. This may be due to the difference between the definition of *age* in the SCF and in databases with information on individuals.[14] Because SCF respondents are asked about the financial status of their household, participation in a 401(k) means that someone in the household has a 401(k) account. Household age is determined by the age of the household head, which is a noisy measure of the age of actual participants. This could weaken the relation between age and the behavior of participants as measured in the SCF.[15]

percent for those between forty-one and fifty, and 52.3 percent for those over sixty) and the fraction who allocate more than 60 percent of their contributions to equities (36.7 percent for the twenty-one to thirty group, 30.7 percent for those forty-one to fifty, 18.8 percent for those over sixty, and 31.4 percent of the entire sample).

14. Bajtelsmit and VanDerhei (1996) analyze asset-allocation decisions in a single large defined-contribution plan and find some evidence that both younger and older workers are more likely to hold assets in fixed-income instruments than are middle-aged workers. This result may be driven by their use of a quadratic specification in modeling the age dependence of asset holdings or by special characteristics associated with the defined-contribution plan under analysis.

15. Another possibility is that Goodfellow and Schieber's data set reflects an unrepresentative sample of 401(k) participants, but we have no way to address this issue.

Table 9.8   **Allocation of Funds in 401(k) Investment Plans**

Investment Category	Income Group (thousands)							
	< 15	15–25	25–35	35–45	45–60	60–75	75–100	100 +
Stock funds	24.6	21.5	19.5	18.6	25.3	42.2	45.4	52.0
Company stock	6.5	7.6	8.2	6.6	7.6	10.6	7.9	2.3
International stock funds	.6	.8	1.7	1.6	2.0	3.9	6.1	10.2
Fixed-income funds	62.1	63.0	61.6	66.7	53.2	32.2	26.0	27.2
Balanced funds	5.9	7.2	9.0	6.5	12.0	11.1	14.7	8.4

Source: Goodfellow and Schieber (1996).

It is difficult to evaluate IRA and 401(k) asset-allocation choices in the absence of a benchmark, derived either from theoretical analysis of the return distributions and consumption needs confronting investors or from other sources. One possible comparison is the current asset mix in these plans relative to that in defined-benefit pension plans. In 1994, Bernstein Research (1995) reports that these plans held 46 percent of their assets in domestic equity, 11 percent in international equities, 28 percent in bonds, 5 percent in GICs, 3 percent in real estate, and 7 percent in other assets. IRA and 401(k) investment patterns thus reflect a much greater holding of GICs and a somewhat lower level of equity investment, but they are not dramatically different from the asset allocations of defined-benefit pension assets.[16]

9.3 Asset Allocation in Two Retirement Saving Systems

The discussion so far has considered asset allocation in individual retirement accounts, which are available (at least in some form) to all individuals with current earned income, and 401(k) plans, which are broadly available in the private sector. In this section, we draw on the experience of two more specialized retirement saving programs, the Thrift Savings Plan for federal government employees and the TIAA-CREF system for employees of educational institutions, to address similar issues of asset allocation.

9.3.1 Asset-Allocation Experience in the Federal Employee Thrift Savings Plan

The federal government's retirement system includes an option for voluntary contributions to the federal Thrift Savings Plan (TSP), which is structured along the lines of most 401(k) plans. In early 1995, the TSP had 2 million participants and nearly $27 billion under management (according to Hinz, McCarthy, and Turner 1996). Employee contributions to the TSP are made on a

---

16. The merits of this comparison may be questioned on the grounds that defined-benefit plan assets are managed to achieve objectives of an infinitely lived agent, the plan's corporate sponsor, and are insured by a government agency, the Pension Benefit Guaranty Corporation.

pretax basis. The federal government matches, dollar for dollar, employee TSP contributions up to 3 percent of salary and fifty cents on the dollar for the next 2 percent of salary. Contributions to the TSP are constrained by the same contribution limits as 401(k) contributions at private-sector employers, although there are no nondiscrimination rules constraining the distribution of contributions to the TSP.

Table 9.9 shows the percentage of workers choosing to make contributions to the TSP in 1993. In contrast to the private-sector experience with 401(k) plans, where participation in these plans conditional on eligibility exceeds 60 percent even at low income levels (see Poterba, Venti, and Wise 1995), participation in the TSP is below 50 percent at income levels below $20,000 per year and rises to 96 percent at income levels above $70,000. The federal government automatically contributes 1 percent of salary to the TSP for all employees; this is not considered "participation" in this table.

The federal Thrift Savings Plan historically offered more limited investment options than many private 401(k) plans.[17] Until 1987, all TSP contributions had to be invested in a federal government securities fund. This requirement was gradually phased out between 1987 and 1991. Since 1991, TSP assets can be allocated between three different funds, without restriction. Participants are allowed to reallocate assets that have accumulated from pre-1987 contributions as well as to allocate new contributions among three funds: a government securities fund that earns the average market return on marketable Treasury securities with more than four years to maturity; a large-capitalization stock fund that invests in the S&P 500; and a fixed-income fund that invests primarily in a Shearson Lehman Hutton commingled government/corporate bond index fund. The U.S. General Accounting Office (1995) reports that, at the beginning of 1995, 70 percent of the assets in the federal thrift plan were invested in the federal securities fund and that 6 percent were held in a commercial bond fund and 24 percent in the corporate equity fund. The equity fund is currently attracting a higher share of contributions (35 percent in August 1994) than its share of assets, but participants have apparently made little use of a post-1990 provision permitting reallocation of funds that were contributed during the period when all contributions were directed to the government bond fund.

9.3.2   Asset Allocation in TIAA-CREF

TIAA-CREF is the retirement saving system for employees of colleges, universities, and some other nonprofit institutions. It includes university faculty as well as staff. Many TIAA-CREF participants, like employees of the federal government, are better educated than randomly selected individuals in the population, so analysis of their retirement saving behavior may not be completely representative of all who might participate in a mandatory, economy-wide saving system. Nevertheless, one important benefit of analyzing the TIAA-CREF

---

17. Hinz, McCarthy, and Turner (1996) provide an overview of the federal Thrift Savings Plan.

Table 9.9   **Participation in, and Salary Deferral Rates in, the Federal Employee Retirement System**

Salary Range (thousands)	Percentage of Federal Employees Making Voluntary Contributions	Deferral Rate if Making Voluntary Contribution (%)
10–19	45	4.4
20–29	69	5.2
30–39	81	6.0
40–49	89	6.5
50–59	93	6.9
60–69	93	7.2
70 +	96	7.2
All	73	5.7

Source: U.S. General Accounting Office (1995).

data is that we can obtain individual-level data as well as aggregate information on asset-allocation choices.

Because TIAA-CREF is a financial service provider, individual data records suffer from the same limitations as participant records in 401(k) plans, notably the lack of information on demographic characteristics and household income. However, two special databases, the 1993 Premium Paying Research Panel and the 1988 Participant Survey, have been collected in recent years, and each of these databases has detailed information on individual attributes. Both surveys include a set of questions about participant retirement and financial planning, and they provide valuable information for studying participant decisions. The decision we focus on is the choice between allocating funds to TIAA accounts, which are invested in portfolios of fixed-income instruments, and CREF accounts, most of which are invested in equities.[18]

Table 9.10 presents information on the current asset-allocation choices of TIAA-CREF participants as well as the allocation of existing balances between CREF and TIAA accounts. In 1993, TIAA accounts attracted 38 percent of contributions (contributions to TIAA-CREF are frequently referred to as *premiums*).[19] There is a clear link between age, income, and the fraction of contributions allocated to fixed-income instruments. The TIAA share is 32 percent for those under the age of thirty-five. It rises to 38 percent for those between the ages of forty-five and fifty-four and then to 53 percent for those over the age of sixty-five who are still making contributions to TIAA-CREF. The fraction devoted to TIAA declines by more than 15 percentage points as we move from individuals with incomes under $25,000 to those with incomes over $100,000.

18. Since 1988, CREF has offered a money market account, and, since 1990, CREF has offered a bond market account. When the survey data were collected in 1988, however, virtually all CREF assets were invested in equities.

19. CREF attracted 43 percent of premiums, with the other 19 percent of premiums allocated to hybrid accounts or other specialized accounts.

Table 9.10   Bonds versus Equity: Current Investment Decisions and Asset Balances of TIAA-CREF Participants

Age or Income in 1993	Percentage of Contributions in TIAA Accounts	Percentage of Assets in TIAA Accounts
Total	38	44
Age:		
< 35	32	37
35–44	37	44
45–54	38	45
55–64	44	49
65 +	53	57
Income (thousands):		
< 25	50	53
25–34	41	45
35–49	39	46
50–74	39	44
75–99	35	42
> 100	34	40

Source: Unpublished tabulations from the 1993 Premium Paying Research Panel, TIAA/CREF Participants, courtesy of Brett Hammond.

The fraction of total TIAA-CREF assets held in TIAA accounts is remarkably similar to the asset-allocation mix of current contributions. This reflects the combined effect of an increase over time in the share of contributions that participants have allocated to CREF accounts and the greater return on equities than on bonds. The first effect would cause the contribution share going to TIAA to fall below the share of existing assets held in TIAA accounts, while the second effect works in the opposite direction.

9.3.3   Participant-Level Evidence on Allocation Decisions in TIAA-CREF

To further explore the factors that affect asset-allocation choices, we obtained data from the 1988 TIAA-CREF Participant Survey. This unique database has been used by Laitner and Juster (1996) to study the determinants of intergenerational altruism; the data are described in detail in Juster and Laitner (1990). In addition to information on the percentage of TIAA-CREF accumulation held in each type of account, drawn from participant records, the database also includes information on participant and other family income, financial assets and other components of net worth, and various demographic characteristics. We use this information to estimate simple regression equations of the following form:

$$\%\mathrm{TIAA} = \alpha_0 + \alpha_1 \times \mathrm{AGE} + \alpha_2 \times \mathrm{MARRIED}$$

(1)
$$+ \alpha_3 \times \mathrm{FEMALE} + \alpha_4 \times \mathrm{INCOME}$$

$$+ \sum \alpha_{5,j} \times \mathrm{EDUC}_j + \sum \alpha_{6,j} \times \mathrm{WEALTH}_j + \varepsilon.$$

EDUC$_j$ denotes a set of indicator variables for particular ranges of education, and WEALTH$_j$ similarly denotes a set of indicator variables for net worth in various categories. *Net worth* is defined as the sum of all financial assets net of debts, plus the reported value of housing, other real estate, boats, autos, life insurance, trusts, and businesses owned. INCOME corresponds to family income, so it includes both income that the TIAA-CREF participant may earn outside the educational institution as well as income earned by others in the household. The median asset share in TIAA for this sample is 43 percent, and the mean is 52 percent. These values are higher than in the 1993 data shown in table 9.9 above, consistent with the view that TIAA-CREF participants have become increasingly equity oriented over time.[20]

Table 9.11 presents the results of estimating these regression models. The table shows three different specifications with respect to education and wealth. The only demographic variable that affects asset allocation in all three specifications is the gender of the respondent; women systematically invest approximately 4 percent more of their accumulation in TIAA accounts.[21] Family income, education, and household net worth are also related to asset-allocation choices. With respect to family income, the only category indicator that enters the equations in a statistically significant fashion is that for family income above $100,000. Participants from such households allocate between 5 and 7 percent less of their TIAA-CREF assets to TIAA than do participants from households with incomes below $50,000 per year. These results are consistent with earlier evidence from 401(k) plans and IRAs suggesting that higher-income households are more likely to choose equity investments. With respect to education, the only important distinction is between those TIAA-CREF participants with twelve or fewer years of schooling and those with more than twelve years of schooling. The former group allocates more than 10 percent more of its portfolio to TIAA than does the combined more highly educated group.

9.3.4 Interpretation

Similar asset-allocation patterns emerge with respect to household net worth. Participants from households with net worth above $250,000 allocate approximately 4 percent less of their TIAA-CREF accumulation to TIAA, but there are no statistically significant differences in the asset-allocation patterns of participants from households with net worth below this level. The results in table 9.11 support the evidence from other sources that suggest that high-income, high-net-worth individuals are more likely to allocate retirement sav-

20. Assets in CREF accounts can be transferred into a TIAA account, but, once assets have been placed in a TIAA account, they may not be reallocated to a CREF account. This places constraints on the speed with which the aggregate TIAA-CREF portfolio can shift from bonds to stocks.

21. This finding also appears in other data sets; see, in particular, Hinz, McCarthy, and Turner's (1996) analysis of data from the federal Thrift Savings Plan.

Table 9.11   Participant-Level Models for Share of TIAA-CREF Assets in TIAA

Constant	67.33	49.19	62.81
	(6.68)	(4.99)	(6.92)
Age	−.07	.05	.02
	(.08)	(.09)	(.09)
Married	−.05	.88	.28
	(2.02)	(2.02)	(2.03)
Female	4.07	4.76	3.70
	(1.84)	(1.79)	(1.86)
Family income (thousands):			
25–50	2.12	2.02	2.02
	(2.14)	(2.14)	(2.15)
50–100	−1.86	−1.48	−1.11
	(2.12)	(2.14)	(2.15)
> 100	−6.76	−5.92	−5.21
	(2.70)	(2.79)	(2.79)
Education:			
12–16 Years	−10.15		−9.54
	(5.04)		(5.04)
16 Years	−11.97		−10.76
	(4.78)		(4.79)
> 16 Years	−13.88		−12.31
	(4.26)		(4.29)
Net worth (thousands):			
50–100		2.13	2.11
		(3.23)	(3.23)
100–250		.52	.42
		(2.22)	(2.22)
250–500		−4.94	(4.24
		(2.33)	(2.34)
> 500		−5.66	−4.84
		(2.54)	(2.56)
Adjusted R^2	.0275	.0260	.0306

Note: All equations are estimated on a sample of 1,190 observations in the 1988 TIAA-CREF Participant Survey. Standard errors are shown in parentheses.

ing assets to equities than are their counterparts from lower-income, lower-net-worth households.

Our ubiquitous finding that lower-income, less-educated individuals allocate a smaller share of retirement plan assets to equities can be interpreted in either of two ways. First, it is possible that these individuals are more risk averse than higher-income, better-educated individuals and that they are choosing different asset allocations because of this underlying difference in preferences. The second, alternative, interpretation is that these individuals do not correctly perceive the higher expected returns associated with equity investing and that they are making an optimization error by holding too large a share of their portfolio in fixed-income assets.

One way to distinguish between these alternative views might involve studying how participant education affects asset-allocation choices. If 401(k) and other retirement plan participants in low-income classes choose to hold a higher fraction of their assets in equity after they have been exposed to information on portfolio returns, then the optimization-error view may receive some support relative to the risk-aversion explanation. The Employee Benefit Research Institute (1996a) reports that asset allocation is one of the most frequently covered topics in participant education programs at firms with 401(k) plans or similar retirement saving options. The effect of this education on asset choices is an important issue for further investigation.[22]

9.4   Evidence on Annuity Demand

The extent to which individuals would use the proceeds accumulated in mandatory saving accounts to purchase annuities is another important issue in evaluating and designing such plans. Relatively few household surveys explicitly inquire about income received from individual annuity contracts. The Health and Retirement Survey did include such a question, but, since the respondents were typically in their fifties, it is not surprising that the resulting prevalence of annuity income, 1.57 percent, was low.[23] Perhaps more relevant, in the HRS sample only 8.0 percent of respondents who had previously worked for an employer with a defined-contribution plan reported that they had selected an annuity as the method of payout for their accumulated defined-contribution plan assets. Other possible responses to this question included withdrawing the money, rolling it over into an IRA, and allowing it to accumulate.

9.4.1   Would Current Retirees Choose to Purchase More Annuity Coverage?

A more valuable source of information on potential annuity demand is the 1988 TIAA-CREF survey of annuitants, which paralleled the survey of TIAA-CREF contributors discussed above but was administered only to annuity recipients.[24] Annuities are only one of the ways TIAA-CREF participants can withdraw their accumulated account balances. Although rare during the time period corresponding to this survey, participants could also choose lump sum payouts or withdrawals of several substantially equal payments. The 1988 survey focused only on those participants who had reached the distribution phase

---

22. Milne, VanDerhei, and Yakoboski (1996) present some information on the asset-allocation choices of individuals in 401(k) plans with different types of participant education systems, but they do not report "before and after" asset-allocation patterns.

23. The mean annual annuity payout reported by those who indicate that they receive annuity income is $13,496.

24. The asset-allocation patterns between TIAA and CREF in the participant and annuitant surveys are similar. At the lowest education and net worth levels, there is a pronounced tendency for greater investment in TIAA rather than CREF.

of their saving plan and who had chosen the annuity option.[25] TIAA-CREF offers a variety of potential annuity options, including participating annuities (with a low guaranteed payout rate but historically substantial dividends) for TIAA participants and variable annuities based on a range of different portfolios for CREF participants.

One of the questions on the TIAA-CREF annuitant survey was, "If you unexpectedly received $100,000, what would you do with it?" Just over one-quarter of the respondents, 26.5 percent, indicated that they would purchase an annuity. This fraction did not vary substantially as a function of respondent age. Roughly the same fraction, 24.5 percent, indicated that they would either spend roughly $16,000 per year (which would exhaust the windfall in about eight years) or $10,000 per year (windfall exhausted in about twelve years). Thirty-seven percent of the respondents indicated that they would consume only the income from the windfall, and about 12 percent reported that they would spend less than the annual income from this windfall.

It is important to recognize three features of the TIAA-CREF annuitant group that makes them special for the purpose of analyzing annuity demand. First, all the survey participants have both a real annuity from social security and another annuity payout from TIAA-CREF.[26] Their responses may, consequently, not describe the responses of retired households who do not have annuity coverage beyond social security or the responses that would be observed if the current social security system were pared back. Second, most of the respondents are drawn from the upper quintile of the U.S. income and wealth distributions (see Laitner and Juster 1996), although they are not likely to represent the very highest income and wealth strata of the population. If the demand to bequeath assets is related to lifetime income, then this group may provide a guide to the annuity demands of only a part of the population. Third, the TIAA-CREF participants may have access to annuities on more favorable terms than individuals in the private marketplace and may be assuming that they would purchase additional annuities on such terms.

While recognizing these limitations, we explored the factors that affect the respondent's answer regarding how a windfall would be allocated.[27] Our approach follows the regression strategy that we used above to investigate the share of assets that TIAA-CREF participants hold in TIAA accounts. We now estimate linear probability models for each of the possible responses to the

---

25. Some participants might have stopped contributing to TIAA-CREF but not yet begun to withdraw their accumulation. They would not be included in the survey.

26. TIAA-CREF participants who purchase standard annuities can choose between simple nominal annuities and "graded" policies in which the stream of payments is backloaded in part to offset the effects of inflation. Thus, TIAA-CREF annuitants are not necessarily holding simple nominal annuities in addition to their social security real annuity.

27. One difficulty with surveys of this type is "surveyor preference bias": respondents attempt to provide what they believe the survey taker believes is the "correct" answer. It is difficult to know how important biases of this type are likely to be in this data set.

questions on windfall use, illustrated, for example, by BUYANNUITY, which equals unity if the respondent indicated that he or she would purchase an annuity with the windfall proceeds:

$$\text{BUYANNUITY} = \beta_0 + \beta_1 \times \text{AGE} + \beta_2 \times \text{MARRIED}$$

(2) $$+ \beta_3 \times \text{FEMALE} + \beta_4 \times \text{SOCSEC} + \beta_5 \times \text{KIDS}$$

$$+ \sum \beta_{6,j} \times \text{EDUC}_j + \sum \beta_{7,j} \times \text{WEALTH}_j + \varepsilon.$$

The family income variable from the earlier specification is now replaced with a variable measuring the household's social security benefits, which proxy for a ranking of lifetime labor income. We also augment the earlier specification with a variable indicating whether the household has children since that may be a proximate determinant of annuity demand.

The results of estimating this equation are shown in table 9.12, and they suggest that it is difficult to find simple patterns in the responses to these questions. The only robust empirical finding is that TIAA-CREF participants with children are less likely to choose an annuity or a rapid "spend-down" plan, and more likely to pursue policies that preserve their capital, than are participants without children. There is some evidence that married respondents are less likely to annuitize a windfall than are other respondents; this may indicate a belief that the question is limited to individual annuities, which terminate at the death of the annuitant (a married couple could also choose a joint and survivor's annuity). There is also weak evidence that respondents in the lower portion of the net-worth distribution are more likely to say that they would spend their windfall than are those in the higher parts of the distribution. One puzzling feature is that the prevalence of spending down among those with the lowest net worth, under $50,000, is lower than among those in the $50,000–$250,000 net-worth range. The estimates in the last column of table 9.12, which correspond to the response that recipients would spend less than the current income from the windfall, do not show any robust patterns.

9.4.2   Current Annuitization Patterns at TIAA-CREF

One issue that TIAA-CREF data can enlighten is the type of annuity contracts that individuals purchase when they do purchase annuities. TIAA-CREF retirement annuity contracts can be written on a single life or two lives (typically to provide for the participant and a spouse), and these contracts can be written as simple annuities, in which the payouts cease when the annuitants die, or as annuities with guarantees that payments will be made for a certain period even if the annuitants do not survive for this period.[28] In a standard life-cycle setting without bequest motives, the simple annuity, which provides a

---

28. "Years-certain" annuities are life annuities with a guarantee that payments will be made for at least some number of years.

Table 9.12   TIAA-CREF Annuitant Responses to "How Would You Spend a
$100,000 Windfall?"

	Buy an Annuity	Spend the Amount over 8–12 Years	Annually Consume No More than Income
Constant	.295	.411	.294
	(.265)	(.254)	(.292)
Age	.002	−.002	.0002
	(.004)	(.004)	(.004)
Married	−.096	.171	−.075
	(.071)	(.068)	(.079)
Female	−.049	.116	−.067
	(.064)	(.061)	(.070)
Social security benefit	.025	−.081	.056
receipts (/1,000)	(.067)	(.064)	(.074)
Have kids?	−.095	−.208	.303
	(.071)	(.068)	(.078)
Education:			
12–16 years	.083	−.028	−.054
	(.112)	(.107)	(.123)
16 years	−.022	−.076	.099
	(.115)	(.110)	(.127)
> 16 years	−.011	−.015	.026
	(.102)	(.098)	(.113)
Net worth (thousands):			
50–100	.041	.189	−.231
	(.102)	(.097)	(.112)
100–250	−.059	.164	−.105
	(.073)	(.070)	(.080)
250–500	−.140	.061	.079
	(.080)	(.077)	(.088)
> 500	−.022	.073	−.052
	(.080)	(.076)	(.088)
Adjusted R^2	.0049	.0404	.0590

Note: All equations are estimated on 310 observations with complete data on annuity demand in the 1988 TIAA-CREF Participant Survey. Standard errors are in parentheses.

higher monthly payout in each period when the annuitant is alive than any of the guaranteed options, dominates the other choices.[29]

Table 9.13 presents information on the choice of annuity policy by TIAA-CREF participants who contracted for annuities in 1978 and in 1994. The table shows both single-life and joint-life annuity policies. King (1996) reports that, in 1978, 44 percent of the annuities contracted for by male TIAA-CREF participants were single-life policies, compared with 26 percent of such policies in

29. This assumes that the available annuity policy is actuarially fair for the potential purchaser. In practice, since TIAA-CREF uses a unisex life table to price annuities, it could be the case that policies other than a simple annuity are optimal for some participants.

Table 9.13   **Annuity Choices of TIAA-CREF Annuitants, 1978 and 1994 (%)**

Annuity Type	1978	1994	1978	1994
	Male Single-Life Annuitants		Female Single-Life Annuitants	
Single life:				
Without guarantee	33.6	33.8	46.0	35.0
Ten-year certain	38.2	25.8	30.5	29.8
Fifteen-year certain	.0	16.2	.0	15.0
Twenty-year certain	25.1	23.8	21.0	19.5
Installment refund	3.2	.4	2.6	.7
	Male Primary Annuitants		Female Primary Annuitants	
Joint life:				
Full annuity to survivor:				
Without guarantee	5.6	13.3	2.2	11.7
Ten-year certain	32.3	9.9	30.0	11.1
Fifteen-year-certain	.7	13.0	.0	14.6
Twenty-year certain	63.1	63.8	67.8	62.6
Half annuity to survivor:				
Without guarantee	7.2	14.2	2.4	12.6
Ten-year certain	37.0	8.9	45.9	12.3
Fifteen-year certain	1.0	12.2	.0	22.2
Twenty-year certain	54.7	64.7	51.8	52.9

Source: Personal communication from Francis P. King at TIAA-CREF.

1994. For women, the respective percentages of single-life policies were 81 and 68 percent.

The table shows that simple annuities without guarantee provisions account for only about one-third of all single-annuity policies but less than 15 percent of joint-life policies. Policies with certain payout periods of fifteen years or more account for more than one-third of the single-life annuities chosen by both men and women in 1994 and nearly two-thirds of the two-life policies. Since the guarantee provisions in annuity contracts become operative only when the annuitant dies, in the case of single-life policies, or when *both* annuitants die, in the case of two-life policies, the widespread choice of annuities with guarantees casts doubt on the value of the simple life-cycle model as a starting point for describing household annuity demand.

9.4.3   Theoretical Estimates of the Utility Gain from Annuitization

To provide some perspective on the utility consequences of choosing to annuitize a given amount of wealth, we present illustrative calculations similar to those in Kotlikoff and Spivak (1981) and Friedman and Warshawsky (1990). We consider an individual who derives utility from consumption each month according to a standard isoelastic utility function, $U_t = (C_t^{1-\beta} - 1)/(1 - \beta)$, where β is the coefficient of relative risk aversion. When $\beta = 1$, this utility function yields the special case of logarithmic utility. We assume that an individual faces a probability of death each month that corresponds to the annual mortality rates reported in the 1996 social security actuary's cohort life table for men born in 1930 (i.e., sixty-five-year-olds in 1995). We assume that no one lives beyond age 115 and that lifetime expected utility for a man aged sixty-five is given by

$$(3) \qquad\qquad V = \sum_{t=65}^{115} P_t \times (1 + \delta)^{-t} \times U(C_t),$$

where P_t denotes the survival probability (to age t) for a sixty-five-year-old white man, and δ is the individual's time preference rate.

We first compute the expected lifetime utility associated with a "homemade annuitization" policy that involves consuming an amount in each period that equals current wealth divided by life expectancy.[30] This implies that wealth evolves according to

$$(4) \qquad\qquad W_{t+1} = (1 + r)W_t - (1/L_t) \times W_t,$$

where r is the real rate of return. We assume that an individual has accumulated assets of 100 at age sixty-five and find the value of V (which we denote V_{homemade}) that corresponds to this consumption strategy.

Next, we assume that the individual can purchase an actuarially fair real annuity at age sixty-five. We find the level of wealth at age sixty-five that would generate the same lifetime expected utility as the homemade annuity applied to wealth of 100 at age sixty-five. The ratio of this wealth to 100 indicates how much the wealth of the sixty-five-year-old could be reduced, while leaving him at the same lifetime expected utility level, if he had access to an actuarially fair annuity market. We perform a similar calculation assuming that only nominal annuities are available but again maintaining the assumption that these policies are actuarially fair.

Finally, we consider the effect of allowing for preexisting real annuity policies in this setting. We assume that the sixty-five-year-old man has both 100 in accumulated assets and the claim to a real annuity with an expected present value of 100; that is, half his wealth is annuitized. We then repeat the calculation allowing this individual to purchase a real or nominal annuity and find the

---

30. This does not represent the optimal consumption policy in the presence of lifetime uncertainty, except in special cases. When period-by-period utility is given by $U = \log c_t$ and the individual's time preference rate is zero, e.g., the optimal consumption profile involves consuming wealth/ (life expectancy) in each period. We focus on this consumption rule even in cases when it is not optimal because it is a simple rule, analogous to some withdrawal rules from retirement saving accounts such as IRAs, that individuals might easily implement. In calculations not reported here, we have discovered that there can be substantial differences in the lifetime utility accruing to individuals who follow optimal, and suboptimal, consumption paths. Thus, the current calculations may overstate the gains from annuitization for such optimizers, especially in the case with substantial preannuitized wealth.

reduction in wealth that would lead to the same expected utility level if the annuity market were available.

Table 9.14 presents the results of these calculations. The upper panel considers the case in which real annuities are available in the private market, and the lower panel considers the case of nominal annuities. The first entry, for the log utility ($\beta = 1$) case, shows that with a 3 percent real interest rate and an annual discount rate of 1 percent, with no "preexisting" annuity, an individual would receive the same lifetime expected utility whether he had wealth of 100 and no access to a real annuity market or wealth of 64.0 and access to such a market. A sixty-five-year-old man would be prepared to give up 36 percent of his wealth if he could purchase a real annuity rather than consume according to the reciprocal life expectancy rule. This finding, and the other results in the table for different parameter values, is broadly consistent with the results from the Kotlikoff and Spivak (1981) study. Higher risk aversion values increase the share of wealth that the individual would be prepared to give up to obtain access to an actuarially fair annuity market.[31]

The lower panel of table 9.14 presents results for nominal rather than real annuities. The wealth equivalent results are similar to those for the real annuity case, although individuals would not be prepared to forgo as much wealth if they could purchase nominal annuities as if they could purchase real annuities. The effect of allowing for a preexisting real annuity stream on the wealth equivalent measure is small, as can be seen from the differences between the wealth equivalents in the first and second columns of table 9.14.

While these findings are based on a stylized model, they generally suggest that individuals receive substantial expected utility benefits from purchasing annuity contracts, at least in standard models. They draw attention to the limited fraction of TIAA-CREF annuitants who report that they would use a lump sum windfall to purchase an additional annuity.

9.5   Conclusions and Extensions

More than half of U.S. households between the ages of fifty-one and sixty-one currently participate in some form of self-directed retirement saving account. The financial management decisions of households with these accounts can provide some evidence on the how households might manage funds in a mandatory private saving system. We consider two aspects of financial management: asset allocation between stocks and bonds and demand for annuities. With respect to the choice between stocks and bonds, we find that the aggregate fraction of 401(k) or IRA assets that are held in stocks is smaller, by approximately 10 percentage points, than the equity fraction held by defined-

---

31. Further analysis of the utility gain from annuitization, along with updated information on the actuarial present discounted value of currently available individual annuity contracts, may be found in Mitchell et al. (1998).

Table 9.14   Wealth-Equivalent Value of Annuities Compared to "1/Life Expectancy" Consumption Plan

	No Real Annuity Baseline	Preexisting Real Annuity Equal Half of Net Worth
Annuity market offers real annuities:		
Log utility ($\beta = 1$) case:		
$r = .03, \delta = .01$	.640	.665
$r = .03, \delta = .03$	.666	.684
$r = .05, \delta = .03$	.672	.681
$\beta = 2$ case:		
$r = .03, \delta = .01$	.501	.656
$r = .03, \delta = .03$	.567	.677
$r = .05, \delta = .03$	.618	.677
Annuity market offers nominal annuities, inflation = .03:		
Log utility ($\beta = 1$) case:		
$r = .03, \delta = .01$	.672	.688
$r = .03, \delta = .03$	.679	.689
$r = .05, \delta = .03$	.700	.702
$\beta = 2$ case:		
$r = .03, \delta = .01$	.538	.684
$r = .03, \delta = .03$	.591	.687
$r = .05, \delta = .03$	.659	.703

Note: Each entry shows the wealth required at age 65 to achieve the same expected lifetime utility as in the case without an annuity market, with a wealth at age 65 of 1, and when the individual consumes (wealth/life expectancy) each period.

benefit pension fund managers. One notable feature of 401(k) investment patterns is that they involve more holdings of own-company stock, and less investment in diversified portfolios of common stocks or international equities, than defined-benefit plan portfolios. The share of 401(k) and IRA assets allocated to equities, either via direct stock holding or through investment with intermediaries such as mutual funds, has increased significantly since the late 1980s. There are clear age-related and income-related patterns in asset allocation: higher-income households and younger participants in retirement saving plans tend to hold a higher fraction of their assets in equities.

While these findings provide some evidence on asset allocation, they must be interpreted with caution for two important reasons. First, plan participants do not have complete investment discretion with respect to all assets in 401(k) plans, as they do with assets in individual retirement accounts. Some 401(k) plans involve restrictions on asset choice, such as rules that employer contributions must be invested in employer stock. A related issue may arise in analyzing allocations for TIAA-CREF participants, some of whom face restrictions on the allocation of account inflows. Asset-allocation patterns in IRAs may therefore provide a better indicator of unconstrained asset choice than decisions in existing employment-linked retirement saving plans.

A second difficulty in interpreting existing asset-allocation decisions is that these decisions are made in an environment in which individuals expect to receive a real annuity, social security, which provides a floor on their consumption opportunities. Because some mandatory saving plans would scale back at least part of the existing social security system, it is possible that portfolio allocation decisions in such an environment would differ from those under the current system. This is an issue that can be analyzed under specific assumptions about the nature of individuals' utility functions, the distribution of returns available to them, and the nature of social security.

This paper also presents some evidence on the demand for annuities by participants in the TIAA-CREF system, which provides retirement benefits for employees of educational institutions. Roughly one-quarter of TIAA-CREF annuitants in the late 1980s, a group of individuals who already receive income from annuities, indicated that, if they received a $100,000 windfall, they would use these funds to purchase an *additional* annuity. Our analysis of a cross-sectional survey of these TIAA-CREF annuitants reveals few strong correlates of this demand for additional annuities; married individuals are less likely to demand an additional annuity, and there is weak evidence that those with higher levels of net worth would be less likely to annuitize a windfall.

An important issue, one that we have unfortunately been unable to find data to analyze, concerns the choice between annuities and other payout options by individuals who have accumulated assets in retirement saving plans. Participants in the Health and Retirement Survey, who were between the ages of fifty-one and sixty-one, report that, in 8 percent of the cases when they left previous employers who had offered defined-contribution plans, they chose to distribute plan assets by purchasing an annuity. This sample is too young to provide a clear perspective on the decisions made by individuals who reach retirement with substantial assets accumulated in a self-directed retirement saving account.

Even if it were possible accurately to measure the fraction of assets that are annuitized in this way, it is not clear how this information would bear on individual choices under a system of mandatory saving accounts. For precisely the reasons noted above, any proposal that scales back the real annuity associated with the existing social security system may affect individual demand for annuities. It is not clear what model to use in evaluating this issue. In simple life-cycle models, individuals with access to actuarially fair annuity markets should annuitize all their wealth at retirement. However, these models may not provide a realistic guide to individual behavior. In models with bequest motives, private annuity markets that do not offer actuarially fair annuities, and uncertainty regarding future health risks and associated consumption needs, individuals might choose not to annuitize fully. Analyzing how individuals would decide between annuities and other distribution options requires a model that incorporates these features. In addition, as Diamond (1994) notes, one of the key questions about a system of privately managed saving accounts is what annuity policies will be offered by private insurers in this setting. Considering general equilibrium effects in the annuity market complicates the analysis even further.

References

Access Research. 1995. *Marketplace dynamics.* Windsor, Conn.
Bajtelsmit, Vickie L., and Jack L. VanDerhei. 1996. Risk aversion and pension investment choices. In *Positioning pensions for the twenty-first century,* ed. Michael Gordon, Olivia Mitchell, and Marc Twinney. Philadelphia: University of Pennsylvania Press.
Bernstein Research. 1995. *The future of money management in America: 1995 edition.* New York: Sanford C. Bernstein.
Bodie, Zvi, Robert Merton, and William Samuelson. 1992. Labor supply flexibility and portfolio choice in a life-cycle model. *Journal of Economic Dynamics and Control* 16:427–49.
Diamond, Peter. 1994. Privatization of social security: Lessons from Chile. *Revista de análisis económico* 9:21–33.
Diamond, Peter, and Salvador Valdés-Prieto. 1994. Social Security Reform. In *The Chilean economy,* ed. B. Bosworth, R. Dornbusch, and R. Laban. Washington, D.C.: Brookings.
Employee Benefit Research Institute. 1996a. Participant education: Actions and outcomes. Issue Brief no. 169. Washington, D.C.
———. 1996b. Worker investment decisions: An analysis of large 401(k) plan data. Issue Brief no. 176. Washington, D.C.
Feldstein, Martin S. 1996. The missing piece in policy analysis: Social security reform. *American Economic Review* 86 (May): 1–14.
Friedman, Benjamin M., and Mark J. Warshawsky. 1990. The cost of annuities: Implications for saving behavior and bequests. *Quarterly Journal of Economics* 105:135–54.
Goodfellow, Gordon P., and Sylvester J. Schieber. 1996. Investment of assets in self-directed retirement plans. In *Positioning pensions for the twenty-first century,* ed. Michael Gordon, Olivia Mitchell, and Marc Twinney. Philadelphia: University of Pennsylvania Press.
Hinz, Richard P., David D. McCarthy, and John A. Turner. 1996. Are women conservative investors? Gender differences in participant-directed pension investments. In *Positioning pensions for the twenty-first century,* ed. Michael Gordon, Olivia Mitchell, and Marc Twinney. Philadelphia: University of Pennsylvania Press.
Ibbotson Associates. 1995. *Stocks, bills, bonds, and inflation: 1995 yearbook.* Chicago.
Investment Company Institute. 1995. *Mutual fund 1995 fact book.* Washington, D.C.
Juster, F. Thomas, and John Laitner. 1990. The TIAA-CREF data base: A special purpose data set for the analysis of life-cycle saving behavior. Working paper. Institute for Social Research, University of Michigan.
King, Francis P. 1996. Trends in the selection of TIAA-CREF life-annuity income options, 1978–1994. TIAA-CREF Research Dialogues, no. 48. New York: TIAA-CREF, July.
Kotlikoff, Laurence J., and Avia Spivak. 1981. The family as an incomplete annuities market. *Journal of Political Economy* 82:372–91.

Laitner, John, and F. Thomas Juster. 1996. New evidence on altruism: A study of TIAA-CREF retirees. *American Economic Review* 86 (September): 893–908.

Milne, Deborah, Jack VanDerhei, and Paul Yakoboski. 1996. Participant education: Actions and outcomes. Issue Brief no. 169. Washington, D.C.: Employee Benefit Research Institute.

Mitchell, Olivia M., James M. Poterba, Mark J. Warshawsky, and Jeffrey R. Brown. 1998. New evidence on the money's worth of individual annuities. Working paper. Department of Economics, MIT.

Poterba, James M., Steven F. Venti, and David Wise. 1994a. 401(k) plans and tax-deferred saving. In *Studies in the economics of aging,* ed. D. Wise. Chicago: University of Chicago Press.

———. 1994b. Targeted retirement saving and the net worth of elderly Americans. *American Economic Review* 84 (May): 180–85.

———. 1995. Do 401(k) contributions crowd out other personal saving? *Journal of Public Economics* 58 (September): 1–32.

———. 1998. Lump sum distributions from retirement saving plans: Receipt and utilization. In *Inquiries in the Economics of Aging,* ed. David A. Wise, 85–105. Chicago: University of Chicago Press.

RogersCasey and Institute of Management and Administration. 1995. *RogersCasey/ IOMA 1995 defined contribution survey.* Darien, Conn.: RogersCasey.

Samuelson, Paul A. 1989. A case at last for age-phased reduction in equity. *Proceedings of the National Academy of Sciences* 86 (November): 9048–51.

———. 1990. Long-run risk tolerance when equity returns are mean-regressing: Pseudoparadoxes and vindication of "businessman's risk." In *Macroeconomics, finance, and economic policy: Essays in honor of James Tobin,* ed. W. Brainard, W. Nordhaus, and H. Watts. Cambridge, Mass.: MIT Press.

Siegel, Jeremy J. 1994. *Stocks for the long run: A guide to selecting markets for long-term growth.* Burr Ridge, Ill.: Irwin Professional.

U.S. Department of Labor. Pension and Welfare Benefits Administration. 1996. *Private Pension Plan Bulletin: Abstract of 1992 form 5500 annual reports.* Washington, D.C.: U.S. Government Printing Office.

U.S. General Accounting Office. 1995. *Federal pensions: Thrift savings plan has key role in retirement benefits.* GAO/HEHS-96-1. Washington, D.C.

———. 1996. *401(k) pension plans: Many take advantage of opportunity to ensure adequate retirement income.* GAO/HEHS-96-176. Washington, D.C.

Comment   Jack L. VanDerhei

The paper by Poterba and Wise sheds considerable light (empirical and otherwise) on two of the more vexing policy issues that will be encountered by privatization proposals that contain mandatory private savings accounts: (1) whether restrictions need to be placed on asset-allocation options and (2) the risk of outliving one's resources after retirement.[1]

Jack L. VanDerhei is a professor at Temple University and a fellow of the Employee Benefit Research Institute.

1. Actually, there may also be an interaction that the authors would want to consider, namely, do fixed annuity options force participants to ratchet down their equity allocations as they approach retirement age?

To address the first policy question, the authors provide new regression results as well as a valuable summary of previous literature that analyzed behavior of participants in various participant-directed savings plans. Although they point out that participants generally have higher incomes than nonparticipants, it is quite likely that this will be the only type of data available to answer questions of how individuals would behave in a system of mandatory savings accounts. Although the paper had a considerable discussion of the participation and contribution literature, I am assuming that, under the mandatory savings accounts referred to in this paper, the participants would not have any freedom in determining whether they would contribute and, if so, at what rate. Therefore, in discussing the accumulation phase of the paper, I focus my remarks on asset-allocation results.

Comments are warranted on a few of the points brought up in the first section of the paper since they are crucial to a proper interpretation of the results. First, the authors mention that available investment options in 401(k) plans are plan specific. It should be noted that the effect of this can be enormous. Figure 9C.1 shows the variation in percentage of investors with no GIC (guaranteed investment contract) holdings (among those offering this option) in Goodfellow and Schieber (1997). This suggests that the various options (as well as their relative attractiveness in the case of GICs) may explain a great deal of interplan variation. Figure 9C.2 shows the tremendous difference in three large plans with a total of nearly 200,000 participants that were the focus of a recent EBRI issue brief (Yakoboski and VanDerhei 1996). Plan C was one in which the employer stock investment option was extremely popular.

There are two points of information that need to be corrected in this section. The paper mentions that, since 1993, Department of Labor guidelines require all 401(k) plans to offer at least three investment options. It should be noted that this applies only to those plans seeking 404(c) protection.[2] The paper also implies that assets can be withdrawn from a 401(k) plan at any time; however, in most cases, the 401(k) assets are subject to strict withdrawal constraints.[3]

---

2. An unfortunate consequence of providing investment flexibility for participants is that, in their capacity as fiduciaries, sponsors could be considered liable for investment "losses" suffered by the participants, even though such losses are a direct result of the participants' own investment choices. However, Section 404(c) of the Employee Retirement Income Security Act of 1974 may allow the sponsor to shift the liability for investment decisions from plan fiduciaries to plan participants.

3. The value of elective contributions in a 401(k) plan may be distributable only on death, disability, separation from service, the termination of the plan (provided no successor plan other than an ESOP [employee stock ownership plan] or a SEP [simplified employee pension] is established), or certain sales of businesses by the employer. Distributions of elective contributions will be permitted after the employee has attained age 59½ or before this age in the case of a hardship. For hardship withdrawals, however, the amount available is limited to the elective contributions themselves; investment income on such contributions can be included only to the extent earned prior to 31 December 1988 (for calendar-year plans). Also, it should be noted that, if employer contributions have been included in the ADP (actual deferral percentage) test, the withdrawal restrictions on these amounts are even greater; any such contributions and any investment income earned on such contributions can be withdrawn for hardship only to the extent made or earned before the end of the last plan year ending before 1 July 1989.

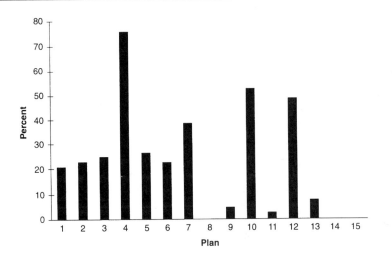
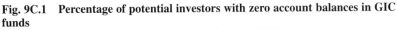

Fig. 9C.1   Percentage of potential investors with zero account balances in GIC funds
Source: Authors' tabulations from Goodfellow and Schieber (1997).

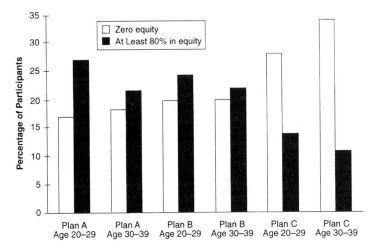
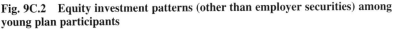

Fig. 9C.2   Equity investment patterns (other than employer securities) among young plan participants
Source: Yakoboski and VanDerhei (1996).

This may be important if employees perceive the constraints as essentially limiting the prospect of withdrawal to termination of employment. Note, however, that loans may be made available, and this may be an important determinant of asset allocation in terms of both plan-specific design (whether loans are offered) and the employees' utilization up to the tax limit.[4]

4. A loan to an employee will be treated as a taxable distribution unless certain requirements are met. These requirements involve the amount of the loan (or accumulated loans) and the time

The next section of the paper provides a useful summary of existing information on the asset allocation of retirement saving plans. However, some points should be considered when interpreting the results. In table 9.3, it is difficult to determine the extent to which the SRA (salary-reduction arrangement) information is participant directed and how employer securities differ from diversified equities. Similarly, table 9.5 provides findings from 401(k) plan data from Access Research and the Institute of Management and Administration showing a substantial percentage of equity in the aggregate, somewhere between 21 and 55 percent, depending on treatment of employer stock and balanced funds.

While I agree with the authors' comments in note 9 on the importance of individuals' adjustments to company stock, it is not clear what the breakdown of participant-directed choices should be. Most important, it is not correct to assume that 100 percent of the employer stock is due to mandatory elections from employer matches.[5]

The authors also note the substantial increase in equities between 1991 and 1995. I believe that they are correct in suggesting that much of this may be due to a run up in the equity markets during that period, especially compared with the alternatives of reallocating contributions or transferring existing account balances. My preliminary research on 401(k) contributions shows that, even though new contributions are far less "sticky" than reallocating existing balances, they show very little movement from year to year. The small use of transfers is consistent with the findings in the federal Thrift Savings Plan discussed in section 9.3 of the paper.

Table 9.6 provides conditional probabilities of use of an investment option. The authors conclude that roughly 60 percent of individuals make at least some use of equity mutual funds when those funds are included in the opportunity set. Although I am not familiar with the report cited, I would suggest that the authors reconsider this conclusion since many plans will provide more than one such fund option; therefore, the probability of at least some use of equity mutual funds will actually be much larger. In fact, the Employee Benefit Research Institute is currently analyzing in excess of one thousand 401(k) plans in a somewhat different way by looking at the percentage of account balance, not simply whether it was used. We are attempting to analyze how the "menu" of investment choices available to the employees affects the percentage of equities in both account balances and asset allocation for current contributions. It

period for repayment. The maximum amounts that can be borrowed without being considered a distribution depend on the amount of the employee's vested interest in his or her account balance. If it is (1) $10,000 or less, the entire vested interest is available; (2) between $10,000 and $20,000, $10,000 is available; (3) between $20,000 and $100,000, 50 percent of the vested interest is available; or (4) $100,000 or more, $50,000 is available. The $50,000 limitation on loans from qualified plans is reduced by the excess of the highest outstanding loan balance during the preceding one-year period over the outstanding balance on the date a new loan is made.

5. For example, more than 40 percent of the participant-directed assets for plan C in Yakoboski and VanDerhei (1996) were invested in employer stock.

is too soon to give definitive results; however, preliminary research reveals a tremendous interactive effect between the equity percentage and whether GICs and/or employer securities have been offered.

Earlier work that I have done (Bajtelsmit and VanDerhei 1997) suggests that there appears to be a great degree of substitution between fixed-income investments and employer securities. This is consistent with the authors' findings in note 12 when they compare Goodfellow and Schieber's findings with those of Access Research. Moreover, for the few plans where information is available, the terms of the GIC and the recent experience of the employer security also have important implications for the overall asset allocation. This should be viewed as a cautionary note with respect to using this type of data to extrapolate to a social security reform proposal, a universe in which neither GICs nor employer securities may be available.

Table 9.7 summarizes the Goodfellow and Schieber study, which shows that younger workers are more likely to invest in equities and employer securities than are older workers. The authors note that this is a much more significant result than is suggested by their Survey of Consumer Finances findings and wonder whether it may be due to an unrepresentative sample of 401(k) participants. Figure 9C.3 compares the age-specific equity allocations (other than employer securities) for three large 401(k) plans with those of Goodfellow and Schieber. It would appear that the Goodfellow and Schieber results are certainly within a range suggested by the three large plan results and indeed very close to company B, the only plan without employer securities.

Table 9.8 illustrates the Goodfellow and Schieber findings that higher-income workers allocate a larger percentage of funds to "stock funds." However, above a threshold level of income ($60,000–$75,000), the increase in stock funds is directly offset by the fact that company stock decreases with higher income. This is probably due to a better appreciation of the merits of diversification plus a higher likelihood of having stock options with the employer.

The third section of the paper analyzes the asset-allocation experience of the TIAA-CREF system. A major advantage of these data is that, in most cases, they are likely to represent the entire employer-sponsored retirement benefit.[6] All three of the large 401(k) plans that I have studied, and probably many of those in the Goodfellow and Schieber study, were secondary plans or at least plans where employees had a defined-benefit plan also.

It is difficult to compare the authors' tabulations of TIAA-CREF experience in table 9.10 with either Goodfellow and Schieber or Yakoboski and VanDerhei, given the lack of information on how the hybrid and specialized account assets are distributed over the various age groups and whether any of them are

6. It is difficult to ascertain whether these data are limited to employees with 100 percent of their account balance in TIAA-CREF, however. To the extent that this is one of a menu of choices, employees may elect TIAA as their "GIC" alternative and put their equity holdings into mutual funds.

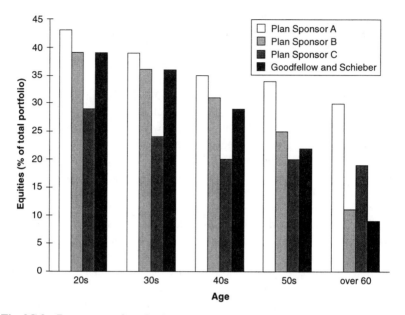

Fig. 9C.3   Percentage of equity funds (other than employer securities) in 401(k) investment plans, by participant age
Source: Authors' tabulations from Goodfellow and Schieber (1997) and Yakoboski and Van-Derhei (1996).

invested in equities. Controlling for these uncertainties,[7] and comparing the asset allocations with 401(k) participants also covered by a defined-benefit plan, may provide an initial estimate of the equity allocation expected if the defined-benefit component of the social security program were at least partially replaced with participant-directed individual accounts. Another interesting finding of this experiment would be to determine whether there is a less-pronounced tendency to transfer from equities to a fixed-income investment as individuals approach retirement age, perhaps owing to the availability of variable annuities for TIAA-CREF participants.

In the fourth section of the paper, the authors report some interesting results on the applicability (or lack thereof) of a simple life-cycle model in predicting annuity demand. Unfortunately, it appears that research in this important area is still desperately in need of a database providing participant decisions on the choice of (1) lump sum distributions versus annuitization and (2) consumption (or perhaps distribution) patterns after retirement if a lump sum distribution is chosen. Moreover, it would be very useful if this type of data could be limited to those situations in which the plan is the exclusive (or at least primary) retirement plan provided by the participant's employer.

7. Note that there are constraints on the transfers from TIAA to CREF that may result in lower TIAA contributions than otherwise.

In the conclusion, the authors suggest that asset-allocation patterns in IRAs may provide a better indicator of unconstrained asset choice than decisions in existing employment-linked retirement savings plans. While this may be true, I would suggest that the real question is whether they would better represent the asset-allocation choices made if social security were privatized. I would argue that, to the extent that preretirement withdrawals were effectively eliminated under a reform proposal *and* to the extent that we learn how adequately to control for the effect of employer securities, the 401(k) asset allocation would likely be a better indicator owing to the withdrawal restrictions based on these assets.[8]

The authors acknowledge the difficulty in interpreting existing asset-allocation decisions made in an environment in which individuals expect to receive a real annuity from social security that provides a floor on their consumption opportunities. They state that this issue can be analyzed under specific assumptions about the nature of individuals' utility function, the distribution of returns available to them, and the nature of social security. The ability to simulate participants' results under various reform proposals will be greatly enhanced by such an undertaking.

Although this paper accomplishes its objective of providing evidence on how households might manage funds in a mandatory private saving system, there are several extensions to this paper that would be useful in determining the effect of a privatized social security system on individual asset allocation.

First, one might look at employers' reactions with respect to the qualified retirement plans they sponsor. The entire concept of integrated plans under a partially privatized social security system would need to be reexplored in terms of both the legislative and the regulatory amendments to Internal Revenue Code section 401(l) and the sponsor's reaction to such modifications.[9]

Second, would there be a greater demand for employer-sponsored defined-benefit plans if at least a portion of the current defined-benefit-type social security promise were replaced with an individual account plan? If so, how would asset allocation in social security defined-contribution accounts change in response?

The final set of extensions is empirically based. Obviously, it would be quite useful to integrate a micro-level asset-allocation database from a 401(k) plan

---

8. It should be noted that, technically, these withdrawal restrictions apply only to certain elective contributions; some contributions to what are generally referred to as 401(k) plans may have less restrictive withdrawal restrictions.

9. A plan will not be discriminatory merely because it uses a benefit formula that provides a larger percentage of benefits for earnings in excess of some amount, such as the social security taxable wage base, than it does for earnings under this amount. However, if the benefit formula is in any way integrated with social security benefits, certain requirements are imposed to prevent discrimination in favor of the highly compensated employees. The basic concept of these requirements is that the benefits from the employer's plan must be dovetailed with social security benefits in such a manner that employees earning over the taxable base will not receive combined benefits under the two programs that are proportionately greater than the combined benefits of employees earning under this amount. For a complete explanation, see Allen et al. (1992, chap. 14).

with household asset-allocation information.[10] Other important limitations would be overcome if longitudinal micro-level data were available from the 401(k) plans. Currently, the best information available is in essence a snapshot of the asset allocation at a particular point in time. If future data are provided in a form that will allow linkages with previous investigations, researchers will eventually be able to explore the following important issues: how asset allocation changes over time; how asset allocation changes as a function of changing market returns; how employees react to a termination/modification of defined-benefit or defined-contribution plan; and how employees react to changes in educational programs.

References

Allen, Everett T., Jr., Joseph J. Melone, Jerry S. Rosenbloom, and Jack L. VanDerhei. 1992. *Pension planning: Pensions, profit sharing, and other deferred compensation plans.* Homewood, Ill.: Richard D. Irwin.

Bajtelsmit, Vickie L., and Jack L. VanDerhei. 1997. Risk aversion and pension investment choices. In *Positioning pensions for the twenty-first century,* ed. Michael Gordon, Olivia S. Mitchell, and Marc Twinney. Philadelphia: University of Pennsylvania Press.

Goodfellow, Gordon P., and Sylvester J. Schieber. 1997. Investment of assets in self-directed retirement plans. In *Positioning pensions for the twenty-first century,* ed. Michael Gordon, Olivia S. Mitchell, and Marc Twinney. Philadelphia: University of Pennsylvania Press.

Yakoboski, Paul J., and Jack L. VanDerhei. 1996. Worker investment decisions: An analysis of large 401(k) plan data. Issue Brief no. 176. Washington, D.C.: Employee Benefit Research Institute.

Discussion Summary   Jeffrey Liebman and Andrew Samwick

One participant said that the main reason people do not buy annuities is that they are not indexed for inflation. So far they are all nominal. In response, Poterba said that the simulations reported in the paper indicate that the wealth equivalent difference between real and nominal annuities is quite small.

Another participant said that it was puzzling that young investors do not hold a greater share of their portfolios in stocks. He also asked if there is any information on differences in asset allocations between defined-contribution and defined-benefit plans. Poterba responded that, on average, defined-benefit plans hold 5–10 percent more in equities than do defined-contribution plans.

Another participant pointed out that, in looking at people's choices within

---

10. One of the more troubling aspects of using these data is the potential bias from liquidity or tax effects. For example, what if participants, especially the higher-income employees, prefer to hold their equities outside the qualified plan for capital gains treatment? Alternatively, what if just the opposite happens because they want to hold munis?

401(k) plans, it is important to consider how much time has passed since firms altered the investment options available to their employees. This explains why people still hold lots of GICs (guaranteed investment contracts).

A member of the group suggested that the authors take the data on where people invest and then simulate returns over a lifetime. What is really important, he said, is the performance in the tails, not the means. He also questioned whether the investment choices by the lowest-income 401(k) investors are representative of those who do not have 401(k) accounts.

Another participant pointed out that investors who hold assets both inside and outside tax-favored plans should hold bonds within the plans since bonds are more heavily taxed than stocks (stocks benefit more from the lower tax rate on capital gains). He noted, however, that only a small fraction of investors have significant wealth both inside and outside such plans.

Someone suggested that the data on asset holding from the HRS presented in the paper are not representative of lifetime portfolio choices since people are likely to shift to less risky assets as they approach retirement.

An audience member asked if there are data on the composition of equity holding rather than on the split between equities and bonds. He said that it would be interesting to know whether people are diversified in their equity holdings. It was also pointed out that it is difficult to separate age and cohort effects in asset holdings.

Poterba said that there are two theories of what would happen if a lot of extra money were invested in equities. One is that there is a big world capital market to absorb the additional investments and that therefore there would be little effect. This is what he thinks is most likely. Another theory is that there are segmented capital markets and that there would therefore be large relative price changes between stocks and bonds.

Poterba said that a major difficulty in learning more about retirement portfolio behavior from investment fund providers is that the researcher can see only part of the investor's total portfolio in cases in which the investor has accounts with a number of different providers.

Poterba also argued that, while one view says that equities have little long-term risk, the U.S. experience in the twentieth century may be atypical. Poterba recommended Stephen J. Brown, William N. Goetzmann, and Stephen A. Ross's "Survival" (*Journal of Finance* 50, no. 3 [July]: 853–73) on the survival of stock markets that provides evidence on this issue. An investor in 1900 who invested in a well-diversified global portfolio would have invested in German stocks, Russian stocks, and Argentinean assets. Many of these markets performed poorly or ceased to exist.

10 Administrative Costs in Public and Private Retirement Systems

Olivia S. Mitchell

> Literally every dollar which is unnecessarily or uneconomically
> expended on administration is a dollar which could otherwise go
> to the plan participants. (Hoexter 1970, 134)

> The question may well be raised as to whether the administrative
> expenses are too low, with the result that the insured persons are
> not receiving adequate service. . . . [Social security] beneficiaries
> deserve better service and could well be willing to bear the slight
> additional amount needed. (Myers 1992, 16)

Looking across countries, government-managed old age social security systems differ widely in the level of benefits they provide, their methods of financing, and their overall extent of redistributiveness. Despite these differences, a feature common to most of these old age income programs is that they are heading toward insolvency. As a result, there is increasing interest in and support for moving toward a mostly private retirement system, one that relies at least in part on investing retirement assets in private capital markets.[1]

This paper addresses a possible concern arising from a move toward a privatized retirement system, namely, whether administrative costs in a privately managed system would be expected to be higher or lower than those found in national, centrally run social security systems. The particular focus I take is that of the U.S. social security system, asking the following questions: What are the administrative costs of the current U.S. retirement system? Does the United States spend too much on administering its old age social security system? What are the administrative costs of prominent alternatives to social security systems? Would a privately managed retirement system cost more or less than the current old age income system?

I analyze available evidence on costs associated with the U.S. and other

Olivia S. Mitchell is the International Foundation of Employee Benefit Plans Professor of Insurance and Risk Management at the Wharton School of the University of Pennsylvania and a research associate of the National Bureau of Economic Research.

Useful comments were provided by Jonathan Dickson, Robert Luciani, Phillip Lussier, Dennis Mahoney, Jerry Rosenbloom, and William Shipman, although none of these persons is responsible for errors or omissions. Opinions are solely those of the author and not of the institutions with which she is affiliated.

1. In the United States, this topic was the subject of a Senate Finance Committee hearing (on 25 March 1996) that reviewed options for privatization as described by members of the Social Security Advisory Council as well as the chairs of the technical panels reporting to the council (see also Quinn and Mitchell 1996).

national social security systems and compare them to expenses reported by various other institutions that might be seen as alternative means to supply retirement protection.

To preview the conclusions, I find that administrative costs of publicly run social security systems vary greatly across countries and institutional settings. Some are less expensive to manage than others, and it is clear that scale matters: larger publicly managed old age programs cost less than do smaller public plans. It is also clear that quality varies across programs: some public systems have low expenses but deliver few and/or poor-quality services. While public-system administrative costs could in some cases be reduced, cutting expenses cannot save an insolvent plan, and cost pressure could lessen service quality. I also examine the possibility of replacing a publicly managed retirement system with privately managed alternatives in the United States and conclude that a privately managed old age retirement saving program would probably be more costly than the current publicly managed social security program. Nevertheless, a privately managed system is likely to offer better and more diverse services in exchange for these higher costs, including the opportunity to self-direct pension asset investments, the possibility of investing in higher-return assets, the likelihood of more frequent reporting to participants, and possibly greater satisfaction with the system as a whole.

10.1   An Overview of Government-Run Social Security System Administrative Costs

It is useful to begin by recalling the objectives of a national social security system before hoping to understand whether the costs associated with managing one can be altered or reduced. Looking across countries, it is clear that two (at times competing) objectives are common to most countries' programs: providing earnings replacement for retirees and providing welfare support for the elderly indigent. In this section, I first review available data on publicly run, government-managed social security systems from developed and developing countries; I then turn to a more detailed look at the U.S. old age retirement income system.[2] Finally, I offer an evaluation of the factors that influence social security administration costs in a multivariate framework.

10.1.1   International Perspectives on Social Security Costs

Social security systems around the world approach the twin goals of welfare and earnings insurance in numerous ways and with weights that differ across countries. For instance, in the United States, the social security program concentrates mainly on old age, survivor, and disability benefits, while, in Europe,

---

2. This section draws on Reid and Mitchell (1995) and Sunden and Mitchell (1994). It should be emphasized that the present paper focuses on the provision of retirement income, not health care and welfare/social assistance. Also, disability benefits are treated only in passing.

medical and unemployment insurance programs are also included under the social security umbrella.[3] The form of the benefit varies a great deal across countries, too; some follow a defined-benefit formula, wherein the benefit payment is linked to years of service and earned income, while others follow a defined-contribution approach, tying payments to assets accumulated in an investment account.

Because my focus is on the expenses associated with running a retirement system, it is useful to define *social security administrative expenses* as the costs of providing these retirement benefits. That is, I focus, not on the tax and/or investment revenue used to pay benefits, but rather on the expenses incurred in collecting the funds, managing the records, investing the money, determining eligibility, and paying out benefits.

An economic measure of this concept would include the full resource costs of producing these services, which is not necessarily the charges that government agencies report. A discrepancy sometimes occurs because government services are often not valued at their economic resource cost—particularly when public agencies do not purchase their inputs in a competitive market.

As an example, many government-managed social security systems use public buildings and land. Reported social security administration costs under such a system will not reflect economic scarcity values. Nor will reported public-sector provision costs be an accurate estimate of the likely costs that private-sector counterparts would charge in performing the same services. Similarly, government contracts to install computer systems are awarded on a noncompetitive basis in many countries, and, in other cases, the public pension agency may obtain its mail and telephone services at a subsidized rate. Depreciation and fringe benefits often do not appear on a government agency's budget, and costs of collecting the payroll tax are often shouldered by the central tax authority.

For all these reasons, publicly managed old age programs would be expected to appear less expensive than they actually are, relative to privately managed plans. Conversely, when services are contracted through private firms, administrative costs will probably appear higher than in public plans because market prices for inputs will have to be paid. The resulting public/private cost differential may therefore be more apparent than real.[4]

Keeping these caveats in mind, I next review reported social security administration costs from almost fifty developed and developing countries around the world.[5] Table 10.1 reveals that OECD countries spent an order of magni-

---

3. A discussion of the rationale for retirement systems is offered by Atkinson (1987, 1989) and Barr (1992), among others.

4. Private pension plans must also recognize a premium to cover the longevity, inflation, and interest rate risks they assume, whereas most government-run retirement systems will instead implicitly bear the costs and raise taxes if the need arises (see Mitchell and Sunden 1993; Mitchell, Sunden, and Hsin 1994; Reid and Mitchell 1995).

5. Where possible, only old age retirement programs were included in table 10.1, but social security costs were not always broken down by type in developing countries.

Table 10.1   Administrative Costs as a Percentage of Social Security
              Benefit Expenditures

Latin America/Caribbean		OECD	
Mean	27.78	Mean	3.12
Standard deviation	31.16	Standard deviation	1.28
Argentina	2.30	Australia	1.22
Bahamas	30.75	Austria	2.48
Barbados	5.56	Belgium	4.55
Belize	89.49	Canada	2.80
Bolivia	21.39	Denmark	2.98
Brazil	7.00	Finland	3.36
Chile	8.00	France	4.18
Colombia	81.80	Germany	2.86
Costa Rica	4.75	Greece	6.72
Dominica	46.97	Iceland	1.71
Dominican Republic	31.72	Ireland	4.88
Ecuador	13.55	Italy	2.20
El Salvador	33.40	Japan	1.79
Grenada	9.85	Luxembourg	2.74
Guatemala	12.72	Netherlands	3.10
Guyana	22.66	New Zealand	2.42
Honduras	18.25	Norway	1.00
Jamaica	6.40	Portugal	4.86
Mexico	23.55	Spain	2.81
Panama	5.88	Sweden	4.24
Peru	130.98	Switzerland	3.04
St. Lucia	48.31	Turkey	2.62
Trinidad and Tobago	15.29	United Kingdom	3.10
Uruguay	6.51	United States	3.28
Venezuela	17.46		

Source: Mitchell, Sunden, Hsin, and Reid (1994).

Note: Data may reflect expenditures on pensions in all cases; in some, additional functions as the provision of health services are included.

tude less on social security costs at the end of the 1980s—3 percent of their annual system budgets—as compared to the developing nations of the Latin American and Caribbean (LAC) region, where administrative costs ran 28 percent of annual expenditures.

One of the least costly programs on the list in table 10.1 is the U.S. old age program, whose reported administration costs in 1990 stood at less than 1 percent (0.7 percent) of old age benefit expenditures, after falling by a third during the 1980s. By contrast, the LAC countries with the lowest reported administration costs as a fraction of benefit expenditures included Argentina, with reported administration costs for its public plan at 2.3 percent of benefit expenditures, Costa Rica, with 4.8 percent of benefit expenditures devoted to administration costs under the old age and disability insurance, and Chile, with an 8 percent expense rate for its public plan overall (Sunden and Mitchell 1993).

Part of the explanation for the marked differences in social security administrative costs across countries is that program objectives vary internationally, in terms of the particular mix of social assistance (benefits tied to need) and insurance (benefit tied to contributions), the degree to which the programs are government run or privately managed, and even the types of payments offered, including cash and in-kind transfers to the elderly, survivors, the disabled, the sick, new mothers, the unemployed, and so forth. For example, in both Argentina and Chile, the range of government programs is wide and includes old age, survivor, and disability benefits, cash sickness and maternity benefits, medical care and work injury coverage, an unemployment insurance system, and a family allowance plan. In Costa Rica, by contrast, unemployment and family allowance plans are not included in the social security system design. For this reason, cross-national data on administrative costs are somewhat treacherous to interpret.[6]

A related issue is how one should handle measurement problems that arise when assessing social security costs. Ideally, the administration costs would be normalized by a direct measure of the service being provided—namely, social security administration. Unfortunately, there is no simple measure of this multidimensional service. Normalizing by total benefit expenditures, as in table 10.1, tends to make costs look lower in more generous systems as well as in mature systems with more beneficiaries than contributors. Conversely, costs appear lower in systems paying high benefit levels when one normalizes program expenditures by beneficiaries. Normalizing by assets is meaningless when the publicly managed plan has few assets (as in pay-as-you-go systems), although this is the statistic of choice often given by private pension plans and mutual funds. Normalizing program expenditures by per capita income tends to make richer countries with more generous programs look more cost effective. Clearly, there is no perfect or universally accepted normalization method to use in reporting retirement system costs.

At least one useful approximation to a measure of social security administration services is the number of clients a system serves. In other words, one could sum contributors and beneficiaries, ideally appropriately weighted to reflect the relative contribution of each client type to the administrative service demands placed on the social security agency. Lacking a simple, defensible method of assigning weights to client types, the common practice is simply to assign equal weights.

The effect of using different cost measures across social security administering agencies is not trivial. Table 10.2 offers data on administrative retirement

---

6. I do not investigate here whether a social security program is consistent with national goals of growth and income distribution, although some systems are probably more conducive than others to these objectives (see World Bank 1994).

Table 10.2 **Annual Social Security Administrative Costs per Financial Flow Measures (%)**

Year	Chile: AFP, Admin. Charges per Contribs.	Chile: INP, Admin. Costs per Benefit	Costa Rica: CCSS, Admin. Costs per Benefit	Argentina: ANSeS, Costs per Benefit — Without Collection Costs	Argentina: ANSeS, Costs per Benefit — With Collection Costs	United States: SSA, Cost per Benefit — OASI	United States: SSA, Cost per Benefit — Disability
1980						1.1	2.0
1981							
1982							
1983							
1984							
1985				1.7		.9	2.8
1986				1.8			
1987	25			2.7	5.3		
1988	24			2.2	4.1		
1989	20			2.3	5.5		
1990	18	1.1		3.3	5.6	.7	2.4
1991		1.3		2.7	5.1	.7	2.4
1992	17	1.6	5.1	4.7	7.4		
1993		1.9					

Source: Reid and Mitchell (1995).

Note: Data in this table reflect only pension-related social security functions.

system costs in Chile, Costa Rica, Argentina, and the United States normalized by financial flows (either contribution or benefit payments). Data on four public plans were developed by Reid and Mitchell (1995), namely, Chile's public-sector INP (Instituto de Normalizacion Previsional) system, Costa Rica's public CCSS (Caja Costarricense de Seguridad Social) system, Argentina's publicly run (Administracion Nacional de la Seguridad Social) ANSeS system, and the U.S. OASI (old age and survivors insurance) system. Across these four public systems, administrative costs range from about 1 to 7 percent of benefit payments, with the lowest being for the U.S. OASI program.[7] In addition, data are provided on Chile's private-sector pension agencies, known as the AFP funds. These have been criticized as having high administrative costs, and certainly table 10.2 indicates that they are the most costly of those shown, with 1993 administration costs equaling 17 percent of contributions. However, it should be noted that these AFP costs have fallen steadily from a high of 25–30 percent of contributions at the system's inception in the early 1980s.[8]

To show how different normalization methods change perceptions of system expenses, table 10.3 offers other variants. During the early 1990s, for example, expenses under Chile's privately managed AFP program were roughly equivalent to those incurred by that country's public social security system (INP) on an active contributor basis—around U.S.$50.00 per year. The figures would be even lower if one used total rather than active contributors since there are many inactive accounts under the Chilean AFP system. On a total contributor basis, the administrative costs of Chile's privately managed pension plan stood at between U.S.$23.00 and U.S.$45.00, only two-thirds the level of Chile's public INP per member costs (1992 U.S. dollars).[9] Clearly, privately managed retirement systems are not necessarily more expensive than their public-sector counterparts.

Another interesting finding from table 10.3 concerns the wide range of public-system costs. At the low end of the range are U.S. retirement system costs at $12.00–$14.00 per covered worker per year and the Costa Rican system's reported expenses of less than $10.00.[10] At the upper end among the

---

7. In the case of Argentina, there was some question as to the proper cost to assess for payroll tax collections. The data given assume that average tax collection costs should be charged to the public pension system for the collection of social security taxes; while this is probably too high a charge, no other figures are available (see Reid and Mitchell 1995).

8. High administrative expenses have also been experienced under Argentina's new private defined-contribution system modeled after the Chilean regime; here, administrative charges currently amount to 32 percent of contributions (personal communication, Rafael Rofman, 1996). However, the Argentine private pension system is only in its second year of operation, and charges would be expected to decline over time.

9. It should also be noted that there are important differences in services rendered across systems in Chile; most private pension (AFP) members are not retired, while most public plan (INP) participants are.

10. It should also be evident that system cost comparisons are sensitive to the measure of participants used. For instance, normalizing by beneficiaries yields U.S. system cost estimates more than three and a half times higher than those generated by normalizing with contributors.

Table 10.3   Administrative Costs per Participant Measures (constant 1992 U.S. dollars)

| | Chile | | | | Argentina: ANSeS, Cost per Member | |
| | AFP | | | | | |
Year	Per Active Contributor	Per Contributor	INP, per Plan Member	Costa Rica: CCSS, per Plan Member	Without Collection Costs	With Collection Costs
1980						
1981						
1982	71.0	44.7				
1983	55.0	35.8				
1984	50.0	29.5				
1985	43.0	24.9			6.7	
1986	42.0	24.2			8.9	
1987	39.0	22.6			11.0	21.5
1988	44.0	24.5			8.5	15.7
1989	42.0	23.2			5.4	12.9
1990	45.0	31.8			16.8	28.4
1991	46.0	27.8	44.2		20.7	39.1
1992	49.0	29.8	47.7	7.6	46.0	72.6
1993			40.8		39.2	65.2

| | United States: SSA | | | | |
| | OASI Cost Per: | | Disability Insurance Cost Per: | |
	Pensioner	Covered Worker	Beneficiary	Covered Worker
1980	62.2	17.0	114.9	5.5
1981				
1982				
1983				
1984				
1985	58.6	16.2	175.9	6.5
1986				
1987				
1988				
1989				
1990	43.8	11.7	151.7	5.7
1991	47.7	13.0	148.2	6.1

Source: Reid and Mitchell (1995).

Note: For similar data on forty-two countries worldwide, including some of the above, see World Bank (1994, table A.9).

cases studied is the Argentine public system, where annual per member costs total about $70.00 (1992 U.S. dollars).[11] In any event, the Chilean public as well as private system figures appear to be about mid-range in absolute dollars and certainly not outliers in terms of available data.[12]

Some lessons may be drawn from the discussion thus far. First, data problems limit comparisons that can be made across systems, and no cost normalization is ideal for all purposes. When comparing costs across countries, it is likely that normalization by the number of participants comes closest to capturing trends in the levels of administrative expenses, although it cannot account for differences in the services provided—a flaw shared by all the typical normalization procedures. Second, it would be useful to have service-specific cost accounting, identifying the specific functions performed by a social security system as well as the costs incurred in undertaking them.

10.1.2   A Closer Look at U.S. Social Security System Functions and Administrative Expenses

The U.S. social security system is a large and complex institution. Its four main programs include the old age (OA) retirement program, the disability insurance (DI) program, the hospital insurance (HI) program, and the supplemental medical insurance (SMI) program (Social Security Administration 1995). Most proposals to privatize the retirement portion of the social security system have focused almost exclusively on the OASI program; hence, the discussion here will be mainly concerned with the costs of administering that program. In contrast, the Medicare and disability components will not concern us further except when data limitations require it.

Turning to table 10.4, it is useful to gain a working familiarity with the size and scope of what is generally known as the retirement component of the social security system in the United States. The OASDI program is a mandatory, virtually universal program, collecting tax revenues in 1994 from some 139 million workers annually, and paying benefits to 37 million retired plus 6 million disabled persons each year. OASDI system revenues in 1994 totaled $380 billion, or about 12 percent of covered earnings ($2,700 in contributions and interest per covered worker per year in 1994). OASDI system benefits came to $317 billion in 1994, paying an annual retired-worker benefit averaging $8,400—approximately 35 percent of covered payroll—and a disabled-worker benefit of about $7,900. Because the nation's social security system is mostly

11. This high figure assumes that average rather than marginal tax collection costs should be assessed against the public plan. While this is no doubt unrealistic, more precise data do not exist.

12. Salvador Valdés-Prieto notes that the figures for Chile are not exactly comparable with those reported in other countries since Chile's system exacts a one-time fee when the defined-contribution monies are contributed and no additional fees are charged on the accruing assets (personal communication, 1996). Larry Kotlikoff argues that it is more appropriate to spread the Chilean one-time up-front fee over the pension accrual phase in order to determine its effect on annualized returns, which he estimates at approximately eighty basis points per year for younger contributors (personal communication, 1996).

Table 10.4   **Facts and Figures about OASDI (1994 dollars)**

	Quantity	Source
Revenues and tax base:		
OASI revenues ($million)	328,271	SSA 1995, table 4.A1
DI revenues ($million)	52,841	SSA 1995, table 4.A2
Workers with taxable earnings (million)	139	SSA 1995, table 4.B1
Workers fully insured (million)	173	SSA 1995, table 4.C1
Covered earnings ($million)	3,229,100	SSA 1995, table 4.B1
Average earnings/covered worker ($)	23,231	Author's calculations
OASI revenues/covered worker ($)	2,362	Author's calculations
OASI revenues/covered earnings (%)	10	Author's calculations
OASDI revenues/covered worker ($)	2,742	Author's calculations
OASDI revenues/covered earnings (%)	12	Author's calculations
Beneficiaries and benefits:		
OASI benefits paid ($million)	279,068	SSA 1995, table 4.A4
DI benefits paid ($million)	37,704	SSA 1995, table 4.A4
OASI recipients (million)	37	SSA 1995, table 5.A4
DI recipients (million)	6	SSA 1995, table 5.A4
Average annual retired worker benefit ($)	8,368	SSA 1995, table 3.C4
Average retired worker benefit/average covered earnings (%)	36	Author's calculations
Average disabled worker benefit ($)	7,940	SSA 1995, table 5.A1
Covered workers + OASDI recipients (million)	182	Author's calculations
Trust fund accumulation:		
OASI fund year end 1994 ($million)	413,460	SSA 1995, table 4.A1
DI fund year end 1994 ($million)	22,925	SSA 1995, table 4.A2
OASI fund/revenues (%)	126	Author's calculations
OASDI fund/revenues (%)	115	Author's calculations
OASDI funds/participants ($)	2,399	Author's calculations
Annual OASDI administrative costs:		
Administrative costs ($million)	2,600	SSA 1995, 14
Administrative costs/covered worker ($)	19	Author's calculations
Administrative costs/participant ($)	14	Author's calculations; active and retired workers
Administrative costs/benefits paid (%)	.93	Author's calculations
Administrative costs/trust fund (%)	.63	Author's calculations
Administrative costs/contributors (%)	.68	Author's calculations
Annual OASI administrative costs:		
Administrative costs ($million)	1,600	SSA 1995, 14
Administrative costs/covered worker ($)	12	Author's calculations
Administrative costs/participant ($)	9	Author's calculations; active and retired workers
Administrative costs/benefits paid (%)	.57	Author's calculations
Administrative costs/trust fund (%)	.39	Author's calculations
Administrative costs/contributors (%)	.42	Author's calculations
Administrative data (all OASDHI included in counts):		
No. of SSA employees	64,234	SSA 1995, table 2.F2

(*continued*)

Table 10.4   (continued)

	Quantity	Source
No. of SSA offices:		
Field and regional offices	1,412	SSA 1995, table 2.F1
Appeals/hearings offices	146	SSA 1995, table 2.F1
Service centers	6	SSA 1995, table 2.F1
Data operations center	1	SSA 1995, table 2.F1
Claims information:		
Processed claims/year (thousands)	3,206	SSA 1995, table 2.F4
Accuracy rates, OASI (%)	99.80	SSA 1995, table 2.F7

a pay-as-you-go account, the difference between system revenues and annual outlays is quite narrow. The excess revenue has been deposited into so-called trust funds projected to grow and then be depleted as the baby boom cohort ages. In 1994, the OASI trust fund amounted to only about 125 percent of one year's annual outlays, or $2,270 on a per participant basis. Thus, the OASI trust fund could not guarantee a robust flow of retirement income if it were to be allocated among participants covered by the system today, contrary to some popular opinion.

In approaching the question of how expensive the current social security system is to administer, table 10.4 shows that costs totaled $1.6 billion in 1994. This may be broken down to an annual $12.00 per covered worker (or $9.00 per participant, including retirees). As a fraction of benefits paid, these administrative costs equaled 0.6 percent of benefits paid, or 0.4 percent of contributions. Computed administrative costs as a fraction of system assets would amount to 0.39 percent, or thirty-nine basis points; although this computation is the usual one reported for mutual funds, it is meaningless to report figures this way since the system is mostly unfunded.[13]

One fact to point out regarding social security administrative costs is that they have apparently fallen over time quite substantially. This pattern is explained partly by the fact that, as a system grows, fixed costs can be spread over larger participant pools and partly by the fact that benefit payouts and retiree numbers rose over time. Robert Myers (1992) traces the time path of administrative expenses since the social security program's inception, concluding that costs in the early days of the program were over ten times greater than they are now. His analysis used total OASDHI costs, which during the period 1940–44 amounted to 22 percent of benefits; at the beginning of the 1990s, these total costs stood at just 1 percent of benefits paid (Myers 1992, 16). This

13. For the combined OASDI program, total administration costs amounted to $2,600 million in 1994, or $19.00 per worker (and $14.00 per participant). As a percentage of benefits paid, administrative costs for this segment of social security came to 0.93 percent of benefits, or 0.68 percent of contributions, and 0.63 percent, or sixty-three basis points, of the combined OASDI trust funds.

trend conceals cross-program differences, however (table 10.5). Costs for the old age and survivors program were halved between 1980 and 1994, falling from 1.07 percent of benefits paid to 0.59 percent. In contrast, administrative expenses for the DI program rose substantially over the same period, from 2 to 2.7 percent of benefits. It seems fair to conclude that the retirement component of the social security system has become more cost effective over the period but that the disability program has not.[14]

A different approach to measuring costs under the U.S. retirement system is to assess the ways in which the system allocates its administrative expenditures (Mitchell and Sunden 1993). It is probably not surprising to learn that the OASI system devotes the lion's share—93 percent—of its administration expenses to the benefit function. This benefit function entails the determination of eligibility for prospective retirees, spouses, and survivor recipients, along with the actual payment of benefits. Because most of the payroll tax revenue is collected by the Internal Revenue Service, a relatively small amount—on the order of 7 percent of administrative expenses—is devoted to revenue collection. In this sense, the social security system benefits from substantial externalities by piggybacking on the IRS collection mechanisms and enforcement structure. Finally, a tiny fraction of expenses—less than one one-hundredth of a percent—is currently allocated to the money-management function. This is because the social security system's trust funds are by law required to be invested in special issue Treasury bills. Clearly, under current regulations, there is no need for a large financial management staff, and the system's costs are held down because of this condition.

10.2 Determinants of Social Security Retirement System Administrative Expenses

10.2.1 Measuring Inputs and Outputs

The question of whether social security expenses are at the "right" level (or too high, or too low) is a difficult one to address since often a nation's social security system is run as a government monopoly producing outputs that are not competitively priced. As a result, it is difficult to determine whether levels of output produced, costs incurred, and services generated by the government agency are comparable to or differ from what one might anticipate if the system were operated by the private sector.

As an example, the U.S. social security retirement program currently provides benefits that are in part earnings insurance and in part redistributive welfare payments. It is debatable whether a private market could, and would, substitute for a mandatory system with an equally strong redistributive bent,

14. The fact that disability claims require the collection of medical data and subsequent medical assessments probably helps explain why the process is more cumbersome.

Table 10.5   **U.S. Social Security Administration Costs over Time (per capita, 1994 dollars)**

Program	Administrative Cost per Beneficiary	Administrative Cost per Covered Worker
OASI:		
1980	65.72	35.95
1985	61.91	17.13
1990	46.25	12.35
1994	44.10	11.83
DI:		
1980	121.43	5.77
1985	185.85	6.86
1990	160.28	5.98
1994	259.19	7.40
HI:		
1980	136.34	8.16
1985	165.39	9.25
1990	129.59	6.20
1994	164.03	9.09
SMI:		
1980	61.59	9.68
1985	58.00	10.45
1990	63.55	12.95
1994	57.56	12.22

Sources: 1980–90 figures from Mitchell and Sunden (1993). 1994 data from SSA (1995, tables 4A1 and 2, 4B1, 5A4, 8B1 and 2).

particularly if participation were voluntary (Mitchell and Zeldes 1996). If one thought that private producers could replicate the social insurance program, then private-sector costs could be used to compare with government costs, in order to assess whether the government program was paying an appropriate level of administrative expenses. On the other hand, if no private group could replicate the government program, it might be impossible to ascertain whether current levels of administrative costs are equal to those that would prevail in a competitive market.

In addition, of course, social security system expenses should properly be assessed in the context of a model that specifies production inputs, constraints, and the available technology with which these can be combined to produce desired outputs. In practice, it is difficult to develop such a model using real-world data since the system produces many outputs using a range of inputs, all of which are difficult to measure empirically.

To illustrate this point, it is helpful to turn to some aggregate output data on the U.S. retirement system. Annually, some 43 million recipients receive OASDI benefit checks, and about 4.8 million new cases are filed (Social Security Administration 1995, table 2.F). The Social Security Administration (SSA) also collects contributions for 139 million workers and tracks the earnings records of more than 200 million people over time.

These aggregate performance measures aside, it is far more difficult to determine whether the system is providing optimal levels of service for the costs incurred. In particular, the retirement-system portion of the SSA has several different responsibilities, including issuing all workers (and, most recently, children) social security numbers, maintaining earnings records, and determining eligibility and paying benefits in a timely manner. The agency has set itself internal standards, which it has been meeting to a greater or lesser degree. For example, as table 10.6 notes, 98 percent of applicants filing for social security numbers receive them within twenty-four hours and obtain their cards within five days; there appears to be little error in this process. This is a massive task, inasmuch as the SSA issued 17 million new numbers per year in the early 1990s (personal interviews with SSA staff). (That the system has upgraded service from the early 1980s is evident from the fact that, a decade ago, obtaining a social security number took six weeks [Sunden and Mitchell 1994].)

Nevertheless, the system seems to be slow in tracking earnings and contributions. Under current law, employers furnish reports of wage earnings to the SSA (the self-employed report pay via their income tax reports). Annually, something on the order of 227 million earnings reports are received. Of late, there has been some delay in the recording of earnings within the agency's own recommended time line; for example, only 70 percent of earnings were posted within six months of the tax-year end in 1991 (although accuracy rates were 99.2 percent [as per Mitchell and Sunden 1993]). This performance is within the agency's standards and is certainly a vast improvement since the early 1980s, when updating of earnings records took two to three years (Doggette 1988). Nevertheless, it might be suspected that delays in posting earnings would be quite problematic if the system were to move toward an individual account–type program. Indeed, when lags of ninety days were recently detected for privately sponsored 401(k) accounts, the U.S. Department of Labor deemed this period unusually and unacceptably long (Limbacher 1995).

Since benefit payments are the major activity of the SSA, it is here that performance data are most critical. One performance statistic (see table 10.6) indicates that about 95 percent of all initial benefit payments are correctly determined each year. Overall, around 7 million new claims are registered per year (counting all OASDHI applicants), and meeting this workload is a substantial task. A different way the SSA judges its performance is by its new claims accuracy rate, which in 1993 stood at 99.8 percent for OA benefits and 94.2 percent for DI benefits (Social Security Administration 1995, table 2.F7). A further performance standard is the computed "accuracy of lifetime benefits per award," which has been reported at close to 100 percent for some time. Finally, the agency monitors whether benefits are received on time. On average, it takes seventeen days from the time a retiree files for benefits for the first

Table 10.6   U.S. Retirement System Performance Standards and Quality Measures

Service Provided	Output Measure	Standard	Quality of Service
Issue social security numbers	Approximately 7–8 million issued per year	Assign social security number within 24 hours of receiving documentation	98% get social security number in 24 hours, cards within 5 days
		Issue social security number correctly	99.8% of social security numbers correct
		Correct social security problems in under 30 days	Not measured
Pay benefits correctly	Benefit expenditures	100% accuracy goal, initial payment	94.8% of initial payments correct
		100% accuracy goal, lifetime payment	99.8% of lifetime dollars correct
		Accurate DI determinations	96.7% DI accuracy rate
Pay benefits on time		First benefit check within 15 days of filing for old age benefits	17 days average payment time
		Regular old age benefits paid on schedule	99.9% of regular payments on schedule
		DI benefits paid within 6 months of disability or 60 days of filing	90 days average to process disability cases
		Denied claims noticed within 60 days, 120 days for hearings, 90 days for review of appeal	229 days average to process hearing, 239 for appeals case; 13.2% of hearings with decision within 120 days of filing

Personal contact	Number of telephone calls, letters, visitors	15 minutes or less waiting time in field office with appointment, 30 minutes without	87.5% with appointment seen in 15 minutes or less, or else 82.3% seen in 30 minutes or less; 4.7% without appointment seen in 30 minutes or less
		Accurate handling of phone calls within 24 hours	92.9% of callers can access 800 number in 24 hours or less; 12.5 days for handling inquiries
Maintain accurate earnings records	Number of contributors, amount of contributions	Post earnings accurately	99.2% of reported earnings posted accurately
		Earnings posted within 6 months of end of tax year	70% of reported earnings posted within 6 months of tax year end
		Resolve earnings differences within 30 days	Not presently measured

Source: Adapted from Sunden and Mitchell (1994).

payment to be received, a figure slightly higher than the performance target of fifteen days. The agency also reports that it makes 99.9 percent of retirement benefit payments on the scheduled delivery dates, a statistic that is certainly consistent with reliable service.

In providing these services, the agency is aware of and seeks to reduce system fraud. As in all programs, some level of investigation is required to determine whether new applicants are in fact eligible for benefits and whether current beneficiaries should continue to receive payments. Common forms of deception include failure to notify the agency when recipients change eligibility status (owing to marriage or death, e.g.); also, some participants have more than one social security number, potentially enabling them to receive multiple benefit checks. As the SSA has upgraded its computer files and systems in the last decade, more careful and extensive cross-checks have become feasible. In addition, in recent years, the SSA has required beneficiaries to recertify their eligibility periodically and actively pursues allegations of fraud through the office of the inspector general (Sunden and Mitchell 1994).

Whether the optimal level of output (including service and fraud control) is being expended by the SSA is difficult to determine given available data. What we do know is that the agency has faced substantial cutbacks in its workforce over the last decade, now employing some 64,000 full-time employees, or 0.37 employees per 1,000 active participants, down from 0.68 workers per 1,000 insured in 1980 (table 10.4 above; and Sunden and Mitchell 1994). Downsizing was made possible by the introduction of a new computer system that helped reduce reported administrative costs by about one-third over the last couple of decades (Doggette 1988). Computerization also permitted better cost accounting for each separate agency function, including tracking of personnel salary and benefits (accounting for approximately 60 percent of SSA expenses). One potentially troublesome area identified by the U.S. General Accounting Office is the fact that it is not always possible to detect poorly performing SSA employees; hence, federal government employees' tenure is not readily rescinded in such cases (U.S. General Accounting Office 1989).

How do U.S. system performance levels compare to those of other nations?[15] With regard to collecting tax contributions, for instance, the Chilean private system reports an error rate of 0.8–1 percent in posting contributions to individual accounts, similar to the U.S. SSA's error rate of 0.8 percent in posting contributors' summary earnings records.[16] The Chilean private pension system appears to do better updating accounts, reporting only 6 percent delayed accounts within a one-month window (in the United States, there is a 30 percent incidence of nonupdated accounts within six months of the close of a tax year).

---

15. The data in this and the next two paragraphs are taken from Reid and Mitchell (1995).

16. As might be expected, many developing countries' national social security systems do not regularly provide data on the accuracy and timeliness of tax and benefit functions. This was true, e.g., in a recent analysis of the Costa Rican national retirement system (the CCSS), the Argentine program (the ANSeS), and the Chilean public retirement system (the INP).

Another issue is system evasion, an increasingly serious problem around the world. Argentina reports that as many as half of all eligible contributors do not pay into the system, and, in Uruguay, the figure is estimated at 44 percent (Reid and Mitchell 1995). Having a computerized database of covered earnings greatly facilitates this supervisory task, as in the United States and many other developed nations. It is likely that a system will be more efficient when the revenue collection and record-keeping functions are handled by a single agency, and, thus, when Mexico developed its new individual account retirement system, it opted for centralized computer technology to track taxes paid and benefits delivered.

Performance can also be compared with regard to the effectiveness of delivering retiree benefits. This complex of tasks is handled rather inexpensively by the U.S. social security system since initial payments are in error only 5 percent of the time and a mere seventeen days are required to process an old age pension claim (it takes ninety days to process a disability claim). In contrast, the Chilean privatized pension system reports a 27 percent error rate in benefit determinations, and processing of normal retirement pension determinations requires seventeen days, that of early retirement and survival pensions sixty-five and seventy-four days, respectively, and disability pensions 146 days. Public plans in other countries fare poorly on this criterion as well: in Costa Rica, 20–50 percent of old age pension determinations are appealed annually, after 60–150 days to process an old age pension and 150–80 days to process an invalidity pension. The public pension system in Argentina, ANSeS, requires 60–150 days to process pension claims, and almost one-third of all benefit determinations are appealed. One positive finding is that the Chilean public pension (INP) system was successful in its effort to halve its determination times between 1990 and 1993, as a result of concerted effort on the part of the government and international lending agencies. In general, both privately and publicly run retirement systems could improve service quality to program beneficiaries (Reid and Mitchell 1995).

A third function that both public and private retirement systems bear responsibility for is the management of contributed funds. It seems reasonable to expect that assets held in a partially (or fully) funded system should be invested prudently, following accepted money management (and possibly fiduciary) practices. By law in the United States, social security trust fund investment practices are sharply constrained, but, in other countries, more flexibility is evident, and performance has been widely variable. Overall, it appears that private pension system managers subject to competitive market pressures often tend to generate higher real rates of return on average than do publicly managed funds. For example, the Chilean private defined-contribution system reported returns of 13 and 9.2 percent over the periods 1980–85 and 1985–90, respectively (Valdés-Prieto 1994); this exceeded returns of 7.7 and 9.6 percent achieved by the U.S. SSA fund over the same periods as well as the 7.8 percent return in large U.S. private pension funds and the 9.2 and 7.3 percent returns earned by public funds in eight industrial countries.[17] Even worse, Costa Rica's and Peru's public pension funds reported negative real rates of return over the decade of the 1980s—as have large numbers of other public pension systems around the world (World Bank 1994).

To sum up thus far, assessing the efficiency of the U.S. government–run social security system is problematic because it is a government monopoly, providing services for which there are no precise private market counterparts. In any event, administrative expenses for the U.S. Social Security Administration's old age retirement program are moderate in terms of international comparisons and also have declined over time. U.S. annual retirement system administration costs currently run under $15.00 per worker; these equal 0.42 percent of contributions, or 0.57 percent of benefits paid. As a percentage of system assets, costs sum to 0.39 percent, or thirty-nine basis points; this figure is not directly comparable with privately managed plans, however, since the system is only very partially funded. Also, inasmuch as social security taxes are collected by the IRS and the SSA trust funds are invested in treasuries, the majority of administrative costs can be attributed to the benefit function.

Although it is debatable whether the system spends "enough" or "too much" on administrative expenses, it seems clear that determination of eligibility for old age benefits is handled with alacrity and that payments are made on time. These costs have trended down in part because fixed costs are now amortized over a larger participant pool and also because of computerization and the subsequent downsizing of the agency. The fact that workers' earnings take a while to be posted to their social security earnings file does not materially influence the system as it is structured now; however, such a delay would certainly be more troublesome in an individual account system. The DI system appears to be experiencing relatively more administrative difficulties; costs including DI are under $20.00 per worker, 0.68 percent of contributions, 0.93 percent of benefits, and 0.63 percent of the combined OASDI trust funds.

10.2.2   Multivariate Models of Social Security Costs

A more systematic assessment of social security costs is facilitated with a multivariate model linking production costs to output. While a cost function methodology is most familiar to those examining firms operating in a competitive market framework, it has also been applied to the study of government units in order to determine whether scale economies exist in the production of government services and to ascertain which technological factors most influence measured costs.[18]

---

17. Some would argue that the Chilean market's return should not be compared to those of developed countries since the Chilean AFPs were initially restricted to holding mainly government paper and still are very heavily concentrated in Chilean firms. Hence, their investment universe had very different risk/return characteristics than U.S. or European markets.

18. For examples of this literature, see Borcherding, Pommerehne, and Schneider (1982) and Mehay and Gonzales (1985), among others.

In the context of the social security question, analysts have used a general cost model relating system administrative costs to output levels, input prices, and indicators of program characteristics and technology, as follows:

(1)
$$\text{social security costs } = $$
$$f(\text{output, input prices, program characteristics, technology}).$$

The idea is that social security costs, usually measured as reported administrative expenses somehow normalized, should be influenced by output (proxied by benefit measures such as system expenditures), holding constant other factors. Depending on the country and system under study, one would want to control such other factors as input prices (for labor, land, and capital) and program characteristics varying by locale (including, e.g., whether the program is means tested, whether it is centrally run or decentralized, and other related aspects of the program itself). Additionally, when one looks across systems and countries, it is clearly important to try to control for differences in technology, including the degree to which computerization has been achieved by the system, the degree to which the system relies on a modern communications and banking infrastructure, and the overall literacy (and perhaps financial literacy) rate in the population. Finally, as Valdés-Prieto (1993, 1994) has pointed out in a case-study analysis of Chile, the United States, Malaysia, and Zambia, it is important, but extremely difficult, to control for quality differences in services provided across public pension systems.

For all these reasons and others relating to data limitations, only a few studies have estimated a multivariate model of social security administration costs. The few economic studies that do adopt a simple Cobb-Douglas cost specification, relating social security administration expenses across a set of developed and developing nations to output measures (Mitchell, Sunden, and Hsin 1994; Mitchell, Sunden, Hsin, and Reid 1994; Palacios 1994). In this framework, both costs and output are measured in natural logs so that the estimated coefficient a_1 in the following equation is interpreted as a measure of scale economies:

(2)
$$\text{social security expenses } = a_0 + a_1 \text{ output measures } + a_2 \text{ input prices}$$
$$+ a_3 \text{ program characteristics}$$
$$+ a_4 \text{ technology } + \varepsilon.$$

That is, if a_1 proves to be less than unity, it would be concluded that larger systems would be less expensive to operate than smaller systems. One problem with this prediction is that only rarely do countries report expenses for their old age programs separately from their other programs and that overall costs would therefore be anticipated to rise when the social security system has many different social insurance program obligations. Hence, the empirical models seek to control for the fact that in some countries the social security agency is responsible for retirement payments as well as the provision of health care, unemployment insurance, maternity care, etc. It is likely that cash payments to general retirees are less costly to deliver than are means-tested and noncash benefits like health care and food stamps.

Another hypothesis tested with this framework is that social security systems may be more costly to operate when more agencies are involved. Unlike in the United States, in some countries the federal, state, municipal, and even smaller units of government are involved in the collection of revenue and the disbursal of social security benefit payments. Looking across countries, it is also important to control the degree to which the population is integrated into a national financial system; in practice, this is often done with a proxy variable measuring the fraction of the population that is rural dwelling, which probably is inversely correlated with computerization, integration into a banking system, literacy, and so forth. Finally, it is useful to control differential input prices across countries, although in practice obtaining a good measure of this proves difficult; one approach is to include a measure of GDP per capita to capture cross-country differences in pay.

Turning to the empirical findings, Mitchell, Sunden, Hsin, and Reid (1994) use as a dependent variable social security administration costs expressed as a percentage of GDP (to control for exchange rate differences) and regress this against social security benefit expenditure (also standardized by GDP).[19] The analysis uses cross-sectional data for forty-three countries, including all the OECD nations as well as those in the Latin American and Caribbean region. For this sample, the authors find evidence of substantial scale economies, irrespective of the other control variables included in the equation. Across the sample as a whole, a 1 percent increase in output measured by benefit expenditures is found to be associated with 0.5 percent increase in system administration costs. Further refinements indicate that a modification of this overall conclusion is required. One is that the OECD nations have very large social security systems and appear to face constant returns to scale; hence, only the Latin American and Caribbean nations in this sample face increasing returns given the small social security programs they currently support. Second, for the subset of nations able to furnish cost data on the national retirement system separately from their overall social security program, the evidence is consistent with constant returns to scale, rather than increasing returns. These findings are robust to the inclusion of controls for other program characteristics, and none of the other factors is consistently significant in the empirical analysis.

As far as I know, the only other multivariate study of social security costs is that of Palacios (1994; summarized in James and Palacios 1995). Here, the focus is on system administrative costs for forty nations surveyed by the International Labor Organization around the year 1986. Social security system ad-

---

19. Benefits and system membership were too collinear to permit including both in the same equation.

ministrative expenses are regressed on the size of the participant pool, a parameter indicating whether the system offers a universal demogrant sort of benefit versus an earnings-related benefit, and a special variable to account for unusual costs experienced under Chile's privately managed national defined-contribution system. Of most interest is the finding of scale economies once again: a 1 percent increase in participants raises social security retirement system costs by only 0.6–0.9 percent. There is also evidence that a universal, demogrant system is significantly less costly to administer than a means-tested or earnings-related program. Controls measuring the country's level of technology include energy consumption, which proves to be strongly negatively correlated with costs, suggesting that more developed countries manage their systems less expensively. Finally, the "Chile effect" is positive but only marginally significant (at the 10 percent level), suggesting that, given the small size of the system, costs are not terribly out of line.

10.2.3   Further Considerations Regarding Social Security System Costs

After reviewing social security costs around the world, I find that U.S. system administrative expenses are in the middle of the range for developed nations, at 3 percent of total expenditures, and are on the order of ten times lower than the developing-country average. The U.S. system's costs per active participant appear to be quite low (under $15.00 per worker per year) compared to those of many other countries. For example, in Chile, annual per contributor costs totaled about $30.00 under the private system and $41.00 under the public system, and, in Argentina, the public system expenses ran $40.00–$60.00 annually.

Nevertheless, there are important, and very difficult to answer, questions about whether the funds are well spent and whether output levels and output quality are as good as they could be given available funds and technology. In many countries, including the United States, for instance, service could be improved by cutting the delays experienced in posting earnings to the social security records. In many countries' systems, evasion of social security taxes is an important and growing problem, as in Japan and in Chile, where some 30–50 percent of earnings are believed to be outside the purview of the payroll tax (Watanabe 1996; Valdés-Prieto 1994). Another difficulty is that plan participants are beginning to expect private market rates of return on their contributions to the social security system, despite the fact that usually most government old age pensions are defined-benefit rather than defined-contribution promises. This expectation has not been met by public pensions around the world producing zero or negative real rates of return on assets over the last decade (World Bank 1994).

As a result of these issues, serious questions are now being raised about the ability of conventional government-run social security programs to produce high-quality money management, benefit delivery, and other services in countries around the world. Therefore, I turn next to an examination of costs of possible alternatives to a publicly managed social security agency, with the intention of comparing potential costs across sectors.

10.3   Administrative Costs of Alternatives to Social Security

One reason to assess expenses incurred in running the government-run social security system is that market alternatives might be expected to result in lower costs and/or greater services provided. Costs could be high in publicly provided plans if, for example, there were diseconomies of scale in production or if private institutions could select more efficient technologies and inputs than government bodies. Also, under some scenarios, privately managed financial institutions might generate outputs more to participants' liking than did the public sector. In this sense, it is of interest to ask whether financial institutions such as mutual funds, pension funds, and/or life insurance companies might be able to provide lower-cost (but equivalent or better) service than the government-managed program.

To address this question, I examine what is known about some of these alternative financial institutions and offer some tentative conclusions about the findings. The specific institutions analyzed are the mutual fund industry, the pension industry, and the life insurance industry.

10.3.1   Mutual Fund Industry Costs

The U.S. mutual fund industry has been in existence for at least five decades: recently, mutual funds have become the second largest financial intermediary after commercial banks (ICI 1995b). In mid-1996, the industry held over $3 trillion in assets.

As U.S. mutual funds have grown in size and influence, financial market analysts have devoted substantial attention to assessing their investment performance, ranking individual funds, and exploring anomalies.[20] Analysts agree that understanding mutual fund costs requires delving into two general categories of charges, namely, loads and expenses.[21] *Loads* refers to commissions that are levied at the time the investor purchases or sells fund shares or that may be exacted when the investor reallocates fund shares across holdings in a "fund family." For example, a fund's front-end load is computed by subtracting the price at which one may purchase a fund share (the buy price) from the price at which one may sell the fund share (the sell price); this figure divided by the buy price equals the front-end load. Commonly seen loads or commissions range from 4 to 8.5 percent of invested assets; no-load funds do not charge this fee. In *back-loaded* funds, the term generally refers to a commission associated with redeeming a fund investment, which may be a flat rate or a percentage of

20. For example, a compilation of mutual fund returns and expenses appears weekly in the *Wall Street Journal,* and frequent updates are available from Lipper Analytical Services and Morningstar Mutual Fund Reports, among others.
21. The discussion in this paragraph draws on Vanguard (1995a, 2).

Table 10.7   **Mutual Fund Expense Ratios by Fund Type (funds with assets above given levels)**

Type of Fund	Dollar-Weighted Average Expense Ratio (%)			Average Account Size ($)
	Average	Lowest Quartile	Highest Quartile	
Equity index (assets above $100 million)	.324	.150	1.640	20,968
Money market (assets above $1 billion)	.613	.150	1.000	43,276
Fixed income (assets above $1 billion)	.876	.280	2.000	34,530
Growth (assets above $500 million)	1.043	.500	2.460	16,800
Growth and income (assets above $500 million)	.834	.390	1.840	22,027
Balanced (assets above $250 million)	.895	.350	1.910	15,360
Global (assets above $250 million)	1.250	.840	1.380	14,686

Source: Lipper Report, dollar-weighted expense ratios for samples of mutual funds of designated size, fiscal years ending 1994–95. Expense ratio defined as fraction of assets devoted to fund administrative expenses annually.

assets. A mutual fund employing this type of load may levy a 5–6 percent charge if the funds are withdrawn during the first year of the investment, with the rate declining to zero over six or seven years. Additionally, some funds charge an exchange or transaction fee when dividends are reinvested and/or impose a fee when assets are shifted across different fund types.

These loads are reported in fund prospectuses in accordance with regulations devised by the Securities and Exchange Commission but are typically not included in expense ratio information. Instead, *expense ratio* refers to the fraction of investor assets expended annually in fees and charges. Included in this tally are operating expenses attributable to investment advisory/management fees and costs attributable to fund administration. In addition, mutual funds must report so-called 12b-1 expenses, or distribution costs that may be charged to fund assets. Under SEC rules, such fees and charges must be included in the expense ratio information reported by mutual funds. However, the fact that loads are not incorporated in expense ratio data should be kept in mind when comparing expense ratios across funds, particularly in the retail or individually purchased mutual fund arena. (No-load funds are more common in the institutional market.)

Table 10.7 summarizes categories of fund expenses from a recent Lipper Analytical Services survey of individually purchased mutual funds. Expense ratios for some of the larger mutual funds in this class appear in table 10.8, again for the retail market. Perhaps not surprisingly, table 10.7 indicates that the "index fund" group reports the lowest expense ratios of all those repre-

Table 10.8　　　　**Large Mutual Fund Portfolio Expense Ratios and Other Data**

	Expense Ratio (% of assets)	Size of Fund ($million)	Turnover Rate (%)
Fidelity funds:			
Market Index[a] (S&P index)	.45	288	2
Blue Chip[b] (blue chip stock fund)[c]	1.02	2,229	182
Fidelity Fund[d] (long-term capital growth)	.64	1,592	157
Disciplined Equity[e] (undervalued S&P)	.96	2,088	221
Contrarian[f] (undervalued stock)	1.00	8,694	235 .
Vanguard funds:			
Total stock portfolio (Wilshire 5000 index)	.25[g]	786[h]	2[i]
500 Portfolio (S&P index)	.20[j]	9,356[k]	6[l]
Value Portfolio (large-cap index)	.20[m]	297[n]	32[o]
Balanced Index (60/40 stocks/bonds)	.20[p]	403[q]	16[r]
Total bond portfolio (bonds)	.20[s]	1,731[t]	33[u]

[a] *Fidelity Market Index Fund Prospectus,* June 1995. Also an additional $10.00 account fee charged per account per year and a 0.50 percent redemption fee charged on shares held less than 180 days. Redemption fee not included in returns figure given.

[b] Assumes annual account larger than $2,500, else $12.00 annual account maintenance fee charged. Total returns do not include one-time sales charge.

[c] *Fidelity Blue Chip Growth Fund Prospectus,* November 1995.

[d] *Fidelity Fund Prospectus,* August 1995. See also note a.

[e] *Fidelity Disciplined Equity Fund Prospectus,* December 1995 See also note a.

[f] *Fidelity Contrarian Fund Prospectus,* February 1995.

[g] Vanguard (1995a). Includes $10.00 annual account maintenance fee charged to account smaller than $10,000.

[h] 1994 year end (*Vanguard Index Trust Prospectus,* revised September 1995).

[i] 1994 year end (*Vanguard Index Trust Prospectus,* revised September 1995).

[j] Vanguard (1995a). Includes $10.00 annual account maintenance fee charged to account smaller than $10,000. Also portfolio transaction fee of 0.25 percent per dollar invested assessed in 1995 (not included in expense ratio).

[k] 1994 year end (*Vanguard Index Trust Prospectus,* revised September 1995).

[l] 1994 year end (*Vanguard Index Trust Prospectus,* revised September 1995).

[m] Vanguard (1995a). Includes $10.00 annual account maintenance fee charged to account smaller than $10,000.

[n] 1994 year end (*Vanguard Index Trust Prospectus,* revised September 1995).

[o] 1994 year end (*Vanguard Index Trust Prospectus,* revised September 1995).

[p] Vanguard (1995a). Includes $10.00 annual account maintenance fee charged to account smaller than $10,000.

[q] 1994 year end (*Vanguard Balanced Index Fund Prospectus,* revised April 1995).

[r] 1994 year end (*Vanguard Balanced Index Fund Prospectus,* revised April 1995).

[s] Vanguard (1995a). Includes $10.00 annual account maintenance fee charged to account smaller than $10,000.

[t] 1994 year end (*Vanguard Bond Index Fund Prospectus,* revised September 1995).

[u] 1994 year end (*Vanguard Bond Index Fund Prospectus,* revised September 1995).

sented: these funds reported average costs of 0.32 percent of investor assets.[22] This relatively low expense ratio may be compared to several benchmarks, one being the next lowest rate in the table, which is for money market funds. This latter group reported almost double the index fund level of costs (0.61 percent of assets). Another comparison group is the all-fund average of 1.05 percent of investor assets reported for 1994 (Vanguard 1995b, 4). These cost differentials are striking because of the fact that index funds are relatively new and hence relatively small: index funds on the Lipper list start at asset levels of $100 million, with an average account size of $21,000, whereas there are numerous money market funds on the list with over $1 billion, and average account size is double the index fund amount ($43,000 in 1994).

To the extent that there are scale economies (and Baumol et al. [1990] have reported that there are—costs rise by only 0.4–0.9 percent as assets grow in the mutual fund industry), one might expect the much larger money market portfolios to be more cost effective than index funds. However, at least at this aggregate level, expense ratios for larger, more actively managed funds are higher than those for the smaller, more passively managed set. Expense ratios reported for so-called growth and global funds are even higher, at over 1 percent of assets per year. A possible explanation for these higher expense ratios is that the more actively managed funds tend to provide different service levels and restrictions over investor behavior, as compared to the passive index funds. These include differential access to check-writing privileges, limits on trades over given time periods, and other such factors.

A cost metric that appears to generate somewhat different rankings uses annual dollar expenses per account, figures appearing in the last column of table 10.7. Not surprisingly, the equity index fund again comes in with the lowest costs, at $68.00 per account per year. But now the per account costs of money market and fixed-income funds are far higher, between $265 and $300 annually, a result stemming from their higher expense ratios and larger average account size. Even costs for the "balanced" portfolio totaled around $140 per year (these funds seek a mix of equity and fixed income).

One possible explanation for the relatively low index fund costs is that managers in this fund group hold broadly diversified portfolios designed to match the investment returns of the overall market; on the whole, they devote relatively little time and effort to stock picking.[23] This does not directly explain the differences because commissions tend not to be reported in the administrative cost figures (rather, lower commissions from a more passive management style would be capitalized in the mutual fund's share price). Nevertheless, it

22. Between 1981 and 1994, the expense ratio for the lowest-cost family of mutual funds fell 48 percent, from 0.58 to 0.30 percent, although for the mutual fund industry as a whole expense ratios rose 42 percent, from 0.65 to 0.92 percent of assets (Vanguard 1995b, 3).

23. Mutual funds as a whole averaged yearly portfolio turnover rates of 76 percent, much higher than the 2–6 percent rates for prominent index funds such as Fidelity's Market Index, Vanguard's Total Stock Portfolio, and Vanguard's 500 Portfolio (Vanguard 1996, 2; see also table 10.8).

appears that, as turnover rises, so do fund expenses: thus, a positive (but not precisely measured) response of turnover on expenses is also reported by Baumol et al. (1990, 185).

This matters because higher expenses would be expected to lower *net* rates of return on the more actively managed funds, to the extent that markets are efficient. Evidence supportive of an inverse expense/returns relation was offered in an analysis of U.S. retail mutual funds that concluded that better-than-average returns earned by high-performing mutual funds were offset by higher fund expenses (Ippolito 1989). More extensive trading and investment research did appear to generate higher returns, but higher costs were associated with generating these returns.[24]

A far lower estimate of mutual fund expenses appears to characterize those funds serving the institutional market, targeted to large investment pools such as employer pension plans. Because of their considerable size, these plans would be expected to benefit from some economies of scale. Nevertheless, obtaining clearly comparable estimates of expenses in this market is difficult since the larger mutual funds tend to tailor an institutional plan to a particular employer's specification and each custom component can alter expenses in important ways. Two examples for which data were gathered include the Institutional Index Fund at Vanguard, which reported a 1995 expense ratio of six basis points for a minimum $10 million investment (down from seven to eight basis points the previous four years), and the same firm's Employee Benefits Index Trust (EBIF), which charges an initial ten basis points in expenses down to one basis point for funds over $200 million (a transaction fee is also charged of 0.15 percent on net cash flows over $4 million) (Vanguard, *Prospectus*, 23 April 1996; Joel Dickson, personal communication, May 1996). After reviewing similar figures, Dickson concluded that the marginal cost of money management would be even smaller for a large, centrally held mutual fund invested primarily in equities: "Total fees charged by an investment adviser for managing a broad equity index . . . would be considerably less than 1 basis point per year. If the money manager were allowed to earn profits through securities lending activities, investment management expenses would be bid down to zero. If securities lending were prohibited, then management fees might total ¼ to ½ of 1 basis point per year" (Dickson 1996, 9). To these money-management costs must be added annual per capita record-keeping fees for individual accounts of around $30.00–$35.00 (Dickson 1996).

In sum, data on mutual fund administrative expenses suggest several conclusions: (1) The least costly retail mutual funds report expense ratios of twenty to thirty basis points at their current level of operation. They appear to be those

24. The Ippolito data were reanalyzed by Elton et al. (1993), who conclude that mutual funds did not earn higher-than-average returns. Analysis by Lakonishok, Shleifer, and Vishny (1992) suggests that average mutual fund performance lagged behind index fund performance by seven to eighty basis points over the Ippolito study period (1964–85) but detects evidence of better mutual fund performance over the period 1983–89.

offering a portfolio consisting of a broad cross section of the capital market. (2) Mutual fund products aimed at the institutional market report significantly lower expenses, at under ten basis point annually for money-management fees (excluding administrative expenses, thought to be around $30.00–$35.00 per year per participant). (3) Until very recently, mutual funds have perceived their mission as investment companies rather than full-service retirement plan administrators, so their expenses may fall as they learn the new market.[25]

10.3.2   Costs of Managing Pension Plans

Employer-sponsored pension plans are an institution that some believe offers a viable and cost-effective alternative to a government social security retirement program. Like the government system, a pension plan collects contributions, manages funds, keeps records, and is in charge of disbursing benefits. Pension plans also have functions and responsibilities that differ from those of a social security system, which in the United States include reporting and disclosure requirements to plan participants, the government, and shareholders (in publicly held firms) and monitoring and compliance with nondiscrimination laws; in the case of a defined-benefit pension, the plan must also pay annual premiums to the Pension Benefit Guaranty Corporation (see Hustead, in press).

Private-Sector Pension Plan Cost Levels

Establishing pension plan total expenses has been an interest of regulators for many decades, although it remains the case that it is much more difficult to obtain good data on the investment fees and record-keeping costs of pensions than on those of mutual funds. The standards for reporting are less clear, and employers sponsoring a single-firm pension plan tend to underreport their pension costs since much of the record-keeping, payroll, and benefits-payment work is handled in house and not necessarily billed to the pension plan as an expense (Hoexter 1970).

It is sometimes argued that pension costs are most reliably reported in the case of multiemployer pension plans since these plans are run by a joint union/management board that pays expenses centrally. Early evidence supportive of this notion was offered by Hoexter (1984), who found that per member total expenses for the multiemployer plans were over six times higher than for single employer plans. She also found substantial scale economies among these plans, such that costs grew by only 2.5 when membership rose by 100 and costs grew by two-thirds when assets were 20 times larger (Hoexter 1984). Expense ratios stood at 1.6 percent of assets for multiemployer plans with under $2.5 million but only 0.4 percent for plans with assets over $50 million.

---

25. Within the last year, Fidelity Investments announced that it would be the first mutual fund group to provide a full menu of benefit offerings for companies considering benefits outsourcing (see Shutan 1995).

More recently, the U.S. Department of Labor has released tabulations on private-sector pension plans from form 5500 data (U.S. Department of Labor 1996). Required to be collected by law, the form includes reports on plan expenses, participants, assets, and liabilities. Here again, it must be kept in mind that single-employer pension plan expenses will tend to be underreported, inasmuch as the sponsoring companies absorb some portion of the plan's administrative costs rather than charging them directly to the pension plan. Among multiemployer pensions, where the pension plans cover employers of several different companies, reported expenses would be expected to be higher partly because a fuller accounting of costs is ensured in the multiemployer group. On the other hand, multiemployer pension costs may be unduly high inasmuch as these plans have recently faced substantial legal expenses, incurred as they seek to obtain delinquent contributions from small employers.

Private-sector pension plan total expenses are summarized in table 10.9 for plan year 1992, which reports expenses for pensions with at least one hundred participants.[26] Single-employer plans in the sample held approximately $1.6 trillion in assets, versus $214 million for the multis in 1992. Nevertheless, because 63 million participants were in the single-employer plan pool and 10 million in the multiemployer pool, net assets per participant were similar, at $26,000 and $21,000, respectively. Annual contributions were quite different, standing at $1,500 in the single-employer plan and around half that, $900 that year, in the multiemployer pension system. Defined-benefit pensions for both employer types held more assets than did the defined-contribution plans, although contribution levels in both sectors were higher than for the defined-benefit plans, attesting to the relatively mature status of the defined-benefit plans in both cases (generally, contributions decline as the workforce matures and moves into retirement).

Turning now to expenses, the data reveal that, among defined-benefit pensions, reported per capita total expenses were between $90.00 and $150 per participant per year (1992 dollars). By contrast, defined-contribution plan expenses were much lower, at $31.00 per year for singles and $97.00 per year for multis. The fact that they were lower is due in part to lower actuarial costs and in part to the fact that defined-contribution plans do not pay premiums to the Pension Benefit Guaranty Corporation (PBGC) for pension insurance. These expenses totaled 11 percent of contributions for single defined-benefit plans and 17 percent of contributions for multiemployer defined-benefit plans. Defined-contribution plans experienced lower expense rates, but again a sectoral difference is evident: expenses came to 2 percent of contributions for single-employer defined-contribution plans and 10 percent for the multis. In terms of assets, expenses came to 0.65 percent and 0.82 percent, respectively, for multiemployer defined-benefit and defined-contribution plans.

The data also show that both types of plans devoted a similar proportion of

26. Under ERISA, small plans do not face the same annual reporting requirements.

Table 10.9   Private Pension Plan (over 100 participants) Administrative Expenses (1992)

	Single Employer Plans			Multiemployer Plans		
	Total	Defined Benefit	Defined Contribution	Total	Defined Benefit	Defined Contribution
Expenses ($million):						
Salaries and allowances	70	41	29	161	140	21
Accounting fees	176	36	140	41	33	8
Actuarial fees	287	269	18	59	55	4
Contract administrator fees	188	103	85	142	123	19
Investment advisory and management fees	1,471	1,159	312	566	508	58
Legal fees	39	26	13	89	76	13
Valuation/appraisal fees	15	7	8	2	1	0
Trustee fees/expenses	463	293	169	20	17	4
Other administrative expenses[a]	1,073	835	238	352	286	66
Total Expenses	3,782	2,769	1,012	1,432	1,239	193
Expenses as % of:						
Contributions	4.00	10.76	1.47	15.76	17.20	10.27
Total assets	.23	.30	.15	.67	.65	.82
Net assets	.24	.30	.16	.68	.66	.83
Expenses/participant ($)	60.30	91.48	31.18	141.59	152.36	97.33

Source: U.S. Department of Labor (1996): assets: table C5, single; table C6, multis; expenses and contributions: table C10, single; table C11, multis; participants: table B.4.

the overall total expense to investment advisory and management fees—on the order of 40 percent of the total. Single-employer defined-benefit plans reported costs almost 20 percent lower than multiemployer plans. For defined-contribution plans, the single-multiemployer differential was even larger, with single-employer plans reporting costs about one-third those of the multiemployer plans. One reason that these costs differed so is that multiemployer plans spend more on legal fees, for reasons already explained. They also devoted more money to contract administration and salaries, as compared to single-employer plans.

More systematic studies of private pension plan administrative costs have been conducted by two research teams that focused on multiemployer pension fund expenses (Caswell 1976; Mitchell and Andrews 1981). Using multivariate econometric analysis, both studies concluded that economies of scale were prevalent in the pension industry. The former was limited to the construction industry; the latter examined a broader range of multiemployer plans using a cost function of the form

(3)   expenses = f(participants, assets, % retired, % pooled),

where annual plan expenses were regressed on the number of plan members and dollars of plan assets as well as the fraction of members retired and the fraction of the assets held in pooled funds. Data from the late 1970s were obtained from reporting forms filed under the Employee Retirement Income Security Act of 1974.[27] The results provided evidence of statistically significant scale economies in this set of defined-benefit plans. Specifically, holding constant the number of plan participants, increasing the plan's asset size by 1 percent (holding participants constant) was predicted to increase costs by only 0.27 percent; in other words, adding to existing pension plan asset pools is relatively inexpensive. Mitchell and Andrews (1981) also showed that, raising the number of plan participants by 1 percent (holding benefits payable constant) would raise pension administrative costs by 0.8 percent, or less than 1 percent. In other words, increasing the size of the participant pool by adding new members with comparable assets would raise costs less than proportionally.

An important reason to ask about variation in pension plan costs, of course, is because such variability in costs might correlate with fund performance. A multivariate regression study relating equity management fees to five-year annualized pension fund performance found that lagged strong returns were only weakly associated with higher subsequent fees (Lakonishok, Shleifer, and Vishny 1992). Nevertheless, the same study concluded that the equity portion of pension portfolios underperformed mutual funds by fifty to one hundred basis points between the mid-1960s and the mid-1980s, suggesting that high expenses might reduce fund performance.

27. Because the market for pension professionals was assumed to be national in scope, the lack of cross-sectional data on input prices was not deemed critical.

Costs of 401(k) Pension Plans

Over the last decade in the United States, a new breed of retirement saving vehicle has grown up, namely, 401(k) pensions. These plans are often thought of as a type of defined-contribution pension but have in fact become increasingly distinct in character from the old employer-directed defined-contribution pension accounts.

In a 401(k) plan, generally the sponsoring employer will select a set of investment vehicles to which participating contributors may direct their contributions; individual plan participants often have substantial flexibility over subsequent asset allocations. For example, many funds permit participants to inquire about their account balances and alter their accruals as well as new contribution flows via a twenty-four-hour telephone service center. In addition, many employers allow participants to take loans from their 401(k) plans, a feature that increases these plans' popularity but one that would also be expected to raise their operating expenses (Mitchell 1992). In addition, the 401(k) rubric encompasses a wide range of plan types and structures, including those funded by profit sharing, those with or without employer pretax match amounts, and thrift plans. Finally, given the fact that employers are concerned about liability for participants' investment choices, substantial funds are devoted to investor education efforts as well as periodic statements of accounts to participants.

In contrast to the old corporate (and public-sector) pension model, at the time of retirement participants in a 401(k) plan may select from a variety of different payout options (Mitchell 1992). One is to take the accruals in a lump sum (and perhaps roll it over into a tax-qualified individual retirement account); another is to use the funds to purchase an annuity; and a third is to accept a graduated payout in accordance with IRS requirements. Because these and other feasible payout options are tailored to the individual retiree, one might anticipate that 401(k) administrative costs would exceed those of conventional defined-contribution plans.

Evidence on the cost effect of plan flexibility is as yet preliminary. Assets in 401(k) plans total more than half a billion dollars. The ICI (1995a) data indicate that 401(k) plans have on the order of 18 million participants, with assets per participant running about $26,000 (median $16,000) and median overall contribution rates of $2,286 per year (with 35 percent contributed by employers). Median record-keeping expenses reported by 401(k) plans in 1993 totaled $66.00 per account per year, or 3 percent of annual contributions. Of course, to the extent that administrative fees are sometimes charged to the 401(k) plan sponsor, reported administrative expenses may appear unduly low (ICI 1995a). Nevertheless, one might anticipate that 401(k) plans would require somewhat more administration than individually purchased mutual funds, inasmuch as the tax-qualified plans permit participant involvement in the asset-allocation process and also require monitoring for tax purposes. On average, 20 percent of the 401(k) plans permit daily reallocation of accruals or new contributions; 12 percent permit monthly exchanges; 40 percent permit quarterly adjustments; and only 20 percent limit changeovers to once or twice a year (ICI 1995a, 10). While permitting more transactions is attractive to many participants, industry experts point out that the practice raises costs. Also, almost three-quarters of the plans give out quarterly statements of participants' asset allocation and performance, and most devote substantial effort to marking their assets to market, many on an hourly basis.

Table 10.10 indicates average total expenses charged by 401(k) pension plans, costs generally attributable to start-up fees, annual per person service charges, loan fees, annual reporting fees, transaction charges, and approximately five to ten basis points for trustee charges, presumably mostly insurance (ICI 1995). As a matter of practice, money-management fees are not included in these tallies and must be added to obtain total expenses. The data indicate that average record-keeping expenses range from a low of 80 basis points in the short-term bond fund to 188 basis points in international equity funds, with the mid-range for equity funds around 140–150 basis points per annum. On an annual basis, the average per participant cost of administering a 401(k) plan appears to be between $5.00 and $55.00 annually, including nondiscrimination testing, quarterly statements, and investor information.[28]

One of the most difficult issues in the 401(k) field is that the 401(k) plans often offer a life annuity at retirement, with the result that the product provided is distinct conceptually from a simpler money-accumulation plan. Figuring out what additional expense the insurance annuity adds, as distinct from the money-management and record-keeping costs, is not a simple matter. Some modest evidence in this direction compares expense ratios for small and mid-sized 401(k) plans with and without an annuity product embedded in the offering (see table 10.11). (Not reported are record-keeping and administrative fees, which are similar for both plan types.) Not surprisingly, it appears that administrative expense ratios are higher for 401(k) plans offering insurance annuities: the additional asset-based charge over the mutual fund investment options appears to be six to thirty-two basis points.[29]

Public and International Pension Plan Administrative Cost Comparisons

It is useful to compare the private pension plan costs reported thus far with a range of other plans, as a method of gaining some perspective on the range of figures. Comparing expenses of large U.S. corporate plans with U.S. public-sector pension plans and endowment/foundation funds shows that fees paid to

---

28. The range of record-keeping costs for 401(k) plans suggested by industry experts is $15.00–$30.00 per year.

29. What is interesting is that, in the 401(k) plan containing only an index fund, adding the annuity costs increases costs by thirty-two basis points, while the annuity raises costs by only three to eight basis points for the money market, balanced, and equity accounts. This may be explained by the fact that few mutual funds offer an annuity product in the large institutional 403(b) marketplace and that reported data may therefore be skewed by an overweighting of smaller retail plans. Hence, adding the annuity charge appears to raise expense ratios by a low of 4 percent to a high of double, depending on the fund.

Table 10.10   Expenses for 401(k) Plans Holding Mutual Funds

	Exp. Ratio (%)	Assets ($billion)
Short bonds	.84	46
Intermediate bonds	1.01	131
Long bonds	1.16	71
Balanced/total return	1.41	132
Income/utility	1.36	99
Growth/income	1.27	290
Long-term growth	1.44	340
Aggressive growth	1.58	136
Global bonds	1.54	39
International/global equity	1.88	175

Source: "Fund Scoreboard" (1996).

Table 10.11   Expense Ratios[a] for Small and Midsized 401(k) Pensions with and without an Annuity Product (basis points)

Type of Fund	Life Insurance Fund (401[k] with annuity) (1)	Mutual Fund (401[k], no annuity) (2)	Difference (1) − (2)	Ratio (1)/(2)
Equity	1.13	1.07	.06	1.06
Balanced	.85	.82	.03	1.04
Fixed income	.84	.66	.18	1.27
Money market	.5	.42	.08	1.19
International	1.53	1.32	.21	1.16
Index	.6	.28	.32	2.14

Source: Driscoll and Springsteel (1995).
[a]Asset-based charges (investment expenses) equal fiscal year operating expenses divided by average net assets. Both plans also levy record-keeping and administrative fees on plan sponsors.

outside managers totaled thirty-four basis points among public funds, as opposed to forty-five among the larger corporate funds in 1994 (Greenwich Associates 1995a, 1995b, 1995c). While the government-run plans are somewhat less expensive, there is little evidence of scale economies among this set of public plans examined: public funds with over $1 billion in assets paid thirty basis points, as opposed to thirty-seven basis points for plans with less than $100 million, whereas, in the corporate sector, plans with over $1 billion in assets paid thirty-three basis points in expenses, as opposed to those with under $100 million in assets, which paid fifty basis points (Greenwich Associates 1995a, 26). Nevertheless, no formal model was used in that study holding other factors constant; more will be said on this below.

As has been noted, corporate plan sponsors are not required to account for all pension expenses separately, in contrast with more complete reporting in public plans. For instance, in 1994, 68 percent of U.S. corporate pension plans reported that the plan sponsor (typically a private employer) directly paid a portion of pension plan staff costs rather than charging the pension plan, but only 42 percent of public-sector plan sponsors devoted staff time to pension fund activities (Greenwich Associates 1995a, 35). The smallest public/private reporting differential found is in the area of investment-management fees, where 76 percent of the private pension funds and 77 percent of public plans reported that their investment-management fees were charged to the pension plan (Greenwich Associates 1995a, 35). Overall, fewer corporate funds charge actuarial fees, pension-consulting fees, and performance-measurement fees to the pension fund, as compared to the public plans. In general, then, the higher fees paid by U.S. private plans are probably still underreported.

Other data sets offer distinct comparisons between U.S. corporate funds and Canadian and British pension plan costs. Across these three groups, the U.S. mean (median) private pension expenditure on annual money-management fees is systematically the highest, at forty (thirty-eight) basis points, compared to Canadian corporate funds, which pay thirty (twenty-eight) basis points, and U.K. private funds, where the mean is twenty-two (eighteen) basis points. An examination of these countries' corporate pension fund–management expenses reveals that U.S. plans had higher average expenses, as compared to the two comparator nations (where funds reported expenses over fifty basis points only rarely) (Greenwich Associates 1995a, 26).

Other places to seek evidence on pension expenses are in the nonprofit as well as government pension plans. In the former case, complete expenses are reported only to the extent that the plan is charged full cost for expenses incurred in its behalf. A rather interesting case is that of the College Retirement Equity Fund (CREF), the nation's largest defined-contribution pension plan, covering employees in higher education and research institutes. It is a nonprofit institution and, for historical reasons, receives special treatment under ERISA law. CREF is a national plan, covering people in many different institutions, and employers participating in the system tend to cover most of the payroll-based costs as part of their own benefits function. This suggests that the CREF plan would appear to have lower costs as compared to a plan where all benefits and payroll-related costs were charged to the plan. The system is also quite responsive to individual participating employers, permitting cross-employer differences in contribution levels, rules regarding lump sum versus annuity payouts, and asset-allocation choices; these differences may drive up expenses. Additionally, CREF contributions include the value of annuity insurance since, strictly speaking, participants in the contributory phase purchase a deferred variable annuity. For this reason, costs would not be expected to reflect or to be directly relevant to those experienced by corporate pensions. In any event, it is of interest to inquire about CREF's expense structure because of its large scale and because some have suggested that this might be a viable model if social security should be partly privatized.

CREF costs are reported in table 10.12, where it will be seen that total expenses (including money management and record keeping) ranged from 0.29 percent of assets per annum for the money market fund to 0.42 percent for the growth fund (plan year ending December 1994). This narrow differential can be attributed to CREF's application of identical administration and distribution expenses (0.21 and 0.03 percent of assets, respectively) to all funds. As a result, the only source of reported cross-fund variation is due to investment advisory fees, which vary from 0.05 to 0.18 percent. Certainly, these are low levels of cost, and the differentials narrow in light of the expenses reported for other funds described above. It is possible that these lower figures, five to eighteen basis points, would characterize money-management fees if a large-scale funded government program modeled on CREF were to replace the current, mostly unfunded, social security system.

A different pension plan outside the corporate sector is the federal government retirement system, known as the Federal Retirement Thrift Investment Fund. This civil service retirement plan is reasonably large, including over 2 million participants and $36 billion in assets, and is a contributory defined-contribution plan that may be allocated at the participant's behest into a stock fund, a bond fund, and/or a government securities fund. The 1996 annual report indicates that administrative expense ratios in this system total nine basis points; however, this figure excludes costs associated with collections of employer and employee contributions since an individual agency's or office's payroll system handles these separately. Even more striking is the low reported level of investment expenses—computed at under one basis point. This figure is indicative of the extent of scale economies feasible in a centrally managed, large defined-contribution pension plan that restricts its investment choices to a very small set of indexes (see table 10.13).

U.S. state and local pension plans afford another data point on large pension plan costs, but here defined-benefit systems are generally the norm.[30] In a recent study of more than three hundred public employee retirement systems with assets of $791 billion and 10.6 million active members in 1992, administrative expenditures for these public employee pension plans averaged 9 percent of total pension contributions; median per participant expenses were $130 per year (1992 dollars; Hsin and Mitchell 1994). This is comparable to private plan costs reported above (yet private plan figures may be biased downward for reasons already noted).[31]

---

30. In the last few years, however, a handful of states and municipalities have offered a defined-contribution alternative. For example, the city of Westminster, Colorado, provides defined-contribution plans for its police, firefighters, and general city employees, holding plan assets, $43 million, for some 770 participants. Expenses per participant are reported at $248 per year per person (1994 dollars). On a percentage basis, annual expenses total 0.45 percent of assets, or 5.4 percent of contributions. These expenses are allocated roughly two-fifths to operational expenses and three-fifths to money management costs.

31. These public plan costs could still be understated, to the extent that public-sector pensions probably do not fully account for collection costs, the use of public land and buildings, and benefits provided by other government agencies.

Table 10.12   1994 College Retirement Equity Fund (CREF) Administrative Expenses (%)

Type of Fund	Total Expenses	Investment Advisory Fees	Administrative Expenses	Distribution Expenses
Equity index	.32	.08	.21	.03
Stock account	.34	.10	.21	.03
Growth	.42	.18	.21	.03
Global equities	.41	.17	.21	.03
Social choice	.33	.09	.21	.03
Money market	.29	.05	.21	.03
Bond market	.30	.06	.21	.03

Source: CREF (1995)—data cover year ending December 1994.

The econometric analysis recognized that public-sector pensions might not operate on the economically efficient feasible frontier with minimum possible expenditures, inasmuch as public retirement systems usually are not subject to market pressures. Hence, a frontier cost model was estimated using a general multiproduct cost function of the form

(4)   administrative costs$_i$ = f(output vector, input prices; α) + ε_i,

where α is a vector of parameters, and ε_i is an error term made up of two independent components ($\varepsilon_i = v_i + u_i$, where v_i captures random error, and $u_i \geq 0$). Of particular relevance to the present work is the finding of substantial scale economies: among public-sector pension plans, a 1 percent increase in the number of plan participants raised pension administrative expenditures by 0.74 percent, holding assets per participant constant, and a 1 percent increase in assets ceteris paribus raised costs by less than half a percent. A more troubling finding was that some 30 percent of reported administrative expenditures was attributed to inefficiencies, although this figure was lower than those reported by other public-sector agencies.

Having measured pension plan inefficiency gaps, the analysis then explores factors associated with measured inefficiencies. The evidence suggests that public plans were more efficient when investment services were contracted out to private money managers. It was also found that granting pension boards authority over their administrative budgets reduced administrative efficiency, particularly when administrative budgets were picked up by the sponsoring employer (as opposed to having the pension fund cover its own costs). In general, therefore, administrative costs of public pension plans could probably be reduced somewhat, perhaps by as much as a third, with somewhat different reporting and management structures.[32]

32. In related work, Mitchell and Hsin (1994) and Mitchell and Smith (1994) found that public plan funding and investment performance was related to the composition and responsibilities of the pension boards managing the plans. Specifically, funding and returns were lower when a pension plan had more participants on the board, when in-state investments were required, and when board members were not required to carry liability insurance. (See also Hsin and Mitchell 1997.)

Table 10.13 Federal Retirement Thrift Investment Board Financial Data (1995 dollars)

Summary Data, Federal Thrift Plan (year end 1995)		Data by Fund Type	
Average account size ($)	16,500	U.S. Government Securities Investment Fund:	
Total participants (million)	2.2	Assets ($billion)	12.8
Investments ($billion):		Administrative expenses ($billion)	.024
Total investments	26.5	Administrative expenses/assets (%)	.19
Net assets	36.3	Wells Fargo Equity Index Fund:	
Contributions ($billion)	5.6	Assets ($billion)	11.5
Participant	3.8	Administrative expenses ($billion)	.008
Employer	1.8	Administrative expenses/assets (%)	.07
Administrative expenses ($billion)	33.4	Wells Fargo U.S. Debt Index Fund:	
As % of net assets	.09	Assets ($billion)	2.2
As % of total contributions	.59	Administrative expenses ($billion)	.002
Investment expenses ($billion)	.002	Administrative expenses/assets (%)	.09
As % of net assets	.006		
As % of total contributions	.03		

Source: Arthur Andersen LLP (1996).

Note: Expenses associated with collection of payroll contributions not included in expense figures. Fiduciary insurance premiums set at zero in 1995. Investment expense ratio not available on a per fund basis.

Trends in Pension Administrative Costs over Time

Estimates of trends in pension plan administration costs over time are relatively few, but one source is a recently revised and updated report on defined-benefit and defined-contribution pension plans over the period 1981–96 (Hustead, in press). Table 10.14 summarizes annual defined-benefit costs on a per person basis (in 1996 dollars) as computed from an actuarial simulation for a hypothetical plan and real cost trends over time.

The results indicate that average per participant costs rose rapidly for all sizes of plans and for both plan types, particularly during the latter half of the 1980s. Whereas annual private plan expenses stood at about $23.00–$26.00 per participant in larger pensions in 1981 (1996 dollars), by the mid-1990s the cost has risen almost three times for the defined-benefit pension plan and by almost double for the defined-contribution plan. Similar percentage changes characterized small pension plans, although the levels of administrative expenses for both plans are much higher because the smaller plans could less ably capture scale economies. In 1981, small plans of both types experienced per participant costs of under $200 per year per participant in 1981, but, by 1996, defined-contribution costs were $287 and defined-benefit costs higher than $600 per participant per year. Large plans reported administrative costs of $68.00 (defined benefit) and $49.00 (defined contribution) per year in 1996. (It should be noted that these administrative expenses exclude investment management fees but that they do include Pension Benefit Guaranty Corporate premiums for the defined-benefit pension plan figures.)

Several explanations have been offered for the increasing cost levels as well as the rising differential between defined-benefit and defined-contribution plans; most prominent explanations are the increasingly complex nondiscrimination rules that plan sponsors must meet and the rising cost of insurance premiums for defined-benefit pension plans (Hustead, in press; Clark and McDermed 1990).

Table 10.14   Actuarial Analysis of Defined-Benefit Pension Administrative Costs per Person (1994 dollars)

	Size of Pension Plan					
	15 Participants in Plan			10,000 Participants in Plan		
Year	DB ($)	DC ($)	DC/DB (%)	DB ($)	DC ($)	DC/DB (%)
1981	184	131	71	22	24	110
1985	456	374	82	31	32	104
1991	518	259	74	62	46	74

Source: Author's calculations from Hay/Huggins (1990), 31, 39.

Note: DB = defined benefit. DC = defined contribution.

Overview   ·

This investigation into pension plans of different types and in different sectors suggests several conclusions regarding pension administrative cost levels, differentials, and trends: (1) Large corporate pension plans reported total administrative costs of $68.00 (defined benefit) and $49.00 (defined contribution) per year in 1996. These costs have risen steadily in real terms over time. (2) Scale economies are significant for pension plans. Total administrative costs are much higher—perhaps five to ten times as high—on an annual per person basis, in company pension plans with fifteen versus ten thousand participants. (3) Overall pension plan expenses appear to be split approximately two-fifths to advisory and money-management fees and three-fifths to contract administration and salaries. Paying benefits in the form of an annuity adds additional costs, roughly six to thirty-two basis points over a mutual fund investment. (4) U.S. corporate pension plans report substantially higher money-management fees than do their Canadian and U.K. counterparts, at about forty basis points instead of twenty to thirty basis points. Corporate U.S. pension plans also report higher outside management fees than do public U.S. pension funds (where the latter devote about thirty-three basis points to outside fees). (5) Public- and nonprofit-sector pension plan expenses tend to be lower than corporate plan costs. For example, the CREF plan covering employees in higher education and research institutes reports devoting twenty-nine to forty-two basis points to expenses, with a constant fraction devoted to record keeping and distribution (twenty-four basis points) across plans. The Federal Thrift Retirement plan devotes nine basis points to administrative costs and less than one basis point to money-management costs. These figures should not be directly extrapolated to the private-sector arena, however.

10.3.3 Administrative Expenses in the Insurance Industry

Another line of inquiry pertains to the question of how well insurance firms could supply retirement annuities in the event that social security benefits were scaled down substantially. In this regard, it is important to address two issues: First, how efficient are privately managed insurance firms? Second, how well does the insurance market work as a whole? Presumably, the appeal of social security privatization would increase if private firms could be anticipated to fill the gap and to do so at relatively low cost.

In terms of the life insurance business in the United States, the American Council on Life Insurance (1995, 37) reports that life insurance firms in 1994 received some $453 billion in annual premiums and investment earnings. On a per dollar of asset basis, expenses totaled 11 percent of annual income (16 percent of annual contributions) and amounted to some 2.6 percent of the asset base of almost $2 trillion in 1994. Some 45 percent of the total expense dollar is devoted to selling costs or agents' commissions.

To date, much of the insurance economic literature has explored efficiency in the property-casualty market (e.g., Cummins and Weiss 1995). As a rule, these studies estimate cost functions, and the availability of firm-level panel data has permitted the estimation of quite flexible functional specifications. A persistent problem acknowledged across all these studies is that it is difficult to measure insurance firm output and quality. Hence, persistent cost differentials over time between different lines of insurance and different distribution systems for the same insurance product turn out to be quite difficult to interpret (see Berger, Cummins, and Weiss 1995). Nonetheless, looking across the available literature, it appears that firms in the U.S. property-casualty insurance sector are operating inside their efficient production frontier by significant margins, suggesting room for reductions in system administrative expenses.[33]

In addition to the general efficiency question just raised is a serious concern regarding how seriously adverse selection and moral hazard pose important real-world obstacles to the privatization of retirement annuities. Allowing individuals to elect whether to take their retirement accounts as a lump sum or as an annuity suggests that there are some potentially troubling weaknesses in the market for annuities. One influential study concluded that expected annual yields on individual life insurance policies were approximately 2 percentage points lower than on group policies owing to adverse selection (Warshawsky 1988). Other evidence suggests that purchasing individual annuities costs approximately two-thirds more than group purchase (Diamond and Valdés-Prieto 1993). These findings, along with the high and not necessarily efficient annual costs reported above, suggest that privatization of the insurance portion of the system would raise costs beyond current public provision of the old age annuity.

10.4   Relating These Findings to a Privately Managed Old Age Retirement System

How these findings might be relevant to a privatized social security system in the United States depends on the exact institutional structure that would be implied under such a reform. One option, dubbed the *maintain benefits* option by members of the Social Security Advisory Council, is to simply invest a portion of the existing social security trust fund in equities. This approach would leave intact the current revenue-collection mechanism, the Social Security Administration's record-keeping and benefit-payout functions, and all else; the only change would be that the government would now invest a portion of the fund, probably in an index portfolio (Quinn and Mitchell 1996).

Whether or not purists would deem this a real step toward privatization, it is nevertheless seen by many as a viable political possibility. Supporters argue that the SSA could earn higher rates of return than on Treasury bills; detractors

---

33. For studies of life insurance industry costs and efficiency, see Grace and Timme (1992), Fields and Murphy (1989), Gardner and Grace (1993), Yuengert (1993), and Zi (1994).

point to the fact that system participants may be forced to confront greater capital market risk than under the current defined-benefit plan (Mitchell and Zeldes 1996). In any event, it is plausible to argue that system expenses would increase as the government took on an additional money-management function, but the additional costs would probably be relatively small. If the trust fund were simply deposited in an indexed, passively managed mutual fund, administrative expenses would rise by as little as one to as many as twenty basis points, with the likeliest number being at the lower end of the range.

This figure relies on cost figures currently experienced by large, passively managed mutual funds; it could rise if more actively managed portfolios were chosen. Some analysts have expressed concern that political pressures would be brought to bear on a government-managed pension account worth, eventually, several hundred billion dollars.[34] To the extent that this did occur, expenses would be higher and investment performance lower than the returns offered by competitive privately managed mutual funds (Mitchell and Hsin 1994). This estimate also assumes that the government would continue to collect revenues, maintain records, and disburse benefits as now; in other words, the investment fee would be the only incremental charge over the system's current expenses.

A different approach to social security privatization is the proposal to establish a "personal saving account" (PSA).[35] This plan would require all participants to deposit a portion of their payroll taxes into individual private pension accounts managed by regulated but private fund administrators.[36] These pension managers would then invest participants' assets and pay out benefits at retirement. An important question regarding how such accounts might work in the United States has to do with how much self-directed investment would be permitted in the PSAs and how interfund competition would be regulated since the system's inception. In Chile, for instance, private pension fund asset-allocation decisions have been heavily restricted. There, workers may change pension allocations only three to four times per year (and must hold all their funds in a single pension fund at any given time), and fund managers face extensive regulation regarding asset composition, permissible (and prohibited) commission charges, and reserves. Although early in that nation's privatization drive administrative costs were quite high (about 23 percent of contributions or 14 percent of assets), these costs have dropped more recently (to 15 and 2.3 percent, respectively). It is, of course, inevitable that costs would be higher initially; the subsequent downward cost trend results partly from competition

34. Testimony of Sylvester Schieber before the Senate Finance Committee, 25 March 1996.

35. For further discussion of the Chilean system, see Diamond and Valdés-Prieto (1993) and World Bank (1994).

36. There is debate over whether this plan would be mandatory or optional and how funds would be collected. If contributions were collected at the individual level instead of continuing to use the Internal Revenue Service, collection costs could also be expected to rise substantially. Many of the issues raised in this discussion are taken up in Technical Panel on Trends and Issues in Retirement Saving (1995).

and partly from scale economies as assets have grown. Still, however, after fifteen years, the Chilean AFP pension system is relatively small by U.S. standards, having assets of around U.S.$25 billion (Edwards, chap. 1 in this volume).

If a PSA system were mandated in the United States, system administrative expenses would clearly rise, but probably not as much as the high end of the costs experienced in Chile. Inevitably, specific cost rates would depend on specific plan design details, such as what investors are permitted to do with their funds, how often they can reallocate their investment portfolio, and what restrictions on fees and other rules are instituted. An optimistic assessment would take the Federal Thrift Plan numbers, where it will be recalled that only three relatively passively managed options are permitted. In that system, administrative expense ratios were nine basis points (excluding collection costs), and money-management expenses are estimated at less than one basis point. Obviously, fund charges could be higher if people opted for more actively managed accounts; recent research on 401(k) plans has concluded that the first cohort to have access to these plans chose fixed-income and guaranteed insurance company holdings, but younger participants have chosen equity funds by substantial margins (see table 10.15). The CREF plan offers many additional options and has estimated expense figures of thirty to forty basis points annually (including record keeping).

A PSA account system that required investors to place their contributions with mutual funds would probably experience higher administrative and record-keeping fees and would also probably incur costs associated with providing annuities. In terms of the former expense, if individual pension accounts were offered as add-ons to existing company-sponsored 401(k) plans, administrative costs would probably be on the order of $50.00–$60.00 per year. This assumes that the plan does not require (or offer) that benefits be paid out in an annuity. If one were additionally to require that benefits be paid as an annuity, costs would probably rise by an extra 10 percent of contributions, or $100 per participant per year, extrapolating from multiemployer defined-

Table 10.15   **Defined-Contribution Asset Holdings by Participant Age (%)**

Proportion of Assets Held In:	Age of Plan Participant				
	21–30	31–40	41–50	51–60	61+
Fixed-income funds	41	43	49	62	85
Domestic equity funds	39	36	30	22	10
Balanced funds	6	8	11	8	1
Company stock funds	11	9	6	6	3
International equity funds	3	3	4	3	1

Source: Derived from Schieber and Goodfellow (forthcoming, table 4).

Note: Columns may not sum to 100 percent owing to rounding error.

contribution plan costs. This figure might be lower if, as the annuity market grew, private insurance firms experienced substantial scale economies; it might be higher if substantially greater adverse selection resulted from optional annuity purchases.

10.5   Conclusion

Opponents of social security privatization argue that privately managed systems are more costly to manage than public systems, and this is a charge that advocates must evaluate carefully. This paper contributes to the discussion by exploring a range of evidence on public and private pension system administrative expenses as well as the determinants of retirement system administrative efficiency in the United States and elsewhere.

The research shows that the administrative costs of providing old age retirement benefit services through a public system are often difficult to measure with precision. Conceptually, a comparison of public administration costs with private plan costs requires not only assessing the expenses incurred in delivering pension services but also controlling for the quality of services delivered. Available data fall far short of the desired measures. Nevertheless, evidence from international sources indicates that there are wide differences in retirement system administration costs from plan to plan and from country to country. Some of these differences are due to the level of privatization, but most appear to be attributable to particular institutional structures and management practices.

For example, the U.S. Social Security Administration manages a very large old age system at costs that are mid-range among developed nations, but these costs are low compared to smaller systems in smaller countries. Using several different metrics, these costs may be alternatively described as 0.7 percent of benefit expenditures, 0.4 percent of contributions, $12.00–$14.00 per covered worker per year ($9.00 per participant in 1994), or 0.39 percent of system assets (the latter figure is, however, misleading because the system is mostly unfunded). In exchange for these costs, the U.S. social security system appears to do some things quite well. Focusing on the provision of benefits, for instance, there is reason to believe that most eligible retirees receive the benefit amounts to which they are entitled on time. On the other hand, the posting of workers' earnings to system computer files could be improved, although this delay causes no particular problem under current rules. Under current rules, the U.S. social security system bears relatively small expenses for the collection of revenues and virtually nothing for money management since funds must by law be invested in special issue Treasury bills.

These figures were compared with expenses reported by a range of other financial institutions that might be potential players in a privatized social security system. Data from both retail and institutional mutual funds, private and nonprofit pension plans, and insurance companies were collected. Each of these private alternatives produces a somewhat different mix of outputs, with varying types of participant tailoring and service. The data suggest that adding a privately managed individual savings account to existing mutual fund or 401(k) plans would be relatively low cost, with money-management fees potentially ranging between one and twenty basis points (for a passively managed indexed portfolio) and administrative costs of perhaps $50.00 per year. Money-management costs could be substantially higher for more actively managed funds.

If a group model were taken as the likely prototype of a privatized system, such as a national TIAA-CREF-type or Federal Thrift–type plan (and the range of options were limited quite substantially), investment costs have been estimated to be on the order of a basis point or less per year. Administration costs would be potentially on the order of twenty to thirty basis points, judging from available evidence. In addition, one must add the costs of providing longevity insurance if annuities are to be guaranteed.[37]

Even if a privately managed defined-contribution system would result in somewhat higher administrative costs compared to the current pay-as-you-go system, these higher expenses would have consequences that many would find appealing. These additional expenses make possible a system that handles the pension system's necessary functions with greater alacrity while permitting workers to undertake more active asset management in their retirement portfolios. A variant of this approach has been suggested by several members of the 1994–96 U.S. Social Security Advisory Council: under this scenario, the government would offer and manage three to four funds among which plan participants could choose. This approach would also result in higher administrative costs as compared to the current social security system, but it would still permit some of the advantages of having individual accounts.

All the privatization options considered here would be expected to cost somewhat more in administrative expenses than the current publicly run plan in the United States, but the precise level of administrative costs in a privatized social security system will depend crucially on the specifics of the plan proposed. Costs will rise, experts believe, if actively managed funds are permitted, if twenty-four-hour call-up access were allowed, and if participants can obtain loans from the funds. Some of the variants would also entail higher collection costs, reporting expenses, and insurance annuity costs. A lower-cost system would require only a few investment options with little hands-on participant access and infrequent reporting. Offsetting these additional costs, of course, are potentially substantial economic benefits flowing from having a privately managed system (Feldstein and Samwick, chap. 6 in this volume; Kotlikoff, chap. 7 in this volume; Quinn and Mitchell 1996; Mitchell and Zeldes 1996).

---

37. This is one aspect of the current social security retirement account that might continue to be managed by the government, although encouraging the formation of groups for insurance purposes may suffice.

These benefits could include the opportunity for participants' contributions to earn a higher rate of return than that feasible under the public program, the possibility that labor supply and savings disincentives would be diminished, and a reduction in the political risk regarding future benefits.

References

American Council on Life Insurance. 1995. *Life insurance fact book supplement.* Washington, D.C.

Arthur Anderson LLP. 1996. *Report of independent public accountants to the executive director of the federal retirement thrift investment board.* Atlanta, 15 March.

Atkinson, Anthony B. 1987. Income maintenance and social insurance. In *Handbook of public economics,* vol. 2, ed. A. J. Auerbach and M. Feldstein. New York: Elsevier Science/North-Holland.

————. 1989. *Poverty and social security.* New York: Harvester Wheatsheaf.

Barr, Nicholas. 1992. Economic theory and the welfare state: A survey and interpretation. *Journal of Economic Literature* 30 (June): 741–803.

Baumol, William J., Stephen M. Goldfeld, Lilli A. Gordon, and Michael F. Koehn. 1990. *The economics of mutual fund markets: Competition versus regulation.* Rochester Studies in Economics and Policy Issues. New York: Kluwer Academic.

Berger, Allen, J. David Cummins, and Mary Weiss. 1995. The coexistence of multiple line systems for financial services: The case of property-liability insurance. Working paper. Wharton School, Center for Research on Risk and Insurance, March.

Borcherding, Thomas E., Werner W. Pommerehne, and Friedrich Schneider. 1982. Comparing the efficiency of private and public production: The evidence from five countries. *Journal of Economics,* suppl. 2:127–56.

Caswell, Jerry. 1976. Economic efficiency in pension plan administration: A study of the construction industry. *Journal of Risk and Insurance* 4, no. 2 (June): 257–73.

Clark, Robert, and Ann McDermed. 1990. *The choice of pension plans in a changing regulatory environment.* Washington, D.C.: American Enterprise Institute Press.

College Retirement Equities Fund (CREF). 1995. *Prospectus.* New York: TIAA-CREF.

"CREF cuts charges." 1996. *Participant* (May), 6.

Cummins, J. David, and Mary A. Weiss. 1995. Measuring cost efficiency in the property-liability insurance industry. *Journal of Banking and Finance* 17:463–81.

Diamond, Peter, and Salvador Valdés-Prieto. 1993. Social security reforms. In *The Chilean economy: Policy lessons and challenges,* ed. B. Bosworth, R. Dornbusch, and R. Laban. Washington, D.C.: Brookings.

Dickson, Joel. 1996. Analysis of financial conditions surrounding individual accounts. In *Report of the 1994–6 Social Security Advisory Council,* vol. 2. Washington, D.C.: Social Security Administration.

Doggette, H. 1988. Technological change and its impact on the management of social security agencies. *International Social Security Review* 41, no. 4:355–67.

Driscoll, Mary, and Ian Springsteel. 1995. Focus on 401(k) performance. *CFO Magazine* (October), 23.

Elton, Edwin J., Martin Gruber, Sanjiv Das, and Matthew Hlavka. 1993. Efficiency with costly information: A reinterpretation of evidence from managed portfolios. *Review of Financial Studies* 6, no. 1:1–22.

Fidelity Investments. Various dates. *Prospectus.* Boston.

Fields, J., and N. Murphy. 1989. An analysis of efficiency in the delivery of financial services: The case of life insurance agencies. *Journal of Financial Services Research* 2, no. 24:323–56.

"Fund Scoreboard." 1996. *Plan Sponsor* 4, no. 1 (February): 64.

Gardner, Linda, and Martin Grace. 1993. X-efficiency in the US life insurance industry. *Journal of Banking and Finance* 17, nos. 2/3:497–510.

Grace, Martin F., and S. Timme. 1992. An examination of cost economies in the US life insurance industry. *Journal of Risk and Insurance* 59:72–103.

Greenwich Associates. 1995a. *Eleven thorny problems.* Greenwich Report. Greenwich, Conn.

———. 1995b. *Investment management 1995: Statistical supplement.* Greenwich Report. Greenwich, Conn.

———. 1995c. *More equities, greater diversification, sensible shifts.* Greenwich Report. Greenwich, Conn.

Hay/Huggins Co. 1990. *Pension plan cost study.* Report prepared for the Pension Benefit Guaranty Corporation. Washington, D.C., September.

Hoexter, Elsie. 1970. *Administrative expenses of welfare and pension plans.* U.S. Department of Labor, Labor Management Services Administration. Washington, D.C.: U.S. Government Printing Office.

Hsin, Ping-Lung, and Olivia S. Mitchell. 1994. The political economy of public pensions: Pension funding, governance, and fiscal stress. *Revista de análisis económico* 9, no. 1 (June): 151–68.

———. 1997. Are public pension plans administratively efficient? In *Positioning pensions for the 21st century,* ed. M. Gordon, O. S. Mitchell, and M. Twinney. Philadelphia: University of Pennsylvania Press/Pension Research Council.

Hustead, Edwin C. In press. Retirement income plan administrative expenses: 1981 through 1996. In *Living with defined contribution plans,* ed. O. Mitchell and S. Schieber. Philadelphia: Pension Research Council/Wharton School.

Investment Company Institute (ICI). 1995a. *401(k) plans: How plan sponsors see the marketplace.* ICI Research Report. Washington, D.C.

———. 1995b. *Mutual fund 1995 fact book.* Washington, D.C.

Ippolito, Richard A. 1989. Efficiency with costly information: A study of mutual fund performance, 1965–1984. *Quarterly Journal of Economics* 104, no. 1 (February): 1–23.

James, Estelle, and Robert Palacios. 1995. The cost of administering publicly-mandated pensions. *Finance and Development* 32, no. 2 (June): 12–15.

Lakonishok, Josef, Andrei Shleifer, and Robert Vishny. 1992. The structure and performance of the money management industry. *Brookings Papers on Economic Activity: Microeconomics,* 339–91.

Limbacher, Patricia. 1995. ERISA reform hidden agenda in 401(k) furor. *Pensions and Investments* (December), 1.

Mehay, Stephen, and Rodolfo Gonzalez. 1985. Economic incentives under contract supply of local government services. *Public Choice* 46, no. 1:79–86.

Mitchell, Olivia S. 1992. Trends in pension benefit formulas and retirement provisions. In *Trends in pensions 1992,* ed. J. Turner and D. Beller. Washington, D.C.: U.S. Department of Labor, Pension and Welfare Benefits Administration.

Mitchell, Olivia S., and Emily Andrews. 1981. Scale economies in private multi-employer pension systems. *Industrial and Labor Relations Review* 34, no. 4 (July): 522–30.

Mitchell, Olivia S., and Ping-Lung Hsin. 1994. Public sector pension governance and performance. Working Paper no. 4632. Cambridge, Mass.: National Bureau of Economic Research, January.

———. In press. Managing public sector pensions. In *Public policy toward pensions,* ed. John Shoven and Sylvester Schieber. New York: Twentieth Century Fund.

Mitchell, Olivia S., and Robert Smith. 1994. Public sector pension funding. *Review of Economics and Statistics* 76, no. 2:278–90.

Mitchell, Olivia S., and Annika Sunden. 1993. *An examination of social security administration costs in the United States.* Report to the Public Sector Management Division, Latin America and the Caribbean Region Technical Department, World Bank. Washington, D.C.

Mitchell, Olivia S., Annika Sunden, and Ping-Lung Hsin. 1994. Social security costs in Latin America, the Caribbean, and OECD Nations. *Journal of International Compensation and Benefits* 2, no. 4 (January–February): 59–64.

Mitchell, Olivia S., Annika Sunden, Ping-Lung Hsin, and Gary Reid. 1994. An international appraisal of social security administration costs. Report to the Public Sector Management Division, Latin America and the Caribbean Region Technical Department, World Bank. Washington, D.C., May.

Mitchell, Olivia S., and Steven Zeldes. 1996. A framework for analyzing social security privatization. *American Economic Review* 86, no. 2 (March): 363–67.

Myers, Robert J. 1992. Can the government operate programs efficiently and inexpensively? *Contingencies* (March/April), 15–17.

Palacios, Robert. 1994. Determinants of administrative costs in publicly managed pension schemes. Washington, D.C.: World Bank. Mimeo.

Quinn, Joseph, and Olivia S. Mitchell. 1996. Prospects for social security reform. *American Prospect,* no. 26 (May–June): 76–81.

Reid, Gary, and Olivia S. Mitchell. 1995. *Social security administration in Latin America and the Caribbean.* Report to the Public Sector Modernization and Private Sector Development Unit, Washington, D.C.: World Bank, March.

Schieber, Sylvester, and Gordon Goodfellow. 1997. Investment of assets in self-directed retirement plans. In *Positioning pensions for the 21st century,* ed. M. Gordon, O. S. Mitchell, and M. Twinney. Philadelphia: University of Pennsylvania Press/Pension Research Council.

Shutan, Bruce. 1995. Fidelity pursuit changing face of total benefits outsourcing. *Employee Benefit News* 9, no. 5: 1, 18–19.

Social Security Administration (SSA). 1995. *Social Security Bulletin, Annual Statistical Supplement, 1995.* Washington, D.C.: U.S. Government Printing Office.

Sunden, Annika, and Olivia S. Mitchell. 1994. *An examination of social security administration costs in the United States.* Report to the Public Sector Management Division, Latin America and the Caribbean Region Technical Department, World Bank, and Pension Research Council Working Paper. Wharton School.

Technical Panel on Trends and Issues in Retirement Saving. 1995. *Final report to the 1994–95 Advisory Council on Social Security.* Washington, D.C.: U.S. Social Security Administration, September.

U.S. Department of Labor. Pension and Welfare Benefits Administration. 1996. *Abstract of form 5500 data financial reports.* Bulletin no. 5. Washington, D.C., Winter.

U.S. General Accounting Office. 1989. *Poor performers: How they are identified and dealt with in the Social Security Administration.* Washington, D.C.: U.S. Government Printing Office, January.

Valdés-Prieto, Salvador. 1993. Administrative costs in the Chilean pension system: Evidence from an international comparison. Santiago: Instituto de Economía, Pontificia Universidad Católica de Chile, January. Mimeo.

———. 1994. Administrative charges in pensions in Chile, Malaysia, Zambia, and the United States. Policy Research Working Paper no. 1372. Washington, D.C.: World Bank, October.

Vanguard. 1995a. *Facts on funds for your retirement.* Valley Forge, Pa., December.

———. 1995b. *Ten reasons to index* (marketing brochure). Valley Forge, Pa.

————. 1996. *Plain talk about index investing* (marketing bulletin). Valley Forge, Pa.

————. Various years. *Prospectus* (various funds). Valley Forge, Pa.

Warshawsky, Mark. 1988. Private annuity markets in the United States: 1919–1984. *Journal of Risk and Insurance* 55 (September): 518–28.

Watanabe, Noriyasu. 1996. Private pension plans in Japan. In *Securing employer-provided pensions: An international perspective,* ed. Z. Bodie, O. S. Mitchell, and J. Turner. Philadelphia: University of Pennsylvania Press/Pension Research Council.

World Bank. 1994. *Averting the old-age crisis: Policies to protect the old and promote growth.* Policy Research Report, Policy Research Department. Washington, D.C.: World Bank, June.

Yuengert, Andrew M. 1993. The measurement of efficiency in life insurance. *Journal of Banking and Finance* 17, nos. 213:483–96.

Zi, Hongmin. 1994. Measurement of cost efficiency in the US life insurance industry. Working paper. University of Pennsylvania, Wharton School.

Comment   Sylvester J. Schieber

In her paper, Olivia Mitchell presents an extensive analysis of the costs of administering a wide range of retirement programs. She investigates the costs of administering programs operated under several different structures. She looks at public and private plans as well as defined-benefit and defined-contribution plans. Finally, she evaluates U.S. plan administration costs and those of national retirement plans around the world.

I draw conclusions from Mitchell's paper and from the discussions in and about other papers presented at the conference and apply them in sketching out possible administrative structures for a U.S. personal investment option of the sort considered by the Social Security Advisory Council in their deliberations during 1995 and 1996. I also look at some of the existing models and explore their relevance as appropriate administrative structures for personal investment accounts.

One of the major conclusions that comes from this paper and other discussions at the conference is that there are tremendous opportunities to realize economies of scale in administering retirement plans. We see that the relative costs of administering the U.S. social security system have fallen over the years as coverage and benefits have expanded. Sebastian Edwards showed us (chap. 1 in this volume) that the costs of administering Chile's plan, as a percentage of assets in the personal accounts, has fallen significantly over the life of the plan now operating there. Mitchell shows us the same kinds of economies of scale in the administration of private and public employer-based retirement systems in this country.

In order to put into context the potential size of the system that might arise if the United States were to allow personal accounts of the sort included in

Sylvester J. Schieber is vice president of research and information for Watson Wyatt Worldwide.

the personal saving account (PSA) proposal considered by the Social Security Advisory Council, we can compare the potential here in the United States with the situation in Chile. For example, Edwards has told us that Chile's system has accumulated $25 billion over one and a half decades of operation. By comparison, if the PSA proposal were implemented on 1 January 1998, the PSA accounts would hold roughly $25 billion by the middle of March of that year. In today's dollars, these accounts would surpass $0.5 trillion within five years, $1 trillion within nine years, and $2 trillion within seventeen years. Once again, by way of comparison, James Poterba and David Wise (chap. 9 in this volume) tell us that 401(k) assets equal $600–$700 billion today. Under the PSA proposal, employees' annual contributions to their individual accounts would equal two to three times current contributions to 401(k) plans. In other words, the PSAs would become a very large collection of personal retirement assets in a relatively short time. If nothing else, the size of the accumulations would make it important that we be efficient in the administration of the program.

In developing an administrative structure to support a program like that envisaged in the PSA proposal, we would have certain advantages over many of the countries that have set up mandated individual retirement programs. For example, when Chile began its program, it had no long-term bond markets. Indeed, it found it necessary to create a whole new system of funds for the investment of the personal accounts that developed under the new system. In our case, we already have a highly developed marketplace of asset types and funds available for the investment of the funds that would result from the adoption of a personal account proposal. And, as Mitchell has documented, many of these are operating at levels of administrative costs, at least on the asset-accumulation side of the system, well within the range of assumed costs of one hundred basis points per year used in developing the PSA proposal now before the Social Security Advisory Council.

In her paper, Mitchell points to some existing systems as potential administrative models for the personal account system that we might adopt here in the United States, namely, TIAA/CREF and the Federal Retirement System (FERS). The thing that is attractive about both these systems is that they operate with extremely low administrative costs. While low costs are important, the costs of services should not be the only consideration in setting up whatever administrative structure we might adopt if we move forward with a PSA-type proposal. In recent years, dissatisfaction with the range of investment options, with flexibility to move assets, and with the level of services provided by TIAA/CREF has led a number of participating institutions in that program to offer an alternative set of investment and annuity options. The FERS system has been held out as a potential model for management of the individually accumulated funds in some U.S. reform proposals. FERS has an extremely limited set of investment options that many participants do not find sufficient to meet their needs and is currently considering a more typical set of offerings provided by employer sponsors of these types of plans.

While TIAA/CREF or FERS might not be the exact models that we would want to adopt under a personal account system, I believe that we should structure a system that would allow most workers to invest through group arrangements. In the consulting that Watson Wyatt does with employers on the administration of their 401(k) plans, we find that workers often prefer to use their employer plans as a means to consolidate their retirement savings into a coordinated set of investment options. I believe that the licensing of many existing investment offerings would allow employers to offer sets of widely available existing investment options to their employees in coordination with 401(k) offerings already being offered by those same employers. I believe that licensing is important because many employers will be reluctant to take on the fiduciary obligations of selecting and validating such plans on their own.

In discussing potential administrative costs with some of the organizations that would administer PSAs if we were to adopt such a program here in the United States, I have been told by several of them that, if the government were to impose annual administrative cost limitations of fifty or seventy-five basis points, we would still see many firms offering their funds for PSA investments. Even without those limits, we might expect PSA administration costs to be less than current 401(k) costs for several reasons. As noted earlier, PSA contributions under the option considered by the Social Security Advisory Council would be about two to three times the level of contributions to 401(k) plans. Another would be because the PSAs would not be required to do the same kind of discrimination modeling and testing that are required of 401(k) plans. Finally, costs would likely be lower because of the revolution going on in the administration of these types of plans. The ability to move money between funds, to get balances in accounts, etc. without the intervention of a human being on the administration end of plans is expanding rapidly. These technological advances will significantly reduce the cost of individual account plans in the future.

On the annuity front, there is still much work to be done. The proponents of the PSA proposal at the Social Security Advisory Council did not develop this facet of the proposal as fully as others. The whole issue of requiring annuitization is one that was discussed and garners a wide range of opinions. The thinking in not requiring annuitization of the personal accounts in the PSA proposal flowed from the analysis of benefit levels provided through the floor of protection in the flat benefit. Specifically, the analysis indicated that, for the prototypical "low-wage workers," the flat benefit alone would provide a level of real benefits roughly comparable to the level of benefits provided under current law. For the "average"- and "maximum"-wage workers, the flat benefit would dip below the poverty line by up to $100 per month for a ten- to fifteen-year period but would exceed current poverty levels beyond that. The question faced in developing the PSA proposal was at what level it was appropriate to set a required annuity floor of protection. Some people would clearly set it higher than the PSA proponents did.

Mitchell's paper pulls together a great deal of information on retirement plan administration costs. It makes an important contribution to the discussion about personal retirement account policy options. The issue of reasonable administrative cost assumptions was one of the most acrimonious elements of the Social Security Advisory Council's deliberations over PSAs. While this paper does not tell us definitively what these costs might be, it helps us understand some of the reasonable boundaries that we face.

Discussion Summary   Jeffrey Liebman and Andrew Samwick

The discussion began with a participant noting a trade-off that exists in other countries' public retirement schemes. A means-tested first tier of benefits is very expensive to administer but relatively cheap to fund. In contrast, a high flat-rate benefit for the first tier is cheap to administer but expensive to fund. Since no one is actively proposing either one of these plans for the United States, the author also pointed out a similar trade-off that exists in disability insurance programs: the government can spend more on screening and less on benefits to those who are marginally eligible for the program, or it can spend very little on screening and wind up paying out greater sums to beneficiaries. Both examples served to highlight the possible interactions between the administrative and the funding costs of retirement schemes.

Questions then began to focus on the cost data that were reported in the paper. A suggestion was made that it would be useful to have information not just on average total costs but on the breakdown of the whole cost function into, for example, fixed and variable costs. Two other ways of presenting the cost data were also suggested: the marginal cost of another dollar of assets under management and the marginal cost of another person in the fund. A question was raised as to whether the author was double-counting costs in mutual funds or 401(k) plans because many of those funds waive the record-keeping fees. It was also noted that the figures presented are *charges,* rather than costs.

The participants commended the author's emphasis on the distribution of costs. Quoting the *ranges* of costs is important because the money-management and insurance industries are composed of imperfectly competitive markets. It was then noted that the Social Security Advisory Council had assigned costs of five, ten, and one hundred basis points to the MB (maintenance of benefits), IA (individual account), and PSA (personal security account) plans, respectively. These figures are all within the ranges presented in the paper for analogous schemes, but it was also pointed out that privatized plans like the PSA plan that do not completely eliminate the current system would have all the current system's administrative costs *plus* these other costs.

The last point of discussion was that an additional cost of a privatized system would be that of regulating the management of the funds. One proposal that has been associated with the IA plan is to allow the federal government to set up its own fund that would follow a passive investment strategy and therefore have low administrative costs. Many participants expressed concern that, although this default option could put competitive pressure on private funds to keep their charges low, there was a grave risk of the government fund abusing its soft budget constraint.

Contributors

Alan Budd
HM Treasury
Parliament Street
London SW1P 3AG, England

Nigel Campbell
HM Treasury
Parliament Street
London SW1P 3AG, England

Joaquín A. Cottani
Argentina Financial Office
1901 L Street NW, Suite 606
Washington, DC 20036

David M. Cutler
Department of Economics
Harvard University
Cambridge, MA 02138

Gustavo Demarco
Superintendencia de AFJP
Tucuman 500
1049 Buenos Aires, Argentina

Richard Disney
Department of Economics
Queen Mary and Westfield College
London E14 NS, England

Malcolm Edey
Head of Economic Analysis
Reserve Bank of Australia
65 Martin Place
Sydney NSW 2000, Australia

Sebastian Edwards
Andersen Graduate School of Business
University of California at Los Angeles
110 Westwood Plz., Suite C508
Box 951481
Los Angeles, CA 90095

Martin Feldstein
NBER
1050 Massachusetts Avenue
Cambridge, MA 02138

Alan L. Gustman
Department of Economics
Dartmouth College
6106 Rockefeller
Hanover, NH 03755

Laurence J. Kotlikoff
Department of Economics
Boston University
270 Bay State Road
Boston, MA 02215

Jeffrey Liebman
John F. Kennedy School of Government
Harvard University
Cambridge, MA 02138

Olivia S. Mitchell
University of Pennsylvania
The Wharton School
3641 Locust Walk, 304 CPC
Philadelphia, PA 19104

457

John Piggott
School of Economics
University of New South Wales
Sydney NSW 2052, Australia

James M. Poterba
Department of Economics
MIT
E52–350
Cambridge, MA 02139

Carlos Sales-Sarrapy
Protego and ITAM
Sta. Catarina 267
Mexico, DF 01060, Mexico

Andrew Samwick
Department of Economics
Dartmouth College
6106 Rockefeller Hall
Hanover, NH 03755

Thomas J. Sargent
Hoover Institution
HHMB-Room 243
Stanford University
Stanford, CA 94305

Sylvester Schieber
Watson Wyatt Worldwide
6707 Democracy Blvd., Suite 800
Bethesda, MD 20817

Anita M. Schwarz
The World Bank
1818 H Street, NW
Washington, DC 20433

John B. Shoven
Dean's Office of Humanities & Sciences
Building One
Stanford University
Stanford, CA 94305

John Simon
Reserve Bank of Australia
GPO Box 3947
Sydney NSW 2000, Australia

Fernando Solís-Soberón
Consar and ITAM
Camino Sta. Teresa 1040
Mexico, DF 14210, Mexico

Thomas L. Steinmeier
Department of Economics
Texas Tech University
Lubbock, TX 79409

Aaron Tornell
Department of Economics
Littauer M-6
Harvard University
Cambridge, MA 02138

Jack L. VanDerhei
Temple University
School of Business Management
Philadelphia, PA 19122

Alejandro F. Villagómez-Amezcua
Department of Economics
CIDE
Carr. Mexico Toluca 3655
Mexico, DF 01210, Mexico

David A. Wise
Kennedy School of Government
Harvard University
Cambridge, MA 02138

Stephen P. Zeldes
Graduate School of Business
Columbia University
3022 Broadway, Uris 605B
New York, NY 10027

Author Index

Subject Index

Administrative costs: Australian superannuation, 96; new Chilean pension system, 45–46, 50–52, 59; U.K. pension systems, 129–30

Advisory Council on Social Security (1994–96), United States: personal security account plan of, 262; proposal to use payroll tax to finance IRA and social security, 316; Technical Panel on Trends and Issues in Retirement Savings, 313; trust fund investment option, 444

AFJP (private pension fund management), Argentina, 186–87, 192f; commissions charged, 198; investments and capitalization, 193, 195f, 196–99

AFOREs (Administradora de Fondos para el Retiro), Mexico: capital, reserves, and investments of, 152; evaluation of, 153–54; of IMSS under new system, 156; pension fund management, 146, 150–51; programmed withdrawals from, 147

AFPs (administradoras de fondos de pensiones), Chile: administrative costs of, 44–46, 409–12; companies managing individual retirement accounts, 39–40, 61; conditions for liquidation of, 46–47; fees and commissions charged by, 45; investment reserves of, 44; investments by, 41–44; mandatory and voluntary contributions to, 41–42; participants switching among, 61; profitability of, 46; regulation of, 59

AIME. *See* Average indexed monthly earnings (AIME)

AK model. *See* Auerbach-Kotlikoff model (AK model)

Annuities: Australian deferred life annuity, 93–94; Australian superannuation funds, 70, 93–94, 97; available in Chilean pension system, 47–49, 93; CREF pension plan, 438; market in United Kingdom, 115–16, 133; under Mexico's reformed pension system, 147; options for IRAs and 401(k)s, 366–67; proposed inflation-indexed Australian, 93; provided by social security, 11; TIAA-CREF, 383–87, 391; wealth of nominal and real, 400

Annuitization: estimates of utility gain from, 387–89, 391–92, 398; in 401(k) plans, 367; savings plans requiring, 364–65; TIAA-CREF patterns, 385–87

ANSES (Administración Nacional de la Seguridad Social), Argentina, 190, 191f, 192f, 409–12

APPs (approved personal pension accounts), United Kingdom: contributions of members, 131–32; earnings of members, 131; employee choice of (1987–88, 1994–95), 128, 131; National Insurance contribution rates to, 128–29

Argentina: basic universal pension, 186, 188–89, 201; decision to reform social security, 177, 179–85; evaluation of reformed pension system, 207–11; evolution of